Democracy amid Crises

DEMOCRACY AMID CRISES

Polarization, Pandemic, Protests, and Persuasion

The Annenberg IOD Collaborative

The Annenberg IOD Collaborative members are:

MATTHEW LEVENDUSKY
JOSH PASEK
R. LANCE HOLBERT
BRUCE HARDY
KATE KENSKI
YOTAM OPHIR
ANDREW RENNINGER
DAN ROMER
DROR WALTER
KEN WINNEG
KATHLEEN HALL JAMIESON

OXFORD
UNIVERSITY PRESS

OXFORD
UNIVERSITY PRESS

Oxford University Press is a department of the University of Oxford. It furthers
the University's objective of excellence in research, scholarship, and education
by publishing worldwide. Oxford is a registered trade mark of Oxford University
Press in the UK and certain other countries.

Published in the United States of America by Oxford University Press
198 Madison Avenue, New York, NY 10016, United States of America.

Library of Congress Cataloging-in-Publication Data
Names: Annenberg IOD Collaborative, author
Title: Democracy amid crises : polarization, pandemic, protests, and
persuasion / the Annenberg IOD Collaborative.
Description: New York, NY : Oxford University Press, [2023] |
"The Annenberg IOD Collaborative members are: Matthew Levendusky, Josh Pasek,
R. Lance Holbert, Bruce Hardy, Kate Kenski, Yotam Ophir, Andrew Renninger,
Dan Romer, Dror Walter, Ken Winneg, and Kathleen Hall Jamieson." |
Includes bibliographical references and index.
Identifiers: LCCN 2022042308 (print) | LCCN 2022042309 (ebook) |
ISBN 9780197644690 (hardback) | ISBN 9780197644706 (paperback) |
ISBN 9780197644720 (epub) | ISBN 9780197644737
Subjects: LCSH: Presidents—United States—Election—2020. |
United States—Politics and government—2017-2021. |
Elections—United States—Public opinion. | Americans—Attitudes
Classification: LCC E915 .A56 2023 (print) | LCC E915 (ebook) |
DDC 324.973/0933—dc23/eng/20221025
LC record available at https://lccn.loc.gov/2022042308
LC ebook record available at https://lccn.loc.gov/2022042309

DOI: 10.1093/oso/9780197644690.001.0001

1 3 5 7 9 8 6 4 2

Paperback printed by Sheridan Books, Inc., United States of America
Hardback printed by Bridgeport National Bindery, Inc., United States of America

Contents

Preface

ON JANUARY 6, 2021, we were on a Zoom call vetting questions for the last wave of the panel data underlying *Democracy amid Crises*. We expected that day to complete the questionnaire for the study's final wave and to do so (symbolically) on a day certifying the results of the 2020 election we had set out to study two years before. Partway through the call, however, we began to receive news alerts on our phones that a mob of Trump supporters had stormed the US Capitol. The expressions we saw on each others' faces suggested that even the most jaded among us had not anticipated that a riot would follow the speech the incumbent president gave at the Ellipse that day. Or that any of us would ever witness a mob marching though the Capitol chanting "Hang Mike Pence," or see a Confederate battle flag paraded through its corridors. Collaboratives collaborate—but not dumbstruck, horrified ones. So we suspended the Zoom session to immerse ourselves in the media that we both study and consume. Given the centrality of January 6 to the story we tell in the pages that follow, there is a dark irony to our having met on that day.

The Annenberg Institutions of Democracy (IOD) Collaborative draws on the expertise of scholars from five disciplines to help us make sense of the 2020 election and its aftermath. Its members included a political scientist (Matt Levendusky), four communication scholars (Lance Holbert, Bruce Hardy, Kate Kenski, and Josh Pasek), a rhetorical critic turned sometime social scientist (Kathleen Hall Jamieson), a psychologist (Dan Romer), a survey researcher (Ken Winneg), and a geographic data expert (Andrew Renninger). Off-screen but working away on social media data and so also enmeshed in the moment were two other members of the team, both communication scholars (Yotam Ophir and Dror Walter). Since the IOD Collaborative is a project of the Annenberg Public Policy Center (APPC) of the University of Pennsylvania, it will come as no surprise that five members of the team are graduates of the university's Annenberg School for Communication or that two of us are on the faculty there.

This book, and the survey on which it is based, was truly a collaborative effort. Every team member contributed questions. Ken managed the survey. Andrew prepared and integrated the geographic data that we use throughout the book. Josh focused on data analysis and racial attitude measures, and produced the striking visuals that readers will encounter in all of our empirical chapters. Lance developed media measures. Matt was in charge of fundamentals and legitimacy. Kathleen tracked the messaging. Bruce focused on campaign events, Kate on early voting. Dan concentrated on conspiracy theories. Yotam and Dror sleuthed through social media messaging. A bit more biographical detail on the individuals in the Zoom squares on the screen that day can be found in the contributor list that follows the preface.

Dictionaries define a collaborative, a word that until recently was thought to serve only as an adjective, as an organized group effort. Although sometimes more effortful than organized, ours was both. For us, the word "collaborative" is also a solution to a problem. Crediting *Democracy amid Crises* to the Annenberg IOD Collaborative not only recognizes the Annenberg Public Policy Center endowment from which its funding came but also is a way of avoiding crowding the cover of a book with ten names. It also resolves the question and vaudeville gag line, "Who's on first?" Although individual chapters credit those who put fingers to computer keyboards, the book as a whole would not exist were it not for the work of every individual who was part of the collaborative. Accordingly, we consider the group as a whole the author of the book. This is particularly important since, as we pruned the manuscript to ensure that its length did not rival *War and Peace*, entire blocks of pristine prose by many of its members were sidetracked into other forms of publication.

Still, someone needs to be on first. So we have listed Matt, Josh, and Lance as the first three authors in the collaborative list to recognize that Matt did a disproportionate amount of the writing; Josh the cleaning, organizing, and analysis of the data, and virtually all of the work reflected in the figures; and Lance the heavy lifting of theorizing, instrumenting, analyzing, and writing up the media findings. Kathleen is listed at the end because she initiated the project and, as the firstborn in her family, thought that she should be last for a change. The order in which authors are listed atop each individual chapter credits as first author the person who assumed primary responsibility for conceptualizing its arguments and organizing its evidence.

After more weekly meetings than any of us care to count, *Democracy amid Crises* is our answer to the question "What will ten researchers from seven different universities (Penn, Temple, University of Michigan, University of Arizona, University of Buffalo, Georgia State University, and University College, London) in seven cities spread across two continents make of a data set housing the answers to more than a thousand questions asked over fourteen waves of a panel study to more than 9,000 individuals drawn from four battleground states about the 2020 presidential election and its aftermath?" Whether the years of planning, surveying, analysis, and writing paid off is for the reader to judge.

Over a three-year period, we all change, in ways both big and small. But from 2019 to 2022, that truism was pushed to its limits. We struggled to figure out how to shift our courses online and still provide our students with a great educational experience. Some of us fell ill with COVID-19. Some had family members who contracted the disease, necessitating complicated quarantine procedures. Some had friends and relatives die from it. Many of us scrambled as childcare vanished and schools closed while we continued to teach and do research. We began the process meeting in the third-floor conference room at the APPC building, but we ended it at home on Zoom. In light of all of this, our first and deepest thanks as a team are to our families, for all of their help and support during this process. This line is in most, if not all, academic books, but it was never more true than in this period.

But we also owe much to many others as well. We thank the more than 9,000 respondents who took the time to answer our surveys and stuck with us even when our questionnaires were long and frequent. Some even took time to flag questions they found wanting, unclear, biased, or needless, and in the process helped us improve our instrument. We think of our Oxford University Press editor, Dave McBride, as our collaborator-in-chief. He also deserves our thanks for shepherding more Annenberg data into book form than any other editor on the planet and for serving as the godfather of the two APPC books, *The Obama Victory* and *Cyberwar*, that have received awards from the Association of American Publishers. We are grateful as well to our copy editor (Sue Warga) and our indexer (Judith Linwood), the APPC guardians of the manuscript, Samantha Fox and Emily G. Maroni, and our eagle-eyed proofreaders, Michael Rozansky and Karen Riley. We also thank Paige Betoff, Anna Lisa Lowenstein, Mia Vandermeer, and Summer Wylie, the undergraduate research team that tamed the campaign's messages so that we could survey our respondents about them, and the APPC research support team of Zachary Reese, Gary Gehman, Dan Corkery, Ruthie Fields,

Molly Des Jardins, Karen Riley, Ellen Iwamoto, and Tim Duff. There would be no book had they not wrangled data, tracked content, coded, retrieved the unretrievable, and archived ads, news, and social media messaging. We gratefully acknowledge the role that Patrick E. Jamieson played in crafting key questions for the COVID, conspiracy, and handling batteries. We also owe a special thanks to our APPC budget officer, Lena Buford, who kept us within budget and handled the complexities of contracts, as well as Jennifer Su, Chintan Turakhia, Kyle Berta, and the rest of the SSRS team, who managed a complicated sampling procedure, fielded the survey, and provided a critical additional check on question wordings and survey logic.

Two anonymous reviewers gave us constructive, detailed suggestions on ways to improve the prospectus and sample chapters. Additionally, Larry Bartels, Chris Wlezien, Vince Hutchings, and Talia Stroud not only read the first draft in the middle of a busy semester but also pointed to numerous landmines and suggested ways to disarm them. Thank you all. An extra shout-out to Larry Bartels, who also played an indispensable role in the development of *The 2000 Election and Foundation of Party Politics* (by Richard Johnson, Michael Hagen, and Kathleen Hall Jamieson) and *The Obama Victory* (by Kate Kenski, Bruce Hardy, and Jamieson), two earlier books based on large Annenberg election data sets.

We finalized this manuscript in January 2022. In the months since then, many of the questions we raised about the norms that sustain our institutions and our democracy have only become more relevant, not less. As the House's Select Committee to Investigate the January 6th Attack on the Capitol and the Department of Justice continue to explore these topics, no doubt we will learn even more about the ways in which our democracy was stress-tested in 2020. This gives this book more resonance than any of us anticipated or, frankly, wanted. May you live in interesting times indeed.

As we rushed to meet that January 2022 deadline, we paused to observe the one-year anniversary of a day that none of us will forget. The congressional commemoration of January 6 included a speech by the nation's first female vice president and the statements of two septuagenarians that may mark the opening salvo of the 2024 presidential contest. In Biden's speech in Statuary Hall, the forty-sixth president labeled the forty-fifth "the defeated former president," indicted him for the lies he continued to advance about the outcome of the 2020 election, and condemned his contention that Election Day 2020 was the insurrection and January 6 the protest. Responding in a written statement, the defeated former president appropriated the language routinely used to dismiss his claims that the election was stolen. The "Big Lie" was not the claim of voter fraud, he asserted, but rather the November 3 election itself, echoing the sort of delegitimizing rhetoric we track in this book.

In the months that followed, the contrast persisted. For example, in a September 1, 2022 interview concerning the judicial travails of January 6 rioters, Trump revealed that he would "look very, very favorably about full pardons if I decide to run." His rambling answer also forecast the possibility of "full pardons with an apology." On the same day, standing before Independence Hall in Philadelphia, Biden declared that "Donald Trump and MAGA Republicans represent an extremism that threatens the very republic."

Mindful of these exchanges, we dedicate this book to those who heroically protected the integrity of the 2020 election before, during, and after January 6.

Matt Levendusky, Josh Pasek, Lance Holbert, Bruce Hardy,
Kate Kenski, Yotam Ophir, Andrew Renninger, Dan Romer,
Dror Walter, Ken Winneg, and Kathleen Hall Jamieson
January 2022

List of IOD Collaborative Members

DEMOCRACY AMID CRISES is the work of the Annenberg IOD (Institutions of Democracy) Collaborative. Here we provide a brief biographical sketch for each of the members.

MATTHEW LEVENDUSKY is Professor of Political Science (and, by courtesy, in the Annenberg School for Communication), the Stephen and Mary Baran Chair in the Institutions of Democracy at the Annenberg Public Policy Center, and the Penny and Robert A. Fox Director of the Fels Institute of Government, all at the University of Pennsylvania. He has published widely on polarization, partisan media, and other topics in political behavior and political communication.

JOSH PASEK is Associate Professor of Communication & Media and Political Science, Faculty Associate in the Center for Political Studies, and Core Faculty for the Michigan Institute for Data Science at the University of Michigan. His research explores how media, identities, and psychological processes each shape political attitudes, public opinion, and political behaviors.

R. LANCE HOLBERT is Professor of Communication and Social Influence with Temple University's Klein College of Media and Communication, as well as a Distinguished Research Fellow at the University of Pennsylvania's Annenberg Public Policy Center, an International Communication Association Fellow, and Editor-in-Chief for *Journal of Communication*. He studies persuasion-based media effects in political contexts.

BRUCE W. HARDY is Associate Professor of Communication and Social Influence with Temple University's Klein College of Media and Communication, as well as a Distinguished Research Fellow at the University of Pennsylvania's Annenberg Public Policy Center. He researches political, science, and health communication. Hardy is the co-author with Kenski and

Jamieson of *The Obama Victory: How Media, Money, and Message Shaped the 2008 Election* (Oxford University Press, 2010), winner of the National Communication Association's Diamond Anniversary Book Award, the International Communication Association's Outstanding Book Award, and the American Publishers' Association PROSE Award as Best Book in Government, Policy, and Politics.

KATE KENSKI is Professor of Communication at the University of Arizona, as well as a Distinguished Research Fellow at the University of Pennsylvania's Annenberg Public Policy Center. She studies political communication, presidential campaigns, and incivility in online spaces. Kenski is the co-author with Hardy and Jamieson of *The Obama Victory*.

YOTAM OPHIR is Assistant Professor of Communication at the University at Buffalo, State University of New York, and a Research Fellow at the Annenberg Public Policy Center at the University of Pennsylvania. His research, which focuses on media effects, persuasion, and misinformation, combines computational tools for automated content analysis with experimental and survey designs, in order to study media content and its effects on audiences.

ANDREW RENNINGER was a researcher at the Wharton Geospatial Initiative and the Annenberg Public Policy Center until August 2021. He holds master's degrees in urban planning and spatial analysis from the University of Pennsylvania and is currently pursuing a Ph.D. at University College London.

DAN ROMER is the research director of the Annenberg Public Policy Center. His research focuses on adaptive decision-making, civic engagement, and healthy development, especially in young people, and, more recently, on the role of conspiratorial thinking in response to the coronavirus pandemic.

DROR WALTER is Assistant Professor of Digital Communication at Georgia State University's Department of Communication, and is also a Research Fellow at the University of Pennsylvania's Annenberg Public Policy Center. His research is centered on the intersection between media effects theories and computational social science methods, focusing on contexts related to political communication, political/health misinformation, and political extremism.

KEN WINNEG is Managing Director of Survey Research at the Annenberg Public Policy Center of the University of Pennsylvania. He is responsible for surveys conducted by the Annenberg Public Policy Center, including the Annenberg Institutions of Democracy surveys and the Annenberg Science Knowledge survey.

KATHLEEN HALL JAMIESON is Professor in the Annenberg School for Communication of the University of Pennsylvania and director of its Annenberg Public Policy Center. Including *Packaging the Presidency* (1984), five of Jamieson's ten authored or co-authored Oxford University Press books have won awards in the communication or political science field. Most recently, *Cyberwar: How Russian Hackers and Trolls Helped Elect a President* (Oxford University Press, 2018) received the 2019 R. R. Hawkins Award from the Association of American Publishers.

I

An Election Shaped by Crises

The Annenberg IOD Collaborative

A nation in crisis faces a critical moment in history this election.
—CNN headline from November 2, 2020[1]

THOUGH FEW REALIZED it at the time, the opening salvo of the 2020 election actually took place in 2017. That February, the Charlottesville, Virginia, city council had voted to remove a city-owned statue of Confederate general Robert E. Lee and to rename the eponymous park in which it stood. In August of that year, as part of a "Unite the Right" rally, a group of torch-carrying white nationalists and white supremacists marched toward that statue, determined to prevent the city from removing it. The slogans they chanted—which included "Blood and soil," "White lives matter," "You will not replace us,"[2] and "Jews will not replace us"[3]—will figure prominently in our arguments in subsequent chapters. Counterprotesters awaited their arrival. In the melee that ensued, self-avowed neo-Nazi James Alex Fields Jr. drove his car into a crowd of pedestrians, killing counterprotester Heather Heyer and injuring more than thirty others.[4] Asked about the event, Trump remarked, "You also had people that were very fine people, on both sides."[5] That remark, which drew considerable criticism at the time, was noteworthy as well because of the response it elicited from Joe Biden, the former vice president and US senator. "With those words, the President of the United States assigned a moral equivalence between those spreading hate and those with the courage to stand against it," Biden said in the April 2019 video announcing his run for the presidency. "And in that moment, I knew the threat to this nation was unlike any I'd ever seen in my lifetime."[6]

But Charlottesville did more than just inspire Biden to run for the nation's highest office: it foreshadowed the violence that would course through 2020. Indeed, the 2020 election began and ended with acts of violence: on one end, the tumult in Charlottesville; on the other, the riot at the US Capitol on January 6. Those at the Capitol that day were motivated by Trump's false claims of massive voter fraud. Academic experts, state and local officials, the US Department of Justice, and more than sixty judges—many of them Republican appointees—had investigated these claims and found them to be utterly without merit.[7] Nevertheless, Trump, his allies, and supporters in conservative media continued to promulgate them. Backed by misinformation and conspiracy theories both online and off-, and egged on by Trump's argument that "if you don't fight like hell, you're not going to have a country anymore,"[8] his supporters stormed a citadel of democracy that had been forcibly breached only once before in the nation's history. But unlike that earlier assault, US citizens—not foreign troops—were now the marauders.

Trump and Biden's views of January 6 were as dissimilar as were their takes on Charlottesville. Where Biden saw it as "the worst attack on our democracy since the Civil War,"[9] Trump said that those arrested for their activities on January 6 were being "persecuted so unfairly" and termed their actions a "protest concerning the Rigged Presidential Election."[10]

Democracy amid Crises tells the story of the tumultuous final year of Donald Trump's presidency. Importantly for us, this is not just a book about the 2020 election and why voters balloted the way they did. To be sure, that is an important part of our story. But equally important is what happened afterward, and how Trump's efforts to delegitimize Biden's victory led not only to the events at the Capitol on January 6 but also to a more pernicious undercutting of democratic legitimacy among many of his supporters. The effects of the 2020 election will linger for years to come.

In the chapters that follow, we use an eleven-wave panel survey of more than 9,000 respondents spread across four swing states to show how the four interrelated crises of the 2020 election season shaped the election and what followed: the COVID-19 pandemic, the economic crash and uneven recovery, the debate over racial justice and policing sparked by the death of George Floyd, and the crisis of democratic legitimacy brought about by Trump's efforts to discredit Biden's victory in the November election. From confrontational stand-offs over stay-at-home orders and mask mandates, to clashes between protesters, counterprotesters, and law enforcement officers during the protests over policing and racial justice, to the riot of January 6, the threat of violence churned like an undercurrent through each of these crises. Indeed, as we discuss in later chapters, worrisome numbers of people now agree that to defend "the American way of life" and redress their grievances, disaffected citizens may need to take up arms. For them, deliberation and debate may not be up to the task of protecting values they cherish or the kind of nation in which they wish to live. Instead, violence and force might be needed, an ominous possibility.

Both the Democratic and Republican presidential contenders agreed with our epigraph: the nation was in crisis in 2020. They just focused on different crises. Where the challenger argued that Trump's handling of the pandemic and the economic fallout was the crisis, the incumbent argued that there would be a stock market crash and explosion of crime in the suburbs should the challenger win. Pointing to "the worst pandemic in over 100 years. The worst economic crisis since the Great Depression. The most compelling call for racial justice since the 60's" in his convention acceptance speech, Biden called on Americans to "just judge this president on the facts: 5 million Americans infected by COVID-19. More than 170,000 Americans have died. By far the worst performance of any nation on Earth. More than 50 million people have filed for unemployment this year. More than 10 million people are going to lose their health insurance this year. Nearly one in six small businesses have closed this year."[11]

In contrast, in his acceptance speech, Trump argued that "this election will decide whether we SAVE the American Dream, or whether we allow a socialist agenda to DEMOLISH our cherished destiny. It will decide whether we rapidly create millions of high paying jobs, or whether we crush our industries and send millions of these jobs overseas, as has foolishly been done for many decades . . . whether we protect law abiding Americans, or whether we give free reign [*sic*] to violent anarchists, agitators, and criminals who threaten our citizens . . . whether we will defend the American Way of Life, or whether we allow a radical movement to completely dismantle and destroy it."[12] In sharp contrast to Biden's, Trump's speech made little to no mention of the ongoing pandemic. These convention addresses foreshadowed the themes and arguments that would last through the fall campaign, as we argue in the chapters that follow.

The Four Crises of 2020

One has to go back to 1918 or even 1864 to find years in which the United States faced as many crises as it did between January 20, 2020, and January 20, 2021, the final year of Donald J. Trump's presidency.

In 1864, civilians in the American South "rioted for bread and salt," outbreaks of measles, smallpox, and tuberculosis flared,[13] and by its close in 1865, the Civil War had claimed 620,000 American lives.[14] To silence dissenters, in 1861 Lincoln suspended habeas corpus from the District of Columbia to Philadelphia, an action legitimized by congressional authorization in 1863. With that approval in hand, the sixteenth president imposed the suspension throughout the Union.[15]

In 1918, an influenza pandemic ravaged the country, ultimately claiming an estimated 675,000 US lives.[16] On the battlefields of World War I, the United States would suffer another 115,000 deaths.[17] At home, gross domestic product (GDP) dropped by 1.5 percent and consumption by 2.1 percent.[18] Under the 1917 Espionage Act, antiwar presidential candidate Eugene Debs was jailed in 1918.[19] The same act sanctioned the arrest of 2,000 protesters for "inspiring resistance to military recruitment." Extremists rampaged through the country as well. "The American Defense Society, a right-wing vigilante group, pulled anti-war speakers off soapboxes in New York City."[20]

On January 1, 2020, prognosticators did not anticipate that the events of the coming year would later be analogized to those that occurred during either of those earlier war years. Instead, Americans rang in the new year blissfully unaware that just over the horizon lurked a pandemic that would affect the lives of all Americans, severe economic dislocation, a national reckoning on racial justice, protests and counterprotests of previously unseen scale, mobilizations of the National Guard and the deployment of federal forces in response to civil unrest, and an assault on our presuppositions that elections register the public will and a peaceful transition of power is inevitable when an incumbent loses.

In the pages that follow we will show that these crises upended lives, stress-tested the resilience of democratic structures, shaped the contours of the 2020 election and its aftermath, and reshaped the 2022 and 2024 electoral landscape.

The COVID-19 Pandemic

Awareness that something was amiss emerged in late 2019, as reports filtering out of Wuhan, China, indicated that a new respiratory infection was spreading in the city. Initial reports suggested that the outbreak was small and confined to a few who had visited the Huanan wholesale seafood market.[21] However, in short order it became clear that that was not the case. Instead, the virus was spreading rapidly throughout the city, even among those who had no links to the market. In short, human-to-human transmission of severe acute respiratory syndrome coronavirus-2, SARS-CoV-2, was occurring.

By January 11, 2020, Chinese officials reported their first death from this novel coronavirus. Nine days later, on January 21, the first case was diagnosed in the United States.* On January 23, Chinese officials locked down the city of Wuhan, forcing individuals to quarantine inside their homes—a grim preview of what was to come. The World Health Organization (WHO) declared the newly identified virus to be a global health emergency on January 30, and the following day, the Trump administration restricted travel into the United States by those who had been in China in the last fourteen days. At this point, however, the situation in the United States looked manageable. The word from the White House was reassuring. At a late January press conference, President Trump responded to a question about whether he was worried about the possibility of a pandemic: "No, not at all. We have it totally under control. It's one person coming in from China. We have it under control. It's going to be just fine."[22]

On February 11, the World Health Organization added a new term to the international lexicon by naming this airborne disease COVID-19. The coming weeks and months would show how unprepared the United States actually was to deal with it. On March 11, the WHO declared COVID-19 to be a global pandemic.[23] Two days later, President Trump declared it to be a national emergency.[24] On March 19, California became the first state to issue a stay-at-home order, requiring citizens to remain within their residences unless they were traveling to obtain necessary supplies (such as food or medicine) or going to an essential job; forty-two other states and territories would ultimately follow suit.[25]

Meanwhile, the nation watched anxiously as New York City hospitals struggled to deal with COVID-19 patients for whom they had neither treatment nor cure. With the sound of sirens becoming white noise in the city that never sleeps, New Yorkers emerged at 7:00 PM each evening to bang pots and pans in a show of support for, and solidarity with, healthcare workers struggling with the virus.[26] At the time, Dr. Anthony Fauci, director of the National Institute of Allergy and Infectious Diseases, one of the nation's leading infectious disease experts and a member of President Trump's coronavirus task force, estimated that perhaps 100,000 to 200,000 Americans might eventually die from the disease.[27] In a statement that set expectations against which his performance could be judged, the incumbent president said in March 2020 that "if we have between 100,000 and 200,000 we've all together

---

*. For a timeline of events related to COVID-19, see https://www.nytimes.com/article/coronavirus-timeline.html.

done a very good job."[28] While at the time those numbers seemed preposter-
ously high, the nation would surpass them in short order. More than 100,000
had died from the disease by May 2020, and by Election Day, over 232,000
Americans had been felled by COVID-19.[29] Grim new death tolls became a
regular part of the news during 2020.

As states that had imposed stay-at-home orders in March and April 2020
began to lift them in late spring, some people began to try to resume a (somewhat) normal life. But soon after the first wave of the virus that prompted the
stay-at-home orders in the spring subsided, a new one emerged, centered in
the South and Southwest. The nation—once again—saw hospitals overrun,
this time in Texas rather than New York. But by late summer, it looked as if
the country was slowly getting the virus under control. US daily infections
peaked at roughly 70,000 on July 22 and by mid-August had fallen to roughly
42,600 per day. The percentage of tests returning positive readings declined
from 8.5 percent to 6.2 percent over that same period.[30] All of this suggested
room for cautious optimism.

By the time of the fall election campaign, a third wave of COVID-19 had
crushed that optimism. Although the death rate among those hospitalized
was lower than it had been in spring due to improved therapies and the
changing demographics of those being infected, the COVID-19 situation
had once again become worrisome. By the end of October, the United States
had set a new world record for the number of cases reported in a single day
(100,000)—a pattern that would be repeated with alarming frequency in the
months to come. In the weeks leading up to Election Day, forty-seven of fifty
states were experiencing an upswing in cases.[31] Indeed, with the final day of
balloting only three days away, Dr. Fauci accurately predicted a grim winter,
saying, "All the stars are aligned in the wrong place as you go into the fall and
winter season, with people congregating at home indoors. You could not possibly be positioned more poorly."[32]

Unsurprisingly, the pandemic became one of the central issues in the campaign, with Biden and Trump arguing over how best to combat the virus and
how well the incumbent had done so. From the beginning of the crisis, the incumbent downplayed its threat. Even after he contracted and allegedly nearly
died from COVID-19 (the latter fact not reported at the time),[33] and despite
characterizing it as the "plague,"[34] Trump argued that the severity of COVID-
19 had been overblown. And as we discuss in Chapter 5, he also alleged that a
"deep state" within the Centers for Disease Control and Prevention (CDC)
and Food and Drug Administration (FDA) was exaggerating its severity,
sidetracking effective therapies such as hydroxychloroquine, and stalling the

development of a vaccine to undermine his reelection. Although on April 3 the CDC recommended that Americans wear face masks to reduce the spread of the disease, Trump was rarely seen wearing one, and he also held numerous in-person events with minimal social distancing. Trump focused not on COVID-19 but on reopening the economy on the grounds that the latter was more important to the country.

In contrast, Biden argued that the virus was the main challenge the nation faced. Biden's chief claim against Trump was that his handling of COVID-19 and the ensuing economic fallout were an indictment of his leadership, and the rationale for denying him a second term. Biden argued that we could reopen the economy only if stringent public health policies were in place, including testing and personal protective equipment (PPE) for all called back to work.[35]

The two campaigns embodied their candidates' respective perspectives on COVID-19. Until the fall, Biden made most of his electoral appeals from his Delaware basement; when he did appear in public, he stood physically distanced from his advisors and audiences and, like his staff and spouse, was masked. While Trump held large, in-person rallies, Biden's supporters cheered him on from their cars in parking lots. As we detail in later chapters, the behaviors and beliefs of Biden's and Trump's supporters mirrored those of their preferred candidates.

An Economic Crisis, for Some

At the close of 2019, the US economy appeared to be in good shape. During President Trump's time in office, unemployment had fallen to 3.5 percent,[36] GDP had grown at 2.5 percent per year on average, and the stock market had soared to ever greater heights.[37] Unsurprisingly, in January 2020, 63 percent of Americans approved of the incumbent's handling of the economy, the highest for an incumbent in an election year since Bill Clinton.[38] President Trump and his team felt confident that this strong economic record would lead voters to reelect the president that fall.

However, once the nation locked down in March to halt the spread of the pandemic, the economy spiraled into crisis as well. Retail sales dropped 8.7 percent in March, the worst decline since record-keeping began in 1992.[39] As an analysis by St. Louis Federal Reserve Bank vice president David Wheelock showed, "the drop in economic activity during the second quarter of 2020 was larger than any quarterly decline during the Great Depression."[40] The second quarter of 2020 saw the single biggest drop in GDP in the post–World

War II period—9.5 percent in real terms and more than 30 percent on an annualized basis. In summer 2020, the International Monetary Fund (IMF) predicted that the United States would experience an 8 percent (annualized) drop in GDP during 2020.[41]

With most of the economy shuttered, the country veered from having the lowest unemployment rate since the Korean War[42] to the highest since the Great Depression.[43] In April 2020 alone, 20 million Americans lost their jobs, and the unemployment rate—which had been 3.5 percent at the end of February[44]—rose to 14.7 percent.[45] In some areas, more than three in ten residents were out of work.[46] In response, Congress swiftly passed the historic Coronavirus Aid, Relief, and Security (CARES) Act, which allocated approximately $2.2 trillion to fight the virus, protect businesses, and provide unemployment assistance and direct cash payments to American families to help them weather the shutdown. To put this figure in perspective, the amount was "larger than the economies, or gross domestic products (GDPs), of all but six other nations."[47]

Although the third-quarter GDP figures, released on October 29 by the Bureau of Economic Analysis, showed a marked improvement,[48] the economy still had a long way to go to return to its pre-COVID level. In July, the Congressional Budget Office forecast that from 2020 to 2030, the GDP would be 3.4 percent lower, on average, than it had projected in January.[49] It also estimated that the annual unemployment rate from 2020 to 2030 would average 6.1 percent.[50] In August, the Department of Labor indicated that 27 million workers were unemployed, making the unemployment rate 10.2 percent—down from the springtime highs, but still far above where it had been at the end of 2019. Although new unemployment claims fell to just under 1 million in the week in August in which Trump accepted his party's renomination, that week was the twenty-third in which new jobless claims were near or above one million.[51]

While the unemployment rate continued to fall as early voting began in mid-September, it remained at historically high levels, at least relative to recent years.[52] Trump's claim during the fall campaign was that the nation had weathered the worst of the coronavirus pandemic and its economic fallout and was experiencing a "V-shaped" recovery, with pre-pandemic employment levels on the horizon. But many economists—and Joe Biden—argued that the recovery was instead "K-shaped," with those at opposite ends of the pre-pandemic income spectrum experiencing radically different economic trajectories.[53] Upper-income voters—who owned stocks and homes—saw those assets appreciate rapidly, while lower-wage workers were more likely to experience continued unemployment,[54] the threat of eviction or foreclosure,[55] and other economic distress. The title of a report by Brown University economist John Friedman summarized the state of the economy in mid-2020 well: "Recession Has Nearly Ended for High-Wage Workers, but Job Losses Persist for Low-Wage Workers."[56] Indeed, upper-income earners actually increased their savings over the course of 2020, while lower-wage workers saw theirs fall.[57]

Of course, this economic disparity predated the COVID-linked shutdowns. Income inequality had been steadily rising for years, a reality documented by a Pew Research Center study released in January 2020, which found that "the growth in income in recent decades has tilted to upper-income households. At the same time, the US middle class, which once comprised the clear majority of Americans, is shrinking. Thus, a greater share of the nation's aggregate income is now going to upper-income households and the share going to middle- and lower-income households is falling."[58] Those with higher incomes were well positioned to ride out the economic collapse that accompanied the COVID-19 pandemic.

Not so those at the bottom of the economic ladder. Instead, some in that precarious and vulnerable state experienced truly desperate times. "Nearly 26 million adults—12 percent of all adults in the country—reported that their household sometimes or often didn't have enough to eat in the last seven days," according to data gathered between October 28 and November 9, 2020, by the US Census Bureau's Household Pulse Survey.[59] Food pantry lines stretched for miles, as millions of Americans were now unable to afford food or to pay for other basic necessities.

Just as with the coronavirus, the economic visions of the two campaigns had little in common. There were two dimensions to the economic debate, as we show in Chapter 6. First, Trump argued that he should be judged on pre-pandemic growth, which for most voters had indeed been quite strong, whereas Biden emphasized the ongoing pain of 2020, especially for those who had less. Second, Trump and Biden clashed over whether the economy was experiencing a V-shaped or K-shaped recovery, a conflict that got to the heart of who had escaped the pandemic largely unscathed and who had suffered its worst consequences.

Civil Unrest and a Reckoning over Racial Justice

In 2013, Trayvon Martin, an unarmed Black seventeen-year-old, was shot and killed by George Zimmerman, a White neighborhood watch captain. On the argument that he had acted in self-defense, Zimmerman was acquitted of murder charges. In response, activists formed the Black Lives Matter (BLM) movement to protest systemic racism and dismantle white supremacy. In the years since, the movement has had regular occasion to protest the deaths of Black Americans at the hands of the police and others. Those killed by police officers included forty-three-year-old Eric Garner in Staten Island, New York, who was suffocated by an officer while in custody for allegedly selling loose cigarettes in 2014; teenager Michael Brown, who was shot by a police officer in Ferguson, Missouri, later that year; seventeen-year-old Laquan McDonald, who was shot in Chicago, Illinois, in 2014; Tamir Rice, a twelve-year-old boy who was shot by an officer while playing with a pellet gun in Cleveland, Ohio; Walter Scott, fifty, who was shot in the back after a routine traffic stop in North Charleston, South Carolina; Samuel DuBose, forty-three, who was shot after he allegedly started to drive away from officers carrying out a routine traffic stop in Cincinnati, Ohio, in 2015; Freddie Gray, twenty-five, who died of spinal injuries sustained in police custody in 2015; and Philando Castile, 32, also shot by an officer during a routine traffic stop in Minneapolis, Minnesota, in 2016.

Lethal violence against Black citizens continued in 2020. In late February, twenty-five-year-old Ahmaud Arbery was jogging in Brunswick, Georgia, when he was shot and killed by two White men (abetted by a third) who said they thought he was a burglar. On March 13, 2020, while trying to serve a no-knock warrant in the middle of the night, multiple Louisville, Kentucky, police officers shot and killed Breonna Taylor, a twenty-six-year-old Black woman. The person for whom the warrant was intended no longer lived at Taylor's address.

In late May 2020, the country faced what the mainstream press cast as a "racial reckoning"[60] after a viral video taken by a passerby showed the death of George Floyd, a forty-six-year-old Black man, handcuffed and pinned to the ground facedown by White Minneapolis police officer Derek Chauvin, who knelt on Floyd's neck. Floyd gasped that he could not breathe, as bystanders begged the officer to stop. Floyd's alleged crime was tendering a counterfeit twenty-dollar bill to purchase a pack of cigarettes at a convenience store.

When the video of Floyd's death was replayed online and on broadcast and cable networks, outrage mounted. It not only refuted the initial police report of Floyd's death but also demonstrated the transformative power of cellphones and social media.[61] On Twitter, within the three days after Floyd's death, "more than eight million tweets tagged with #BlackLivesMatter were posted on the platform," according to a *New York Times* account. "By comparison, on Dec. 4, 2014, nearly five months after Eric Garner died at the hands of a police officer on Staten Island, the number of tweets tagged with #BlackLivesMatter peaked at 146,000."[62]

As emotions swelled, so too did what may have been the nation's largest protest movement. On June 6 alone, "half a million people turned out in nearly 550 places across the United States."[63] In the summer of 2020, protests, rallies, and demonstrations occurred not just in the nation's largest cities but in many suburbs and small towns as well. While the vast majority were peaceful, some did turn violent.[64] Throughout the summer and fall, that subset would be heavily featured on conservative media outlets and in Republican advertising.

Counterprotesters, among them some in paraphernalia bearing Trump's MAGA ("Make America Great Again") campaign slogan and some who argued that they were there to keep the peace, organized as well. In August 2020, protesters, counterprotesters, and some agitators took to the streets of Kenosha, Wisconsin, after Jacob Blake, a Black man, was paralyzed after being shot seven times in the back by White police officers. During one of the clashes that ensued, Kyle Rittenhouse, a teenage White counterprotester armed with an AR-15 assault-style rifle, killed two White individuals and seriously injured a third.

Clashes played out not just in Kenosha but around the country as well. State and local officials responded: at least twenty-one states activated the National Guard and cities announced curfews. In the process, in an echo of the 2017 confrontations in Charlottesville, members of anti-immigrant and white supremacist groups joined the fray. The all-male, anti-immigrant group known as the Proud Boys clashed with Black Lives Matter protesters in New Port Richey, Florida, in summer 2020.[65] At a pro-Trump rally in December 2020, Proud Boys chairman Enrique Tarrio burned a Black Lives Matter flag stolen from a historically Black church in Washington, DC.[66]

Some of those counterprotesters were opportunists bent on magnifying tensions and instigating conflict. In Minneapolis, for example, a man "accused of helping incite riots and looting in the aftermath of George Floyd's police-involved death" was identified by police "as a member of a white supremacist group that aimed to stir racial tensions amid largely peaceful Black Lives Matter protests."[67] Consistent with that revelation, the Anti-Defamation League (ADL) reported the spread online of "disinformation about antifa and Black Lives Matter protesters organizing violent attacks in suburban communities." "Despite the lack of evidence of any such impending attacks, these types of rumors affected communities across the country, often in connection with false reports about busloads of protesters," noted the ADL.[68]

Among the accounts disabled by Twitter was one "linked to a white nationalist group which was posing as Antifa and encouraging violence in white, residential neighborhoods around the country."[69]

Threats posed by white nationalists concerned the Department of Homeland Security as well. After attributing violence in Portland, Oregon in particular to "violent opportunists," in September, acting Homeland Security Secretary Chad Wolf called out violence perpetrated by "white supremacist extremists" and "anarchist extremists." In the same address, he described "how protesters had attacked federal officers with sledge-hammers, pipes, fireworks, homemade bombs and other weapons."[70]

The slogans from the 2017 Charlottesville "Unite the Right" rally that we highlighted in the introduction to this chapter—"You will not replace us," "Jews will not replace us," "Blood and soil," and "White lives matter"— suggested that the messengers felt threatened by the nation's shifting demographics, including the reality that by midcentury, Americans of European descent would no longer be the majority of the nation, with the United States becoming a majority-minority country. While demographers note that this demographic shift is complex and analytical nuance is required to do justice to the phenomenon, this process and what it portends for political power in America underlie the norm-breaching behavior of some affiliated with groups involved both in the counterprotests to the Black Lives Matter movement and in the January 6 riot.

Trump and Biden disagreed about the lens through which to see the protests and counterprotests. Trump stressed law and order, famously tweeting that "when the looting starts, the shooting starts."[71] In stump speeches in the fall, the incumbent claimed, as he had in the passage from his acceptance speech we quoted earlier, that if Biden and the Democrats won, lawlessness, chaos, and violence would invade the suburbs. While condemning violence and looting, Biden argued that the protests were a cry for justice. As we will show in Chapters 7 and 8, these themes mattered in very different ways to their respective constituencies.

Not Three Pre-Election Crises, but One

But in many ways, as we will discuss throughout the book, the COVID-19 pandemic, the economic collapse and K-shaped recovery, and the protests over racial justice were fundamentally linked to one another. As we noted above, the economic crisis was largely precipitated by the decision to shut down the economy to limit the spread of a deadly virus. The nation's racial reckoning, while sparked by concerns about race and policing, also exposed the racial inequalities of both COVID and the ensuing economic fallout. By late spring, it had become clear that the toll of COVID-19 was falling disproportionately on people of color, with Black and Hispanic Americans far more likely to be infected and more likely to be hospitalized or die than Whites were as a result of COVID-19.[72] The sources of these racial disparities were legion. Not only did people of color disproportionately live in the urban areas that were hit earliest in the pandemic, but they also tended, for various socioeconomic reasons, to have worse underlying health profiles than did Whites (e.g., greater rates of obesity and diabetes), and they were often not as well served by the medical establishment.[73] At the same time, they were more frequently employed in positions that required them to interact in person with others, a status that increased both susceptibility and likely viral load.[74] As a result, while we treat these crises separately for expository reasons, they are deeply and inextricably linked, a fact we emphasize in our later chapters.

Challenges to Democratic Legitimacy

Our fourth and final crisis—the crisis of democratic legitimacy—has its roots in Trump's 2016 rhetoric. "The election is absolutely being rigged by the dishonest and distorted media pushing Crooked Hillary—but also at many polling places," Trump tweeted shortly before Election Day 2016.[75] His efforts to delegitimize the 2016 popular vote outcome continued while in office, as he claimed that he would have won the popular vote—and not just the Electoral College—had millions of illegal votes not been cast for the Democrats. An Election Integrity Commission that he established disbanded after finding no such evidence,[76] a finding echoed in academic analyses of the election.[77] Nonetheless, a majority of Trump's base believed the false allegation[78] and hence was primed to accept his 2020 claims that Democrats would—once again—use fraud to try to steal the election from him, this time through mail-in balloting instituted widely in response to the pandemic (providing a link between this fourth crisis and the ones discussed above).

The available evidence confirms that there was no significant voter fraud either in 2020 voting or in the counting process. Not only were the Trump campaign's more than sixty court challenges dismissed, but a number of them elicited rebukes from Republican-nominated judges. Election administrators in the states concurred.[79] So too did the US Cybersecurity and Infrastructure Security Agency, which after a post-election review declared that the 2020 presidential election was "the most secure in American history."[80] Even Attorney General Bill Barr noted that there was no evidence of a significant problem.[81] Nevertheless, Trump and his allies continued to push the false-hood that the election had been stolen. This mendacity undermined a core tenet of democracy: that free and fair elections determine our leaders.

But it was not just that Trump cast the election as illegitimate, a claim his voters accepted. As we argue in Chapter 9, his arguments and rhetoric called into question the claim that dialogue, not violence, is how Americans resolve their conflicts. This crisis would culminate, but not end, in the January 6 assault on the Capitol.

Two Key Arguments

In the chapters that follow, we illustrate how these four crises shaped the discourse of the election, voters' evaluations of the candidates, the election outcome, and perceptions of the events that followed. We show that Americans saw the crises of the pandemic, the economy, and the protests over racial justice, as well as the crisis regarding the election's legitimacy and the broader legitimacy of democracy itself, through the lens of their polarized partisan predispositions filtered by their preferred media sources and affected by the media options they were incentivized to seek out or avoid. This argument rests on two key claims—first, that there are multiple electorates, and second, that making sense of them requires a communication lens.

Claim #1: There Are Multiple Electorates

Our first presupposition is premised on the realization that the polarized perceptions of partisans make talking in terms of one electorate problematic. As a result, throughout *Democracy amid Crisis* we will advance the case for the existence of multiple electorates, defined not only by their partisan affiliations but also by their patterns of media use. These electorates were exposed to different informational environments, whose divergent messages shaped not only their vote choice but also how they made sense of each of the four crises.

Although we found a great deal of stability in our panelists' attitudes, persuasion did take place throughout the contest and its aftermath. While many voters are locked in place by their partisan priors, many others wavered, and needed some reinforcement or persuasion before they decided their vote. Importantly, the specific sets of beliefs and attitudes that Americans adopted over the course of the campaign reflected the different informational contexts in which these electorates immersed themselves.

As we show in the chapters that follow, these different electorates behave in quite dissimilar ways; Trump and Biden's staunchest voters are attitudinally different from those with weaker attachments to their own side. To understand the dynamics of the election, we need to understand these differences not just between Trump and Biden supporters but also within each candidate's supporters.

Claim #2: Understanding These Electorates Requires a Communication Lens

A key component is the communication environments enveloping voters: messages that matter include those from the campaigns, from their family and friends, and from those in mass and social media. This explains why some individuals waivered in their presidential preferences or in the surety of their preference while others did not, and why some saw the economy, COVID-19, or the protests over racial justice as a focal concern while others did not. Understanding who was persuaded, when, and why requires unpacking the messages they received. To identify those messages, we need to fathom the fundamentally different communication environments in which different groups of voters (Biden vs. Trump vs. other, wavering vs. unwavering) resided.

These media environments are distinct and distinctive as well as complex and varied. Most citizens consume a wide variety of sources, including various types of mainstream local and national news. But what they read, see, or hear, and how varied it is, differs across our electorates. Indeed, there is a small group of voters who consume only news that fits with their partisan priors, without any news from countervailing outlets; these people are in what is commonly called an echo chamber. While this group is relatively small, that does not mean it is unimportant.

Knowing someone's media diet alone is not enough; we also need to know how they consumed it. Some people actively seek information from particular sources, while others try—unsuccessfully—to avoid them (i.e., they encounter them but did not choose to do so). We show that these action tendencies—seeking versus avoiding, and being successful or unsuccessful—shape how respondents react to particular sources. In turn, this suggests that communication scholars have developed an oversimplified understanding of the nature of exposure. In particular, although scholars have focused on incidental exposure through social media, it occurs much more broadly through many other outlets.

To outline the path that we will take to chronicle our respondents' views of the crises, their electoral choices, and the events of January 6, we now preview the coming chapters.

A Brief Overview of the Book

The chapters that follow can be divided into three main parts. In the first part of the book, Chapters 2 through 4 lay out the basic contours of our argument. In Chapter 2 ("What Fundamental Factors Shape Elections?"), we review the core phenomena that shape elections, and show how one needs to understand both core political ones—such as presidential popularity, the state of the economy, and the balance of partisanship—as well as the media and communication environment. In short, both political media forces matter. We also explain how the unique environment of 2020 shaped the ways in which these factors affected and were affected by the crises on which the book focuses.

Throughout the book, we draw on an eleven-wave panel survey of more than 9,000 respondents spread across four key battleground states: Florida, Michigan, Pennsylvania, and Wisconsin. In the interest of narrative flow, we relegate such details as how we constructed the sample and why we targeted those states to the Appendix ("Appendix: Our Data and Analytical Strategy"). There we also explain the analytical strategy we used to understand and model the campaign dynamics of this unique year. We encourage readers to consult the Appendix to better understand the panel data and analyses that undergird this book. In particular, we walk readers through the types of graphical analysis that they will encounter in the book.

In Chapters 3 and 4, we lay out our argument that to make sense of this election, we need to understand that there are multiple electorates in the US, and that each exists in a different communication environment. In Chapter 3 ("Not One Electorate, but Many"), we explain how we segmented voters into the different electorates, and how their demographics, attitudes, and experiences of 2020 differ. In Chapter 4 ("The Electorates' Communication Dynamics"), we show how each of these segments of the public exists in a different communication ecosystem, defined both by distinct patterns of media consumption and by different ways of getting that content, some of it sought out, some of it encountered incidentally, and some of it avoided, both successfully and unsuccessfully.

In the second part of the book, Chapters 5–9, we explore how the crises— the pandemic, the economic crash, the clash over racial justice and policing, and the crisis of democratic legitimacy—shaped the 2020 election and its aftermath. In Chapter 5 ("Did the COVID-19 Pandemic Sink Trump's Reelection?"), which focuses on the meaning of and messaging about the COVID-19 pandemic, we show that even Trump's own voters tended to give him relatively poor marks on the pandemic (relative to other issues) and that these perceptions likely did cost him some electoral support. One might have anticipated that the death of nearly a quarter of a million Americans before Election Day would have dramatically damaged the incumbent's vote share, but that was not the pattern we found. Instead, we show that while the pandemic did affect the election, its effect was limited by the divergent ways in which Trump and Biden voters perceived it. We show that a core contrast in the election was whether voters chose to prioritize the pandemic (as Biden argued), or instead the economy (as Trump claimed).

In Chapter 6 ("The Best of Times, the Worst of Times"), we trace the effects of the economic dislocation on the election. In the spring of 2020, after the nation stayed at home to fight the virus, the bottom fell out of the US economy. Throughout the campaign, Biden and Trump sparred over whether the recovery from the coronavirus would be V-shaped, with a quick return once the lockdowns ended (Trump's claim), or K-shaped, with very different paths for the haves and the have-nots (Biden's claim). Overall, most of our voters saw this as a K-shaped recovery, a conclusion that was influenced as much as by their political views as by their economic well-being. But there is a special tragedy in this for those at the very bottom of the economic ladder. Consistently 10–15 percent of our sample experienced genuine financial hardships, unable to afford basic necessities such as rent, utilities, or enough food. These individuals were markedly less likely to turn out and vote, and those who did were much less likely to vote for Trump, a conclusion that suggests that economics does powerfully shape political attitudes.

In contrast to the COVID-19 pandemic, all voters—even Biden's supporters—agreed that the economy was one of Trump's stronger issues. It is unsurprising, then, that throughout the campaign, Biden emphasized the pandemic and Trump stressed the economy. Rather than a debate over who best could handle the key issue of the campaign, the debate between Biden and Trump was about which issue voters should prioritize.

In Chapter 7 ("Law and Order vs. Law and Order with Racial Justice"), we show how the protests over racial injustice and policing shaped the election. The clash between Trump and Biden over whether they were about racial justice or law and order affected voters' views. These debates both primed and shifted respondents' prior racial attitudes, making racial attitudes one of the fundamental determinants of vote choice in this election.

In Chapter 8 ("A Deeper Anxiety: Was Status Threat at Play in 2020?"), we show that racial attitudes in 2020 were not simply beliefs about whether minority groups face discrimination; intimately connected to them is the argument that majority groups are being discriminated against as well. This latter concept—termed status threat by social scientists—focuses on the belief that the relative position of White Americans, particularly White men, is declining, and it is an important part of why racial attitudes are so powerful.

Chapter 9 ("'Stop the Steal'") explains how Trump's false claims of rampant voter fraud and his efforts to overturn the election results magnified beliefs among his supporters that electoral victory had been stolen from him. Early in the campaign season, Trump and Biden voters were equally likely to believe the election would be free and fair. But by October, those opinions had diverged. In the intervening months the incumbent had forecast that the Democrats would rig the election against him. His voters took this message to heart. Post-election, the gap in perceptions became a chasm. By the end of our study, nearly all Biden voters believed that Biden was legitimately elected, while few Trump voters did.

But we show that there is more to the story. The view that the election was stolen was strongest among those who think minority groups face little discrimination and majority groups face comparatively more. These same attitudes also predicted support for the actions of Trump supporters at the Capitol on January 6, as well as support for violence in defense of the American way of life. Beliefs about race and status threat not only shape vote choice but also fundamentally shape attitudes toward the fourth crisis. In many ways, the post-election crisis of legitimacy was, at its core, about the changing demographics of America and who holds political power.

In the third part of the book, which contains the tenth and final chapter ("A Republic, if You Can Keep It"), we summarize our findings and ask what they portend for future elections and the well-being of the body politic. Underlying this chapter are concerns that the effort to overturn the 2020 outcome may portend even more sinister and effective actions in 2024 or beyond. The chapter also details the guard rails that held in 2020 and 2021 and ways that their tensile strength might be enhanced.

Of course, all of this assumes familiarity with the individuals contesting for the presidency and vice presidency in 2020. Readers who command the relevant details may want to skip the remainder of this chapter. But for the benefit of those who might dust off a copy of *Democracy amid Crises* many years from now, we set the stage with a few reminders about the biographies and records of the four individuals responsible for the messaging on which *Democracy amid Crises* focuses.

The Two Tickets

Few took Donald Trump seriously when he descended an escalator in Trump Tower in June 2015 to announce that he was a candidate for president. Critics—including his Republican opponents—suspected he was running for office to boost either his brand or his appeal as a reality TV star. They would be humbled. Trump emerged victorious from the primaries and proceeded to score an upset victory over Hillary Clinton in the general election. While the Democratic nominee amassed over 2.8 million more votes than the Republican contender, narrow victories in several key states—notably Pennsylvania, Michigan, and Wisconsin, which Trump won by a combined total of less than 80,000 votes—secured him the Electoral College majority, and with it the presidency. His unorthodox candidacy broke from traditional Republican positions on trade and support for international organizations such as NATO and adopted populist stances that favored the working class on healthcare (e.g., allowing Medicare to negotiate drug prices), education (e.g., easing student loan debt), and the environment (e.g., prioritizing the coal industry) and diverged from those of traditional Republican standard-bearers.

In his presidency as in the campaign, Trump stressed his role as an outsider skilled in "the art of the deal," saying that he alone could succeed where previous presidents had failed. He declared in his inaugural address, "For too long, a small group in our nation's capital has reaped the rewards of government, while people have borne the cost." Trump also vowed to "drain the swamp" and put federal government back in the hands of the people.

He promised to nominate conservative judges, build a wall on the southern border for which Mexico would pay, deregulate, lower taxes, protect the suburbs from the lawlessness and disorder of "Democrat cities," and "Make America Great Again." How he would govern was anyone's guess. Trump had spent his career constructing or branding skyscrapers, hotels, golf courses, and casinos, publishing ghostwritten advice on how others could achieve equivalent success, and hosting a reality TV show in which he famously fired contestants who failed to satisfy his expectations.

In office, President Trump continued his pattern of unorthodox behavior. Not only did the country's forty-fifth president shatter presidential norms with his "Manichean, evidence-flouting, accountability-dodging, and institution-disdaining claims,"[82] but, during his time in office, policy announcements were often delivered via the incumbent's personal Twitter account rather than through carefully vetted speeches and statements (though Trump would eventually be banned from Twitter in connection with the events of January 6). Nonetheless, Trump also kept many of his major campaign promises, with some help from happenstance: a Republican-controlled House and Senate in the first half of his term and a Senate majority in his party's hands in his final two years in the White House.

Across his tenure in office, he delivered three Supreme Court nominees and roughly three hundred judges to the federal courts, signed a trillion-dollar tax cut, built a portion of the proposed wall along the southern border with Mexico, and, in his first three years in office, presided over an economy with record low unemployment and stock market highs. Indeed, he was especially proud of the stock market's performance, bragging about it in tweets more than 150 times during his presidency.[83] As one might expect from someone who pledged an "America First" foreign policy that disdained the value of international agreements, he withdrew the United States from the Paris Climate Accords, the Iran nuclear deal brokered by his predecessor, and the Trans-Pacific Partnership.[†] But, consistent with his unorthodox approach to politics, he also took actions more likely to be championed by the left than the right, including signing a major criminal justice reform package, banning bump stocks after they were used in mass shootings, increasing funding for historically Black colleges and universities (HBCUs), championing the creation of opportunity zones in urban centers, and suspending student loan payments. On the foreign policy front, he recognized Jerusalem as the capital of Israel and brokered a Middle East accord between Israel and the United Arab Emirates.

For soliciting the investigation of his presumed Democratic opponent by the president of Ukraine while withholding vital military aid to that country, Trump joined Bill Clinton and Andrew Johnson in the history books as the third president to be impeached but not convicted. After the Democratic-controlled House of Representatives impeached him for abuse of power and obstruction of justice, the Republican-controlled Senate acquitted him on both charges.

---

†. While the United States and the other parties had signed the Trans-Pacific Partnership in 2016, when Trump withdrew the United States from the deal in 2017, it could not go into effect. The remaining countries then banded together to form the Comprehensive and Progressive Agreement for Trans-Pacific Partnership in 2018.

Although the investigation by Special Counsel Robert Mueller into the role of Russian intervention in the 2016 US presidential campaign found that the interventions were "sweeping and systematic" and that the Trump campaign welcomed and used the help, that report concluded, "[W]hile this report does not conclude that the President committed a crime, it also does not exonerate him." After Trump proclaimed that the report "exonerated" him,[84] in a statement to the press Mueller said, "If we had confidence that the president clearly did not commit a crime, we would have said that. We did not, however, make a determination as to whether the president did commit a crime."[85]

Throughout all of this, former Indiana governor Mike Pence served as vice president in a fashion whose hallmark was loyalty. A self-proclaimed "Christian, a conservative and a Republican, in that order," Pence's electoral value to the thrice-married Trump was his appeal to evangelical voters. In making the case for the reelection of the Trump-Pence ticket, the former Indiana governor reminded evangelicals that Trump had nominated Judge Neil Gorsuch to the Supreme Court seat formerly held by the revered conservative Antonin Scalia, supported anti-abortion measures, moved the American embassy in Israel to Jerusalem from Tel Aviv, enacted tax reform, and secured the releases of Christian hostages from North Korea.[86]

At the head of the Democratic ticket was Joe Biden, a senator from Delaware from 1973 to 2009, who, before leaving the Senate to serve as vice president under President Barack Obama, had chaired both the Senate Foreign Relations Committee and the Senate Judiciary Committee. In the latter role, he superintended the defeat of Robert Bork's nomination to the Supreme Court and facilitated the placement of Clarence Thomas on it. In Thomas's confirmation hearing, a former member of his staff, Anita Hill, testified about incidents of sexual harassment by Thomas; this testimony was treated skeptically by a Judiciary Committee entirely composed of White men.

Legislative highlights of the Delawarean's time in the Senate included passage of the 1994 Violent Crime Control and Law Enforcement Act, which would prove controversial as policing tactics and criminal justice sentencing came under scrutiny in the 2016 and 2020 contests, and the 1994 Violence Against Women Act.

Prior to 2020, Biden had been a presidential also-ran. His first bid for the presidency in 1988 was derailed by charges that he had plagiarized a passage from a speech by British Labor Party leader Neil Kinnock. His second lasted until January 3, 2008, when he withdrew after placing fifth with less than 1 percent of the votes cast in the Iowa caucuses. The most memorable moment of that bid came during a 2007 debate when NBC's Brian Williams quoted a statement from the *Los Angeles Times* that said, "In addition to his uncontrolled verbosity, Biden is a gaffe machine," and then asked Biden, "Can you reassure voters in this country that you would have the discipline you would need on the world stage, Senator?" Biden's response earned not only appreciative laughter from the audience but footnotes in histories of presidential debates. "Yes," he said, smiling, before lapsing into silence.[87]

Tapped by Barack Obama to serve as his vice presidential nominee, Biden held his own comfortably in the 2008 vice presidential debate against Alaska Governor Sarah Palin and in 2012 against Wisconsin Congressperson Paul Ryan (R-WI). During Obama's eight years in office, his vice president was seen regularly at the president's side and served as Obama's liaison to their former colleagues in the Senate. Additionally, he supervised the implementation of the infrastructure section of the stimulus package passed to blunt the 2008–2009 recession, led the administration's successful push to gain Senate ratification of the New Strategic Arms Reduction Treaty (START), and played a key role in forestalling default on US debt with passage of the Budget Control Act of 2011.

Widely considered a likely successor to Obama, Biden demurred in 2016, citing his need to grieve the death of his son Beau, a rising star in Delaware politics who served as its forty-fourth attorney general (2007–2015) but succumbed to brain cancer in May 2015. "As my family and I have worked through the grieving process, I've said all along . . . it may very well be that that process, by the time we get through it, closes the window on mounting a realistic campaign for president, that it might close," Biden said. "I've concluded that it has closed."[88]

Many media commentators had counted Biden out of the running early in the 2020 Democratic primary process. Biden came in fourth in the Iowa caucuses, and an even more disappointing fifth in the New Hampshire primary. Although his placement improved in the Nevada caucuses, where he came in second on February 22, what fundamentally changed the dynamics of the race was his victory in the February 29 South Carolina primary. Not only did Biden win a near majority of votes cast, but with the overwhelming support of Black voters and the endorsement of South Carolina icon and House Majority Whip James Clyburn, he also carried every county in the state. After the delegates were apportioned on Super Tuesday, March 3, the former vice president's totals outstripped those of Vermont Senator Bernie Sanders (I-VT). Although Biden did not formally secure the nomination until June, he became his party's presumptive nominee when Sanders suspended his campaign on April 8. The 2020 contest was the nation's first between two septuagenarians, making the vice presidential choices especially important. At age seventy, Trump had been the oldest person to assume the presidency; at seventy-eight by Inauguration Day, Biden would claim that distinction if he won.[89]

After her campaign ran out of funds, California Senator Kamala Harris (D-CA), who had once been seen as a "front-runner"[90] and whose launch had been called "electrifying,"[91] dropped out of the Democratic primary process before the first votes were cast. Before doing so, she had scored debate points with a frontal assault on Biden's support for busing. "There was a little girl in California who was part of the second class to integrate her public schools, and she was bused to school every day, and that little girl was me," Harris said. Biden responded that she had mischaracterized his position and added, "If we want to have this litigated on who supports civil rights, I'm happy to do that. I was a public defender. I was not a prosecutor."[92]

That counterattack referred to Harris's tough-on-crime persona as a prosecutor. Elected district attorney of San Francisco in 2003 and attorney general of California in 2010, she had elicited controversy in 2004 when she refused to seek the death penalty against a person who had killed a police officer. But she earned praise for inaugurating a program giving first-time drug offenders the opportunity to earn a high school diploma and find employment. While attorney general, she also was responsible for $230 million in settlements with the pharmaceutical industry.[93] As part of that effort, she became friends with the attorney general of Delaware, Beau Biden, and in the process was introduced to his father, who at the time was the vice president of the United States.

By winning election to the Senate in 2016, Harris became the second Black woman and the first South Asian American person to earn that distinction. As a member of the Senate Judiciary Committee, she showcased her prosecutorial background in dexterous questioning of former Attorney General Jeff Sessions and Supreme Court nominee Brett Kavanaugh. Whether that record qualifies Harris as liberal or as more centrist depends on whether one focuses on her senatorial career or her prosecutorial career. In the Senate, she supported Medicare for All, a position she modified during her failed bid for the Democratic presidential nomination in 2019. In the 2019 Democratic presidential debates, Harris was the first to endorse the left-of-center Green New Deal.

During the primary season, Biden's promise that a woman would hold the second spot on his ticket was seen by the press as "signaling the importance of women voters to the party."[94] Awareness that the drop in voter turnout among Black Americans in 2016 may have cost Hillary Clinton the presidency[95] heightened the importance of a vice presidential nominee able to mobilize that vote. So too did the increased centrality of the issue of racial justice after the killing of George Floyd. "Harris's nomination, which followed a lengthy vetting process, sends a message about the future of the Democratic Party—and its commitment to women and Black Americans," noted *Vox*.[96] Although White women had previously been nominated to the vice presidential spot by each major party—New York Congressperson Geraldine Ferraro (D-NY) on the Democratic side in 1984 and Alaska Governor Sarah Palin on the Republican one in 2008—neither had been on a winning ticket. As press reports noted, the fifty-five-year-old Harris also gave the ticket "some generational diversity."[97]

Press response to Harris's selection focused on her appeal to those for whom racial justice was a priority. "She emerged as an outspoken voice on race—and the need for police reform—following the death of George Floyd in May and the subsequent protests it sparked around the country," noted CNN about the pick.[98] A California native, Harris recounted that "she was inspired to attend law school after joining civil rights protests with her parents," stated NBC News.[99] "A child of the Civil Rights Movement, whose parents were active in 1960s marches, Harris joined Black Lives Matter demonstrations this summer,"[100] observed *Politico*.

Biden cast his selection of Harris as evidence of his commitment to an inclusive America. "The government should look like the country," Biden said, explaining his selection of Harris. "There's a new law of physics in politics: Any country that does not engage more than half their population in sharing the full responsibilities of governance and power is absolutely going to lose."[101] His awkward inclusion of the words "in politics" and "going to lose" implied that a Democratic ticket that did not include a woman was likely to lose.

"This morning," the putative nominee of the Democratic Party said in his first joint appearance with Harris, "all across the nation, little girls woke up, especially little Black and brown girls who so often feel overlooked and undervalued in our communities, but today, today just maybe they're seeing themselves, for the first time, in a new way—as the stuff of presidents and vice presidents."[102] However, as we will argue in Chapter 7, the thought that a Black woman, an Asian American, the daughter of two immigrants might be inaugurated vice president on January 20, 2021, did not sit well with a discernible bloc of voters who believed that immigrants and people of color were threatening their birthright. Some within them were willing to employ force to protect their interests. Why and how are among the questions we will address in the coming pages.

2

What Fundamental Factors Shape Elections?

Matthew Levendusky, Kathleen Hall Jamieson, R. Lance Holbert, and Josh Pasek

This campaign isn't just about winning votes. It's about winning the heart and, yes, the soul of America.

—Joe Biden's nomination acceptance speech, August 20, 2020[1]

This election will decide whether we save the American dream or whether we allow a socialist agenda to demolish our cherished destiny. . . . Your vote will decide whether we protect law-abiding Americans or whether we give free rein to violent anarchists, agitators and criminals who threaten our citizens.

—Donald Trump's nomination acceptance speech, August 27, 2020[2]

IN 2020, THE country faced a global pandemic in which millions of Americans were infected with a novel disease that, at that time, had neither treatment nor cure. When the nation locked down to fight the virus in March, the country's economy went in a matter of weeks from boom to bust. The murder of George Floyd in May by a White police officer sparked a national reckoning over racial justice, leading to likely the nation's largest protest movement. Donald Trump's false claims of voter fraud and his refusal to accept Joe Biden's victory in the November election sparked a fourth crisis, one of democratic legitimacy. The story of 2020 cannot be told without understanding the impact these interlocking crises had on the campaigns and citizenry.

But equally important to understanding 2020 is a set of fundamental factors that shape every presidential election. Much can be gleaned from the incumbent's performance in office (i.e., retrospective voting), their popularity, and the balance of partisanship. The power of these fundamental factors is what drives the success of electoral forecasting models, which show that scholars can (at least approximately) predict election outcomes months in advance of Election Day based on a few key variables.[3] But these models do not work by magic: they allow scholars to project election outcomes because the candidates and the media environment inform voters about why and how these variables matter.[4] As we show in later chapters, that communication environment is one of the crucial pieces of the puzzle of presidential elections.

This chapter shows how such fundamental factors played out within the context of the 2020 election and helped to shape the election itself. As much as these unprecedented crises reconfigured the landscape in 2020, there was also a great deal of stability induced by underlying structural factors. Continuity, as well as change, is inherent in the story of 2020.

Retrospective Voting: Are You Better Off than You Were Four Years Ago?

In the only debate between the two major party nominees during the 1980 campaign, Ronald Reagan famously asked Americans whether they were better off than they were four years ago. This question encapsulates a truism about American elections: if voters think the incumbent president (or party) has been a good steward of the nation, that party will win another term in office.[5] Such voter assessments typically focus on two concepts, prosperity and peace—voters want a growing economy and a nation free of foreign wars.[6] In the post–World War II era, every incumbent who presided over a period of sustained economic growth and avoided an unpopular war won reelection.[7] And, apart from Al Gore in 2000, so did their heirs apparent. In contrast, if the economy falters or the country becomes bogged down in a foreign war, the incumbent party loses. The only exceptions have been George W. Bush in 2004 (the Iraq War) and Richard Nixon in 1972 (the Vietnam War).[*] Simply put, the incumbent president's stewardship of the nation is perhaps the single biggest factor behind whether or not they remain in office.

---

[*]. Of course, the Nixon case is even more complicated than it appears at first blush, as Nixon drew down US troop levels in Vietnam during his term in office. Given this, voters may have seen Nixon as working to end the war in Vietnam.

The second factor lurking beneath retrospective voting is whether promises made have been promises kept. For example, in 1992, Clinton and Perot reminded voters that George H. W. Bush had broken his 1988 pledge not to raise their taxes (he had done so in 1990 to avoid increasing the federal deficit). By contrast, in 1956 incumbent Dwight D. Eisenhower argued that he had restored peace and prosperity, having ended the war in Korea and continued the unprecedented postwar economic boom. Unable to make the same claim about the Vietnam War, and facing antiwar challengers Senators Eugene McCarthy (D-MN) and Robert Kennedy (D-NY), in 1968 incumbent Lyndon Baines Johnson stepped out of the presidential contest at the end of March.

Of course, voters also evaluate whether incumbents have kept their promises about issues beyond peace and prosperity. In 2020, the Republican Party argued that President Trump had done so in six key areas beyond the economy: promoting the right to life; supporting Israel, especially the movement of the embassy to Jerusalem; appointing conservative judges, including three Supreme Court justices, one just weeks before the election; promoting religious freedom; cutting taxes thanks to the 2017 Tax Cut and Jobs Act; and addressing the opioid crisis. As Trump himself argued throughout 2020, he also had "built the wall" along the southern border with Mexico, or at least three hundred miles of it, and had worked to put "America First." He accomplished this last goal by shifting America's international priorities, most notably by pulling out of the Paris Climate Accords and the Iran nuclear deal, pushing to renegotiate "bad" trade deals such as the North American Free Trade Agreement (NAFTA), and placing tariffs on Chinese goods. From this perspective, Trump delivered on many of his key promises to his supporters.

This was especially important to core demographic groups in Trump's coalition. Religious voters, especially evangelicals, responded favorably to his support for Israel, his promotion of the pro-life cause, and his appointment of conservative justices to the federal judiciary, including the Supreme Court. His corporate and high-income supporters welcomed the Trump tax proposals, which slashed more than a trillion dollars in taxes. His blue-collar supporters valued the renegotiated trade deals, the border wall, and the broader "America First" narrative.

Consistent with his 2016 argument that Black voters had more to gain than lose by supporting his candidacy, in his first term he signed a bipartisan criminal justice reform bill (the FIRST STEP Act), created opportunity zones in urban areas, and increased aid for historically Black colleges and universities. Such points—raised frequently at the Republican National

Convention, especially by speakers of color such as South Carolina Senator Tim Scott (R-SC)—were no doubt meant to appeal to that constituency as well as to suburban White voters, especially White women, who were put off by Trump's racially charged rhetoric (for example, his initial hesitance about disavowing the white supremacists who marched in Charlottesville, Virginia, in 2017). In many ways, at least to his core supporters, Trump had delivered what he said he would during his 2016 election and had a very plausible case for reelection.

Retrospective Voting in 2020

When judging whether the incumbent has delivered prosperity (and hence deserves reelection), most voters look not to their own pocketbooks but rather to the nation's economic health more generally, in what scholars term sociotropic voting.[8] Such patterns are especially strong when the incumbent is seeking reelection.[9] Because of the economic growth seen during his first three years in office—with GDP rising, jobs rising, and unemployment falling—in January 2020 the electoral omens appeared favorable for Trump. Indeed, reviewing the economic and polling data in February 2020, Trump's campaign team confidently predicted that reelection was effectively "in the bag" for the incumbent president, barring some then-unforeseen circumstance.[10]

The unforeseen arrived when the nation locked down to fight the novel coronavirus in March 2020 and the bottom fell out of the economy. As we discussed in Chapter 1 ("An Election Shaped by Crises"), unemployment, which had been at its lowest level since the Korean War, approached highs not seen since the Great Depression of the 1930s. While the unemployment rate fell as the fall campaign approached, it was still twice what it had been before the pandemic.

Trump's claim during the fall campaign was that the nation had weathered the worst of the coronavirus pandemic and its economic fallout and was experiencing a "V-shaped" recovery that would soon return the economy to pre-pandemic levels. Were that in fact the case, it would be good news for Trump. When voters cast their ballots, they consider how the economy performed over an incumbent's entire term in office, but they more heavily weight more recent events,[11] so a V-shaped recovery would benefit the incumbent. Of course, the economic news as the campaign heated up was quite mixed, with some headlines indicating an improving economy, while others were portending continued economic pain.[12]

While Trump argued that the recovery would be V-shaped, Biden—and many economists—argued that it was instead "K-shaped," with those at opposite ends of the pre-pandemic income spectrum experiencing radically different economic trajectories. White-collar workers at the top of the economic ladder—whose jobs could easily pivot to remote work, who owned their own homes, and who owned stocks—saw their economic fortunes improve during 2020. These individuals kept their jobs and, locked down at home, spent less money, bolstering their savings. At the same time, housing prices rose to record levels, and by late summer the stock market had recovered from its pandemic losses (though there would be further ups and downs as Election Day approached).[13] But those at the bottom of the economic ladder, who lost their jobs or were forced to work in person despite the threat of the virus, faced a much grimmer outlook. Workers who were furloughed or laid off or who got sick often quickly exhausted their savings and were facing genuine economic desperation, unable to afford food, rent, and other basic necessities.

These alternative ways of looking back on Trump's economic stewardship paint a complex picture for voters that was at the heart of the debate in the campaign. The Biden team attempted to convince voters that Trump's mismanagement of the coronavirus, and with it the economy, led to an unprecedented downturn, and hence was a key reason to remove him from office. According to Democrats, Trump inherited a growing economy from President Obama, overinflated it with a massive tax cut that disproportionately benefited the wealthy and corporations, and then wrecked it by failing to act quickly enough to minimize the effects of COVID-19. Indeed, Biden would argue throughout the campaign that it was Trump's failure on COVID that destroyed the economy, which could not be revived until the virus was under control. By contrast, Trump pointed to the strength of the pre-COVID economy as well as to his efforts to restart the economy amid the pandemic in order to argue that he was the better economic steward. He asserted that Democratic governors who were slow to reopen their states were to blame for any economic stagnation. These two messages would battle it out in the fall, with both campaigns trying to convince voters that their path was the best one.

This give-and-take highlights a fundamental truism we return to below: the messages each campaign sends about the economy help explain retrospective voting.[14] But in 2020, it also cuts somewhat deeper. In 2020, the campaigns were, in effect, telling voters to prioritize different sets of issues. Trump—knowing that the pandemic was a liability for him—largely downplayed it and claimed that the worst was behind the nation. Instead, he emphasized his economic performance. In contrast, Biden and his Democratic surrogates sought to increase the salience of the pandemic, where the public assessed Biden's capacities as exceeding Trump's. Biden argued insistently in his ads, in his convention speech, and in an interview with ABC News conducted the day after the convention's close that "in order to keep the country running and moving and the economy growing, and people employed, you have to . . . deal with the virus."[15] Campaigns change not only how voters perceive the various issues but also which issues voters see as the most crucial ones.

However, even to the extent that voters make their choices based on its health, "the economy" is not a single undifferentiated thing. Indeed, different electorates may well experience fundamentally different economies based on who they are and where they live. The most obvious example of this in 2020 is the rift between upper-income and lower-income voters, as we saw earlier in the chapter. This divide could imply that pocketbook voting might be much more likely in 2020 than in past years. Decades ago, scholars first noted that the lack of evidence for pocketbook balloting could be explained by the fact that in most cases we cannot determine whether people's personal financial circumstances changed due to government policy or because of some other idiosyncratic factor.[16] In 2020, the cause was clear. The scale of the economic collapse due to COVID-19 was unprecedented in the post–World War II United States, with millions thrown out of work as the economy shut down to slow the spread of the virus. This increased the potential that voters could credit—or blame—Trump for their own economic circumstances.

Further, it is not just one's own economic fortunes that matter for economic voting; the economic fortunes of one's geographic area are also important.[17] Indeed, midyear estimates suggested that while some areas of the country had maintained near pre-pandemic levels of unemployment, in others the jobless rate had surged to more than 30 percent.[18] As this pattern replicated nationally, voters responded differently to "the economy" depending on who they were and where they lived, reinforcing the potential heterogeneity of economic perceptions and of economic voting overall.

Of course, as we noted above, retrospective voting is not limited to economic evaluations: in 2020, Trump's handling of the COVID-19 crisis was also on the ballot. If the nation managed to get the virus under control by the election, would Trump get credit for improving the trend line, or would he face voters' wrath for the high overall levels? And would areas that saw more deaths from the virus punish the incumbent more heavily? These questions highlight that, yet again, local context might matter here as well.

Attributions of Responsibility

The attributions of responsibility that voters make for both positive and negative developments during a president's term are crucial to understanding retrospective voting. As noted above, the Trump campaign made a point of taking credit for the positive economic trends of the first three years of his presidency while dismissing those in 2020 as the product of the pandemic. Although the Trump administration was initially supportive of attempts to close businesses to keep the virus at bay, this position shifted quickly. By mid-April, federal support for lockdowns had evaporated and responsibility for most aspects of pandemic management had been transferred to the states. For example, in May, the Department of Health and Human Services released a memo asserting that states, not the federal government, bore the responsibility for testing and contact tracing: "State plans must establish a robust testing program that ensures adequacy of COVID-19 testing, including tests for contact tracing, and surveillance of asymptomatic persons to determine community spread."[19] Governors and state public health departments therefore were often the ones deciding when and how to reopen the economy and what rules would be necessary for public health.[20] This allowed the Trump administration to blame state-level actors for coronavirus outbreaks as well as for the economic fallout from mitigation efforts. At the same time, Democrats countered that this shifting of responsibility showed the failure of the Trump administration to lead during the pandemic.[21] Because American voters are quite bad at distinguishing the roles and responsibilities of state versus federal officials,[22] it is likely that voters could accept either account.

Starting in April, Trump asserted that the lockdowns were harming the economy and urged governors, particularly Democratic governors, to lift restrictions. This constituted an attempt by the president to redirect the blame for the economic fallout. By not lifting restrictions, Trump contended, they were principally responsible for harming the economy. To the extent that voters bought this narrative, they might not regard the current economic situation as a failure for the president.

Shifting responsibility for pandemic management to the states also likely had implications for evaluations of how well the president handled the pandemic. On one hand, if the governors were principally at fault, they would bear the brunt of the blame for COVID-related deaths. Yet in states with especially large outbreaks—such as Florida, Arizona, and Texas—voters may have continued to blame the president for not acting more decisively, even if governors also deserved some share of the blame. This gave the

Biden campaign an opening to persuade voters that Trump's handling of the COVID-19 pandemic—economic effects aside—was another reason to vote him out of office.

The desire to redirect blame also helps make sense of Trump's switch in position on the role of China in the spread of the virus. While initially the president praised China for its handling of the virus,[23] he also ignored warnings from Chinese officials that the pandemic was real and was spreading. China formally notified international health authorities on December 31, 2019, that a pneumonia outbreak had been identified in Wuhan, and confirmed on January 7, 2020, that those cases were associated with a novel coronavirus.[24] Once the virus began to spread in the United States, President Trump labeled it the "Wuhan virus" or the "China virus" (despite criticism that such labeling was xenophobic), and in early February 2020, he banned travel from China. During the campaign, he would repeatedly claim that had he not taken this position, a position he argued Biden had opposed, the pandemic would have been even worse.

The final unknown with respect to the pandemic was whether Operation Warp Speed—the Trump administration's plan to rapidly produce a vaccine for the coronavirus—would pay off before the election. While Trump claimed that a vaccine would soon be available, the success of the Pfizer-BioNTech vaccine was not announced until November 9, six days after the election and two days after the media projected that Biden would become the nation's forty-sixth president.[25] That said, however, as Trump trumpeted the likely success of a vaccine throughout the fall campaign, that prospect may also have weighed in Trump's favor with some voters.

Peace: Keeping Us out of (Literal and Figurative) War

Perhaps the most critical noneconomic factor bearing on a president's popularity is his ability to avoid unpopular foreign conflicts. When incumbents instigate wars that later prove unpopular—as was the case with George W. Bush and the Iraq War by 2004—voters punish them at the polls, even if they win reelection.[26] While the fight against COVID-19 was not an actual war, Trump invoked a wartime analogy by using the Defense Production Act to increase the supply of ventilators and N95 masks.[27] When he sent federal forces onto the streets of Portland, Oregon, in July, ostensibly to protect a federal courthouse from damage, the wartime analogy became inescapable. The incumbent repeatedly invoked "law and order" rhetoric after the racial justice protests began in early June, tweeting that "when the looting starts,

the shooting starts," voicing support for military-style police tactics to suppress protests, and even considering invoking the Insurrection Act to send
active-duty US military personnel into the streets.[28] He also cast protestors
as "anarchists, criminals, rioters, looters and flag burners,"[29] and, in his acceptance speech at the Republican convention, asserted that if Joe Biden was
elected, "no one will be safe."[30] The Trump campaign's conviction that it was
advantaged by a "law and order to quash chaos and violence" frame was evident on August 27, when Trump's White House aide Kellyanne Conway told
Fox and Friends, "The more chaos and anarchy and vandalism and violence
reigns, the better it is for the very clear choice on who's best on public safety
and law and order."[31]

While the forty-fifth president frequently employed "law and order" rhetoric in his 2016 campaign against Hillary Clinton, brandishing these themes
as the incumbent is quite different from doing so as a challenger completely
outside of government. In their first debate, when challenged by Trump to
say the words "law and order," Biden responded that he stood for "law and
order with justice where people get treated fairly."[32] This set up another fundamental contrast between Biden and Trump that played out throughout
the election: Trump used the protests following George Floyd's death to emphasize the theme of law and order, while Biden countered that racial justice
needed to be a key part of the mix as well. Given the nation's long history
of discrimination against Black Americans—especially at the hands of the
police—this suggests that voters' preexisting attitudes about race and discrimination would shape how they perceived these issues.

Presidential Popularity

Of course, retrospective voting is not the only factor that determines whether
a president is reelected—presidential popularity also influences the outcome.
Simply put, even controlling for economic conditions and other factors,
the more popular a president is—indicated by higher approval or better
performance in the horse-race polls—the more likely that person is to win
reelection.[33]

One limitation to this metric in 2020, just as in 2016, is that the polls
proved to be unreliable in forecasting the spread between Biden and Trump
in key states,[34] and hence Trump may well have actually been more popular
than he appeared to be. A second limitation is that it is difficult to separate
popularity from a strong economy. The better the economy is doing, net of
other factors, the more popular a president tends to be.[35] Indeed, even during

a campaign, as the economy does better, so do the incumbent's prospects.[36] But both of these effects appear to operate simultaneously—that is, even after accounting for the performance of the economy, the incumbent's popularity helps to explain election outcomes.[37]

However, even assuming that he was underpolling throughout, the striking disconnect between approval of Trump and the strong economic indicators that characterized his first three years in office upended the assumption that one was invariably yoked to the other. "Trump's approval rating is about 15 points lower than we'd predict from the historical relationship between economic evaluations and presidential approval," observed political science professor John Sides in December 2019. "Right now, about 43 percent of Americans approve of the job Trump's doing, even though unemployment is lower than economists once thought possible."[38] Treated separately from the economy, Trump's low favorability seemed to spell his political doom, as the percentage of those regarding him favorably hovered in the 30s or 40s throughout his first term in office. In general, incumbents situated below 50 percent approval tend not to win reelection, suggesting a tough campaign for President Trump.[39] Of course, as we discuss below, the polarization of the electorate means that this may no longer be as significant a factor as it once was, because—no matter the state of the economy—fewer voters will cross party lines in a high-profile election.

The Balance of Voters' Partisanship

At the macro level, retrospective factors are perhaps the most important considerations that shape whether a president wins reelection. But at the micro level, a voter's partisanship—whether they think of themselves as a Democrat, a Republican, or an independent—is the predictor of vote choice that carries the greatest weight,[40] and that relationship has strengthened considerably over time.[41] According to the 2016 exit polls, 89 percent of Democrats backed Hillary Clinton, and 88 percent of Republicans backed Donald Trump,[42] levels similar to the 2008[43] and 2012[44] elections as well.[†]

[†]. In an earlier era, with less elite polarization, there was some evidence that incumbency conditioned the effect of partisanship on vote choice, as some people would defect from their party to support the incumbent president, especially if he was popular. This view is encapsulated in Herbert F. Weisberg, "Partisanship and Incumbency in Presidential Elections," *Political Behavior* 24, no. 4 (December 2002): 339–360, doi:10.1023/A:1022558810957. But in 2020, this would almost certainly not apply given the incredible polarization of views of President Trump by party.

The same is true of 2020, with approximately nine in ten voters backing their party's nominee.[45] This individual-level pattern also holds in the aggregate, with the balance of partisanship in the electorate (i.e., the macro-partisanship) strongly predicting election outcomes.[46]

While this relationship is true, it is also somewhat reductive to say that partisanship measured on Election Day—after a months-long campaign—predicts vote choice. After all, part of the reason it does so is that campaigns are designed to prime (that is, make more salient) and shape voters' partisan loyalties. As political scientist James Campbell succinctly puts it, "Campaigns remind Democrats why they are Democrats rather than Republicans, and remind Republicans why they are Republicans rather than Democrats."[47] Part of the job of the campaign and the messaging from both sides is to "drive home" their partisans to their natural base,[48] and campaign events—such as conventions, debates, et cetera—do just that over the course of the campaign.[49] So while partisanship is a stable, long-term factor,[50] it also evolves over time. Indeed, faced with an unpopular president, some voters will even go so far as to switch their partisan identifications.[51] The fact that the proportion of survey respondents who identify as Republicans fell during the first six months of 2020—from 47 percent of the public to 39 percent (including partisan leaners), according to Gallup[52]—may suggest that some former Republicans decided that they were now independents because they were embarrassed by the president.[‡] To study the relationship between partisanship and electoral choices, we need to examine it across the scope of the campaign.

But the power of partisanship does not simply stop at vote choice. Indeed, especially in an era of polarization, partisanship fundamentally colors how individuals see the political world. Even if Democratic and Republican voters see the same objective events on the ground, they can perceive them quite differently. Because of their affiliations, Democrats and Republicans were predisposed to experience the crises of 2020—the economy, the pandemic, the protests over racial injustice, and the election's legitimacy—quite differently. Consistent with this view, CBS-YouGov polling from late August found that 67 percent of Republicans considered the state of the economy to be good, while only 11 percent of Democrats felt the same. A similar divide occurred in assessments of the acceptability of the number of COVID-19 deaths at the

---

‡. This could also be a case of differential responsiveness to surveys: Republicans are more likely to respond to surveys when the Republican candidate is doing well, and less likely to do so when he is doing poorly. On this idea, see Andrew Gelman et al., "The Mythical Swing Voter," *Quarterly Journal of Political Science* 11, no. 1 (April 2016): 103–130, doi:10.1561/100.00015031.

time. Where 57 percent of Republicans found the number acceptable, just 10 percent of Democrats did, as did 33 percent of independents.[53] Partisanship provides a fundamental lens through which voters saw these crises.

The Messaging and Media Environment

These broad structural factors—the health of the economy, whether the nation is at war or peace, the president's popularity, and the balance of partisanship in the electorate—largely drive campaign outcomes. But if voters simply looked at the confluence of these factors to make their decisions, their preferences would be static and would shift only in response to changes in these variables. Instead, polling data tend to track numerous changes in preferences during the pre-election period. To explain this apparent discrepancy, political scientists Robert Erikson and Christopher Wlezien note that "it is the campaign itself that somehow primes and/or enlightens voters about the economy."[54] In other words, campaigns provide a learning environment where individuals pick up cues about the fundamental variables that help them arrive at their decisions. And here the next key structural variable enters the picture: the campaigns' messages and media coverage. If we want to understand *how* these factors drive electoral choices, we need to attend to the media environment.

As an example of this phenomenon, political scientist Lynn Vavreck explains why incumbents typically win when they are advantaged by the economy:

> The economy matters because the candidate who benefits from it talks about it a lot during the campaign, and this makes voters more aware of the condition [of the economy] and this candidate's relationship to it. Why is it so difficult for a challenger to defeat an economically advantaged candidate? Because finding the right issue onto which the electoral agenda can be reset is difficult, and candidates are challenged by it.[55]

When a candidate fails to prime the country's strong economic performance under an administration of which he was a part, as was the case with Democratic nominee Al Gore, that person will fail to benefit from it to the extent that political science models anticipate.[56] Economic factors thus shape election outcomes in part because the campaigns spend so much time and effort ensuring that they do. Media messages help shape consumer sentiments,[57] which in turn shape electoral choices. The messages that campaigns promulgate—which are reinforced by the mass media[58] and received by susceptible potential voters—shape how the structural factors map back onto voters' decision rules.

Messages can also facilitate or frustrate efforts to paint the opposing candidate as an extremist. In 1972, McGovern lost control of the messaging environment after the Nixon campaign painted him as the candidate of "acid, amnesty, and abortion"; in 2020, Biden attempted to thwart Republican efforts to employ similar tactics. When "Defund the police"§ became a rallying cry to Black Lives Matter protesters, the former vice president went out of his way to emphasize that he did not support that policy but instead advocated tougher accountability for police, and he noted that Trump's proposed budget would cut police funding. Likewise, in the face of claims that he was a puppet of the left wing of his party, Biden remained steadfast in opposition to decriminalizing illegal entry into the United States and did not support a "Medicare for All" health insurance plan, instead arguing that the country should build on the existing Affordable Care Act.

The consensus from the literature is that messaging effects matter. However, because communication effects generated in the hypercompetitive context of a presidential campaign tend to be small and short-lived,[59] such effects exist primarily on the margins.[60] That said, if a single message from a candidate or a campaign ad does not have much of an effect,[61] the aggregation of messages can be decisive, especially in a close election.[62] As the campaigns press a particular theme—for example, that Trump should be reelected because of his handling of the economy, or should be voted out of office because of his handling of the pandemic—it can alter electoral choices. Decisions concerning which issues to raise and how to frame those issues—for example, whether the summer's Black Lives Matter protests are about a quest for racial justice or about law and order—shape what issues become most salient and how voters perceive those issues. To understand how voters make up their minds, we need to carefully study the messages coming from the campaigns.

Of course, the message environment is not singular but multifaceted and complex, in at least two key ways. First, because presidential elections

---

§. While the phrase "defund the police" was used somewhat differently by different activists, in general, it refers to efforts to shift funding currently allocated to police departments to other social service agencies. For more on the background of this term, see Rashawn Ray, "What Does 'Defund the Police' Mean and Does It Have Merit," Brookings Institution *FixGov* blog, June 19, 2020, https://www.brookings.edu/blog/fixgov/2020/06/19/what-does-defund-the-police-mean-and-does-it-have-merit/.

are decided by the Electoral College and not the national popular vote, candidates focus their messages on a small set of battleground states.[63] As Hillary Clinton found to her dismay in 2016, even if you win the national popular vote by more than 2.8 million votes, you will not become president if you do not assemble an Electoral College majority. As a result, campaigns focus much of their messaging—and other campaign activities—on a particular set of states, because their voters are the ones needed to become president.

Second, it is not just the messages from campaigns themselves that matter, but how they are covered and carried in the press. Trump and Biden can speak directly to voters through digital platforms such as their websites, their social media accounts, their own apps, paid advertising, and campaign media events (e.g., debates, conventions). While such direct channels are important, for most voters information about the candidates and their campaigns is filtered through the news media. But unlike in an earlier era, "the news media" is not just one thing anymore, and different outlets will cover the election quite differently.[64] As a result, it is essential to know which types of media people consume (recognizing, of course, that such consumption decisions are endogenous to people's preferences). For example, partisan outlets—such as Fox News, Breitbart, or MSNBC—cover some issues extensively and ignore others, and tend to slant their campaign coverage, favoring one side or the other, as befits their more partisan nature.[65]

We also know that the coverage offered in legacy print outlets (and their digital representations)—especially high-quality newspapers such as the *New York Times*, the *Washington Post*, and the *Wall Street Journal*—is far more detailed than what is available on television,[66] and hence voters who are more ensconced in traditional print outlets exist in a quite different information environment. And of course, as we forecast in Chapter 1 and will argue at greater length in Chapter 4 ("The Electorates' Communication Dynamics"), the mix of sources voters consume may matter as well. Citizens who consume a wide variety of media outlets offering a diversity of perspectives approached the 2020 presidential campaign from a unique vantage point compared with those who were enveloped in a one-sided, highly partisan information world. In short, voters' media diets affect their decision-making in an election season.

What Factors Make 2020 Unique?

The factors that we discussed to this point—the economy, whether the country is at war or peace, the president's popularity, voter partisanship, and the messaging environment—have mattered in every election during the post–World War II period. As a result, any serious study of election outcomes must carefully consider their influence. But in the unique electoral landscape of 2020, there is another set of factors that takes on even greater importance in this election than in previous contests.

The Increasing Salience of Partisan Identification

It is a truism to remark that America is increasingly ideologically divided, especially at the elite level (i.e., among elected officials).[67] Such elite polarization has, in turn, made partisanship become more salient to ordinary voters.[68] Americans' partisan identities are now sufficiently important that they color how we see the political world and engage with political facts,[69] even seemingly objective ones such as the state of the economy.[70]

As a result, voters perceive the actual fundamentals, especially the state of the economy, through the lens of their partisanship and expected vote choice.[71] This means that in the case of 2020, even as the economy was recovering, many Democrats likely were not disposed to give Trump credit for it. Likewise, even as the economy performed well below the levels set before the pandemic, many Republicans may well have remained committed to their belief that, compared to Biden, Trump was better able to handle the economy.[72] Following the same logic, other factors—such as the incumbent's handling of the pandemic, or the protests, or any other issue—also likely reflect the influence of partisanship and vote choice. Because partisanship is so powerful, it may have muted the influence of other structural factors on vote choices in 2020.

This pattern has played out with respect to presidential approval more generally in recent years. As previously discussed, presidential approval has historically been a function of the health of the economy and whether the nation was at war or peace.[73] But more recently this relationship has become weaker, with those from the president's party approving and those from the other party disapproving of the incumbent, regardless of the true state of the world.[74] This same tendency exists more broadly, and it likely shapes how citizens interpret the government's response to the pandemic at both the national and state levels. Republicans will be more likely to credit Trump for his successes in the pandemic (such as banning travel from China, or Operation Warp Speed), whereas Democrats will focus on his failures. Similarly, voters may also be more likely to approve of state-based action if the governor is of their party. Perception, more than reality, may well be the key issue here.

This has another important implication: the strengthening of partisanship and related group primes may render other fundamental factors somewhat less important. Because partisanship so strongly predicts vote choice in contemporary elections, there is simply less room for other factors to matter. Further, because partisanship shapes perceptions of these other factors (the state of the economy, presidential popularity, etc.), voting is overdetermined. In other words, it is very difficult to pull apart which factor causes someone to vote a particular way, because these factors are all so interconnected (we return to this point, and its implications for our study, in Chapter 3, "Not One Electorate, but Many").

But there is another consequence of this point as well: partisanship and candidate choice (which, again, are fundamentally linked) will likely shape how voters perceive our crises. As we discussed earlier in this chapter and the last, Trump and Biden framed the crises in starkly different terms. Given this, voters will likely perceive them in ways in line with their partisanship and these candidate messages. In short, part of the effect of each crisis is not simply whether it affected the election but how it did so, and how that varies based on voters' underlying partisan and other identities.

Stronger Group Identity Priming

Not only is partisanship increasingly salient, but so too are our group identities, especially in an election with President Trump as a candidate. To say that these identities shape our vote choice is nothing new: such claims can be found from the earliest academic studies of campaigns and elections up through those conducted today.[75] Traditionally, scholars looked at how membership in various sociodemographic groups shaped vote choice (e.g., how social class shapes vote choice). More contemporary scholarship tends to focus on identification with various groups and how this affects vote choice and attitudes—what political scientists Christopher Achen and Larry Bartels call the "group theory of democracy,"[76] noting that while membership in and identification with a particular group overlap, they are not synonymous. It is those identities, more than the particular group memberships per se, that matter.

Perhaps the most obvious group identity in politics is one's partisan identity, which powerfully shapes vote choice both directly (as discussed earlier) and indirectly through the media outlets people choose to consume,[77] the levels of partisan-motivated reasoning in which they engage,[78] and so forth.

So, for example, Republicans were more likely to be pessimistic about their own economic prospects during the Obama years than during the Trump administration, consistent with our argument above.

Nevertheless, there are still many politically relevant identities beyond partisanship.[79] During the 2016 campaign, Trump worked hard to prime White identity—a sense of common fate among non-Hispanic Whites.[80] This was made most clear in Trump's slogan: he declared that he would "Make America Great Again," harking back to a more traditional period when White Christians were the unquestioned majority in the nation, and the only ones controlling the levers of political power. He also promised that his agenda would put "America First," reviving a nationalist and isolationist tag line long associated with anti-immigrant tendencies. The incumbent further implied that Whites were losing out in the contemporary United States by emphasizing the threats posed by immigrants from Latin America and majority-Muslim societies, as well as foreign adversaries such as China, Iran, and North Korea. Indeed, one of the best predictors of whether someone would vote for Trump in 2016 (aside from partisanship, of course) was this sense of racial and ethnic animus among Whites,[81] as well as the sense that once-dominant groups (i.e., White men) were losing out, also known as status threat.[82] In the 2020 campaign—especially with debates over police brutality, the Black Lives Matter movement, and the role of race in American history— these identities once again came to the fore. As we show in the chapters that follow, attempts by Trump and Biden to prime and de-prime racial identity, as well as a sense of status threat, shaped not only electoral choices in 2020 but also how voters perceived the broader crisis of democratic legitimacy that followed.

Questions About Electoral Legitimacy

In normal times, one does not need to question whether presidential election results will be accepted as legitimate by both parties. Indeed, even in the wake of elections that may have been tainted by fraud (e.g., the 1960 election, especially in Illinois) or were affected by ballot design errors (e.g., the 2000 election in Florida),[83] the losing candidate graciously accepted the outcome. President Trump, however, called such norms into question. Though he won the 2016 election, Trump promulgated the false claim that millions of illegal ballots were cast for Hillary Clinton. During a September 2020 press conference, he forecast that he might not accept the 2020 election outcome if he lost. Even after states had certified their votes and Biden was the clear winner of the election, President Trump refused to acknowledge this outcome, setting up our fourth and final crisis: the crisis of democratic legitimacy.

In the months leading up to the 2020 election, Trump regularly asserted—without evidence—that mail-in ballots were rife with fraud. This rhetoric would create a perfect storm in November. Republicans, less worried about the pandemic and skeptical about voting by mail given Trump's claims, were more likely to cast their ballots in person on Election Day. Democrats, who were more worried about COVID-19 and hence more nervous about voting in person, disproportionately voted by mail.

Because mail-in ballots take longer to verify and count than those cast in person, the early returns on election night had Trump up in key states. But as those states counted their mail-in ballots in the days that followed, Biden took the lead and won the critical states to secure the Electoral College majority. Election experts and officials noted that the election night totals would change as mail ballots were counted, and preliminary totals on November 3 would likely be misleading.[84] But this argument also fit into Trump's claims about voter fraud: to his supporters, Trump's victory was being stolen from him with fraudulent mail-in ballots. This pattern led many Trump supporters to view Biden's election as illegitimate, with important consequences that we will discuss in Chapter 9 ("'Stop the Steal'").

But as we argued in Chapter 1, it is not simply that Trump undercut the legitimacy of the election; he also fueled and fanned the flames of intolerance in ways that intersected with this delegitimization. He did so by fomenting racial animus throughout his presidency, and by legitimizing violence: telling rally-goers to "knock the crap" out of protestors, telling police to rough up criminal suspects, and tweeting that "when the looting starts, the shooting starts,"[85] a phrase initially uttered by a police chief during the civil rights era. His initial refusal to condemn white supremacists in Charlottesville and his rhetoric in the first debate—telling the Proud Boys to "stand back and stand by"—invite the possibility that taking things into their own hands, with violence if need be, was an option his supporters thought was on the table.

The world saw these fears dramatically play out in real time on January 6, 2021, when a mob of Trump supporters stormed the US Capitol to disrupt the pro forma certification of Joe Biden as the winner of the 2020 election. So just as the 2020 election was birthed in violence in Charlottesville, it closed in violence at the Capitol. Even after it was clear that Biden had won, and more than sixty courts had rejected as baseless the Trump campaign's lawsuits alleging election tampering and fraud, President Trump continued to claim that the election had been stolen from him. Because the president continued to promote this false narrative, and it was amplified by right-wing media and social media, Republicans became convinced that he was correct and that Biden was a usurper. Some of the president's most ardent supporters took this argument to its logical end and attempted to prevent certification of Biden as president, with tragic consequences: the 2020 election ended the United States' long run of peaceful transitions of power. As we discuss in the final chapters of the book, this means that the consequences of this election leave us in a fundamentally different, and darker, place than the other elections in living memory.

3

Not One Electorate, but Many

THE MULTIPLE ELECTORATES OF 2020

Josh Pasek and Matthew Levendusky

*I could stand in the middle of Fifth Avenue and shoot some-
body and I wouldn't lose voters.*
—Donald Trump, January 23, 2016[1]

PUBLIC POLLING THROUGHOUT 2020 revealed remarkable stability.
National measures of presidential job approval and vote choice hewed to a
tight range and seemed only weakly responsive to the crises and events that
characterized a tumultuous year (Figure 3.1). Even looking back across the
entirety of the Trump presidency, presidential favorability and approval were
essentially static.* Despite all that happened during Trump's four years in
office—the Muslim ban, Charlottesville, the crisis along the southern border,
the Mueller Report, Trump's impeachment, and much more—the president's
approval ratings changed only at the margins. This consistency echoed a
long-standing theme of the contemporary political era: Americans are highly
polarized and deeply entrenched, and few—if any—voters were left to be
persuaded. From this perspective, Trump's claim that he "could stand in the
middle of Fifth Avenue and shoot somebody and . . . wouldn't lose voters,"
cited in the epigraph to this chapter, seems prescient.

---

*. Figure 3.1 is based on all polls gathered from FiveThirtyEight.com. The site assembled 10,009
polls of job approval during the Trump presidency and 1,628 polls of two-party vote preferences
from the 2020 election. Job approval is calculated as (Approval / (Approval + Disapproval))
and two-party vote preferences is calculated as (Biden / (Trump + Biden)). Polls were weighted
based on the square root of their sample sizes. Trend lines are based on generalized additive
models, better known as GAMs (for more on GAMs and our modeling strategy more generally, see the Appendix).

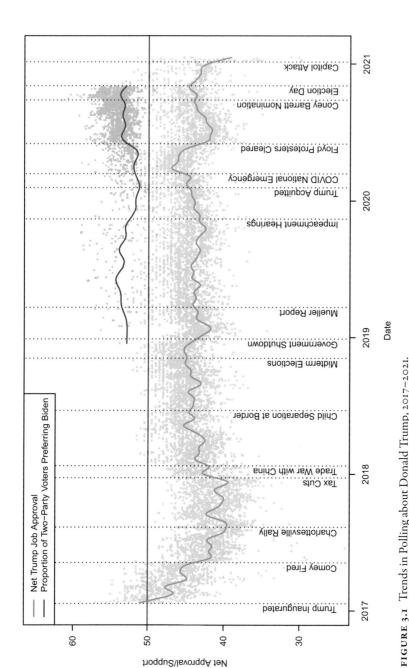

FIGURE 3.1 Trends in Polling about Donald Trump, 2017–2021.
Historical polling data on presidential approval and 2020 vote preferences throughout the Trump presidency. Green dots show net approval ratings for Donald Trump calculated as (approve − disapprove)/(approve + disapprove) and purple dots show the proportion of two-party votes favoring Biden in surveys presenting Biden and Trump as the opposing candidates. The green line tracks the average approval rating for President Donald Trump across his term, based on a GAM regression, weighted by the number of respondents in the survey. The purple line shows the average proportion of two-party voters preferring Biden in pre-election polls. Key events of Trump's term are shown with dashed lines. Data come from FiveThirtyEight.com.

The reasons behind the vast and stable contemporary partisan cleavage have been the subject of considerable scholarship. Researchers have noted the growth of affective polarization,[2] the central importance of partisan identity,[3] and the increasing alignment of issue attitudes and identity groups with political party affiliation,[4] as we discussed in Chapter 2 ("What Fundamental Factors Shape Elections?"). These trends have been further fueled by declining institutional trust,[5] geographic segmentation,[6] the availability of polarized media outlets,[7] and digital tools that have enhanced Americans' ability to both interact with like-minded others[8] and seek viewpoint-reinforcing information.[9] The result is an environment in which Americans are less likely to know those across the political divide and less likely to respect information that challenges their own viewpoints.

Further, Trump himself was a polarizing figure. His rhetoric and actions in office were loved by some and reviled by others, while few were indifferent to him. With the incumbent the presumptive Republican presidential nominee, the presidential vote of many was locked in place regardless of the identity of the Democratic standard-bearer. We saw evidence of this when we first recruited our panelists in late 2019 and early 2020. At that time, we asked them which candidate they planned to support in the November 2020 presidential election. Because the Democratic Party's primaries had not yet even begun when we started recruiting our panelists, we asked them to select from three possibilities: (1) "I am almost certain to vote for Donald Trump no matter who the Democrats nominate for president," (2) "I am almost certain to vote against Donald Trump no matter who the Democrats nominate for president," or (3) "I may vote for or against Donald Trump depending upon whom the Democrats nominate for president." In a subsequent wave, we asked how they had voted in 2016: had they supported Hillary Clinton, Donald Trump, or a third-party candidate, or had they not voted? We can use these two measures to get a sense of how much preferences changed across our study.[†] In Table 3.1, we show the percentage of each group who ultimately backed either Trump or Biden in the November 2020 election; we also include their responses from the first wave of the study, shortly after Biden clinched the nomination.

---

† Technically, the 2016 recall item is a measure of how much they changed since that election. But because we asked the item more than three years after that election (in early 2020), it may well be subject to some imperfect recall, and hence better reflects what subjects thought as of early 2020.

Table 3.1 Candidate Preference Stability over Time.

Ultimate 2020 Decision	Response at Recruitment			Choice in 2016				Preference in Wave 1		
	For Trump	Against Trump	Depends	Trump	Clinton	Neither voter	Nonvoter	Trump	Biden	Neither
Trump voter	93.0%	3.2%	47.6%	90.3%	4.6%	32.8%	32.5%	88.3%	3.1%	22.6%
Biden voter	1.6%	88.1%	34.8%	7.0%	92.3%	55.0%	38.4%	4.5%	90.7%	39.2%
Neither voter	0.7%	1.3%	2.5%	1.0%	0.6%	6.6%	1.8%	1.0%	0.5%	7.1%
Nonvoter	4.7%	7.4%	15.2%	1.7%	2.5%	5.6%	27.4%	6.2%	5.7%	31.1%
Total	100.0%	100.0%	100.0%	100.0%	100.0%	100.0%	100.0%	100.0%	100.0%	100.0%
N	15453	18662	11068	16700	14795	2697	11088	21070	19669	4540
% in category	34.2%	41.3%	24.5%	36.9%	32.7%	6.0%	24.5%	46.5%	43.4%	10.0%

Cell entries indicate who voted for a particular candidate in 2020, based on their candidate preferences at recruitment (left-hand panel), how they said they voted in 2016 (middle panel), and their response in wave 1 (right-hand panel). Cells give column percentages.

Despite everything that happened in 2020, vote preferences changed little over that year. Even before Joe Biden had won a single Democratic primary, many voters knew how they would cast their ballots. In our recruitment study, 68.2 percent both knew whether they would vote for or against Trump and did not change from this point through the election, despite all that happened in the interim—the emergence of COVID, the economic collapse, the racial reckoning, and the debate about the legitimacy of the election and so forth. And 90.3 percent of those who had expressed a preference for one of the two candidates in the recruitment wave ultimately voted that way. The same pattern emerges looking at the 2016 behavior: 63.4 percent reported both selecting one of the major-party nominees and holding to that preference in the two elections, and 91.2 percent of those who reported voting for a major-party nominee in 2016 reported a vote for the same party's nominee in 2020. By the time Democrats settled on a nominee, 80.5 percent of our respondents expressed preferences that matched their final choices.

Few would be surprised by a finding that stability more than change characterizes voters' preferences, as it fits with our discussion in Chapter 2 about the dominance of partisanship in contemporary political behavior. It is noteworthy, however, that Trump started with slightly more support than Biden. But over the course of the election, not only were Biden voters slightly more loyal, but more of those who had not expressed a preference at the outset moved toward Biden. This phenomenon highlights the importance of understanding the campaign dynamics that we address in this book, and the changes that occur, even in an era of stability. Yet, despite this seeming stability, the winner and loser were far from preordained, especially in a year with so much upheaval. Instead, the predetermination with which large segments of the public entered the campaign served to highlight the groups that were, in fact, open to changing their minds. Those people whose attitudes and votes could be persuaded may have been few in number but were great in consequence exactly because small shifts in their decisions about whether and how to vote were disproportionately consequential. Hence, uncommitted voters were at once elusive and seminal.

Who Are These Distinct Electorates, and How Can We Identify Them?

In making sense of the 2020 election, it helps to distinguish those who were susceptible to persuasion—either because they were not sure they would turn out to vote or because they were not certain which candidate they would support—from those who were sure of both. Our panel design makes it possible to tease these groups apart, thereby revealing the attributes of solidified voters as well as the nature of those who were susceptible to influence. To do so, we adopted an epidemiological approach that focused on voting behavior as a key outcome. In short, we aimed to understand the differences between people who voted in different ways rather than the factors that "caused" them to vote a particular way (see the Appendix for more discussion of this point).

We initially grouped individuals into four categories based on whether they voted for Trump (44.7 percent), voted for Biden (45.4 percent), voted for a non-major-party candidate (1.4 percent), or did not vote (8.5 percent).[‡] Among those who voted for Trump or Biden, we differentiated those who were rock-solid in their support from those who wavered. We did so by examining responses to three items that were asked across every pre-election wave: (1) how likely they were to vote in the general election, (2) whom they would vote for "if the election were held today," and (3) how certain they were that they would end up voting for that candidate. Respondents were classified as unwavering supporters if the answers to these three questions consistently indicated that they would definitely be voting, that they were very certain for whom they would vote, and that their choice at every point in time reflected their eventual behavior. Once early voting had begun, respondents who indicated that they had already voted for their preferred candidate were treated as definite voters who were certain about their preferences.

This approach provides what is likely a conservative estimate of the number of individuals who were fully committed to one candidate or another. Respondents who completed all waves needed to provide a specific pattern of answers for as many as twenty-two questions to be considered an unwavering supporter of their preferred candidate.[§] Nonetheless, 43.8 percent of weighted respondents could be classified this way, composed of 48.1 percent of those who voted for Trump (totaling 21.5 percent of weighted respondents) and 49.1 percent of those who voted for Biden (totaling 22.3 percent of

---

‡. People who voted but left the presidential ballot blank were classified as nonvoters. All percentages were calculated with weights.

§. Individuals who failed to answer one or more of these questions had their values imputed before the measure was calculated (for details on the imputation procedure, see the Online Appendix). Individuals who had already voted were treated in subsequent waves as certain voters who were definitely going to vote, with a preference matching the person they reported voting for.

weighted respondents). Respondents who did not report a consistent un-wavering preference for a single candidate were instead regarded as wavering voters. Notably, around half of these unwavering respondents expressed less-than-confident preferences before Biden was selected as the Democratic nominee (24.3 percent of all respondents, composed of 11.8 percent who de-cided on Trump and 12.6 percent who decided on Biden around this time). It is unclear, however, whether these preferences were actually settled by Biden's choice as the Democratic nominee or would have solidified similarly regard-less of who was nominated.

The wavering category included many individuals who were relatively set in their choices. For instance, 11.0 percent of respondents wavered by only a single answer from this pattern of responses (e.g., by saying in a single wave that they "probably" instead of "definitely" would vote), and an additional 6.2 percent wavered with only two different answers. The wavering group also includes the 1.5 percent of respondents who never mentioned an intention to vote for either of the two major-party candidates, a position that could also be regarded as fixed in preference. Yet some individuals were more fluid in their responses: 8.5 percent of respondents vacillated between the two major-party candidates even after Biden won the primaries. Although by this measure there weren't many classic "swing" voters in our study, the propor-tion there was far larger than the election margin in any of the states on which we focused.

For the purposes of analysis, wavering individuals could be sorted into four distinct groups: people who were persuaded to vote for Biden, people who were persuaded to vote for Trump, people who ended up voting for a minor-party candidate (more commonly known as a third-party candidate), and people who did not vote for president. Among wavering Trump and Biden supporters, we can also further subdivide them into two groups: those who were inconsistent or uncertain in their preferences (Wavering—Choice) and those who wavered only in their self-reported likelihood of voting (Wavering—Turnout). Since these groups were similar in most respects, that distinction was not relevant for most of our analyses, and unless otherwise noted, we collapse across them in our analyses.

Overall, 21.5 percent of weighted respondents were unwavering Trump voters, 23.2 percent were wavering Trump voters (8.0 percent Choice and 15.2 percent Turnout), 23.1 percent were wavering Biden voters (9.8 percent Choice and 13.3 percent Turnout), 22.3 percent were unwavering Biden voters, and the remaining individuals were either nonvoters (8.5 percent) or minor-party voters (1.4 percent). Because the group of nonvoters and the group of minor-party voters are quite modest in size and demographically similar, unless otherwise noted we group them together in our analyses. Categorizing voters by whether they vacillated only in their propensity to turn out or also in their choice reveals that around a third of the wavering voters for each candidate were at least somewhat uncertain about their choices. While the proportions of individuals voting for Trump and Biden differed slightly due to different overall state vote shares, the segments that could be identified in each of these categories were similar (Figure 3.2).

In the rest of this chapter, we consider how these groups of Americans— unwavering and wavering Trump or Biden voters, as well as minor-party voters and nonvoters—differ in composition, political affiliation, experiences, attitudes, patterns of media use, and so forth. We also explore how and when they settled on their ultimate decision and cast their ballots.

Demographic Composition of the Electorates

The different electorates are characterized by distinct groups of individuals. Consistent with work by political science professor Liliana Mason,[10] we find that Americans are increasingly sorted not only on partisan grounds but also with respect to other social identities. In addition to race, religion, and ethnicity, which have historically been important sources of political cleavage,[11] there are stark newer differences by gender and education level. However, while upper- and lower-income voters once differed dramatically in their partisan preferences,[12] that pattern is no longer as true as it once was.

In Figure 3.3, we show how various demographics map onto electorate membership. On the left-hand side (the bar chart), we show how a given demographic varies by electorate. On the right-hand side, we show the relationship between the Trump-Biden split (x-axis) and what fraction of the group wavered in their choice (y-axis). Together, these tell us not only how a demographic affects candidate choice but also how certain that group was. Take, for example, gender, which is the first row of Figure 3.3. The left-hand side shows that men were more likely to prefer Trump, while women were more likely to prefer Biden, consistent with arguments about the gender gap. The right-hand side shows that both genders were equally likely to be unwavering in their support for their candidate. In the second row, where we show the effects for education, we see not only that Biden voters were better-educated on average but also that those better-educated voters were more likely to be unwavering than less-educated groups. So, Biden's better-educated voters were somewhat more locked in for him, even if they were fewer in number.

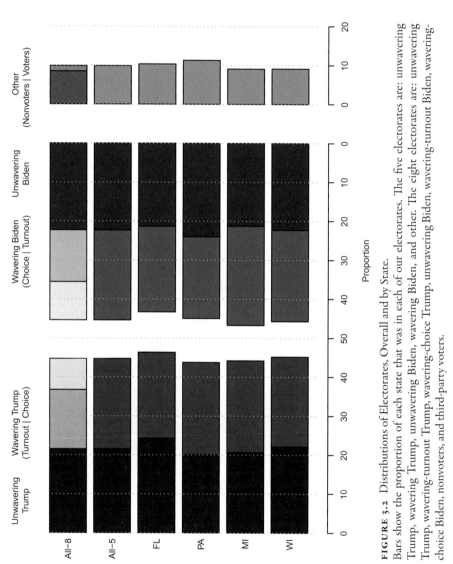

FIGURE 3.2 Distributions of Electorates, Overall and by State.
Bars show the proportion of each state that was in each of our electorates. The five electorates are: unwavering Trump, wavering Trump, unwavering Biden, wavering Biden, and other. The eight electorates are: unwavering Trump, wavering-turnout Trump, wavering-choice Trump, unwavering Biden, wavering-turnout Biden, wavering-choice Biden, nonvoters, and third-party voters.

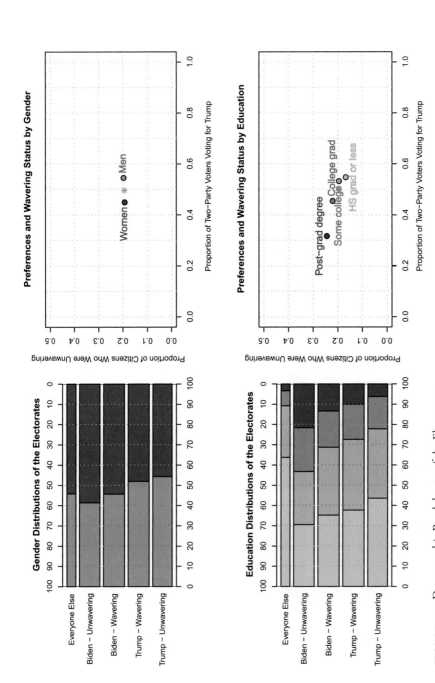

FIGURE 3.3 Demographic Breakdowns of the Electorates.
In the left-hand column, we show the demographic composition of each electorate. In each row, we show this distribution for a different demographic trait (e.g., gender, education, etc.). In the right-hand column, we show what fraction of each demographic group was wavering vs. unwavering in their support (y-axis), and the proportion of the two-party vote share in that group that was cast for Trump.

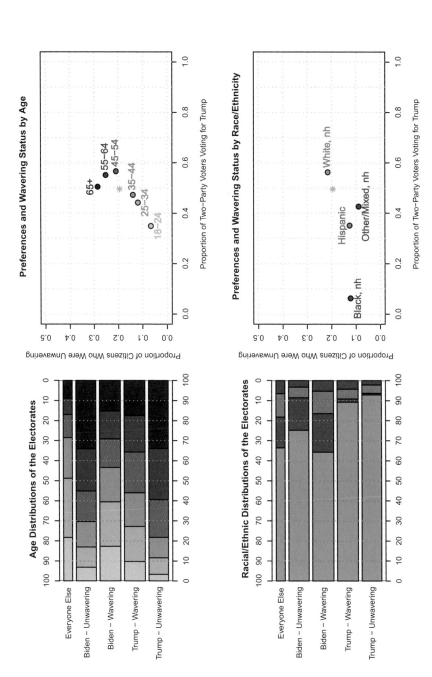

FIGURE 3.3 *Continued*

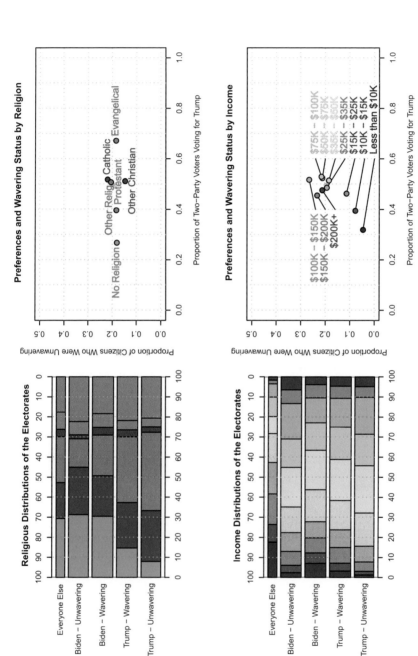

FIGURE 3.3 *Continued*

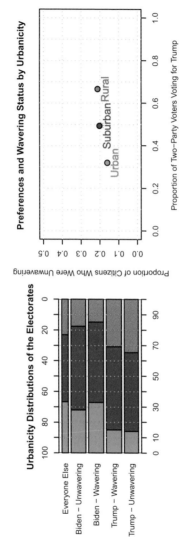

FIGURE 3.3 *Continued*

And while increases in age were closely linked with unwavering preferences, choices of Americans of different age groups reflected a curvilinear relationship, with the youngest Americans most likely to support Biden, middle-aged individuals tending to support Trump, and older individuals splitting relatively evenly in their preferences (row 3; as we discuss in the Appendix, "Our Data and Analytical Strategy," while the oldest voters favored Biden, those just slightly younger favored Trump, producing this net even split).

Demographic differences between the candidates' supporters in 2020 typically served to reinforce preferences for each party that had emerged in prior years. There was nothing novel about the fact that most non-White voters preferred Biden, for instance (Figure 3.3, row 4), nor that evangelical Christians strongly backed Trump (row 5). The proportion of White Americans supporting Republicans has been growing since the 1960s,[13] and a religiosity gap was already widening by the early 1990s.[14] Some of the differences observed during this cycle did, however, reflect the changing composition of the parties, such as the relatively modest and nonlinear relationships between income and preferences (row 6) and the growing divide on urbanicity (row 7). But if there was a theme in the relations between demography and choice in 2020, it was that the year would evidence an ever-deepening identity divide between the parties.

The distinctions between wavering and unwavering individuals who eventually supported each of the candidates reflect a mixture of a few key tendencies. For instance, the relatively static choices of older Americans likely stem from a sort of path-dependence in their preferences. Habitual support for a particular political party over a lifetime coupled with experience navigating the voting system may have instilled in these individuals a confidence in their choices and likelihood of turnout not yet developed in younger citizens. The tendency of Black voters to waver in their reported preferences, as we discuss in Chapter 7 ("Law and Order vs. Law and Order with Racial Justice"), likely illustrates increased uncertainty that they would make it to the polls and a lack of confidence in Biden earlier in the campaign cycle. It also could reflect the suasory power of Trump's attacks on Biden's championing of the 1990s crime bill, the Republican ads suggesting that Biden was taking Black voters for granted, and Trump's reiterations of his record of accomplishments for the Black community. These uncertainties and the push and pull of the messaging increased the susceptibility of Black voters even though their behaviors could be largely predicted in advance.

A good deal of political science theory, going back to foundational works from the postwar period, led us to expect that those most likely to be unwavering would have the most consistent set of demographic identities—for example, a southern White male evangelical Christian, as all of those identities should push him toward voting for Trump.[15] In contrast, those who were cross-pressured (i.e., a highly educated woman living in a rural area) or ambivalent should have a harder time deciding how and whether to vote, while those whose preferences are consistent and clear should have an easier time making up their minds.

Indeed, as expected, some demographics or combinations of demographics made it easy to predict whether voters would prefer Trump or Biden, presuming that they did indeed vote for one of the two. But some individuals with a predisposition to vote for Biden or Trump might end up not voting or might be inconsistent in their support. Recognizing this allows us to test how demographic cross-pressures relate to wavering and unwavering support as well as to the tendency to turn out for a particular candidate. The cross-pressures theory would suggest that individuals with the strongest demographic propensity to vote for one candidate or another would disproportionately fall into our unwavering category, whereas wavering voters would be overrepresented among those whose demographic identities yielded a moderate probability of supporting each nominee.

To test how cross-pressures related to our electorates, we estimated a logistic regression predicting whether voters who turned out for one of the major-party candidates had selected Trump as a function of their demographic attributes.[**] We then generated estimates for how likely it was that each respondent to the survey would have voted for Trump presuming that they voted for one of the two major-party nominees. That is, we calculated predicted probabilities for all survey respondents regardless of whether they voted or for whom. And finally, we estimated the likelihood that individuals with any given set of preferences would fall into each of our electorates.

Here, and throughout the book, we use generalized additive models (GAMs) to study how our variables relate to one another. The advantage of using a GAM-based approach is that it allows us to model a flexible (i.e., potentially nonlinear) relationship between the variables of interest. In the Appendix, we describe the advantages of this GAM-based approach in much more detail, and we refer interested readers there for more detail. For readers

---

**. Demographic variables were inserted both individually and in all possible two-way interactions. Data were subsetted to respondents who voted for one of the two candidates to calculate parameters, but predicted probabilities were generated for all respondents regardless of vote status.

uninterested in the details, we simply note that one chief advantage of this approach is that we can present straightforward graphical displays of our results, rather than asking readers to slog through lengthy tables of regression coefficients. This makes our results much easier, and more straightforward, to understand. Figure 3.4 presents one such graphical display.

These findings provide mixed support for the notion that more consistent directional group memberships will yield unwavering voters. As expected, individuals who were predicted to vote for Biden based on their demographic attributes were indeed more likely to do so; a parallel pattern emerges for those predicted to vote for Trump. Of course, because the model uses demographics to predict vote choice, this is hardly a surprise. But the results did not consistently validate the expectation that voters whose identities pushed most strongly in a consistent direction would be disproportionately likely to express unwavering support compared with those

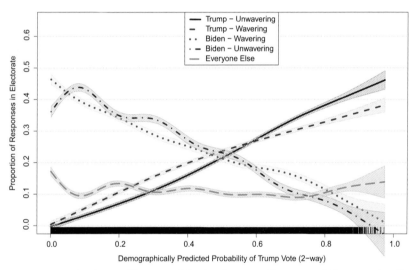

FIGURE 3.4 Predicting Electorate Membership as a Function of Demographically Derived Preferences.

This figure shows the distribution of electorates depending on whether individuals' demographic attributes pushed consistently toward one candidate or the other. Differences in the solid and dashed red lines illustrate how individuals with similar demographic tendencies to vote for Trump (vs. Biden) were more or less likely to waver in their choices if they eventually chose Trump; differences in the dotted and mixed blue lines illustrate how individuals with similar demographic tendencies to vote for Trump (vs. Biden) were more or less likely to waver in their choices if they eventually chose Biden; and variability in the wide-dashed green line illustrates how the tendency not to vote for either candidate varied depending on how we might otherwise have expected individuals to behave based solely on their demographics.

whose identities were cross-cutting. Instead, this anticipated pattern is apparent for only one of the two candidates. In estimates of Trump support, we indeed see that the relative likelihood of being an unwavering Trump supporter (as opposed to a wavering one) increased as more identities (race, gender, religion, etc.) pushed a respondent toward voting for Trump. This is apparent from the growing gap between these two lines toward the right side of Figure 3.4. But among those pushed toward Biden, this pattern is not apparent. Instead, the relative likelihood of being an unwavering Biden supporter (as opposed to a wavering one) has no clear pattern for those respondents whose demographics indicate a likely Biden preference (compare the gap between Biden lines on the left side of Figure 3.4). These results indicate that the demographic groups supporting Biden appear to have been less consistent in their support than those whose attributes were associated with voting for Trump.

Two explanations for this result seem likely. First, it is possible that Joe Biden, regarded by many as a centrist candidate, initially alienated some left-leaning voters and had to work to draw them to his cause (e.g., because they might otherwise have voted for a third-party candidate). It is also possible that the Democratic Party coalition is by nature simply more fragile than the Republican one, relying more heavily on groups that may be less confident about voting or more difficult to turn out. The fact that Black Americans, younger Americans, and low-income individuals disproportionately voted for Biden and also tended to be wavering voters accords with this latter explanation (see Figure 3.3). This also reaffirms our decision throughout to look more closely at identities, rather than just at group membership, when we analyze how voters understood the election and its implications.

Political Self-Identification and the Electorates

If the literature on affective polarization and motivated reasoning has taught political scientists anything, it is that partisan identity is a potent force. It is therefore unsurprising that partisanship and ideology tell us a lot about how people will end up voting and thus which electorate they find themselves in. Among those identifying as strong Republicans, 95.5 percent reported voting for Trump and a mere 2.4 percent said they voted for Biden (the other 2.1 percent did not vote for either one). Similarly, strong Democrats overwhelmingly cast their ballots for Biden (91.2 percent vs. 4.2 percent for Trump). Many of these strong identifiers also never wavered in their selections: 70.8 percent of unwavering Trump supporters identified as strong Republicans and

62.7 percent of unwavering Biden supporters said they were strong Democrats (Figure 3.5).

But the fact that partisanship and behavior are correlated does not imply that we should view the electorates and partisan self-identification as synonymous. There are two key reasons we shy away from a partisan frame in favor of this epidemiological approach. For one, some individuals in each partisan group did not behave in the ways we might have expected. Understanding these factors is critical to making sense of their decisions. For another, long-standing research in public opinion has shown that partisan self-identification is itself subject to change over time.[16] Some individuals might self-identify as Republicans not as a basis for making their decisions but instead because they had already planned to vote in a particular way. Handling this endogeneity by simply attributing behavior to partisanship has the potential to miss key variables that may be affecting choices.

The disconnect between partisanship and decision-making can be seen in the fact that strength of partisan identification was virtually unrelated to the likelihood of supporting a party's nominee and tended principally to influence whether individuals were wavering or unwavering in that support. In addition, those individuals who did not associate with a political party but leaned toward one were somewhat more likely to vote for that party's nominees and to be unwavering supporters of those nominees than were those who said they identified with a party but not strongly (Figure 3.5, row 1). And although self-reported ideology was closely associated with the electorates among Trump voters, this was true to a far lesser degree for Biden voters, where individuals who self-identified as somewhat or very liberal were equally likely to be his unwavering supporters (row 2).

Attitudes of the Electorates

It should come as no surprise that members of each electorate regarded their chosen candidate as preferable across a host of issues or that answers to questions, such as whether they approved of the job President Trump was doing, diverged sharply across these groups. From the beginning of our study, virtually no unwavering Trump supporters disapproved of his job performance (0.5 percent) and only 14.2 percent of the wavering Trump supporters expressed disapproval (Figure 3.6). These patterns were almost perfectly reversed among wavering and unwavering Biden voters (with 16.1 percent and 1.2 percent expressing approval, respectively). Among those who did not vote for either candidate, most did not have strong views of Trump's performance

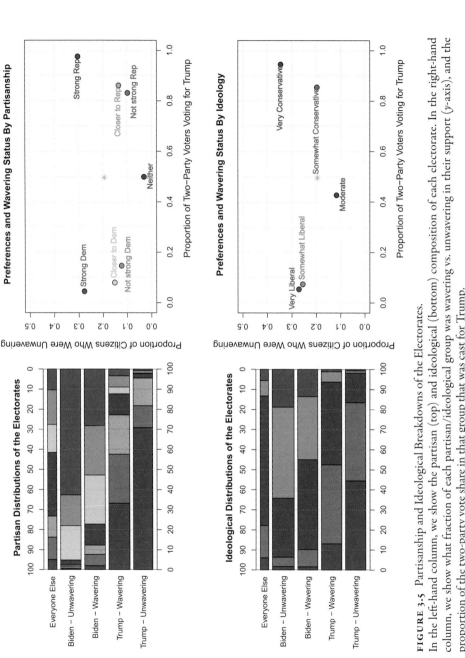

FIGURE 3.5 Partisanship and Ideological Breakdowns of the Electorates.
In the left-hand column, we show the partisan (top) and ideological (bottom) composition of each electorate. In the right-hand column, we show what fraction of each partisan/ideological group was wavering vs. unwavering in their support (y-axis), and the proportion of the two-party vote share in that group that was cast for Trump.

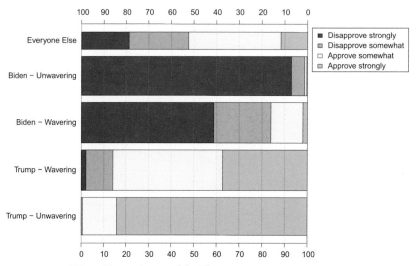

FIGURE 3.6 Wave 1 Trump Approval, by Electorate.
Bars show the distribution of Trump approval in each electorate during wave 1 of the
survey (May 2020).

in wave 1 (67.0 percent said they only somewhat approved or disapproved)
and their overall perceptions were relatively evenly split.

By comparing initial levels of approval in each electorate with those same
attitudes shortly before the election, we can see how these attitudes shifted
over time. To simplify this comparison, we calculate the mean value of approval in each electorate when the values of presidential approval are recoded
to range from 0 to 1.[††] The comparison is shown in the top row of Figure 3.7,
with arrows pointing from each electorate's approval in wave 1 (W1) to their
approval in wave 7 (W7). Overall, presidential approval did not change much
across the entire electorate, but there were changes in particular groups over
time. In particular, wavering Biden voters and individuals who would not end
up voting for either of the major-party candidates reported lower levels of
presidential approval as the election drew nearer.

In general, assessments of Trump tended to be relatively stable, whereas
evaluations of Biden became more polarized across electorates over time. This
pattern can be seen clearly in evaluations of the two candidates' favorability
(rows 2 and 3 of Figure 3.7). In wave 1 of our study, almost all unwavering

---

††. That is, "disapprove strongly" was coded as 0, "disapprove somewhat" was coded as 0.33, "approve somewhat" was coded as 0.67, and "approve strongly" was coded as 1. A similar recoding
strategy was used for all other measures in Figure 3.7.

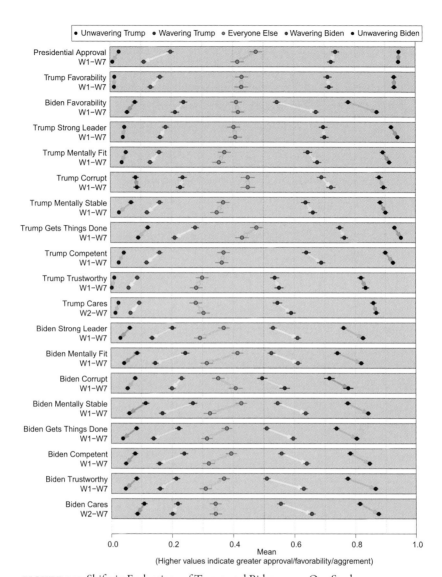

FIGURE 3.7 Shifts in Evaluations of Trump and Biden across Our Study.

Each row shows how each electorate changed their evaluation of Trump or Biden on a given measure between wave 1 (May 2020) and wave 7 (October–November 2020). The direction of the change is given by the arrow. Shifts to the right (left) of the figure indicate that the electorate grew more (less) more likely to say that they approved of Trump's performance, favored each candidate, or thought that the trait fit the target candidate for that item. Horizontal lines show 95% confidence intervals.

Biden supporters reported that they had "very unfavorable" views of Trump (95.8 percent), whereas the vast majority of unwavering Trump supporters said their views were "very favorable" (77.7 percent). These numbers were virtually unchanged in wave 7 (at 97.4 percent and 78.6 percent, respectively). Wavering supporters shifted slightly, with wavering Biden voters expressing slightly less favorable preferences and wavering Trump voters expressing slightly more favorable ones (row 2 of Figure 3.7). In contrast, the favorability of Biden shifted notably over time across our electorates. While unwavering Biden supporters viewed their nominee more favorably than unwavering Trump supporters, this gap increased from .70 to .82 when both were coded on a 0-to-1 scale (see row 3 of Figure 3.7). Wavering supporters of each candidate diverged even more, shifting from an initial difference of .30 to an ultimate pre-election gap of .46.

These differences in favorability also are reflected in patterns of responses for the vast majority of trait assessments for Trump and Biden. Evaluations of Trump as "a strong leader," "mentally fit," "corrupt," "trustworthy," and as someone who "cares about people like me" changed little in any of the electorates across the campaign cycle. Voters across the electorates diverged slightly in evaluations of how well each of the traits "mentally stable," "gets things done," and "competent" described the incumbent. Evaluations of Biden polarized considerably for all these traits, as his eventual supporters came to view him more positively and wavering Trump supporters, in particular, came to view him more negatively (Figure 3.7).

When voters were asked to indicate which candidate they thought would do a better job on various issues, they again reported perceptions in line with their eventual vote choices. Across the board, Biden voters (and particularly unwavering Biden voters) thought their candidate was preferable on each of the issues we queried, while Trump voters (and particularly unwavering Trump voters) were far more likely to say that their candidate would do a better job. In fact, it seems as if virtually no unwavering voters would even entertain the notion that the two candidates could be equally able to handle many issues. Figure 3.8 shows the difference between the proportion of individuals in each electorate who asserted that Biden would do better on each issue and the proportion who thought that Trump would do better on that same issue. In line with the notion that wavering voters were still deciding on their preferred candidate, these individuals appear to have adopted the view over time that their candidate would be better on most issues. The only exception to this pattern was for handling of the coronavirus pandemic, where Trump voters became more likely to assert that the two candidates

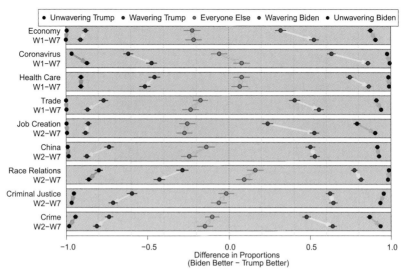

FIGURE 3.8 Shifts in Perceptions of Candidate Issue Competence.
Each row shows how each electorate changed their evaluation of whether Trump vs. Biden could better handle various issues between wave 1 (May 2020) or wave 2 (July 2020) and wave 7 (October–November 2020). The direction of the change is given by the arrow. Shifts to the right (left) of the figure indicate that the electorate thought that, across our study, Biden (Trump) could better handle that issue.

were equivalent as Election Day drew closer (Figure 3.8, row 2). We will come back to these patterns—especially as they relate to the coronavirus pandemic and the economy—in later chapters.

Experiences of the Electorates

The different electorates also began 2020 with different evaluations of the Trump years. As we illustrate in Chapter 6 ("The Best of Times, The Worst of Times"), Trump voters—both wavering and unwavering—disproportionately asserted that they and their communities were in better financial shape just before COVID hit than they had been when Trump was elected in 2016 (Figure 3.9). While the other electorates were less bullish on the performance of the economy during Trump's first three years in office, it is worth noting that even for these individuals, they were unlikely to think that the pre-COVID economy had gotten worse. This suggests that most voters—even Biden supporters—saw the economy as growing, or at least not shrinking, during Trump's first three years in office, a theme we return to in Chapter 6.

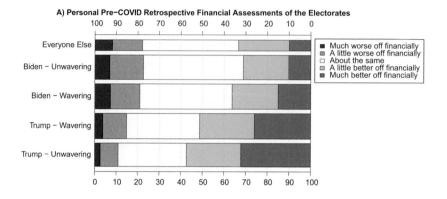

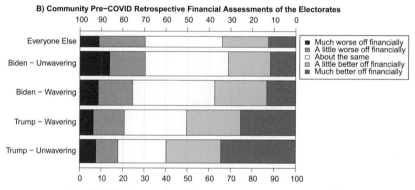

FIGURE 3.9 Pre-COVID Personal and Community Retrospective Evaluations.
Bars show each electorate's retrospective evaluations of how their personal (panel A) and community's (panel B) economic health had changed between 2016 and the start of the COVID-19 pandemic.

The electorates diverged more sharply during 2020 in their assessment of the virus's effect, the economic turbulence, and the push for racial justice. Biden voters were more likely to report direct personal effects from the pandemic, disproportionately saying that they knew people who were infected by COVID and who had died of coronavirus throughout the crisis (Figure 3.10). Figure 3.10 presents the results of generalized additive models estimating the proportion of individuals within each electorate who, over time, reported knowing someone who had been infected (panel A) or had died (panel B) of COVID. In the immediate post-election survey, 42.6 percent of unwavering Biden voters and 41.9 percent of wavering Biden voters reported that they knew someone who had died of COVID. In contrast, 29.5 percent of wavering Trump voters and a mere 21.5 percent of unwavering Trump voters reported

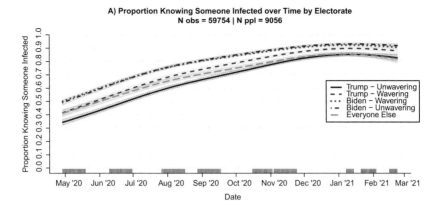

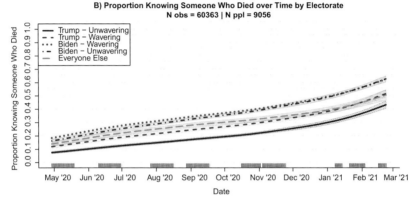

FIGURE 3.10 Personal Knowledge of COVID-19 Infection and Death.
Lines show the estimated proportion of respondents in each electorate that knew someone who had been infected with COVID-19 (panel A), or who had died from COVID-19 (panel B), across the study.

that someone they knew had died of the disease (among those who did not vote for either candidate, 29.7 percent reported knowing someone who had died). We discuss the implications of these differences in Chapter 5 ("Did the COVID-19 Pandemic Sink Trump's Reelection?"), in terms of both attitudes toward the pandemic itself and eventual vote choice.

The economic impacts of the coronavirus pandemic (such as job losses and food insecurity) were felt widely, but also varied across electorates. A majority of the households in our study (52.8 percent) reported a furlough or job loss between the beginning of the pandemic and the second wave of the study in late June. As the COVID-driven problems in the economy persisted, by our final pre-election wave 60.4 percent of our respondents indicated that they had been furloughed or lost a job at some point since the start of the pandemic. And at any given time, 11 to 15 percent of households reported having trouble paying for food, 12 to 17 percent were finding it difficult to cover utilities, and 9 to 13 percent reported struggling to pay their rent or mortgage in the last thirty days. Economic hardships were felt most acutely by wavering voters, but especially by nonvoters, those who did not end up voting for a major-party candidate, and those who wavered and eventually voted for Biden. These tendencies can be seen in the plots in Figure 3.11; we take up these effects in Chapter 6.

Finally, Biden voters, both wavering and unwavering, were more likely to participate in the racial protests that characterized the summer of 2020. Overall, we estimate that 9.6 percent of our respondents lived in households

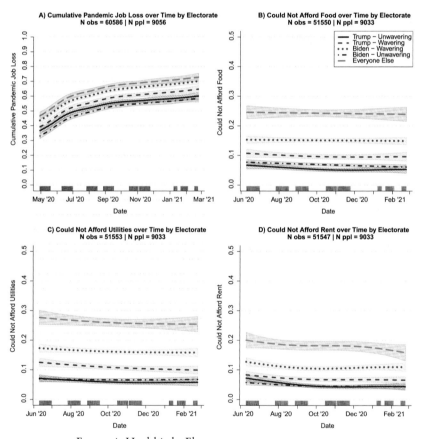

FIGURE 3.11 Economic Hardship by Electorate.
Lines show the estimated proportion of each electorate reporting that they had lost a job (panel A), could not afford enough food (panel B), could not afford their utilities (panel C), or could not afford their rent/mortgage (panel D), across the study.

with at least one individual who participated in these protests between June and August 2020 (waves 2–4; see Chapter 7). The Biden-supporting electorates had far greater participation, at 17.2 percent for unwavering supporters and 16.3 percent for wavering ones, where the Trump electorates had participation rates of 4.4 percent among wavering supporters and a mere 1.7 percent among unwavering ones (6.6 percent of the respondents who did not vote for either candidate participated). The events that framed the debate about racial justice and policing were more proximal to voters in some electorates than in others; we take up these effects in Chapter 7.

Binding these experiences together was the fundamental interrelatedness of these three crises. As we noted earlier, the economic crisis was largely precipitated by the need to shut down the economy to limit the spread of a deadly virus. The nation's racial reckoning was about more than use of lethal force by police against Black citizens. The video of George Floyd's death "captured an individual tragedy," noted NPR. "But it's set against a backdrop of poverty and discrimination that have long colored relations between law enforcement and the African American community."[17] By late spring, it had become clear that the toll of coronavirus differed along racial lines, with Black and Hispanic Americans more likely to be infected by COVID-19, to be hospitalized because of it, and to die of the disease.[18] The sources of these racial disparities were legion: non-White Americans disproportionately lived in the urban areas that were hit earliest in the pandemic; they tended for various socioeconomic reasons (i.e., the structural determinants of health) to have worse underlying health profiles than did Whites (e.g., greater rates of obesity and diabetes);[19] they were often not as well served by the medical establishment;[20] and they were more likely to be classified as essential workers and hence had to work in person during the pandemic, putting them at greater risk of contracting COVID-19.[21] All of this magnified the racialized toll of the pandemic, as we can see in Figure 3.12.

It is little surprise, then, that Black and Hispanic Americans were far more likely to report that someone in their family had become sick or that they knew someone who had died of COVID throughout the study (panels A and B of Figure 3.12). The latter effect was especially strong: among Black respondents, more than a third reported that they knew someone who had died of coronavirus by the first wave of the study and more than half reported knowing a decedent by August. In contrast, White respondents did not report a similar impact on their communities until well after Election Day.

Non-White communities also suffered the steepest economic hits of the pandemic. Compared to Whites, Black and Hispanic Americans were

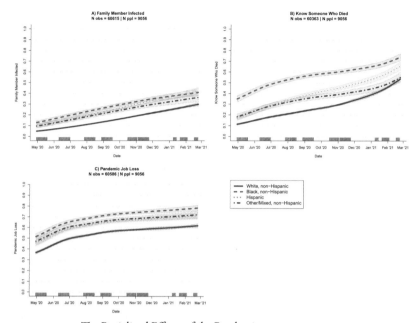

FIGURE 3.12 The Racialized Effects of the Pandemic.
Lines show the estimated proportion of respondents in each electorate who had a family member infected with COVID-19 (panel A), know someone who died from COVID-19 (panel B), or experienced a job loss (panel C) across our study, broken down by race/ethnicity.

more likely to lose their jobs (panel C of Figure 3.12) and also to face economic hardship. These too reflect the legacy of a wealth and class gap across American racial groups.[22] The acute conditions that non-White Americans were experiencing during the pandemic provided tinder to already smoldering grievances that would form the basis for the summer's racial protests. Further, because non-Whites constituted such a large portion of the Democratic Party's voter base (see Figure 3.3 above), these racial issues would have disparate influence on the different electorates.

Collectively, then, the different experiences of the electorates highlight the potential for the series of pre-election crises to affect the outcome of the election and the events that followed. In later chapters, we show how these crises shaped—in fundamental and profound ways—voters' ultimate decisions in 2020.

What Issues Did Voters Prioritize?

Perhaps not surprisingly, given these stark differences in voters' experiences in 2020, our electorates viewed various key issues in dissimilar ways. During the fall campaign (waves 5–7, August–November 2020), we asked respondents which issue was most important to them as they made up their minds: the economy, the coronavirus pandemic, race relations, crime, health care, or some other issue. After the election, in wave 8 (November 2020), we followed up with individuals who said they had voted to ask them which issue had factored most heavily into their decision. In a slight change from the pre-election measure, we removed the "other" response category and added options for both climate change and the Supreme Court to our post-election battery. Figure 3.13 shows which issue was most important to each electorate and how the assessments changed over time.

The data in Figure 3.13 reveal two key patterns over time. First, there is a striking divide between Trump and Biden voters. Trump voters thought that the economy was the most important problem, and that perception grew throughout the fall campaign. Alternatively, Biden voters were much more likely to prioritize the pandemic. While some voters selected other options, these tended to shrink in importance somewhat over time. The key contrast between the electorates—and the campaigns—was in attitudes toward the pandemic versus the economy. Trump voters saw this election through the lens of the economy; Biden voters saw it through the lens of the pandemic.[‡‡]

In our post-election survey, in addition to the most important issue, we asked respondents for their second- and third-most-important ones as well. While the most important issue gives us some insight into the main frame in the election, asking about these additional items adds nuance. These responses clarify perceptions of the third crisis: the debate over racial justice versus law and order. As we can see in Figure 3.14, a majority of both wavering and un-wavering Trump supporters named crime as one of their top three issues, but only 7 percent of wavering or unwavering Biden supporters did the same. Where 41.3 percent of wavering and unwavering Biden supporters named race relations, only 13 percent of Trump supporters did so. Consistent with Trump's and Biden's messaging on this issue, Biden voters saw the summer's protests as being about racial justice, while for Trump and his supporters they were much more about crime and the need for law and order.

Pulling back, we see that in deciding their vote, our respondents prioritized the three pre-election crises differently depending on whether they supported the challenger or the incumbent. For the pandemic and the economy, the battle

---

‡‡. The smaller number of people in the "everyone else" category post-election in Figure 3.13 is due to the fact that this question was asked only of voters, so this category includes only third-party voters (nonvoters are excluded here).

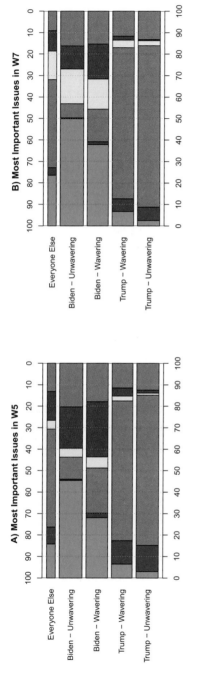

A) Most Important Issues in W5

B) Most Important Issues in W7

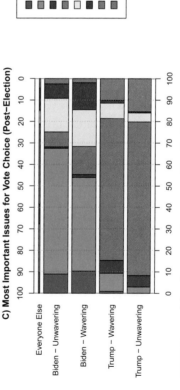

C) Most Important Issues for Vote Choice (Post-Election)

- Climate Change* (Only Asked Post–Election)
- COVID
- Crime
- Economy
- Healthcare
- Race Relations
- Supreme Court* (Only Asked Post–Election)
- Other* (Only Asked Pre–Election)

FIGURE 3.13 Most Important Issue across Our Study.
Bars show the issues voters perceived to be the most important one, by electorate, in wave 5 (August–September 2020; panel A), wave 7 (October–November 2020; panel B), and wave 8 (November 2020, post-election; panel C).

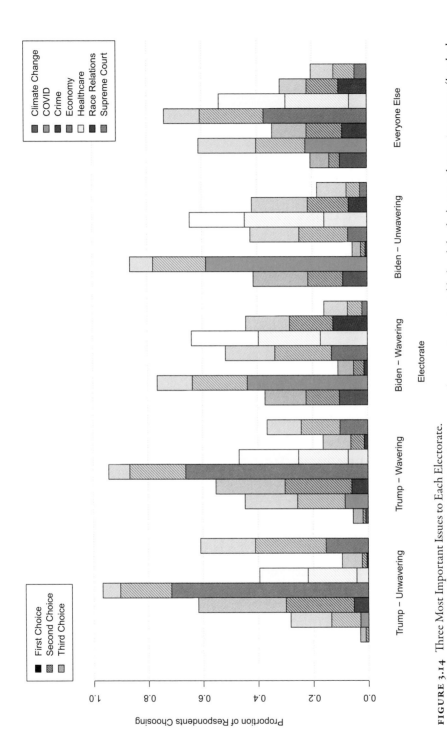

FIGURE 3.14 Three Most Important Issues to Each Electorate.
Bars show the proportion of each electorate that selected an issue as the most important (dark solid color), second most important (hatched color), or third most important issue (light solid color) in the election. Responses are from wave 8 (November 2020, post-election).

between the candidates, and their voters, was about which issue was central. However, for our third crisis, it was about how to frame it. In Chapters 5–7, we will develop our arguments about these differences in greater depth.

When Electorates Made Up Their Minds

As one would expect, as the campaign went on, those who wavered (eventually) made up their minds. For each wavering voter, it is possible to estimate the point at which they settled on their candidate (i.e., the point at which they no longer varied in whom they would support or whether they would vote). Since there is a time gap between waves of the survey, we define each person's vote as settling sometime between the last time that voter expressed uncertainty or a preference that differed from their final one. These bounds are imperfect at an individual level, but in the aggregate they are highly indicative of when choices were made and by which demographic types of people. Notably, imprecision in choice dates could occur either because voters underestimate the extent to which they are committed to one candidate or another (e.g., by expressing some uncertainty where there really was none, a phenomenon political scientists have long observed with partisan leaners)[23] or because they wavered briefly in their confidence during a window between surveys. But we should be able to detect these shifts because we collected relevant answers regularly. Hence, we can model the extent to which voters within groups settled over time.

To do this, we use the same GAM-based modeling approach described in the Appendix and referenced in Figure 3.4 above. We model whether someone had settled by a particular wave as a function of their attitudes/demographics, allowing us to estimate which groups of voters had settled on their candidate by a particular date.[§§] Importantly, this allows us to discern whether particular events (such as the debates) played a role in solidifying voters' choices.

In general, wavering Biden voters made up their minds earlier than did wavering Trump ones (Figure 3.15). The median wavering Trump voter decided

---

§§. To model this, we treat each respondent wave as a separate observation, and regress a dummy variable indicating whether the respondent had settled or not on an interaction of survey date and attributes of interest (most importantly, the respondent's electorate). Because we are estimating a GAM, we can account for the nonlinear dynamics of settling, where few people might settle in one range of dates, but many others might settle in another (i.e., around a pivotal moment like a debate or convention). Given the setup of our model, we should not see the number of people who have settled go down. Should such reductions appear, it would suggest that our model had incorrectly identified some voters as settled when their choices were still in doubt (this corresponds to the possibility that we might be missing some evidence of wavering between waves). Where such evidence can be found, the results suggest that some event may have pushed voters who were about to settle away from their preferred candidate temporarily.

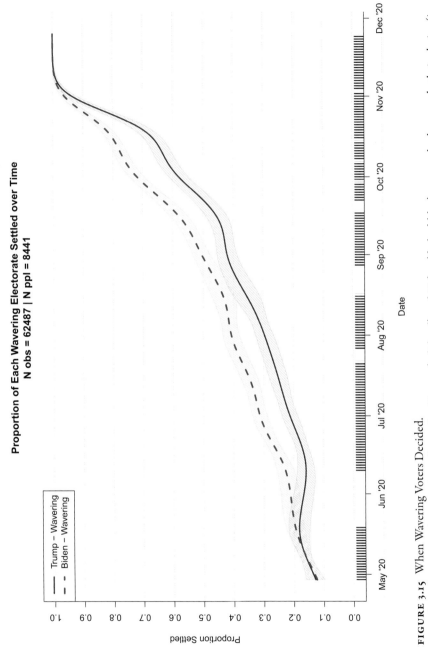

FIGURE 3.15 When Wavering Voters Decided.
Lines show the estimated proportion of wavering Trump (solid red) and Biden (dashed blue) voters who have made their choice (i.e., settled), by date.

whom to vote for between September 21 and October 17. On the other hand, the median wavering Biden voter came to a decision a few weeks earlier, between September 5 and October 8.[***] This put the first debate, on September 29, within the window for the median settling of voters who would support each candidate and the second one, on October 22, in the window for neither. One reason for the earlier settling of Biden voters was a large difference that emerged in 2020 in the process of voting for each of the candidates. As we discuss below, Biden's voters—in large part due to their concerns about the implications of voting in person during a pandemic—were far more likely to cast their ballots by mail than Trump's voters, who were repeatedly told by the president that mail-in voting was insecure and would be rife with fraud. This meant that a large portion of Biden's votes were cast before Election Day, thereby locking in voters' choices at a somewhat earlier date.

The implications of early voting explain some of the difference in vote settling between wavering Biden voters and wavering Trump voters, but not all of it. Wavering Biden voters were also more likely to settle in their choices during the early part of the campaign, whereas many Trump voters took longer to make up their minds. This difference in preference formation, clear from the density plot in Figure 3.16, among electorates of relatively similar sizes suggests that many of the events during the campaign served to help Biden voters solidify their choices more than they did for Trump voters. The prevalence of vote settling at the very end of the campaign among Trump voters, in contrast, may indicate that these individuals were mobilized by the campaign's get-out-the-vote operation (though, of course, we cannot know this for sure).

When Electorates Cast Their Votes

Early and absentee voting was far more prevalent in the 2020 election than in years prior. This occurred for three distinct reasons. First, 2020 continued a long-standing trend wherein many states expanded the availability and use of no-excuse absentee balloting and in-person early-voting locations. Second, election officials in a number of states modified rules to make it easier for individuals to vote early or absentee during the coronavirus pandemic. And third, voters were more likely to take advantage of the chance to cast early and absentee ballots because they received them by mail as part of expanded mail-in voting.

[***]. This is presented as a range because we can conclude only that they settled between the points in time at which they were interviewed.

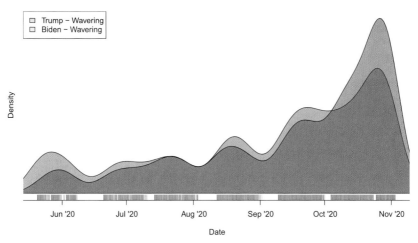

FIGURE 3.16 Distribution of Settling Dates.
Kernel density plot of the approximate settling date for Trump (red) and Biden (blue) voters.

Across our states, the rates of early and absentee voting varied widely. According to official statistics, 37.9 percent of Pennsylvania voters voted early or absentee, compared to 81.8 percent of Florida voters. In both Michigan and Wisconsin, majorities of voters cast their ballots ahead of the election (51.2 percent and 58.4 percent, respectively). Rates of early voting among our respondents closely match these proportions (76.3 percent in Florida, 56.7 percent in Michigan, 41.0 percent in Pennsylvania, and 59.2 percent in Wisconsin).[24] These state differences were associated with each state's history of allowing no-excuse absentee or early voting. In Florida, early and no-excuse absentee voting had long been an option, and more than two-thirds of voters had voted before Election Day in the 2016 presidential election. In Wisconsin, no-excuse absentee voting, but not early voting, had also been available for a number of years. Michigan had enabled both early voting and no-excuse absentee voting by ballot initiative in 2018.[25] But no-excuse absentee voting, and some limited early voting, became possible in Pennsylvania only with the passage of Act 77 in 2019,* which was still being challenged in the courts at the time of the 2020 election.[26]

Beyond the availability of voting options before Election Day and the awareness of these options, there were major differences in vote timing by

---

*. ˙ Pennsylvania does not allow traditional early in-person voting, but does allow voters in some counties to pick up, and immediately vote with, an absentee ballot up to fifty days before Election Day.

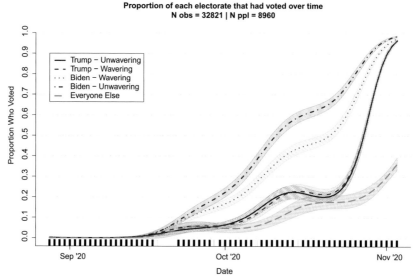

FIGURE 3.17 When Our Panelists Voted.
Lines show the estimated proportion of each electorate that had voted by a given date.

electorate (Figure 3.17). Biden supporters were much more likely to take advantage of early and absentee voting options. They were also far more concerned than Trump voters about the implications of voting in person during a pandemic. More than a third of each of the Biden electorates was somewhat or very worried that the government would use voting locations to conduct arrests, almost half expressed concerns that militias might show up at polling places, and about 60 percent were worried that those voting in person risked infection with COVID-19 (Figure 3.18). Trump supporters didn't share those concerns. Less than a quarter of those in the Trump electorates expressed concerns about any of these possibilities. In deference to voter concerns, the Biden campaign made a strong push to encourage voters to use early and absentee options and thereby avoid the potential risks associated with casting ballots in person. The focus on early and absentee voting was coupled with a decision to eschew the traditional political "ground game" by the Biden campaign, which had fewer field offices than Trump's campaign, did less door-to-door canvassing,[27] and relied on digital tools to remind people to vote.[28] The Trump campaign ran a far more traditional Election Day operation.[29]

Messaging by the Trump campaign and by the president himself also reduced the extent to which his voters adopted mail-in voting. At a number of times throughout the election cycle, Trump asserted that mail-in voting

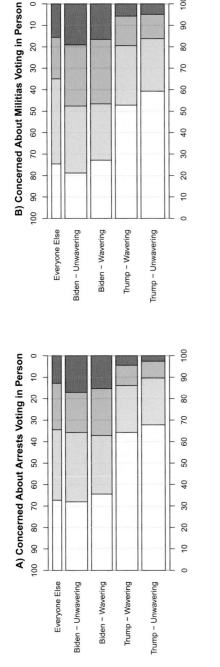

A) Concerned About Arrests Voting in Person

B) Concerned About Militias Voting in Person

C) Concerned About COVID Voting in Person

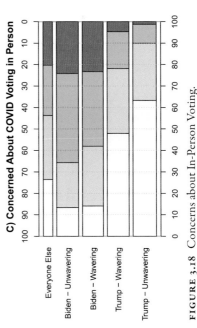

- Not at all concerned
- Not too concerned
- Somewhat concerned
- Very concerned

FIGURE 3.18 Concerns about In-Person Voting.

Bars show how worried each electorate was about various risks stemming from in-person voting: being arrested (panel A), physical violence or having an armed militia show up to your polling place (panel B), or contracting COVID-19 (panel C).

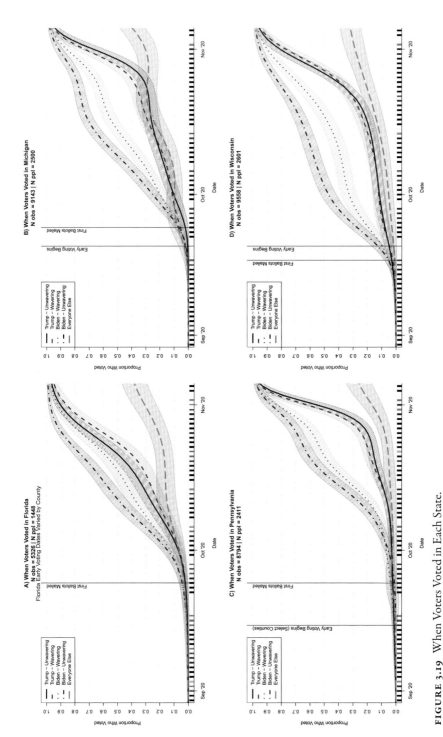

FIGURE 3.19 When Voters Voted in Each State.

Lines show the proportion of each electorate that had voted by a given date, broken down by state. The first date for early in-person voting and the first date for mail-in voting in the state (if applicable) are shown with vertical lines. In Florida, we do not list a specific date for early voting because it varies by county.

was rife with fraud—though, somewhat ironically, Trump himself voted by mail in the 2020 Florida primary election. Indeed, attacks on mail-in voting were a principal component of the election fraud narrative that would dominate the post-election period, as we discuss in Chapter 9 (" 'Stop the Steal' "). These arguments affected not only when and how voters cast their ballots but also how they viewed the legitimacy of this election.

Florida was the state where Republicans were the most inclined to vote by mail. Figure 3.19 shows that these differences in voting methods and timing across electorates were apparent in each of our states.

Electorates and Behaviors

The campaigns and crises of 2020 sometimes shaped and sometimes reinforced the attitudes and behaviors of the electorates. In the following chapters, we focus on how the crises affected them, their attitudes, and their electoral choices. By simultaneously examining our electorates and the factors that affected their choices, we can gain a better understanding of the identities they brought to the voting booth and to their assessment of January 6 and the ways in which their partisanship affected both. But so too did their media menus and patterns of exposure. In Chapter 4, we add this critical final piece of the puzzle to the mix, before we turn to an analysis of each of our crises.

4

The Electorates' Communication Dynamics

R. Lance Holbert, Yotam Ophir, Dror Walter, Josh Pasek, and Kathleen Hall Jamieson

@FoxNews weekend afternoons is the worst! Getting into @CNN and MSDNC territory. Watch @OANN & @ newsmax instead. Much better!
—Tweet by Donald Trump, July 5, 2020

CITIZENS TODAY ARE awash in a sea of political media options. Not only can they watch local and national broadcast and cable news, but they can read legacy print ranging from national outlets such as *USA Today*, the *Wall Street Journal*, the *New York Times*, and the *Washington Post* to local outlets such as the Madison, Wisconsin, *Capital Times* and the Harrisburg, Pennsylvania, *Patriot-News*; they can listen to national radio ranging from Pacifica on the left to Dan Bongino, Mark Levin, and Sean Hannity on the right; and they can use a variety of social media platforms and apps. The political issues a given voter prioritizes are in part a function of the media outlets an individual encounters. So too is the way in which that voter sees (or frames) issues such as: Is the economy or the pandemic the central concern? Were the summer 2020 Black Lives Matter protests lawless or peaceful? Did Donald Trump win or lose the 2020 election? In this chapter, we explore the media diets of those citizens in the electorates identified in Chapter 3 ("Not One Electorate, but Many").

The media consumed by citizens depend, in part, on the options available to them. As 2020 illustrated, the media choices on offer are not fixed. For example, social media platforms such as Parler, Telegram, and Gab and extremely conservative cable outlets such as Newsmax and One America News Network

(OANN) grew their audiences by providing a safe harbor for the conspiracy theories being advanced by Trump and his advocates about COVID and the election. Among the platforms that benefitted was Parler, which had emerged in 2018 as a response to curbs on misinformation instituted by platforms such as Twitter and Facebook and was characterized by the *Wall Street Journal* as a "libertarian-leaning social network." In one week in October, Parler was "the most downloaded app on both Android and Apple devices."[1]

Conservatives' anger at Fox News—a reaction that Trump fueled—was another factor incentivizing some in the network's audience to seek content in the more extreme venues. On election night, Fox News was the first to project that Arizona's Electoral College votes would go to Biden. "Trump supporters chant down a Fox News reporter in downtown Phoenix," the website Arizona Central reported the next day.[2] Even as the number of votes that separated the two tickets in that crucial state narrowed in the following days, Fox News stood by its Arizona projection. The other networks would not call Arizona for Biden until eight days later, after Biden had secured the Electoral College votes needed for victory elsewhere. When all the ballots had been counted, Biden had won Arizona by 10,457 votes.[3] Adding to the grievances against Fox News voiced by Trump advocates, that network joined the other major ones in announcing on November 7 that the Biden-Harris ticket had won the election.

Trump responded to all of this by retweeting the posts of disaffected Fox viewers who were urging others to join them in switching to alternative outlets such as Newsmax.[4] "Hundreds of thousands of new viewers have tuned into Newsmax programs that embrace the president's debunked claims of voter fraud and insist that Mr. Trump can keep the White House," noted the *New York Times* on November 22. "Until recently, the network's top shows attracted a paltry 58,000 viewers. On Thursday night, the network drew its biggest audience ever, notching 1.1 million viewers at 7 p.m."[5]

One America News Network, an outlet that had begun covering Trump rallies in 2015 and which Trump in his last two years in office touted to his 88 million Twitter followers at least 120 times,[6] began aggressively courting the Trump base as well. OANN's "online audience soared in November, after conservative mainstay and OANN competitor Fox News affirmed Joe Biden's victory," noted John Shiffman, of Reuters. "Trump and his camp blasted Fox. A record 767,000 people installed the OANN app that month, nine times as many as in October, according to data firm Sensor Tower. In January, Trump supporters, including at least one carrying an OANN flag, stormed the US Capitol. That month, app installs spiked again to 517,000."[7]

These arguments highlight the central role of the media in this, and every, election. Especially in a book whose authors include numerous communication scholars, it would hardly be a surprise to find considerable attention paid to citizens' media diets. While we too focus on our panelists' patterns of media exposure, *how* we do that is unique. In this chapter, we outline the strategy we use to study the distinct communication environments of our electorates. In particular, we argue that it is important not only to understand what media voters consume but also how they consume it: do they actively seek out a source, or do they encounter it despite trying to avoid it? Throughout the book, we will explore whether how voters encounter media outlets shapes their attitudes and behaviors.

Here, we outline three key findings that help to structure our analyses of the role of media and messages in shaping the 2020 election and its aftermath. First, we show that our electorates existed within different communication environments. While we defined our electorates in terms of their vote choice and turnout intention (see Chapter 3), their communication environments were also quite distinct. Our different electorates consumed fundamentally different media diets, and these diets reinforced their differing candidate choices and turnout intentions. Put slightly differently, part of why some Trump supporters wavered while others did not is their differential media behaviors (though parsing cause and effect here is, of course, incredibly challenging).

Second, merely knowing how much someone attends to a given outlet is not enough. To really understand the role that media play, we need to know *how* they read, watch, or listen to it: do they actively seek it out, or do they instead just casually come across it? As we show in later chapters, these different types of exposure have quite different effects on behavior.

Third, we also feature the role, if any, of echo chambers in the contemporary media environment. We discuss the concept at greater length later in the chapter, but in brief, an echo chamber is a media environment in which someone proactively consumes only media that are consistent with their existing beliefs while effectively avoiding all others (i.e., a conservative who only watches Fox News and listens to conservative talk radio, and is able to avoid other types of media sources). The literature is correct that echo chambers do not really exist at scale in the mass public. But that does not mean that no one is ensconced in them; we show that a group, made up primarily of unwavering Trump supporters, actually is. While not a large group, as we show in later chapters, it is distinctive in a number of ways, with important implications for our understanding of the 2020 election, its aftermath, and the functioning of our democracy moving forward.

Measuring Media Exposure in a High-Choice Environment

The 2020 electorates were defined by unique patterns of political behavior encompassing vote intention, candidate support certainty, and vote choice. But this is not all that differentiates them: so too do their media diets, as the media they consumed reinforce and strengthen these attitudinal differences. It is not just what they consume that matters; also important is how they consume it. Because of today's high-choice media environment and Web 2.0, we need to study the motivations that drive individuals to seek out particular sources. Observations of audience action tendencies (i.e., the seeking and/or avoiding of particular content) and their relative levels of success in seeking or avoiding underscored the existence of clear political communication divisions within the US population that shape how a presidential election is conducted, the nature of the election's outcome, and its aftermath. Just as the 2020 electorates display unique patterns of exposure, so too do they reflect distinct patterns of seeking, avoiding, and incidental exposure to mediated political information.

Collecting observations of media exposure in combination with audience desires to seek and/or avoid a wide range of political media content is a departure from the more typical exposure-only methods used to assess mediated political communication activities. Drawing on 2008 Annenberg data, political communication scholars Suzanne Dilliplane, Seth Goldman, and Diana Mutz[8] advocate the use of a yes/no check system for a wide range of individual television outlets to determine what political content respondents consume "regularly" (i.e., at least once a month)[9]; this method has been expanded for use with other types of media.[10] Political scientists Michael LaCour and Lynn Vavreck offer support for the "program-count" approach through their analyses of its construct and convergent validity, and the Democracy Fund + UCLA Nationscape project[11] employs a similar series of dichotomous (i.e., yes/no) media exposure measures in its instrumentation as well.[12] The strength of such a move is its capacity to measure whether individuals consume a given outlet. However, this measure does not tell us how they approach it.

Other scholars take a more nuanced approach to the study of media effects. Because they treat whether someone is exposed to a given message or outlet as a necessary but not sufficient condition for it to have an effect, they advocate the capture of additional audience data. From this vantage point, communication scholars Kim Anderson, Claes de Vreese, and Erik Albaek encourage the use of "list-frequency" that incorporates not only whether an outlet has been encountered but also the degree to which it is used (e.g., number of days per week).[13] When assessing media influence in an election (or any other context), there is added predictive value in being able to differentiate occasional from more habitual consumers of a given program, outlet, or platform. For this reason, frequency of exposure was a key element of our approach to the communication dynamics of the 2020 electorates.

Building on this approach, we accompanied a measure of exposure with an assessment of individual-level action tendencies (i.e., the desire to seek and/or avoid different types of political media). Recent attention given to how best to tackle the persistent challenge of measuring political media exposure stems from a recognition that citizens now function within a high-choice media environment.[14] If the impetus for this work is the need to better understand the "choice" component, then it is important to gain an understanding of how audience members navigate an ever-expanding, diverse range of options.

An assessment of communication influence that focuses only on levels of exposure stops short of addressing the motivations that underlie and, in part, shape media behaviors (i.e., how people function within their communication environments). In addition, a sole focus on exposure has the potential to embed a set of faulty assumptions. Most prominently, just because a citizen indicates a certain level of exposure to a specific piece of political media content does not mean that this activity was intended or desired. Unsurprisingly then, scholars are paying increased attention to the potential importance and prevalence of incidental exposure (i.e., encountering a piece of media content without actively having sought it out).[15] Renewed interest in this classic concept stems from a recognition that audience members, no matter what tools they have at their disposal, are unable to have complete, effective control over the media messages they encounter. Incidental exposure is central to understanding how the 2020 electorates differentiate themselves communicatively.

However, as we will show in this chapter, there are two very distinct types of incidental exposure. First, there is the *casual consumption* of political media. This type of inadvertent contact stems neither from audience members actively seeking nor actively avoiding a specific source. For example, a voter may be scrolling through her Facebook feed and encounter a friend's post about a news headline from CNN. Although she is neither seeking nor avoiding CNN, simply encountering this headline can have an agenda-setting effect on what she perceives to be the major issues of the day.

The casual consumption of political media as one form of incidental exposure needs to be contrasted against the *unsuccessful avoidance* of content. Unsuccessful avoidance is defined as an instance in which there is some level of exposure to a type of political media even though the audience member indicates (1) a desire to avoid this content and (2) no desire to seek it out. Once again, just because someone wants to avoid one type of media does not mean that outlet will not be encountered in some form or fashion over the course of an election season. Our hypothetical citizen scrolling through a news aggregator on her smartphone may have a strong desire to avoid CNN since her preferred candidate, Donald Trump, singled it out as an example of "fake news." Nevertheless, if her news aggregator includes some CNN content, she may scroll through this material while taking note of a headline or two and may even engage in some sustained attention to this material if it is presented in a manner that piques her interest (e.g., asking herself, "What lies are they telling about Trump this time?"). The ability to distinguish between incidental exposure that results from casual consumption and unsuccessful avoidance comes only from studying a combination of exposure *and* multiple action tendencies. Incidental exposure, as scholars have previously analyzed it, is actually two distinct phenomena, which need to be disaggregated. Our study of media exposure in combination with corresponding action tendencies reveals the need to shift from the generic use of incidental exposure as a concept.

National News Media Exposure

We captured self-report estimates of news media exposure at four different points in our study: wave 1 (April–May 2020), wave 2 (June 2020), wave 5 (August–September 2020), and wave 6 (September–October 2020), spanning the spring, summer, and fall of 2020. Wave 1 was in the field as the COVID-19 pandemic was taking shape in the United States, and few other topics were garnering much attention. Wave 2 fielded during the Black Lives Matter protest movement sparked by the May 25 murder of George Floyd. Because respondents were providing answers in waves 5 and 6 as the news media began to focus in earnest on the general election, we were able to track media usage and possible effects at key points in that contest, including the two parties' conventions and presidential debates.

Rather than presupposing a common definition of concepts such as "conservative" or "legacy media," we signaled categories of media use by specifying a limited number of exemplars with high reach. For example, to measure exposure to conservative outlets, we asked respondents how often they get information from "sources such as Fox News Channel or Rush Limbaugh."[16] We used this strategy to assess exposure to conservative, liberal, moderate, and legacy print sources. The conservative and liberal media exposure items included dominant mainstream ideological outlets as exemplars (e.g., Fox News for conservative, MSNBC for liberal). The moderate classification was focused primarily on traditional television news broadcasts (e.g., ABC News) but also included *USA Today* since audiences perceive it as one of the more neutral/centrist sources of national news.[17] Legacy print outlets were exemplified as historically print-based newspapers that are now digital as well, with the primary outlet anchors being the *New York Times* and the *Washington Post*.

In waves 1, 2, and 5 we asked respondents how often they got information from each of our types of outlets, using a 5-point Likert scale running from "never" to "all the time." The referents varied by wave, with wave 1 asking about "the coronavirus pandemic," wave 2 asking about "the most important issues of the day," and wave 5 asking about "the 2020 U.S. Presidential election." The wave 6 instrument utilized a very similar media classification approach, but with a slightly different set of exemplars to match those used in other studies.[18] In addition, rather than asking about the degree to which respondents encountered the various types of news media, subjects were asked about how much information they received from each media type on a 6-point scale ranging from "no information" to "a lot of information." The respective four-item media exposure scales (conservative, liberal, moderate, and legacy) retain sufficient reliability, with Cronbach's α estimates exceeding 0.81 in all four cases.

An assessment of the frequency of exposure to various classifications of national political news media revealed that the 2020 electorates were quite distinct from each another (see Figure 4.1). Of those in the unwavering Trump electorate, 32.5 percent consumed conservative media the equivalent of often or all the time (panel A).* This comprised 74.5 percent of all heavy conservative media users (i.e., the vast majority of heavy conservative media users were unwavering Trump supporters). Levels of exposure to conservative media also served to differentiate the Trump wavering and unwavering electorates. Unwavering Trump voters were more habitual users of conservative outlets: while the vast majority of those in the unwavering Trump electorate had the highest levels of conservative media exposure, only 6.5 percent of the wavering Trump electorate match this description. In contrast, few Biden supporters, whether wavering or unwavering, consumed much conservative media. Three-quarters of unwavering Biden voters indicated no exposure,

---

*. This is equivalent to scoring 0.80 or higher on the 0–1 scale depicted in Figure 4.1. Those having no exposure are 0.15 or below on that same scale.

while the wavering Biden electorate had more contact with conservative media than their unwavering peers did (51.4 percent had some exposure). For the electorate unaffiliated with either of the major-party candidates, most had some conservative media exposure (71.9 percent) but few reported doing so often or more (9.8 percent).

The unwavering Biden electorate contained the majority of citizens who indicated very high levels of liberal news media exposure (78.6 percent of these individuals; see panel B of Figure 4.1). In contrast to unwavering Trump

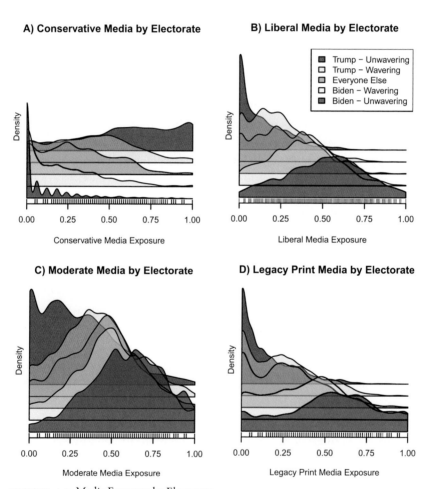

FIGURE 4.1 Media Exposure by Electorate.
Panels show density plots of exposure to various media sources by electorate, where higher values indicate greater exposure. Panel A shows exposure to conservative media, panel B, exposure to liberal media, panel C exposure to moderate media, and panel D exposure to legacy print media.

supporters, however, only 10.9 percent of unwavering Biden ones fell into this group. It is important to note that the unwavering Biden electorate's frequency distribution for exposure to liberal news was normal. This shape is distinct from the more skewed distribution formed by the unwavering Trump electorate in relation to its level of conservative media exposure (see panel A of Figure 4.1). The remaining electorates functioned as predicted, with diminishing exposure as we moved from the wavering Biden folks on through to the unwavering Trump group.

The greatest national news overlap among electorates occurred, as predicted, in the moderate media exposure category (see panel C of Figure 4.1). However, this communication activity revealed some separation between seemingly like-minded groups. For example, much of the unwavering Trump electorate indicated very little, if any, exposure to moderate national news. The percentage of the unwavering Trump electorate that indicated minimal exposure to moderate news (32.0 percent) far exceeded what was evident in the wavering Trump electorate (13.4 percent). Most members of the wavering Trump electorate, while retaining lower levels of exposure to moderate news than the unaffiliated/nonvoters or either of the Biden electorates, had at least some contact with moderate national news media. Whether or not moderate media were consumed is a key line of delineation between the unwavering and wavering Trump electorates.

Legacy media consumption (e.g., the *New York Times* and the *Washington Post*) further demarcates the 2020 electorates. The unwavering Trump electorate had little contact with these sources, and the wavering Trump electorate and the "everyone else" electorate (that is, those who did not vote or supported a third-party candidate) also had relatively limited exposure. While the wavering Trump electorate's low exposure levels likely reflected a lack of trust in these outlets, the "everyone else" electorate likely did not consume them because of a lack of political interest, as the more taxing task of reading may be a sufficient barrier to exposure for the politically disengaged. In contrast, the unwavering Biden electorate clearly comprised avid consumers of print-based political information: more than half of this electorate indicated that they read these sources at least some of the time (58.2 percent), versus only 3.9 percent of the unwavering Trump electorate. It is therefore appropriate to define the unwavering Biden supporters as generally made up of readers (more so than any of the other electorates). Before asking what difference any of this makes, we now consider the action tendencies of the various electorates.

Action Tendencies

As we argued earlier in the chapter, it is not simply enough to know how often someone consumed a given type of media; we need to know how they approached it. As a result, in wave 8 (November 2020), we asked panelists to indicate whether they sought out and/or avoided each of the various national political media classifications. More specifically, we asked which of the news media types they "actively seek out for political information" and, separately, which media types they "actively avoid for political information." The ordering of the "seek" and "avoid" batteries was randomized. Subjects could select as many of the news media classifications as they wished, creating a series of dichotomous (yes/no) "seek" and "avoid" items for each media type. A cutoff of .15 (between "never" and "rarely," but closer to "never") on a 0–1 media exposure scale was used to establish whether there was meaningful exposure to a particular type of national news media. The media exposure measures consisted of four items, and the utilization of a hard zero exposure cutoff for scales constructed for people who generally said "never" but said "rarely" even once was deemed artificially strict. An acknowledgment of measurement error alone requires identifying some level of exposure in these scales to determine what is a meaningful level of exposure.

A 2 × 2 × 2 classification (yes/no for exposure, active seeking, and active avoidance) yielded eight groups that represent different types of media activity.[†] Of these eight groups, five represented a large percentage (i.e., over 90 percent) of people residing in each of the five 2020 electorates: successful seeking, successful avoidance, unsuccessful avoidance, disengaged, and casual consumption. There are very few unsuccessful seekers for a desired form of national news media. Overall, people know where to go in the media environment to find desired political media content. Unsuccessful avoidance far exceeds unsuccessful seeking for all electorates. In addition, both forms of ambivalence (i.e., seeking *and* avoiding) toward all types of political media were rarities. Though the five 2020 electorates distinguished themselves on levels of media exposure alone, a more nuanced approach that included an assessment of "seek" and "avoid" action tendencies brought into sharper focus the need to treat these groups as distinct communication entities.

For conservative media, the unwavering Trump electorate was dominated by individuals who were successful seekers (see Figure 4.2; note that this figure parallels Figure 3.3 in Chapter 3, where there are more details on this

---

†. See the Online Appendix for a summary of the group types.

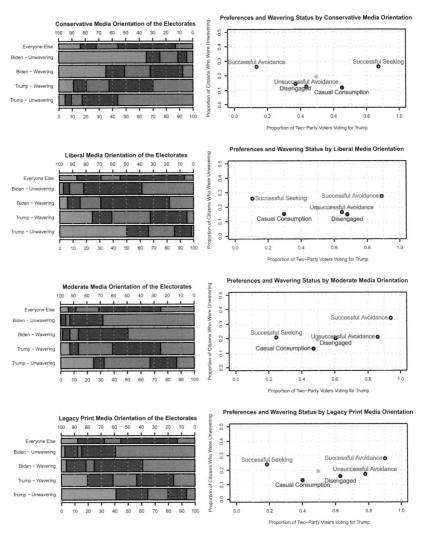

FIGURE 4.2 Media Orientations by Electorate.
In the left-hand column, we show the media orientations for each electorate. In each row, we show those tendencies for a different type of media (e.g., conservative, liberal, etc.). In the right-hand column, we show what fraction of each orientation was wavering vs. unwavering, and the two-party vote share for Trump.

figure type). A majority (56.1 percent) of this electorate fell into this classification. In addition, a further 26.5 percent were casual consumers of it. In contrast, only around 30 percent of the wavering Trump electorate consisted of successful seekers of conservative media (29.9 percent), and roughly the same percentage were casual consumers of it (32.6 percent). The relative balance of successful seeking versus casual consumption of conservative media is a dividing line between the two Trump electorates.

The Biden electorates were practically the mirror image of their Trump counterparts. The unwavering Biden electorate was dominated by successful avoidance, while the wavering Biden electorate was much more evenly dispersed among the action tendency types. Interestingly, more than 20 percent of the wavering Biden electorate were casual consumers of conservative media (24.5 percent), outpacing the unsuccessful avoidance group (18.9 percent). Roughly half of the wavering Biden electorate reported some level of meaningful exposure to conservative news media, and a little more than 70 percent of the everyone else electorate did so as well.

The Biden electorates' engagement with liberal media was marked by higher levels of casual consumption than successful seeking. This was notably different from the pattern evident in the Trump electorates' relationship to their own ideologically preferred outlets in the conservative media realm. Only 38.5 percent of the unwavering Biden electorate were successful seekers of liberal media, and this fell to 18.1 percent for the wavering Biden folks. The Biden electorates were far less ideologically driven in their media use than the Trump electorates.

When comparing the action tendency types for nonvoters and third-party supporters (the "everyone else" electorate) across both conservative and liberal media, there was a consistent pattern. The everybody else electorate was dominated by casual consumption, with a relatively equal distribution of the remaining individuals falling into the other four action tendency types. In short, a decent percentage of citizens untethered to the two major parties had some contact with both types of ideological national political media, but this exposure was not driven by some internal desire to consume messaging from either side of the political spectrum.

When focusing on consumption of moderate media (primarily broadcast television news) and legacy media (primarily national print outlets like the *New York Times* and the *Washington Post*), the unwavering Biden electorate retained similar action tendencies. There was a high percentage of successful seekers (higher than what we see with this electorate for liberal media) as well as a decent percentage of casual consumption. Only 4.0 percent of the unwavering Biden electorate had no exposure to moderate media and only 12.4 percent had no exposure to legacy print media. The wavering Biden electorate also successfully sought out moderate and legacy media more than liberal media. In addition, notable percentages (around 35 percent) of this electorate were casual consumers of both moderate and legacy print media.

The biggest action tendency differences between moderate and legacy print media were evident with the two Trump electorates. Trump-affiliated citizens registered higher percentages of successful avoidance of legacy print media as compared to moderate media. It is easier to steer clear of the historically print-based sources, an insight further supported by the lower percentages of unsuccessful avoidance of legacy media compared to moderate media. The unwavering Trump electorate retained a discernible percentage (a little over 30 percent) of citizens who were unsuccessful avoiders of moderate media.

Echo Chambers

Measuring exposure, seeking, and avoiding of a variety of national news media types allows us to identify potential echo chambers. In light of the literature's emphasis on patterns of media reliance,[19] we focused our attention there (and, as we show below, functionally only a conservative echo chamber exists). We described a panelist as a member of a conservative media echo chamber if (1) that person reported at least some minimal level of meaningful exposure to conservative media, (2) this exposure was driven by the active and successful seeking of that content, and (3) the person failed to cross a threshold of meaningful exposure for all other types of national news. By this measure, only 4.2 percent of all respondents ($N = 377$) were classified as members of a conservative media echo chamber (see Figure 4.3).

These individuals resided in each of the two Trump-favoring groups, not just the unwavering Trump electorate. However, 17.0 percent of those in the unwavering Trump electorate had constructed a conservative media echo chamber for themselves. A much smaller percentage of the wavering Trump electorate could be characterized as evincing this unique media exposure-action tendency (2.1 percent); virtually no members of any other electorate were in this echo chamber. Indeed, we cannot include this predictor in our models of vote choice because it perfectly predicted voting for President Trump. As we will note in later chapters, this was a group worthy of additional attention given the 2020 election outcome and the series of events that led to the January 6, 2021, storming of the US Capitol.

For purposes of comparison, we operationalized the construction of a possible liberal media echo chamber to see if there was a similar group of respondents on the other side of the political spectrum. For individuals to be members of a liberal media echo chamber, (1) they would have to have at least some minimal level of meaningful exposure to liberal media, (2) this exposure would need to be driven by the active and successful seeking of that content, and (3) they would need to fail to cross a threshold of meaningful exposure

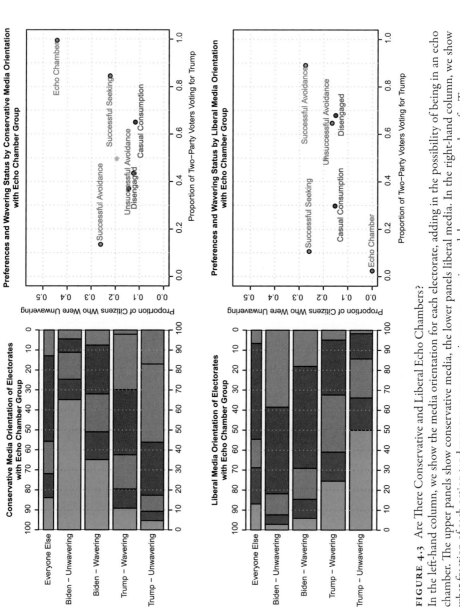

FIGURE 4.3 Are There Conservative and Liberal Echo Chambers?

In the left-hand column, we show the media orientation for each electorate, adding in the possibility of being in an echo chamber. The upper panels show conservative media, the lower panels liberal media. In the right-hand column, we show what fraction of each action tendency group was wavering vs. unwavering, and the two-party vote share for Trump.

for all other types of national political media. We did not find evidence of a liberal echo chamber. Only two respondents matched this description: one who was in the wavering Biden group and one who reported voting for a third-party candidate. In short, in our dataset, media isolation is a phenomenon found on only one end of the political spectrum.

This result helps to explain an important matter of contention in the literature on media effects. A number of scholars and much popular commentary about the contemporary media environment have highlighted the possibility that Americans might be living in echo chambers. This hypothesis raises the possibility that the cloistering of like-minded individuals in divergent, fundamentally incompatible media environments and carefully curated filter bubbles might lead to serious problems for democracy.[20] Numerous studies attempting to identify cloistered publics have suggested that this is not a common phenomenon.[21] Our evidence bridges both accounts. Echo-chambered individuals constituted only a small group. However, the content trafficked in those chambers (which we detail in later chapters) may reinforce problematic forms of division and precipitate worrisome action. As we will see through the rest of the book, individuals in the conservative media echo chamber were distinct in ways that would be consequential after Election Day.

Very Conservative National News Media

The identification of a small but meaningful conservative media echo chamber necessitates an assessment of the consumption of national news media that rests further to the right of mainstream conservative outlets like Fox News. As we discussed at the outset of this chapter, the audiences for these outlets expanded in 2020. We asked respondents in wave 9 (December 2020) to indicate their levels of exposure to national news media "sources such as Newsmax, One America News (OANN), The Gateway Pundit, or Parler." We included this item in response to a growing rift between President Trump and Fox News over the latter's Election Day coverage, following the network's election night projection that Joe Biden would win Arizona. When Trump officials contacted the network to have it retract the call, it refused to do so. In the wake of this event, Trump began to urge his followers to abandon Fox and move to these other outlets, which offered even more pro-Trump coverage.

The existence of a conservative media echo chamber is a foundation that can be expanded to include outlets that are even more conservative. It is clear that a discernible portion of Trump supporters desired a national news media environment that pristinely presented a preexisting worldview. As a result, the existence of potentially dissonant coverage of the election in more main-stream conservative sources (e.g., coverage of the Trump campaign's failed legal challenges or of the certification of contested state-level election results) could lead some individuals to shift to outlets that were claiming more openly that Biden's victory was fraudulent.

The wave 9 exposure measure reveals that the audience consuming very conservative media consisted primarily of individuals who were members of the unwavering Trump electorate (see Figure 4.4, panel A). However, it is notable that the audience for these outlets also included some individuals from the wavering Trump electorates and from the electorates unaffiliated with either major party candidate (i.e., everyone else). Although these two groups registered lower levels of exposure than the unwavering Trump supporters, their media behavior patterns reveal some meaningful contact with this very conservative material. The Biden electorates, especially the unwavering Biden one, had little to no exposure to these outlets. Very conservative media offered a diet that included misinformation able to reduce the cognitive dissonance generated by Trump's defeat at the polls.

It is little surprise, then, that conservative media orientations were closely related to the later adoption of these very conservative sources, as we see in Figure 4.4, panel B. Successful avoiders of conservative media, disengaged

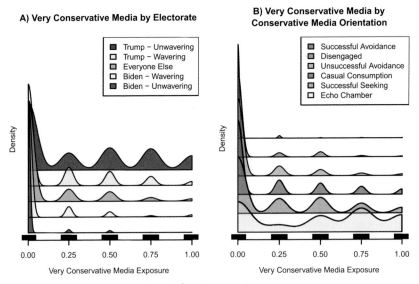

FIGURE 4.4 Very Conservative Media Consumption.
Panels show the density plots of very conservative media consumption, broken down by electorate (panel A) and by conservative media orientation (panel B).

individuals, and unsuccessful avoiders were more likely to say that they never saw content from places like Newsmax, OANN, or Gateway Pundit than that they rarely did. Those who casually consumed conservative media and successful seekers of conservative content who were not in the conservative media echo chamber also reported that they were rarely exposed to such sources, averaging .18 and .24 on the 0–1 scale. Echo-chambered individuals, however, were considerably more likely to encounter this content, saying on average that they sometimes were exposed (M = .47). Indeed, to a large extent, those who consumed this very conservative content were the ones ensconced in the echo chamber, yielding another indication of the extent to which these individuals enveloped themselves in a media bubble.

Communication Convergence

Adding data on "seek" and "avoid" action tendencies to our analysis of national news media exposure reinforces our overarching argument that the 2020 electorate reflected several quite distinct voter groups. While these groups did vary in important ways when it comes to the consumption of national political media, they were more alike than different in their approaches to local news media and social media. As with the national news media outlets, we focused on earlier levels of exposure to political information in local news and social media collected in waves 1, 2, 5, and 6. In addition, "seek" and "avoid" measures were captured in wave 8.

Local news media outlets were the one place where the varied electorates, from the unwavering Trump voters to the unwavering Biden ones, were most likely to consume the same political content (see Figure 4.5). Sizeable percentages of each electorate were exposed to discernible quantities of local media, and this empirical insight stems in no small measure from local news being a more trusted source than any national news outlet.[22] The levels of reported exposure to political information in social media were generally lower than what exists for local media, but the distributions also were consistent across electorates. Although, uniquely, the unwavering Biden electorate tended to report lower levels of social media use than the other groups, the difference, which was not huge, was somewhat offset by the fact that a solid percentage of wavering Biden voters engaged social media for political information, behind only those who did not vote for a major-party candidate or chose not to vote (i.e., everyone else). Nevertheless, the electorates showed far more similarities in local news media and social media exposure than they did in any of our national political media exposure dynamics.

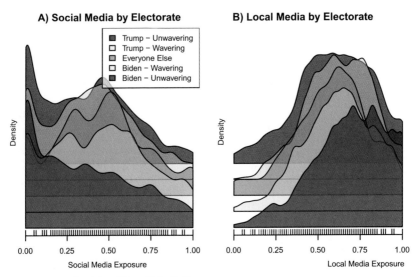

A) Social Media by Electorate

B) Local Media by Electorate

Legend:
- Trump – Unwavering
- Trump – Wavering
- Everyone Else
- Biden – Wavering
- Biden – Unwavering

Social Media Exposure

Local Media Exposure

FIGURE 4.5 Social and Local Media Exposure.
Panels show density plots of exposure to social media sources (panel A) and local media (panel B), broken down by electorate.

Between-electorate similarities for local and social media were even clearer when we considered the "seek" and "avoid" action tendencies (see Figure 4.6). For local news media, more than one-quarter of each electorate reported seeking out this content. The unwavering Biden electorate was particularly high in this regard, but all five electorates consumed this information with some regularity. All five electorates reveal high levels (over 30 percent of any one electorate) of the casual consumption of local news. And vanishingly few individuals reported no contact with local media, whether as a result of successful avoidance or disengagement (5 percent or less).

The greatest similarities between the five electorates can be found in their social media action tendencies. A relatively small percentage of each electorate (less than 20 percent) consisted of successful social media seekers of political information. Instead, engagement with political information on social networking sites was driven by incidental exposure, both casual consumption and unsuccessful avoidance. More than half of those in any of the electorates fell into a combination of the two incidental exposure categories. The two unwavering electorates had higher percentages of individuals who reported being able to successfully avoid political content in their social media feeds, but these percentages hovered around 20 percent for each group. Most people did encounter politics as part of their social media landscape, but it was clearly not something that many of them were proactively seeking.

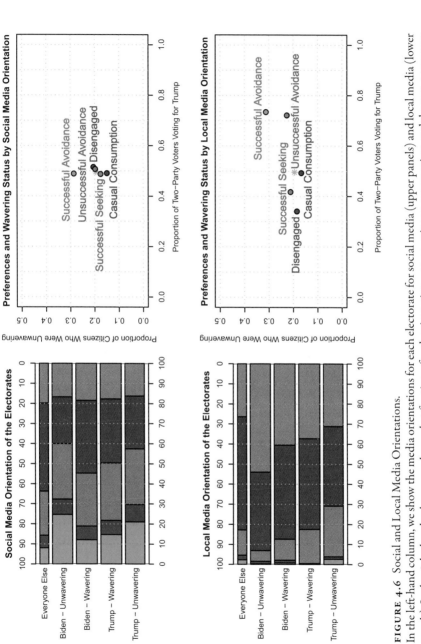

FIGURE 4.6 Social and Local Media Orientations.

In the left-hand column, we show the media orientations for each electorate for social media (upper panels) and local media (lower panels). In the right-hand column, we show what fraction of each orientation was wavering vs. unwavering, and the two-party vote share for Trump.

Using Twitter Activity to Support Our Self-Report Measures

To gain additional insight into the social media behavior of our wavering and unwavering electorates, we asked survey participants for their consent to analyze their Twitter behavior (and corresponding linguistic patterns).

As expected, most participants reported having a Twitter account. In wave 4, 1,415 individuals in our sample (19.1 percent) reported that they had one and that it was intended for personal use. We obtained consent from 522 participants to collect data from their accounts. Of these, 118 accounts were not retrievable because of incorrect usernames, suspended accounts, blocked content, and the like. This yielded a total of 384 accounts for which we could track survey respondents' Twitter use.[†] Overall, data were available for fewer Trump supporters (23 wavering and 24 unwavering) than Biden ones (94 wavering and 161 unwavering). The remaining 82 individuals were not members of any of the candidate-affiliated electorates. For these 384 users, we measured the volume of tweets posted between November 3, 2019, and November 3, 2020, the full year leading up to Election Day. When examining the content (topics and broader themes) of tweets, we limited the sample to users who tweeted at least once during this one-year period ($N = 302$). We can then use these Twitter accounts to assess their communicative behavior.

To be clear, because so few of our respondents allowed us to use their Twitter data, our analyses here are necessarily circumscribed. We cannot claim that our data are in any way a representative sample, and so we are not drawing the sort of inferences here that we do elsewhere in the book. But we view this as a useful descriptive analysis that could serve as a launching pad for future efforts to more fully integrate social media and survey data.[23]

Volume

First, to validate the self-reported social media consumption habits, Figure 4.7 presents the volume of tweets posted by participants with different social media action tendencies. Our expectation would be that those who actively seek out this content, or at least do not avoid it, would have the highest levels of Twitter activity.

---

†. These data were analyzed separately from survey data and only aggregate results from Twitter were connected to the survey, per an arrangement reviewed by the University of Pennsylvania IRB.

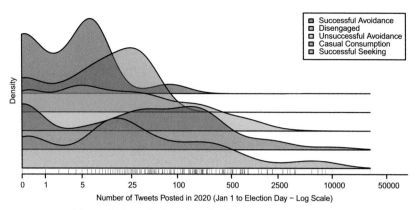

FIGURE 4.7 Twitter Volume by Social Media Orientation.
The figure shows density plots of the observed number of tweets posted by Twitter users who gave us permission to link data, broken down by social media orientation.

As expected, Twitter posting frequency differed by group, with the lowest activity recorded for participants in the successful avoidance group (who posted an average of 8.6 tweets in the prior year) and the highest posting activity for those in the successful seeking group (who posted an average of 383.7 tweets). Those who signaled a desire to avoid politics in social media and reported being successful at doing so were least active on the Twitter platform, and those who successfully embraced politics being a part of their social media environment were among the most active in this mediated space.

To understand how posting behaviors varied across the electorates, we conducted two separate comparisons. Because we were only able to get Twitter data from forty-seven Trump supporters, we cannot say much of anything about the differences in behavior between Biden and Trump ones. But pooling Biden and Trump adherents makes it possible to say something about the differences between those who were wavering and unwavering. Here, since greater conviction should predict activity, our expectation was that unwavering voters—who are more firmly anchored to their candidate—would post more tweets, and in general should be more active on social media. Comparing those in the wavering and unwavering electorates, we found that wavering voters posted an average of 74.9 times in the prior year compared to 380.0 times for unwavering voters, a large and statistically significant difference that was robust to removing outliers and to nonparametric analysis techniques (bootstrap $p < .001$). Overall, individuals who were firmer in their political convictions were more active posters on social media, just as we would expect *ex ante*.

Themes

Our wavering/unwavering and action tendencies distinctions should matter not just for how much individuals post but also for what they post about. To assess this, we examined the content and thematic composition of tweets posted by the 302 participants who tweeted at least once during the year leading up to the elections. We identified and qualitatively analyzed two distinct themes.[§]

One theme was clearly political, focusing on Trump, the Democrats, and debates around issues such as taxes, healthcare, and the Israeli-Palestinian conflict. The second cluster was much more diverse and included discussions of topics ranging from sports, fashion, recipes, and food to other Twitter-related ads, competitions, giveaways, inspirational quotes, and quizzes. Given these breakdowns, we labeled these themes "political" and "non-political," respectively.

The question, then, is whether our unwavering voters posted more about politics. Figure 4.8 presents the distribution of proportions of tweet language coded as political for the wavering and unwavering groups. As the figure shows, unwavering voters not only were more active on Twitter but also, when tweeting, focused more on political topics than did the wavering group. To further probe this finding, we compared the extent to which unwavering and wavering accounts talked about politics. Although not sizeable, the differences between these groups were clear. Unwavering voters posted more frequently on politically relevant topics than did wavering ones (40.6 percent vs. 38.0 percent; bootstrap $p < .001$).

Taken as a whole, these results showed that at least these individuals fit the pattern that we would expect: unwavering electorates tweeted more than wavering ones and were more likely to engage with political content when posting or retweeting. These results are consistent with the self-reports elicited by the survey and highlight that our self-reports do meaningfully capture variation in observable behavior, at least of these individuals.

Communication Electorates

An exposure-frequency-activity approach to the study of political media use reveals the 2020 electorates to be distinct communicatively in relation

---

§. See the Online Appendix for the details of the process through which we identified these themes.

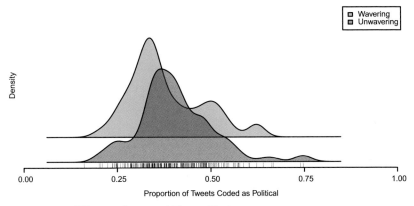

FIGURE 4.8 Wavering Status and Twitter Topics.
The figure shows the density plot of the proportion of tweets that were political, broken down by wavering (green) vs. unwavering (purple) voters.

to national political media. A sizeable percentage of the unwavering Trump electorate resided at the high end of conservative media exposure range but rested at the lower end of the frequency distributions for all other national news media types. The unwavering Biden electorate consumed sizeable quantities of all types of non-conservative national political media. However, this group's media exposure anchors are not ideological. There was a decent percentage of the unwavering Biden electorate at the highest levels of liberal news media exposure; even larger percentages of this group were at the higher register for moderate media and legacy print media. Also, the incorporation of properly realized frequency distributions allowed for important distinctions to be made between the wavering and unwavering peer groups tied to the respective candidates. The unwavering Trump electorate had far less contact with non-conservative media (especially moderate media) than their wavering Trump peer group, and the wavering Trump electorate was also defined more by its tempered levels of exposure to conservative media. For the Biden electorates, the unwavering group consumed more legacy print than its wavering peer electorate.

The unwavering Trump electorate was defined by its successful seeking of conservative media content and relative effectiveness in avoiding any national political media that do not share the same ideological orientation. At the same time, members of the wavering Trump electorate were more casual consumers of conservative media, and this group retained a far higher percentage of citizens who would at least dip their toes into moderate national political media. The Biden-affiliated camps were less ideologically oriented in their national political media activities than the Trump supporters were. Biden supporters, even members of the unwavering Biden electorate, were defined by their successful seeking out of moderate and legacy media more so than of liberal media. The unwavering Biden electorate's attachment to legacy, historically print media was particularly noteworthy. Members of the unaffiliated electorate were, for the most part, casual consumers of a diverse range of national media, showing no preference for outlets with a particular ideological orientation or set of journalistic standards.

Our exposure-frequency-activity methodology provides new insights into the all-important concept of incidental exposure. It makes the case that its casual consumption and unsuccessful avoidance dimensions need to be disaggregated. Incidental contact can result from happenstance or a failure to act effectively on one's desire to avoid some kinds of material deemed undesirable. The dynamics of how citizens come to experience this incidental exposure are unique across the two types, and may well generate distinct media effects.

The measures collected for this study also allow us to identify respondents enveloped in a small but meaningful conservative media echo chamber and to confirm that there were virtually no respondents inhabiting a corresponding liberal one. While only a small percentage of respondents seem to have surrounded themselves exclusively with like-minded national political media content, some in the unwavering Trump electorate fell into this classification. One-sided message environments of this kind have the potential to induce jarring levels of cognitive dissonance when real-world political events fail to turn out as expected (e.g., Trump losing the 2020 US presidential election). The result can be political unrest like that witnessed on January 6 and further retreat into the darker recesses of a political media landscape rife with outlets all too willing to traffic in misinformation, disinformation, and conspiracy theories. In the chapters that follow, we explore whether and how these patterns of media use—and particularly orientations toward conservative media—played an important role in shaping what people thought about the crises and how they made sense of the election.

Did the COVID-19 Pandemic Sink Trump's Reelection?

HOW TRUMP AND BIDEN APPROACHED THE PANDEMIC

Kathleen Hall Jamieson, Matthew Levendusky, Josh Pasek, and Andrew Renninger

And we're prepared, and we're doing a great job with it [COVID-19]. And it will go away. Just stay calm. It will go away.

—President Donald Trump after a meeting with Republican senators, March 10, 2020[1]

No rhetoric is needed. Just judge this president on the facts. 5 million Americans infected with COVID-19. More than 170,000 Americans have died. By far the worst performance of any nation on Earth. More than 50 million people have filed for unemployment this year. More than 10 million people are going to lose their health insurance this year. Nearly one in 6 small businesses have closed this year. If this president is re-elected we know what will happen.

—Joe Biden, acceptance speech, Democratic National Convention, August 21, 2020[2]

ON FEBRUARY 25, roughly a month after the first known US case of COVID-19 was confirmed in a Washington State resident who had visited Wuhan, China,[3] Dr. Nancy Messonnier, the director of the National Center for Immunization and Respiratory Diseases, predicted that COVID-19 spreading throughout the United States was not "so much of a question of if this will happen anymore, but rather more a question of exactly when this will happen." In the same news briefing, she suggested that businesses make plans for employees to work from home and that cities plan to implement social distancing measures. "We are asking the American public to work with us to prepare in the expectation that this could be bad," she concluded.[4]

Coronavirus is "under control in our country," responded the incumbent president. "We have very few people with it, and the people that have it are, in all cases, I have not heard anything other—the people are getting better, they're all getting better."[5] At that point, according to the *New York Times*, "the United States has just 57 cases, 40 of them connected to the Diamond Princess, the cruise ship overwhelmed by the coronavirus after it docked in Japan."[6] But it was not under control. Even then, COVID-19 was spreading across the country, though few people realized it at the time. In the weeks and months that followed, the nation would watch in horror as the virus overwhelmed New York City and other early epicenters. In mid-March, much of the nation locked down to fight the virus, which would spark the economic crisis we cover in Chapter 6 ("The Best of Times, the Worst of Times"). In the months that followed, wave after wave of the virus would sweep across the nation, straining the hospital system and pushing the death toll ever higher.

Biden and Trump's approaches to the virus could hardly have been more different. As the epigraph with which we opened this chapter attests, throughout his time in office the incumbent sought to downplay the virus and reopen the economy following the spring lockdowns. Alternatively, the Democrat contended that the economy would not thrive until the virus was brought under control. Whereas Trump argued that the country had rounded the corner and the pandemic would fade into the rearview mirror, Biden argued that much more needed to happen before that was true. Whereas Trump was almost never seen wearing a mask and held numerous in-person rallies and events, Biden rarely left his Delaware home for much of the campaign, and when he did emerge, was masked. When the former vice president did hold rallies, they were in parking lots, with his supporters honking their admiration from their cars.

Perhaps nothing better illustrated the candidates' contrasting approaches to the COVID-19 crisis than their party's respective conventions. In the late spring, Democrats confirmed that they would have a virtual convention with almost no in-person events.[7] During their convention, Democrats laced their message with reminders that the country was in the midst of a pandemic. Most speakers were fully virtual, and Biden and Harris delivered their acceptance speeches to an empty auditorium, with the crew socially distanced and wearing masks.

In contrast, the Republicans' convention sought to downplay the pandemic. After shifting from their original location of Charlotte, North Carolina, because the Democratic governor and mayor imposed COVID-related restrictions that they found to be too onerous, the Republicans attempted to hold an in-person convention in Jacksonville, Florida. When that proved not to be possible, they pivoted to a hybrid model at the last moment. Where the Democrats had no in-person audiences, the Republicans held two large-scale, in-person events. Vice President Pence spoke from a stage at the Fort McHenry National Monument before a crowd of several hundred largely maskless supporters, and President Trump accepted his party's nomination on an elevated stage in front of the White House. At Trump's event, there were fifteen hundred fans, most of whom were not wearing masks, seated arm to arm on folding chairs on the lawn. As we will show in the second part of this chapter, these competing treatments of COVID-19 spilled over into how their supporters assessed the pandemic.

In the pages that follow, we draw on the work of others to show that the president was well aware of the nature and severity of the pathogen. We then contrast the positions taken by the two contenders on the future of the pandemic, lockdowns, masking, and the advice provided by public health officials such as Dr. Anthony Fauci. In the process we note that Trump tried to deflect blame for mishandling the pandemic by redirecting it to China and the mass media or by claiming that it had been overblown and would soon fade away.

Before launching into our arguments in this chapter, we need to provide more information about the somewhat unusual structure of the chapters that cover our four crises: Chapter 5 (the pandemic), Chapter 6 (the economy), Chapter 7 (the debate over race and policing), and Chapter 9 (electoral and democratic legitimacy). In each of these chapters, we split the chapter into two parts to better help structure it for our readers. In Part 1 of each chapter, we provide the narrative explanation that covers the key elements of each crisis, which sets up the key questions to be addressed empirically. In Part 2, we use our data to answer the questions raised in Part 1, allowing us to understand how our electorates saw these crises and their implications not only for the election but for American democracy more broadly. We hope this bifurcation makes it easier for readers of all types to get what they need from these chapters. Those readers whose primary interest is in the history and rhetoric can concentrate their attention on the first part and skim the subsequent analyses. Alternatively, those more interested in the empirics can skim the narratives and focus on the data and results.

Stay at Home or Reopen the Economy?

On March 19, California became the first state to issue a stay-at-home order, requiring citizens to remain at home unless they were traveling to obtain necessary supplies (such as food or medicine) or going to an essential job. In the weeks that followed, a total of forty-two states and territories would impose similar orders to help flatten the curve and prevent the health care system from being overwhelmed.[8]

While Trump was initially supportive of such measures, he quickly reversed himself, arguing that the nation should focus on the economy and lift the stay-at-home orders and other restrictions. Emblematic of the new position was Trump's tweet in late March: "WE CANNOT LET THE CURE BE WORSE THAN THE PROBLEM ITSELF."[9] He argued as well that "our country wasn't built to be shut down."[10] In early May, as governors debated lifting the stay-at-home orders, he noted that "we have to get our country open again," and continued, "People want to go back, and you're going to have a problem if you don't do it."[11]

Indeed, there were problems resulting from the stay-at-home orders. As anger over the lockdowns grew, Trump famously tweeted "LIBERATE MINNESOTA," "LIBERATE MICHIGAN," and "LIBERATE VIRGINIA" in the span of a few minutes on April 17.[12] All three states had Democratic governors who had imposed relatively restrictive stay-at-home orders, which led to protests. Those in Michigan verged on violence, offering a grim foreshadowing of January 6. "Dozens of heavily armed militiamen crowded into the Michigan Statehouse [in April 2020] to protest a stay-at-home order by the Democratic governor to slow the pandemic," noted the *New York Times*. "Chanting and stomping their feet, they halted legislative business, tried to force their way onto the floor and brandished rifles from the gallery over lawmakers below."[13]

But this was not the only time that events in Michigan during 2020 offered a grim foreshadowing of January 6. In October, the FBI charged thirteen individuals who had ties to a paramilitary group known as the Wolverine Watchmen with attempting to kidnap Michigan governor Gretchen Whitmer and try her for treason over the state's COVID-19 restrictions, a chilling preview of rioters walking through the halls of the Capitol chanting "Hang Mike Pence." Whitmer asserted that Trump's actions—his support of the earlier protests and his failure to condemn violence—were a tacit endorsement of their tactics: "When our leaders meet with, encourage, or fraternize with domestic terrorists, they legitimize their actions and they are complicit. When they stoke and contribute to hate speech, they are complicit," she said.[14]

While most protests over lockdowns did not turn violent, the case that economic activity needed to ramp up was a compelling one. Disruptions caused by the pandemic included slowdowns in the supply chain that would continue to plague the country well into the second year of the Biden administration. Throughout the campaign, Donald Trump focused on the costs to businesses rather than the health consequences of the virus. Some argued that much of Trump's thinking about the COVID-19 lockdowns was influenced by their effect on stocks.[15] As we will see in Chapter 6 ("The Best of Times, The Worst of Times"), Trump's campaign repeatedly emphasized that the nation should lift the stay-at-home orders, return to work, and see the country's economy return to normal.

But Biden took a very different approach to the stay-at-home orders. He hewed to the guidance from most public health experts and argued that the economy should restart only when public health protections were in place. "An effective plan to beat the virus is the ultimate answer to how we get our economy back on track," said the Democratic Party nominee. "So we should stop thinking of the health and economic responses as separate. They are not."[16]

His pledge to follow the science took a controversial turn in the first joint interview he and Harris gave after he picked her as his running mate. Asked whether he would shut down the country again if scientists recommended it due to the twin risks of COVID-19 and the flu, Biden responded, "I would listen to the scientists."[17] Faced with Republican attacks for appearing to support another lockdown, Biden backtracked in the coming days to argue that he did not anticipate the need, would follow the science, and wanted everyone coming in contact with others in public to mask.[18]

Capitalizing on what the Republicans viewed as a significant Biden gaffe, in his convention acceptance speech a week later Trump contended that "instead of following the science, Joe Biden wants to inflict a painful shutdown on the entire country. His shutdown would inflict unthinkable and lasting harm on our nation's children, families and citizens of all backgrounds." Reframing a shutdown as a public health risk, the incumbent also contended that "the cost of the Biden shutdown would be measured in increased drug overdoses, depression, alcohol addiction, suicides, heart attacks, economic devastation and more. Joe Biden's plan is not a solution to the virus, but rather a surrender."[19]

Biden shot back at Trump, arguing that it was Trump's failures that kept key institutions closed. In the October 22 debate, he said, "It's his ineptitude that caused the country to have to shut down in large part, why businesses have gone under, why schools are closed, why so many people have lost their living, and why they're concerned."[20] Biden repeated his claim that the US economy could not restart in a meaningful way until the virus was under control: "I'm going to shut down the virus, not the country." But when debate moderator Kristen Welker asked whether Biden was ruling out a future lockdown, Biden demurred: "I'm not shutting down today," he said, "but there are . . . Look, you need standards."[21] Where Biden was equivocal, Trump was categorical. "No, we're not going to shut down. And we have to open our schools," he said. The contrast could hardly have been starker.

Mask Wearing

The candidates' competing positions on mask wearing and public events were emblematic of this same contrast. On April 3, when the CDC recommended Americans mask in public settings to reduce the spread of the pathogen, Trump noted that such guidance was voluntary and that he would not be following suit: "You can do it—you don't have to do it. It's only a recommendation. . . . I don't think I'm going to be doing it."[22] Trump was rarely masked, even in locations that mandated it. Many of his rallies featured tightly packed audiences with few mask-wearers in attendance. "I wear masks when needed. When needed, I wear masks," he remarked during the first debate. "I don't wear a mask like him. Every time you see him, he's got a mask."[23]

Trump offered the media images of enthusiastic partisans and their leader apparently unaffected by a raging pandemic. He also hosted large-scale rallies and in-person events—including the September 26 Rose Garden ceremony for Supreme Court nominee Amy Coney Barrett in which little social distancing or mask wearing was in view. In the words of Dr. Anthony Fauci, that was "a superspreader event," with at least eight people who attended the event testing positive for COVID-19 soon afterward, including the president and First Lady.[24]

Even in the days leading up to Trump's own diagnosis with COVID-19, the White House downplayed the importance of masking to prevent the spread of the illness.[25] After the election, evidence would emerge that he had participated in the first debate on September 29 despite a positive COVID-19 test three days earlier, then followed by a negative one his team decided to consider dispositive,[26] even though it was not, as he needed to be hospitalized for the disease on October 2.[27] When offered masks by their Cleveland Clinic hosts at the September debate, Trump's family flouted agreed-upon rules and refused to wear them.[28]

Indeed, even after Trump was released from the hospital—where doctors confirmed that he had been much sicker than he or his staff acknowledged at the time[29] and that he allegedly needed experimental drug treatments to save his life[30]—he continued to downplay the disease, telling the public, "Don't be afraid of Covid. Don't let it dominate your life. . . . I feel better than I did 20 years ago!"[31] In contrast, Joe Biden was regularly photographed wearing a mask and socially distanced from his aides and supporters.

Who Was Responsible for the Pandemic?

Throughout 2020, Biden's argument was that Trump had mismanaged the pandemic and that his failure to control it was a reason to vote him out of office, as the second epigraph to this chapter suggests. Biden claimed that Trump's was a policy failure—he failed to plan and coordinate a federal response—and that the incumbent had done "next to nothing" to fight the virus.[32] Biden declared that the president should focus on coordinating the federal government's response with states, distributing tests to help flag infected individuals, and developing plans for vaccine distribution, which he said the incumbent had not done.[33]

Trump, by contrast, sought to shift blame to others, most notably China and the media. He also argued that COVID's severity had been overblown, especially by Democrats and the media, and the nation would soon round the bend and the virus would disappear from our lives. In this section, we review their contrasting arguments about responsibility for the pandemic.

What Did the President Know, And When Did He Know It?

With mounting evidence that the novel coronavirus was spreading around the world, a journalist asked President Trump on January 22, 2020, whether he was worried about the possibility of a pandemic. "No, not at all," the incumbent replied. "We have it totally under control. It's one person coming in from China, and we have it under control. It's going to be just fine."[34] Trump knew at the time that the virus posed a serious threat. So too did his staff and advisors. In a taped February 7 conversation with Bob Woodward—which would become public when Woodward and Robert Costa's best-selling book *Peril* was published in September 2020—Trump characterized the novel coronavirus as "deadly stuff" transmitted through the air. "It's a very tricky situation," said Trump. "It goes through air, Bob. That's always tougher than the touch. . . . That's a very tricky one. That's a very delicate one. It's also more deadly than even your strenuous flus."[35]

In that same interview, Trump explained that he would "play it down" and not tell the public about the true danger of COVID (to avoid causing a panic, he said). Accordingly, in March, Trump suggested that COVID-19 was less dangerous than the flu, tweeting: "So last year 37,000 Americans died from the common Flu. It averages between 27,000 and 70,000 per year. Nothing is shut down, life & the economy go on. At this moment there are 546 confirmed cases of CoronaVirus, with 22 deaths. Think about that!" Testifying before a House committee later that week, Anthony Fauci countered that "this is 10 times more lethal than the seasonal flu."[36]

This point—that Trump deliberately downplayed the severity of the virus—was a persistent Biden theme throughout the campaign. "Donald Trump knew that COVID-19 was dangerous. He knew it was deadly. And he purposely downplayed it. Now, nearly 200,000 Americans are dead," the Democratic Party nominee tweeted on September 9.[37] "President Trump knew how deadly COVID-19 was back in January and did nothing to control it," Biden noted in late October,[38] a theme Biden also emphasized in both their first and second debates.[39] This assertion—that Trump's inaction cost lives—fit into Biden's general argument that Trump had mismanaged COVID.

In the first debate, the Democrat suggested that Trump was protecting himself but not others in public settings, a comment that would be belied by the incumbent's COVID diagnosis days later. "A reporter came up to him to ask him a question," noted Biden of Trump, "he said, 'No no. Stand back. Put on your mask, put on a mask. Have you been tested? I'm way far away from those other people.' That's what he said. 'I'm going to be okay.' He's not worried about you. He's not worried about the people out there." "We've had no negative effect, and we've had, 35, 40,000, people at some of these rallies," Trump responded.[40]

Unspoken in that exchange was the name of Trump enthusiast and 2012 Republican presidential contender Herman Cain, who had died of COVID-19 in July 2020.[41] Cain had attended Trump's largely maskless rally in Tulsa, Oklahoma, several weeks earlier, leading some to speculate that he contracted the virus there. While it is impossible to know whether Cain, or anyone else, contracted the virus there, it is known that many areas where Trump held large, in-person rallies subsequently experienced outbreaks of the virus.[42]

Shifting Blame to China

"China has been working very hard to contain the Coronavirus," Trump noted in a January 24 tweet. "The United States greatly appreciates their efforts and transparency. It will all work out well. In particular, on behalf of the American People, I want to thank President Xi!"[43] That position was short-lived. If anyone was to blame, Trump would later contend, it was China. Speaking at a ceremony in the Rose Garden in May, Trump noted that "the world is now suffering as a result of the malfeasance of the Chinese government. . . . Countless lives have been taken, and profound economic hardship has been inflicted all around the globe." This was a theme he returned to repeatedly throughout the year.[44] Speaking to Bob Woodward, Trump employed the same blame-and-exoneration frame: "The virus has nothing to do with me. It's not my fault. It's—China let the damn virus out."[45]

Throughout the campaign, not only would Trump argue that China was to blame for the virus, but he would also contend that his decision to ban travel from China early in the pandemic saved lives. On January 31, 2020, Trump issued a proclamation banning travelers who had been in China in the previous fourteen days from entering the United States,[46] a policy later extended to cover other nations where COVID-19 was spreading rapidly. In his acceptance speech at the summer's Republican convention, he said, "When I took bold action to issue a travel ban on China, Joe Biden called it hysterical and xenophobic. If we had listened to Joe, hundreds of thousands more Americans would have died."[47] This same view resurfaced in the first debate, when Trump argued, "And if you [Biden] were here [in the Oval Office], it wouldn't be 200 [200,000 people dead from COVID-19], it would be two million people because you were very late on the draw. You didn't want me to ban China, which was heavily infected. You didn't want me to ban Europe."[48] While some scholars were skeptical that the travel ban did much to slow the spread of the virus,[49] Trump was not.

Blaming the Media for Exaggerating COVID-19

More generally, Trump argued that the risks of COVID-19 had been overblown, especially by the media, who he declared were exaggerating the pandemic to harm him and boost their own ratings. "Low Ratings Fake News

MSDNC (Comcast) & @CNN are doing everything possible to make the Caronavirus [*sic*] look as bad as possible," President Trump tweeted on February 26,[50] a sentiment he would repeat throughout the year. It is also worth noting that he refers to MSNBC as "MSDNC," a subtle prime to his audience of the linkages between the mass media and the Democratic Party (DNC), underscoring a long-running conservative argument about liberal media bias and reinforcing such inferences among his supporters.

This was not the only time Trump claimed the media were emphasizing COVID-19 to harm him. Later in the year, he argued that the media focus on the virus' spread was an attempt to influence the election, tweeting, "The Fake News is talking about CASES, CASES, CASES. This includes many low risk people. Media is doing everything possible to create fear prior to [Election Day] November 3rd."[51] Several days later, he suggested that because COVID-19 coverage was designed solely to deny him reelection, the topic would shift after the election, tweeting: "[COVID-19 coverage is] A Fake News Media Conspiracy . . . Corrupt Media conspiracy at all time high. On November 4th, topic will totally change."[52] While the post-election topic did change—to Biden's victory and Trump's refusal to recognize it, as we discuss in Chapter 9 ("'Stop the Steal'")—COVID-19 also remained in the news.

Trump's argument about COVID-19 being overblown was covered skeptically in mainstream media but less so in conservative outlets. As studies showed, those who relied on conservative media such as Fox News were more likely to be misinformed about the pandemic[53] and less likely to follow social distancing guidelines.[54] In the second part of the chapter, we explore the role of conservative media consumption and orientation on attitudes in more depth.

But more broadly, the argument that the media were exaggerating the risks of COVID-19 fit with another Trump claim: COVID-19 would soon disappear altogether. At least thirty-eight times during 2020, Trump asserted that COVID would simply vanish at some point.[55] Perhaps most famously, in February 2020 he remarked, "It's [COVID] going to disappear. One day—it's like a miracle—it will disappear."[56]

When the spread of the virus persisted in the final months of the election, Trump launched a related but distinct claim: that the United States was rounding the bend on COVID-19 and the worst of the virus was behind us. He first voiced this claim in late August 2020 at a rally, when he declared that the nation was "rounding the final turn," a phrase he would repeat, with some minor alterations, thirty-nine times before the election.[57] The argument was that the worst of the pandemic was over and, with the vaccines approaching, the virus would soon recede into the background. Complicating this argument that fall was that cases and deaths continued to increase rapidly. Although we did not know it then, in the fall of 2020 the United States was indeed rounding a curve, but it was the intensifying curve of the third wave, which would not peak until that winter at the cost of thousands of additional lives.

The Politicization of Public Health Authorities

In the face of a novel virus infecting millions of Americans and killing hundreds of thousands of them, one might expect that public health authorities would be seen by all sides as valorous, apolitical sources of advice. In the COVID-19 pandemic, that was not to be the case. Public health authorities clashed, quite publicly, with President Trump throughout the pandemic. For example, various experts disputed both the incumbent's claims that the death rate from COVID was being exaggerated by the CDC[58] and his touting of the efficacy of hydroxychloroquine (HCQ), an antimalarial drug that he cast as a potential "game changer."[59] Although the incumbent reported in May that he was taking the drug prophylactically,[60] when he was admitted to the hospital in October with COVID-19, it was not included in his treatment regimen. In the interim, randomized controlled studies had shown it to be ineffective for those who were hospitalized with the virus.[61]

Perhaps no relationship evidenced this antagonism better than the one between Trump and Dr. Anthony Fauci. Early in the pandemic, Trump referred to Fauci as a "major television star," perhaps the highest praise that one could receive from the reality TV star turned president.[62] But their relationship turned testy after Fauci rebutted some of Trump's claims about the pandemic, drawing Trump's ire. In April, Trump retweeted a call to fire Fauci,[63] while in late June Biden pledged, "If I'm elected, I'll immediately reach out to Dr. Fauci and ask him to continue his incredible service to our country."[64] Indeed, while Trump pushed back against Fauci's recommendations, Biden, as we noted above, said that we needed to listen to science, implicitly inviting his supporters to rally to Fauci's defense and increasing the chances that Trump's supporters would view Fauci with disdain.[65]

Fauci and Trump's relationship took a particularly rocky turn in October. With Fauci earning higher favorability ratings than the incumbent president,[66] in early October a Trump campaign ad misleadingly implied that the NIAID director had applauded the forty-fifth president's handling of the pandemic. Just as President Trump was recovering from the coronavirus, so too was America, said the ad. Not only were seniors getting lifesaving drugs in record time, but Trump was "tackling the virus head on as leaders should." The spot then suggested that Fauci agreed. As his words were superimposed on the screen, he is shown in a March Fox interview saying, "I can't imagine that . . . anybody could be doing more." Fact-checkers quickly pointed out that Fauci's statement referred to his own efforts and those of the White House task force on which he served. "Since the beginning that we even recognized what this was," he had said in the Fox News interview, "I have been devoting almost full time on this. I'm down at the White House virtually every day with the task force. It's every single day. So, I can't imagine that under any circumstances that anybody could be doing more."[67] As Trump campaign spokespersons[68] and a Trump tweet both contended that the ad quoted Fauci's own words, the NIAID director insisted, "In my nearly five decades of public service, I have never publicly endorsed any political candidate. The comments attributed to me without my permission in the GOP campaign ad were taken out of context from a broad statement I made months ago about the efforts of federal public health officials."[69] The tense back-and-forth continued. In a mid-October call with reporters about campaign plans, Trump reportedly said of Fauci, "Every time he goes on television, there's always a bomb, but there's a bigger bomb if you fire him. This guy's a disaster."[70]

With new infections on the rise in forty-two states, at the end of October Fauci elicited outrage in the Trump campaign with his blunt assessment that "all the stars are aligned in the wrong place as you go into the fall and winter season, with people congregating at home indoors. You could not possibly be positioned more poorly."[71] Fauci also observed that Biden "is taking it seriously from a public health perspective," while Trump is "looking at it from a different perspective," specifically by focusing on "the economy and reopening the country,"[72] giving what some Republicans viewed as a de facto endorsement of Biden. Responding to a chant from a rally crowd to "fire Fauci," Trump said, "Don't tell anybody but let me wait 'til a little bit after the election."[73]

Nor were the national health agencies insulated from Republican claims that they were acting against the interests of the incumbent. As the forty-fifth president urged schools to reopen for in-person classes in August, a leaked email showed Trump administration advisor Dr. Paul Alexander berating CDC scientists for supposed "hit pieces" and for exaggerating the risk COVID-19 posed to children in order to "hurt the President."[74] In a similar vein, on August 22, Trump tweeted, "The deep state, or whoever, over at the FDA is making it very difficult for drug companies to get people in order to test the vaccines and therapeutics. Obviously, they are hoping to delay the answer until after November 3rd."[75] And in early October, the incumbent accused the FDA of engaging in a "political hit job" for establishing a vaccination authorization process that he assumed would delay the okaying of a coronavirus vaccine until after the November election.[76] Given this sustained exchange, it is possible, indeed probable, that evaluations of these public health figures would polarize across the course of our study.

The Questions to Be Answered in Chapter 5, Part 2

The COVID-19 pandemic and the incumbent's handling of it were destined to be at issue in the 2020 election. In this first part of Chapter 5, we showed how Biden and Trump laid out strikingly distinct approaches to the pandemic. While Trump argued that the worst was behind the United States and COVID would soon recede into the rearview mirror, Biden claimed that much more needed to be done to fight the virus. While Trump claimed that we should reopen the economy, Biden said that we could not restart the economy until the virus was under control. While Biden rallied his supporters from their cars, Trump held large, in-person rallies. While Biden religiously wore a mask in public, Trump almost never wore one. Simply put, Biden and Trump provided fundamentally different outlooks on the pandemic.

With this context in mind, in the next part of Chapter 5 we ask and answer four questions. First, how did voters evaluate Trump's handling of the pandemic? Second, how did evaluations of his performance, as well as voters' personal experiences with the pandemic, affect their candidate preferences? Third, how did Trump and Biden supporters see the pandemic—for whom was it a central issue, and why? And finally, did evaluations of ostensibly apolitical medical sources such as Anthony Fauci and the CDC become polarized over the course of the campaign? Together, answering these questions helps us understand how the COVID-19 pandemic shaped the 2020 election and its aftermath.

5.2

Did the COVID-19 Pandemic Sink Trump's Reelection?

HOW THE VIRUS SHAPED THE ELECTION

Matthew Levendusky, Josh Pasek, Andrew Renninger,
and Kathleen Hall Jamieson

IN PART I of this chapter, we saw that Trump and Biden took fundamentally different approaches to the pandemic throughout the campaign, with Trump arguing the worst was behind us and stressing the need to restart the economy, while Biden emphasized that we had to get the virus at bay before we could move forward with the economy or anything else. We have already chronicled some of the effects of these divergent responses in Chapter 3 ("Not One Electorate, but Many"), where we saw that Biden's voters viewed the election as a referendum on Trump's handling of the virus and Trump's voters perceived it as a referendum on his handling of the economy. But that conclusion neither accounts for the divergence in perceptions nor identifies the factors that shaped those attitudes.

Turning from the messaging that was the focus of Part I of this chapter to the meaning voters made of it, we draw four conclusions here. First, many voters—even some of Trump's most ardent ones—thought his handling of the pandemic was a weakness of his, not a strength. Our panelists soured on Trump's handling of the pandemic during 2020, even relative to their overall assessments of him. Among the more than twenty other issues we asked about, the pandemic emerged as the one on which the incumbent was most vulnerable.

Second, how Trump handled the pandemic did, in fact, hurt his prospects. Tracking our panelists over time, we can see those who are skeptical of his handling of the pandemic moving away from him and toward Biden. As they watched the pandemic play out, even some who started off in Trump's camp at the outset became disaffected.

While these effects are real, they are also modest. Most of those who initially supported Trump ultimately balloted for him even if they were unimpressed with the ways in which he dealt with the pandemic. Our third finding explains why: Trump and Biden voters perceived the pandemic fundamentally differently. Biden's voters were more concerned with the virus, and reported higher levels of anxiety about it. They also more frequently checked the news for information about it, and were more worried about its effects on their health (or the health of a loved one) should they become infected with the virus.

Trump supporters squared their perceptions that he performed relatively poorly in this area with their support of his candidacy by discounting the importance of the pandemic. For them, the pandemic was not the central issue in the election. The economy (an area where Trump was stronger) mattered more. In line with that conviction, they forecast that the worst of it was already behind us. And they focused on aspects of the pandemic they thought Trump handled well, such as an early ban on travel from China and the development of vaccines through Operation Warp Speed. In short, Trump's supporters—and his campaign—recognized the pandemic as an area of weakness, and worked to deemphasize and reframe it as a result.

Finally, and perhaps most troublingly, we show that the crisis politicized perceptions of public health experts such as Dr. Anthony Fauci and agencies such as the Centers for Disease Control. As Trump called their recommendations into doubt (and as they pushed back on some of Trump's statements about the pandemic), his supporters came to see them as less trustworthy sources of information. In contrast, Biden's supporters came to trust them more. This politicization of public health figures and agencies—paralleling trends in other types of scientific communication such as climate change—has dangerous consequences not only for the COVID-19 pandemic (which is arguably becoming endemic) but for other future public health emergencies as well.

How Do Voters Evaluate Trump's Handling of the Pandemic?

There is no question that who could better quell the COVID-19 pandemic was a central issue in the campaign. Indeed, it is hard to imagine a global health crisis that left almost a quarter of a million Americans dead by Election Day not having an effect. To help understand how voters' views of the pandemic shaped their vote choice and attitudes, in each wave of our study we asked respondents whether they approved or disapproved of Trump's handling of the coronavirus pandemic, utilizing a 4-point scale ranging from "strongly disapprove" to "strongly approve." In these polarized times, we of course expected their evaluations of Trump's performance on this issue to be strongly shaped by their party/candidate support.[1] The real question was how responsive they would be to real-world conditions: did they change their evaluations of President Trump's handling of the crisis as the events on the ground changed?

Unsurprisingly, Figure 5.1 illustrates vast, stark gaps in approval between our different electorates (as a reminder, for a discussion of the analytical strategy that we use throughout the book, including this type of graph, please refer to the Appendix, "Our Data and Analytical Strategy"). Both wavering and unwavering Trump supporters approved of the incumbent's performance, whereas wavering and unwavering Biden supporters disapproved. However, we do see some change over time. In particular, all groups—even the unwavering Trump voters—soured on his performance over the first four waves of

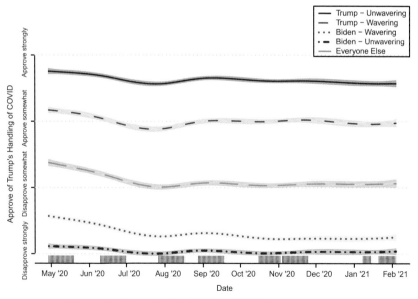

FIGURE 5.1 Approval of Trump's Handling of COVID-19.
Lines show the average level of approval of Trump's handling of the COVID-19 pandemic across our study, broken down by electorate.

our study (May 2020 through August 2020), though the trend flattens there-after. Voters updated their beliefs about Trump's handling of this issue after the United States had surpassed 100,000 deaths from the pandemic (on May 28), the country had reached 3 million diagnosed COVID-19 infections (July 7), some states had begun to postpone their reopening plans in the face of rising cases (mid-July), and the second wave of the virus had crested, largely in southern states (July). After that, it seems that people's perceptions of Trump's handling of the pandemic were more stable.

Because we also tracked respondents' overall approval of Trump, we can compare it to their response to his handling of the COVID-19 pandemic. Doing so, we find that most voters evaluated Trump's overall performance very similarly to his handling of the COVID-19 pandemic. But to the ex-tent that there is a gap, voters—especially Trump ones—tend to evaluate him more negatively on his handling of this issue. This finding is consistent with claims by the Trump campaign that the pandemic was a liability for the incumbent.[2]

How Voters Assessed Trump's and Biden's Ability to Handle the Pandemic Relative to Other Issues

Beyond this approval data, we asked, more broadly, which candidate would better handle twenty-one different issues ranging from taxes and trade to cli-mate change and the COVID-19 pandemic (voters could say Trump would handle the issue better, Biden would handle the issue better, or there would be no difference between them; see also our discussion of Figure 3.8).[3] Since this handling battery allows us to assess how voters perceived Trump and Biden on the issues, here we compare (1) what fraction of these groups thought Trump would better handle the COVID-19 pandemic (relative to Biden) and (2) how this compares to other issues. No one would be surprised to find that Trump's supporters thought that he, not Biden, would better handle the pandemic; after all, if they didn't, they wouldn't have been Trump supporters. However, their assessment relative to other issues is more telling.

First, consider the over-time trend in how voters assessed whether Trump or Biden would better handle the pandemic. In Figure 5.2, as elsewhere in the book when discussing these items, we plot the proportion of each electorate that thought Trump would handle the issue better minus the percentage that thought Biden would do so. Here, higher values (closer to 1) mean that more voters in that electorate think that Trump would handle the issue better, whereas lower values (closer to −1) indicate that more in that electorate think

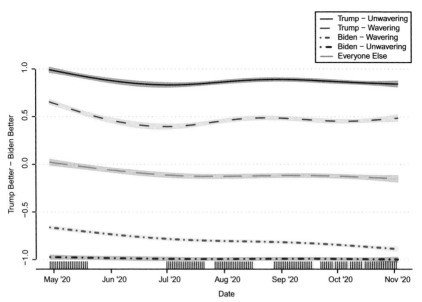

FIGURE 5.2 Believe Trump Could Better Handle COVID-19.
Lines show whether each electorate believes Trump or Biden could better handle the COVID-19 pandemic across our study. Higher (lower) values indicate that the group believes Trump (Biden) could better handle pandemic.

that Biden would. Values close to 0 mean that the group is relatively evenly split between the two.

Consistent with the story of Figure 5.1 above on Trump's COVID-19 approval, we see that voters grew increasingly skeptical of his pandemic response over the first few waves of our study. Notably, we observe this pattern even among Trump's unwavering supporters. But this does not mean that they thought Biden would do a better job. Rather, they simply began to say that there would be no difference between them. While Trump supporters' assessment of his handling of the pandemic did improve somewhat later in the campaign (likely due to campaign messaging), it never recovered to its earlier levels, suggesting that all voters—even Trump supporters—doubted his ability to manage the pandemic.

To determine how this compares to voters' perceptions of other issues, we computed the percentage of each electorate that thought Trump would be better able to handle each of our issues. Doing so makes it possible to compare handling the COVID-19 pandemic to these other issues to assess how voters perceived Trump's competence (relative to Biden's) on COVID-19 in relative terms. In Figure 5.3, which presents the results, values represent the difference

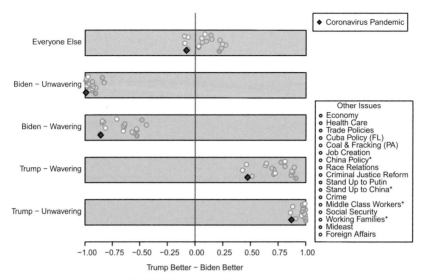

FIGURE 5.3 Better Handle COVID-19 vs. Other Issues.
Each symbol shows the fraction of each electorate that thinks Trump rather than Biden could better handle various issues. Starred items indicate measures that were asked of a random half of respondents. Respondents were asked either about which candidate was better for "China Policy" or about which would better "Stand up to China" and were also asked about who was better either for "Middle-class workers" or for "Working families." Values to the right (left) mean that they think Trump (Biden) can better handle the issue in question. The COVID-19 pandemic is indicated by the dark red diamond.

between the proportion of each electorate asserting that Trump would better handle issues and the proportion reporting that Biden would do so. The value for COVID-19 in each electorate is identified with a red diamond, and other issues are presented as circles (asterisks denote issues that were asked of a random half of respondents).

Figure 5.3's conclusion is clear: voters, even Trump supporters, viewed this issue as a relative liability for President Trump. Unwavering Trump voters are illustrative. Averaging across all other issues in our battery, they thought that President Trump would better handle a given issue 96.7 percent of the time. But only 87.0 percent felt that way about the COVID-19 pandemic: seeing Trump's performance, even his staunchest supporters were less enthusiastic about his handling of the pandemic. The really stunning comparison occurs among wavering Trump supporters. On other issues, they thought that Trump could better handle the issue 77.9 percent of the time, but only 56.4 percent of them felt that way about the pandemic. To be clear, it is not that Trump voters thought that Biden would be better (virtually none of the incumbent's unwavering supporters said this, and only 9.0 percent of his wavering supporters answered this way). Instead, they reported that there would be no difference (12.9 percent of unwavering supporters and 34.6 percent of wavering ones), as we saw in Chapter 3. But this is still a notable shift in light of their patterns of response on other issues. Third-party supporters, nonvoters, and Biden voters likewise expressed less support for Trump on this issue compared to other issues (though they obviously were less enthusiastic about Trump overall).

Across these analyses, a clear picture emerges: all voters, even Trump's strongest backers, rated his pandemic performance poorly (relatively speaking). Rather than a strength to be emphasized, this was an issue to play down during the campaign.

Did COVID-19 Affect Voters' Electoral Decisions?

These data show that voters saw the pandemic as a potential liability for the incumbent president. The panel nature of our data allows us to answer the question: did this, in turn, affect how they voted? In each wave of our study, we asked respondents whether they intended to vote for president, and if so, whether they would support Trump, Biden, or someone else. To determine whether those who disapproved of Trump's handling of the pandemic early in our study—but still said that they intended to vote for him—ultimately cast their ballot for him, we modeled respondents' ultimate vote choice as a function of their wave 1 (April–May 2020) vote choice, their approval of Trump's handling of the pandemic in wave 1, and the interaction of these two elements. Here, we separately predict voting for Trump and Biden, which also allows us to consider the extent to which this set of choices encourages some voters to move out of the electorate (for more discussion of this type of figure and how we will use it throughout the book, please refer to the Appendix, especially the discussion of Appendix Figure 6).

Begin with the upper left-hand panel of Figure 5.4. Here, we plot the probability that someone ultimately votes for Trump as a function of their approval of Trump's handling of the pandemic (in wave 1) and their initial candidate support (also from wave 1). Those who supported President Trump in wave 1 are shown with dashed red lines, those who supported President Biden are indicated with dotted blue lines, and those who supported someone else (or said they would not vote for president) are shown with a solid green line. Looking at President Trump's initial supporters (a red line), we see that approval of Trump's handling of COVID-19 early in the pandemic had a significant effect on their ultimate choice at the ballot box. Among these voters, moving from the "approve somewhat" to the "disapprove somewhat" category

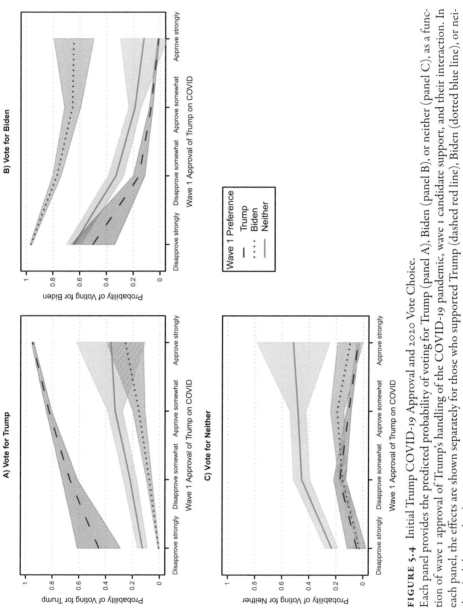

FIGURE 5.4 Initial Trump COVID-19 Approval and 2020 Vote Choice.
Each panel provides the predicted probability of voting for Trump (panel A), Biden (panel B), or neither (panel C), as a function of wave 1 approval of Trump's handling of the COVID-19 pandemic, wave 1 candidate support, and their interaction. In each panel, the effects are shown separately for those who supported Trump (dashed red line), Biden (dotted blue line), or neither (solid green line) in wave 1.

leads to a 15.7 percentage point reduction in the predicted probability of voting for Trump, a stunning shift. In the upper right-hand panel, we see parallel Biden vote results. Among those who initially intended to vote for President Trump, strongly disapproving of his handling of COVID-19 makes them as likely to vote for President Biden as to maintain their preference for Trump. In short, among Trump's initial supporters, disapproval of his handling of the pandemic cost him votes. To be clear, there are not many Trump voters who disapproved of his handling of the pandemic, as we saw in Figure 5.1 earlier in the chapter. But among those who did, it eroded the incumbent's support.

In some ways, there is a parallel to this shift among those who initially supported Joe Biden. In the top right-hand panel of Figure 5.4, those who initially supported the challenger but approved of Trump's handling of COVID-19 became less likely to ultimately vote for Biden. We see in the top left-hand panel, however, that these individuals did not largely vote for Trump. Instead, many of them cast a third-party ballot or chose not to vote (see the bottom left panel). An initial Biden supporter who strongly approved of Trump's handling of COVID-19 has a predicted probability of voting for Biden of 64.4 percent, but a predicted probability of voting for Trump of only 25.8 percent. However, for the initial Trump supporters who strongly disapproved of his performance, the figures are 45.3 percent and 50.0 percent for Trump and Biden, respectively. In effect, Trump's COVID performance eroded his own support more than it converted Biden voters to his camp. Hence, in the end, the pandemic became a burden that weighed down Trump's performance.

It is not just those who disapproved of Trump's handling of the pandemic who may have shifted away from him during the election season. As the narrative in Part 1 of the chapter suggests, Trump consistently downplayed the health risks of the virus, emphasized the need to reopen the economy (even if some would get sick or die), refused to wear a mask, and held large, in-person events with largely mask-less crowds and minimal social distancing. His behavior was at odds with advice from public health officials, who stressed the need for masking, social distancing, and caution with respect to this lethal virus. Indeed, as we noted earlier, President Trump told people not to worry about COVID-19 shortly after contracting—and by some accounts nearly dying from—the virus. Seeing this, someone who started off as a Trump supporter but was worried about the health risks of the virus early in the pandemic might ultimately abandon him, just as those who disapproved of his handling of the pandemic did.

As above, we model respondents' ultimate support for Trump or Biden as a function of their wave 1 (April–May 2020) candidate preference, their worry about the health effects of COVID-19 (measured in wave 2 in June 2020, the first wave in which we asked about it), and the interaction of these two factors. The results are presented in Figure 5.5. As we move from left to right in the figure (and the respondent's level of worry increased), respondents became less likely to vote for Trump.* This effect is especially large for those who initially indicated that they would support President Trump. In the top right-hand panel, we see that most of those who defected from Trump ultimately backed Biden; note too that there is a parallel but smaller shift among initial Biden supporters who were not at all worried about the health effects of COVID. Concern about COVID also drove some of those who initially did not have a preference toward the Biden candidacy (compare bottom left panel with top right panel). Again, Trump's downplaying of the health risks of COVID-19 appears to have eroded some of his initial support.

Does Personal Experience with the Pandemic Matter?

The findings so far in this section highlight how the pandemic helped to shape vote choice, in some surprisingly powerful ways. But these effects are based on Trump's overall handling of the pandemic, not the respondent's personal experiences. Many voters experienced the coronavirus pandemic in a direct and visceral fashion: they or their family members were infected with the disease, or they knew someone who died from it (not even accounting for the economic toll, which we consider in Chapter 6, "The Best of Times, the Worst of Times"). These voters—even some of Trump's initial supporters— might have punished him for his handling of the pandemic. In other words, what mattered may be not just one's assessment of Trump's overall handling of the pandemic but also one's personal experience with it.

To assess this, we adopt the same strategy as above and test whether personal experience with COVID-19 moved those who initially said they would vote for Trump to ballot for another candidate. In Figure 5.6, we plot the predicted probability of voting for Trump for those who have personal experience with COVID versus those who do not.

---

*. Note that this analysis excludes a small number of respondents whose health had already been negatively affected by the virus. While this number would grow over the course of the study, it was still relatively modest in wave 2 (from which these data come).

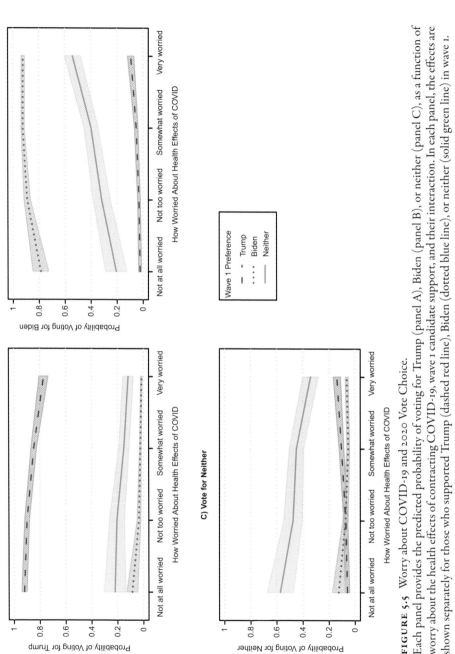

FIGURE 5.5 Worry about COVID-19 and 2020 Vote Choice.
Each panel provides the predicted probability of voting for Trump (panel A), Biden (panel B), or neither (panel C), as a function of worry about the health effects of contracting COVID-19, wave 1 candidate support, and their interaction. In each panel, the effects are shown separately for those who supported Trump (dashed red line), Biden (dotted blue line), or neither (solid green line) in wave 1.

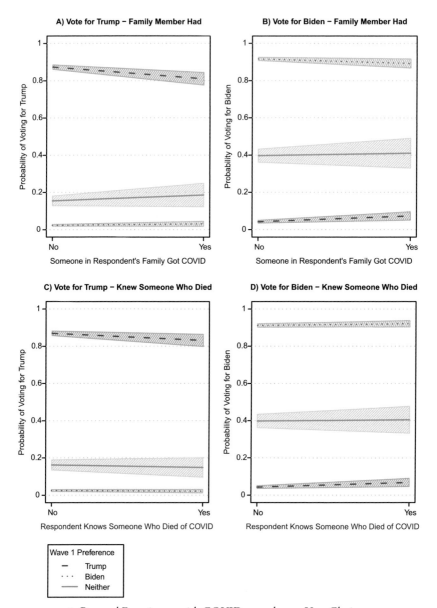

FIGURE 5.6 Personal Experiences with COVID-19 and 2020 Vote Choice.
Each panel provides the predicted probability of voting for Trump (left-hand column) or
Biden (right-hand column) as a function of experience with COVID-19, wave 1 candidate
support, and their interaction. In the top row, the experience is you or a family member
contracting the virus; in the bottom row, it is knowing someone who died from COVID-
19. In each panel, the effects are shown separately for those who supported Trump (dashed
red line), Biden (dotted blue line), or neither (solid green line) in wave 1.

The top half of Figure 5.6 shows that having been infected with COVID-19 or having an immediate family member diagnosed between wave 1 and the election had only modest effects on vote choice. For those who initially supported Biden or who did not prefer either nominee, there was basically no effect. Among those who supported Trump in wave 1, there was a small but statistically significant decline in intention to vote for him. Specifically, those who contracted COVID between wave 1 and the election, or lived with someone who did, went from having an 87.3 percent chance of voting for Trump to an 81.0 percent chance. To be clear, this was a very modest effect; this sort of direct experience with COVID peeled away only a small number of voters from Trump. Moreover, our use of a dichotomous measure is likely masking some heterogeneity in these effects. Perhaps only those who became seriously ill punished the incumbent for it. Because we do not have questions assessing those differences in COVID status, we cannot determine whether that is in fact the case.

Surprisingly, regardless of initial candidate preference, knowing someone who died of COVID-19 had no significant influence on ultimate vote choice (bottom row of Figure 5.6). This is a bit puzzling in light of our earlier findings, but the non-finding here may stem from a similar source: it may depend on who died from COVID, their preexisting conditions, and the like. Again, we lack the data needed to fully test the hypothesis.

Perhaps it is not just one's direct personal experience with COVID-19 that matters; the severity of the local outbreak might also affect balloting decisions. By the time of the election, no part of the nation was untouched by the pandemic. However, some areas had been hit more severely than others. Data on COVID cases, which were available at the county level, made it clear that in some places few were infected and died, while in other areas deaths mounted. Perhaps voters who lived in especially hard-hit areas (those with high numbers of COVID-19 deaths) were more likely to defect from President Trump.

To assess this, we measured the total number of deaths from COVID (per 1,000 people) that had occurred in each county by the date someone voted; recall from Chapter 3 that thanks to the expansion of vote-by-mail in our states, most of our voters cast their ballots prior to Election Day. After calculating the number of deaths, we employed the same modeling strategy as above. Because counties experienced dramatically different numbers of COVID-19-related deaths, even on a population-adjusted basis, we use the log of deaths in our model.

The effects in Figure 5.7 show that the local context did shape vote choice, but the effect is relatively limited. The local death toll had no effect on those

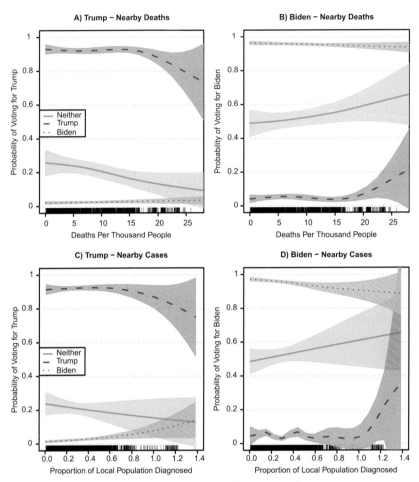

FIGURE 5.7 Local COVID-19 Death Rates and 2020 Vote Choice.
Each panel provides the predicted probability of voting for Trump (left-hand column) or Biden (right-hand column) as a function of population-adjusted COVID-19 death rate (top row) or case rate (bottom row) in the respondent's county, wave 1 candidate support, and their interaction. In each panel, the effects are shown separately for those who supported Trump (dashed red line), Biden (dotted blue line), or neither (solid green line) in wave 1.

who had initially supported President Biden: they voted for him whether their county was hard-hit or largely spared from the pandemic. However, those who initially supported a third-party candidate (or planned not to vote) did shift their behavior: as the death toll in their county climbed, they moved away from Trump and toward Biden. It is worth noting that individuals in the counties with the highest death tolls were more likely than not to support Joe Biden to start with, but of course the standard error on that estimate is quite large. We see that for those who initially supported President Trump, there is an effect, but only for those living in counties especially hard hit by the pandemic. In counties where there were 20 deaths per 1,000 people or more, those who initially supported Trump did become less likely to vote for him and more likely to vote for the Democratic nominee, though again, because there is not much data here, the standard error is quite large. Why this effect is concentrated in this way is an important topic for future research, but it is clear that voters in especially hard-hit areas moved away from the incumbent.

Did the Pandemic Change When Voters Made Up Their Minds?

These analyses highlight how perceptions of, and experiences with, the pandemic shaped ballot decisions. But did they also shape *when* respondents decided on Trump, Biden, or a third-party candidate (or not to vote at all)? This sort of influence could occur in one of two ways. First, perhaps wavering Biden voters who saw the pandemic as particularly important settled on him earlier (i.e., viewing the pandemic as important locked in their support for Biden earlier in the campaign). Alternatively, perhaps wavering Trump voters who viewed the pandemic as particularly important took longer to reach a decision, consistent with arguments about the effects of cross-pressures.[4] To test this, we can look at whether wavering Trump or Biden voters who viewed the pandemic as more important to their vote choice in (the post-election) wave 8 were quicker or slower to make up their minds; this analysis is shown in Figure 5.8.

We find a strong effect for Biden's supporters, but not for Trump's. Among wavering Biden voters, there is a large and notable gap: those who said the pandemic was very important to their decisions settled on Biden earlier than those for whom it was a less important issue. If this was central to Biden voters' decision-making, they settled on their support for him earlier in the campaign. On the other hand, for Trump voters, there was no difference in when people settled based on the importance of this issue. These results suggest that voters who ultimately cast their ballots for Trump found a way to square their views of his handling of the pandemic with their vote for him. As we will see later in the chapter, they employed a number of different strategies to do so. For those who would eventually vote for Biden, COVID seems to have driven their decision-making.

Together, these models help us make sense of how the coronavirus pandemic influenced voters' decision-making in 2020, in terms of both how people voted and when they made up their minds. The effects were not so

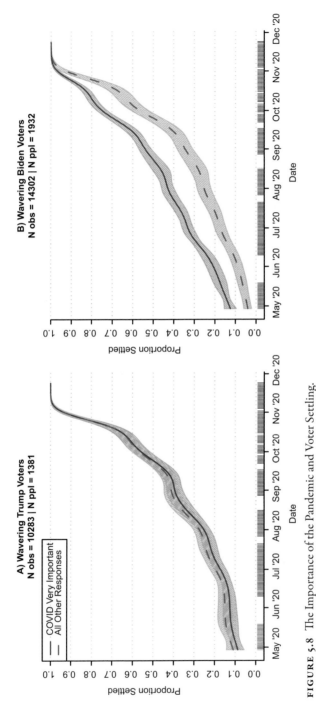

FIGURE 5.8 The Importance of the Pandemic and Voter Settling.
Each panel provides the proportion of wavering voters who had settled on their choice, based on whether they thought that the COVID-19 pandemic was a very important issue to their vote (solid red line) or did not (dashed blue line). Wavering Trump voters are shown in the left-hand panel, wavering Biden voters are shown in the right-hand one.

much about voters' direct personal experience with the pandemic; those were relatively modest. The larger effects are more about assessments of how Trump handled the pandemic (as well as among those living in the areas hardest hit by the virus). Trump's management of the COVID crisis and dismissal of its health risks eroded his initial base of support. To be clear, most of Trump's initial supporters did ultimately back him: recall from Table 3.1 in Chapter 3 that 93.0 percent of those who favored Trump when we recruited them in late 2019 and early 2020 wound up voting for him, despite all that happened in the intervening months. But our finding does suggest that the pandemic hurt Trump. Given the number of states that were razor-close in 2020, this may well have made the difference (though, as we note below, we cannot really know with certainty).

The limitation here and in the analyses in subsequent chapters is that we cannot neatly separate the effects of the pandemic from the economic collapse and the racial reckoning sparked by the Black Lives Matter protest movement (see our discussion of this in Chapter 1 in the section entitled "Not Three Pre-Election Crises, but One"). Because all three crises occurred contemporaneously and were affected by overlapping forces, no data can really unpack their distinct effects; in many ways, in all of these chapters we are dealing with a complex hybrid "treatment" of all three crises occurring during this election year. Nevertheless, these data and those in subsequent chapters make clear that these crises affected this election.

These data also leave us with something of a puzzle. The pandemic cost Trump votes, but those losses were more modest than one initially might have expected given the tumult caused by the pandemic. As we saw earlier, even Trump's own supporters rated him poorly on this issue, relative to their assessment of him on others. Most voted for him nonetheless. To determine why, we need to understand how citizens made sense of the pandemic, a task to which we now turn.

How Do Biden and Trump Voters Perceive the Pandemic?

As we discussed in Part 1 of this chapter, Trump and Biden reacted to the pandemic in starkly different ways. Biden, from the outset, argued that Americans needed to wear masks, practice social distancing, and leave their homes only when necessary. Trump, in contrast, rarely masked and downplayed the severity of the virus, even after he himself became infected and extremely ill.

Paralleling the presidential candidates' behavior, Democratic and Republican governors took very different approaches as well. Democratic governors imposed stricter (and swifter) stay-at-home orders and related measures to halt the spread of the virus[5] than did Republican ones, and these differences were reported in media coverage of the pandemic (and hence would have been visible to voters).[6] For example, when Wisconsin's Democratic governor, Tony Evers, attempted to extend the state's stay-at-home order in late April, Republicans in the state legislature sued, saying he lacked the authority to do so under the state's constitution; the state's Supreme Court then sided with the Republican legislators.[7] While other nations' leaders unified over the crisis, treating it as a moment to come together to fight the virus,[8] America's leaders politicized it and splintered along party lines.

This suggests that Biden supporters, much more so than Trump's, should have been attentive to news about the pandemic and more anxious about COVID-19. In wave 1 (April–May 2020) and in wave 10 (January–February 2021), we asked respondents how closely they were following the news about the COVID-19 pandemic: not closely at all, not too closely, somewhat closely, or very closely. To examine partisan differences in news attentiveness over time, Figure 5.9 breaks down their responses (in each wave) by electorate.

There are important wave and electorate differences in attentiveness to the pandemic. Unsurprisingly, all groups were markedly more attentive to pandemic-related news during wave 1, when the outbreak was still in its relatively early stages: the modal response in *every* group was to follow this news very closely. But even then, we see differences across groups, with Biden supporters, whether wavering or unwavering, more likely than Trump supporters to say that they were doing so. But by early 2021 (wave 10), Biden's voters were still following coronavirus-related news very closely, while the other groups were only following it somewhat closely. Indeed, over this nine-month period, the fraction of unwavering Biden supporters who followed the news about the coronavirus very closely fell by only 10.5 percentage points (a 13.5 percent relative decline), but among unwavering Trump voters those closely following coronavirus news fell by 32.2 percentage points (a 56.7 percent relative decline). So not only were Biden voters more attentive to the news at the outset, but their interest persisted throughout our study.[†]

---

†. We asked a parallel question about how often respondents were checking online, including social media, for information about the pandemic. The results for this item directly parallel the results in Figure 5.9 and so we omit them here in the interest of brevity.

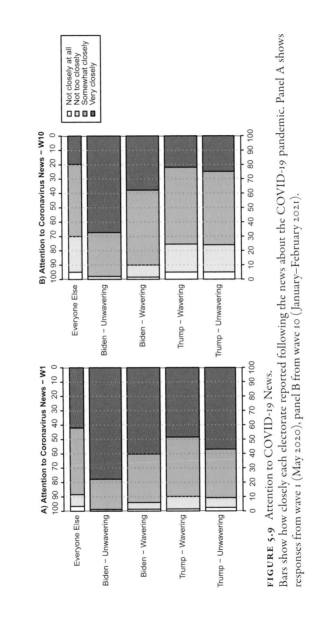

FIGURE 5.9 Attention to COVID-19 News.

Bars show how closely each electorate reported following the news about the COVID-19 pandemic. Panel A shows responses from wave 1 (May 2020), panel B from wave 10 (January–February 2021).

We also asked respondents in wave 1 how often they were experiencing various emotions in response to the pandemic (i.e., how often they felt fear, anger, and anxiety in the past seven days in response to the coronavirus pandemic: not at all, a little, a moderate amount, a lot, or a great deal).[‡] Figure 5.10 shows the distribution of these emotions in each of our electorates.

Here we see that, in general, Biden voters experienced more negative emotions about the pandemic (i.e., they were more fearful, angrier, and—especially—more anxious) than did Trump voters. The differences in fear and anger were relatively modest, but Biden voters experienced much higher levels of anxiety. Relative to unwavering Trump supporters, unwavering Biden ones were more than twice as likely to report "a lot" or "a great deal" of anxiety about the pandemic. (Though the differences are less stark among the wavering electorates, parallel gaps emerge there as well.) So not only were Biden voters more attentive to the news about COVID-19 but they also felt more anxiety surrounding the pandemic. These two phenomena are likely linked. Anxiety, after all, increases the desire to seek information,[9] especially threatening information,[10] such as that about a potentially lethal virus. Their greater news attentiveness is a manifestation of the greater anxiety among Biden voters.

Likewise, when we asked our respondents about how worried they were that their health or the health of someone in their family would be seriously affected by COVID-19, we again see large, persistent gaps in worry between the electorates. Respondents answered on a 4-point scale: not at all worried, not too worried, somewhat worried, or very worried.[§] As Figure 5.11 indicates, Biden voters were nearly one full scale point more worried than Trump ones, and that pattern persists across the entire course of our study.

On average, unwavering Trump supporters were largely "not too worried" about the impact of a COVID-19 infection on their family's health. Both wavering and unwavering Biden supporters were (on average) "somewhat worried," and a good number were "very worried." However, as vaccines came online toward the end of our study, that worry level began to decline.

---

‡. Our respondents' answers about two positive emotions—hope and compassion—evinced more muted differences. Very few were especially hopeful about the pandemic, though Biden voters generally scored higher on compassion than did Trump voters.

§. This analysis excludes a small number of respondents who report that their health, or that of a family member, already had been negatively affected. This number grew from a minimal portion to around 3 to 5 percent of respondents who provided this answer in later waves.

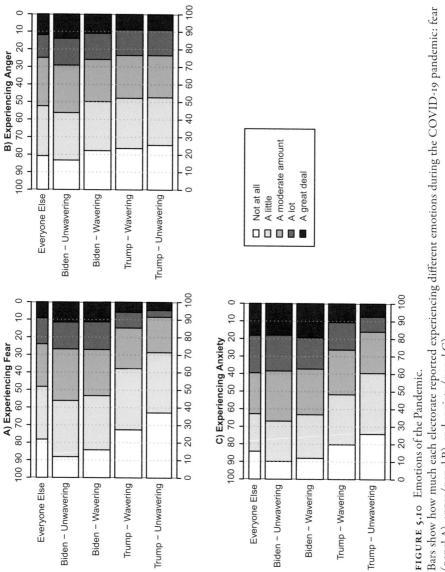

FIGURE 5.10 Emotions of the Pandemic.

Bars show how much each electorate reported experiencing different emotions during the COVID-19 pandemic: fear (panel A), anger (panel B), and anxiety (panel C).

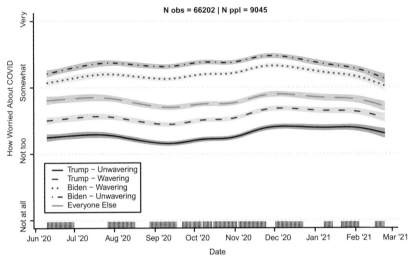

FIGURE 5.11 Worry about the Health Effects of COVID-19.
Lines show how worried each electorate was about the health effects of they themselves or a family member contracting COVID-19 across our study.

Paralleling our results about anxiety, Biden supporters also were more worried about COVID's possible effects on their family's health.

Is the Worst Behind Us?

Our just reported results, as well as the contrasting candidate messages we reviewed in Part 1 of this chapter, might lead one to expect Trump and Biden voters to see the future of the pandemic very differently. Beginning in wave 4 (August 2020), we asked respondents whether the worst of the COVID-19 pandemic was behind us or was yet to come. Unsurprisingly, the views of Trump and Biden supporters diverged on where the nation was heading with respect to the pandemic. Figure 5.12 shows the percentage of respondents who thought the worst of the pandemic was behind us over time, broken down by electorate.

Two important trends emerge in this figure. First, during wave 4 (August 2020), almost all respondents—even the unwavering Biden supporters— became somewhat more cautiously optimistic, though this pattern is starkest for the unwavering Trump supporters. At the time, coronavirus infections were dropping across all of our states. As COVID-19 cases crested later that fall, that optimism dissipated. Trump himself was hospitalized with the virus in early October (though he contracted the virus in September), and

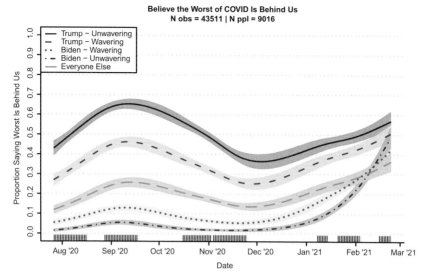

FIGURE 5.12 The Worst of the Pandemic Is behind Us.
Lines show the proportion of each electorate who believed the worst of the pandemic
was behind us, across our study.

in this period the United States reported more than 100,000 new infections
in a single day for the first time. Faced with this grim reality, most voters—
including the unwavering Trump supporters—became increasingly pessimistic about the pandemic's course. That trend reversed when the vaccines
began to be distributed in early 2021 (waves 9–11 of our study). At that time,
all groups became more optimistic (notably, our study ended several months
before the delta variant lead to a fourth wave of the virus during the summer
of 2021). Although perceptions of the trajectory of the pandemic reveal important between-electorate differences, these findings suggest that all of our
electoral groups were sensitive to the dynamics of the pandemic.

Trump and Biden supporters also envisioned the outbreak's future in very
different ways. Where both wavering and unwavering Biden supporters were
convinced that the worst was yet to come, Trump supporters—especially
the unwavering ones—were largely convinced that the darkest days were behind us. The larger gap between wavering and unwavering Trump supporters
compared to wavering and unwavering Biden ones fits with the data showing
that Biden supporters of all stripes were more worried about the pandemic, more anxious about it, and more attentive to the news about it (see
Figures 5.9–5.11). Although Trump voters were more dismissive of the outbreak, it was the unwavering Trump ones who stand out in this respect.

The Reinforcing Role of Conservative Media Orientations

How did these unwavering Trump voters get the impression that the pandemic was essentially over by late August 2020 or come to the decision that it wasn't worth worrying about? The likely answer is messaging telling them so. In particular, conservative media outlets were reflecting the president in downplaying the extent and lethality of the virus and exaggerating the likely efficacy of unproven treatments. To be certain, most Americans—even most Americans who supported Trump—were concerned about the pandemic and responded to facts on the ground, especially in the fall as the third wave of the virus spread across the nation. But for those individuals who only received their media from conservative outlets, the story was quite different. The individuals in the conservative media echo chamber group were far less worried about coronavirus throughout 2020, even relative to those who were avid consumers but got at least some information from elsewhere (left side of Figure 5.13). Likewise, those in the conservative echo chamber remained more likely than not to say that the pandemic's darkest days were over (right side of Figure 5.13). Across both measures, those in this echo chamber, who only get conservative media messages with no cross-cutting information, saw the coronavirus as a less lethal threat, consistent with the messages promulgated on those outlets.

A Surprising Point of Cross-Party Commonality

Although Trump and Biden supporters saw the pandemic through very different lenses, there was one area where they agreed: by the end of our study, all of our electorates become more likely to report wearing a face mask when they were out in public. Although the CDC initially discouraged ordinary Americans from wearing face masks, they reversed course and advocated wearing them on April 3, 2020.[11] Beginning in wave 2 (June 2020) and continuing throughout the remainder of the study, we asked respondents how often they wore a mask when they left their homes: never, rarely, sometimes, often, or always.[**] Figure 5.14 shows the patterns over time.

While there are the expected differences—unwavering Biden supporters were consistently the most likely to report mask wearing, whereas unwavering Trump supporters were least likely to do so (and overall, Biden supporters were notably more enthusiastic about mask wearing than Trump ones)—the

---

[**]. This analysis excludes a tiny number of respondents who report that they did not go out in public.

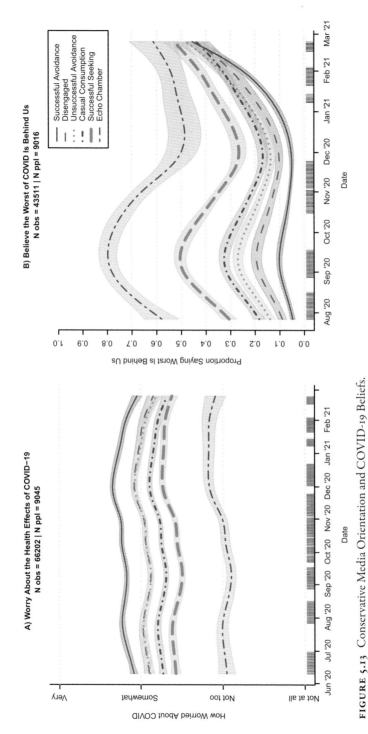

FIGURE 5.13 Conservative Media Orientation and COVID-19 Beliefs. Lines show the proportion of each conservative media orientation reporting that they worried about the health effects of COVID-19 (panel A) and believed the worst of the pandemic was behind us (panel B) across our study.

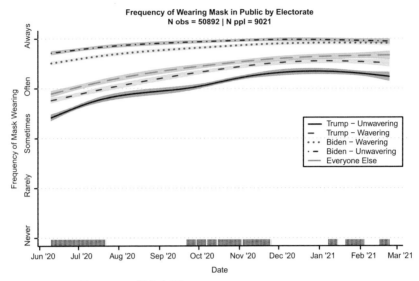

FIGURE 5.14 Frequency of Mask Wearing.
Lines show how often each electorate reported wearing a mask when they left their homes across our study.

change over time is the more important story. Over time, all groups, regardless of candidate preference, reported greater levels of mask wearing. By the end, even Trump supporters were wearing masks most of the time, paralleling trends observed in other surveys as well.[12]

While masks remained a political totem, this obscures this broader, and quite important, behavioral change over time: most people, even most Trump supporters, became more likely to report wearing a mask. The small number of vocal anti-mask advocates greatly skews public perceptions on this issue, as it does on many others.[13] But it also highlights that while the political class was busy fighting over masks, ordinary voters were, to an overwhelming extent, simply putting them on and going about their business, just as public health authorities recommended.

But despite the common acceptance of masks, the clear story across these analyses is that Biden and Trump supporters saw the pandemic in fundamentally different terms, a conclusion consistent with other work on the pandemic.[14] Throughout 2020, the unwavering Biden electorate persisted in believing that the worst was yet to come, a pattern that did not change until Biden was in office and vaccines were being distributed to the public. Even among the wavering Biden supporters, there was no point in 2020 at which more than 15 percent thought that the worst of the pandemic was behind us;

for Trump supporters, it never dipped below 25 percent. This fits with the pattern in Figure 5.11 above: Biden voters were more anxious about the pandemic and feared that we were not yet out of the woods, while Trump voters were more confident that it would soon be in the rearview mirror.

This finding helps us answer the question we posed at the end of the last section: how did Trump voters square their support of him with the view that he performed (relatively) poorly on the pandemic? Theories of motivated reasoning would suggest that they would shift their attention to another issue, downplay the COVID-19 pandemic, or find aspects of Trump's COVID-19 performance that they could celebrate.[15] We saw clear examples of the first two responses in earlier findings. In Chapter 3, we saw that Trump voters downplayed the pandemic as an issue in their vote choice, instead prioritizing the economy, where Trump had a more plausible claim to success (as we explore in Chapter 6).[††] In Figure 5.12 above, we saw that Trump's supporters downplayed the pandemic, saying that the worst was already behind us, even at times when case counts were rising. Both of these responses helped them square their support for Trump with their perception that his handling of the pandemic was less than stellar.

Finding Areas of Success for President Trump: The Travel Ban and Vaccines

Another strategy was available to Trump's supporters to square support for him with their assessment that his pandemic performance was (relatively speaking) not strong: highlight praiseworthy actions that his administration took. As we argued in Part 1 of the chapter, Trump touted two such successes. First, he argued that his early decision to ban travel from China slowed the spread of the virus in the United States and helped to save lives. Second, he contended that Operation Warp Speed would soon produce a pandemic-ending COVID-19 vaccine, perhaps even before the election.

Beginning in wave 2 (June 2020), we asked respondents which of two statements came closer to their view: that Trump's early ban on travel from China saved lives, or that Trump's failure to act early to address the pandemic cost lives (respondents could also say both or neither were true). If our argument about motivated reasoning is correct, then we should see Trump supporters agreeing that his travel ban saved lives, and, as time passes, the

---

†. Motivated reasoning likely also drove Biden supporters to focus on COVID-19: it was a Trump policy failure, so it made sense for them to make it central to their vote choice.

reinforcing messages of the Trump campaign and its surrogates should increase their belief that that was indeed the case. The data in Figure 5.15 confirm the existence of the pattern we expected: not only did Trump supporters, especially the unwavering ones, think that his travel ban saved lives, but the share concurring with that conclusion increased, albeit slightly, over the course of the fall campaign (Figure 5.15, panel A).

The success of the travel ban helped Trump's supporters square their support for him with his faltering performance on the pandemic overall.[‡‡] As the election approached, this message also appears to have buffered his supporters from the countervailing narrative that Trump's initial failure to treat the pandemic seriously increased the number of Americans who died (Figure 5.15, panel B).

Operation Warp Speed performed a similar role. Announced in mid-May, this program was designed "to accelerate the development, manufacturing, and distribution of COVID-19 vaccines, therapeutics, and diagnostics (medical countermeasures)."[16] Indeed, as we noted in Part 1 of this chapter, in early September, federal spokespersons fueled hope that the end of the pandemic was on the horizon with a request that state and local health departments prepare for delivery of a vaccine as soon as November 1, and in the second debate, Trump asserted that a vaccine was only weeks away.[17]

Less than a week after Election Day, Pfizer and its partner BioNTech announced, "based on early and incomplete test results," that its vaccine might be 90 percent effective.[18] That revelation, noted the *Associated Press*, "brought a big burst of optimism to a world desperate for the means to finally bring the catastrophic outbreak under control."[19] Had the announcement come a week or two earlier, an election decided by roughly 43,000 votes in three states might have swung to the incumbent. Although Pfizer was not part of Trump's Operation Warp Speed, on November 13, in his first public remarks after losing the presidency to Joe Biden, Trump took credit for that vaccine's development.[20] If credit was due Trump, it was because his administration had brokered the $1.95 billion agreement between the pharmaceutical giant and the federal government to provide 100 million doses of the vaccine to Americans if the FDA approved its vaccine after completion of clinical trials.[21] More good news arrived the following week with word that Moderna's

---

‡‡. In light of this pattern of results, and Trump's more general attacks on China, we might ask whether Trump supporters grew more negative toward China overall. Although they did, the general pattern across our study is that all respondents—regardless of candidate choice— became more anti-China during our study.

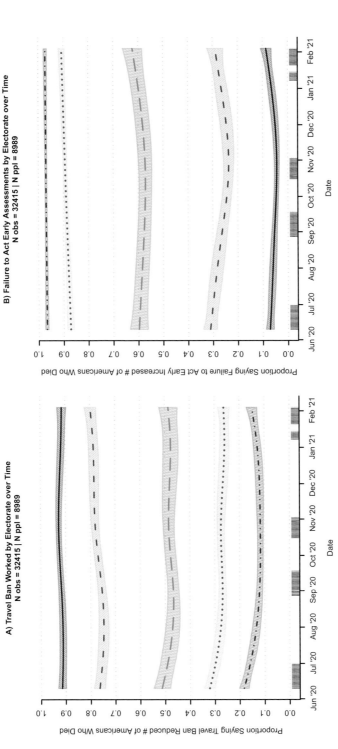

FIGURE 5.15 Belief That Trump's Travel Ban Worked.
Lines show the proportion of each electorate who believed that Trump's ban on travel from China saved lives (panel A), and the proportion who believed that Trump's failure to act early cost lives (panel B).

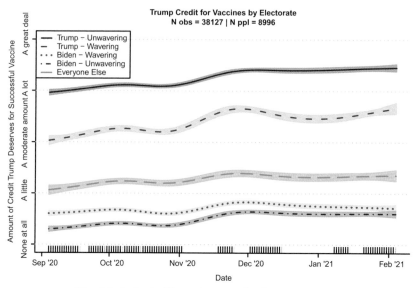

FIGURE 5.16 How Much Credit Trump Deserves for the Vaccine.
Lines show how much credit each electorate thinks Trump deserved for the vaccine across our study.

vaccine (which had been funded by Operation Warp Speed) had also proven to be effective, highlighting that Trump had delivered on his promise to promote development of a COVID-19 vaccine in record time.

Beginning in wave 5 (August–September 2020), we asked respondents how much credit President Trump would deserve if a safe and effective vaccine for COVID-19 became available to the public: none at all, a little, a moderate amount, a lot, or a great deal.[§§] Their answers are digested in Figure 5.16.

Not only did Trump voters give him an increasing amount of credit for the vaccine program over time, but they also responded much more favorably to the post-election news about the vaccines' development than did our other electorates. While all voters thought Trump deserved more credit in the post-election waves than they did prior to the election, the jump among Trump supporters was larger, just as we would expect. Although Biden voters acknowledged that President Trump succeeded here, their partisan

---

§§. Before the Pfizer-BioNTech announcement, we asked respondents how much credit President Trump would deserve if a safe and effective vaccine became available to the public by the end of the year. After the announcement of the vaccine availability to the public in early 2021, we changed the question to ask about how much credit he deserved for the development and distribution of the vaccines. We combine the two questions here, as the underlying patterns of responses are very similar.

priors prevented them from giving him the level of credit accorded him by his supporters (or, frankly, the level of credit that he probably deserved). At the same time, for Trump's supporters, the success of Operation Warp Speed compensated for his failures elsewhere in the pandemic, even if it did not come in time to swing the election.

Overall, then, we see a clear pattern in these data. Voters in each of our electorates—even Trump's backers—thought he mishandled the pandemic. His supporters sustained their enthusiasm for his reelection by prioritizing issues on which Trump was advantaged (such as the economy), downplaying the pandemic's severity (saying the worst is behind us and that it was not that serious), and finding other dimensions of the pandemic (such as the travel ban and vaccines) for which they could more unreservedly praise Trump. In this manner, Trump's supporters found ways to square their support of him with how he managed the pandemic.

Do Scientific Sources Become Politicized?

We saw above that Trump and Biden voters, unsurprisingly, evaluated the incumbent's handling of the crisis differently. But was the same the case in their evaluations of the performance of supposedly apolitical scientific actors, such as the CDC, the FDA, and Dr. Anthony Fauci, the most visible governmental spokesperson on the pandemic? One might expect that voter partisanship would have little effect on such assessments. But as we showed in the first part of this chapter, that is not likely to be the case, since these authorities disagreed—often quite publicly—with the incumbent. Accordingly, it is likely that attitudes toward them would polarize across our study.

To determine whether this was the case, we asked our respondents how much they trusted the information various sources provided them about the coronavirus pandemic: not at all, a little, a moderate amount, a lot, or a great deal. Here, we focus on voters' assessments of three key scientific actors: Fauci, the CDC, and the FDA. Figure 5.17 reports the patterns over time.

The data show that perceptions of these public health actors became increasingly politicized over the course of the election and its aftermath. Even at the outset of our study, Biden voters were more trusting of all three than were Trump supporters. This finding is consistent with research findings that Trump supporters are generally less trusting of institutions overall and less trusting of scientific authorities as well.[22]

Over time, we see politicized perceptions emerge about all three actors, but most clearly Fauci, who, as we discussed in Part 1 of the chapter, sparked

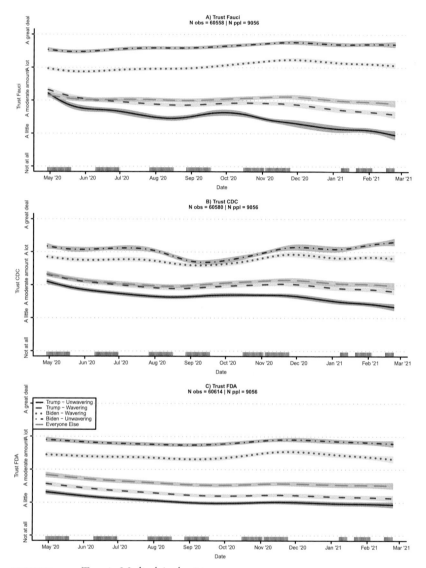

FIGURE 5.17 Trust in Medical Authorities.

Lines show how much trust each electorate has in the information coming from Dr. Anthony Fauci (panel A), the Centers for Disease Control (panel B), and the Food and Drug Administration (panel C), across our study.

visibly with the incumbent president throughout 2020 and whose comments about Trump's management of the pandemic spawned partisan controversy. Unwavering Trump supporters' average trust in Fauci fell by more than one full scale point over the course of our study: while at the outset they had (on average) "a moderate amount" of trust in the information he provided to them, by February 2021, when we closed our study, that had fallen to just "a little." In opposite fashion, unwavering Biden supporters started off trusting the NIAID director at lot and inched toward "a great deal." Their slope is less steep than that of the Trump supporters largely because of a ceiling effect; most of this group fully trusted Fauci's information from the outset of our study. We see similar but less pronounced patterns among the wavering Trump and Biden supporters, a finding consistent with research showing that those more committed to their candidate react most strongly to political signals from elites.[23]

One other somewhat ironic factor is of note here. Even as Trump and his surrogates were accusing the health agencies and their spokespersons of making decisions designed to defeat him, he and his appointees were trying to manipulate their findings for their own political ends. In September 2020, journalists learned that Trump appointees had "reportedly worked to suppress reports on the ineffectiveness of hydroxychloroquine (a drug Trump has routinely touted as being effective against COVID-19), as well as to have the agency change published reports on the risks of the coronavirus and on who might be blamed for infections."[24]

Evidence that their efforts bore fruit appeared in February 2021 when the Democrat-controlled House Select Subcommittee on the Coronavirus Crisis released emails and documents showing that "Trump appointees succeeded on several occasions in changing language and influencing the tone of the Centers for Disease Control and Prevention's Morbidity and Mortality Weekly Reports, which offered weekly public updates on scientists' findings."[25] Additional documents disclosed later showed that the Trump administration softened CDC guidance on religious services, removing language calling for virtual gatherings (rather than in-person ones).[26] Disaffected former Trump administration officials later confirmed that the incumbent's appointees more broadly had tried to sidetrack politically inconvenient COVID-related scientific data,[27] and the former NIH director reported that various Republican officials urged the president to fire Dr. Fauci.[28]

The Pandemic's Ultimate Effect

Key takeaways from Chapter 5, Part 2 include our findings that:

- Voters saw Trump's handling of the pandemic (relatively speaking) as a liability for him. Compared to other issues, even Trump's own supporters were less likely to say that the pandemic was an issue that Trump would handle better than Biden.

- COVID-related factors that reduced the likelihood of voting for Trump included: disapproval of Trump's handling of the pandemic, worry about the health consequences of contracting COVID-19, contracting COVID-19 or living with someone who did, or living in an area with relatively high numbers of COVID deaths. These effects were relatively modest in size.

- Wavering Biden voters who said that the pandemic was very important to their vote choice were more likely to decide earlier that they would cast their vote for Biden.

- Consistent with the messages from the Trump and Biden campaigns, their respective voters saw the pandemic in starkly different terms. Biden voters monitored COVID-related news more closely, experienced more negative emotions about COVID, and were more convinced that the worst of the pandemic was ahead (at least until Biden took office and the vaccines became available to the public).

- Trump voters squared their support for the incumbent with their poor ratings of his pandemic performance by (1) shifting attention to other issues on which Trump was stronger, such as the economy, (2) downplaying the pandemic, saying the worst was behind us, and (3) focusing on areas Trump touted as successes, such as his ban on travel from China and Operation Warp Speed's vaccine development. These moves help to explain the modest effects on vote choice seen in the chapter.

- Finally, perceptions of national health experts and agencies became polarized during the pandemic. Over time, Trump supporters grew increasingly distrustful of Dr. Anthony Fauci, the CDC, and the FDA, while Biden supporters came to trust them more. Agents and agencies once assumed to be neutral and apolitical became political symbols.

Together, these results highlight the fundamental ways in which the pandemic shaped the election, just as it shaped so many other aspects of life in 2020.

But we have still not answered the question posed by the chapter's title: did the pandemic sink Trump's reelection chances? While one cannot definitively answer such a broad question, our data point to two ways in which the pandemic helped to shape the election outcome, one more obvious than the other. First, the pandemic did cost Trump votes among those who initially supported him. But as we noted a moment ago, those effects were muted by the fact that most Trump voters found ways to reconcile their poor assessment of his pandemic performance with their support for him. Ironically, even when voters were not deciding on the pandemic, this justification process meant that their pandemic-related perceptions were central to their decisions.

But there is a second, and more indirect, way in which the pandemic likely helped seal Trump's fate. As one of the epigraphs with which we opened Part 1 of this chapter indicates, Joe Biden's case that the election was a referendum on Trump's competence pivoted on the assumption that the incumbent's botched response to the pandemic disqualified him from holding office. We cannot know what would have happened had the coronavirus pandemic not struck the United States in the spring of 2020. But if the economy had continued growing as it had over the first three years of Trump's term, it is hard to see how Biden would have dislodged it as the most important issue in the election. This would have been particularly problematic for Biden because, as we show in Chapter 6, voters across our electorates granted Trump's competence on the issue, and hence he might well have won reelection as a result. The pandemic allowed Biden to shift voters' focus to an issue on which virtually all agreed the incumbent fared poorly. To be clear, not all voters accepted Biden's reframing: after all, he very narrowly won the critical Electoral College states, even if he carried the national popular vote by an overwhelming margin. But without the pandemic, or some other major disruption, Biden would have faced a steeper climb. In that sense, by shifting what the election was about, the pandemic helped Biden to carry the day.

6.1

———————

The Best of Times, the Worst of Times

THE 2020 ECONOMY AND THE 2020 ELECTION

Kathleen Hall Jamieson, Matthew Levendusky,
Josh Pasek, and Andrew Renninger

> *We're in a good place. Just don't make a mistake and you've*
> *got this [reelection] in the bag.*
>
> —Brad Parscale, Trump's then campaign manager, speaking to him
> after reviewing polling and economic data in February 2020[1]

> *This is his economy, it's been shut down. The reason it's shut*
> *down is because—look[,] you folks at home. How many*
> *of you got up this morning and had an empty chair at the*
> *kitchen table because someone died [of] COVID[?] How*
> *many of you are in a situation where you lost your mom or*
> *dad and you couldn't even speak to the nurse holding the*
> *phone up so you could in fact say goodbye[?]*
>
> —Joe Biden, September 29, 2020, presidential debate[2]

IN JANUARY 2020, by most indicators, the US economy was in good shape. As we noted in Chapter 1 ("An Election Shaped by Crises"), unemployment had fallen to 3.5 percent, GDP had grown at 2.5 percent per year, and the stock market had soared to ever-greater heights. In January 2020, 63 percent of Americans approved of the incumbent's handling of the economy, the highest for an incumbent in an election year since 1996, when Bill Clinton handily won reelection.[3] "Americans' overall satisfaction with the country's direction is at its highest point since 2005," reported Gallup's pollsters.[4]

In light of these sentiments, Trump's advisors were confident, as the first of this chapter's epigraphs attests. Not only did voters feel their economic situations had improved, but they credited President Trump for the improvement.[5] While conceding that many voters might not like Trump's style, his advisors believed that low levels of unemployment, rising incomes, and growing retirement accounts had put the incumbent on a glide path to reelection. Of course, no one then foresaw the havoc that COVID-19 would bring to the nation's economy. As we argued in Chapter 5 ("Did the COVID-19 Pandemic Sink Trump's Reelection?"), the COVID-19 pandemic and efforts to control it reshaped both the country and the economy.

In this chapter, we explore how the economic crisis affected the 2020 election. In this first part of the chapter, we outline its twists and turns throughout 2020 and the quite different pictures that Trump and Biden painted of the economy's health and future outlook. Reassuring Americans that the worst of the pandemic either was or soon would be over, the incumbent told them that only he could return it to pre-COVID levels. Biden, by contrast, reminded voters that the pandemic was raging and predicated economic recovery on control of COVID-19, which he argued Trump had mishandled. As we will see in the second part of the chapter, those competing messages helped shape voters' perceptions of the effects of the economy in the 2020 election.

The Economic Crisis of 2020

On January 31, 2020, Health and Human Services secretary Alex Azar declared the novel coronavirus a national public health emergency. In the ensuing month, the economy peaked and then fell into recession.[6] "Economic activity in the United States began to contract sharply at the very end of February and into early March as the coronavirus spread across major metropolitan areas, like New York City, Chicago and Atlanta," noted the *New York Times*. "Shops closed, travelers canceled flights and diners began avoiding restaurants, even before some states issued formal stay-at-home orders."[7]

In a nationally televised March 11 speech to the nation, the forty-fifth president advised nursing homes to suspend all medically unnecessary visits, suggested that older Americans avoid nonessential travel in crowded areas, and reported that his administration had issued guidance on school closures, social distancing, and reducing large gatherings. He declared, "This is not a financial crisis, this is just a temporary moment of time that we will overcome together as a nation and as a world."[8] As news of the coronavirus spread, on March 12 the S&P 500 had its biggest sell-off in over three decades, a nearly 10 percent drop.[9] The following day, the incumbent issued emergency declarations, freeing $50 billion in federal funds to combat what he termed the "China virus"[10] and providing small businesses with access to $7 billion in low-interest, long-term loans.[11] Days later, the number of reported COVID deaths in the United States reached 100.[12]

On March 19, California became the first state to issue a stay-at-home requirement. In short order, forty-two states and territories followed suit.[13] As these orders went into effect, the economy was transformed almost overnight. While some businesses could pivot to adapt to these orders—for example, some restaurants shifted to delivery and takeout options, and grocery stores made it easier to stock the fridge through curbside pickup—others could not. Many businesses that operate in person, such as gyms, hair salons, and so forth, had no choice but to close their doors, and schools of all levels moved classes online.

Of course, not all businesses were shuttered: those deemed essential were required to remain open. Employees at these businesses—including hardware stores, grocery stores, pharmacies, health care facilities (hospitals, nursing homes, etc.), farms, and public safety organizations (such as police and fire departments)—had to continue to work in person, despite the risks. Many of these essential workers were lower-income, less well educated, and more likely to be people of color.[14] This set up a sharp contrast: while better-educated workers—largely white Americans—safely Zoomed in to work from the comfort of their living rooms, many Black and Hispanic workers risked contracting the virus when they went to work every day. Not only were these in-person workers typically making less money, but they were also exposing themselves to greater risk of COVID-19 while doing so.

Many nonessential businesses closed, uncertain of when they could reopen, and laid off or furloughed workers in droves. During the week of March 14, before the first stay-at-home order went into effect, 256,000 first-time unemployment claims were filed. The week of March 28, there were 5,985,000, and the following week, there were 6,149,000, breaking all records for single-week claims. Indeed, there would be more than 1,000,000 first-time claims filed each week until the second one of the last month in summer.[15] The unemployment rate peaked at 14.8 percent in April and was still nearly 7 percent on Election Day, double what it had been before the pandemic.[16] The change meant that the rate went from the lowest since the Korean War to the highest since the Great Depression, with more than three in ten residents estimated to be out of work in some areas.[17] The public health crisis had triggered an economic one.

Responding to the economic collapse and soaring unemployment rate, the nation's leaders authorized unprecedented governmental action. On March 27, Congress passed, and President Trump signed, the Coronavirus

Aid, Relief, and Economy Security (CARES) Act, which authorized $2.2 trillion to fight the economic slowdown and the virus. This legislation gave one-time cash payments (also known as Economic Impact Payments or stimulus payments) to many, expanded unemployment assistance, created the Paycheck Protection Program to keep employees on company payrolls, and gave billions to state and local governments to help prop up their finances. This enormous cash infusion helped dampen the worst effects of the recession. According to the US Bureau of Economic Analysis, real disposable income increased 6.2 percent in 2020.[18] Despite the enormous GDP contraction, and the millions who lost their jobs, in aggregate Americans' incomes actually increased. As we see in what follows, however, these gains were distributed very unequally throughout society.

In mid-April, the White House released guidelines for a phased reopening of the economy, calling for states to begin lifting their stay-at-home orders and restarting economic activity. By the beginning of the third week in May, all of the states had at least partially done so.[19] By May 25, the economy was beginning to show signs of life. "Truck loads are growing again. Air travel and hotel bookings are up slightly. Mortgage applications are rising. And more people are applying to open new businesses," noted the *Wall Street Journal*. "These are among some early signs the US economy is, ever so slowly, creeping back to life."[20] While the economy did begin to recover in the summer, it still had a long way to go to return to its pre-COVID levels. At issue in the fall election was how long it would take for our various electorates to experience the level of economic security they had felt prior to the pandemic.

Would the Recovery Be V-Shaped or K-Shaped?

According to the incumbent, the spring's economic pains would be short-lived. Trump argued that the economy would soon come roaring back once the stay-at-home orders were lifted. This would be a so-called V-shaped recovery: a sharp drop in the spring post-lockdown, but an equally rapid rise by the fall as the economy reopened. Trump's argument that a V-shaped recovery was in the offing was predicated on the assumption that his tax cuts, deregulation, and policies toward China had and would "Make America Great Again." In a speech to the Economic Club of New York on October 14, he noted, "Under my continued leadership, we will continue our V-shaped recovery and launch a record smashing economic boom. . . . [We will] create 10 million jobs in the first 10 months of 2021, where we're going to have a phenomenal year, and we will soon be announcing[,] in my opinion, a phenomenal, a phenomenal record setting third quarter and quickly return[] to full employment."[21]

For most upper-income Americans, declines in employment or wages were largely transitory, and home prices, savings accounts, and the stock market had more than recovered by the fall. Most of these Americans could also work safely from home and simply order their groceries and essential supplies online. For the well-to-do, any economic pain felt in the spring was gone by Election Day; their recovery was indeed V-shaped.

This was especially true for those who owned stocks, a group of individuals that skews heavily toward the wealthy.[22] Although US stocks shed more than a third of their value in February and March 2020, they had recovered from most of these losses by mid-August.[23] Even as the Dow dropped on the news of rising COVID-19 infection rates in the days before the election, the stock market overall had performed well.[24] It is also worth noting that Trump himself argued that the market's performance during his time in office—especially in 2020—was a key reason to reelect him.[25] "They say the stock market will boom if I'm elected," Trump declared in the October 22 general election debate. "If [Biden's] elected, the stock market will crash."[26]

Recognizing its centrality to Trump's reelection, Biden focused on the stock market's benefits to the wealthy. Trump instead stressed its value to retirees. "The idea that the stock market is booming is his only measure of what's happening," the Democrat said of Trump in the October 22 presidential debate. "Where I come from in Scranton and Claymont, the people don't live off of the stock market. Just in the last three years, during this crisis, the billionaires in this country made, according to Wall Street, 700 billion more dollars. 700 billion more dollars. Because that's his only measure. What happens to the ordinary people out there? What happens to them?" "401(k)s are through the roof," Trump responded. "People's stock are through the roof."[27]

For those not at the top of the economic ladder, for those who did not own stocks or their own homes, the economic pain continued to be sharp and severe throughout the fall. If anything, their economic distress deepened over the course of 2020. According to data from Harvard economist Raj Chetty, those in the bottom 25 percent of the earnings distribution had lost three times as many jobs as those in the top 25 percent.[28] Millions of low-wage workers, especially those who only had a high school diploma, remained out of work, with few prospects of being rehired, as Election Day approached.[29] According to Federal Reserve chair Jerome Powell, approximately 12 percent of college-educated "prime-age" Americans were laid off from their jobs in 2020, versus 20 percent among those without a college degree.[30] Food pantry lines stretched for miles, as millions of Americans faced genuine economic desperation.[31] Almost 20 percent of Americans lost all of their savings during the COVID pandemic, losses concentrated primarily among low-income workers.[32] In states that had expanded Medicaid eligibility under the Affordable Care Act, enrollment in the program surged. In Pennsylvania, the program's rolls grew by 13.7 percent in 2020, as hundreds of thousands of state residents found themselves impoverished and desperate for health care during the pandemic.[33]

Given this sharp contrast between the top and the bottom of the economic ladder, Joe Biden—and many economists—argued that the economic recovery would be K-shaped: those at the top of the economic heap would emerge from the recession stronger than they were before, while those at the bottom would be even worse off than they had been pre-COVID.[34] Biden argued that Trump's economic policies—such as the 2017 Tax Cut and Jobs Act—benefitted those at the very top at the expense of middle-class families. This echoed long-standing Democratic Party arguments about the people versus the powerful. When asked in the September 29 presidential debate by moderator Chris Wallace to explain the difference between a V- and K-shaped economic recovery, the former senator from Delaware responded that "millionaires and billionaires like him [Trump] in the middle of the COVID crisis have done very well. . . . But you folks at home, you folks living in Scranton and Claymont and all the small towns and working-class towns in America, how well are you doing? . . . [H]e's going to be the first president of the United States to leave office, having fewer jobs in his administration than when he became president."[35]

As the preceding description suggests, there was some truth to both Biden's and Trump's claims, and the picture one got of the economy depended, in part, on which indicators one used to define it. Where a gain frame favored Trump, a loss one benefitted Biden. By the numbers, a story built on the upward trend in GDP, increasing numbers employed, and the trajectory of the stock market favored Trump. But other indicators—stressing the overall decline in GDP, the continued high rate of unemployment, and the numbers experiencing deprivation, hunger, and prospective homelessness—favored Biden.

Which vision of the economy—Trump's V-shaped recovery or Biden's K-shaped one—was correct was a central point of contention in the election. While the economy matters in every election, the depth and complexity of the economic fallout in 2020 gave it special importance in this year.

The Importance of the Virus and the Economy

And, of course, Trump and Biden saw the economy in fundamentally different terms vis-à-vis the coronavirus. Throughout the campaign season, the

Democratic and Republican nominees clashed over how the pandemic could be contained without further jeopardizing the economy. In their final debate, on October 22, Trump declared that "we can't keep this country closed" and that "the cure cannot be worse than the problem itself." Biden argued that "I'm going to shut down the virus, not the country," and grimly forecast "a dark winter," arguing that Trump had "no clear plan" to fight the virus. If "you hear nothing else I say tonight, hear this," the Democratic nominee said in that debate. "Anyone [who] is responsible for that many deaths should not remain as president of the United States of America."[36] When Trump asserted, "I say we're learning to live with it. We have no choice. We can't lock ourselves up in a basement like Joe does," Biden countered, "He says that we're learning to live with it. People are learning to die with it."[37] As we will show in Part 2 of this chapter, this core difference over whether the virus or the economy was the central issue of the campaign framed and reflected how Trump and Biden supporters saw the contest.

The Questions to Be Answered in Chapter 6, Part 2

In every election, the economy is an important issue, although, as the 2000 contest indicated, not necessarily the central one.[38] In 2020, however, its collapse and unevenly shared recovery raised the possibility that its effects might be different this year than in past ones. In particular, because the economy recovered much more quickly and completely for those at the top of the economic ladder than it did for those at the bottom, those on different rungs of the income ladder might have very different perceptions of it.

To understand how the economy shaped perceptions of the candidates in the 2020 election, in Part 2 of this chapter we ask whether voters balloted retrospectively in 2020: that is, did their views of the economy shape their vote choice? At the same time, we dig into whether the recovery really was K-shaped, paying special attention to the perceptions of those at the bottom of the economic ladder who faced economic desperation (i.e., those who were unable to afford necessities such as food, utilities, or housing). Finally, we explore voters' perceptions of Trump's and Biden's ability to handle the economy and related issues. Taken together, our answers to these questions will help us determine whether and, if so, how the unique economic circumstances in which voters found themselves in 2020 shaped their views of the candidates and likelihood of supporting one ticket over the other.

6.2

The Best of Times, the Worst of Times

PERCEPTIONS AND EFFECTS OF THE ECONOMY

Matthew Levendusky, Josh Pasek, Andrew Renninger, and Kathleen Hall Jamieson

It was the best of times, it was the worst of times, it was the age of wisdom, it was the age of foolishness, it was the epoch of belief, it was the epoch of incredulity, it was the season of light, it was the season of darkness, it was the spring of hope, it was the winter of despair.

—Charles Dickens, *A Tale of Two Cities*

THE OPENING LINES of Charles Dickens's *A Tale of Two Cities* are often quoted but rarely apt. After all, how often are the times truly both the best and the worst? But there is a case to be made that these classic lines do, in fact, apply to the state of the economy in 2020. As we reviewed in the first part of the chapter, there were bright spots, especially for those at the upper end of the economic ladder. But there was also plenty of pain, especially for those who were less well-off. Confronted by all of this, how did voters make sense of the economy, and how did it shape their electoral choices in 2020?

In Part 1 of this chapter, we tracked the economy's unique contours during 2020; here we ask what effect they had on voters' perceptions and vote preferences. To begin, we consider whether pre-pandemic economic growth, plus the fall recovery (spurred, at least in part, by the government stimulus), convinced voters to support the president. We show that many did vote retrospectively, as in so many previous elections: their perceptions of the economy's course during Trump's term helped to shape their vote choice. Self-reported perceptions of the economy confirm this conclusion, as do more objective indicators of economic health.

Voters' beliefs about their personal finances coincide with their place within the K-shaped recovery. Those at higher income levels were much more optimistic about their economic health than those of lesser means. Although most suffered economically as the economy locked down in the spring to combat the virus, by the fall the pain remained much more concentrated among those at the bottom of the income distribution. But, as in earlier studies, we find that political attitudes as well as economic factors shaped these perceptions.[1] Even after controlling for objective economic differences between Trump and Biden supporters, the former but not the latter thought that their financial situation had improved. While objective conditions mattered, politics also played a strong role in shaping economic perceptions. In a campaign context, we cannot separate politics and economics.

But that does not mean that economic assessments are mere partisan projections. For those at the very bottom of the economic ladder, the economic crisis carried genuine desperation. Throughout our study, approximately 15 percent of our sample could not afford necessities such as food, utilities, or rent. While some in each of our electorates experienced economic desperation, wavering Biden voters and nonvoters were especially likely to do so. This finding highlights an often overlooked but important dimension of pocketbook voting in this election, as well as the ways in which economic hardship can demobilize or mobilize certain segments of the public.

Finally, we show that the economy was one of Trump's stronger issues, if not his strongest overall. Every group in our study—Trump voters, Biden voters, third-party voters, and nonvoters alike—saw Trump as stronger on the economy relative to other issues in the campaign. This helps to explain why the incumbent emphasized the economy in his campaign: on this issue, voters saw him as especially qualified. In contrast, as we demonstrated in Chapter 5 ("Did the COVID-19 Pandemic Sink Trump's Reelection?"), because voters saw Trump as uniquely unqualified on the pandemic, Biden focused his attention there. Obviously, there is a push and a pull, and voters' perceptions were shaped by campaign messages. But these differences also highlight what each campaign saw as its unique strength and its path to victory. The battle between these two competing messages would ultimately help to determine the election's outcome.

How Did Voters Perceive the Economic Landscape in 2020?

To assess how voters perceived the economy in 2020, we asked four retrospective items throughout our study. In wave 1 (April–May 2020), we asked respondents to think back to the period before the COVID-19 pandemic and ascertain whether their economic fortunes, as well as those of their community, had improved over Trump's first three years in office (we first discussed this data in Figure 3.9). Shortly before Election Day in wave 7 (October–November 2020), we asked whether the nation's economy as a whole, as well as their own economic circumstances, had improved since the 2016 election. Their responses make it possible to assess how several different economic perceptions varied: voters' own financial circumstances, both pre-pandemic and across the whole of Trump's term, as well as the nation's economic health and that of their local communities. Because economic growth differed locale to locale, when casting a ballot for president, the question about their communities is particularly important, as voters are especially attentive to their own community's economic health.[2]

Figure 6.1 presents the distribution of each of these variables for each of our electorates.

The data here explain why President Trump spent so much time emphasizing pre-pandemic economic growth: most voters thought that their own financial circumstances, as well as those of their communities, had improved during his first three years in office (top row of Figure 6.1; note in particular the strong sense of a growing pre-COVID economy among the Trump electorates). Indeed, only about a fifth of voters thought that their fortunes, or those of their community, had declined. Of course, it is worth remembering that we asked this question in April–May 2020, during the sharp economic downturn. This timing raises the possibility that the answers are shaped, in part at least, by a contrast effect created by the dissimilarity between the pre-COVID period and the one in which the question was being answered. Nonetheless, these numbers suggest that most voters thought that their economic fortunes, as well as those of their communities, had improved during Trump's first three years in office.

In contrast, looking back across Trump's entire term, we see a starker divide between personal assessments and those of the nation as a whole, and an overall grimmer picture (bottom row of Figure 6.1). First, looking at the national picture, the overwhelming consensus among our sample was that the nation's economy had deteriorated during the Trump administration. Since voters consider an incumbent's entire economic record but put somewhat more weight on more recent economic performance when casting their ballots,[3] this was not good news for the Trump campaign. It also helps to explain why he emphasized his pre-pandemic economic record and argued that there would be a V-shaped recovery, in which the nation would soon see strong economic growth once again.

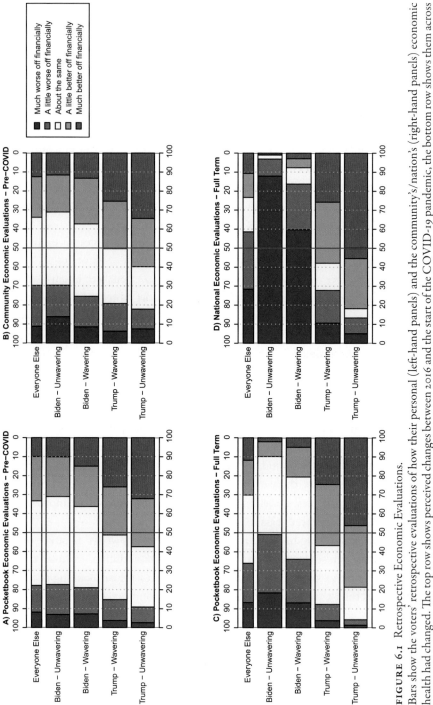

FIGURE 6.1 Retrospective Economic Evaluations.

Bars show the voters' retrospective evaluations of how their personal (left-hand panels) and the community's/nation's (right-hand panels) economic health had changed. The top row shows perceived changes between 2016 and the start of the COVID-19 pandemic, the bottom row shows them across Trump's entire term in office.

Assessments of personal financial circumstances show a rosier picture. Indeed, these retrospective evaluations don't look that different from respondents' pre-pandemic assessments. This finding suggests that even when our respondents thought the nation's fortunes had sunk, they didn't necessarily think their individual ones had done so (the exception would be Biden supporters, but those assessments may well be partially driven by political factors).

While the question wordings of the two personal retrospective items are not identical, they are close enough to permit comparison. Doing so lets us determine how voters perceived their economic well-being to have changed over 2020. So, for example, if our respondents were more optimistic about the economic circumstances in October 2020 than they'd been pre-COVID, we would conclude that they thought their economic circumstances had improved during 2020. Comparing these two variables, we found quite a bit of divergence among voters. While some voters (36.6 percent) thought their fortunes had sunk during 2020, others (28.2 percent) believed theirs had improved (the remaining 35.2 percent reported that they were unchanged). This lends some initial credence to the idea of a K-shaped economic recovery, where some respondents experienced very different economic outlooks during 2020. To understand these differences, we now turn to a more detailed exploration of our data.

Was There a K-Shaped Economic Recovery in 2020?

As we discussed in Part 1 of the chapter, economists argued that the United States experienced a K-shaped recovery in 2020: for those who were relatively financially well-off, the pandemic's economic consequences were short-lived and not terribly severe. But for those lower down on the economic ladder, the economic pain dragged on from 2020 into 2021, with longer-lasting unemployment and ensuing economic hardship.

Our data allow us to speak in several different ways about whether our respondents can be parsed into the two halves of the K. If there was a K-shaped recovery, we should see the economic well-being of most slide in the spring of 2020, when the country goes into lockdown, but then in the summer and fall, as the economy begins to reopen, the fortunes of higher-income voters should diverge from those of people who were at lower income levels before the crash. Put simply, those at the top should see their incomes return to their pre-pandemic levels, while those at the bottom should continue to experience unemployment or lower wages. As an initial indicator of the state of the economy in the spring of 2020, in wave 1 (April–May 2020), we asked respondents whether they or someone in their household had had their hours cut or their salary reduced since the start of the coronavirus pandemic and whether they had lost their job. In that first wave, a majority of our sample said one of these had happened to them or someone in their household. While this is simply one indicator, it points to the fact that the economic pain of the COVID-19 pandemic was widespread in the spring of 2020.

Beginning in wave 2 (June 2020), we asked whether the salary or hours that had been cut had been restored and also whether those who had lost their job had found a new one. Their responses provide an indicator of the extent and duration of the economic dislocation. They also make it possible to distinguish respondents who had had their hours or salary cut but rapidly restored from those whose cuts were sustained through the end of our study. We also asked those who had gotten a new job whether it was better, worse, or about the same as their previous one. Collectively, we use these items to assess what fraction of various groups' wages had returned to a pre-pandemic level (i.e., what fraction of the group either never had their salary cut or never lost a job, had a salary cut restored, or got a new position that was at least as good as the previous one). In Figure 6.2, we plot this pattern over the course

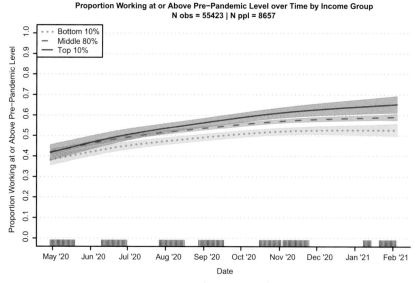

FIGURE 6.2 Return to Pre-COVID Employment Levels.
Lines show the proportion of those who, having lost their job or had their hours cut, had their hours restored or found a job at least as good as the one they had pre-COVID, across our study. Estimates are provided separately for the bottom 10%, middle 80%, and top 10% of the income distribution.

of our study. In light of claims that the United States experienced a K-shaped recovery, we plot separately the bottom 10 percent of the income distribution in our sample (those earning $25,000 or less in 2019), the middle 80 percent of our sample, and the top 10 percent of our sample (those earning $200,000 or more in 2019).

As the figure indicates, at the top of the income ladder, there was significant economic disruption in the spring of 2020: among high-earning households, more than half experienced some negative effects on their earnings. But for these individuals, the pain was transitory and many saw their positions restored by Election Day. The middle of the income distribution saw a similar, though not quite as complete, return to normal. But there was considerably less upward change for those at the bottom of the income scale: their economic loss largely persisted into the fall and winter (and likely even beyond the close of the study).

We see this same pattern in aggregate data from Opportunity Insights at Harvard University.[4] In Figure 6.3, we use these data to plot the monthly change in employment in each of our states, broken down by income tercile, across 2020.

In each of our four states, there was a sharp fall in employment across all income levels in March and April 2020. But two patterns stand out. First, the dip was quite modest for those in the top third of the income distribution: in no state was this change more than 10 or 15 percent from January 2020's levels for this group. By contrast, for the bottom third, this drop was seismic, with their employment falling by at least 30 percent in every state, and by 50 percent in Michigan. Second, for higher-income earners, the crisis was over by the late summer; indeed, by December their levels of employment had increased relative to January 2020. But among those at the bottom of the income scale, unemployment continued unabated throughout 2020. These data reinforce the message from our survey data above: while those at all income levels felt economic pain in the spring of 2020, the fortunes of the top and the bottom of the economic ladder diverged as the year went on.

Did Some Voters Experience Economic Desperation in 2020?

Saying that the recovery was K-shaped does not capture the full extent of the economic fallout in 2020. For those at the bottom of the economic ladder, the damage wrought by the pandemic was severe. Not only did these Americans disproportionately lose their jobs, but some among them lost the ability to pay for basic necessities, such as food, utilities, and rent. We argue that those

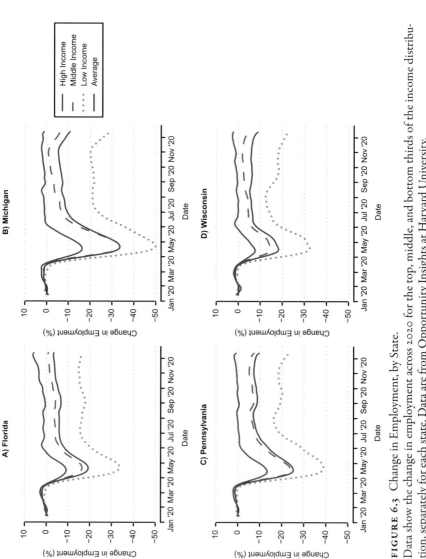

FIGURE 6.3 Change in Employment, by State.
Data show the change in employment across 2020 for the top, middle, and bottom thirds of the income distribution, separately for each state. Data are from Opportunity Insights at Harvard University.

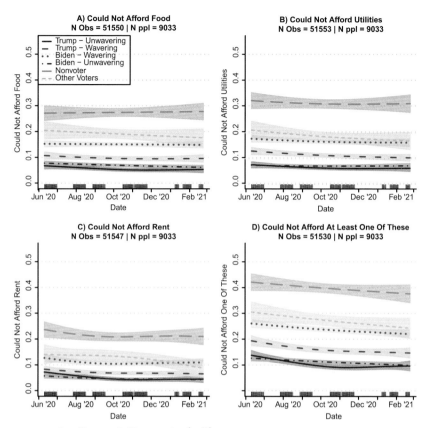

FIGURE 6.4 Economic Desperation by Electorate.
Lines show the proportion of each electorate that cannot afford enough food (panel A), cannot afford their utilities (panel B), or cannot afford their rent/mortgage (panel C), or at least one of these three (panel D), across our study.

who cannot afford one or more of these necessities are experiencing economic desperation, and we expect them to behave quite differently than others in our study. Figure 6.4 (echoing parts of Figure 3.11) shows what percentage of each of our electorates reported not being able to pay for rent, food, or utilities in each wave of our study, along with those who indicated an inability to afford at least one of them.

Figure 6.4 shows us that, by each of these metrics, a nontrivial fraction of the public experienced economic desperation in 2020. In each wave, approximately 15 percent of respondents reportedly could not afford to pay for at least one of these key necessities (rent, food, or utilities). While there are some minor differences across items (e.g., respondents reported more difficulty paying utilities than rent), the key takeaway is that a noteworthy fraction of those in each of our states experienced real economic hardship and desperation during this period.* Expanding on our measures of economic dislocation, in waves 3 (July 2020) and 6 (September–October 2020), we asked respondents if they had required assistance to get the food they needed. For example, had they turned to a food pantry, food distribution from their local school district, or the Supplemental Nutrition Assistance Program (the successor program to food stamps)? In both waves, roughly one-quarter of the sample had received food from one of these entities during the pandemic, with SNAP being the most common source of nutritional help. These findings underscore the depth of desperation brought on by the coronavirus pandemic. This is a reminder that while most of our respondents—and most Americans—experienced some economic pain and dislocation in 2020, for some that pain was much more acute than for others.

This desperation was distributed very unevenly across our electorates. Overall, desperation levels ranged from an average of 9.2 percent across waves among unwavering Trump voters to an average of 39.8 percent among those who did not end up voting for president. The unwavering electorates (for both candidates) were the *least* likely to experience desperation (13.6 of unwavering Biden voters reported desperation). For individuals who were wavering, desperation was considerably higher. Among those who voted, wavering Biden voters were the most likely to report it (26.8 percent of these voters did so), with those who did not vote for a major-party candidate less so (21.8 percent), and wavering Trump supporters even less likely (17.5 percent). It therefore seems that economic suffering was associated both with some level of uncertainty about vote choice and with a general preference for Biden.

The likely impact of desperation comes into further relief once we go beyond disaggregating the electorates into wavering and unwavering groups and also tease out those who vacillated in their choices from those who only wavered with respect to whether or not they would vote. Rates of desperation were far higher among those who were unsure of their preferences across the election cycle. Biden and Trump voters whose preferences were consistent but who varied in their likelihood of turning out were far less likely to experience desperation than those who were at least somewhat uncertain about their choices (with desperation affecting 23.1 and 16.3 percent of wavering Biden

---

*. One limitation is that because our data began in 2020, we do not know which voters were struggling to pay for these necessities before the coronavirus pandemic. While some families were undoubtedly having these challenges in prior years, given the dislocation caused by the pandemic, at least some of this suffering can be attributed to the events of 2020.

and Trump voters with steady candidate preferences vs. 31.8 and 19.9 percent of voters whose choices were in doubt). These results suggest that desperation may have actually swung some voters by shifting their choices over time (we return to this point later in the chapter).

A second pattern that calls for explanation is the disproportionate rates of desperation among those who voted for Biden compared to Trump. It is possible that this pattern is mostly an expression of demographics—the younger, non-White Americans who supported Biden were hit much harder by the coronavirus pandemic and the ensuing economic fallout.[5] But coupling this difference with evidence that Biden voters who experienced desperation disproportionately wavered in their choices, it seems likely that some amount of persuasion was happening as well. Not only is this another reminder that the pain and consequences of the pandemic were distributed unevenly, but it also underscores the finding that Biden's voters prioritized the pandemic as the key issue in the election. The pandemic was presumably more salient to those who suffered more as a result of it. It suggests as well that the negative personal retrospective evaluations for Biden voters seen in Figure 6.1 may not have been motivated by partisanship or vote choice but instead reflected genuine economic pain.

Overall, Biden's voters were in a more economically precarious position than were Trump's. This parallels trends seen in 2016 as well: while the initial post-election narrative in that year was that Trump's voters were experiencing economic anxiety, careful data analysis showed that the opposite was true.[6] In both elections, Trump voters were, if anything, less economically disadvantaged, contrary to the popular narrative. His voters were experiencing anxiety of a different kind, however, as we discuss in Chapter 8 ("A Deeper Anxiety").

So far, we have focused on Biden and Trump voters. But another group stands out in Figure 6.4: the nonvoters. At any given time, roughly 40 percent of nonvoters were struggling to pay for at least one essential item; 15 percent were struggling to pay for all three. Nonvoters experienced economic desperation at much higher levels than other groups, and, likely as a result, were largely disengaged from the political system (we return to this point below).[7] This should serve to remind us that discussions of pocketbook voting (i.e., voting based on how one's personal finances have done; see the discussion in Chapter 2, "What Fundamental Factors Shape Elections?") largely overlook the most vulnerable Americans, whose economic desperation is associated with disengagement from the political system. If we broaden our understanding of pocketbook voting to include these potential voters, we can see that their desperation may lead them to feel disengaged and push them away from voting, a central act of American citizenship.

Across these analyses, a clear pattern emerges. "The economy" was not one thing in 2020: what you experienced depended on your pre-COVID socioeconomic situation. For those of means, 2020 was a good year financially: their investments increased in value, they kept their jobs (shifting office meetings to online videoconferencing systems), and they ended the year financially more secure than they were before the pandemic began. But for those lower down the economic ladder, especially those at the very bottom, the picture was grim. Such differences, in turn, suggest that the economy might factor into these individuals' vote choices in very different ways.

How Did the Economy Impact Vote Choices in 2020?

To this point, our analyses show that in 2020 "the economy" meant different things to different people. But did it affect Americans' ballot preferences? Perhaps the most fundamental economic effect is retrospective voting: when a president presides over a growing economy, he is likely to win reelection, all else being equal. To begin the investigation of the economy's effects in 2020, first we consider how our panelists' retrospective assessments were related to their vote choice in 2020. Were those who thought that the nation's economy, or their own personal finances, improved during Trump's term more likely to cast their ballot for him? In Figure 6.5, we present a graphical summary of regression results testing whether these economic retrospective evaluations, either individually or in combination, predict vote choice, as theories of retrospective voting contend that they should. For a discussion of this type of graph, and our approach to using this style of analysis throughout the book, please see our discussion in the Appendix ("Our Data and Analytical Strategy"), especially our discussion of Appendix Figure 5.

As in other regressions in the book, we present results predicting voting for Biden separately from voting for Trump (as we explained in Chapter 5, this allows us to identify how the predictors shift support for either candidate). Unsurprisingly, we find a strong relationship between retrospective economic evaluations and vote choice. No matter what measure we use, those who thought the economy had done better under Trump were more likely to vote for him, even controlling for partisanship and various demographic measures. When both sets of predictors are included in the model, however,

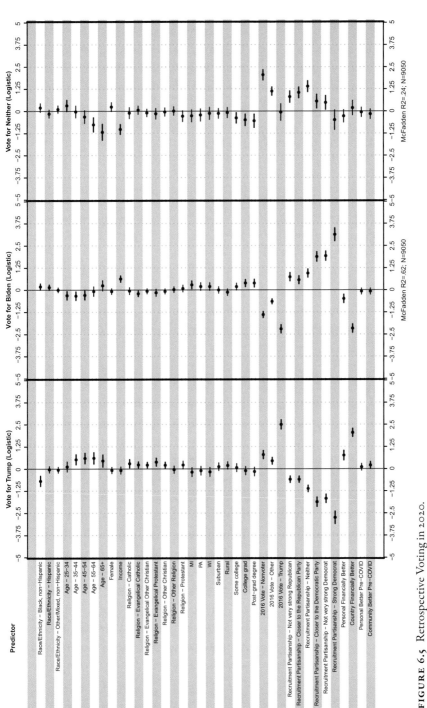

FIGURE 6.5 Retrospective Voting in 2020.
Standardized regression coefficients from logistic regressions predicting voting for Trump (left column), Biden (center), or neither (right). For each variable, standardized coefficient estimates are given as circles with 95% confidence intervals as black lines. Bolded coefficients are statistically significant at the $p < 0.05$ level.

it is clear that assessments across Trump's entire term in office seem to account for the impact of pre-pandemic personal circumstances. That is, our respondents didn't seem to evaluate Trump on the pre-pandemic economy so much as on how it fared during his whole time in office. His argument that the economic turbulence of 2020 was not his fault—while possibly rendered moot by the recovery—does not seem to have been a persuasive one. The takeaway from Figure 6.5 is that economic retrospection shaped vote choice in 2020, just as it has in so many other contests.

Is Retrospective Voting Simply a Matter of Perceptions?

One criticism of the results in Figure 6.5 is that those economic perceptions are subject to a great deal of political projection. Rather than showing that those who thought the economy expanded were more likely to vote for Trump, perhaps what they show is that those who planned on voting for Trump were more likely to rationalize that decision by reporting that the economy had grown during his time in office. Put differently, this may be a case of politics shaping economic views, rather than the reverse; indeed, later in the chapter, we show this is at least partially true.

An alternative way of assessing retrospective voting is to use measures of actual economic output and determine whether voters who live in areas where the economy was doing better were more likely to vote for Trump. Whereas Figure 6.5 tests whether voters who *say* that the economy is doing better are more likely to vote to reelect him, we are now looking for the answer to a slightly different question: were voters who *lived in areas where the economy had actually improved* more likely to vote for the president?

Complicating this move, as we noted earlier in the chapter, is that there is no agreed-upon metric with which to assess "the economy." Nor are metrics used to make sense of a usual economy necessarily suited to one as odd as 2020's, where stock-market highs coincided with high levels of unemployment and even desperation. To surmount this challenge, given the importance of the local economy for vote choice, we looked at how the economy performed in voters' very local area.

To gauge that economic performance in 2020, we used a measure of how many people visited local businesses over the course of that tumultuous year. Using data from SafeGraph,˙ we constructed a measure of foot traffic at the

---

˙.˙ For more details on this data (as well as other data types), see the Online Appendix at https://osf.io/487jk/.

twenty businesses that were closest to each respondent's home address. Using GPS data from approximately 10 percent of the nation's mobile phones, SafeGraph records visits to points of interest across the country, allowing us to estimate foot traffic at each of these businesses in each of our waves. With this dataset, we can see the extent to which foot traffic changes across the course of the pre-election period: for all areas, foot traffic fell precipitously in wave 1 (April–May 2020) relative to where it had been pre-pandemic. However, in some locales, it effectively rebounded to pre-pandemic levels by the fall, while in others it continued to lag. To measure economic change over 2020, we looked at the difference between foot traffic measured in wave 1 and wave 7 (November 2020).[†] Were voters who live in areas in which foot traffic recovered more fully by the election more likely to vote for President Trump, relative to those who live in areas where it did not? Figure 6.6 presents the results using this more objective measure of local economic performance.

In Figure 6.6, we see that voters *do* respond to changes in the economic conditions of their local area when casting their ballots. Positive changes in foot traffic were associated with an increased likelihood of voting for President Trump. However, individuals who preferred Trump in wave 1 but whose neighborhoods had far less foot traffic in October than they had in May (dashed red lines in Figure 6.6) were somewhat more likely to defect from the incumbent. And voters who did not prefer either candidate in wave 1 seemed to make their decisions at least in part in relation to the vibrancy of the local recovery (solid green lines in Figure 6.6). For at least some voters, the strength of their local economy may have increased the likelihood of supporting the incumbent's reelection.

One might point out, however, that the effect of the local economy is rather weak, at least compared to the effect of perceptions. This is doubtless attributable to the fact that political factors and economic perceptions are endogenous to each other, and, as other results have shown, perceptual measures overstate the true effect of the economy on vote choice.[8] That said, it is

---

[†] This is scaled by the general amount of foot traffic that nearby businesses have, measured as the average of the pre-pandemic traffic and the amount of traffic in wave 7. A decrease of .5 implies that foot traffic dropped by 50 percent of this average value between waves 1 and 7, while an increase of 1.0 implies that the amount of foot traffic doubled between these waves. Values of less than −1.0 (a 100% decrease) were observed in eight cases where foot traffic increased considerably between the baseline in January and wave 1 (likely due to new stores opening) before subsequently dropping.

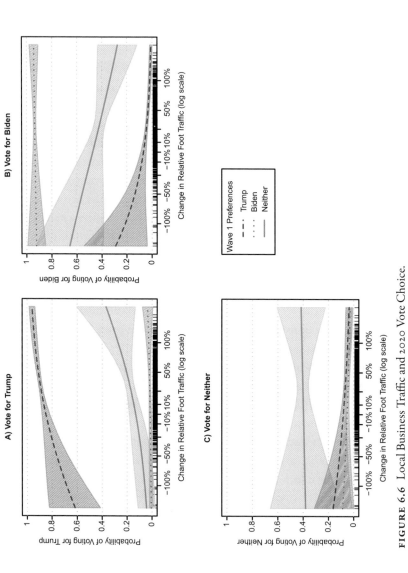

FIGURE 6.6 Local Business Traffic and 2020 Vote Choice.

Each panel provides the predicted probability of voting for Trump (panel A), Biden (panel B), or neither (panel C), as a function of the change in local business foot traffic, wave 1 candidate support, and their interaction. In each panel, the effects are shown separately for those who supported Trump (dashed red line), Biden (dotted blue line), or neither (solid green line) in wave 1.

worth noting that voters do indeed seem to respond to changes not just in the perceived economy but also in the actual one.[‡]

How Did Personal Economic Circumstances Shape Voting in 2020?

In the unique economic environment of 2020, we might expect to find evidence that one's personal economic circumstances help to explain how one votes. Normally, the effect of personal economic circumstances—pocketbook voting—is weak because voters do not know how to map their economic status back to government policy. But the COVID-driven shutdown of the economy made the linkage in 2020 more direct, especially for those at the bottom of the economic ladder. If you worked at a business that had to shut down during the COVID lockdowns, and therefore you lost your job or had your hours cut, you could draw a clear connection between your economic pain and government policy. It is not just economic pain that matters, however; some voters might also see how their economic fortunes *improved* due to government policy. Because the government provided direct stimulus payments to many voters, their improved circumstances can also be attributed, in part, to governmental policy. Thus, both gains and losses might have driven pocketbook voting in the 2020 election.

To begin, consider the most direct—and visible—economic boost most people got from the federal government: the Economic Impact Payments authorized by the CARES Act, better known as stimulus payments. Since this direct cash payment provided a lifeline to many struggling families, those who got such a payment and credited President Trump for delivering it may well have become more likely to vote for him. To determine whether this is the case, we model a respondent's ultimate vote choice as a function of their initial candidate choice, whether or not they reported receiving a stimulus payment, and the interaction of these two measures. Here, we use the final engagement wave as our measure of baseline preferences, rather than wave 1 as we usually do, because some families received stimulus checks before wave 1 and this could bias our result. Because stimulus payments depended in part on income levels, we also interacted both of these with income to ensure that this did not confound any results. Our interest here is in knowing whether

---

‡. Notably, there were no residual influences of objective economic conditions on vote choices after accounting for perceptions in a combined model, so these effects were not entirely distinct.

those who initially supported Biden or a third-party candidate instead shifted toward Trump as a result of receiving this payment.

In Figure 6.7, we show only a small effect of getting a stimulus check on voting for either Trump or Biden. For most initial preferences, the dashed lines (tracking the behaviors of those who reported receiving the payment) and the solid lines (indicating the behaviors of those who did not) were not significantly different. The differences that did emerge, however, were telling. While there was no appreciable effect among those who initially preferred Trump or Biden, there was an effect among those for whom the identity of the Democratic nominee mattered. It appears that the primary effect of the stimulus was not so much to shift choice as to enable some individuals to get out and vote (presumably because it reduced hardship in other areas). Indeed, the biggest difference we observe between those who did and did not get a stimulus payment was in terms of whether the lowest-income individuals who lacked a preference at the beginning of the study would actually report voting. Because these individuals marginally preferred Biden when they did vote, the stimulus does not appear to have benefitted Trump much electorally.[§]

But given the nature of the economic dislocation in 2020, if there were pocketbook effects, they were likely to be concentrated among those who felt economic pain. Of those who lost their job or had their hours cut but not restored (see Figure 6.2), we asked whether they became less likely to vote for President Trump, in effect holding him responsible for their economic dislocation. In particular, did those who initially supported President Trump but then experienced economic dislocation shift away from him? As in Figure 6.7, we once again measured initial candidate support in our final engagement wave because so many of those who would lose their job had already done so by the time of our wave 1 interview.

In Figure 6.8, we see that there were some notable effects of job loss, though they were concentrated among those at the lowest income levels. Among panelists who initially supported Trump, those who had not found a job at least as good as the one they had pre-COVID (labeled "Not Yet Fully Employed" on the graph and shown with the dotted red line in panel A) were more likely to defect from the incumbent than those who had done so (labeled "Fully Employed" on the graph and shown with the solid red line). This effect, however, was predominantly concentrated among those with lower

§. The apparent drop in support for Biden among individuals who got the stimulus and said at recruitment that their preferences depended on the nominee are not particularly meaningful, as there were almost no people in this group.

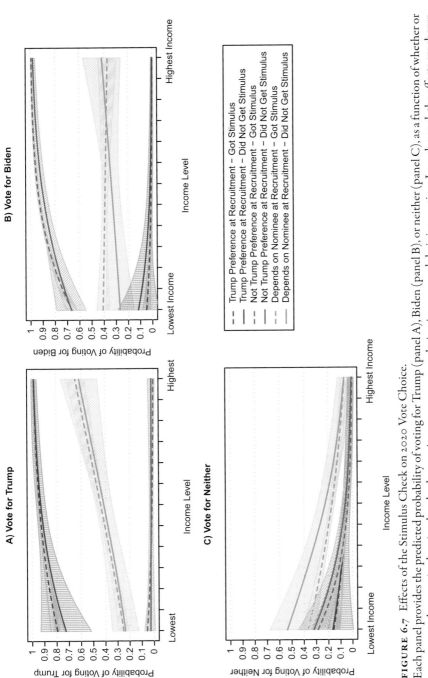

FIGURE 6.7 Effects of the Stimulus Check on 2020 Vote Choice.

Each panel provides the predicted probability of voting for Trump (panel A), Biden (panel B), or neither (panel C), as a function of whether or not a respondent received a stimulus check, recruitment survey vote choice, income, and their interaction. In each panel, the effects are shown separately for those who supported Trump (red line), did not support Trump (blue line), or said their choice depended on who the Democratic nominee was (green line) in our recruitment survey. Dashed lines indicate individuals who received a stimulus check and solid lines indicate individuals who did not receive a stimulus check. Recruitment survey preferences were used here because some respondents received their stimulus checks before the wave 1 survey.

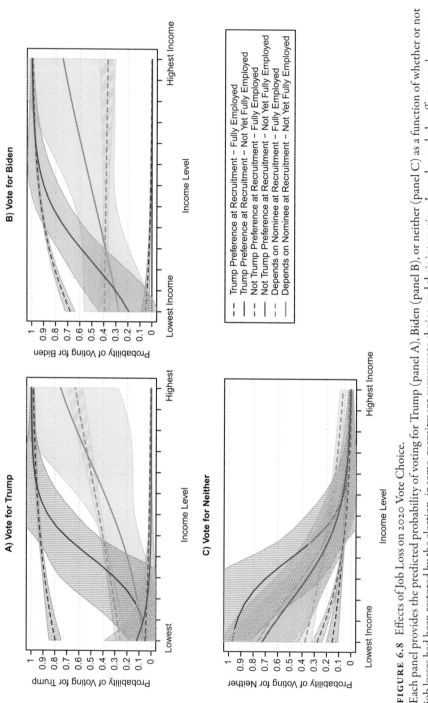

A) Vote for Trump

B) Vote for Biden

C) Vote for Neither

- - - Trump Preference at Recruitment – Fully Employed
──── Trump Preference at Recruitment – Not Yet Fully Employed
- - - Not Trump Preference at Recruitment – Fully Employed
──── Not Trump Preference at Recruitment – Not Yet Fully Employed
- - - Depends on Nominee at Recruitment – Fully Employed
──── Depends on Nominee at Recruitment – Not Yet Fully Employed

FIGURE 6.8 Effects of Job Loss on 2020 Vote Choice.

Each panel provides the predicted probability of voting for Trump (panel A), Biden (panel B), or neither (panel C) as a function of whether or not job losses had been restored by the election, income, recruitment survey vote choice, and their interaction. In each panel, the effects are shown separately for those who supported Trump (red line), did not support Trump (blue line), or said their choice depended on who the Democratic nominee was (green line) in our recruitment survey. Dashed lines indicate individuals who had lost salary or jobs and had not returned to full employment, and solid lines indicate individuals who either did not lose these, had their salaries restored, or had a job at least as good as their previous one by the wave 7 survey. Recruitment survey preferences were used here because many respondents had lost their jobs before the wave 1 survey.

incomes (i.e., roughly the bottom third of the income distribution). Further, note that these individuals did not vote for Biden: in panel B, we see that these individuals, regardless of their employment status, were almost certain not to vote for Biden (i.e., both red lines run along the *x*-axis in panel B). Rather than switch their vote, individuals who were not fully employed did not ballot for either candidate and instead largely sat out the election (see panel C).

There is a parallel finding for Biden voters in panel B. Those who initially said they would not support Trump in our engagement study and who had not yet gotten a job equal to their pre-COVID one were much less likely to vote for the Democratic nominee (relative to those who had returned to their pre-COVID employment level; these are the blue lines in panel B). But once again, these effects exist only for voters with low to moderate incomes, and rather than switching to Trump, these respondents also largely sat out the election. This parallels the effects we observed about economic desperation above: for those at the lowest income levels, the economic pain of 2020 likely helped to push them out of the electoral system.

Does Economic Desperation Affect Electoral Outcomes?

As we discussed earlier in the chapter, some voters experienced genuine economic hardship in 2020, insofar as they could not afford basic necessities such as rent, food, and utilities. This sort of especially significant economic pain was poised to produce effects on vote choice. So, did it? In Figure 6.9, we predict the likelihood that individuals would support each of the candidates based on the proportion of times they reported difficulty paying for one or more of these items.[**]

We see striking effects of desperation on vote. Among those who initially supported Trump when we contacted them in wave 1 (April–May 2020), experiencing desperation dramatically reduced their probability of actually voting for him (see the red line in the top left panel). Evidence that Trump supporters were less likely to experience desperation (see Figure 6.4) may be largely attributable to the fact that those who experience desperation shifted away from him. Indeed, among individuals who did not experience any desperation, 91.4 percent of those with an initial Trump preference reported

---

[**]. For this measure, we considered three questions about whether respondents had trouble affording food, utilities, and rent in the past month that were asked in each of five waves: wave 2, wave 4, wave 5, wave 7, and wave 8. The *x*-axis represents the proportion of times that respondents answered that they had trouble.

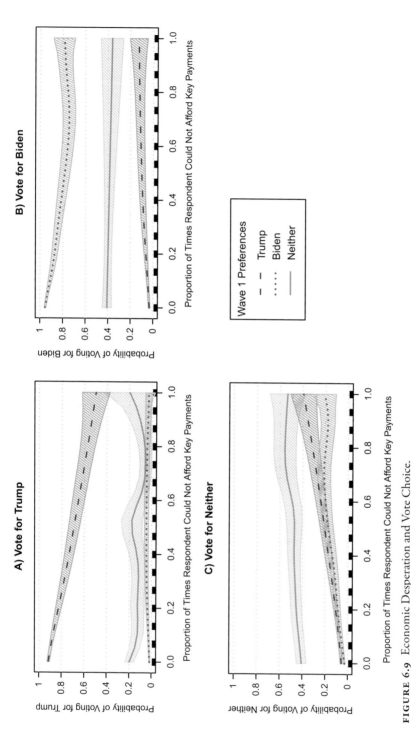

FIGURE 6.9 Economic Desperation and Vote Choice.

Each panel provides the predicted probability of voting for Trump (panel A), Biden (panel B), or neither (panel C), as a function of the frequency of their inability to pay for rent, utilities, and food, wave 1 candidate support, and their interaction. In each panel, the effects are shown separately for those who supported Trump (dashed red line), Biden (dotted blue line), or neither (solid green line) in wave 1.

balloting for him. Among initial Trump supporters who experienced an average of one of the three measures of desperation, only 76.3 percent did the same. And among those whose desperation was the most severe, most initial Trump supporters did not end up voting for him. Even though not many Trump voters experienced much desperation (relative to our other electorates), those who did were more likely to become disaffected with his candidacy.

But it is not enough to say that desperation decreased their likelihood of voting for President Trump. When we look at the red line in the top right panel, we see that desperation made those who initially supported Trump modestly more likely to vote for Biden. But there was a much more notable effect of desperation: many of these prospective voters became nonvoters (bottom left panel). This pattern emerges even more strongly among Biden's initial supporters. Biden voters who experienced desperation became markedly less likely to vote for him (top right panel, blue line), but there was little effect on their likelihood of voting for Trump (top left panel, blue line). Instead, most of these potential voters simply did not ballot (bottom left panel).

This underscores an important, but often overlooked, point about pocketbook voting. There are certainly cases in which voters experienced economic dislocation and punished the incumbent; we see some evidence of this in Figure 6.7. But true economic hardship (economic suffering to the point where life's necessities become difficult to afford) apparently yields political disengagement—possibly, as Maslow's hierarchy of needs[9] would suggest, because taking the time to navigate voting is not a high priority under those circumstances. This dropout effect ironically reduces the likelihood that politicians hear from, and respond to, those in need of government assistance.

These analyses suggest that the effects of the economy on vote choice were complex in 2020. Those who perceived a growing economy or lived in an area in which it was recovering were more likely to reward Trump with a second term. But for those who suffered greater financial hardship, and especially those who experienced genuine economic desperation, there was a move away from Trump, though not inevitably toward Biden. If Trump wanted to be reelected, he needed to ensure that his likely voters would not experience economic dislocation. Presumably had Trump supporters suffered additional hardship, his loss would have been even more pronounced.

Does Politics or Economics Explain Changes
in Economic Perceptions?

In the discussion thus far, we have seen evidence that economic factors shaped political attitudes and behaviors: those who thought the economy improved during Trump's tenure in office, or who lived in an area with a growing economy, were more likely to support his reelection, and those who experienced economic desperation were less likely to vote for him. But of course, we also know from many earlier studies that political factors influence economic perceptions as much as the reverse. If we look at our data, do we see any evidence of political factors shaping respondents' economic perceptions?

To answer that question, we examine how our panelists' perceptions of their personal financial circumstances changed over the course of 2020. As we noted above, we asked respondents for their personal financial retrospective evaluations at two different points in time: in wave 1 (April–May 2020), we asked them to think back to the time before the pandemic and assess how their financial situation had changed during Trump's first three years in office, and then in wave 7 (October 2020), we asked them to do the same while thinking back across Trump's entire term. Comparing the answers to these two questions makes it possible to assess how respondents think their economic fortunes changed in 2020. The dependent variable here is the difference between the wave 7 retrospection (across Trump's entire term in office) and the wave 1 one (covering the pre-pandemic period). Here, higher values mean that the respondent thought their financial situation improved in 2020, and negative values mean that they thought it declined.

Analyzing this variable provides us with a way to test the relative power of economics and politics to influence each other. We saw earlier that for the economy as a whole, the recovery was K-shaped, with upper- and lower-income workers experiencing different economic effects. If economic perceptions were more driven by economic factors, then we should see that upper-income voters thought their fortunes improved during 2020, while lower-income ones should believe their fortunes declined. Of course, such evaluations can be colored by partisanship. If that explains these results, Trump voters— regardless of income—would say that their fortunes improved, while Biden voters would say that theirs declined. Across the course of our panel, we have a large number of indicators of a respondent's economic health:

- We asked respondents for two different measures of their income. In our recruitment wave, we asked for their household's income in 2019, and then in wave 10 (February 2021) for their *expected* income in 2021. We can look at current income (in 2019) with the expectation that high-income individuals will be more bullish about their economic outlook (given the strong K-shaped recovery). We can also examine the difference between these two to look at changes in expected income, with our expectation being that those who think that their future income will be higher than it was in the past will be more optimistic about their economic situation.

- We asked whether they were employed full-time at the time they were recruited and again during wave 5 (August–September 2020). Employed individuals were expected to evaluate the economy more positively.

- We asked whether they received a stimulus payment (Economic Impact Payment) in the spring of 2020. Since that boost had a large effect on individuals' finances in 2020,[10] we expected those who received the checks to be more optimistic about their financial situation.

- We asked whether they owned stocks, and if so, whether their portfolio's value increased during the pandemic. We asked about the change in the value of their portfolio in wave 8 (November 2020). Since the S&P 500 gained 16 percent during 2020, if their portfolio tracked the market, it would have increased considerably in value.[11] As a result, we expected those who owned stocks to be more optimistic about their financial health, especially those whose portfolios had increased in value.

- We asked whether members of their household had had their hours cut or salary reduced at any point since the start of the pandemic, and whether they lost their job during this period as well as whether the hours were restored, or they found a new job (see Figure 6.2). Obviously, those who had had their hours cut or lost their job were expected to be more pessimistic.

- We asked whether they depleted their savings during the pandemic, with the expectation that such draw-downs would make respondents less optimistic about their economic fortunes.

- We asked whether they experienced desperation during 2020 (i.e., they were unable to pay for their rent, utilities, or food at any point during the pandemic) and how frequently this happened (see Figures 6.4 and 6.9). We created a scale of these items (Cronbach's $\alpha = 0.92$), with higher values indicating more frequent difficulty in paying for these life necessities. We expected those experiencing this sort of economic desperation to be more negative about their economic prospects.

- Finally, we used our measure of foot traffic recovery at local businesses to ascertain whether the local economy in their area had recovered, with the expectation that an objective local recovery might improve personal evaluations.

In Figure 6.10, we present regression results using these factors, along with partisanship and conservative media use, to predict changes in respondents' perceptions of their personal finances.

In Figure 6.10, we see that those who lost full-time employment, had their hours or salary cut, or experienced economic desperation more frequently (i.e., could not pay for rent, utilities, or food) became less optimistic about

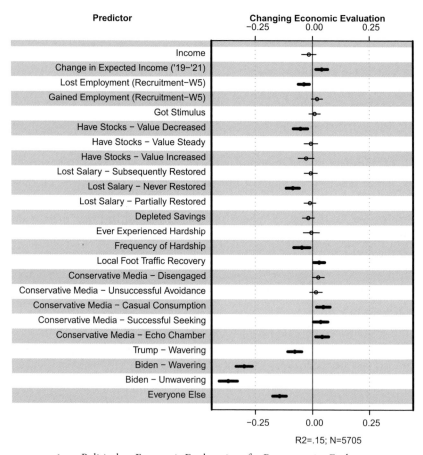

FIGURE 6.10 Political vs. Economic Explanations for Retrospective Evaluations. Standardized regression coefficients from an OLS regression model predicting changes in retrospective economic evaluations. For each variable, standardized coefficient estimates are given as circles with 95% confidence intervals as black lines. Bolded coefficients are statistically significant.

their economic fortunes over time (those who depleted savings were slightly but not significantly less optimistic). In contrast, those who lived in areas where the local economy recovered more fully in 2020 (as measured through foot traffic) became more optimistic.

Interestingly, there was no effect of respondents' 2019 incomes; this was largely due to the fact that high-income individuals were more bullish about their prospects in both waves, so the net change was effectively zero. But that does not mean that income was unrelated to changes in economic outlook. It was not a respondent's 2019 income but rather the change in their expected income from 2019 to 2021 that predicted more positive economic assessments. This makes sense, as rising income suggests that their economic fortunes were improving. We also observe the odd result that owning stocks was slightly negatively correlated overall with changes in personal financial assessments (though not significantly so). This is puzzling in light of the stock market's sharp increase during the pandemic. But this odd result is clearly explained when we look at the performance of individuals' portfolios. The negative coefficient is driven by those who own stock portfolios that lost money feeling especially pessimistic about their changing finances.

Two variables matter above and beyond these economic ones: a respondent's intended vote choice and their media consumption. Viewers who successfully sought out conservative media sources, and especially those in the conservative media echo chamber, were more optimistic about the economy. This conclusion fits with the argument that this type of media presented a pro-Trump picture of the economy.[12] But a respondent's vote choice matters even more. The unwavering Trump voters were the most optimistic—by far—about how their economic fortunes changed in 2020. Note that because they are the baseline category here, the negative and statistically significant coefficients on the other electorates imply that all other respondents were more pessimistic about their outlook. Indeed, both wavering and unwavering Biden voters were more than one full scale point more pessimistic about their economic fortunes in 2020 relative to Trump voters. Importantly, the fact that wavering Biden voters reported more economic hardship than unwavering ones suggests that some of what made individuals wavering Biden voters may have been the economic experiences they had during the election.

The other variable that had a notable impact on vote choices was the hardship that individuals experienced during the election period (see Figures 6.4 and 6.9). Accordingly, we explored whether and, if so, how these variables included in Figure 6.10 predicted whether individuals experienced economic hardship during 2020 (i.e., the inability to pay for food, utilities, or housing). Figure 6.11 presents these results.

We find that the predictors of economic hardship function largely as one would expect. Individuals who had lower incomes, whose expected future incomes were lower, who became unemployed during 2020, who did not own stocks, who lost their salaries, and who depleted their savings were more likely to report economic hardship during the study. The relations linking hardships with conservative media orientations and with our electorates should of course be viewed as endogenous, but nonetheless, they help to illustrate who was experiencing hardships at the time. The fact that hardships, unlike economic perceptions, were much more closely linked to measures of direct economic impacts suggests that this measure, more so than more perceptual ones, may more accurately tap how the real-world economy can influence voters.

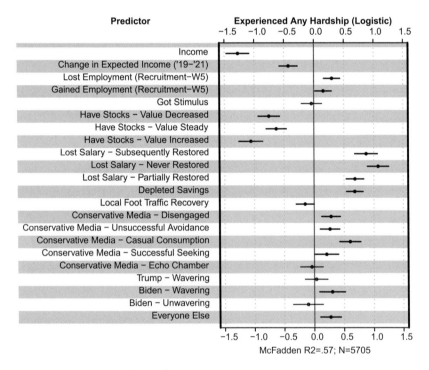

FIGURE 6.11 Factors That Predict Economic Desperation.
Standardized regression coefficients from a logistic regression model predicting whether a voter ever experienced economic desperation (i.e., could not afford rent, food, or utilities). For each variable, standardized coefficient estimates are given as circles with 95% confidence intervals as black lines. Bolded coefficients are statistically significant.

In the end, then, our survey data show that vote choice, as much as or more so than economics, shapes how voters saw their economic fortunes in 2020. While political preference does not override genuine economic hardship (such as a job loss, exhausting one's savings, or experiencing economic desperation such that you cannot afford basic necessities), for most voters it was their political attitudes, not their economic fates, that colored how they perceived the economy in 2020. This shows us not only the power of partisanship, as past studies have argued, but also the power of campaign messaging. It is not simply that Trump's voters saw the world through their support for him (though, obviously, this is a central part of the story). It is also that Trump voters heard his campaign's messages about the economy (and its strong growth during the Trump administration) and updated their beliefs accordingly. Campaign messages prime and activate voters' predispositions.[13]

Did Voters Think Trump or Biden Would Better Handle the Economy?

The data we provided so far do not answer a fundamental question: which candidate did voters think would better handle the nation's economy? As in every election, the economy was an issue in 2020. But the economy's swings over the election year and the candidates' sharply divergent messages about how best to restart it invested the issue with added resonance.

As we discussed in Chapter 5, to measure perceptions of handling of the economy, in each of the pre-election waves of our study we asked respondents which candidate (if either one) would better handle a long list of issues—including the economy, the coronavirus pandemic, race relations, and crime, among others. To begin, consider whether voters thought Trump or Biden could better handle the economy, which could better handle job creation (obviously closely related), and, in Pennsylvania only, which candidate could better handle policies related to coal and fracking, as well as how all three change over time. Figure 6.12 plots the percentage of voters, broken down by electorate, who think that Trump (rather than Biden) could better handle each of these aspects of the economy.

Unsurprisingly, for both items asked to all respondents, the unwavering Trump and Biden voters were largely locked in place: Trump's were convinced that he could better handle the economy and create jobs, and Biden's felt similarly about their candidate. Given the centrality of the economy to the messaging in the campaign, this should hardly be a surprise, as it effectively says

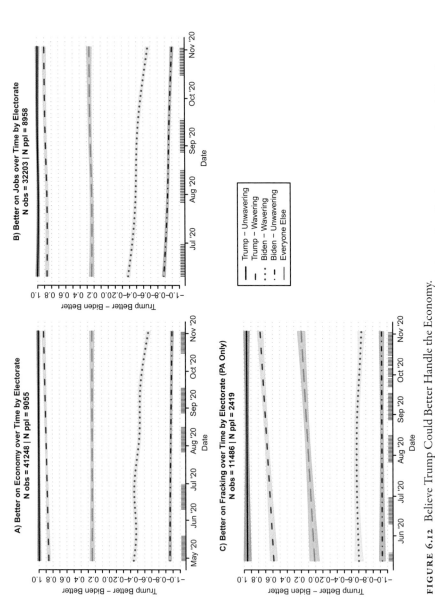

FIGURE 6.12 Believe Trump Could Better Handle the Economy.

Lines show whether each electorate believes Trump or Biden could better handle the economy (panel A), job creation (panel B), or coal and fracking (panel C, PA only). Higher (lower) values indicate that the group believes Trump (Biden) could better handle the issue.

that on an issue that both candidates knew was central and messaged heavily on, unwavering voters championed their candidate's competence. But the wavering voters are much more interesting. On both measures, we saw persuasion over the course of the campaign, with wavering Biden voters moving away from Trump and toward Biden, and wavering Trump voters doing the reverse, a finding that suggests that the campaigns and their messages helped bring them to their eventual decisions (these shifts are especially notable for the Biden respondents). And as one might suspect, consistent with them not really favoring Biden or Trump, those in the other category—those who supported a third-party candidate or did not vote—split relatively equally over time on which could better handle the economy and employment. Their slight preference for Trump on these issues may have reflected a sense that this was an especially strong area for him (we return to this point below).

We also asked voters in Pennsylvania about a salient economic issue in their state: which candidate would better handle policy toward coal and fracking. Fracking (hydraulic fracturing) is a method that extracts natural gas trapped deep underground in shale rock formations. As a result of fracking, in 2019, Pennsylvania was the second-largest producer of natural gas in the country, behind Texas; the industry employs roughly 20,000–50,000 Pennsylvanians.[14] The issue came to the fore in the vice presidential debate, when Vice President Pence argued that "they [Joe Biden and Kamala Harris] want to abolish fossil fuels and ban fracking," leading Senator Harris to counter that "Joe Biden will not ban fracking, he's been very clear about that."[15] The issue emerged again in the final presidential debate on October 22, when President Trump argued that Biden had been inconsistent on fracking and would ban the procedure once in office: "He [Biden] was against fracking. He said it. I will show that to you tomorrow. 'I am against fracking,' until he got the nomination, went to Pennsylvania than [*sic*] he said—You know what, Pennsylvania? He'll be against it very soon because his party is totally against it." Biden responded that he would only ban fracking on federal land (all fracking in Pennsylvania—and most in other states—occurs on private land).[16]

Did this exchange—or the fact that the issue played out over time in the messages from the campaigns—change which candidate Pennsylvania voters felt would better handle this issue?[††] The bottom panel of Figure 6.11

---

†† In the fall waves (waves 5–7), we asked all voters—not just Pennsylvania voters—this item, and we see the same pattern. We focus on the Pennsylvania sample here because we asked this throughout the study, so we can track the evolution of these attitudes over time with much greater precision.

provides the answer. Biden voters evinced little change over time on this issue; few, if any, thought Trump would better handle it. Fascinatingly, however, we see that for third-party voters and nonvoters, as well as wavering Trump voters, there was a notable shift, though it began early in the campaign, long before either debate. Over time, everyone but Biden's voters came to believe that this was another issue where Trump was the superior candidate.

To make sense of these shifts, we need to know how voters' evaluations of Trump and Biden on the economy compared to the other issues included in our battery. Accordingly, we calculated the fraction that thought Trump would better handle every noneconomic issue in our battery in the final pre-election wave, and then compared that to the percentage who felt that way about the economy overall, job creation, and coal/fracking (again, the last of these just in Pennsylvania). This is the same procedure we used in Chapter 5 (see Figure 6.3). The question here is whether the economy was "just another issue" and looks like everything else, or whether voters saw this issue as uniquely advantaging one of the candidates. Figure 6.13 presents these results. In it, the proportion of respondents in each electorate who think that Biden will better handle each issue was subtracted from the proportion that said Trump would do so. Distinctions between these values for economic and other issues are indicated with diamonds and circles, respectively.

We see a revealing pattern here, and a rare example of cross-party agreement: relative to other issues, voters thought that Trump—much more than Biden—would better handle the economy. As above, unwavering voters are less interesting; both blocks of them thought that their preferred candidate would do the better job. But some of the wavering voters, especially wavering Biden ones, defy this partisan pattern. Averaged across issues, 5.9 percent of wavering Biden voters thought Trump would do a better job handling various noneconomic issues, but more than twice as many (12.6 percent) felt that way about the economy. Likewise, wavering Trump voters thought he would do a better job handling noneconomic issues 73.6 percent of the time, but that jumps to 87.8 percent on the economy (and we see a similar shift among nonvoters and third-party voters as well). The pattern is less pronounced on fracking, but even there, modestly more Biden supporters thought Trump could better handle fracking, relative to noneconomic issues. But for practical purposes, nearly *all* voters saw the economy as an especially strong issue for Trump.

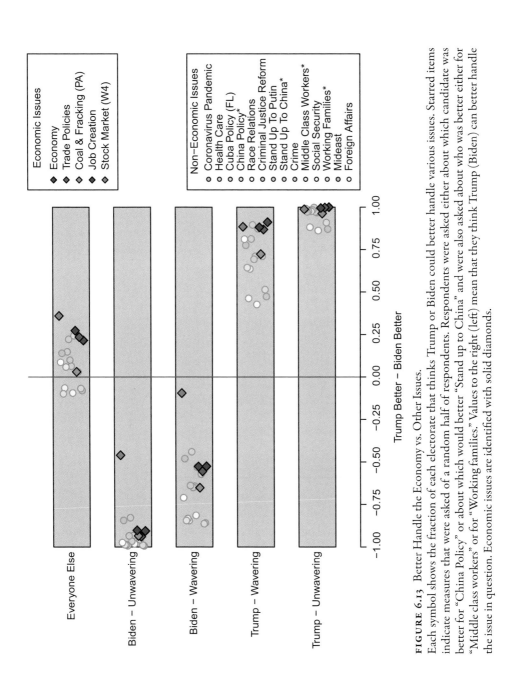

FIGURE 6.13 Better Handle the Economy vs. Other Issues.

Each symbol shows the fraction of each electorate that thinks Trump or Biden could better handle various issues. Starred items indicate measures that were asked of a random half of respondents. Respondents were asked either about which candidate was better for "China Policy" or about which would better "Stand up to China" and were also asked about who was better either for "Middle class workers" or for "Working families." Values to the right (left) mean that they think Trump (Biden) can better handle the issue in question. Economic issues are identified with solid diamonds.

Trump's Strongest Issue: The Stock Market

There is one additional economic issue that President Trump made central to his campaign: his handling of the stock market. Evidence that it thrived under Trump is incontrovertible: all three major indices (the Dow Jones Industrial Average, the S&P 500, and the NASDAQ composite) recorded near-record levels of annualized growth during his presidency.[17] The answers we got in wave 4 (July–August 2020) to the question "Which candidate (if either) would be better for the growth of the stock market?" revealed that market performance was by far the incumbent's most potent selling point.

Paralleling but exceeding the results of the other economic handling measures, voters thought Trump would better handle the stock market overall (orange diamond in Figure 6.13). While the characteristic differences emerge between the electorates, the key pattern is that—relative to other issues—this is an issue on which the overwhelming share of voters, even Biden ones, gave Trump the edge. Averaging across the noneconomic issues, less than 1 percent of unwavering Biden voters thought that Trump would better handle those issues, but 8.8 percent of them felt that way about the stock market. Obviously, unwavering Biden voters still favored Biden's handling of it. But they too recognized that this is an issue on which Trump was well positioned. We see the same pattern among the other electorates as well: relative to other issues, handling the stock market was Trump's strongest card.

The pattern becomes even starker once we look at those who own stocks. In every electorate, those who did so were more likely to say that Trump, rather than Biden, would do a better job handling the stock market (the exception is the unwavering Trump electorate, but that is because even those who did not own stock effectively all agreed he would be better). We observe especially large effects among wavering Biden voters, as well as nonvoters and third-party voters. For all but unwavering voters, stock ownership increased the belief that Trump would better handle the market by a substantial amount. Simply put, this is by far the strongest issue for Trump. Little wonder, then, that he messaged it so heavily on Twitter,[18] in his speeches, and, as we noted in Part 1 of this chapter, in the debates.

Did Trump's Handling of the Economy Affect When Voters Made Up Their Minds?

This difference in perceptions of Trump's handling of the economy may also have affected Americans' decisions to settle on one candidate rather than the other. To find out whether that is the case, we examined whether the importance voters attached to different issues played a part in helping them make up their minds—in particular, did wavering Trump voters who thought the economy was an especially important issue settle on Trump earlier in the campaign?

Wavering Trump voters who said that the economy was very important to their vote did in fact decide that their ballot would go to the incumbent earlier than did those who did not prioritize the economy (see Figure 6.14). This finding parallels the ones we reported in Chapter 5 for the COVID-19 pandemic and a decision to ballot for Biden. These two issues helped wavering voters on each side nail down their choices.

Together, these findings help us to better situate the finding that Trump voters saw the economy as the most important issue in the election, whereas Biden voters thought it was the COVID-19 pandemic. They suggest that both contenders played to their forte. Of course, there is a push and a pull here, and part of why voters saw the economy as such a strong issue for Trump was that he messaged it very effectively (but of course that messaging depended on a relatively strong pre-COVID economy as well). As we saw in Chapter 5, the issue of the COVID-19 pandemic was, in many ways, the mirror image of the economy issue, with voters seeing Biden as relatively more qualified to handle that crisis. Not only did the two candidates compete to convince voters that they could better handle the issue that was their strong suit, but the ebb and flow of 2020, with its multiple crises, gave Trump advantages at some points and did the same for Biden at others.

But there is perhaps an even more important implication here. In Chapter 5 we argued that the coronavirus pandemic was important to Biden's victory in that it provided him an opportunity to argue that Trump was unqualified to be president: Biden contended that Trump's mismanagement of the pandemic justified voting him out of office. This argument allowed him to successfully dislodge the economy—otherwise the dominant issue in every election—from enough voters' minds to win the election. The fact that all of our electorates recognized the economy as Trump's strong suit reveals just how difficult Biden's electoral prospects would have been had the pandemic not intruded on the issue agenda. Not only is the economy a perennially important issue, but it is also one that voters—even amid an unprecedented economic downturn—said was the incumbent's forte. While we can never know what would have happened had the pandemic not arrived, Biden's victory would almost certainly have been less likely without it.

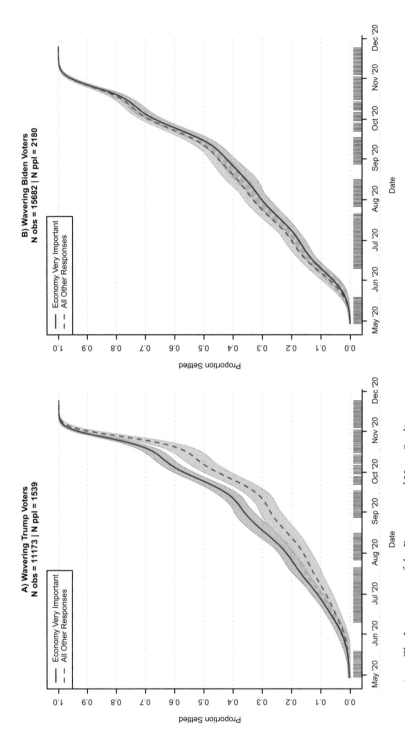

FIGURE 6.14 The Importance of the Economy and Voter Settling.
Each panel provides the proportion of wavering voters who had settled on their choice, based on whether they thought that the economy was a very important issue to their vote (solid red line) or did not (dashed blue line). Wavering Trump voters are shown in panel A, wavering Biden voters are shown in panel B.

The Economy's Impact in 2020

As in Chapter 5, before wrapping up the chapter, we telescope our findings:

- On balance, the electorates thought the pre-COVID economy was doing well. They thought their own finances, as well as those of their communities, had, by and large, improved during Trump's first three years in office. Once 2020 was factored into the mix, however, their assessments were grimmer. This helps to explain why Trump emphasized the strength of the pre-COVID economy and argued that the recovery from the lockdown would be V-shaped, with the nation soon returning to its pre-COVID footing.

- Consistent with the view of most economists that in 2020 the economic recovery was K-shaped, we found that those whose income levels were higher did indeed recover more quickly from the spring's economic tumult. However, some of those who were less well-off experienced what we characterized as economic desperation. Approximately 15 percent of our sample was unable to afford at least one of such basic necessities as food, shelter, and utilities at some point during our study.

- Our respondents' partisanship and vote choice were strong predictors of their assessments of their personal financial situation. In an election context, we cannot fully separate partisanship from economic perceptions.

- As in many other elections, voters did vote retrospectively. Those who thought that the economy improved during President Trump's term in office or who lived in areas where the economy recovered more fully in 2020 were more likely to vote for him.

- Wavering Trump voters who prioritized the economy settled on a vote for the incumbent earlier than those who prioritized other issues. This parallels our finding for wavering Biden voters and the pandemic in Chapter 5 ("Did the COVID-19 Pandemic Sink Trump's Reelection?"). In effect, the voters who agreed with their candidate's issue priority locked into place sooner, just as we would predict.

- We also find evidence of pocketbook voting, whereby a voter's personal economic circumstances affected their choices at the ballot box. Using different metrics—receipt of a stimulus payment, not being fully employed, and suffering economic desperation—we find that one's personal finances have a modest effect on whether one ballots for Trump or Biden. But they have a larger effect on whether one turns out at all: those who experience hardship are less likely to do so. When voters suffer significant economic hardship, the likelihood that they become disengaged from the electoral system increases (arguably for a good reason, as they need to attend to their more pressing personal needs).

- We also saw that respondents in general thought that the economy was an issue that Trump more so than Biden would handle well. Just as the pandemic advantaged Biden, the economy advantaged Trump.

Taken together, these findings help us make sense of how the economy, with its many twists and turns throughout the year, shaped the 2020 election. The economy did matter, and economic growth did help President Trump, even if it did not ultimately secure him reelection, as his advisors predicted it would before the spring's economic meltdown.

But much like the pandemic, the ultimate effect of the economy was more about agenda setting than individuals' balloting choices. The unique environment of 2020 meant that the candidates did not merely compete over which of them could better handle a single most important issue; each also sought to get voters to prioritize the issue that advantaged his candidacy. Biden and Trump gave fundamentally contrasting messages about which issues mattered and why. Rather than telling voters why they could better handle the same issue, Biden and Trump drove them toward different ones.

Where this chapter and the last concentrated on an agenda-setting contest pitting the economy against the pandemic, the next one focuses on our third crisis. There, the issue is an alternative framing of the same sets of events, namely, how to interpret the summer's Black Lives Matter protests. While Trump championed a "law and order" message, Biden argued for "law and order with justice." As we will see, these contrasting messages had strong effects on voters as well.

Law and Order vs. Law and Order with Racial Justice

DEBATING HOW TO UNDERSTAND THE SUMMER'S PROTESTS

Josh Pasek and Kathleen Hall Jamieson

"THE PEOPLE OF this country want and demand law and order and you're afraid to even say it," Trump declared in the first presidential debate on September 29, 2020. Later in the debate the incumbent asked his challenger, "Are you in favor of law and order?"

"Law and order with justice, where people get treated fairly," Biden responded.[1]

That Trump-Biden exchange digests the dissimilar ways in which the two campaigns framed the third of the four crises on which this book focuses. The issue of racial injustice in policing gained national and international headlines when millions of Americans turned out to take part in what may have been the nation's largest protest movement.[2] As the numbers who took to the streets grew, "Black lives matter" and Floyd's plea, "I can't breathe," became mantras expressing what many in the press cast as a racial reckoning. "Protesters called for police reform, defunding the police or outright abolition; for an end to qualified immunity for officers; for reinvestment in underfunded communities; for schools, companies and communities to address their own complicity in racial inequity," noted NPR.[3]

Although Trump would argue throughout the general election that Biden endorsed defunding the police, the former vice president contended instead that he would condition "federal aid to police based on whether or not they meet certain basic standards of decency and honorableness ... [and] are able to demonstrate they can protect the community and everybody in the community."[4] Biden asserted that it was Trump who proposed "cutting a half a billion dollars of local police support,"[5] a reference to the administration's proposed cut of $465.8 million in the budget of the Office of Justice Programs, which supports community safety.[6]

In real time, national news covered the demonstrators' peaceful demands for change, the counterprotesters, and the violent encounters between them, as well as the clashes between protesters of both kinds and law enforcement that occurred in cities such as Minneapolis, Portland, Seattle, Philadelphia, and Washington, DC. "The nation was rocked again on Saturday as demonstrators clashed with police from outside the White House gates to the streets of more than three dozen besieged cities, as outrage over the death of George Floyd in Minneapolis traversed a razor's edge between protest and civic meltdown," noted the *New York Times* on May 30. "The escalating violence and destruction felt like a warning that this moment could be spinning out of control both because of the limitations of a largely spontaneous, leaderless movement and because, protesters and officials warned, there were indications it was also being undermined by agitators trying to sabotage it."[7] On June 7, the *New York Times* posted video of protests from across the country—Philadelphia to Los Angeles, Tampa to Atlanta to Indianapolis.[8] In the aftermath of Floyd's death, as the murders of other Black Americans killed by police became more widely known, "protests and unrest ... rocked Minneapolis and other cities," reported the *New York Times*, which went on to observe on July 10 that "since the death of Mr. Floyd, protests have erupted in at least 140 cities across the United States, and the National Guard has been activated in at least 21 states."[9]

According to the US Crisis Project, a joint effort by the Armed Conflict Location and Event Data Project (ACLED) and the Bridging Divides Initiative (BDI) at Princeton University, militias and other "nonstate actors" such as antifa, the Not Fucking Around Coalition, the New Mexico Civil Guard, the Patriot Front, the Proud Boys, the boogaloo bois, and the Ku Klux Klan were involved in more than a hundred demonstrations, most often in response to Black Lives Matter protests.[10] Although their report found that 93 percent of the 10,600 demonstrations held across the United States between May 24 and August 22 were peaceful and nondestructive, in roughly 220 locations events turned violent.[11] Meanwhile, by the end of the first week in June, "at least 9,300 people [had been] arrested in protests," according to the Associated Press;[12] according to ABC News, curfews were in place in nearly eighty localities and thirty-one states, and the District of Columbia had activated seventy-five thousand National Guard soldiers and airmen.[13] Whether their presence and actions exacerbated or extinguished the violence was a matter of contention. Biden's supporters saw them as instigators, and a problem; Trump's, as defenders of the law, keepers of order, and a solution.

In conservative media venues and Republican campaigns ads thereafter, the protests became synonymous with police in riot gear, overturned police cars, buildings ablaze, stores vandalized, and violent clashes. By contrast, Democratic ads and mainstream news recalled the protests as serene nonviolent marches and somber candlelit vigils. The same form of polarized amnesia would affect media coverage of the January 6, 2021, riot at the Capitol.

Just as the 2017 clash in Charlottesville spoke to more than whether a statue of Robert E. Lee deserved a place of honor in a city park, a number of what ACLED and BDI characterized as "violent or destructive demonstrations" focused on monuments "seen to represent the country's legacy of racist violence, such as monuments celebrating colonial figures, slave owners, and Confederate leaders."[14] In response, President Trump claimed that "key targets in the violent extremists' campaign against our country are public monuments, memorials, and statues. Their selection of targets reveals a deep ignorance of our history, and is indicative of a desire to indiscriminately destroy anything that honors our past and to erase from the public mind any suggestion that our past may be worth honoring, cherishing, remembering, or understanding."[15] This remark from the president is noteworthy for two reasons. First, President Trump links efforts to reckon with the legacy of slavery and racism with a destructive "ignorance of our" history; we will explore this theme in more detail in Chapter 8 ("A Deeper Anxiety"). But it is also noteworthy because of his argument that clashes over preserving or warehousing monuments justify federal intervention.

Promising prison time for anyone who destroyed a statue that the federal government owned,[16] on June 26 the incumbent signed an executive order "directing federal law enforcement agencies to prosecute people who damage federal monuments—and to withhold portions of federal funding to cities that don't protect statues from demonstrators."[17] Five days later, the Department of Homeland Security announced that it had established the Protecting American Communities Task Force (PACT), to coordinate "departmental law enforcement agency assets in protecting our nation's historic monuments, memorials, statues, and federal facilities."[18] In nearly one in ten instances, the protests were met with some level of government intervention.[19] "Facing Protests over Use of Force, Police Respond with More

Force," read an end-of-May headline in the *New York Times*. "Videos showed officers using batons, tear gas, pepper spray and rubber bullets on protesters and bystanders."[20]

Asserting that they were necessary to "protect Federal property" and contain "civil unrest," Trump dispatched federal law enforcement officers to cities such as Portland, Oregon; Chicago; and Milwaukee.[21] Several of the mayors and governors objected to their presence. Between Floyd's death on May 25 and August 22, more than fifty-five federal and National Guard deployments occurred across the United States.[22] Governmental responses may have worsened the situation. "Although federal authorities were purportedly deployed to keep the peace, the move appears to have re-escalated tensions," ACLED and BDI reported. "Prior to the deployment, over 83 percent of demonstrations in Oregon were non-violent. Post-deployment, the percentage of violent demonstrations has risen from under 17 percent to over 42 percent."[23]

Local responses to the protests included reconsiderations of what and who deserved a place of honor in community memory, a focus of Chapter 8. "Of the estimated 208 schools in the U.S. named after figures with ties to the Confederacy, at least 39 have initiated the renaming process while 25 are considering a rebrand following months of global anti-racism protests," reported *Forbes*.[24] Meanwhile, Biden argued that Confederate statues should be housed in museums, not public squares.[25] Efforts to rename military installations that honor Confederate generals gained momentum as well.*

At the same time, the incumbent president claimed that chaos reigned in Democratic-run cities, derided some of the protesters as anarchists and antifa supporters, and forecast that violence would infect the suburbs—not just big cities—if Biden were elected. Because police treatment of Black Americans was a central issue in the protests, the role of law enforcement in society at large and in response to the events at hand became a subject of contention and the object of the competing frames featured at the start of this chapter— the distinction between "law and order" and "law and order with justice."

Each of the major party nominees carried baggage into the law-and-order debate. Trump had based his political rise in part on an overt appeal

---

*. As part of the National Defense Authorization Act (NDAA), the Republican-controlled Senate and Democratic-controlled House passed an act to create the Commission on the Naming of Items of the Department of Defense That Commemorate the Confederate States of America or Any Person Who Served Voluntarily with the Confederate States of America (known as the Naming Commission). When Trump vetoed the act, Congress overrode the veto.

to racial animus and fear of crime. This thread ran from his earliest political engagements, including his call for the death penalty in the 1989 case of the Central Park Five (five Black and Latino teenagers who were convicted of the rape of a jogger in Central Park and later exonerated), to a 2020 tweet that proclaimed "when the looting starts, the shooting starts," echoing a white police chief during the civil rights era.[26] Nonetheless, as president, he signed prison reform into law, increased support for historically Black colleges and universities (HBCUs), and could correctly claim that Black unemployment had reached record lows.

Part of Biden's history with the Black community dogged him throughout the campaign as well. Although he argued that the 1994 Violent Crime Control and Law Enforcement Act, which he authored, did not increase incarceration of Black men, the two Black Democratic candidates also vying for their party's 2020 nomination disagreed. "That crime bill was shameful, what it did to black and brown communities like mine (and) low-income communities from Appalachia to rural Iowa," noted New Jersey Senator Cory Booker (D-NJ) in 2019. "It was a bad bill." "It did contribute to mass incarceration in our country," said California Senator Kamala Harris (D-CA). "It encouraged and was the first time that we had a federal three-strikes law. It funded the building of more prisons in the states."[27] They were not alone in that view. "One thing is clear," concluded an August 2020 report by the left-leaning Brookings Institution, "the 1994 bill interacted with—and reinforced—an existing and highly problematic piece of legislation: The Anti–Drug Abuse Act of 1986, which created huge disparities in sentencing between crack and powder cocaine. . . . While the Fair Sentencing Act of 2010, enacted under the Obama-Biden administration, reduced the crack/powder cocaine disparity from 100:1 to 18:1, the damage had been done, and its effects continue to this day."[28] "The bill . . . is now roundly criticized by nearly all Democrats and some Republicans and blamed for locking up a generation of non-violent offenders," noted CNN in 2019.[29] "Anyone associated with the 1994 Crime Bill will not have a chance of being elected," Trump tweeted in May 2019. "In particular, African Americans will not be able to vote for you. I, on the other hand, was responsible for Criminal Justice Reform, which had tremendous support, & helped fix the bad 1994 Bill!"[30] In the nationally televised October 15, 2020, town hall in Philadelphia, Biden finally bowed to political reality. Asked by moderator George Stephanopoulos whether his support of the 1994 Violent Crime Control and Law Enforcement Act was a mistake, Biden answered, "Yes, it was." However, he added, the worst effects were the result of state decisions, not federal ones.[31] During the campaign, the Democratic nominee also promised to repeal mandatory minimum sentences,[32] and he advocated halving the prison population,[33] improving educational opportunities in prisons,[34] and eliminating jail time for drug use.[35]

In this chapter, we examine the roles of race and racial attitudes in shaping Americans' beliefs and vote choices. First, we explore Trump and Biden's past remarks on race and racialized issues, to explain how their positions changed and evolved over time, as that helps to situate their responses to the summer's protests and the attendant racial reckoning. We then explore how the two candidates responded to the protests. For the incumbent, the protests that summer were exemplified by mayhem that menaced the communities in which they occurred, and he believed the appropriate response was use of force in service of law and order. While condemning violence, the Delawarean argued that racial inequities urgently needed to be addressed: "And after two weeks of daily protests, with thousands of people coming out to march for racial justice in the midst of a pandemic, with gatherings in all 50 states and Washington, D.C., and in communities of every size, the American people have shown the world exactly where we stand in this battle," wrote Biden in an op-ed published in *USA Today* in June. "We know the nation we want to be. Now we have to deliver on this moment to achieve fundamental changes that address racial inequalities and white supremacy in our country."[36]

Trump and Biden both pointed to the part of the protests that advantaged their framing of the issue. As we show in Part 2 of this chapter, these contrasting frames—and the summer's racially charged events—affected voters' attitudes and eventual balloting decisions.

A Racialized Presidency

At key moments in his ascent to power, Mr. Trump gave voice to those who held racial animus. Not only did he advocate the death penalty for the Central Park Five, but he also refused to apologize for that view when it was revealed they were wrongly convicted.[37] Trump also attempted to delegitimize the presidency of the nation's first biracial president by promulgating the false "birther" allegation that Barack Obama was born outside the United States. As his birth certificate attests and as a contemporaneous birth announcement in a Honolulu newspaper confirms, Obama was born in Hawaii and hence is a natural-born US citizen.[38] Both partisanship and anti-Black attitudes predicted acceptance of the false claim promulgated by Trump.[39]

In the 2015 speech that launched his candidacy for president, the real-estate-developer-turned-reality-TV-star descended a golden escalator in

Trump Tower to allege that, instead of sending America its best, Mexico was "sending people that have lots of problems, and they're bringing those problems with us. They're bringing drugs. They're bringing crime. They're rapists." He then added, "And some, I assume, are good people."[40] When Trump became president, among his first policies was a restriction on visas for travelers and immigrants from predominantly Muslim countries, a policy popularly known as the "Muslim ban." At the same time, one of his goals in office was the construction of a wall on the southern border with Mexico—a key rallying cry from his 2016 campaign—which was widely regarded as more symbolic than effective.[41]

As we noted earlier in the book, when clashes broke out in Charlottesville, Virginia, in 2017 between those attending a white supremacist march and counterprotesters, President Trump was quick to assert that there were "very fine people on both sides," though under pressure he partially walked back the statement.[42] He would continue to use racially charged rhetoric throughout his presidency and the 2020 campaign. These factors led to Ta-Nehisi Coates's widely read *Atlantic* magazine article deeming him "The First White President"[43] and to Biden asserting that when he heard Trump's response to the events in Charlottesville, that was the "moment [he] knew [he] had to run."[44]

Nonetheless, during his time in office, Trump provided what, to some supporters, was a credible answer to the question he asked of Black voters in 2016: "What have you got to lose [by supporting me]?"[45] He did so by championing and passing the First Step Act, which shortened some mandatory minimum prison sentences and helped reduce sentences for many prisoners, who are disproportionately Black. Additionally, as we noted earlier, in conjunction with Congress, his administration increased support for HBCUs. He also argued that his administration saw record low levels of Black unemployment.[46] While these actions predate the 2020 campaign, they provide important context for questions about race because they were talking points for Trump and his surrogates and were highlighted in ads addressing communities of color. Trump argued that these accomplishments meant that he "ha[d] done more for the black community than any President since Abraham Lincoln."[47]

A Racial Evolution

Although Biden was generally regarded by contemporaries as a racial liberal, in the 1970s, in the words of the *New York Times*, he "led an effort in the Senate to end court-ordered busing."[48] Earlier we noted the problematic elements in the 1994 crime bill that he authored.[49] Nor was his rhetoric problem-free. In 2007 he characterized fellow presidential aspirant Barack Obama as "the first mainstream African-American who is articulate and bright and clean and a nice-looking guy";[50] in Iowa in 2019 he alleged that "poor kids are just as bright and just as talented as white kids."[51] In fact, Biden at one point even mocked the very phrase he would adopt during the 2020 debate, stating in a 1994 Senate floor speech, "Every time Richard Nixon, when he was running in 1972, would say, 'Law and order,' the Democratic match or response was, 'Law and order with justice'—whatever that meant. And I would say, 'Lock the S.O.B.s up.'"[52]

Nonetheless, as vice president for eight years to the nation's first Black president, Biden earned accolades from many in the Black community. In 2020, Black Americans were the base that effectively secured him his party's nomination. After he underperformed in early primaries (finishing fourth in Iowa and fifth in New Hampshire, and barely eking out second place in Nevada), a resounding win among South Carolina's overwhelmingly Black Democratic voters—prompted by a last-minute endorsement from Representative Jim Clyburn (D-SC), the sole Democratic member of the state's congressional delegation—positioned Biden as the standard-bearer for the moderate wing of the party and the eventual nominee. Notably, even before the events of the summer, racial justice constituted an important pillar of the Biden campaign, with the candidate regularly highlighting the dangers of institutional racism and America's continuing legacy of hate.

By selecting Kamala Harris as his running mate, Biden not only could claim a link to the nation's first Black president but also, if elected, would play a key role in putting the nation's first Black vice president in the line of succession. As we discuss in Part 2, Harris's presence on the ticket was not only symbolically but also practically important in this election.

The Racially Charged Events of 2020: The George Floyd Protests

It was not just Trump and Biden's histories and rhetoric that shaped how race would play out in 2020: A series of racially charged events also shaped the campaign.

First, as we noted earlier, was the death of George Floyd. On May 25, 2020, Floyd was arrested in Minneapolis for allegedly trying to spend a counterfeit

$20 bill at Cup Foods, a local convenience store. Four officers, including White Minneapolis police officer Derek Chauvin, arrived on the scene in response to a 911 call from a store clerk. Chauvin killed Floyd while the latter was in custody; a bystander captured this tragedy on video. Night after night, the news replayed the video of Chauvin kneeling on Floyd's neck for what at the time was reported as 8 minutes and 46 seconds (though video evidence later showed that it was 9 minutes and 29 seconds) as his three fellow officers stood by. Those listening to the tape could hear the words of the cooperating detainee, forced face down in the street, repeatedly pleading that he couldn't breathe, until finally there was silence. In response to this and other unprovoked deaths of Black individuals at the hands of police, Black Lives Matter protests drew record numbers into the streets in cities and towns across the nation. Amid the pandemic and economic slowdown, the country confronted its legacy of racial inequity. In April 2021, Derek Chauvin, the officer in question, was convicted of second-degree unintentional murder, third-degree murder, and second-degree manslaughter; in February 2022, the other police officers at the scene were convicted of violating Floyd's civil rights.

Although Floyd's death was the culminating event lighting the spark in a national and global wave of protests, it was far from the first death of an unarmed Black American in recent years, many of them at the hands of police officers or individuals who thought force was justified because they imagined that the victims were threatening. The Black Lives Matter movement began in 2013 after neighborhood watch coordinator George Zimmerman was acquitted for the fatal 2012 shooting of Trayvon Martin, an unarmed Black teenager. The movement became more coordinated after the deaths of Michael Brown and Eric Garner at the hands of police in 2014. And two prior incidents in 2020 received widespread attention as well—the killing of Ahmaud Arbery, who was pursued by a former police officer and two other men while jogging in February, and the shooting of Breonna Taylor in a botched police raid in March. Protesters highlighted these deaths in addition to Floyd's in asserting that "Black lives matter," calling for police reform, and proposing that American cities should "defund the police."

What Americans Heard About the Protests

As these protests expanded in scale, headlines characterized the moment as one of racial reckoning or focused on what was cast as civil unrest. As indictments of "structural racism" gained currency on social media, worldwide attention followed. Addressing "the English-speaking faithful" at one of his general audiences, Pope Francis said, "I have witnessed with great concern the disturbing social unrest in your nation in these past days, following the tragic death of Mr. George Floyd. . . . We cannot tolerate or turn a blind eye to racism and exclusion in any form and yet claim to defend the sacredness of every human life."[53]

In subsequent days, weeks, and months, racial justice and controversies over policing became mainstays of the election. As what the *New York Times* characterized as "huge and sometimes violent protests" erupted in Minneapolis[54] and other cities across the country, Biden made his first major mid-pandemic trip outside Delaware to meet with Floyd's family members who lived in Houston. In a taped message played at Floyd's funeral, the putative Democratic nominee echoed a central line from Martin Luther King Jr.'s most famous speech when he said, "Now is the time for racial justice. That's the answer we must give to our children when they ask why. Because when there is justice for George Floyd, we will truly be on our way to racial justice in America."[55]

Trump's messages were more mixed. In the week following Floyd's death, he spoke with Floyd's family, termed his death "a terrible thing" and "sad and tragic," noted that "the looters should not be allowed to drown out the voices of so many peaceful protesters," and observed that "the family of George is entitled to justice, and the people of Minnesota are entitled to live in safety. Law and order will prevail. The Americans will honor the memory of George and the Floyd family." He also proclaimed, "When the looting starts, the shooting starts"—a phrase that the *New York Times* noted was "coined in the 1960s by a Miami police chief defending crackdowns on black neighborhoods."[56]

As suggested by the debate exchange mentioned at the start of this chapter, the frames that the two major-party candidates brought to the protests and counterprotests were capsulized in an exchange in the section of the first general election debate that Fox News moderator Chris Wallace billed as focusing on "race and violence in our cities."[57] "The people of this country want and demand law and order and you're afraid to even say it," Trump declared, addressing Biden. Later in the debate, as we noted earlier, the incumbent asked Biden, "Are you in favor of law and order?" "Law and order with justice where people get treated fairly," Biden responded, adding, "And the fact of the matter is violent crime went down 17 percent, 15 percent in our administration. It's gone up on his watch."[58]

The same contrastive frame pervaded the advertising on the two sides. So, for example, a Biden ad that aired in August in all four of our battleground states appealed to Black voters to stand up to "this president" "like our ancestors who stood up to the violent racists of a generation ago … We choose to bring back justice, respect and dignity to this country," concluded the ad.[59] And the ad that most clearly conveyed Trump's law-and-order theme, which was titled "President Trump Will Uphold the Law," was among those used to close the Republican campaign. As the announcer intoned, "While America's cities burned, Joe Biden and Kamala Harris fanned the flames, refusing to strongly condemn violence," the ad's video featured close-ups of Biden and Harris superimposed over images of cars and buildings burning. "In Joe Biden's America, we'll all be in danger. . . . If you support the police, support Donald Trump."[60] By contrast, one of Biden's closing ads invoked the theme he struck in his announcement speech to explain how Trump's response to Charlottesville had motivated his candidacy: "I started this campaign saying we're in a battle for the soul of the nation," Biden stated. "I believe that even more deeply today."[61]

Consistent with the alternative frames promoted by the two candidates, incidents of looting and other threats to property were featured on conservative media outlets, but protesters holding candles and calling for racial justice dominated liberal and mainstream ones.

The protests and counterprotests involved some who would reenter the national narrative on January 6. "Shortly before the Capitol riot, the Proud Boys' leader, Henry 'Enrique' Tarrio, was arrested in Washington[, DC,] and ordered to stay out of the city after being accused of vandalizing a Black Lives Matter banner at a historic Black church in December," reported the Associated Press in January 2021.[62]

A Law and Order Narrative

As the president was proclaiming from the Rose Garden on June 1, 2020, that "if a city or a state refuses to take the actions that are necessary to defend the life and property of their residents, then I will deploy the United States military and quickly solve the problem for them," individuals who were peacefully protesting Floyd's death were tear-gassed as they were being pushed out of Lafayette Square, across from the White House, by the DC Metropolitan Police Department.[63] In a subsequent photo op, the incumbent stood before St. John's Episcopal Church with a Bible held upside-down in his hand.

The presumptive Democratic Party nominee tweeted in response, "He's using the American military against the American people."[64] The bishop of that diocese responded to the Trump photo op in even stronger terms: "I am the bishop of the Episcopal Diocese of Washington and was not given even a courtesy call that they would be clearing with tear gas so they could use one of our churches as a prop, holding a Bible, one that declares that God is love and when everything he [Trump] has said and done is to inflame violence," she said.[65] A subsequent investigation by the Interior Department's inspector general released in June 2021 found that, contrary to media reports, the claims of Democrats, and a lawsuit filed by Black Lives Matter, the clearing of protestors was unrelated to Trump's photo opportunity. However, Trump's attorney general, William Barr, had urged that the process be sped up "once Trump had decided to walk through the area that evening."[66]

Images of police using tear gas to clear peaceful protesters from Lafayette Park in the District of Columbia as well as scenes of federal officials and members of the National Guard patrolling cities such as Portland, Oregon, sparked debates about how President Trump was handling the civil unrest. In the process, the incumbent Republican echoed the central theme of his 2016 acceptance speech at the Republican convention and of the 1968 campaigns of Richard Nixon and segregationist George Wallace,[67] stating on June 1 that "I will fight to protect you—I am your president of law and order." Unlike Nixon, he then added, "And an ally of all peaceful protesters," a conclusion belied by his subsequent actions.[68] Central to Trump's rhetoric were allegations that cities led by "radical leftists" were out of control.

We now know that Trump wanted to respond even more forcefully. According to officials present for these discussions, Trump wanted to invoke the Insurrection Act, which would have allowed him to deploy active-duty military troops in American cities to control protests.[69] According to then defense secretary Mark Esper, Trump asked if troops could help control the protests: "Can't you just shoot them? Just shoot them in the legs or something?"[70]

The Racially Charged Events of 2020: A Flashpoint in Kenosha

On August 23, the day before the Republican convention began, officers responding to a domestic complaint in Kenosha, Wisconsin, shot twenty-nine-year-old Black resident Jacob Blake in the back multiple times in front of his three children, leaving him partly paralyzed. This sparked a local explosion of protests and civil unrest in the small city just south of Milwaukee. Kenosha declared an immediate state of emergency, and when peaceful daytime protests were followed by destructive nighttime rioting and arson, the governor called in the National Guard to protect key pieces of infrastructure.

Two days later, members of nearby militia groups and other armed individuals, coordinating their efforts on Facebook, began to filter into Kenosha "to take up arms and defend our City tonight from the evil thugs."[71] One individual who heeded this call from just over the border in Illinois was Kyle Rittenhouse. The seventeen-year-old White male came to Kenosha with an assault-style rifle that had been purchased for him by a nineteen-year-old friend (because Rittenhouse was too young to own a firearm in Illinois). After an altercation, Rittenhouse shot three other White men, two of whom died. Rittenhouse was later charged with homicide and illegal possession of firearms and turned himself in after returning to his home state; he was acquitted on November 19, 2021.

In the weeks that followed, when both presidential candidates made a point of going to Kenosha, their messages differed markedly. Trump's speech during his September 1 visit combined projections of strength with racial dog whistles. Prior to his visit, Trump tweeted, "If I didn't INSIST on having the National Guard activate and go into Kenosha, Wisconsin, there would be no Kenosha right now."[72] "All these problems [with civil unrest] are Democrat cities," said Trump in the Kenosha speech.[73] This pairing of urbanicity and crime draws upon long-standing racial tropes,[74] made more cognitively accessible by the explicit racial messaging of the protesters. Despite his focus on "law and order," Trump made no mention of Rittenhouse and only in passing noted the shooting of Jacob Blake.[75] When asked about Rittenhouse, Trump asserted that the teenager had acted in self-defense.[76] At the same time, the Department of Homeland Security under the Trump administration issued internal talking points that implicitly defended Rittenhouse's actions.[77]

Biden's visit to Kenosha came two days later and could easily have been mistaken for a response to a completely different event. The Democratic nominee made a point of reaching out personally to Jacob Blake,[78] and in his remarks asserted that Trump's rhetoric "legitimizes the dark side of human nature" by failing to condemn white supremacists.[79] Instead of focusing on rioting or disorder, the former vice president concentrated on the need for listening and healing. He too avoided direct mentions of Rittenhouse, though the Democratic campaign featured Rittenhouse in an ad highlighting the unwillingness of Trump to deal with white supremacists.[80] As noted, in November 2021 Rittenhouse was acquitted of all charges in a criminal trial that, in the words of NPR, "divided the nation over questions about gun rights, violence at racial justice protests and vigilantism."[81]

The Questions to Be Answered in Chapter 7, Part 2

As this first part of the chapter suggests, Biden and Trump's messaging, especially around the summer's Black Lives Matter protests and counterprotests, created alternative frames for the issues of race and policing. Although racial attitudes are often at play in contemporary presidential politics, the events of 2020 meant that they would assume a heightened role. In the second part of this chapter, we take up the effect of racial attitudes, as well as voter responses both to the summer's racially charged events and to the presence of Kamala Harris on the Democratic ticket. While we focus on the nationwide Black Lives Matter protests, we also pay special attention to the protests that erupted in Kenosha, Wisconsin, since Kenosha is one of our oversampled counties in Wisconsin (see the Appendix, "Our Data and Analytical Strategy"). We also explore whether and, if so, how our panelists responded to messaging about crime and safety in the suburbs and to the claim that Biden would defund the police. Together, the effects we find confirm that race was on the ballot in 2020.

7.2

Law and Order vs. Law and Order with Racial Justice

THE EFFECT OF THE CAMPAIGN AND RACIALIZED EVENTS ON ATTITUDES AND VOTE CHOICE

Josh Pasek and Kathleen Hall Jamieson

Between 24 May and 22 August, ACLED [Armed Conflict Location and Event Data Project, conducted by researchers at Princeton University] records more than 10,600 demonstration events across the country. Over 10,100 of these—or nearly 95 percent—involve peaceful protesters. Fewer than 570—or approximately 5 percent—involve demonstrators engaging in violence. Well over 80 percent of all demonstrations are connected to the Black Lives Matter movement or the COVID-19 pandemic.[1]

NOT SINCE THE assassination of Martin Luther King Jr. and the ensuing unrest in 1968 had the attention of the nation been as intensely focused on issues related to race as in the 2020 context. In this chapter, we show that racial attitudes themselves mattered in the 2020 election, but so too did specific racialized events cast distinctively by the major-party nominees (distinctions we featured in Part 1 of this chapter). Campaign events—and the messages surrounding them—primed racial attitudes,[2] which in turn further aligned individuals' underlying racial attitudes with their partisanship and vote choice.[3] Racial attitudes divided perceptions of the two major American political parties and their candidates more sharply than other issues, due in no small part to these racialized events. Although these effects moved voters at the margins, the relatively even split on racial attitudes meant that the net effect of these movements was small. But deepening the American racial divide is, in and of itself, a consequential outcome.

Measuring Perceived Cultural Dislocation and Racial Attitudes

To understand how racial attitudes shaped responses to the tumultuous 2020 campaign, we need to measure them, which turns out to be surprisingly complicated. Studying racial attitudes is confounded by the reality that when they are drawn on in contemporary politics, the argument is not typically about overt claims of biological racial superiority but rather about group stereotypes,[4] perceptions of intergroup competition,[5] allusions to implicit biases,[6] and the roles of political and social institutions in reinforcing racial differences.[7] In this environment, group consciousness is often elicited through political dog whistling[8] and messages that blend traditional values with racialized cues.[9]

Whether the changing focus of racial signaling reflects an improvement in racial attitudes, a shift in their nature, or merely redirection in the way that underlying biases are expressed remains a subject of both public and scholarly contestation.[10] Measures capturing various components of racial attitudes, however, continue to suggest that, no matter how such attitudes are assessed, they remain a central cleavage in American political life.[11] Different measures of racial attitudes, based on different theoretical frameworks, capture slightly different yet overlapping facets of the concept; we therefore incorporated components of multiple measures into our approach. Here, we drew on three different but interrelated ways of thinking about the construct. We asked respondents how well each of four stereotypes described Black and White people,* how much discrimination Black and White Americans each face in the United States, and two questions from the racial resentment battery, which measures perceptions of whether Black Americans face distinct racial hardships that require intervention.† Scales generated from all three sets of measures were closely correlated (between .40 and .60) and were

---

*. These stereotypes were "Complaining," "Friendly," "Determined to Succeed," and "Law Abiding."

†. The racial resentment items measured agreement with the statements "Irish, Italians, Jewish and other minorities overcame prejudice and worked their way up, black people should do the same without special favors" and "Generations of slavery have created conditions that make it difficult for black people to work their way out of the lower class."

combined into a single index ranging from −1 to 1, with −1 capturing those who thought that Black people experienced more discrimination than White people, viewed Black people more positively than White people on the stereotypes measures, and thought that Black people faced distinct challenges (Cronbach's α = 0.69). A response of 1 captured those who thought that White people experience much more discrimination than Black people, who stereotyped White people more positively, and who dismissed the notion that Black Americans encounter distinct obstacles.[‡] Perceptions of discrimination against various groups were asked in wave 2 (June 2020), while the initial racial justice protests were ongoing. Stereotypes and racial resentment measures were asked in wave 4 (July–August 2020), shortly before the selection of Kamala Harris as the Democrats' vice presidential nominee and the conventions.

Following the work of Tesler and Sears,[12] we recognize that the political context for contemporary racial attitudes makes it difficult to disentangle adherence to traditional American values from some types of beliefs about race. Answers to the racial resentment items, in particular, can conflate these concepts.[13] In recognition of these concerns, we refer to racial attitudes as ranging from "racially liberal" to "racially conservative." Racially liberal attitudes are those that generally perceive discrimination against Black people as more common than discrimination against White people, stereotype Black people more positively than White people, generally disagree that Black Americans should get ahead without special favors, and agree that generations of slavery introduced additional hurdles for Black Americans. In contrast, racially conservative attitudes are those that broadly perceive discrimination against Black people as less common than discrimination against White people, stereotype Black people more negatively than White people, generally agree that Black Americans should get ahead without special favors, and disagree that generations of slavery introduced additional challenges for Black Americans.

In 2020, racial attitudes also had become conflated with sentiments that were not only about race but also about other identities. The same individuals who said that White Americans experienced more discrimination than Black Americans were prone to claim that men experienced more discrimination than women (correlated at 0.53) and that Christians faced more discrimination than Muslims (correlated at 0.60). That is, there seemed to be

---

‡. Overall, this variable was distributed close to normally, with a mean of −.08 and a standard deviation of .39; Cronbach's α = 0.76.

a sense among some that traditionally privileged groups were now the ones experiencing discrimination. This sentiment, which is reflected in Trump's 2016 campaign slogan, "Make America Great Again" (rebranded as "Keep America Great Again" in 2020), harkens back to a time when White Christian men unquestionably held the reins of political power, and it reflects beliefs that that group's power was waning as that of other groups—the LGBTQIA+ community, racial and ethnic minorities, non-Christians, and women— increased politically, socially, and economically. We discuss these factors in greater depth in Chapter 8 ("A Deeper Anxiety") when we look at the notion of status threat. For our purposes here, it is important to recognize that status threat also is in some ways inseparable from racial attitudes among our respondents in 2020.

Racial Attitudes and Political Preferences

Reflecting scholarship that has demonstrated an increasing alignment between racial attitudes and partisanship over time, we find a close correspondence between racial attitudes and our electorates. On average, unwavering Trump voters scored a 0.27 on the racial attitude scale and unwavering Biden voters scored a −0.41, a gap measuring fully one-third of the entire scale's length (see Figure 7.1). These differences were apparent across all three of the measures used to construct our racial attitude score, though the patterns were different depending on the measure. For the stereotypes measure, in particular, 18.5 percent of respondents assigned identical scores to Black people and White people for all four stereotype measures and another 18.9 percent differed on only a single measure of the four. This tendency to rate both groups similarly led to a spike at 0 for all electorates on this measure. When respondents did differentiate, however, Trump voters were much more likely to associate positive traits with White people than with Black people, whereas Biden voters tended to hold the opposite view.

Racial Attitudes and Vote Choice

Yet racial attitude measures predicted vote choices in ways that went significantly beyond partisanship. While the correspondence between racial attitudes and partisanship was similar to the association between racial attitudes and the electorates (with scale values ranging from −.37 among strong Democrats to .21 among strong Republicans; see Figure 7.2), racial attitudes were a strong unique predictor of 2020 choices. This was true even

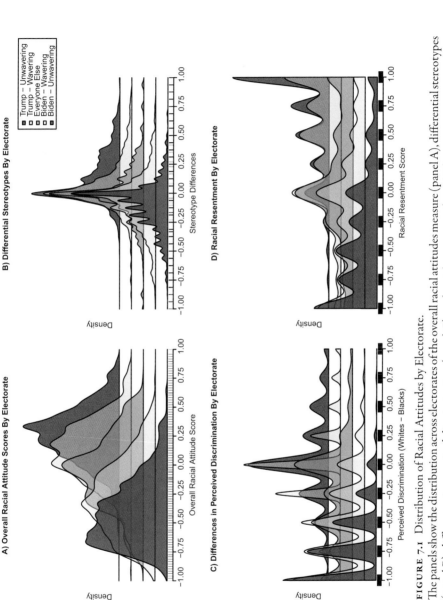

FIGURE 7.1 Distribution of Racial Attitudes by Electorate.

The panels show the distribution across electorates of the overall racial attitudes measure (panel A), differential stereotypes (panel B), differences in perceived discrimination (panel C), and racial resentment (panel D).

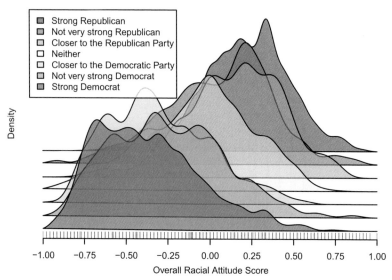

FIGURE 7.2 Distribution of Racial Attitudes by Partisanship.
The figure shows the distribution of the racial attitudes measure by partisanship.

after controlling for demographics (including racial identification), 2016 vote choice, partisanship, presidential approval, and retrospective evaluations of the economy (see Figure 7.3). Across the board, individuals with racially conservative attitudes (higher scores on the racial attitude measure) were much more likely to support Trump, whereas those with more racially liberal attitudes were far more likely to support Biden. Racial attitudes were as strong a predictor as economic attitudes and were weaker only than partisanship and presidential approval.

However, the racial reckoning in the 2020 election was not simply a reminder of the close correspondence between racial attitudes and political behaviors. Instead, it appears to have made these connections even stronger. Changes between candidate preferences expressed in the first wave (April–May 2020) of our study—which occurred before Floyd's death on May 25, 2020—and reported voting behaviors were as strongly predicted by racial attitudes as by just about any other measure (Figure 7.4). Individuals with the most racially liberal attitudes who had expressed a Trump preference in wave 1 of the study were overwhelmingly likely to abandon that preference by the time they voted (indicated by the dashed red lines in Figure 7.4, panel A). Similarly, though to a lesser extent, racially conservative individuals who supported Biden in wave 1 were fairly likely to abandon him by Election Day (dotted blue lines in Figure 7.4, panel B). And racial attitudes were particularly

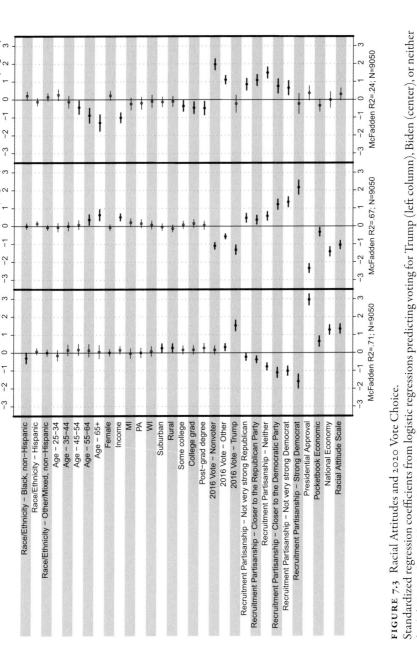

FIGURE 7.3 Racial Attitudes and 2020 Vote Choice.

Standardized regression coefficients from logistic regressions predicting voting for Trump (left column), Biden (center), or neither (right). For each variable, standardized coefficient estimates are given as circles with 95% confidence intervals as black lines. Bolded coefficients are statistically significant.

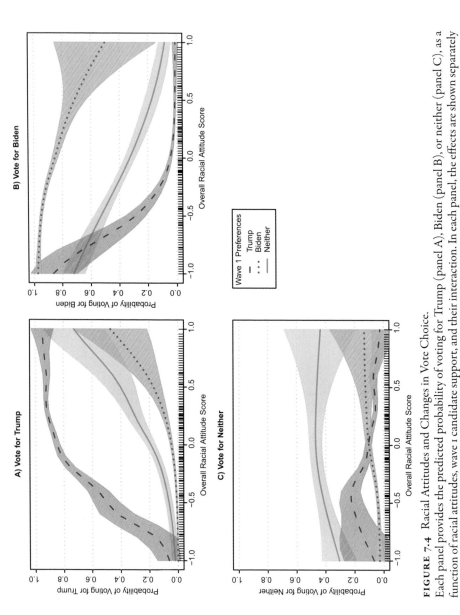

FIGURE 7.4 Racial Attitudes and Changes in Vote Choice.
Each panel provides the predicted probability of voting for Trump (panel A), Biden (panel B), or neither (panel C), as a function of racial attitudes, wave 1 candidate support, and their interaction. In each panel, the effects are shown separately for those who supported Trump (dashed red line), Biden (dotted blue line), or neither (solid green line) in wave 1.

consequential in highlighting the behaviors that could be expected from those individuals who had not expressed a preference for either candidate in wave 1 (solid green lines). Interestingly, unlike economic predictors of choice, racial attitudes seem to have had a greater influence on shifting individuals' support between the two major-party candidates, than on their participation.

As we noted previously, the increasing overlap between racial attitudes and political preferences throughout 2020 suggests that three factors may be at play: racial attitudes may have been made particularly salient by events that occurred during the 2020 cycle, racial attitudes may have been a source of campaign messaging designed to solidify each party's base, or individuals may have adopted racial attitudes during the 2020 campaign that reinforced the partisan divide. As we show in the sections that follow, each of these processes appears to have been at work.

The Effect of Nominating Kamala Harris

The findings that we just reported focus on how racial attitudes overall affected vote choice. But within the context of 2020, there is another way in which racial attitudes might map onto vote choice: the nomination of the first Black and South Asian woman, and the first daughter of immigrants, to be part of a major-party ticket. In the context of 2020, when many pushed Biden to name a Black woman as his vice president in response to the Black Lives Matter protests, Harris's choice was especially important. Additionally, as we noted in Chapter 1, her background as a prosecutor gave her special standing, as well as some potential liabilities,[14] in a year in which crime, law and order, and racial justice were key electoral themes.

Although some argue Sarah Palin's presence weighed down the Republican ticket in 2008,[15] the impact of vice presidential nominees more generally is hard to quantify.[16] However, Harris's presence on the ticket makes racial attitudes especially relevant in 2020, giving us a more direct test of her impact. Including respondents' assessments of Harris in wave 7 (October– November 2020) in a model predicting vote choice significantly improved our ability to estimate the ticket for which our respondents would vote in the 2020 election, even after considering the fundamentals, racial attitudes, attitudes toward the presidential candidates, and other controls. The results are presented in Figure 7.5.

As Figure 7.5 shows, evaluations of Harris predicted vote choices even after controlling for all other variables, including assessments of the presidential candidates. Harris's favorability was almost as strong a predictor of vote preference as Biden's favorability was. Notably, Harris's effect on the election

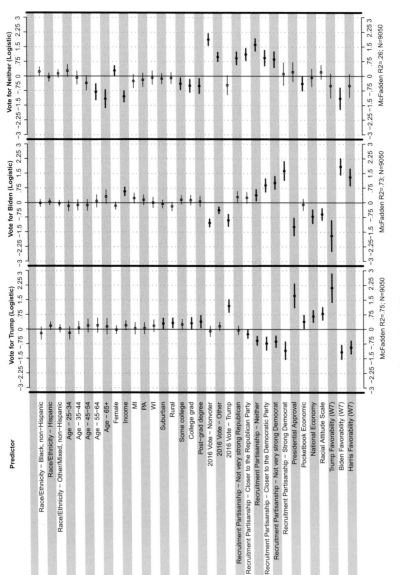

FIGURE 7.5 Kamala Harris Favorability and 2020 Vote Choice.
Standardized regression coefficients from logistic regressions predicting voting for Trump (left column), Biden (center), or neither (right). For each variable, standardized coefficient estimates are given as circles with 95% confidence intervals as black lines. Bolded coefficients are statistically significant.

was relatively static once she was nominated. That is, voters' assessments of Harris in wave 7, just before the election, did not predict vote choice significantly better than their assessments in wave 5 (August–September 2020), shortly after the conventions.

Overall, Harris had a net negative favorability rating across our states, with 45.2 percent of respondents reporting very or somewhat unfavorable opinions of her, 39.1 reporting very or somewhat favorable opinions of her, and 15.7 percent who said their views were neither favorable nor unfavorable.[§] Racial attitudes, again, were a strong predictor of this sentiment. Individuals with the most racially liberal attitudes tended to evaluate Harris slightly more favorably than they rated Biden, those with more neutral racial attitudes tended to evaluate Biden more favorably than Harris, and those who held racially conservative views did not distinguish between the two (Figure 7.6). Racial identification, on the other hand, was not a significant unique predictor of favorability toward Harris. Notably, evaluations of Trump were even more closely associated with racial attitudes than evaluations of Harris or Biden, further indicating the extent to which Trump's candidacy and behavior primed racial attitudes.

This highlights that Harris became yet another vehicle for racial attitudes to function in 2020. Of course, it is impossible to isolate the effect of the party nominating Harris from everything else that happened during the year, but our findings do indicate that the presence of a woman of color on the Democratic ticket underscored the relevance of racial attitudes to vote choice in this tumultuous year.

The Effect of the Summer's Protests

In this section, we explore both who participated in the protests that followed George Floyd's death, and how those protests shaped our panelists' beliefs.

Who Participated in These Protests?

Across our states, 10.0 percent of respondents reported that someone in their household took part in an in-person protest or rally either to "protest the deaths of people like George Floyd and Breonna Taylor" or to support "defunding or reforming police departments." Figure 7.7 shows the

---

§. This was after results were imputed for missing data as well as the 5.5 percent of respondents who said that they did not know enough about her to say.

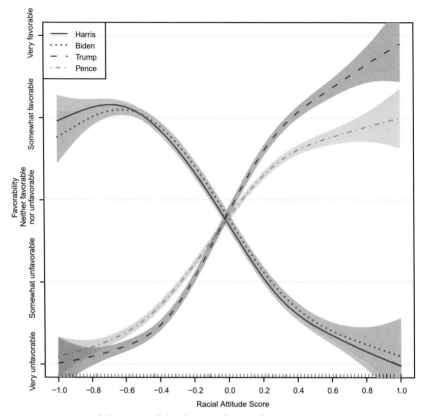

FIGURE 7.6 Candidate Favorability by Racial Attitudes.
Lines show the relationship between racial attitudes and candidate favorability for Trump (dashed red line), Biden (dotted blue line), and Harris (solid purple line).

distribution of all respondents who indicated in waves 2, 3, and 4 of the survey (between June and August 2020) that they protested at least once in favor of one of these issues; dot size corresponds to respondent weight.

But despite the scale of these protests, protesting was still an activity engaged in by a relatively small portion of our sample. To understand the identities of these individuals, we predicted whether respondents ever protested as a function of their prior voting history, demographics, partisanship, and racial attitudes. The results of this regression are presented in Figure 7.8.

A few factors were strongly related to participation in the summer protests (see the model in Figure 7.8). Notably, protesters tended to be younger than other Americans, were more likely to be urban, and were far more liberal in their racial attitudes. However, after accounting for these factors, the effects

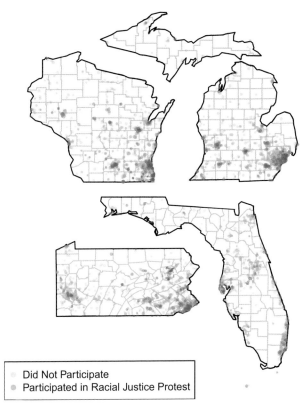

FIGURE 7.7 Locations of Summer of 2020 Racial Justice Protesters.
The light gray dots show the locations of respondents who did not participate in the summer 2020 Black Lives Matter protests; those shown in blue did participate. Dot sizes correspond to respondent weight.

of partisanship and prior support for Trump were weak to nonexistent. Even though Trump's was a highly racialized presidency, his supporters were not less likely than others who held similar views but did not support Trump to show up to these events. Instead, by far, the strongest predictor of attending the summer protests was respondents' racial attitudes, captured by our combined racial attitude measure.

To test whether political orientations affected the likelihood of protesting by shaping whether individuals' racial attitudes translated into this behavior, we interacted racial attitudes with electorates to predict protest attendance. Figure 7.9 presents the results of a generalized additive model with this interaction. With the exception of unwavering Trump supporters, the differences linking racial attitudes and protesting across electorates were minimal. People

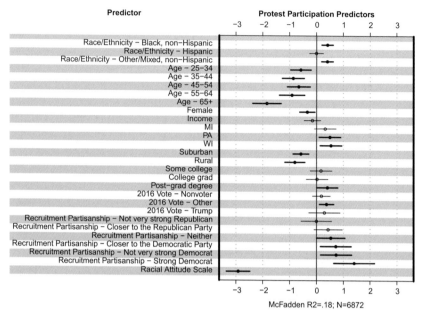

FIGURE 7.8 Predictors of Participation in Racial Justice Protests.
Standardized regression coefficients from a logistic regression model predicting participation in the summer's Black Lives Matter protests. For each variable, standardized coefficient estimates are given as circles with 95% confidence intervals as black lines. Bolded
coefficients are statistically significant.

with more racially liberal attitudes were more likely to protest regardless of
whether or how they voted. The difference for unwavering Trump voters that
can be observed on the left side of Figure 7.9 is less substantive than it might
seem. As Figure 7.1 revealed, few unwavering Trump supporters expressed racially liberal views. It seems as if participation in these protests was about racial attitudes more than anything else.

Did the Protests Change Attitudes?

While most voters did not participate in these protests, that does not mean
that the protests failed to affect Americans' attitudes. Indeed, the media's
and campaigns' contrasting messages about the protests likely ensured that
they would do so. The question of police funding, which became a central
flashpoint over the summer, is illustrative. While some protesters were encouraging cities to "defund the police" and shift resources elsewhere, Trump's
narrative about crime and civil unrest contended that "in many cases local law
enforcement is underfunded, understaffed and under[supported]."[17] In his

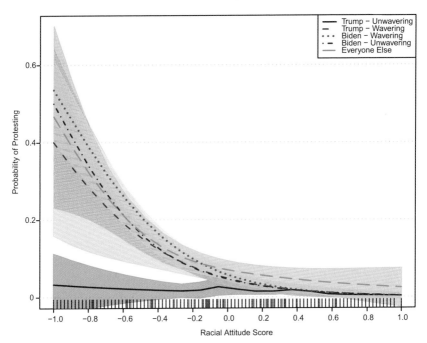

FIGURE 7.9 Racial Attitudes and Protests.
Lines show the predicted probability of participating in a Black Lives Matter protest as a function of electorate membership, racial attitudes, and the interaction of the two.

speeches and ads, as we noted earlier, the claim that Biden would defund the police was front and center.[18] In contrast, Trump proposed increasing police funding and even bringing in federal support. Did this have an effect?

To understand how these messages competed, we looked at the difference between those saying that we should spend more on police funding and those saying that current police funding would be better spent elsewhere over time (Figure 7.10, panel A). In wave 2 (June 2020), during the protests, our panelists were relatively equivocal on the issue. While there was a strong overall divide between the electorates, across all respondents a slight plurality supported redistribution away from police. Over time, however, all groups shifted in the direction of supporting additional funding for police, though the differences between the electorates remained relatively steady. This indicates that the president's countermessage to the protests, focusing on law and order, may have been an effective one. A second indicator that this messaging was effective is apparent in assessments of how well the incumbent had handled civil unrest. Although this was a relatively weak component of the president's job approval, assessments of Trump's performance in this arena went up over

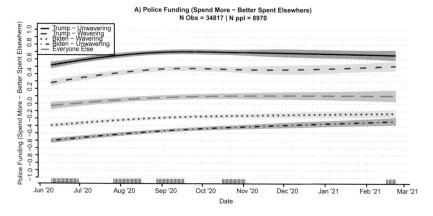

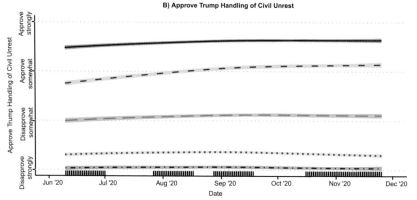

FIGURE 7.10 Police Funding and Trump Approval on Civil Unrest.
The top row shows how much each electorate supported spending more money on the police across our study; higher values indicate supporting more spending, vs. saying that police funding should be spent elsewhere. The bottom panel shows how much each electorate approved of Trump's handling of civil unrest across our study.

time, at least among his supporters (Figure 7.10, panel B). Hence, in comparison to the immediate post-Floyd wave, Trump seems to have improved his standing on these issues over time.

One reason this messaging may have been effective for the president was that he shifted the debate from an issue on which he was relatively weak to one where he was relatively strong. Figure 7.11 highlights three issues of particular salience to the debate between racial justice and law and order: race relations, criminal justice reform, and crime. Americans in each of our electorates consistently thought that race relations was one of the issues for which Biden was the most advantaged (red diamonds in Figure 7.11). Even wavering Trump supporters were relatively equivocal on the performance of the two

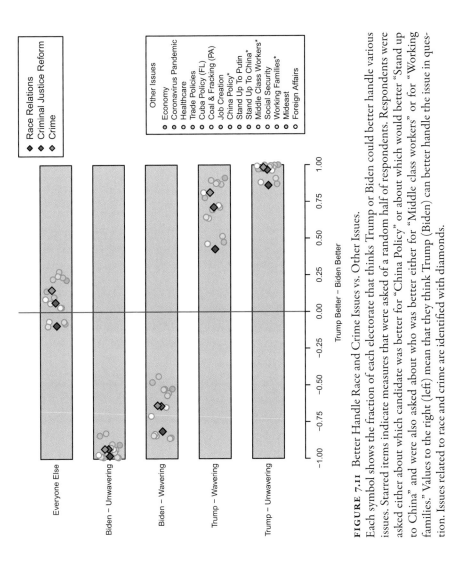

FIGURE 7.11 Better Handle Race and Crime Issues *vs.* Other Issues.

Each symbol shows the fraction of each electorate that thinks Trump or Biden could better handle various issues. Starred items indicate measures that were asked of a random half of respondents. Respondents were asked either about which candidate was better for "China Policy" or about which would better "Stand up to China" and were also asked about who was better either for "Middle class workers" or for "Working families," and were also asked about who was better either for "Middle class workers" or for "Working families." Values to the right (left) mean that they think Trump (Biden) can better handle the issue in question. Issues related to race and crime are identified with diamonds.

candidates. But to the extent that voters would end up focusing on criminal justice reform (blue diamonds) or on crime (green diamonds), they would be considering issues for which Trump was on far firmer ground.

What Effect Did Kenosha Have?

As we noted in Part 1 of the chapter, when a White Kenosha police officer shot and paralyzed Jacob Blake, a Black man, protests, some of them violent, erupted in the city. Our focus on Racine and Kenosha Counties made it possible to explore the effects of these protests on the attitudes of panelists in that locale and in Wisconsin as a whole. Reactions to events in Kenosha reflect the ever-growing polarization of the electorates. In waves 4 (July–August 2020) and 6 (September–October 2020), which bookended the conventions and these events, we asked questions about support for bringing in federal law enforcement to address civil unrest.[**] Although the predictors of support at both times echoed attitudes toward protesters and police more generally, changes between these time points depended on something else entirely: whether respondents resided in Wisconsin and, if so, how far from the events they lived. In Figure 7.12, panel A, the x-axis reports respondents' answers to the wave 4 question about whether federal law enforcement should be sent in; the y-axis corresponds with their answers in wave 6. The 45-degree line shows what would be expected if all respondents gave identical answers in the two waves. Shallower slopes would be expected if there was some regression to the mean in these answers.

The results of this analysis reveal a strong local effect of the events in Kenosha. Changes between waves 4 and 6 in Florida, Michigan, and Pennsylvania are all completely consistent with one another. Because they tend to be higher than the 45-degree line more often than they are below it, we can conclude that individuals in these states became slightly more supportive of dispatching federal law enforcement officers to protests—a reflection of the declining support for the protests over time. But the differences were small. In Wisconsin, however, this effect was far more pronounced (variable purple line in Figure 7.12, panel A). To assess whether this difference was, in fact, due to local experiences, we examined these same patterns in an analysis limited to Wisconsinites, conditioning on how far they lived from the epicenter of

---

[**]. The first question asked specifically about unrest related to the Floyd protests, while the second asked more generally about unrest.

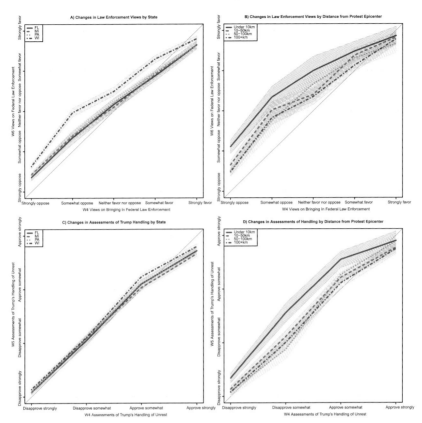

FIGURE 7.12 Attitudinal Effects of the Kenosha Protest.
In each panel, the *x*-axis shows wave 4 measures, and the *y*-axis shows the same item measured in wave 6. Values along the diagonal line indicate identical responses in waves 4 and 6. The top row examines views on bringing in federal law enforcement to handle civil unrest, the bottom panels assess approval of Trump's handling of civil unrest. In the left-hand panels, we show responses separately by state. In the right-hand panels, we show responses based on their distance from the protest epicenter in Kenosha.

the protests (Figure 7.12, panel B).[††] The solid red line in this figure reveals that the influence of the events in Kenosha was far more pronounced among those who lived nearby. Among the 292 unweighted individuals living within 10 kilometers of Kenosha's city center, strong opposition to the use of federal law enforcement fell by 45 percent and strong support more than doubled.

---

††. This was calculated as the geodesic distance from the centroid of the respondent's Census Block Group to the centroid of the protest area.

The events in Kenosha also appear to have improved assessments of Trump's handling of civil unrest among those who lived nearby. When comparing waves 4 (July–August) and 5 (August–September) of the study—again bracketing the events of Kenosha—residents of Wisconsin once more appear as outliers. Their assessments of Trump's handling of the issue improved notably compared to residents of the other three states (Figure 7.12, panel C). And, yet again, these differences were concentrated among those who lived near the epicenter of the events (Figure 7.12, panel D). In short, there appears to be a distinct local component to responses to Kenosha's civil unrest.

But although respondents in Wisconsin became more likely to support federal law enforcement intervention as a function of the incidents in Kenosha, similar effects were not observed on preferences for overall police spending or the sense that Black people were more frequently the victims of unnecessary use of police force (not shown). The shifts that did occur appeared to be all about handling the protests and not about the underlying issues on which the protesters focused.

Media Reliance as a Predictor of Attitudes About the Protests

Collectively, the protests following the death of Floyd were largely peaceful; in dollar terms, however, they were highly destructive. As we noted in Part I of this chapter, roughly 95 percent were neither violent nor destructive.[19] Yet the individuals who were violent or destructive inflicted an estimated $1 billion to $2 billion in property damage.[20]

A violence/destruction frame was among those featured in coverage of the protests.[21] Unsurprisingly, then, although a proportionally small number of protests involved destructive behaviors (and there may have been provocateurs in the crowds),[22] in early summer just over four in ten told Morning Consult pollsters that "Most of the current protesters are trying to incite violence or destroy property, even though some are peaceful and want to bring about meaningful social reform."[23]

From the beginning of the protests, law enforcement often appeared wearing military-style equipment and armed with various crowd control armaments.[24] Social and traditional media shared videos of officers beating, pepper-spraying, and tear-gassing protesters (and sometimes journalists) who were often unarmed and frequently nonconfrontational.[25] In some cities, curfews were imposed, governors called in the National Guard, and, as the Kyle Rittenhouse example suggests, armed citizens joined police in patrolling the streets. This led to a cycle in which interactions between protesters and law enforcement became increasingly contentious.[26] In some places, repressive tactics used by the police were met with destructive behavior by protesters. In Seattle, concerns about these interactions resulted in an unpoliced area of town that became known as the Capitol Hill Occupied Protest or Capitol Hill Autonomous Zone.[27] In Portland, Oregon, nightly clashes between protesters and police continued for months even after it became clear that federal agents in unmarked vehicles were detaining protesters.[28]

President Trump and his supporters in conservative media focused on disruptive and destructive events. In conservative media, Black Lives Matter protesters were portrayed as rioters and looters.[29] Unsurprisingly, then, both Trump supporters and conservative media viewers came to see Black Lives Matter in a strongly negative light. The first two panels of Figure 7.13 show the strongly negative attitudes toward the group among the Trump-supporting electorates and among those who were oriented toward conservative media. Conservative media seekers and especially those in echo chambers held over-whelmingly negative views of the BLM movement. The bottom two panels show similar assessments of the patriotism of Black Lives Matter protesters in wave 10, after the election (January–February 2021). These findings are con-sistent with the Trump messaging, which encouraged law enforcement officers to use aggressive techniques against the protesters while also characterizing them as left-wing extremists and members of antifa.

Following electoral choice and racial attitudes, seeking conservative media and occupying a conservative media echo chamber were the strongest predictors of negative views of Black Lives Matter and of perceptions that protesters were unpatriotic (Figure 7.14).

The Role of Campaign Messages About Race, Crime, and Law and Order

Of course, in addition to these racially charged incidents, there also were a number of campaign themes raised by Trump and Biden that intersected with the ones explored elsewhere in this chapter. In this section, we review their effects.

Would Suburbia Be Threatened by a Biden Presidency?

To his promise to be the "law and order president," Trump added increasingly hyperbolic appeals to suburban women, promising first to save the suburbs from looting and Section 8 housing and then escalating by promising to save

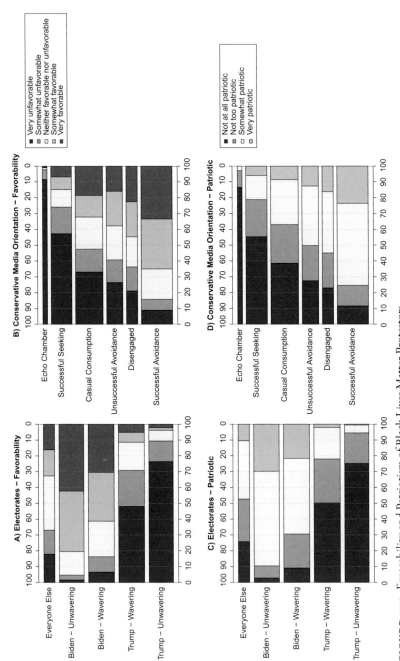

FIGURE 7.13 Favorability and Patriotism of Black Lives Matter Protestors.
Bars show the distribution of favorability (top row) and patriotism (bottom panel) of Black Lives Matter protestors. In the left-hand panels, we show the distribution by electorate; in the right-hand panels, we show the distribution by conservative media orientation.

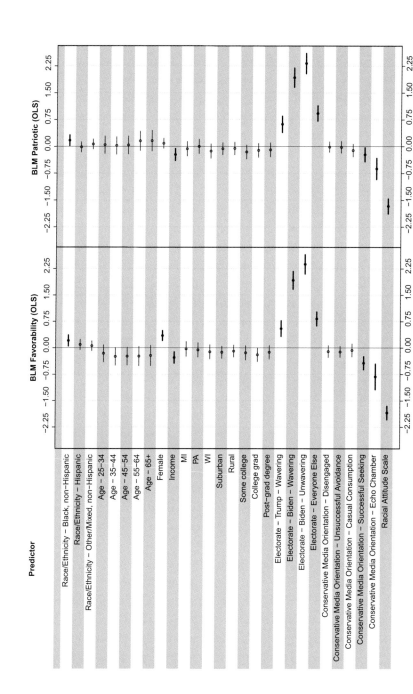

FIGURE 7.14 Predicting Favorability and Patriotism of Black Lives Matter Protestors.
Standardized regression coefficients from OLS regression models predicting favorability (left-hand column) of Black Lives Matter protestors. For each variable, standardized coefficient estimates are given as circles with 95% confidence intervals as black lines. Bolded coefficients are statistically significant.

them from total destruction. In the *Wall Street Journal* in mid-August, Donald Trump and his secretary of housing and urban development, Ben Carson, wrote, "The crime and chaos in Democrat-run cities have gotten so bad that liberals are even getting out of Manhattan's Upper West Side. Rather than rethink their destructive policies, the left wants to make sure there is no escape. The plan is to remake the suburbs in their image so they resemble the dysfunctional cities they now govern. As usual, anyone who dares tell the truth about what the left is doing is smeared as a racist. We won't allow this to happen. That's why we stopped the last administration's radical social-engineering."[30] On August 22 Trump tweeted, "Why would Suburban Women vote for Biden and the Democrats when Democrat run cities are now rampant with crime (and they aren't asking the Federal Government for help) which could easily spread to the suburbs, and they will reconstitute, on steroids, their low income suburbs plan!"[31] In Johnstown, Pennsylvania, in late October he pleaded, "Can I ask you to do me a favor, suburban women? Will you please like me? Please. Please. I saved your damn neighborhood, OK?"[32]

These attempts to instill a fear of crime among suburbanites seemed to have little effect. Starting in wave 5 and running until the election, we asked respondents to select from a list of five issues most central to their voting decision—the economy, the coronavirus pandemic, race relations, health care, and crime (though they could also specify their own issue). Among these five, crime was typically the least important, selected by a mere 5.1 percent of respondents. It held no more sway in the suburbs, where 4.9 percent of our panelists selected the issue. Race relations were deemed the most important twice as frequently. Figure 7.15 shows that the proportion of urban, suburban, and rural voters selecting each of these responses declined over time, indicating that crime, in particular, was not a particularly salient issue and that by Election Day race relations mattered more for all groups. It is of course possible that for some, crime was embedded within their definition of race relations.

Even if Trump's appeals on crime were effective in convincing voters (and suburban ones in particular) that it was an important issue, it is unclear whether Trump would actually gain from this messaging. A plurality of both suburban and urban individuals tended to think that Biden was better than Trump at handling crime, and this difference was relatively steady over time (Figure 7.16). Although Trump appears to have gained a little ground here, his level of improvement was relatively small, though statistically significant. Mirroring this result, when asked in wave 6 whether they thought crime would be lower, higher, or about the same had Biden instead of Trump

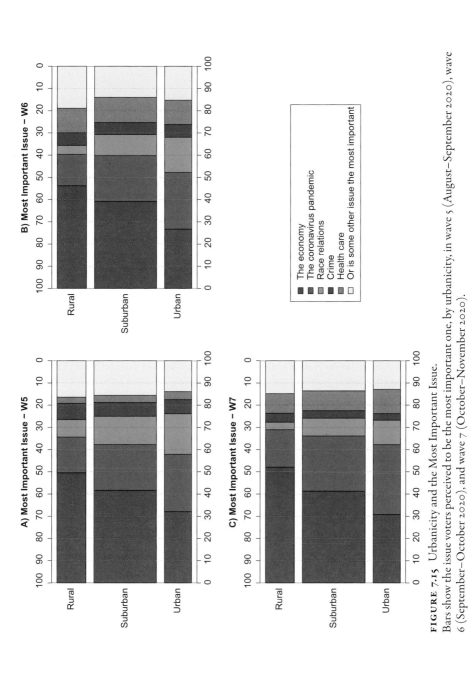

FIGURE 7.15 Urbanicity and the Most Important Issue.

Bars show the issue voters perceived to be the most important one, by urbanicity, in wave 5 (August–September 2020), wave 6 (September–October 2020), and wave 7 (October–November 2020).

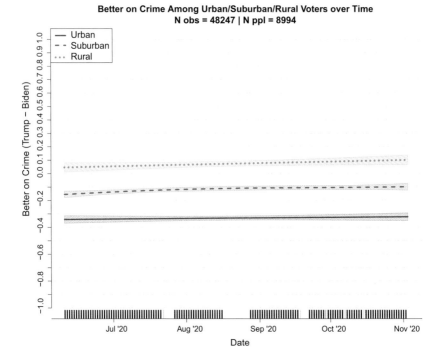

FIGURE 7.16 Believe Trump Could Better Handle Crime.
Lines show whether voters believe Trump or Biden could better handle crime, by urbanicity. Higher (lower) values indicate that the group believes Trump (Biden) could better handle the issue.

been president (Figure 7.17), suburbanites were more likely to say that this counterfactual situation would have produced lower levels of crime (33.3 percent) rather than higher levels of crime (28.7 percent). Trump's argument was simply not a winning one in the suburbs.

These findings are consistent with analysis of the exit polls showing that Trump performed more poorly in the suburbs in 2020 than he had in 2016. The *Washington Post*'s Philip Bump wrote, "Preliminary county-level results show how the average margins in both urban and suburban counties were friendlier to Biden than they had been to Hillary Clinton four years ago, even as rural votes shifted more to the right."[33] That suburban shift was critical: it is estimated that nearly half of the ballots tallied in the election were cast in suburban counties. Biden's picking up 2.3 points on average across those counties made a big difference. "Mr. Trump maintained his strong support in many of the country's less-populous, rural counties while suburban voters collectively swung toward Mr. Biden," noted a study of country voting patterns

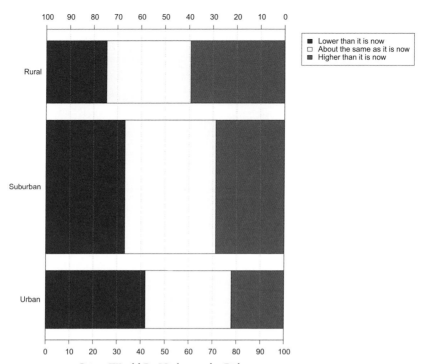

FIGURE 7.17 Crime Would Be Higher under Biden.
Bars show voters' beliefs that crime would be higher, lower, or about the same if Biden (instead of Trump) had been president.

conducted by the *New York Times*.[34] And a Brookings analysis concluded, "The near erasure of Trump's 91,000 suburban vote lead from 2016 played an important part in his Michigan defeat."[35]

Defunding the Police

As we noted in Part 1 of this chapter, throughout the summer some protesters called for "defunding the police." While Trump's speeches, tweets, and ads claimed that Biden embraced the position, the Delawarean had explicitly disavowed it. In a June interview with CBS News, Biden noted, "I don't support defunding the police. . . . I support conditioning federal aid to police, based on whether or not they meet certain basic standards of decency and honorableness."[36] In the first debate, the challenger reiterated, "What I support is the police having the opportunity to deal with the problems they face. . . . [H]is budget calls for a $400 million cut in local law enforcement assistance. They need more assistance."[37]

One result of increasing concern about the protests and their perceived lawlessness can be seen in individuals' desires to provide the police with additional resources. Throughout our study, Trump-supporting electorates, conservative media viewers, and racially conservative individuals were much less likely to believe that police often treated Black people unfairly or that money currently spent on police departments should be redirected. Over time, these views became more common among all but the most racially liberal Americans. What initially appeared to reflect broad support for the demands of protesters shifted to plurality opposition.

In wave 2 (June 2020), shortly after Floyd was killed, 32.2 percent of respondents across our states said that "much of the money currently spent on police departments would be better spent elsewhere," compared to 31.1 percent who said that more money should be used to fund police departments. In wave 7 (October–November 2020), shortly before the election, these numbers were 25.1 percent and 39.0 percent, respectively (see Figure 7.10, panel A, above). To determine what accounted for both initial levels of support for defunding police and changes in that support over time, we present two sets of regressions predicting initial preferences for defunding or increasing police funding from wave 2, while the first sets of protests were ongoing, and also from wave 7, just before the election. In wave 2, we predict these attitudes with demographics, partisanship, and media orientations, along with racial attitudes. In wave 7, we look for the variables that account for changes in these attitudes by controlling for wave 2 answers and examining the same set of predictors. These are presented in Figures 7.18 and 7.19, respectively.

In wave 2, we see that the desire to reduce police funding was more common among Black respondents, younger individuals, those living in urban areas, strong Democrats, those who disapproved of the president, and, most prominently, those with liberal racial attitudes (Figure 7.18). When we look at the factors that account for changes in these views, after controlling for wave 2 answers, some of these predictors persist and others disappear. Changes in police funding preferences over time were associated with respondent age, partisanship, approval of President Trump, and, most notably, racial attitudes (Figure 7.19).

What Were the Effects of These Events and Messages on Voting?

As we have seen, the 2020 campaign had no shortage of racially salient events or racialized messaging. As the unrest of the summer morphed from a racial

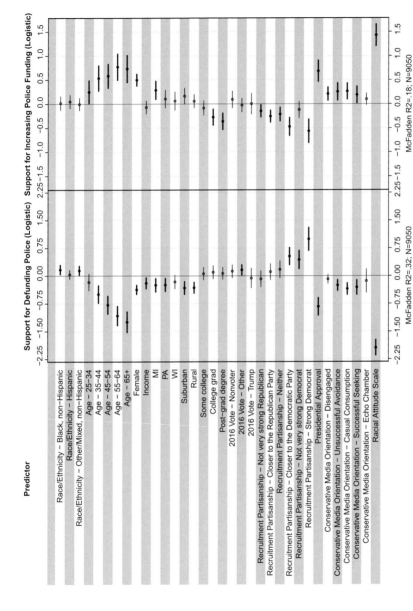

FIGURE 7.18 Predicting Support for Defunding the Police.

Standardized regression coefficients from logistic regression models predicting support for defunding the police (left-hand column) and increasing police funding (right-hand column). For each variable, standardized coefficient estimates are given as circles with 95% confidence intervals as black lines. Bolded coefficients are statistically significant.

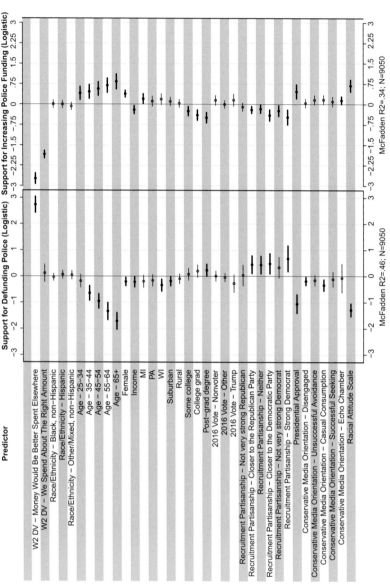

FIGURE 7.19 Changes in Support for Defunding the Police.
Standardized regression coefficients from logistic regression models predicting support for defunding the police (left-hand column) and increasing police funding (right-hand column) in wave 7 controlling the same beliefs in wave 2. For each variable, standardized coefficient estimates are given as circles with 95% confidence intervals as black lines. Bolded coefficients are statistically significant.

reckoning to a contest between two frames—one about race and the other about crime—the candidates were appealing to very different constituencies. If respondents themselves are to be believed, these events were also of considerable importance to the electorates. In AP VoteCast data, more than nine in ten voters said that the protests over police violence were a factor in their decisions, with more than three-quarters calling them an important factor and 19 percent saying they were the most important factor in shaping their vote.[38] Notably, these individuals were relatively evenly split in their preferences, with 53 percent reporting that they voted for Biden and 46 percent opting for Trump. By looking at how the different components of this messaging factored into vote choices, we can examine which of these messages and frames really mattered for individuals' votes and which instead merely served to reinforce existing predispositions.

The regression in Figure 7.20 suggests that many of the forces invoked by this reckoning mattered for the decisions people made, while some did not. Controlling for initial levels of presidential approval, how people voted in 2016, and their wave 1 (April–May 2020) preferences, respondents' own racial identifications did not appear to influence the choices they made. Suburban and rural voters became somewhat more likely to vote for Trump, suggesting that perhaps he did make some gains in these areas, and racial attitudes strongly predicted changes in voting intention. Beyond this, respondents who initially thought that police department funding should be cut were less likely to vote for Trump, and respondents who shifted their views regarding which candidate was better on race or crime became more likely to support those candidates. All of this is in line with what we might expect if the competing narratives had an influence. Further, individuals who sought conservative media shifted increasingly toward Trump, suggesting that these orientations had an impact. Notably, being among the many Americans who attended a protest in the spring was not itself consequential for how individuals voted.

Given the strength of racial attitudes as a predictor of vote choice, as well as the campaign's contrasting messages, activating these attitudes appears to have been the most salient effect of the third crisis on the election. In the end, President Trump's attempt to pivot the question from one about race to a debate over law and order was perhaps strategically wise but not sufficiently effective. Instead, the debate ended up largely about race for most Americans. And when it came to considering which candidate was better on that issue, Biden had a clear advantage (see Figure 7.11 above).

The competition between two divergent narratives from the candidates can be seen in the patterns of vote settling among individuals who said each of these issues was very important (Figure 7.21). Wavering Trump voters

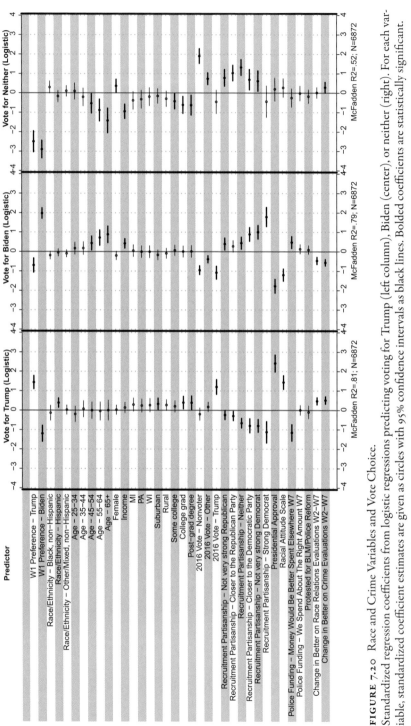

FIGURE 7.20 Race and Crime Variables and Vote Choice.
Standardized regression coefficients from logistic regressions predicting voting for Trump (left column), Biden (center), or neither (right). For each variable, standardized coefficient estimates are given as circles with 95% confidence intervals as black lines. Bolded coefficients are statistically significant.

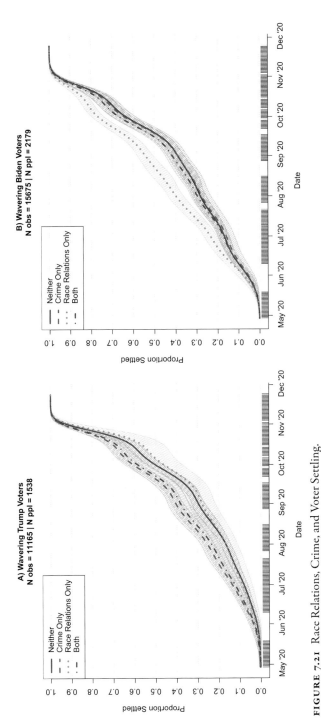

FIGURE 7.21 Race Relations, Crime, and Voter Settling.

Each panel provides the proportion of wavering voters who had settled on their choice, based on whether they thought that race relations, crime, or both were very important issues to their vote. Individuals are identified by whether they thought that neither issue (solid red line), only crime (dashed blue line), only race relations (dotted green line), or both of these issues (mixed purple line) were very important. Wavering Trump voters are shown in panel A, wavering Biden voters are shown in panel B.

tended to make their decisions somewhat earlier if they reported that crime was a very important issue to them than if they did not, and there were no differences between those who asserted that race relations were important and those who did not (left panel). In contrast, wavering Biden voters tended to settle their choices earlier if the only thing they named was race relations (right panel). Interestingly, however, those who cited the importance of both race and crime tended to make their decisions more slowly. Perhaps, then, one of the effects of Trump's crime narrative was to head off the potential that race would be central to the election for some of his prospective voters. Indeed, it appears that if voters had focused only on race relations (instead of crime), Biden likely would have performed even better.

In practice, then, the strong link between respondents' racial attitudes and the shifts in their vote choices confirm the central role of race in American politics and the large partisan divide on the issue. But while Trump's campaign attempted to demonstrate that he was unproblematic on race relations through an impressively diverse lineup of convention speakers and a focus on funding for historically Black colleges and universities, low Black unemployment in the first three years of his presidency, and his passage of the First Step Act on prison reform, these accomplishments could not compete with at least some respondents' preexisting views of the president. The effect of all this, then, was to further sort voting choices on the basis of racial attitudes.

The Implications of a Racial Reckoning

The contest that emerged over race, crime, and policing in the aftermath of George Floyd's murder drew on long-standing tropes of American politics and had important implications for both the election and the events that would follow later. As we did in Chapters 5 and 6, we briefly review the main empirical findings from this chapter:

- Voters in the 2020 election were deeply divided in their racial attitudes, with racially liberal/pro-Black attitudes disproportionately represented among Democrats and Biden-supporting electorates and racially conservative/anti-Black attitudes predominating among Republicans and Trump-supporting electorates.
- Racial attitudes were among the strongest predictors not only of which candidate people would vote for in the election but also of whose preferences would change over the course of the election cycle. This

meant that in the 2020 campaign, the link between racial attitudes and vote choice became even stronger.

- When Kamala Harris was selected as Biden's vice presidential nominee, attitudes toward her selection were shaped by racial attitudes, and assessments of her accounted for some of the influence of racial attitudes on vote choices.

- Around one in ten Americans participated in the summer's protests. This participation was closely related to racial attitudes and not as closely related to candidate support or partisanship.

- Over time, in general, our respondents became less likely to support shifting funds from police departments to other social service agencies and more likely to support using federal law enforcement officers to address civil unrest. This pattern was especially pronounced in Wisconsin, where we used our Kenosha/Racine samples to examine the effects of the protests following the police shooting of Jacob Blake. Those who lived closer to the center of those protests became especially likely to shift in these ways.

As in so many past American elections, issues of racial justice found their way to the center of the campaign—amplified by events and by an already deep correspondence between these attitudes and identification with one or the other of the major political parties. We find in this chapter that although the racial issues that emerged in the campaign nominally favored Biden, Trump developed a compelling, if somewhat weaker, counternarrative that blended racial conservatism with fear of crime and of a changing America (we take up this latter point in Chapter 8). This lens may not have had the intended effect at the ballot box, but it did further radicalize his most ardent supporters. In the end, the events and messages of 2020 deepened the American racial divide, and the longest-running cleavage of American politics remained persistently central to American political life.

8

A Deeper Anxiety

WAS STATUS THREAT AT PLAY IN 2020?

Josh Pasek, Matthew Levendusky, and Kathleen Hall Jamieson

> *Our mission is to defend the legacy of America's founding,*
> *the virtue of America's heroes, and the nobility of the*
> *American character.... [T]he left-wing cultural revolution*
> *is designed to overthrow the American Revolution.*
> —Donald Trump, speaking at the event that launched the 1776
> Commission[1]

AS OUR DISCUSSION in earlier chapters attests, we see a through line from the 2017 Charlottesville, Virginia, "Unite the Right" rally, to the protests about racial justice and policing that spread across the nation in the summer of 2020 following the death of George Floyd, and then to the debates over the legitimacy of the outcome of the 2020 election. Connecting these disparate events are debates over entitlement, power, and their prerogatives driven by the nation's demographic changes. Whereas White Christians once constituted the overwhelming majority of Americans, their share of the population has declined sharply in recent decades, and the nation is shifting toward being what is sometimes called "majority minority." Kamala Harris—a Black and Asian American woman, whose name some conservative lawmakers and pundits delighted in mispronouncing[2]—was a visible signal of this impending shift, especially when contrasted with the Trump-Pence ticket.

From this vantage point, the 2017 Charlottesville clash was only superficially about the statue of Robert E. Lee that stood in that eponymous park. Instead, it was about who was American and who holds power in our society; those marching with tiki torches wanted to preserve a status quo in which White Christian men set and enforced social and political norms. As

we forecasted in Chapter 1 ("An Election Shaped by Crises"), their slogans—
"You will not replace us," "White lives matter," "The South will rise again,"[3]
"Jews will not replace us," and "Blood and soil"[4]—revealed their true aims. So
too did their apparel: "Attendees at the rally also wore Nazi paraphernalia,
carried flags with swastikas alongside Confederate flags, and wore shirts with
quotations by Adolf Hitler," noted a report in *Vox*.[5]

In similar fashion, the emblems of the January 6 rioters included a "Jesus
Saves" sign, a person holding the Bible,[6] a Confederate battle flag, and one
modeled on a Nazi war flag. The sweatshirt of one insurgent read "Camp
Auschwitz."[7] During the January 6 insurrection, when Jacob Chansley—
better known as the "QAnon shaman"—"delivered a prayer thanking God
'for allowing the United States of America to be reborn,'" reported the
Associated Press, "other rioters fell silent in apparent participation."[8] The
sentiments captured in these symbols and slogans reflect a fear that usurpers
were stealing the birthright of the demographic group that traditional historical accounts credit with founding the nation: White Christian—especially
White Protestant—men.

The clash at Charlottesville and the attack on the Capitol had participants
in common. Nicholas Fuentes, described by the *New York Times* as a "white
nationalist, online provocateur, and activist" who is a leader of the "America
First" or Groyper movement and urged his followers at a November 2020
Washington, DC, rally to "storm every state capitol until Jan. 20, 2021, until
President Trump is inaugurated for four more years," was also a marcher at
the Unite the Right rally at Charlottesville in 2017. Among his messages, according to the *Times*, was that "the nation is losing 'its white demographic
core.'"[9]

Long before the 2020 election, social scientists had posited that those
groups experiencing anxiety about their declining status[10] would respond
belligerently (hence they call this general idea "status threat"). When "a
once dominant ethnic-racial group . . . feels threatened by the rise of other
groups," it will move "to create an America that would exclude, expel, or
suppress people of other racial, ethnic, and cultural groups,"[11] forecast political scientist Samuel Huntington in 2004. The rise of the Tea Party proved
Huntington's prescience. Like earlier right-wing reactionary movements, including the Know Nothing Party and the Ku Klux Klan, sympathy for that
movement was grounded in fear that the nation was being stolen from "real
Americans."

For Tea Party activists, Barack Obama was a potent symbol of this shift.
According to a 2010 *New York Times*–CBS News poll, one in four Tea Party

supporters felt that the policies of the Obama administration favored Black people over White people, compared with just over one in ten of the public as a whole.[12] These Tea Party adherents had "a strong sense of out-group anxiety and a concern over the social and demographic changes in America,"[13] and many of them later became some of Trump's strongest backers.[14] Voting for the real estate mogul in 2016 was strongly associated with a sense that once demographically dominant groups were losing ground (i.e., status threat).[15] In the view of Trump enthusiasts, those in the normative race, religion, and language group needed to "protect person, family, culture and country from the tangible threats they believe are posed by outsiders."[16]

In this chapter, we show that status threat shaped vote choice in the 2020 election much as it had in the 2008, 2012, and 2016 ones.[17] While status threat is intertwined with racial attitudes, we argue that elements of each clearly affect how voters perceived the election in 2020. In Chapter 9 ("'Stop the Steal'"), we show that status threat shaped how voters saw the post-election period as well, including the events of January 6. These findings add nuance to the results about the role of racial attitudes that we reported in Chapter 7 ("Law and Order vs. Law and Order with Racial Justice"). It is not simply the belief that racial minorities face discrimination that affects vote choice; so too does the sense that once-dominant groups are on the decline. Put more broadly, this highlights that debates about electoral legitimacy, as well as the Capitol insurrection, are at their heart about who holds political power in America.

What Is Status Threat?

The concept of status threat posits that when a dominant group in society feels threatened, it reacts in ways designed to retain its societal position. Because dominant groups occupy a privileged position in the social hierarchy, being part of one is highly valued. So when the power and attendant prerogatives of a dominant group are threatened or even called into question, members of that group will seek to reassert both—by force if necessary. Doing so may entail working to shore up the preexisting order,[18] strengthening one's justification for existing hierarchical social and political arrangements,[19] expressing more out-group animosity and in-group favoritism, and activating one's authoritarian dispositions.[20] In the process, adherents will attach greater importance to their dominant identities[21] and perceive greater discrimination against these groups, effectively recasting themselves as the persecuted minority.[22] Whether the threat is real or not, such feelings can lead to discrimination against and animosity toward the supposed outsiders.[23] Even if a dominant group's absolute position is unchanged, alteration in its *relative* status can trigger status threat: gains by previously disadvantaged groups are enough to activate it.[24]

In the United States, such debates are intrinsically bound up with the question of what it means to be an American. Unlike European national identities, which are linked to birthplace, American identity is rooted in ideals, but for many it is also tied to Whiteness.[25] Because White Christian men have held—and continue to hold—political, economic, cultural, and social power, they traditionally have been seen as prototypical Americans by the public as a whole,[26] and also have exerted an outsized influence on American society. But that is changing as record numbers of people of color, women, and those of other faiths (or no faith at all) have moved into corporate boardrooms, Congress, state legislatures, and other power centers in society.[27]

Although White Christian men still exert enormous influence, their *relative* position and power have waned in recent years. Demographers estimate that Caucasians will become the numerical minority by the middle of the twenty-first century, a change fueled by immigration from Asia, Latin America, and Africa,[28] though they also note that this considerably oversimplifies the situation, as racial boundaries are in flux and increasing numbers of people identify with more than one race.[29] Moreover, since the 1980s, women have earned more college degrees than men, and now earn more graduate degrees as well,[30] trends suggesting that they may someday outearn men.[31] At the same time, working-class men without college degrees—once the backbone of the American economy—are increasingly struggling to keep up economically, are now more likely than in the past to be adrift and unmoored,[32] and are increasingly dying "deaths of despair" linked to alcoholism and opioid addiction.[33]

As the nation diversifies religiously, the position of Christians is also changing. For much of American history, Christians—in particular, Protestants—were the dominant group. Indeed, all but two presidents have been, at least nominally, Protestants; the other two were Catholic. While anti-Catholic sentiment ran deep in the nineteenth century, over time it has faded; the same is true of animosity toward Mormons, another group that long faced religious discrimination.

While Christians are still the largest religious group in the nation, their share of the population has shrunk rapidly in recent decades. At the same time, more Americans are unaffiliated with any religion: this group has almost doubled in size over the past fifteen years.[34] Democrats were advantaged by this shift. Data from the Pew Research Center found that nonreligious voters made up a quarter of the electorate in 2016.[35] An August 2020 Pew poll found that more than 70 percent of nonreligious voters favored Biden,[36] and these groups disproportionately supported Democrats more generally.[37] So not only has the share of Christians declined, but to the extent that these individuals align with the Republican Party, this shift has been electorally relevant.

In short, even if White Christian men are still among the most privileged groups in American society, their *relative* position is falling compared to, say, where it was in the 1950s. Privileges accorded White men as a matter of course are no longer as readily granted them, a potentially painful loss of status for a once-entitled group.* As a result, some among them see efforts to help historically disadvantaged groups not as an attempt to redress past discrimination but rather as a means of discriminating against those from the dominant group who have worked hard, robbing them of their birthright. As a result, these individuals experience status threat.[38]

How Donald Trump and 2020 Primed Status Threat

Into this shifting demographic plain came Donald Trump with rhetoric—from his 2015 announcement through his statements on January 6—that served to activate and mobilize a sense of status threat among White male Christian Americans. For example, in November 2015, then-candidate Trump retweeted a graphic headlined "USA Crime Statistics—2015" that pictured a dark-complected man, his face obscured by a bandana, pointing a gun. The pictured data dramatically misrepresented the percentage of White murder victims killed by Black perpetrators, putting it at 81 percent, though the best available data suggest that the correct figure is just under 15 percent.[39] In the 2020 campaign Trump wooed White suburban women by claiming that he had protected them from crime and low-income housing: "I'm saving your house. I'm saving your community. I'm keeping your crime way down."[40] The racial subtext of that message became clearer in an appeal he made in a Pennsylvania rally, arguing that suburban women should vote for him because "I'm about having you safe. I'm about having your suburban communities. I don't want to build low-income housing next to your house."[41]

---

*. There is a parallel here to earlier efforts to increase equality throughout the post–Civil War period and into the twentieth century: White political supremacy was so natural that threats to it elicited a violent backlash. See Phillip Klinkner with Rogers Smith, *The Unsteady March: The Rise and Decline of Racial Equality in America* (Chicago: University of Chicago Press, 2002).

His 2016 campaign was not the first time Trump had trafficked in status-threat-laden appeals. Trump was a prominent promoter of the "birther" lie about President Obama, which conflated fears of foreignness and religion to suggest that Obama was doubly other: not only was he a foreigner, but he was also a Muslim (both are untrue). Perhaps somewhat ironically, Trump's promulgation of this rumor helped return him to the national spotlight. Speaking about the false birther rumor, Trump said, "He doesn't have a birth certificate, or if he does, there's something on that certificate that is very bad for him. Now, somebody told me—and I have no idea if this is bad for him or not, but perhaps it would be—that where it says 'religion,' it might have 'Muslim.' And if you're a Muslim, you don't change your religion, by the way."[42] And, consistent with Huntington's account of the way a dominant group deals with status threat, in 2015 the aspiring Republican nominee supported what he characterized as the "complete and total shutdown of Muslims entering the United States."[43] He also explicitly cast his 2016 candidacy as a response to the threats facing Christianity. "I will tell you," Trump informed the audience at a Christian college during the primaries of 2016, "Christianity is under tremendous siege, whether we want to talk about it or we don't want to talk about it." In the same speech, he declared that Christians "don't exert the power that we should have" and promised that if he was elected, "Christianity will have power . . . you don't need anybody else."[44] Although Joe Biden is a practicing Catholic who regularly attends Mass, Trump cast the Democratic Party's 2020 nominee as "against God," "against the Bible," and "essentially against religion."[45]

Trump's 2020 attacks on Democratic vice presidential nominee Kamala Harris, as well as his appeals to suburban women, exhibited both hostile sexism ("antipathy toward women who are viewed as usurping men's power") and benevolent sexism (a "chivalrous ideology that offers protection and affection to women who embrace conventional roles").[46] Not only did he refer to suburban women as "suburban housewives," but he bragged that "we're getting your husbands back to work."[47] Trump also declared that it was not nice to call women tough,[48] characterized Senator Harris (D-CA) as "a monster,"[49] tagged her (as he had his 2016 opponent, Hillary Clinton)[50] as "a nasty woman,"[51] and asserted at a September 2020 rally that Harris "could never be the first woman president. She could never be. That would be an insult to our country."[52] In 2016, non-college-educated White women who endorse hostile sexism and had weaker perceptions of gender discrimination were more likely to vote for Trump,[53] suggesting that these appeals work for at least some women. Trump's reinforcement of traditional gender norms also emerged as a key argument in his favor among some White evangelical Christians.[54]

Trump's slogans in 2016—"Make America Great Again" and "America First"—were, among other things, a repudiation of the country's first Black president. At minimum, "again" refers to a time before the Obama presidency. The phrase "great again" implies that America is no longer great but once was. When was that? Presumably when only White Christian men held the reins of power. The real estate developer's other slogan, "America First," has long historical ties to anti-immigrant and nativist groups.[55] Because White Christian men are seen as the default Americans, the slogan can be heard to say that they should be the ones making the political decisions and asserting power. Unsurprisingly, then, as we noted earlier, scholars found that this sense of status threat was a key predictor of voting behavior in 2016: those who thought their privileged position in society was being usurped were more likely to back Trump.[56] At the same time, the demographic shifts in the United States tilted White Americans' political-party leanings and ideological preferences in a more Republican and conservative direction,[57] and conservative/Republican White people were more likely to feel this sense of status threat.[58] As a result, preference for Trump in 2016 was greater among White Americans whose racial/ethnic identity was more central to them.[59]

Trump's argument that America had lost its way and needed to return to a bygone era was hardly a new one; debates about the country's origins and destiny have raged with surprising regularity throughout American history,[60] especially with respect to how we teach American history.[61] These issues again came to the fore in 2019, when the *New York Times Magazine* published the 1619 Project, which sought "to reframe American history by considering what it would mean to regard 1619 [rather than 1776] as our nation's birth year."[62] Why 1619? That was the year the first enslaved Africans came to what would later become the United States. Polls suggest that this effort to center the role of slavery in the American story touched a nerve.[63]

The project drew considerable attention—including some pointed scholarly criticism[64]—but notably for our purposes, it led President Trump to launch the 1776 Commission, which its supporters described as an effort to promote "patriotic education."[65] In the eyes of the incumbent, such schooling would "clear away the twisted web of lies in our schools and classrooms, and teach our children the magnificent truth about our country."[66] Rather than focus on the negatives of American history—such as the roles of slavery and racism—it would focus on the greatness of America and the country's role in promoting liberty and advancing freedom. Interestingly, this commission seeking to "cultivat[e] a better education among Americans in the principles and history of our nation"[67] was criticized for, among other things, including no professional historians.[68]

The 1776 Commission can usefully be seen through the lens of status threat: featuring the centrality of enslavement in the founding and development of the nation, as the 1619 Project does, changes the American narrative from one in which the nation was birthed in liberty to one in which it was birthed in bondage. American history is no longer the story of heroic, White, Christian, male founders, but rather now includes others, especially enslaved people. And where there are enslaved people, there are enslavers, including many of the founders themselves.

An effort to promote "patriotic education" and preserve the narrative of exemplary White men in American history speaks to the sense that including others in the narrative changes both national identity and who deserves power in American life. It also helps explain why someone like Arkansas Republican Senator Tom Cotton (R-AR), who opposed congressional efforts to remove Confederate names, monuments, and symbols from military sites,[69] would be the one sponsoring legislation titled the Saving American History Act of 2020. If signed into law, that bill would reduce the federal funding of schools teaching the 1619 Project[70†] by eliminating their access to federal professional development funding intended to improve teacher quality and by barring the federal underwriting of any "cost associated with teaching the 1619 Project, including in planning time and teaching time."[71]

The 1776 Commission was not Trump's only means of fanning the flames of status threat. Earlier in his presidency, he had banned travel from several majority-Muslim countries (the so-called Muslim ban), openly stated that he preferred immigrants from Norway over those from "shithole" countries like Haiti, (partially) built a wall along the southern border with Mexico, initially refused to disavow white nationalists after Charlottesville, and referred to COVID-19 as "Kung Flu." Indeed, looking back at his rhetoric and policies, prominent scholars argue that his actions represent a form of White

---

†. Senator Cotton also wrote an op-ed in the *New York Times* in June 2020 calling for federal troops to be sent into the streets to restore order in the wake of the Black Lives Matter protest movement ("Tom Cotton: Send in the Troops," *New York Times*, June 3, 2020, https://www.nytimes.com/2020/06/03/opinion/tom-cotton-protests-military.html). The association between the use of military force and a desire to ban the teaching of slavery in schools exemplifies the linkage of status threat with the legitimation of violence; we return to this theme in Chapter 9.

protectionism—the idea that White people are central to Americanism and deserve special protection.[72] Trump's arguments were electorally advantageous for him. Because of the demographic sorting that has taken place in recent years, Whiteness and Christianity were increasingly correlated with support for Republican candidates,[73] and White men were more likely to support the GOP than were White women.[74]

Such arguments are an inextricable part of the narrative on conservative media outlets.[75] For example, in 2021, citing a 2015 Biden statement applauding the increasing diversity of the country, Fox News host Tucker Carlson contended: "An unrelenting stream of immigration. But why? Well, Joe Biden just said it, to change the racial mix of the country. That's the reason, to reduce the political power of people whose ancestors lived here, and dramatically increase the proportion of Americans newly-arrived from the third world. And then Biden went further, he said that non-white DNA is the quote, 'the source of our strength.' Imagine saying that. This is the language of eugenics, it's horrifying. But there's a reason Biden said it. In political terms, this policy is called 'the great replacement,' the replacement of legacy Americans with more obedient people from far-away countries."[76] This sense of White people being "replaced" by immigrants who would ensure the Democrats' hold on power sits at the center of the notion of status threat; it was also the language of a long-standing conspiracy theory propagated in white supremacist circles.[77]

The framing of the summer's Black Lives Matter protests had the potential to heighten status threat. While the vast majority of protests were peaceful, as we noted in earlier chapters, a small number of them did lead to violence and looting, especially in cities such as Philadelphia, Chicago, and Portland. As we discussed in Chapter 7, Trump and his surrogates—as well as personalities at conservative media outlets—alleged that the mainstream media downplayed the disorder and refused to condemn the vandalism and violence, a conclusion reinforced by Trump's "law and order" framing. "Left-wing mobs have torn down statues of our founders, desecrated our memorials, and carried out a campaign of violence and anarchy," claimed Trump in 2020.[78]

A Trump ad that aired at high levels in Wisconsin, Michigan, and Pennsylvania from late September through Election Day highlighted this law-and-order framing and its accompanying status threat.[79] That message intercut scenes of burning buildings and looting with images of five White middle-aged men wearing police badges. "I've been a police officer for nearly 32 years. Joe Biden does not have the backs of police officers," says the first. "Joe Biden's silence is encouraging the rioters," reports the second. "If Joe

Biden is elected, it's just going to continue," declares the third. "Joe Biden empowers these people. The more you empower them, the more crime they go to commit," notes the fourth. "In Joe Biden's America we will all be in danger. If you support the police and you want to be safe in your home and you want your children safe, support Donald Trump," observes the fifth. The us-versus-them framing, reinforced by the White men with badges, is inescapable. At the same time, the shadowy, distanced images of the looters invite the audience to fill in any stereotypic assumptions it might have about their race.

The association between Democrats and urban violence in "their cities" was made explicit in a Trump-Pence YouTube ad.[80] Framed by an opening caption reading "Joe and Kamala Lie to Protect the Radical Leftist Mob," assertions by Harris, Biden, their supporters, and a *New York Times* reporter that the protests were peaceful were contradicted by images showing instances in which they were not. Dissonant, anxiety-inflected music and successive scenes of burning buildings and looting increased the likelihood that those images would remain cognitively accessible to viewers and hence their typicality overestimated.[81] "Democrats have ruined their cities," declared the text on the screen at the ad's conclusion. "Don't let them Destroy America."

During the 2020 campaign, Trump explicitly asserted a causal link between what he cast as leftist indoctrination in the schools and the clashes between police and BLM protesters. In remarks at his September 2020 conference on American history, he said: "Far-left demonstrators have chanted the words 'America was never great.' The left has launched a vicious and violent assault on law enforcement—the universal symbol of the rule of law in America. These radicals have been aided and abetted by liberal politicians, establishment media, and even large corporations."[82] The lens of status threat focuses perception on the belief that certain groups—ones favored by the political elites and the media—can engage in vandalism and looting and not be called out or punished for it. Along the same lines, the incumbent argued "the left-wing rioting and mayhem are the direct result of decades of left-wing indoctrination in our schools."[83] This set up a sense that broader sociocultural forces were actively working to change America and, in so doing, disrupt the existing social hierarchy. "This election will decide whether we will defend the American way of life, or whether we allow a radical movement to completely dismantle and destroy it," declared Trump in his acceptance address at the 2020 Republican National Convention. "At the Democrat National Convention, Joe Biden and his party repeatedly assailed America as a land of racial, economic, and social injustice. So tonight, I ask you a very simple question: How can the Democrat Party ask to lead our country when it spends so much time tearing down our country?"[84]

Of course, against this backdrop, Trump also worked to appeal to voters of color. These efforts included a Black Voices for Trump initiative[85] and urban radio ads reminding voters that Trump had increased funding for HBCUs, supported prison reform, and presided over an economy that delivered a historically low rate of Black unemployment.[86] In their addresses at the Republican convention, neurosurgeon Ben Carson, whom Trump had appointed to run the Department of Housing and Urban Development (HUD), and South Carolina Senator Tim Scott (R-SC) celebrated the economic successes of the Trump administration. The NFL's Herschel Walker recalled that Trump joined Walker's family for a trip to Disney World, evidence for him that Trump could not be a racist. In both ads and a convention speech, Alice Johnson, a Black woman who was granted clemency by Trump in 2018, praised Trump for his compassion. In a similar vein, exercising the powers of the presidency during his 2020 convention, Trump issued a pardon on-air to Jon Ponder, a Black man who leads an effort to reintegrate prisoners into society. Ponder had served a five-year prison sentence for robbery. But this outreach, while substantive, did not induce status threat. Easing prison sentences and aiding HBCUs posed no direct threat to the relative status of White Americans. The retired neurosurgeon's role as the only Black member of the Cabinet was similarly nonthreatening precisely because he oversaw HUD, the "urban" cabinet slot more likely than the others to be held by a person of color in the past.

In contrast, the Biden-Harris ticket signaled the reality of demographic and cultural change as surely as had the presidency of the person who both selected Biden as his vice presidential partner and championed the Delawarean's election in 2020. As conservative media hosts such as Tucker Carlson were fond of reminding voters, Biden was on the record stating that he considered it "a source of our strength" that from 2017 onward fewer than 50 percent of those in America would be of "white European stock."[87] Biden's comfort with that transition in national identity was evident in his selection of a history-making vice presidential nominee. As a biracial Asian American woman, former California Senator Kamala Harris incarnated, as had Barack Obama, the multicultural, multiracial identity of the nation. Of particular note is that of the five presidential contests selecting leaders for the twenty-first century, the three won by the Democrats have all had a Black candidate on the ticket. Given these stark contrasts, status threat was likely to be at work in 2020.

Who Experiences Status Threat?

While the concept of status threat is relatively straightforward, measuring it is not. Simply asking White Christian men (or even White people more generally) if they think they are losing their privileged sociopolitical position is unlikely to yield many useful answers. For this reason, most studies rely on proxy measures, such as social dominance orientation,[88] which is whether someone thinks hierarchy among social groups is normal and natural.[89] We take a different approach by instead measuring a key implication of status threat: that people perceive discrimination against dominant groups.[90] Asserting that such groups now face discrimination becomes a way for group members to reassert the group's position (i.e., "if we have lost power, it is because people are biased against us"). In wave 2 (June 2020), we asked respondents how much discrimination there was against men, against White people, and against Christians, and then took the average of these three to measure status threat (Cronbach's α = 0.72). The more people perceived discrimination against these dominant groups, the higher their levels of status threat.

This measure of status threat overlaps with our racial attitudes measure reported in Chapter 7. Since status threat does indeed play a role in Americans' interpretations of race, if we are to account for its unique impact, we need to disentangle key components of our racial attitudes measure from our status threat ones. Consistent with earlier scholarship, we find that the status threat measure is only modestly correlated with racial animus.[91] The correlation between our racial attitude measure and this discrimination measure is 0.51: the two are linked but not identical. But since a conceptual overlap exists, it is important to consider how perceived discrimination against historically privileged groups differs from perceptions of discrimination against historically disadvantaged ones.[‡] This chapter tries to disentangle these factors.[§] That said, because these factors are interrelated, when we consider the effect of status threat, we control for perceived discrimination against minority groups, conservative media action tendencies, and various demographic factors. To be clear, as we reiterate in the following pages, these effects are correlational, not causal.

---

‡. Perceived discrimination against minority groups includes five items asking about discrimination against "black people," "women," "gays and lesbians," "Muslims," and "immigrants." These items were also recoded to range from 0 to 1 and averaged together (Cronbach's α = 0.88).

§. These two factors (status threat and perceived discrimination against minority groups) collectively account for the bulk of our racial attitudes measure (r^2 = 0.74) but are only loosely negatively related to each other (r = −0.19).

Before we examine how status threat relates to key outcomes, however, it is important to understand who felt this sense of reverse discrimination. As Figure 8.1 shows, perceptions of discrimination against privileged groups were far more common among unwavering Trump supporters than in other groups. Similarly, strong Republicans were much more likely than others to assert that there was at least a moderate amount of discrimination against White people, Christians, and men. Biden supporters and Democrats were unlikely to think that there was considerable discrimination against these groups. This pattern was largely reversed for discrimination against minority groups, where Biden supporters and Democrats were far more likely to report that these groups were subjected to discrimination.

When we predict these measures of perceived discrimination as a function of demographics, electorate, partisanship, and conservative media use, a few consistent patterns emerge (Figure 8.2). Individuals who perceive greater discrimination against all three majority groups tend to be members of one or more of those groups, have lower overall incomes, are less educated, are less likely to be members of Biden-supporting electorates or Democrats, and are more likely to be exposed to conservative media (though how they approach those media is less of a factor).** Further, when we control for these variables, the relationship between perceived discrimination against minorities and perceived discrimination against majorities was actually positive, indicating that to endorse one did not necessarily imply rejecting the other (i.e., some people perceived discrimination against both groups).††

Status Threat and Electoral Choice

Next, we examined whether status threat, and the belief that it was majority groups that were facing discrimination, affected vote preferences. In Figure 8.3, we predict vote choice as a function of demographics, partisanship, presidential approval, economic indicators, and our measures of both perceived discrimination and status threat, while controlling for these other important electoral predictors.

**. In addition, we found that individuals who were White, male, or Christian and who rated their Whiteness, masculinity, or Christianity as important to them (measured in wave 4) were much more likely to perceive discrimination against these same groups.

††. It should be noted, however, that both were measured on the same scale, meaning that response style effects could partially explain the residual positive relationship.

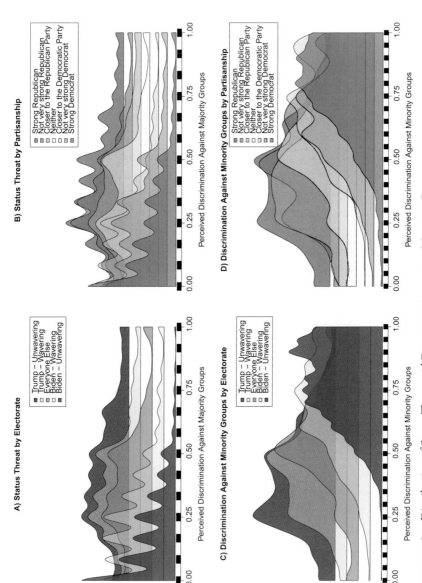

FIGURE 8.1 Distribution of Status Threat and Discrimination against Minority Groups. The panels show the distribution of status threat (top row) and discrimination against minority groups (bottom row), by electorate (left-hand column) and partisanship (right-hand column).

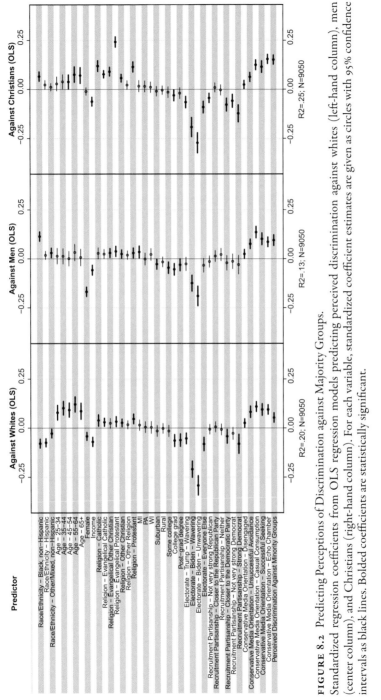

FIGURE 8.2 Predicting Perceptions of Discrimination against Majority Groups.
Standardized regression coefficients from OLS regression models predicting perceived discrimination against whites (left-hand column), men (center column), and Christians (right-hand column). For each variable, standardized coefficient estimates are given as circles with 95% confidence intervals as black lines. Bolded coefficients are statistically significant.

The results in Figure 8.3 show that both status threat and perceived discrimination against minorities are uniquely related to electoral choices. Individuals who believed that there was more discrimination against White people, Christians, and men were more likely to vote for Trump, less likely to vote for Biden, and slightly more likely not to vote than those who thought discrimination against majority groups (so-called reverse discrimination) was less prevalent. Those who perceived discrimination against minorities, in contrast, were less likely to vote for Trump and more likely to choose Biden. Hence, it appears that status threat and perceived discrimination were distinct and important parts of voters' assessments.

In comparing the results from Figure 8.3 with the models predicting voting outcomes using the overall racial attitude scale (Figure 7.3), we find that the two types of discrimination we disaggregate in this chapter account for the same variance that was accounted for by the overall racial attitude scale.[‡‡] In other words, collectively, status threat and perceived discrimination appear to be doing the same work as racial attitudes more generally. This result, along with evidence that the separate measures closely predict the overall racial attitude scale, indicates that while status threat and perceived discrimination are *theoretically* distinct from racial attitudes, in the minds of our respondents these distinctions were not present. With race constituting such a key component of American status, this finding may be unsurprising. As we examine whether status threat operates in the manner we theorize, it is important to keep this conflation in mind.

But this analysis, by itself, shortchanges the ways in which status threat mattered in some voters' decisions. Perhaps it is not simply that status threat is correlated with vote choice, but that status threat and perceptions of discrimination against minorities may be associated with changes in candidate support over time. We test for this in Figure 8.4, where we regress both status threat and perceived discrimination against minorities, interacted with initial preferences, on Election Day choices. The results show how each of these measures, holding the other constant (at its mean), was related to changes from initial intentions to eventual vote decisions over time.

---

‡‡. This can be ascertained by comparing the pseudo-R^2 values for these two sets of regressions. Because all three measures (overall racial attitudes, perceived discrimination against minorities, and status threat) were highly multicollinear, we do not present results with all three at the same time. Notably, however, models including all three can be compared in their goodness of fit to ascertain whether the same variance is being explained by both sets of measures or the variance explained is distinct. The results suggest that the same variance is explained in both regression models, as a model with all measures yields nearly identical total explained variance.

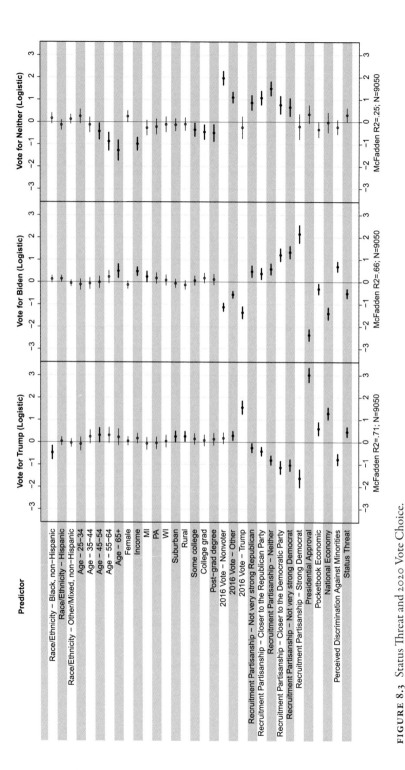

FIGURE 8.3 Status Threat and 2020 Vote Choice.

Standardized regression coefficients from logistic regressions predicting voting for Trump (left-hand column), Biden (center), or neither (right-hand). For each variable, standardized coefficient estimates are given as circles with 95% confidence intervals as black lines. Bolded coefficients are statistically significant.

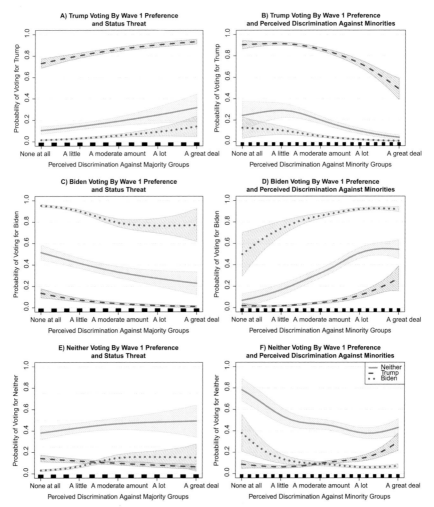

FIGURE 8.4 Status Threat, Discrimination against Minority Groups and Vote Choice. Each panel provides the predicted probability of voting for Trump (top row), Biden (middle row), or neither (bottom row) as a function of perceived discrimination, wave 1 candidate support, and their interaction. In the left-hand column, we use status threat (discrimination against majority groups); and in the right-hand column, we use perceived discrimination against minority groups. In each panel, the effects are shown separately for those who supported Trump (dashed red line), Biden (dotted blue line), or neither (solid green line) in wave 1. Panels in each row were produced using a single regression with both sets of interactions, estimates for status threat reflect marginal effects when perceived discrimination against minority groups is at its mean, and estimates for perceived discrimination against minority groups reflect marginal effects when status threat is at its mean.

Figure 8.4 shows that status threat and perceived discrimination against minorities do indeed operate independently in shaping voters' decisions during the election campaign. The two graphs for each outcome show how the likelihood of each voting choice depends on the interaction of those outcomes and initial preferences. Individuals at the highest levels of status threat were virtually certain to stick with Trump if they preferred him in wave 1 (April–May 2020), whereas those who did not perceive discrimination against White people, Christians, and men were moderately likely to abandon Trump (Figure 8.4, panel A). The reverse was true for those who initially preferred Biden (Figure 8.4, panel C). Likewise, the effects of perceived discrimination against minorities operate in a parallel but even more pronounced fashion (see panels B and D). In other words, we cannot tell the story of 2020 without accounting for perceived discrimination against both majority and minority groups.

Status Threat and Voter Settling

Although racial attitudes became prominent in the election at the beginning of the summer's protests, messages cueing status threat tended to emerge later in the cycle. For example, President Trump's 1776 Commission was launched in September 2020. The kinds of ads highlighting status threat we discussed earlier in the chapter also aired throughout the fall campaign. If status threat played a distinctive role in shaping the 2020 election, we might then expect the voters who most experienced it to have settled on a Trump vote at a somewhat later time than the voters whose decisions were shaped by concerns about discrimination against minorities. To assess this, Figure 8.5 shows when wavering Trump and Biden voters each settled into their choices as a function of their perceptions about whether there was more discrimination against minority groups, more discrimination against majority groups, or equal levels of discrimination against both.

Figure 8.5 shows that wavering voters who believed that majority groups experienced more discrimination than minority ones did tend to settle on Trump earlier than those who reported equivalent levels of discrimination or believed that there was more discrimination against minority group members. This is consistent with the conclusion that these perceptions of discrimination functioned as a factor in their choices. But it is instructive to note that the divergence between those perceiving more discrimination against majority groups and those who reported observing equal levels against majority and minority ones did not appear until mid-August. In contrast, among

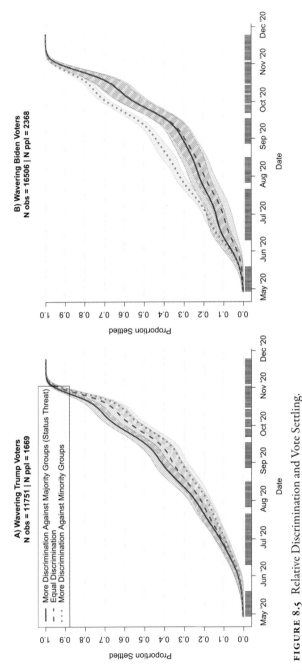

FIGURE 8.5 Relative Discrimination and Vote Settling.
Each panel provides the proportion of wavering voters who had settled on their choice, based on whether they thought that majority groups faced more discrimination than minority groups (solid red line), less discrimination (dashed blue line), or equal amounts of discrimination (dotted green line). Wavering Trump voters are shown in the left-hand panel, wavering Biden voters are shown in the right-hand one.

Biden voters, we see that those who perceived greater discrimination against minority groups were more likely to settle on Biden by wave 2 (June 2020), shortly after the summer's Black Lives Matter protests began. Here we see some evidence that while both types of perceptions largely have the same effects on vote choice overall, the timing of these decisions indicates that status threat and perceptions of discrimination against minority groups were responsive to somewhat different forces, a conclusion consistent with our argument above.

Did Status Threat and Perceptions of Discrimination Affect Each Other over Time?

To this point we have measured both racial attitudes and status threat using the items from wave 2 (June 2020) of our study. But recognizing that the racially charged protests of the summer plus the election and its aftermath could have changed these attitudes, we reasked our questions about perceived prejudice against Black and White people, as well as against men and women, near the close of our study in wave 10 (January–February 2021). How much, if at all, and among whom, if any, did these perceptions change over time?

Take first the question of overall over-time change. Among those individuals who answered the questions at both points, 55.7 percent provided answers suggesting Black people suffered more discrimination than White people in wave 2 (June 2020) compared to 16.6 percent whose answers indicated that White people suffered more discrimination than Black people. The corresponding numbers eight months later were 52.5 percent and 18.3 percent, reflecting a significant increase in White status threat as compared to perceptions of anti-Black discrimination ($p < .001$). The differences between perceptions of discrimination against White people and Black people at the two time points were correlated at 0.72. These numbers both reflect the widespread scholarly sense that racial attitudes are fairly stable[92] and confirm that highly salient attitudes may be subject to some change, as others have more recently argued.[93]

These shifts in relative attitudes were again accompanied by changes in perceptions of discrimination against both groups. In the post-election period, individuals were somewhat more likely to perceive discrimination against White people and less likely to perceive discrimination against Black people than they had been in June, a time just after the murder of George Floyd. Intriguingly, however, these changes in perceptions were not inversely related to each other. Specifically, people who perceived additional discrimination against White people in wave 10 (relative to wave 2) were not the same individuals who reported less discrimination against Black people. Instead, these shifts were slightly positively correlated ($r = 0.11$), indicating that assessments of discrimination were more likely to trend together than not. This provides further evidence that status threat and perceptions of discrimination against minority groups may have been operating at least somewhat independently.

But given the numerous racially charged events of 2020, it may be the case that different groups of respondents moved in opposite directions. For those who were high in status threat at wave 2 (June 2020), perceptions of anti-minority prejudice may well be expected to *decrease* over time. Those individuals might see the treatment of Black Lives Matter protestors and that of January 6 protestors as exemplifying a double standard, reaffirming their belief that many racial and ethnic minorities are more politically powerful than their White counterparts. In contrast, those who perceived low discrimination against majority groups may have seen the Black Lives Matter protests as a stark reminder of the nation's shameful heritage of slavery and its continued relevance today. In short, aggregate stability may mask considerable heterogeneity.

To the extent that perceptions of discrimination did shift over time, we find that these shifts reflected three underlying forces in contemporary American politics. Figure 8.6 shows the results of a regression predicting levels of perceived discrimination in wave 10 (against White people, men, Black people, and women) as a function of lagged dependent variables from wave 2, demographics, partisanship, voting patterns, media orientations, and both the discrimination against minorities and status threat measures.

The results in Figure 8.6 show that across-time changes in perceptions of discrimination against both White people and men increasingly mirror the generalized sense of threat to those in dominant groups, while changes in perceived discrimination against Black people and women reflect more general perceptions of discrimination against those in minority groups. That is, both status threat and perceived discrimination against minorities appear to increasingly consolidate over time. Further evidence of this pattern emerges from the fact that assessments of discrimination against White people and against Black people, and of discrimination against men and against women, themselves became much more closely related over time. Analyzing the 8,140 individuals who completed both waves, the correlation between these difference scores increased from 0.54 in wave 2 (June 2020) to 0.65 in wave 10

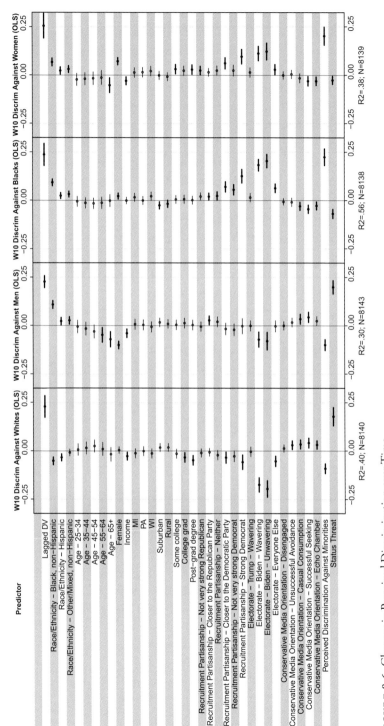

FIGURE 8.6 Changes in Perceived Discrimination over Time.
Standardized regression coefficients from OLS regressions predicting wave 10 perceptions of discrimination against whites (far left), men (middle-left), Blacks (middle-right), and women (far right), controlling for wave 2 measures of the dependent variable. For each variable, standardized coefficient estimates are given as circles with 95% confidence intervals as black lines. Bolded coefficients are statistically significant.

(January–February 2021). The regression results in Figure 8.6 indicate that this increasing correspondence is not simply a function of partisanship or conservative media use, even though these factors are themselves related to changes over time.

Collectively, these results indicate the extent to which perceptions of discrimination feed one another. While these two components of perceived discrimination were only modestly negatively correlated, as we saw earlier in the chapter, they reinforced each other.§§ When someone adopts a status threat perspective, they of course interpret events through that lens. As a result, the dominant group's sense that it is threatened may be heightened by efforts to highlight discrimination faced by minority groups. Alternatively, those without a status threat perspective see events such as the murder of George Floyd as confirmation that those in minority groups are victimized. Where you start shapes where you end up.

Just as we see sorting by the electorates—with Trump supporters tending to see lesser amounts of traditional discrimination over time and Biden supporters seeing more—consistent with earlier studies, we find partisan sorting on racial attitudes and status threat.[94] Few would doubt that race was a significant dividing line pre-2020, but our data illustrate how it became an even deeper one during the tumultuous election year. In an increasingly multiracial, multicultural America, this tighter alignment between race and partisanship has important implications, especially in light of many of the findings we will present in Chapter 9.

Status Threat in a Multiracial Democracy

This chapter underscores the extent to which demographic changes bring with them political ones. As America diversifies demographically and Caucasians make up a smaller share of the American public, some in that demographic feel that their once-dominant group—White Christian men—is no longer afforded the prerogatives that they assume were their birthright. While their absolute levels of privilege may not have changed, they sense that their relative privilege has shifted as other groups have gained social and political power.

---

§§. And the correlations between measures became more strongly negative over time as well. The discrimination against White people and discrimination against Black people items correlated at −0.29 in wave 2 (June 2020) and −0.36 in wave 10 (January–February 2021). Similarly, the corresponding items for gender become slightly more strongly correlated over time, going from a correlation of −0.02 in wave 2 to −0.04 in wave 10.

We show here that status threat is correlated with, but distinct from, other components of racial attitudes. Both factors shape vote choice. In Chapter 9, we show that these same attitudes predict beliefs about voter fraud, electoral legitimacy, and the justifiability of the events of January 6. Because the racial justice and policing crisis in 2020 centered on the role of race in American history, we focused our attention primarily on the role of race in status threat. As our results suggest, this is a key part of the story. But status threat is not just about race; it also encompasses gender and religion.[95] Future work should do more to unpack these effects.

For some Americans, Biden's victory was a triumph over a president with autocratic tendencies and an affirmation that America was a nation of many peoples. For some Trump supporters, it was a reaffirmation that America was changing and that people like them were no longer at the center of the American story. For some in this latter group, fear of loss legitimated violence, a finding with some very dark consequences that we explore in our final empirical chapter.

9.1

"Stop the Steal"

THE RHETORIC OF ELECTORAL DELEGITIMACY

Kathleen Hall Jamieson, Matthew Levendusky, and Josh Pasek

> *He [Joe Biden] only won in the eyes of the FAKE NEWS MEDIA. I concede NOTHING! We have a long way to go. This was a RIGGED ELECTION!*
>
> —Donald Trump, in a tweet the day after Election Day, 2020[1]

> *"I don't f---ing care that they have weapons. They're not here to hurt me. Take the f---ing mags [magnetometers] away."*
>
> —Donald Trump, to aides, instructing them to remove the magnetometers to increase crowd access to his January 6, 2021, speech at the Ellipse, according to Cassidy Hutchinson, senior aide to White House chief of staff Mark Meadows.[2]

ON SEPTEMBER 24, 2020, the US Senate visibly and powerfully buttressed democratic norms by unanimously passing Senate Resolution 718. Authored by West Virginia Senator Joe Manchin (D-WV), the resolution reaffirmed "the Senate's commitment to the orderly and peaceful transfer of power called for in the Constitution of the United States." At the same time, it reiterated the principles on which a democratic system is predicated:

> Whereas the United States is founded on the principle that our Government derives its power from the consent of the governed and that the people have the right to change their elected leaders through elections;
>
> Whereas our domestic tranquility, national security, general welfare, and civil liberties depend upon the peaceful and orderly transfer of power; and

Whereas any disruption occasioned by the transfer of the executive power could produce results detrimental to the safety and well-
being of the United States and its people:

Its resolution clauses made two affirmations that would be
threatened by the post-election conduct of the 45th president:

Now, therefore, be it Resolved, That the Senate—

(1) reaffirms its commitment to the orderly and peaceful transfer
of power called for in the Constitution of the United States; and
(2) intends that there should be no disruptions by the President or
any person in power to overturn the will of the people of the United
States.[3]

That same day, Senate majority leader Mitch McConnell tweeted, "The
winner of the November 3rd election will be inaugurated on January 20th.
There will be an orderly transition just as there has been every four years since
1792."[4] Sadly, McConnell's prediction proved to be inaccurate. Although the
winner was inaugurated, the transition was anything but orderly.

Neither S.R. 718 nor McConnell's tweet mentioned President Donald
Trump by name, but he, of course, was the subject of and intended audience
for both messages. Both the resolution and the statement by the Senate majority leader were reacting to words spoken by the nation's forty-fifth president the evening before. When asked at a White House press conference
whether he would leave the White House peacefully were he to lose the election, Trump had responded, "Well, we're going to have to see what happens.
You know that." Nor, when pressed, would he commit to a peaceful transfer
of power. "We want to have—get rid of the ballots and you'll have a very
peaceful, there won't be a transfer, frankly," Trump stated, adding, "There'll
be a continuation."[5]

Trump's failure to commit to that peaceful transfer of power and his
efforts to delegitimize the election by claiming that Biden's victory was due
to fraud sit at the heart of our fourth and final crisis. What initially was an
unprecedented electoral crisis—an incumbent president saying the election
would be stolen from him, without offering any credible evidence to support
that claim—became a broader crisis of democratic legitimacy as Trump and
his supporters cast doubt on Biden's legitimacy and seemed to sanction violence as a means of resolving conflicts on January 6.

In the first part of this chapter we explain how Trump and his allies
attempted to delegitimize the 2020 presidential election, and in the second
we examine the effects of their delegitimizing rhetoric and actions. After

highlighting Trump's 2020 claims that his opponents were rigging the 2016 election, we will note a few of the conspiracy theories that buttressed his false claims of a stolen 2020 election, explain how the rhetoric of electoral illegitimacy played up concerns about race and status threat, and show how, for some, these assertions expanded to include ones approving of violence to preserve their American way of life. The chapter's second part explains how this rhetoric affected our respondents' attitudes not only about the election but also about Biden's victory.

The Debate over the Legitimacy of the 2020 Election Outcome

Trump's norm-shattering rhetoric was unprecedented for an incumbent, but not for him. During the 2016 election, he made claims directly foreshadowing those in 2020. As we noted in an earlier chapter, in the final 2016 Trump-Clinton debate, moderator Chris Wallace asked Trump if he would accept the result of the election even if he lost. The Republican nominee responded, "I will look at it at the time. I'm not looking at anything now. I'll look at it at the time." When pressed by Wallace to state whether he would respect the election outcome, Trump said, "What I'm saying is that I will tell you at the time. I'll keep you in suspense. OK?"[6] Likewise, during the 2016 election, he argued that Democrats committed vote fraud: "I won the popular vote if you deduct the millions of people who voted illegally."[7] Those invocations also presaged his claims in 2020.

As an internal memo disclosed as part of a defamation suit later confirmed, Trump's own campaign knew that many of their outlandish claims about election theft were inaccurate.[8] Nor was there evidence to support the specific allegation that large numbers of votes had been illegally cast or incorrectly counted.[9] Nonetheless, the incumbent repeatedly advanced conspiracy-based claims that Biden's win was fraudulently secured. Throughout the 2020 contest, the incumbent alleged that Joe Biden's allies would use mail-in voting—greatly expanded in 2020 due to the pandemic—to carry out large-scale voter fraud. In the first debate on September 29, the forty-fifth president claimed, "They're sending millions of ballots all over the country. There's fraud. They found them in creeks. They found some, just happened to have the name Trump just the other day in a wastepaper basket. They're being sent all over the place. They sent two in a Democrat area. They sent out a thousand ballots. Everybody got two ballots. This is going to be a fraud like you've never seen."[10]

This rhetoric, which continued throughout the fall election, came to a head on Election Day. By late that evening, it was clear that Biden would win the national popular vote once all the ballots were counted. But whether he would win the Electoral College as well was unclear. While Trump was ahead in key states such as Pennsylvania and Georgia, this was due, at least in part, to which ballots had already been counted. As we saw in Chapter 3 ("Not One Electorate, But Many"), Republicans were more likely to vote in person, while Democrats tended to do so by mail. Because mail ballots take longer to process, many of the vote totals on election night reflected in-person voting and hence were skewed toward Trump. Experts anticipated that Trump would take an early lead, but that the outcome would likely be decided late in the process when tallying of the mail-in ballots had been largely completed.[11]

Nonetheless, with the count incomplete but after polling places had closed, at 2:00 AM on November 4, the president told supporters gathered in the White House, "We did win this election."[12] That claim was false. As states counted their mail-in ballots, it became clear that the Biden-Harris ticket would assemble an Electoral College majority. On Saturday, November 7— four days after Election Day—the major news networks and the Associated Press projected that Joe Biden would become the forty-sixth president.

However, as the incumbent saw it, the outcome was anything but final. "The simple fact is this election is far from over," Trump stated. "Joe Biden has not been certified as the winner of any states, let alone any of the highly contested states headed for mandatory recounts, or states where our campaign has valid and legitimate legal challenges that could determine the ultimate victor."[13] In the days and weeks that followed, Trump launched a series of lawsuits seeking to overturn the outcome in such key states as Arizona, Pennsylvania, Georgia, and Wisconsin. He would lose all but one of the more than sixty lawsuits they filed, and even that one exceptional ruling would later be overturned by the Pennsylvania supreme court.[14]

Many of these court decisions included sharp rebukes by Republican-nominated judges. "Free, fair elections are the lifeblood of our democracy. Charges of unfairness are serious. But calling an election unfair does not make it so. . . . Charges require specific allegations and then proof. We have neither here," wrote Judge Stephanos Bibas, a Trump nominee, on behalf of a panel of the Third Circuit Court of Appeals.[15] Similarly, in his ruling on November 21, Judge Matthew Brann, a Republican, dismissed President Trump's efforts to overturn the election results in Pennsylvania, noting:

In this action, the Trump Campaign and the Individual Plaintiffs (collectively, the "Plaintiffs") seek to discard millions of votes legally cast by Pennsylvanians from all corners—from Greene County to Pike County, and everywhere in between. In other words, Plaintiffs ask this Court to disenfranchise almost seven million voters. This Court has been unable to find any case in which a plaintiff has sought such a drastic remedy in the contest of an election, in terms of the sheer volume of votes asked to be invalidated. One might expect that when seeking such a startling outcome, a plaintiff would come formidably armed with compelling legal arguments and factual proof of rampant corruption, such that this Court would have no option but to regrettably grant the proposed injunctive relief despite the impact it would have on such a large group of citizens.

That has not happened. Instead, this Court has been presented with strained legal arguments without merit and speculative accusations, unpled in the operative complaint and unsupported by evidence. In the United States of America, this cannot justify the disenfranchisement of a single voter, let alone all the voters of its sixth most populated state. Our people, laws, and institutions demand more.[16]

Not only did the courts reject the Trump campaign's claims, but so too did other agencies in the US government. As we noted in earlier chapters, the Cybersecurity and Infrastructure Security Agency, in its post-election review, said that the 2020 US election was "the most secure in American history," and it found no evidence of election tampering or improprieties.[17] Days after this announcement, Trump fired Chris Krebs, the agency's director.[18] Consistent with scholarship involving earlier elections that found little meaningful voter fraud,[19] a post-election review in which the *New York Times* contacted election officials in every state located no evidence of a level of fraud that could have affected the outcome.[20] Nor did Attorney General William Barr, or post-election investigations by the states,[21] or academic studies of the election.[22] The few cases of voter fraud that were identified did little to bolster the Trump case. One, for example, was perpetrated by a Pennsylvania Republican who, after voting for President Trump using his dead mother's ballot, argued that after listening to "too much propaganda," he had taken it upon himself to counteract presumed Democratic fraud.[23]

A Conspiracy Theory Emerges, but Government Officials Push Back

To accept the claim that the 2020 election was illegitimate and tainted by significant voter fraud required more than disappointment about the election results. To affect a fraudulent outcome, shadowy figures would have needed to infiltrate the nation's highly decentralized voting process not just in one or two places but in many. Moreover, the states in which these machinations would be needed would have to have been known in advance. And since down-ballot Republicans in key states outpolled Trump, these masters of deception would have had to alter only the presidential column and not the vote tallies in other races. Not only that, but their fraud would have had to have gone undetected by state and local election officials from both parties and the many judges who would eventually rule on these cases. Manipulation of this sort would require a conspiracy on a grand scale.

Nonetheless, Trump's lawyers and backers alleged that that is what occurred. On November 7, Rudy Giuliani called a press conference in front of the garage door of Four Seasons Total Landscaping in northeast Philadelphia to outline the Trump campaign's case. The former New York mayor asserted that the count in Pennsylvania and other states was marred by widespread voter fraud, consisting of hundreds of thousands of mail-in ballots manipulated and counted in exactly the places necessary to overturn the result:

> I wanted to give you a flavor of it here in Philadelphia, but we also have to alert the people of Pittsburgh that the same fraud was done to them as here. And I'll also add, the same thing was done in Georgia, the same thing was done in Michigan, the same thing was done in North Carolina; it seems to me somebody from the Democratic National Committee sent out a little note that said "Don't let the Republicans look at those mail-in ballots, at least not in the big Democratic hack cities that we control. We've done a lot to destroy those cities, and now we are going to destroy their right to vote."[24]

As evidence of shenanigans involving vote-counting proved elusive (and was summarily dismissed by the courts), Trump doubled down. On November 12, according to the news aggregation service NewsWhip, the Facebook and Twitter posts with the highest level of engagement were ones in which the incumbent adopted a set of claims from the broadcaster Chanel Rion of the very conservative One America News Network. For example, Trump tweeted this:

"REPORT: DOMINION DELETED 2.7 MILLION TRUMP VOTES NATIONWIDE. DATA ANALYSIS FINDS 221,000 PENNSYLVANIA VOTES SWITCHED FROM PRESIDENT TRUMP TO BIDEN. 941,000 TRUMP VOTES DELETED. STATES USING DOMINION VOTING SYSTEMS SWITCHED 435,000 VOTES FROM TRUMP TO BIDEN." @ChanelRion @ OANN[25]

Not only did Facebook and Twitter flag those claims as false, but Dominion Voting Systems sued some who promulgated them, including OANN and Trump campaign lawyer Sidney Powell.[26]

Another Trump proponent, MyPillow CEO Mike Lindell, claimed that Trump's loss resulted from the "biggest cyber-crime in world history." But election officials in more than a dozen of the counties Lindell pinpointed confirmed instead that "their voting machines are not connected to the Internet, that the results are confirmed by paper ballots, and in some cases that official audits, recounts, or reviews have verified their vote tallies."[27] Ironically, the heightened forms of cyber protection and paper ballot backups cited by these officials were more widespread in 2020 than in 2016 because in the intervening years state and local officials[28] worked diligently to prevent the sorts of intrusions into the electoral infrastructure carried out by Russian hackers in 2016.[29]

Responding to such past threats, Congress had passed and Trump signed into law the Cybersecurity and Infrastructure Security Agency Act of 2018, which created the agency by that name.[30] As we noted a moment ago, not only did CISA confirm the integrity of the election and debunk election-related misinformation, but CISA head Chris Krebs also dismissed the conspiracy theory that the election had been stolen by CIA supercomputers named Hammer and Scorecard. "Seeing #disinfo that some isolated voting day issues are tied to some nefarious election hacking and vote manipulation operation," Krebs noted." Don't fall for it and think twice before sharing!"[31] "To be crystal clear . . . , I'm specifically referring to the Hammer and Scorecard nonsense. It's just that—nonsense," he added.[32] The theory at issue alleged that a CIA computer program named Hammer "cracks into protected networks, while another, called Scorecard, changes vote totals." Like a number of influential conspiracy theories about the pandemic,[33] this one assumes the existence of dozens of anti-Trump partisans engaged in intrigue against him from within the government.

Importantly, several key Republican officials were among those standing up to President Trump and his associates' claims of electoral intrigue. Not only did Attorney General Bill Barr tell the press that the Justice Department had not found evidence of significant voter fraud, but in his resignation letter he wrote, "At a time when the country is so deeply divided, it is incumbent on all levels of government, and all agencies acting within their purview, to do all we can to assure the integrity of elections and promote public confidence in their outcome,"[34] a tacit critique of the president's firing of Krebs and of his attempts to pressure state-level election officials as well as his ongoing assertions that the election had been illegitimately decided. Barr was not alone in ensuring that Trump heard such statements from Republicans. When the incumbent pressured Georgia secretary of state Brad Raffensperger to "find" the 11,780 votes Trump needed to win that state, the Georgian told the president, "Well, Mr. President, the challenge that you have is the data you have is wrong. We have to stand by our numbers. We believe our numbers are right."[35]

Forestalling Use of the Military to Retain Power

Even after the Electoral College voted in favor of the Biden-Harris ticket on December 14, Trump and his allies continued to press their case. In response to all of this, General Mark A. Milley, chairman of the Joint Chiefs of Staff, privately reiterated his determination to thwart any effort by Trump to use the military to retain the presidency. "They may try, but they're not going to f—— succeed," Milley told his deputies as Trump continued to try to overturn the results of the election, according to *Washington Post* reporters Carol Leonnig and Philip Rucker. "You can't do this without the military. You can't do this without the CIA and the FBI. We're the guys with the guns."[36] The importance of Milley's resolve became even more apparent when investigations of January 6 revealed the extent to which those with military training were involved with the storming of the Capitol. According to the Program on Extremism at George Washington University, "At least 87 [of the 723 individuals against whom federal cases involving January 6 were lodged] (12%) have military experience (79 Veterans, 2 National Guard, 4 Reserve, 1 Active Duty, 1 Attending Basic Training)."[37]

Also defending the democratic norm that says that the military has no role in electoral politics was a bipartisan group made up of the living former secretaries of defense. Any involvement of the military in resolving electoral questions would take the nation into "dangerous, unlawful and unconstitutional territory," the group warned in a January 3, 2021, op-ed in the *Washington Post*. As we discuss in Chapter 10 ("A Republic, if You Can Keep It"), this highlights how many officials—including election officials, elected officials, military officers, and others—worked not only to ensure a fair election but also to push back (after the election) on the Trump team's intrigues.

The Tragedy of January 6 as an Echo of Violence

Waking up on January 6, most Americans expected it to be an uneventful day. They thought that Trump's arguments about the stolen election had run their course, Biden's win would be certified, and they could put this all behind them and look forward to the inauguration on January 20. Instead, for some at least, January 6 now holds a place in the American psyche akin to 9/11. The simple mention of each evokes visceral reactions melded to iconic images: A plane flying into one of the twin towers. The towers collapsing into smoldering ruins. A makeshift noose and gallows being erected outside the Capitol. Rioters dragging a police officer down a flight of stairs. Another being beaten with a pole bearing an American flag. Insurrectionists waving the Confederate battle flag inside the Capitol.

At the "Save America" rally near the National Mall, President Donald Trump addressed throngs of cheering fans. In his roughly seventy-minute speech on the Mall, the defeated incumbent reiterated that he had won a landslide victory. In phrases that would then feature in his subsequent impeachment by the House, he added, "All of us here today do not want to see our election victory stolen by emboldened radical-left Democrats which is what they're doing and stolen by the fake news media," "We will stop the steal," "We fight like hell, and if you don't fight like hell you're not going to have a country anymore," and "We are going to the [US] Capitol."[38] When successfully defending him against conviction after his impeachment by the House, his Republican defenders would stress that he also said, "Peacefully and patriotically make your voices heard."[39] As a study by University of Chicago researchers documented, those who marched to the Capitol that afternoon thought that they were doing so at the incumbent's behest.[40] At issue in the impeachment was what the forty-fifth president of the United States expected them to do once they got there.

Responding to his appeals, his supporters raised their voices, showed strength, and fought like hell, storming the US Capitol and disrupting—though not preventing—the certification of Joe Biden as the forty-sixth president of the United States.* As we noted earlier, this marked only the second time that the US Capitol had been overrun in the nation's 245-year history, but this time it was American citizens—not British troops—who were ransacking its halls and chambers.

Had at least some of the rioters gotten their way, the day would have been even more tragic. Acting on a theory concocted by one of his lawyers, Trump in early January tweeted, "The Vice President has the power to reject fraudulently chosen electors."[41] According to this logic, Pence could reject the electoral slates from the battleground states that Trump was contesting and thus activate state and congressional decision-making that could ensure that Trump would remain president. Pence publicly rejected this argument, leading some in the mob to chant "Hang Mike Pence" as they ransacked the Capitol. Had rioters gotten to Pence, it is unclear what would have occurred. Likewise, had the marauders captured members of Congress—especially prominent Democratic ones, such as House Speaker Nancy Pelosi (D-CA)— no one knows what would have happened. Federal prosecutors would later report that one of the women arrested in connection with the US Capitol riot posted a "selfie" video on social media, saying, "We were looking for Nancy to shoot her in the friggin' brain but we didn't find her."[42] So not only had Trump falsely claimed the election was stolen from him and schemed to thwart the peaceful transfer of power, but some of his supporters engaged in violence in service of those ends and even contemplated murder.

---

*. One can debate the extent to which Trump is culpable for the riot at the Capitol (indeed, this was the heart of his second impeachment trial). For example, according to federal investigators, some extremist groups—such as the Proud Boys and the Oath Keepers—had coordinated in advance of January 6 and planned violence (Rachel Weiner, Spencer S. Hsu, and Tom Jackman, "Prosecutors Allege 'Alliance' Between Proud Boys and Oath Keepers on Jan. 6," *Washington Post*, March 24, 2021, https://www.washingtonpost.com/local/legal-issues/oath keepers-proudboys-alliance-capitol-riot/2021/03/24/81e93b48-8cb0-11eb-9423-04079921c91 5_story.html). Other actors also gave incendiary speeches that day, including Rudy Giuliani, who said a "trial by combat" should determine the election's outcome (Ryan Taylor, "Rudy Giuliani Speech Transcript at Trump's Washington, D.C. Rally: Wants 'Trial by Combat,'" Rev, January 6, 2021, https://www.rev.com/blog/transcripts/rudy-giuliani-speech-transcr ipt-at-trumps-washington-d-c-rally-wants-trial-by-combat.). Nevertheless, it seems likely that Trump's words, which included summoning his followers to the event at the Ellipse, did at least contribute to the mayhem at the Capitol. And it is clear that for an extended period he ignored the pleas of members of Congress, his own family, and Fox News hosts urging him to tell the rioters to stand down (Jose Pagliery and Justin Baragona, "Don Jr. and Fox Stars Begged Meadows: Get Trump to Stop Capitol Riot," *Daily Beast*, December 13, 2021, https://www.thedailybeast.com/donald-trump-jr-texted-mark-meadows-begging-his-dad-to-give-an-address-to-halt-jan-6-capitol-riot).

The events of January 6 change the issue from questions of electoral legitimacy to those of democratic legitimacy. They do so by challenging two norms that underlie democracy: first, that elections determine who holds power, and second, that political engagement, not violence, is how citizens and elected officials resolve their differences. Upending these norms undermines not just an election but the very foundations of the government, as it basically asserts that might makes right.

The Foreshadowing of the Violence of January 6

January 6 was a culminating act of disruption and violence. But it was not the first, or only, threat of violence in the 2020 election cycle, as we saw in earlier chapters: from the anti-lockdown protests, to the counterprotesters in Kenosha and elsewhere, to the Wolverine Watchmen and their plot to kidnap, try, and possibly execute Michigan governor Whitmer, the threat of violence threads through all of our crises. Actual violent acts occurred as well.

But there is an even deeper connection than that. Some of the factions that were present on January 6 have long histories of violence. Included among those storming the Capitol that day were individuals with white supremacist ideologies. The danger posed by this ideology was brought home tellingly in September 2020 when FBI director Christopher Wray told the House Homeland Security Committee, "'Racially motivated violent extremism,' mostly from white supremacists, has made up a majority of domestic terrorism threats."[43]

One such group is the Proud Boys, "self-described 'Western chauvinists' who adamantly deny any connection to the racist 'alt-right,'" notes the Southern Poverty Law Center. "They insist they are simply a fraternal group spreading an 'anti-political correctness' and 'anti-white guilt' agenda. The Proud Boys' actions belie their disavowals of bigotry: Rank-and-file Proud Boys and leaders regularly spout white nationalist memes and maintain affiliations with known extremists. They are known for anti-Muslim and misogynistic rhetoric."[44] This "Western chauvinist" group came to national attention during the first presidential debate. When moderator and Fox News anchor Chris Wallace asked Trump whether he would tell white supremacist groups to "stand down," Trump parried by asking Wallace to give him a name. Joe Biden interjected: "Proud Boys." "Proud Boys, stand back and stand by," Trump responded. "But I'll tell you what, somebody's got to do something about Antifa and the left, because this is not a right-wing problem. This is a left-wing problem."[45]

"Many people on social media who identify with the group echoed that language, saying they were 'standing down and standing by,'" reported NBC News. "One known social media account for the group made 'Stand back. Stand by' part of its new logo."[46] Of course, it was not just the Proud Boys but also other groups such as the Oath Keepers and Three Percenters whose members included those who stood by and then stormed the Capitol on January 6.[47]

Threats of Violence Against Elected Officials

The threat of violence also played out more specifically with respect to the election when Trump supporters threatened election officials. "The most turbulent and norm-breaking presidential election of a lifetime has led to an extraordinary spectacle in the United States over the past three days: armed protesters gathering nightly outside offices where workers are counting the votes that will decide who wins the White House," noted the Associated Press. "Some carry shotguns. Some have handguns. Often, they carry black, military-style semiautomatic rifles."[48] "Stop the steal," chanted some protesters, invoking the name and cause of a group that had helped organize the protests. "Arrest the poll workers," chanted others.[49] Responding to calls for violence posted by some of the members of the "Stop the Steal" group, Facebook banned it from the platform.[50] Before that November 5 ban, the "Stop the Steal" group had amassed 360,000 Facebook members.[51]

"Anticipating a crackdown," noted the *Washington Post*, "some of the group's members preemptively shifted their discussions to MeWe, a messaging app favored by militia groups that previously had been banned by Facebook."[52] Meanwhile, the home of Michigan secretary of state Jocelyn Benson was surrounded by armed Trump supporters accusing her of illegally throwing the election to Biden;[53] threats of violence were made against Wayne County, Michigan, election officials;[54] and election officials in Philadelphia received death threats.[55] One threat against Al Schmidt, a Republican city commissioner on the Philadelphia Board of Elections, included the names of his children, his home address, and a photo of the home along with the message, "Tell the truth or your three kids will be fatally shot."[56] In early December, Republican Gabriel Sterling, who supervised the implementation of Georgia's new voting system, said that Trump's disinformation about the election was "inspiring people to commit potential acts of violence" and warned that "someone is going to get hurt."[57]

Electoral Legitimacy and Multiracial Democracy

Not only did Trump and his allies argue that the election was illegitimate, but they did so with appeals linked to racial attitudes and concerns about status threat. Throughout the campaign, Trump argued that Democrats would use voter fraud to steal the election with the help of voters in big cities whose mayors were Democrats and whose populations were racially diverse. Post-election, social media posts also falsely claimed that 22 million undocumented immigrants voted illegally for Biden.[58] This spurious assertion echoes both Trump's 2016 allegation and the Great Replacement theory (promulgated by Tucker Carlson, among others) that Democrats rely on immigrants to try to ensure their victories, a fear appeal we highlighted in Chapter 8 ("A Deeper Anxiety").

Second, as we noted earlier, when Trump spoke about fraud, time and again he singled out cities whose populations are plurality, if not majority, Black, such as Atlanta, Milwaukee, Detroit, and most notably Philadelphia. In the September 29 debate, Trump famously claimed, "In Philadelphia, they went in to watch. They're called poll watchers, a very safe, very nice thing. They were thrown out. They weren't allowed to watch. You know why? Because bad things happen in Philadelphia."[59] Likewise, shortly after the election, Trump tweeted, "In Detroit, there were FAR MORE VOTES THAN PEOPLE. Nothing can be done to cure that giant scam. I win Michigan!"[60] Although Trump never explicitly linked Black Americans to voter fraud, both the symbolism of his campaign and the refrain of voter fraud in big cities employed the kinds of racial tropes that scholars have characterized as implicit racial appeals[61] and had the potential to induce anger, which in turn has been found to boost opposition to racial policies among White racial conservatives.[62]

Trump's disposition to associate fraudulent voting and the Black population persisted in the years following the 2020 election. Speaking to a rally in October 2021, he alleged, for example, that "Joe Biden lost with the African American population [compared] to former President, Barack Hussein Obama in every single State, other than the five swing States. In other words, the only States that were going to determine the election, although I think a lot of other States were corrupt also, but the only swing States, the swing States that determined, that's where Biden won with the African American population."[63]

While Trump singled out battleground cities with large populations of Black citizens when discussing voter fraud, there was a curious lack of attention to the much Whiter locales that helped Biden win these key states.

For example, in Pennsylvania, Trump never talked about fraud in the sub-urban Philadelphia counties, such as Montgomery, Delaware, and Chester, all of which swung sharply toward the Democratic nominee in 2020. Indeed, Trump actually got more votes in 2020 in Philadelphia than he did in 2016; it was shifts in the suburbs and smaller towns that put Biden over the top in that state. Likewise, other Democratic strongholds such as Ann Arbor, Michigan, and Madison, Wisconsin, did not draw Trump's ire to the extent that Detroit and Milwaukee did. This pattern makes the link between race and accusations of fraud hard to ignore.

The implication that Black Americans were engaged in illegal voting invites one of the oldest and most pernicious stereotypes in America: Black criminality.[64] If linking claims of fraud (a crime) and Blackness functions as a racial dog whistle, we would further expect to see that racial attitudes and status threat predict attitudes about the legitimacy of the outcome.

Republican arguments primed status threat not just via race but also through antisemitism and allegations about the subversive behavior of stealthy foreigners and immigrants. The "corrupt, stolen election" was a "left-wing power grab financed by people like George Soros, deeply laid in at the local level," alleged former Republican Speaker of the House Newt Gingrich.[65] Meanwhile, online posts suggested falsely that Soros had been arrested for voter fraud.[66] At the same time, Trump lawyers averred that "communist money" had been insinuated into the election and that those who perpetrated election fraud included not only Soros but also adherents of antifa as well as sinister foreign nationals in countries including Venezuela, Cuba, and China.[67] "The Dominion Voting Systems, the Smartmatic technology soft-ware, and the software that goes in other computerized voting systems here as well, not just Dominion, were created in Venezuela at the direction of Hugo Chavez," claimed Trump attorney Sidney Powell.[68] Chavez had died in 2013. Adding immigrants to the equation, the conservative website Just Facts Daily alleged that Biden was only able to win the Electoral College because noncitizens cast more than 200,000 votes in Arizona, Georgia, Michigan, Wisconsin, Nevada, North Carolina, and Pennsylvania.[69]

Linking January 6 to Status Threat

Not only are these racialized arguments linked to voter fraud and hence elec-toral illegitimacy, but status threats are embedded in the rhetoric Trump employed in the run-up to and on January 6 and associated as well with the legitimation of violence. Speaking at the Ellipse on the morning of January 6, the incumbent evoked status threat by casting the contest over certification of the election as one that at its core was about whether "we" and "you"—his massed supporters—would continue to have a country if they failed to take it back that day. The insinuation of the need for violence came in the words we cited earlier: "You'll never take back our country with weakness. You have to show strength and you have to be strong. . . . And we fight. We fight like hell. And if you don't fight like hell, you're not going to have a country anymore."[70]

Two themes are worth unpacking here. First, the argument that "you" are losing the country (when the "you" was understood to be his supporters) echoes the replacement argument we discussed in Chapter 8. Second, entreaties to "show strength" and to "fight like hell," which featured heavily in Trump's second impeachment trial, hint at the undercurrent of violence or threat of it coursing through the crises of 2020. And because those whose identities were threatened were willing to take steps to reassert them, Trump's arguments can be read to legitimate the means (including use of force) required to reclaim what is rightfully theirs. It is unsurprising, then, that the actions of some in the Capitol on January 6 paralleled those taken in earlier times, including Charlottesville, the planned kidnapping of Governor Whitmer, the anti-lockdown protests, and the clashes that occurred during the Black Lives Matter protests.

The riot at the Capitol on January 6 seemed at first to elicit bipartisan condemnation. Americans watched on television, in real time, as the Capitol building was surrounded, the police officers guarding it were driven back, and a mob entered through broken windows and disarmed doors. But unlike media events of the past, when common imagery drew Americans of different views together,[71] divergent narratives quickly took hold. For some, this was not an assault on the institutions of American democracy but instead a false flag operation or the aberrant behavior of a few. In time, some who in the moment had expressed horror at the events came to dismiss their significance.[72]

Across the months following the assault on the Capitol, the story some conservative leaders and pundits told of what went on there evolved. At first, some conservative and Republican commentators contended that those implicated on January 6 were not exclusively Trump loyalists but included antifa provocateurs bent on discrediting Trump supporters.[73] "Now, they were likely not all Trump supporters, and there are some reports that Antifa sympathizers may have been sprinkled throughout the crowd," noted Fox's Laura Ingraham.[74] In a similar vein, speaking with radio host Candace Owens in December 2021, Trump alleged that there were more than "just—let's call them MAGA people . . . You have BLM and had Antifa people . . . and they were antagonizing and they were agitating."[75] Over time, a growing chorus contended that even if the interlopers were Trump supporters, their actions were misdemeanors, not felonies, and certainly less egregious than the ones attributed to the BLM marchers. In the process, prosecution of the rioters was recast as an assault on the political views of patriots.[†] Trump said that those at the Capitol that day posed "zero threat" to anyone, and Republican member of Congress Andrew Clyde (R-GA) said that their presence appeared similar to a "normal tourist visit." Representative Paul Gosar (R-AZ) argued that the government's ongoing investigations of January 6 amounted to the actions of a police state: "Outright propaganda and lies are being used to unleash the national security state against law-abiding U.S. citizens, especially Trump voters."[76] Gosar referred to those being held in connection to the January 6 attacks as "political prisoners," and asserted that the United States treated terrorists at Guantanamo better than these US citizens.[77]

Indeed, some have contended that punishments meted out to those arrested on January 6 were harsher than for those arrested during the Black Lives Matter protests and that the difference indicated a desire on the part of the government to silence conservative voices,[78] a claim echoing the double standard argument that we discussed earlier. "It's a common refrain from some of those charged in the Jan. 6th riot at the US Capitol and their Republican allies: The Justice Department is treating them harshly because of their political views while those arrested during last year's protests over racial injustice were given leniency," noted an Associated Press article in August 2021. It then added, "Court records tell a different story. An Associated Press review of court documents in more than 300 federal cases stemming from the protests sparked by George Floyd's death last year shows that dozens of people charged have been convicted of serious crimes and sent to prison."[79] There is of course a racial subtext to this debate: where the Black Lives Matter protests were attended "overwhelmingly [by] Black Americans and their allies," the Capitol insurrectionists were "overwhelmingly white Americans."[80]

On Fox News, Tucker Carlson argued that the government's efforts to prosecute those involved with the January 6 riot were an attack on "legacy Americans,"[81] a view he reiterated in a documentary that aired on the Fox

---

† To be clear, these two lines of argument contradict each other: in one, Trump supporters were not involved in the riot; in the other, they were, but as patriots, not lawbreakers (and were not dangerous). We acknowledge this tension but note that this was part of the discourse when we fielded our survey. Over time, however, this second argument has become the dominant one, with claims about antifa fading into the background (though they persist throughout the period we study).

streaming service Fox Nation titled *Patriot Purge*. It contended that January 6 was a false flag operation choreographed by Trump's enemies and instigated by FBI agents pretending to be Trump supporters, all intent on discrediting the forty-fifth president and licensing the tyrannizing of his supporters. The streaming service has over a million subscribers.[82]

In essence, approval of the assault on the Capitol on January 6 signals sympathy for the view that those who supported Trump were legitimately aggrieved about their declining status in America and threatened by shifts in power that would result from a Biden-Harris administration. Their statements harkened back to the same 1776 narrative that Trump's history project celebrated, as we discussed in Chapter 8. In this retelling, MAGA and flag-waving patriots entered the people's House, invited by their president. Concerns about status threat were nothing new, but Trump's actions, as well as the crises, brought them to the forefront of the national dialogue, where they intersected with Trump's rhetoric about a fraudulent election in which "real" Americans were having their voices silenced by those who wanted to fundamentally change the nation and its character. In effect, general concerns over status threat found an outlet in the 2020 election, abetted by Trump's framing of his loss of the election. The march to and assault on the Capitol were the culmination of that process.

Social Media and January 6

At this point, we do not know how much of a role social media (both large-scale platforms such as Facebook and smaller, very conservative ones such as Parler and Telegram) played in making it possible for Trump and his supporters to amass the crowds in Washington, DC, on January 6. However, what can be gleaned from the October 2021 revelations of Facebook whistleblower Frances Haugen is that Facebook suspended some of its pre-election safeguards before January 6. She believes that the change indicated that the platform had returned to prioritizing growth over safety.[83]

Facebook did remove the "Stop the Steal" group two days after it was formed on the grounds that "it contained high levels of hate and violence and incitement (VNI) in the comments." At the time, a Facebook spokesperson reported in a statement, "In line with the exceptional measures that we are taking during this period of heightened tension, we have removed the Group 'Stop the Steal,' which was creating real-world events. The group was organized around the delegitimization of the election process, and we saw worrying calls for violence from some members of the group."[84] Before

Facebook interdicted it, the *Guardian* reported, "the group exploded in popularity on Wednesday and Thursday [November 4 and 5, 2020— the two days following Election Day], racking up more than 730,000 interactions, according to data from CrowdTangle, a Facebook-owned social media analytics platform."[85] An internal Facebook document revealed that in a twenty-four-hour span the group had gained 300,000 members and more than a million people wanted to join.[86] "The document," reported BuzzFeed, which secured a copy, "explicitly states that Facebook activity from people connected to Stop the Steal and other Trump loyalist groups including the Patriot Party played a role in the events of Jan. 6, and that the company's emphasis on rooting out fake accounts and 'inauthentic behavior' held it back from taking preemptive action when real people were involved."[87]

At 4:00 PM on January 6, Facebook announced the "actions that we're taking," which included removing the following from their platform:

- Praise and support of the storming of the US Capitol
- Calls to bring weapons to locations across the US—not just in Washington but anywhere in the US—including protests
- Incitement or encouragement of the events at the Capitol, including videos and photos from the protestors. At this point they represent promotion of criminal activity which violates our policies.
- Calls for protests—even peaceful ones—if they violate the curfew in DC
- Attempts to restage violence tomorrow or in the coming days[88]

At the same time, it reported "updating our label on posts across our platforms that attempt to delegitimize the election results. The new text reads: 'Joe Biden has been elected President with results that were certified by all 50 states. The US has laws, procedures, and established institutions to ensure the peaceful transfer of power after an election.' "[89] The same blog post revealed that over six hundred militarized social movements had been removed from the platform in the days and weeks before. On January 16 another update reported, "We are banning ads that promote weapon accessories and protective equipment in the US at least through January 22, out of an abundance of caution."[90]

Twitter, too, may have played a consequential role. The House of Representatives Select Committee to Investigate the January 6th Attack on the United States Capitol has indicated that

Twitter subscribers reportedly used the platform for communications regarding the planning and execution of the assault on the United States Capitol, and Twitter was reportedly warned about potential violence being planned on the site in advance of January 6th. Further, high-profile Twitter subscribers used the platform for communications amplifying allegations of election fraud even after the December 14 certification of election results by the states, and theories of election fraud in the weeks leading up to the January 6th attack following the December 14 certification of election results by the states.[91]

The same is true of YouTube, where the same committee found that

> YouTube was a platform for significant communications by its users that were relevant to the planning and execution of January 6th attack on the United States Capitol. For example, Steve Bannon livestreamed his podcast on YouTube in the days before and after January 6, 2021, and live-streams of the attack appeared on YouTube as it was taking place.[92]

There were, of course, avenues outside the major platforms that were employed by those who planned the January 6 events. Parler, Telegram, MeWe, and Gab were Trump-friendly venues.‡ Conspiracist Alex Jones of Infowars fame, who helped fund and spoke at a rally in the District of Columbia on January 5, urged his listeners to attend the Trump one the following day. A dark-money group calling itself the Rule of Law Defense Fund, which is tied to the Republican Attorneys General Association, used phone messages to tell listeners where and when to gather for "the march to save America" before informing them that "at 1:00 p.m., we will march to the Capitol building and call on congress to stop the steal. We are hoping patriots like you will join us to continue to fight to protect the integrity of our elections." The call then provided a phone number and web address to consult for additional information.[93]

---

‡. That said, Apple and Google barred Parler's mobile app from their stores, and Amazon Web Services refused to continue to host Parler after reliable information surfaced showing that instigators used Parler to plan some of their activities. See, for example, Kim Lyons, "Amazon Is Kicking Parler Off Its Web Hosting Service," *Verge*, January 9, 2021, https://www.theverge.com/2021/1/9/22222637/amazon-workers-aws-stop-hosting-services-parler-capitol-violence.

Since communication apps such as Facebook's WhatsApp are encrypted, it is all but impossible to know what was happening there. We do know that at least some of those charged with seditious conspiracy for their January 6 activities relied on shielded messaging. A federal indictment notes that the Oath Keepers' founder and leader, Stewart Rhodes, used the encrypted Signal app to send messages that included a November 11, 2020, one saying, "It will be a bloody and desperate fight. We are going to have a fight. That can't be avoided," and "There is no standard political or legal way out of this."[94]

We can never know what would have happened on January 6 had these various platforms stopped such misinformation just after the election, or had they blocked the "Stop the Steal" rallies from organizing on their platforms. But it is at least possible that had they done so, Trump's audience on the Ellipse that day would have been smaller, its responses less perfervid, and the resulting smaller numbers of marchers dispatched to the Capitol less likely to turn into a lawless mob.

The Arguments We Test in Part 2 of the Chapter

In Part 2 of this chapter, we will assess not only Trump and Biden voters' views of the election's legitimacy but also how they changed over time. We will ask how those beliefs are related to conservative media consumption as well as to beliefs about discrimination against minorities and status threat (or, more broadly, the penumbra of racial attitudes). Additionally, we will determine the characteristics of those who endorsed the attempt to disrupt the certification of the election and those who supported violence as a means of protecting the American way of life. Our interest in these questions is driven by the rhetoric from the Trump campaign that, abetted by conspiracy theories circulating online, not only delegitimized the election but also contended that "fighting like hell" would be needed to stop an illegitimate president from hijacking Trump's followers' American dream. Our findings have disturbing implications for our democracy moving forward.

"Stop the Steal"

EFFECTS OF THE ASSAULTS ON ELECTORAL AND DEMOCRATIC LEGITIMACY

Matthew Levendusky, Josh Pasek, and Kathleen Hall Jamieson

IN THE FIRST part of the chapter, we traced the rhetoric that Trump and his supporters used to falsely argue that Biden lost the 2020 election. In so doing, they drew on conspiracy theories and also couched their claims in ways that invoked status threat and primed racial attitudes; these elements were then echoed in conservative media outlets. We suggested that, for some of our panelists, responsiveness to this rhetoric played a role in their rejection of Biden's election win and, for a subset, in their acceptance of the attempt to disrupt the certification of the election and of the possibility that violence would be needed to preserve the American way of life. In this chapter, we put those arguments to the test and explore how the rhetoric at issue shaped our respondents' attitudes.

This chapter documents three key findings. First, beliefs about electoral legitimacy polarized sharply in the aftermath of the 2020 election. At the outset of our study, both Biden and Trump supporters believed that the 2020 election would be free and fair. But as Trump's assertion that Democrats would steal the election from him became a mantra, the supporters of the incumbent and challenger began to diverge in their beliefs about the fairness of the process. After November 3, that pre-election gap became a chasm. By the time of Trump's second impeachment trial in February 2021, Biden's voters were all but certain the election had been free and fair, while Trump's were convinced it was anything but. We also demonstrate that Trump supporters largely thought Biden stole the election and was therefore an illegitimate president;

at the same time, they were also more likely to endorse election-related conspiracy theories.

Second, we show that these beliefs were driven both by media choices and, more importantly, by racial attitudes and the kinds of status threat we detailed in Chapter 8 ("A Deeper Anxiety"). Voters who consumed content from conservative media outlets—especially those who sought out such content and were ensconced in the conservative echo chamber—were more likely to believe that Biden's election was ill-obtained. Voters with racially conservative views, and in particular those who experienced status threat, showed the most skepticism of Biden's victory, underscoring how Trump's rhetoric primed these themes (see Part 1 of this chapter). This set of findings has a more important implication: what, on the surface, are debates about voter fraud, are really reflections of anxieties about perceived shifts in sociopolitical power in United States.

Third, and perhaps most importantly, we show that these same factors also predict both support for the January 6 attacks and for violence more generally. To be clear, few of our panelists endorsed the assault on the Capitol or violence more generally. But those who did so generally experienced high levels of status threat. Not only did conservative media consumption, racial attitudes, and feelings of status threat correlate with beliefs about electoral fraud, but they also spilled over into beliefs that violence to protect the country's identity was legitimate and that the events of January 6 were justified. An electoral crisis was therefore transformed into a crisis of democracy. Some individuals think their country is being taken from them and that they and those like them are losing their grip on power. This leaves our democracy in a precarious place, as we discuss in Chapter 10 ("A Republic, if You Can Keep It").

Beliefs About Electoral Legitimacy Across the 2020 Campaign

Mindful of Trump's rhetoric related to electoral legitimacy (see Part 1), near the outset of our study in wave 2 (June 2020), we began gauging voters' beliefs about whether the 2020 election would be conducted freely and fairly. We asked this item in wave 2, wave 7 (October–November 2020, just before the election), wave 8 (November 2020, just after the election), wave 10 (January 2021), and wave 11 (February–March 2021, after Trump's second impeachment). Figure 9.1 plots the evolution of these attitudes by electorate over time.

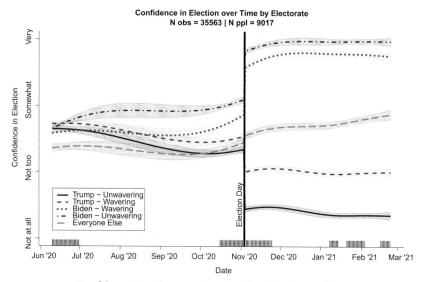

FIGURE 9.1 Confidence That the 2020 Election Would Be Free and Fair.
Lines show the estimated confidence that the 2020 election would be free and fair by
electorate across our study. Election day was treated as a mean-shift discontinuity within
each electorate.

Because the election results were expected to shift perceptions of legitimacy,
we also introduced a discontinuity on Election Day, allowing the trends to be
fitted differently before and after this point.

When we first asked this item in the summer of 2020, there was effectively
no difference between Biden and Trump voters; both were equally confident
that the election would be conducted freely and fairly (both Trump and Biden
voters averaged just a bit below "somewhat confident" on this measure). This
important baseline suggests that the polarization we observe later was not
simply due to preexisting differences between partisans. Rather, these results
indicate that it was the campaign itself—and Trump's false claims of voter
fraud, amplified by the media—that drove perceptions apart. Indeed, by
wave 7, just before Election Day, there was already a gap between Biden and
Trump supporters. Among the unwavering electorates, Biden supporters had
become more confident in the election's legitimacy, Trump's less so. This fits
with other data showing few partisan differences in this belief in the spring,
but larger gaps by the fall.[1]

But immediately after the election, this gap widens dramatically, with
sharply diverging beliefs about the election emerging. Our models confirmed
that a sharp discontinuity appears after Election Day: those in each electorate

abruptly updated their beliefs about the election's legitimacy. In response to the outcome, Biden voters were more likely to become "very confident" that the election was free and fair, and Trump's more likely to say that they were "not too confident" (wavering Trump voters) or "not at all confident" (unwavering Trump voters) that the election had been conducted freely and fairly. The post-election gap between wavering and unwavering Trump voters is especially interesting. Pre-election, there was a modest difference, similar to the one between wavering and unwavering Biden voters. But post-election, the gap between unwavering and wavering Trump supporters grows considerably, a finding that highlights the importance of our wavering/unwavering distinction for understanding these attitudes. We will return to this theme later in the chapter.

Not only did these beliefs diverge on Election Day, but they continued to drift apart in the weeks and months to come. By the time we wrapped up our panel study in February 2021, Biden voters were for practical purposes certain that the election was free and fair, and Trump voters were convinced that the opposite was the case. Trump's rhetoric about voter fraud—and the media coverage in which those voters were enveloped—appeared to have had a major impact.[2]

On some level, the basic tenor of this result is not surprising. In election after election, supporters of the winning candidate have expressed more confidence than those of the loser that the election was free and fair.[3] But two things stand out in the aftermath of the 2020 election. First, the divide was wide.[4] And second, confidence in the conduct of the election among Trump's supporters continued to decline in the post-election period as the forty-fifth president and his allies persistently cast doubt on the outcome even after numerous courts rejected their claims. This suggests that voters did not decide on their own that the election had been stolen. Rather, our respondents adopted this belief because partisan elites and the media sources on which they relied advanced that view. As partisan elites and media figures go, so go their audiences.

Figure 9.1 shows beliefs about the election's fairness overall. Yet even if individuals believe that the overall election was fraudulently decided, they might think their own ballot was counted correctly. In our post-election waves, we asked respondents whether that was the case, as well as how confident they were in their state's electoral results. Figures 9.2 and 9.3 present these results, also broken down by electorate.

Figure 9.2 presents respondents' beliefs about whether their own ballot was accurately tallied. We asked this item in both wave 8, just after the November

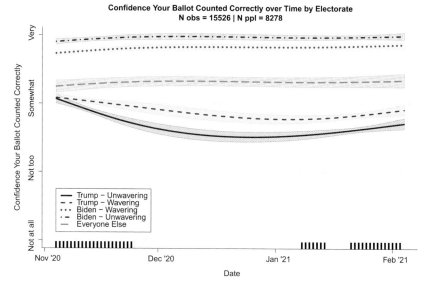

FIGURE 9.2 Confidence That Your Vote Was Counted Correctly.
Lines show the estimated confidence that the respondents' own ballots were counted correctly by electorate across our study.

election, and in wave 10, in January 2021. Consistent with earlier scholarship,[5] the key finding here is that voters are more confident that their own ballot was counted correctly than they are that the election as a whole was free and fair. While most unwavering Trump voters were "not at all confident" that the election overall was free and fair, they were nonetheless "somewhat confident" that the integrity of their own ballot had been protected. These voters thought there was fraud; they just thought it took place somewhere else.

To understand the dynamics of confidence in one's state's vote count, we analyzed respondents by state. The patterns seen in Figure 9.1, above, led us to suspect that voters' levels of confidence in the outcome of their state would be affected by whether their candidate won or lost. Since we only asked this item once, in wave 10 (January 2021), we cannot look at change over time. Still, we see a marked difference across our battleground states (see Figure 9.3).

Biden's supporters across our four states were confident in the fairness and accuracy of their state's vote totals, even in Florida, where Trump had been victorious.[*] Trump's supporters had confidence only in the results in Florida, where their candidate won. And even then, their confidence was far lower

---

[*]. While Biden's supporters in Florida were slightly less confident in their state's vote totals, the differences were very small, especially compared to the gaps for Trump voters.

Confidence in State Vote Count

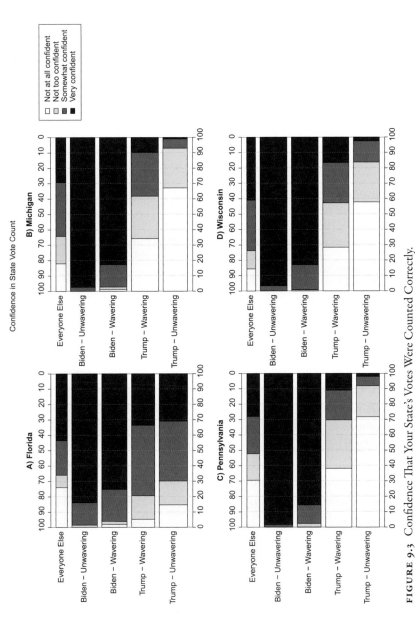

FIGURE 9.3 Confidence That Your State's Votes Were Counted Correctly.
Plots show the level of confidence in the respondent's state's vote count, by electorate, separately for each of our four states.

than that of Biden supporters. When we reanalyzed the data for respondents' beliefs about their own vote counts, we saw the same pattern—Trump supporters in Florida, which the incumbent carried, were more confident that their own ballots were counted correctly. In our federalized election system, this suggests that confidence in the integrity of vote counting in presidential elections is affected not only by whether one's candidate wins the national election but also by whether that person carries one's state.

But there is another, subtler point that might help to explain why Trump voters in Florida were confident of their state's tallies. Florida has made extensive use of mail-in voting for many years, and as we showed in Chapter 3 ("Not One Electorate, but Many"), there was effectively no partisan gap in vote method in Florida (in our other states, especially Pennsylvania, Democrats were much more likely to use mail-in voting than were Republicans, and Republicans were more likely to vote in person; see Figure 3.19). Indeed, President Trump himself voted by mail in the primaries from his Florida address in 2020.[6] Because Florida preprocesses its mail-in ballots and early votes up to twenty-two days in advance of Election Day, it also reports nearly finalized vote totals on election night.[7] Our other three states did not allow for as much ballot preprocessing. Instead, mail-in ballots were counted more slowly and tallied after in-person votes. Pennsylvania—which allowed mail-in ballots without an excuse for the first time in 2020—did not permit *any* processing of ballots before Election Day. So not only was mail-in voting a less familiar voting technology in Pennsylvania, but that state's ballots took days to count. When most Americans went to bed in the early hours of November 4, President Trump was up in Pennsylvania by almost 700,000 votes. As we noted in Part 1 of the chapter, those tallies reflected almost exclusively Election Day balloting, which skewed heavily Republican.[†]

As counties tallied their mail-in ballots in the days that followed, President Trump's lead slipped away. Democratic voters had overwhelmingly voted by mail, especially in the state's largest counties, such as Allegheny, Philadelphia, and Montgomery. In the end, because the mail-in ballots broke so decisively for Joe Biden, he won the Commonwealth of Pennsylvania by 80,555 votes, a little over 1 percent. While the delayed tallying of mail-in votes reflected a

---

†. According to data from the Pennsylvania secretary of state, Trump beat Biden by 1.3 million among votes cast on Election Day, but Biden beat Trump by 1.4 million votes among those who voted by mail. Trump won 66 percent of Election Day votes, but Biden won 77 percent of mail-in ballots, and with that, the election. For the exact totals by mode, see "Pennsylvania Elections—Summary Results," Pennsylvania Department of State, 2020, https://www.election returns.pa.gov/General/SummaryResults?ElectionID=83&ElectionType=G&IsActive=0.

well-known pattern[8] and election experts had warned that this would happen in 2020 as well,[9] one can see why this could have seemed suspicious to Trump supporters, especially in light of the president's claims that Democrats would use mail-in ballots to perpetrate fraud.

In a forty-six-minute video shared widely on social media, on December 2, 2020, Trump reiterated assertions that Pennsylvania and other states were being stolen from him. In it, he claimed that he was winning by a lot in key states until a massive influx of ballots reversed all that to ensure that he would lose by a little. "Large amounts of mail-in and absentee ballots were processed illegally and in secret in Philadelphia and Allegheny County without our observers present," Trump alleged. As numerous fact checkers confirmed, these claims were false.[10] Within an hour, the video, which was flagged by both Facebook and Twitter as problematic, had garnered hundreds of thousands of views on Facebook and was shared by more than 60,000 Facebook users, according to the Associated Press.[11]

Unsurprisingly, then, Trump-supporting Pennsylvanians had the lowest level of confidence in their state's election results of Trump voters in any of our four states. In short, it is not simply whether one's candidate wins the overall contest, or the state itself, that shapes beliefs about electoral legitimacy. Election administration does so as well. Because the practices states employ in processing their ballots affect the speed with which they report their full vote totals, those too affect electoral confidence.

But this finding also highlights, in another way, how state-level policies influence electoral confidence. State leaders were told that without preprocessing, ballots would take days to tally. Although Pennsylvania's election officials warned of this problem months in advance,[12] the Republican-controlled state legislature refused to act.[13] In the future, methods that permit more preprocessing of mail-in votes—which would speed up the vote count and allow for more complete reporting of vote totals sooner—could improve electoral confidence.

Beginning early in the campaign, we also asked how important it was for the loser of the election to publicly acknowledge the winner as the legitimate president of the nation. As we noted earlier, while concessions had been a hallmark of American elections before Trump entered the presidential arena, he threatened this norm in 2016 and violated it in 2020. What did his voters think of this, and did their views evolve across the campaign? To answer this question, we looked at how respondents' assessments of the importance of this norm changed over time across the electorates; Figure 9.4 presents the results.

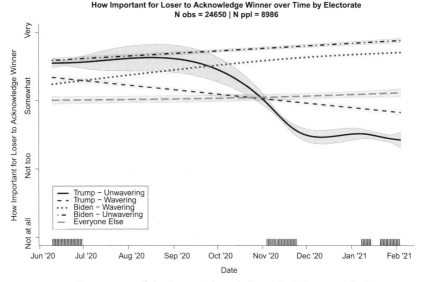

FIGURE 9.4 Importance of the Loser Acknowledging the Winner as the Legitimate President.
Lines show the estimated importance of the loser of the presidential election acknowledging the winner as the legitimate president, by electorate across our study.

Paralleling the results for legitimacy seen in Figure 9.1, early in the campaign there was functionally no difference in the importance Biden and Trump supporters attached to the loser acknowledging the victor as the legitimate winner of the election (see Figure 9.4). If anything, the gap was between wavering and unwavering voters regardless of candidate: both Biden and Trump's unwavering voters attached more importance to this norm than did their wavering counterparts (though at the outset these gaps were small). Early in our study, the average voter, regardless of candidate preference, thought it was between "somewhat" and "very" important that the loser acknowledge the winner's victory. This finding suggests that Trump's 2016 threats to violate this norm did not have a lasting impact on his supporters.

After the 2020 election, however, we observed striking polarization. Biden supporters increased the importance they attached to this expectation (and effectively encountered a ceiling effect), while in contrast, its importance to Trump supporters dropped dramatically, especially for the unwavering ones. Even between waves 8 (November 2020, post-election) and 10 (January 2021), there was further polarization, especially for Trump voters, with the unwavering Trump supporters shifting toward the sense that it was "not too important" for the loser to acknowledge the winner. So not only did the candidates' supporters diverge in their beliefs about the fairness of the election, but they did as well in their support for this norm.

Voter Fraud and the Legitimacy of a Biden Presidency

In wave 8, just after the November election, we asked respondents how much of an impact voter fraud had on the outcome of the election on a scale ranging from "none at all" to "a great deal." If they thought it had at least some impact, they were asked whether the fraudulent behavior benefitted Biden, Trump, or neither of them.[‡]

In the top panel (Figure 9.5, panel A), we see that the overwhelming majority of both wavering and unwavering Biden voters thought that voter fraud had little to no influence on the outcome in 2020. Indeed, 65.1 percent of wavering Biden voters and 86.3 percent of unwavering ones thought that it had no effect at all. In contrast, 60.6 percent of unwavering Trump voters, and 31.4 percent of wavering ones, thought that it had "a great deal" of impact on the outcome.

In the bottom panel (Figure 9.5, panel B), we see that the majority of Biden voters thought that fraud did not help either candidate (consistent with a belief that it had little effect on the outcome), but Trump voters—both unwavering and wavering—overwhelmingly concluded that the voter fraud that occurred conferred large benefits on Biden. The two sides had incompatible views on the influence of fraud on the election's outcome.

To determine whether these beliefs about fraud spilled over into beliefs that Joe Biden legitimately won the election, in our post-election waves we measured whether respondents thought that Biden was the legitimate victor. To do so, we asked each of our panelists in wave 10 (January 2021) whether Biden or Trump won more votes in the election, whether Trump was trying to steal the election, whether Biden was trying to steal the election, and, finally, after Biden had been declared the winner by the Electoral College, whether Biden had been legitimately elected president. We present these data in Figure 9.6.[§]

In all three panels of Figure 9.6, we see sharp differentiation by electorate. Biden voters, even wavering ones, were largely convinced that he had won the

---

‡. Those who reported that it had no impact were presumed to believe that it would not benefit either candidate.

§. We combined the measures about stealing the election into a single item reflecting whether respondents thought Trump, Biden, both, or neither candidate was trying to do so.

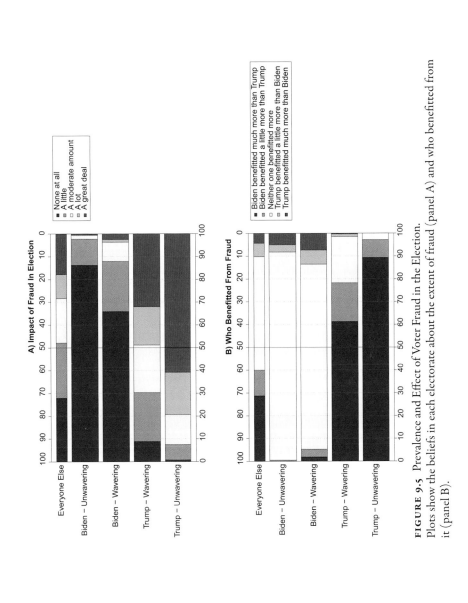

FIGURE 9.5 Prevalence and Effect of Voter Fraud in the Election. Plots show the beliefs in each electorate about the extent of fraud (panel A) and who benefitted from it (panel B).

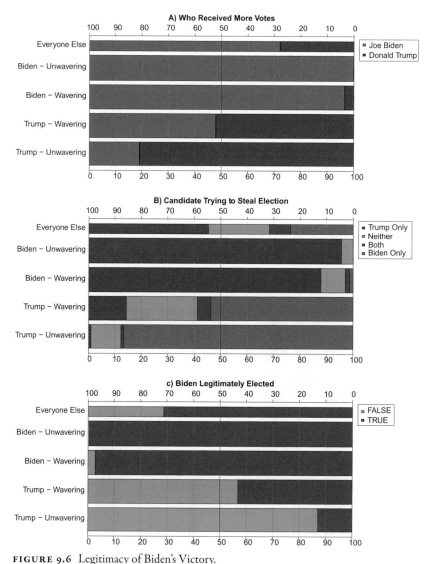

FIGURE 9.6 Legitimacy of Biden's Victory.
Plots show the percentage of each electorate that thinks Trump or Biden got more votes in the 2020 election (panel A), which candidate, if either, was trying to steal the election (panel B), and whether Biden was legitimately elected (panel C).

most votes, that he was not trying to steal the election (although Trump was), and that he was legitimately elected president. Trump voters, especially unwavering Trump ones, by contrast, were much less certain of these facts. Indeed, a minority of wavering Trump supporters—and only 12.9 percent of unwavering ones—thought that Biden was the legitimate winner. The vast majority of unwavering Trump voters (87.5 percent) said that Biden was (or both candidates were) trying to steal the election, and most wavering Trump voters agreed (58.8 percent). And most wavering and unwavering Trump voters asserted that their candidate had received more popular votes, despite final election tallies in which Biden secured 7.1 million more votes than his rival, won 51.3 percent of the votes cast, and prevailed by 4.5 percentage points, each of which reflected the largest margin of victory since 2008. Trump voters' beliefs about voter fraud appear to have translated quite directly into skepticism about the legitimacy of the outcome.

Seeing this, one might wonder whether we are simply finding expressive responding, with Trump voters not necessarily believing that Trump won, but rather signaling their allegiance to their party.[14] In other words, some Trump voters may have known that Biden won, but nonetheless expressed doubt about the legitimacy of his win in order to demonstrate their fealty to the former president. With this type of survey data, we cannot rule out such an explanation, and it is likely that some of our respondents behaved this way, though the magnitude of the effects observed here far surpass any studies of the phenomenon to date.[15] Whether these attitudes are a form of expressive responding or not, they are concerning. Beliefs that elections are freely and fairly conducted, their outcomes accurately reported, and the winner assumes the presidency after a peaceful transfer of power are bedrocks of democracy—indeed, it cannot function without them.[16] Either an expressive belief doubting these precepts or convincing evidence that they are unjustified undercuts the system. As we show later in the chapter, the unwarranted conclusion that the election had been stolen from Trump helped fuel approval of the riot at the Capitol on January 6 and shaped subsequent attitudes toward the events of that day. The beliefs in question are distinguishable from those about whether or not the level of unemployment has changed; they speak instead to confidence in the integrity of core structures of democratic governance.

The Reinforcing Role of Conservative Media

Of course, it was not just President Trump who falsely claimed that he won the election and that Joe Biden had perpetrated fraud. These claims were repeated on conservative media outlets as well, especially on very conservative venues such as Newsmax and OANN—outlets President Trump encouraged his viewers to watch post-election. By contrast, when mainstream media covered Trump's claims that the election was stolen, their hosts and reporters tended to discredit them by noting that they were disputed and unsupported by evidence.[17]

While any media source can be persuasive, conservative media have a unique capacity to influence their audiences. As we saw in Chapter 4 ("The Electorates' Communication Dynamics"), Trump voters—especially the unwavering ones—see them as distinct within the media ecosystem and as uniquely trustworthy.[18] Further, we know that many Trump supporters actively seek out conservative media sources and actively avoid other types of media content, putting a small segment of them into a conservative media echo chamber (an enclaving phenomenon that, as Chapter 4 indicated, we did not find among liberal media users). As a result, a block of his supporters were getting unrebutted messages promoting Trump's claims of voter fraud. Our findings are consistent with others' conclusions that echo chambers do not exist at scale in the mass public, although some on the political right are ensconced in conservative media ones.[19] Such a skewed media diet might play a role in fostering beliefs in voter fraud and electoral illegitimacy.

Accordingly, we suspected that those who sought out conservative media, and particularly those residing within conservative media echo chambers, would have different beliefs about whether the election was free and fair and whether Biden was trying to steal or had stolen the election. Mindful of the results earlier in this chapter, we focused on Trump supporters here (recall that, overwhelmingly, those who consume these media are Trump supporters, as we discussed in Chapter 4).

In the top panel of Figure 9.7, we present beliefs among Trump voters that the 2020 election was free and fair. With the slight exception of those in the conservative media echo chamber, respondents' search/avoidance tendencies had little effect until after the election, when we saw a notable gap emerge. Post-election, we observed a clear divergence for those who actively sought out conservative media sources and particularly those enmeshed in a conservative media echo chamber. This latter group, which effectively had no confidence in the election, is especially important because, as we saw in Chapter 4, it is the one that moved to the very conservative outlets post-election, such as OANN and Newsmax (see Figure 4.4). By doing so, these individuals ensured that they were enveloped in a media ecosphere that presupposed a stolen election and featured little, if any, countervailing discussion.

We see a similar pattern in the bottom panel as well with respect to whether Biden was trying to steal the election: while a majority of all Trump supporters felt this way, more than 90 percent of those in a conservative echo chamber shared this sentiment. These individuals were functionally different

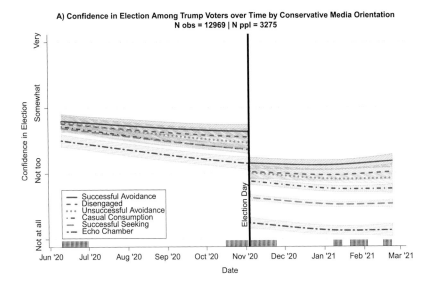

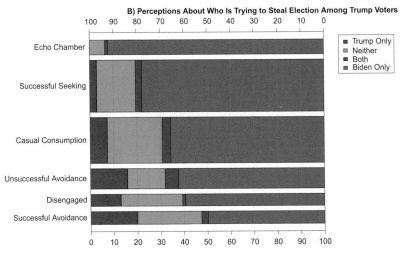

FIGURE 9.7 Effects of Conservative Media Orientations on Electoral Legitimacy. The graph shows the effect of conservative media orientations among Trump voters. Panel A shows the effects on belief that the election was free and fair. Panel B shows the effect on which candidate, if either, was perceived as trying to steal the election.

and held distinctive beliefs, even relative to other Trump voters. Without access to cross-cutting messages, they embraced the perfidy emanating from Trump and his associates on conservative outlets.

These findings reinforce an important point we made in earlier chapters. It is not simply consuming a given outlet that matters, but how individuals

approach that outlet. Mere attention to Fox News is not the main driver of
attitude change here. Instead, it is actively seeking such sources that is the
unique predictor, especially when those are the only ones consumed. Of
course, there is necessarily both a push and a pull, as those who are in these
echo chambers are different from their peers, so we cannot treat these effects
as causal. But the finding underscores the need for scholars to move beyond
exposure to media sources to consider these sorts of action tendencies.

The Role of Electoral Conspiracies

As we noted in Part 1 of this chapter, accepting that the election was marred
by fraud likely required believing in a vast and coordinated conspiracy to rig
the outcome against the incumbent. To examine related beliefs, we focus on
five claims that had circulated widely, primarily online: (1) big tech rigged
the election against Donald Trump; (2) one of the voting systems used by the
states switched as many as 435,000 votes from Trump to Biden and deleted
27 million votes; (3) "deep state" operatives in the government have a secret
supercomputer named Hammer that they used to steal the 2012 election for
Obama and the 2020 election for Biden; (4) Democratic officials from the
Obama era who are part of the "deep state" paid individuals who have communist interests and ties to George Soros to use a secret algorithm to hack
into voting machines in key battleground states and steal millions of votes
from Donald Trump; and (5) in Wisconsin there were more votes cast than
people registered.[**] We asked questions about each of these beliefs in wave 9
(December 2020); the distributions of responses by electorate are presented
for the items in Figure 9.8 and across an index of all five of them in Figure 9.9
(Cronbach's $\alpha = 0.89$).

   Although Biden voters uniformly rejected each of these election-related
conspiracy theories, most appear to have been believed by a plurality, if not
an outright majority, of Trump's voters. Adherence to these beliefs was particularly strong among his unwavering supporters (Figure 9.8 and Figure 9.9).
Further, we can see that orientations toward conservative media predicted
holding these conspiracy beliefs. A plurality of those who did not or tried not
to watch conservative media reported that all of these claims were definitely
false. Groups that casually consumed these media or sought them out were
more likely than not to say that they believed them (and, unsurprisingly, this

---

[**]. Although the last is not technically a conspiracy theory because it does not specify a conspir-
ator, it is difficult to imagine how this scenario could occur without a widespread conspiracy.

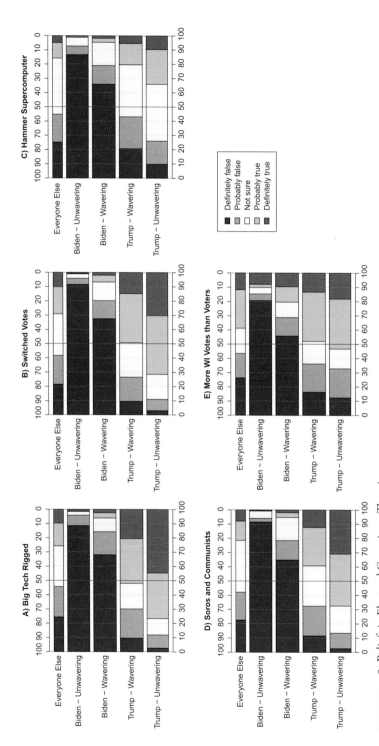

FIGURE 9.8 Beliefs in Electoral Conspiracy Theories.

Bars show distribution of beliefs, by electorate, in each of five electoral conspiracy theories.

A) Election Conspiracy Beliefs by Electorate

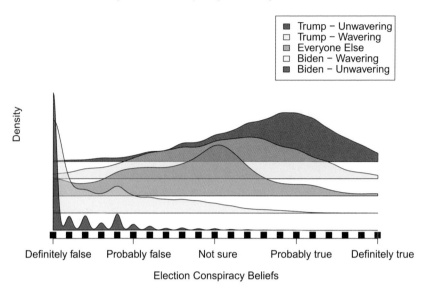

B) Election Conspiracy Beliefs by Conservative Media Orientation

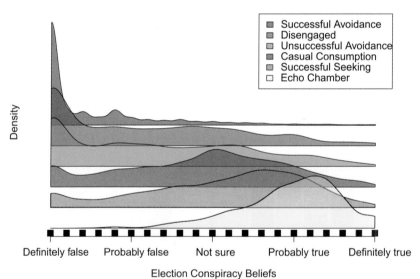

FIGURE 9.9 Distribution of Electoral Conspiracy Beliefs.
The panels show the distribution across electorates (panel A) and conservative media orientations (panel B) of beliefs in the five electoral conspiracy theory items (aggregated into an index).

is most true of those in a conservative media echo chamber). As we will see later in this chapter, such beliefs have important implications for beliefs about January 6 and support for violence.

Does Status Threat Predict Beliefs About Electoral Legitimacy?

In Part 1 of this chapter, we argued that the rhetoric used to attack the legitimacy of the election and to defend the actions of the Capitol rioters on January 6 implicitly and explicitly invoked race and status threat. To test whether status threat and racial attitudes were correlated with beliefs about voter fraud and electoral legitimacy, we examined the measures in our post-election waves that asked respondents whether Biden won more votes than Trump, whether Biden was legitimately elected, the importance of the losing candidate acknowledging the winner as the legitimate president, and how much of an impact voter fraud had on the election outcome (here, we use the measures of all of these items from wave 10, conducted in January 2021), as well as the overall measure of acceptance of conspiracy beliefs. If our hypothesis is correct (controlling for key factors), then racial attitudes, and both the sense of status threat and perceptions of discrimination against minority groups that correspond with those attitudes, should lead respondents (1) to think that Biden did not win more votes than did Trump; (2) to think that Biden was not legitimately elected; (3) to think that it is less important that the losing candidate acknowledge the winner as the legitimate president; (4) to think that voter fraud had a larger effect on the outcome; and (5) to believe that the results were shaped by widespread conspiracies. Figure 9.10 presents the results.

For all of these outcomes, measures of both status threat and perceptions of discrimination against minorities uniquely contributed to beliefs about the election and its legitimacy. Even after accounting for demographics, partisanship, electorate membership, and patterns of media use, individuals who perceived discrimination against dominant groups were more likely to indicate that Trump won more votes than Biden, to claim that Biden was not legitimately elected, to disagree with the notion that the loser should acknowledge the winner, to think that voter fraud had a large impact, and to hold that the election was influenced by widespread conspiracies. Collectively, then, these individuals saw the election outcome as less legitimate. In contrast, those who perceived that minority groups were the object of discrimination were much

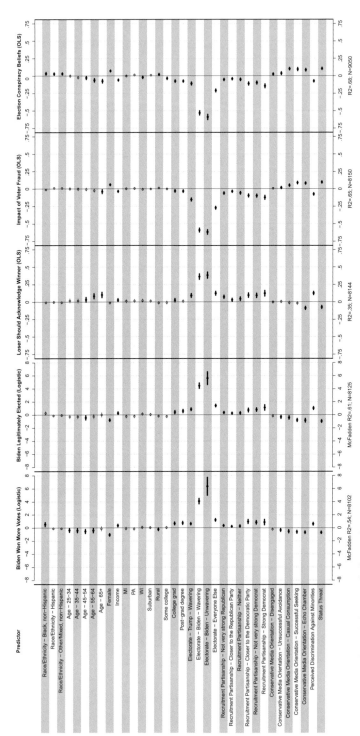

FIGURE 9.10 Status Threat and Electoral Legitimacy.

Standardized regression coefficients from regressions predicting various wave 10 measures of electoral legitimacy. For each variable, standardized coefficient estimates are given as circles with 95% confidence intervals as black lines. Bolded coefficients are statistically significant.

less likely to believe these things. These effects of status threat and perceived discrimination on legitimacy are substantively important as well. Highlighting the central role these factors play in perceptions of the election's legitimacy, these factors have a level of influence similar to that of having a higher level of education, to partisanship, or to seeking out conservative media.

Of course, status threat and perceived discrimination might have different effects for Trump voters and Biden ones. In particular, we might expect these effects to be especially large for Trump supporters, because of the messages coming from his campaign that we discussed in the last few chapters (and the fact that his voters were more likely to hold the attitudes that can be primed by those messages). To test for such differential effects, we reestimated the models underlying Figure 9.10 to include an interaction between our overall racial attitude measure and our electorates variable.[††] The results appear in Figure 9.11.

In Figure 9.11, we see the pattern we predicted: for Biden voters, racial attitude scores had very little effect on these measures of electoral legitimacy, but for Trump voters, as well as those who supported third-party candidates or did not vote, they had much larger effects.[‡‡] This supports our argument that rhetoric from candidates activates and highlights these concerns, which in turn delegitimizes Biden's victory. It is not enough for individuals to hold particular racial views or feel status threat; they need candidates to explain to them how these attitudes should play out politically.

Collectively, these results showcase how race and status threat affected beliefs about electoral legitimacy in 2020. Not all Trump supporters thought the election had been stolen, but those who had racially conservative attitudes and experienced status threat did. Put simply, we cannot understand the post-election crisis of electoral legitimacy on its own, but instead must understand it within these broader patterns of sociocultural anxieties.

Who Supports January 6 and Political Violence?

The findings in this chapter so far focus on electoral legitimacy and understanding which voters thought Biden would rightly assume the presidency.

---

†. As we discussed in Chapter 8, because status threat and perceptions of discrimination against minorities are so strongly predictive of our overall racial attitudes measure, a model interacted with racial attitudes produces nearly identical results to one interacted with status threat and perceptions of discrimination against minorities, but is easier to interpret. This again underscores the extent to which much of what we are observing was multiply determined.

‡. As a reminder, there are very few unwavering Trump voters who hold strongly pro-Black racial attitudes; hence the very large confidence intervals in some of the panels in Figure 9.11.

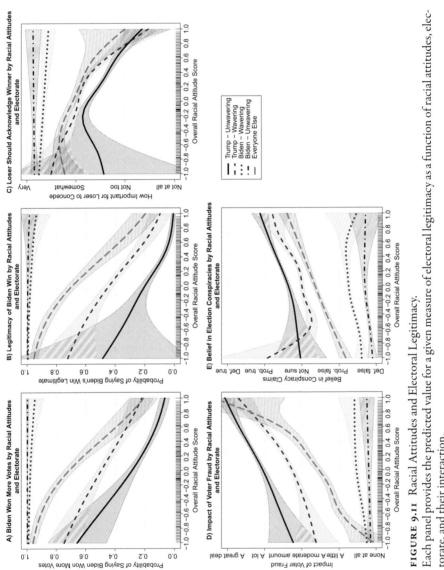

FIGURE 9.11 Racial Attitudes and Electoral Legitimacy.

Each panel provides the predicted value for a given measure of electoral legitimacy as a function of racial attitudes, electorate, and their interaction.

These are important questions. But, as we argued earlier in the chapter, they are not the whole story. The framing of January 6 means that these same factors that predict electoral legitimacy (or, more exactly, the lack thereof) presumably form the basis of support for the events of January 6 and for political violence more generally. To the extent that this is true, the implications are worrisome, as concerns about electoral legitimacy can quickly come to undermine broader democratic legitimacy. If the 2020 election was illegitimately decided, the result should not have determined who holds power; the country is being governed by a usurper. Under such circumstances, violence may be more likely to be seen as a legitimate means of protecting the American way of life and with it the will of "true" Americans (who presumably supported President Trump).

Individuals who doubt the legitimacy of the election would be expected to interpret the January 6 riot and its implications quite differently than most others. Indeed, the individuals who attended the "Save America" rally that played a role in precipitating the events of the day assembled in Washington, DC because they believed the election was illegitimate, a conclusion reinforced by speakers at that rally and the ones that took place the day before. But although tens of thousands of Americans attended the DC event and some among them besieged the Capitol, most Americans were observers, not participants in the rally or assault on the Capitol. In particular, it is important to unpack whether ordinary Americans who may have shared sentiments with some of the individuals in the rally audience at the Ellipse became apologists for the day's subsequent events.

To assess this, we consider both questions regarding beliefs about the activities that occurred on January 6 as well as measures of a more general openness to the view that political violence may sometimes be justified. In service of the former, we asked our panelists two questions in wave 10 (January 2021): (1) whether they approved of the actions of the people who entered the US Capitol to disrupt the process of certifying the outcome of the 2020 presidential general election, and (2) how patriotic they thought those individuals were. We also inquired about perceptions of whether members of the left-wing group antifa were present on January 6, as this was a claim made by Republican elites. To measure the belief that violence may sometimes be justified, we examined a set of beliefs rooted in the notions that the American way of life is threatened and that violence may be necessary and justified its defense.[20] To measure support for violence, we asked respondents in wave 9 (December 2020) two items originally used by political scientist Larry Bartels, examining whether they agreed with the claims "The American way of life is disappearing so fast that we may have to use force to save it" and "A time will come when Americans have to take the law into their own hands."[21] Distributions of each of these measures are shown in Figure 9.12. In further analyses, the two support-for-violence measures were combined into an index (Cronbach's α = 0.81).

Again, perceptions of the events of January 6 and of the legitimacy of using force for political ends differed markedly by electorate. While relatively few Americans either approved of the insurrection shortly after it happened or asserted that the rioters were patriotic, a large majority of those who held these views were in the Trump-supporting electorates (though these sentiments also were fairly common among those who said they did not vote for either candidate). Trump supporters also were convinced that members of antifa were part of the mass storming the Capitol. More general perceptions of when political violence might be justified, however, represented the starkest difference between the electorates. More than half of unwavering Trump supporters agreed with the sentiment that the American way of life was disappearing and that force may be necessary to save it (panel D), and 48.1 percent of these individuals somewhat or strongly agreed that Americans might need to take the law into their own hands (panel E). This latter sentiment was shared by a mere 6.1 percent of unwavering Biden supporters.

But to note that unwavering Trump voters were the most likely to approve of those who breached the Capitol, think insurrectionists were patriotic, believe that antifa members were part of the assault, and believe that force is justified for political ends is neither surprising nor enlightening. Instead, it is important to understand what factors beyond party preferences may have facilitated these beliefs. In particular, we want to know whether the individuals who adopted these points of view were influenced by the messages spreading on conservative media or particularly susceptible to those messages given their racial attitudes and feelings of status threat.

To assess this, in Figure 9.13, we model support for these outcomes.[§§]

We see that they do: the same factors that drove support for believing that the election was illegitimate are associated with these outcomes as well. Those

---

§§. We use ordinal logistic regressions to predict approval of the insurrection and assessments of the patriotism of insurrectionists because endorsement for these beliefs is sufficiently rare that distributional assumptions are violated when using ordinary least squares regression. The results in Figure 9.13 are not sensitive to these decisions, but those of Figure 9.14 are, as we discuss below.

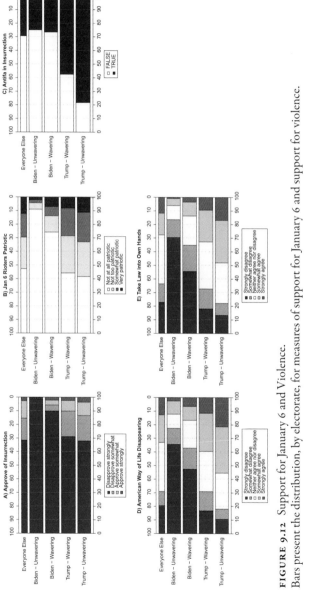

FIGURE 9.12 Support for January 6 and Violence.

Bars present the distribution, by electorate, for measures of support for January 6 and support for violence.

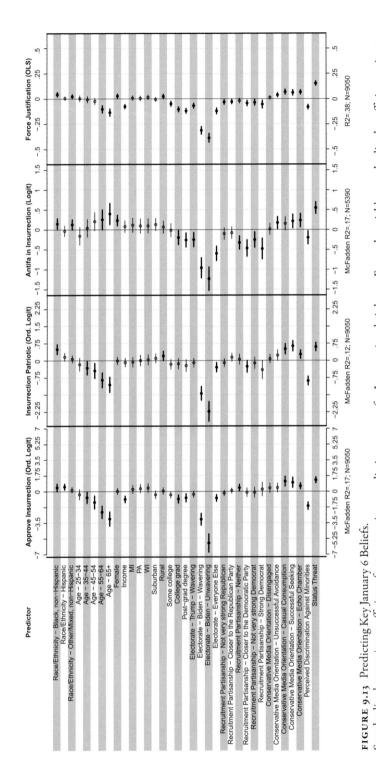

FIGURE 9.13 Predicting Key January 6 Beliefs.
Standardized regression coefficients from regressions predicting support for January 6 and violence. For each variable, standardized coefficient estimates are given as circles with 95% confidence intervals as black lines. Bolded coefficients are statistically significant.

who were experiencing status threat, who thought that minorities did not face much discrimination, or who consumed conservative media were more likely to approve of the January 6 attacks, believe that antifa played a role in them, and assert that force and violence can be justified. The role of status threat is particularly clear here—no other factor was as strong a positive predictor of any of these outcomes. Collectively, then, the factors that imply that Biden and Harris were illegitimately elected are also associated with the perception that violent means would constitute an acceptable recourse.

Seeing these patterns, we might wonder if other factors—electoral conspiracy theories, belief that the results were illegitimate, and support for violence—themselves predict support for the assault on the Capitol on January 6. Logically, they should: if you believe electoral conspiracies saying that the election was stolen, think the results were wrongly decided, and regard violence as justified, then you should be more accepting of a violent effort to prevent an unjust electoral certification. It is not simply that these factors might shape support for January 6; they should also influence perceptions of the players involved in the breach of the Capitol. While the evidence is incontrovertible that Trump supporters stormed the Capitol, some politicians and media outlets attempted to argue (incorrectly) that it was a false flag operation instigated by the FBI or antifa, as we discussed in Part 1 of this chapter. In presence of such assertions, we would expect that those who experience status threat or think that minorities do not face discrimination would be more likely to say that antifa supporters entered the Capitol and less likely to say that Trump supporters did so. In Figure 9.14, we see this pattern of results: all of these factors predict approval for January 6, perceptions that those who breached the Capitol were patriotic, and assertions that members of antifa were present.[***] Support for the January 6 attacks was not high, but it was notably higher among these sets of individuals.

Those who experienced status threat, believed that minorities did not face much discrimination, or were in a conservative media echo chamber were more likely to simultaneously support the Capitol breach and to believe that antifa members stormed the Capitol. This implies that the reactions to the day

---

[***]. Careful readers will note that our model predicts that strong Democrats were *more* likely to approve of January 6, which is very puzzling. But it is ultimately just a model artifact. It reflects the fact that Democrats—who uniformly believed that Biden was legitimately elected, who did not think there was a conspiracy to rig the election, and who were hesitant to justify the use of force—could not oppose the insurrection as strongly as the model predicted they should, because there was simply no available response option for expressing such a high level of disapproval.

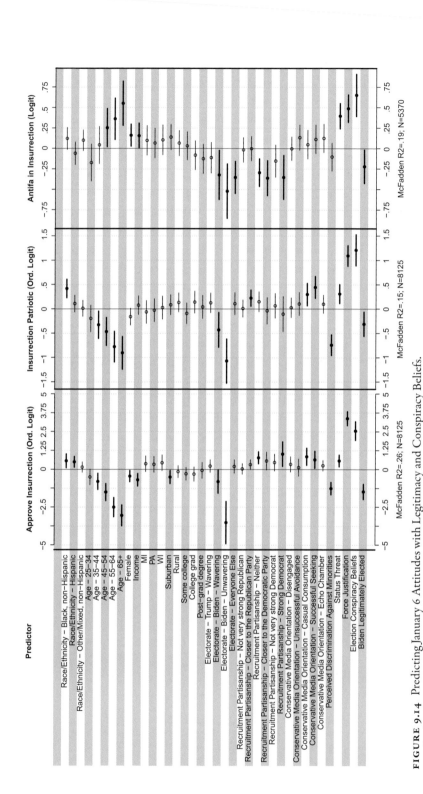

FIGURE 9.14 Predicting January 6 Attitudes with Legitimacy and Conspiracy Beliefs.
Standardized regression coefficients from regressions predicting support for January 6 and force justification perceptions as well as electoral conspiracy beliefs. For each variable, standardized coefficient estimates are given as circles with 95% confidence intervals as black lines. Bolded coefficients are statistically significant.

followed two distinct paths. Some individuals who felt status threat, thought force was justified, and accepted conspiracy beliefs, openly sided with those who attempted to disrupt certification of the election, while a larger group appears to have accepted a counternarrative to the truth, one that centers a nefarious "other" as the instigator of the attack on the certification process. This allows them to see themselves, and their compatriots, as the heroes rather than the villains of this story.

One might argue that perhaps we are focusing too much attention on a small group of relatively extreme individuals. After all, most people in our sample did not support January 6. Additionally, most—correctly—recognized that it was Trump supporters who stormed the Capitol. But in many ways, January 6 shows us that we need to focus both on the population as a whole and on these critical subpopulations. Even if support for some beliefs is rare, it does not take widespread support for them to produce tragic consequences. Further, we measured support for these attacks just after they occurred, when even many Republicans refused to defend them. In the months since, as elites have changed their story, support among Republicans has grown. Since conspiracy theories continue to spread online, support could increase even further. Indeed, in data collected subsequently by the Pew Research Center, the proportion of Republicans who said that it was somewhat or very important to prosecute those who broke into the Capitol declined from 79 percent in March 2021 to 57 percent that September.[22] Such shifts increase the importance of understanding this subpopulation.

Across this set of results, then, we gain insight into why some people support the assault on the Capitol. The debate over the election's outcome, and even over January 6, is not only about an election but also about who will wield power in America. It is about the nation's changing demographics, the sense that once-dominant groups are no longer as dominant, and the feeling that power is slowly beginning to be dispersed more widely.

Perceiving Future Threats

Another factor bodes poorly for the future, beyond even January 6. In wave 7 (October–November 2020, just before the election), in response to government reports arguing that white supremacist groups were the most prominent domestic threat facing the nation,[23] and in light of disagreement between Biden and Trump about the nature and extent of the danger, we asked respondents which posed a greater threat to the nation: activity by white supremacist and militia groups, or activity by antifa (respondents could pick one or the other, say that they were an equal threat, or say that neither one was a threat). While antifa activists do pose some risk, most experts agree that this relatively uncoordinated movement is far less dangerous than white supremacists and self-organized militia groups—indeed, a number of government officials now consider white nationalist groups the most significant domestic terrorist threat.[24] Does this same set of factors, especially status threat and racial attitudes, make it more likely that a respondent will view antifa members, rather than white supremacists and militia groups, as more threatening?

Figure 9.15 shows that it does: those who perceive more discrimination against dominant groups are more likely to think that antifa members pose a greater threat than white supremacists or that the threat levels are similar. To be clear, more of our sample sees white supremacists as the threat, which, according to security experts, is the correct answer: 32.0 percent of our sample says white supremacist groups are more of a threat, 21.6 percent says antifa poses more of a threat, and 40.7 percent says the threats are similar. An additional 5.8 percent says neither poses more of a threat. But a noteworthy number of individuals, and an outright majority of unwavering Trump supporters (52.6 percent), express greater concern about antifa. And perceptions of discrimination against majority and minority groups do seem to drive the sense that white supremacists may be less troubling.

When combined with the support for violence items (described above), as well as support for January 6, this finding reveals a worrisome pattern for our democracy moving forward. Because many of these white supremacist groups explicitly endorse violence, the two interlock, a phenomenon that stands as a reminder that for some Americans, violence, not dialogue, is the way to solve political problems. The crisis of electoral legitimacy is really a crisis of democratic legitimacy pivoting on the question of how we decide who will lead the nation and how we do so.

Electoral Legitimacy, Racial Animus, and the Future of American Democracy

As with our other crisis chapters, we begin our conclusion by briefly summarizing the results of our analyses:

- In the spring of 2020, Biden and Trump voters were equally likely to anticipate that the election would be conducted freely and fairly. By the fall,

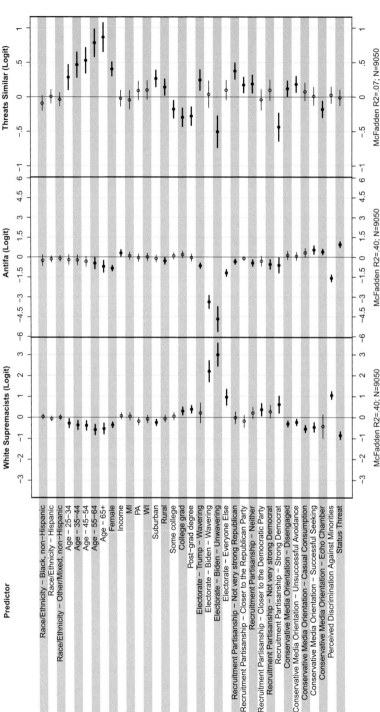

FIGURE 9.15 Is Antifa or Are White Supremacists More of a Threat? Standardized regression coefficients from logistic regression models predicting whether respondents believe antifa is a more of a threat (left-hand panel), white supremacists are more of a threat (center), or they pose similar threats (right-hand panel). For each variable, standardized coefficient estimates are given as circles with 95% confidence intervals as black lines. Bolded coefficients are statistically significant.

their attitudes had begun to polarize, a trend that accelerated dramatically in the post-election period. By the close of our study, Biden voters were convinced that the election was free and fair, while Trump's were skeptical of that claim.

- The incumbent's supporters who lived in states carried by Biden had less confidence in their state's outcome. It was not just the national outcome that drives beliefs in electoral legitimacy but the state-level ones as well.

- Over time, Biden and Trump voters polarized on the importance of the losing candidate acknowledging the winner as the legitimate president. While support for this norm was initially high in both groups, Trump voters became less likely to endorse it over time.

- Trump voters are much more likely to say that there was significant voter fraud in the election and that it benefitted Biden.

- In general, Trump voters are more likely to believe that Biden is an illegitimate president. This is especially true of those who are part of a conservative media echo chamber.

- Trump supporters are more likely to endorse conspiracy theories alleging that the election was rigged against him. Those who believe these conspiracy theories also are more likely to approve of the January 6 attack on the Capitol, as well as to believe that violence can be justified.

- Racial attitudes, as well as status threat and beliefs about the amount of discrimination faced by minorities, predict beliefs about electoral legitimacy. These same attitudes also predict support for the actions on January 6 (and the patriotism of those who entered the Capitol), the belief that antifa members were those storming the Capitol, and endorsement of the possible need for violence.

Although our findings that Trump supporters as a whole are less certain that the election is legitimate and that Biden is a legitimate president are disturbing, they could be discounted as expressive responding, at least in part. But which Trump supporters are the most skeptical is much more telling and important, especially combined with the finding that these same individuals were also more likely to approve of the January 6 insurrection, believe antifa members and not Trump supporters were the ones who entered the Capitol, and more generally think that violence can be justified.

This set of findings is important for two reasons. First, support for the January 6 attacks, and for violence more generally, transforms a crisis of electoral legitimacy into one of democratic legitimacy. When violence, not elections, becomes an appropriate way to determine who holds power, democratic governance crumbles: if the wrong people win elections, the answer is not to organize and try to win the next election but to use extralegal means to ensure that the right people are in office.

Second, this set of findings highlights that debates about election fraud, January 6, and the like are not simply an extension of a contested election; they are fundamentally about who holds power in America and whether America will peacefully transition to a multiracial, multicultural democracy. As we will argue in the book's concluding chapter, the answer to that question is a consequential one.

10

A Republic, if You Can Keep It

The Annenberg IOD Collaborative

Just say that the election was corrupt + leave the rest to me.
—President Donald Trump, speaking on December 27, 2020,
to acting attorney general Jeffrey Rosen and his deputy Richard
Donoghue, according to Donoghue's notes[1]

*I don't f---ing care that they have weapons. They're not here
to hurt me. Take the f---ing mags [magnetometers] away. Let
my people in. They can march to the Capitol from here. Let the
people in. Take the f---ing mags away.*
—President Trump on January 6, according to Cassidy Hutchinson,
a senior aide to White House Chief of Staff Mark Meadows[2]

*Actually, Mike Pence did have the right to change the out-
come . . . he could have overturned the Election!*
—Statement by Donald Trump, January 30, 2022[3]

The Fundamentals, the Crises, and the Election: A Precis of What We Have Learned

We began this book by introducing our four interlocking crises, arguing that one could not understand the election without studying their impact. In Chapter 2 ("What Fundamental Factors Shape Elections?"), we argued that, important as these crises were, a set of fundamental factors shape all elections, including the 2020 election. To open this final chapter, we provide a brief summary of what we have learned across our chapters about how, taken together, these fundamentals and the crises shaped what happened in 2020. Since we included a synopsis of our findings at the end of each chapter, we will not repeat that process here. Rather, we will telescope our conclusions into an overview of what we have learned over the past nine chapters.

Perhaps no fundamental factor is more important to how voters cast their ballots than the sine qua non of voter behavior—their partisanship. To win a bet about whether you can accurately identify how a person typically votes, just ask them their party ID, as the two are effectively synonymous today. Indeed, as we noted in the Appendix ("Our Data and Analytical Strategy"), this partisan-induced stability means that studying voting is much less interesting than studying voters. Hence we adopted the multiple-electorates framework that we outlined in Chapter 3 ("Not One Electorate, but Many").

As we showed in chapter after chapter, our electorates perceived our crises in fundamentally distinct ways. Responses to the pandemic are illustrative. Biden voters were more worried about the virus and its attendant health consequences, more attentive to news about it, and more anxious about it. Throughout 2020, they thought the pandemic's darkest days were still to come. In contrast, Trump voters were less concerned about the virus, less attentive to the news about it, and more likely to say that the worst of the pandemic was in the rearview mirror. Not only that, they polarized during our study in terms of how much they trusted public health figures such as Dr. Anthony Fauci or the CDC, with Democrats coming to trust them more and Republicans moving in the opposite direction. These attitudes mirrored how their candidates approached the pandemic, a finding reflecting the centrality of campaign messages, a theme to which we return in a moment. This sort of dramatic divergence characterized perceptions not just of this crisis but of the others as well: how voters perceived the economy, how they perceived the summer's Black Lives Matter protests, and how they perceived the legitimacy of the election. Partisanship and candidate choice (functionally the same thing) powerfully drove how voters interpreted the disruptive events of 2020.

Although partisanship is the most important factor in shaping vote choice, voters' evaluations of the economy are arguably a close second. Because presidents who preside over a growing economy are likely to win reelection, President Trump and his advisors thought that economic growth would deliver him a second term. But then COVID hit, disrupting the economy and complicating that prediction. Nevertheless, just as in earlier years, how voters perceived the economy mattered: those who thought the economy had improved during Trump's tenure in office, or who lived in areas in which the economy recovered more fully during 2020, were more likely to back the incumbent. The economy did help the president, just not enough to win reelection.

Most scholarship on economic voting focuses on sociotropic voting and argues that voters rely on the strength of the national economy, or at least the economy in their local area, to evaluate the incumbent. Another strand of literature suggests that their focus pivots on the health of their own financial circumstances. Findings of sociotropic effects are common, pocketbook effects less so. Our data show clear effects of both. The pocketbook effects we found are especially interesting. A voter's personal financial circumstances had a modest effect on whether one supported Trump or Biden, but a much larger effect on whether they would vote at all. This directs our attention to the unique economic dislocation of 2020 and the extent to which those at the bottom of the economic ladder experienced true economic pain and desperation in 2020. Our data highlight a conclusion largely overlooked by previous studies: economic pain works to exclude some citizens from the central act of voting, thereby largely disengaging them from the political system.

But in a year such as 2020, retrospective voting was not limited to how President Trump had managed the economy: his handling of the COVID-19 pandemic was also on the ballot. Here too we find evidence of retrospective voting. Those who initially supported President Trump but disapproved of how he navigated the pandemic became much less likely to vote for him; we identified similar results for other pandemic-related assessments. But in the end, those effects were smaller than one might have expected given the millions of infections and more than 200,000 deaths that occurred on his watch.

What dampened them was voters' partisan commitments. By prioritizing other issues, or concluding that the worst of the pandemic was behind the country, or highlighting aspects of Trump's pandemic leadership that they could praise, Trump supporters engaged in classic dissonance-reducing strategies. Partisanship's power mutes the likelihood that other sorts of issues—even a pandemic that killed over 200,000 Americans before the election—will decisively shape how voters make up their minds.

Of course, it is not just the objective conditions of the world that determine the outcome of an election; so too do the messages that voters see and the message environment in which they are received. Trump and Biden's face-off on the pandemic versus the economy vividly illustrates the power of those messages. As we discussed throughout the book, Trump and Biden presented starkly different visions of the pandemic and the economy. For Trump the priority was reopening the economy, whereas for Biden it was control of the pandemic. For Trump, the strength of the pre-COVID economy, the V-shaped recovery, and the resurgent stock market were reasons to give him a second term. Voters responded to these messages: Biden voters, by and large, prioritized the pandemic, while Trump voters featured the economy. In this election, the campaign's rhetoric affected which issue a voter considered most important (we return to this point below).

In Chapter 4 ("The Electorates' Communication Dynamics"), we hypothesized that a voter's action tendencies toward various types of media outlets would shape their attitudes. That is, do those who actively seek out particular types of media behave differently than those who shun those sources? In subsequent chapters, we found support for this argument in only one arena, a finding we will note in a moment. However, we remain convinced that this idea has merit and deserves future study. This is particularly true with respect to social media. As our exploratory Twitter analysis in Chapter 4 indicated, action tendencies there did make a difference.

Action tendencies mattered quite a lot for those ensconced in a conservative echo chamber (those who seek out conservative sources and avoid other media outlets). As we repeatedly observed, these voters saw the world in fundamentally different terms—a finding particularly pronounced with respect to the post-election crisis of legitimacy, when many of those in the echo chamber embraced very conservative outlets such as OANN and Newsmax that were openly dismissive of Biden's victory. Of course, there is a push and a pull here, and more work will be needed to think about treatment vs. selection effects in this context, but this group clearly deserves more careful study.

Although fundamental factors affect all elections, a set of factors unique to 2020 played an important role as well. We already saw one of them above: the power of partisanship, which has become the proverbial eight-hundred-pound gorilla in recent years. But two more deserve special note: the power of group identities, especially racial identities, and assumptions about the legitimacy of the processes involved in casting and counting votes.

Given Trump's rhetoric (see Chapter 7, Part 1, "Law and Order vs. Law and Order with Racial Justice: Debating How to Understand the Summer's Protests"), it is no surprise that racial attitudes mattered in 2020. These attitudes shaped how voters saw the summer's protest movement, as well as their decision to vote for Trump or Biden. But as we discussed in Chapter 8 ("A Deeper Anxiety"), contemporary racial attitudes include two related components: beliefs about discrimination against minority groups and those about discrimination against majority groups (such as White Americans, men, and Christians). This latter set of beliefs, termed status threat by social scientists, affects vote choice, as do beliefs about discrimination against minorities. To understand racial attitudes, we need to understand people's assessments of discrimination against *both* minority and majority groups.

Trump's rhetoric across his career ensured that the legitimacy of the election's outcome would be at issue if Trump lost. Before the election, Trump argued that Democrats would use mail-in ballots to steal the election from him. While there was no evidence that they did, he continued to claim that that was the case, even after sixty courts characterized his assertions as meritless. And over time, Trump began casting the assault on the Capitol as justified action. Although in his late-in-the-day January 6 videotaped address Trump had asserted that "the demonstrators who infiltrated the Capitol have defiled the seat of American democracy," stated that "those who engage in the acts of violence and destruction . . . do not represent our country," and said that those who broke the law would pay,[4] he declared instead at a rally in Conroe, Texas, on January 29, 2022, that "we will treat them [the people from January 6] fairly, and if it requires pardons, we will give them pardons, because they are being treated so unfairly."[5] As we highlight in Chapter 9 ("'Stop the Steal'"), Trump's supporters came to see the election as fundamentally unfair and rife with fraud (benefitting Biden), came to perceive the forty-sixth president as a usurper, and (for at least some of them) viewed the events of January 6 approvingly.

Those who are experiencing status threat and who think that minorities do not experience discrimination believe these things most strongly. This conclusion might seem puzzling at first, as racial attitudes are ostensibly unrelated to electoral legitimacy. However, electoral fraud connects to attitudes about race and status threat when it is framed in that fashion. Trump's rhetoric about who the "real" Americans are and his arguments about where voter fraud occurs (in urban areas with large numbers of Black voters) sent powerful signals to his susceptible supporters.

These same factors predict not just electoral legitimacy but also beliefs about the nature and justifiability of the January 6 attack, the patriotism of those who stormed the Capitol, and, more generally, the possible need for violence to redress grievances. This transforms a crisis of electoral legitimacy into a crisis of democratic legitimacy. It is not simply that some think Biden used voter fraud to steal the election; rather, because of that belief, some think it is acceptable, even praiseworthy, to use violence to overturn the election. Force, rather than the ballot box, becomes the way to resolve disputes—a chilling prospect.

Before we discuss some of the broader implications of our analyses, we wish to highlight two important implications of our arguments for a variety of different literatures in political science and communication.

The Role of Campaign Messages and the Centrality of the Economy and COVID-19

Our data suggest that the Biden campaign's messaging, coupled with the persistent presence of the pandemic, accomplished the unusual feat of displacing the economy as the central issue in many voters' minds. Because the economy is (almost) always one of the key issues in the campaign, as political science scholar Lynn Vavreck notes, the candidate who is advantaged by it emphasizes it.[6] Trump was no exception. But given the fluctuations throughout 2020, he had to prime a particular vision of the economy: the economic recovery would be V-shaped, and the economy would soon return to what it had been pre-COVID.

Instead of legitimizing Trump's focus on the economy, Biden's message downplayed the economy, saying that restoring it required bringing COVID-19 under control. This turned the usual logic on its head: instead of arguing over which one of them could better handle the economy, in effect the candidates debated which issue—the economy or the response to the virus—was the central one in the campaign. The strategy was optimal for each. As our data confirm, even Trump's own voters viewed his handling of the pandemic as a liability for the incumbent, and even some Biden supporters conceded that Trump's economic record was a plus for his candidacy.

This Biden-Trump clash highlights two truisms about elections. First, which issue voters prioritized was in no small part a function of campaign messages (and, of course, partisan predispositions). As our narrative throughout the book makes clear, Biden's message at every turn was that Trump deserved to lose because he had botched the handling of the pandemic. Trump, in contrast, did all he could to downplay the virus, to encourage people to believe that the United States was rounding the corner, or to focus on such pandemic accomplishments and strengths as the prospective vaccine or his decision to ban travel from China. Having done so, the incumbent then pivoted back to the economy and what he cast as its V-shaped recovery.

Second, and equally important, our findings highlight the challenge Biden faced in replacing the economy with concerns about the handling of SARS-CoV-2. It took a global pandemic, with more than 200,000 Americans dead in the United States by Election Day, to dislodge the economy as the issue of central concern in the contest. Biden advisor Anita Dunn was right when she reportedly told an associate, "Covid is the best thing that ever happened" to Biden.[7] As the title of Jonathan Allen and Amie Parnes's *Lucky: How Joe Biden Barely Won the Presidency* suggests, the COVID pandemic and Trump's faltering response to it aligned the stars for the Biden candidacy. Even at that, Biden barely won the pivotal swing states that decided the election.

Of course, had Trump behaved differently—by donning a mask, effectively coordinating the federal response with the states, and showing more empathy and compassion in the face of so much suffering and death, as his advisors were begging him to do throughout the year[8]—Biden's critique would have been less effective. But of course, that would have required Trump to have been a fundamentally different person.

Shifting the economy from its accustomed place in voters' agendas required not just a clear and compelling message but also a particular set of circumstances that allowed a different issue to break through and kept it accessible as voters made up their minds. The anxieties associated with pandemic-driven disruptions of the economy and fears tied to experiences of COVID-19 and its associated hospitalizations and deaths as well as media coverage of them did just that. So too did other alterations in daily life, including mask wearing, physically distancing in public, and contact with colleagues, family, and friends limited to Zoom.

What Is the Vision of America's Future?

The rhetoric and natural constituencies of the Biden-Harris and Trump-Pence tickets set two different visions of the country's past and future in marked relief. The Republican "Make America Great Again" theme implied a return to an earlier time in which White, native-born, Christian men controlled the reins of power, as they had since the earliest days of the republic.[*] Accordingly,

_____

[*]. The title of this chapter also refers back to that time, to a statement allegedly made by Benjamin Franklin when asked what form of government the new Constitution had created. Bartleby, citing *Respectfully Quoted: A Dictionary of Quotations* (1989), no. 1593, accessed 2021, https://www.bartleby.com/73/1593.html.

while explicitly asserting that he was the "least racist" person,[9] Trump none-theless referred to Haiti and a number of African nations as "shithole coun-tries,"[10] retweeted a video in which a supporter shouted "white power,"[11] and in 2016 implied that Indiana native Judge Gonzalo P. Curiel, a Mexican American, was incapable of fairly deciding a Trump-related case.[12] The former star of *The Apprentice* also trafficked in coded antisemitic tropes, asserting in October 2016, for example, that "Hillary Clinton meets in secret with inter-national banks to plot the destruction of U.S. sovereignty in order to enrich these global financial powers, her special interest friends and her donors."[13] Bundling sexism, racism, and xenophobia into the assumption that "our" government was not theirs, Trump also contended that four freshman congresswomen of color "came from countries whose governments are a com-plete and total catastrophe, the worst, most corrupt and inept anywhere in the world . . . [and are] now loudly and viciously telling the people of the United States, the greatest and most powerful Nation on earth, how our gov-ernment is to be run."[14]

In striking contrast, Biden and Harris promised an administration that would look like the country. Biden promised to put a Black woman on the Supreme Court, a promise he fulfilled when he nominated, and the Senate confirmed, Kentanji Brown Jackson to replace Stephen Breyer when he retired from the Court. The Biden-Harris ticket also put a Black and Asian American woman a heartbeat away from the presidency, and Biden told a contentious Black radio host that "if you have a problem figuring out whether you're for me or Trump, then you ain't black."[15] Consistent with his rhetoric during the campaign, in his inaugural address the Delawarean affirmed that "a cry for ra-cial justice some 400 years in the making moves us. The dream of justice for all will be deferred no longer."[16] "We are striving to forge a union with pur-pose, to compose a country committed to all cultures, colors, characters and conditions of man," said the national youth poet laureate, Amanda Gorman, at Biden's inauguration.[17] Her appeal was consistent with the call to "racial solidarity" that former First Lady Michelle Obama offered in her closing video for the Biden campaign: "They're stoking fears about Black and Brown Americans, lying about how minorities will destroy the suburbs, whipping up violence and intimidation—and they're pinning it all on what's been an over-whelmingly peaceful movement for racial solidarity," she said in a message that also labeled Trump's rhetoric "racist."[18]

The Trump and Biden visions could hardly be more different. Where one harkened back to an earlier era, the other embraced America's transition to a more multicultural and multiracial nation. The tension between the two is the most recent incarnation of the dispute about how to achieve the promise of America embedded in our founding documents. As Samuel Huntington's classic work makes clear, this debate has been ongoing since the founding.[19] As Huntington's critics, such as Rogers Smith, argue, because we disagree about what our national ideals actually are, the debate is even more fraught than it appears.[20] If the past is prologue, we should not expect resolution to be easy. But to put it starkly, one could argue that unless America transitions to an egalitarian, multiracial democracy, it may risk its identity as a democracy altogether. A vision of America grounded in ethnonationalism—where "Making America Great Again" requires going back to a halcyon day beyond recall[†]—is incompatible with the realities of an increasingly diverse nation that has pledged itself, in theory at least, both to the equality of all and to political equality. As racial and ethnic minorities become the numerical majority in the country, their access to the ballot should increase the likelihood that their rights and opportunities are no longer circumscribed. With voting power comes status, a reality at play in the ongoing contest over who can vote, how, and how easily, as well as which ballots should be counted, when, and by whom. The extent to which actions in the offing are limiting access of some to the franchise is a topic to which we will return in a moment.

What Broader Lessons Can We Learn?

The premise of the book, captured in its title, is that four consequential crises and their aftermaths continue to test the resilience of our democratic institutions. As we argued in Chapter 1 ("An Election Shaped by Crises"), few other elections have taken place amid so many significant intertwined challenges. Because the four crises on which we concentrated are woven together in different patterns for different individuals, saying that one mattered more than the others overall is a fool's errand. That said, we can still learn a number of lessons from their intersections. Three with implications for our politics moving forward are of special interest here: the normalization of violence, the polarization of public health, and electoral delegitimization.

The Normalization of Violence

Central to America's story of its origins is the notion that recourse to force is justified when other means of securing redress of grievances have been exhausted. In 1970, in a controversial passage, Supreme Court justice William

---

†. As one could correctly note, such days were halcyon only for the privileged. Few who invoke this argument reflect on what they meant for those of lesser status.

O. Douglas drew on that fact to argue that "we must realize that today's Establishment is the new George III. Whether it will continue to adhere to his tactics, we do not know. If it does, the redress, honored in tradition, is also revolution." Although Douglas noted that violence is unconstitutional, he also argued that "where grievances pile high and most of the elected spokesmen represent the Establishment, violence may be the only effective response."[21] Some of the January 6 rioters did indeed identify their actions with those of the American colonists who rebelled against British rule. Of course, the byproduct of that first revolution was the founding of a nation committed to due process and the rule of law, something antithetical to the sort of behavior the nation witnessed during the breach of the Capitol.

The tensions of 2020, however, had spawned violence long before the Capitol insurrection. Ugly confrontations not only emerged during the spring's anti-lockdown rallies but also percolated through the protests and counterprotests in the summer of 2020, as we discussed in Chapter 7 ("Law and Order vs. Law and Order with Racial Justice"). While Biden framed those demonstrations as part of the nation's long struggle for racial justice, Trump argued they were exemplars of chaos abetted by antifa. The irony of the incumbent's law-and-order frame was that his supporters and those aligned with his causes laced the election season with extralegal uses of force, including the clashes between MAGA-flag-carrying counterprotesters and those carrying signs reading "Black Lives Matter," as well as the beatings of police officers in the riot at the Capitol on January 6.

Violence threads through our crises, with events earlier in the year functioning as prologue to and presentiment of those coming later. Accordingly, the Wolverine Watchmen's plot to kidnap, try, and possibly execute Michigan governor Gretchen Whitmer in October foreshadows the noose strung outside the Capitol on January 6. The Watchmen's plot and the mayhem on January 6 chillingly testify to the extent to which some in the nation have normalized and legitimized violence as a means to their political ends.

It is not simply that violence is legitimized; it is also that violence, not politics, is seen by some as the only way to resolve our conflicts. Stuart Rhodes, a leader of the Oath Keepers indicted for seditious conspiracy in connection with the January 6 attack, remarked after Election Day, "We aren't getting through this [the presidential transition] without a civil war." Brian Ulrich, an Oath Keeper who pled guilty for his role in the attack on the Capitol, said, "Trump acts now [to prevent Biden from taking office] a few hundred radicals die trying to burn down cities . . . Trump sits on his hands Biden wins . . . millions die resisting the death of the 1st and 2nd amendment."[22] These remarks are particularly telling, and particularly chilling, because they assume that civil war is inevitable and the only question is what form it will take.

Of course, as we noted in Chapter 1, Trump had sanctioned the threat of violence as early as his 2016 campaign. This licensing continued into 2020, when, for example, he praised those at anti-lockdown protests that had degenerated into violence by saying, in an echo of his controversial response to the Charlottesville tragedy and a forecast of one of his responses to January 6, that "these are very good people, but they are angry. They want their lives back again, safely!" When urged by House Minority Leader Kevin McCarthy to tell his supporters to leave the Capitol on January 6, the incumbent reportedly rationalized the rioters' behavior by responding, "Well, Kevin, I guess these people are more upset about the election than you are."[23] His approval of the rioters was voiced again later in the day when his statement telling them to leave the Capitol affirmed that "we love you, you're very special." He also appeared to justify their behavior, saying, "These are the things and events that happen when a sacred landslide election victory is so unceremoniously & viciously stripped away."[24]

Twenty-four hours after the assault on the Capitol, Trump did, however, issue a video critiquing that day's violence. "The demonstrators who infiltrated the Capitol have defiled the seat of American democracy," he asserted. "To those who engaged in the acts of violence and destruction, you do not represent our country. And to those who broke the law, you will pay."[25] But by March 2021, his version of what had happened that day simply ignored the acts of violence. "Right from the start, it was zero threat," he told Fox's Laura Ingraham. "Look, they went in—they shouldn't have done it—some of them went in, and they're hugging and kissing the police and the guards, you know? They had great relationships. A lot of the people were waved in, and then they walked in, and they walked out."[26] "The Capitol Police were very friendly. They were hugging and kissing. You don't see that. There's plenty of tape on that," he also told two reporters in March.[27] And at another point he said, "There was a lot of love. I've heard that from everybody. Many, many people have told me that was a loving crowd."[28]

As we learned from testimony to the January 6th Committee, and we noted in our second epigraph to this chapter, Trump allegedly knew that some in the crowd had weapons, but he did not care as they were not there to hurt him. That provides a chilling postscript to that day's violence.

The activities at the Capitol are not the only evidence that false claims that the election was stolen have consequences. "At this point, we're living under corporate and medical fascism," said a young man at a Turning Point USA rally in October 2021. "This is tyranny. When do we get to use the guns?" As the audience applauded, he added, "No, and I'm not—that's not a joke. I'm not saying it like that. I mean, literally, where's the line? How many elections are they going to steal before we kill these people?" The presence of applause is as noteworthy as the question, which Turning Point USA's co-founder, Charlie Kirk, promptly denounced.[29]

The legitimation of the threat of violence has infiltrated the language of candidates for office as well as elected leaders. Before her election to the House, Georgia congressperson Marjorie Taylor Greene (R-GA) not only liked a tweet that said "a bullet to the head would be quicker" to oust Democratic House Speaker Nancy Pelosi but also did the same with comments about executing "deep state" FBI agents opposing former president Donald Trump.[30] In November 2021, the Democratic-controlled House of Representatives voted to censure Republican Congressperson Paul Gosar (R-AZ) and strip him of his committee assignments after he posted an animated video on social media depicting him murdering Democratic Congressperson Alexandria Ocasio-Cortez (D-NY).[31] Only two Republicans joined all Democrats in censuring Gosar (one Republican voted present). Sadly, such threats of violence against lawmakers have become increasingly, and disturbingly, common. In 2017, there were fewer than 4,000, but by 2020, that number had risen to 8,600,[32] and it climbed again to 9,600 in 2021.[33]

One might wish to dismiss such rhetoric as bombast and such threats as blowing off steam, but seen against the backdrop of the violence that punctuated the election season, that would be a mistake: underlying the threats is the assumption that violence, not discourse and rule-governed politics, may be the appropriate way to resolve political disagreement.

Despite the *New York Times*'s ominous headline "Menace Enters the Republican Mainstream,"[34] there is no evidence that most Republicans endorse the violence of January 6. But it is true that there are a number of Republican leaders who could have spoken against violence—against the violence at the lockdown protests, against the violence of January 6, or against Gosar's video—but did not. While the legitimation of violence is coming from a small number of leaders, the silence is coming from many more, and that is perhaps the most dangerous part. The whole point of politics is that it is the nonviolent resolution of conflicts; losing sight of this sends the nation down a dark path. Of course, what happens next is not predetermined. As historian Joanne Freeman notes, we are at something of a contingent moment (or, in the language of historical institutionalism, a critical juncture): there is a scenario in which violence becomes normalized, but another in which it is punished and set outside the pale.[35] The prosecution of those who destroyed property and assaulted police in the Capitol is sending the signal that such actions are unacceptable. The rhetoric that casts them as heroic patriots is licensing such behavior.

The Polarization of Public Health

Our findings in Chapter 5 ("Did the COVID-19 Pandemic Sink Trump's Reelection?") showed that Biden and Trump voters saw the pandemic through fundamentally different lenses: for Republicans, it largely had been overblown, whereas for Democrats, it was a clear and present danger. More surprisingly, perceptions of seemingly apolitical public health figures and entities—such as Dr. Anthony Fauci, the FDA, and the CDC—polarized over the course of our study. Although at the outset of the pandemic there were modest gaps in voters' confidence in the information provided by these figures, by the end of our study, after months of politicization—some stemming from the actions of these individuals and agencies, and some resulting from the rhetoric of politicians and media figures—they were seen through partisan-tinted lenses. Across time, modest differences became gulfs. Effectively apolitical scientific institutions became just another set of partisan objects.

To be sure, this is partially due to some of how these actors behaved, and there is justifiable criticism of some of their actions and decision-making processes. For example, the CDC[36] rolled out a flawed coronavirus test kit,[37] and under political pressure the FDA approved the drug hydroxychloroquine for emergency use, an authorization it later withdrew when studies found that the drug was not an effective treatment for COVID-19.[38] Fauci's inadequately explained reversal on masking and comments on Trump's and Biden's pandemic approaches also contributed to this politicization. Nevertheless, the overall effects we find are a function not simply of the rhetoric and actions of these organizations and individuals but also of how they were politicized by political actors. For example, President Trump, his trade advisor Peter Navarro, and their surrogates in conservative media such as Fox News's Tucker Carlson and Laura Ingraham functionally treated them as political operatives rather than scientific experts. While most voters did eventually mask up, masks and vaccines became potent totems of political identity in 2020 and

2021. In October 2021, according to Kaiser Family Foundation polling, the unvaccinated were overwhelmingly Republicans.[39]

In turn, this made fighting the pandemic that much harder. For example, in Arkansas, Republican Governor Asa Hutchinson initially supported and signed into law a ban on mask mandates when case counts were low in the spring of 2021. After the delta variant surged in the state over the summer, he tried to revoke the ban but was blocked by legislators in his own party.[40] Unsurprisingly, in the fall of 2021, the COVID mortality gap between red and blue states grew even wider: red states saw more infections and many more deaths, trends reflecting the differences in attitudes toward the pandemic in their populaces.[41] Indeed, as cases were rising in red states, many Republican governors doubled down on fighting policies (such as mask and vaccine mandates) designed to halt the spread of the virus,[42] even as hospitals filled up and some states—once again—faced the reality of needing to ration medical care.[43] For practical purposes, pushing back against COVID-related rules on vaccine mandates and such became a way for Republican politicians to signal their conservative bona fides; Florida's governor Ron DeSantis serves as a case in point.[44] Heading into the 2022 midterm elections, a number of Republicans have made pointed attacks on Fauci and other public health authorities, further polarizing attitudes toward the pandemic.[45] The politics of the pandemic are likely to persist, and perhaps even accelerate, rather than fade into the background.

The danger is not just that such behaviors complicate bringing the pandemic under control but also that they politicize public health more generally. In 2021, public health experts noted a partisan gap in flu shot uptake: in the past, Democrats and Republicans were equally likely to receive a flu shot, but in 2021, data from the Kaiser Family Foundation found a 25-point gap in flu shot uptake, and an Axios/Ipsos poll found a similar divide.[46] These are just a few polls, but they may be the harbinger of the politicization of other preventative health behaviors. Were that to occur, the nation would find fighting the next pandemic even more difficult from the outset.

Electoral Delegitimization

Trump and his base's response to Republican-sponsored audits that failed to confirm his claim of election theft reveal the extent to which the belief of partisans and the self-protective confirmation bias that protects it insulates them from reality. Also clear is the fact that no amount of evidence has led Trump to abandon his claims that the election was stolen. When the $6 million "forensic audit" of 2.1 million ballots his supporters had funded in Arizona's Maricopa County turned up 99 additional votes for Biden and removed 261 from Trump's column, he ignored the evidence and declared the result "a big win for democracy and a big win for us." By contrast, Arizona Senate President Karen Fann, a Republican, concluded that the tally underscored the results recorded in November. "Truth is truth, numbers are numbers," she declared at a hearing about the review. "Those numbers were close [to the original tally], within a few hundred [votes]."[47] For practical purposes, Trump and Fann ascribe to incompatible epistemologies.

As the first epigraph to this chapter attests, for Trump, reality is simply a rhetorical construction. In the process of creating his reality, the former president is willing to employ action unsanctioned by the Constitution if it advances his cause. As one of Trump's lawyers argued before January 6: "The main thing here is that Pence should do this without asking for permission—either from a vote of the joint session or from the Court. Let the other side challenge his actions in court."[48] This is eerily close to Nixon's famous phrase "When the president does it . . . that means that it is not illegal."[49] In both scenarios, the president and his surrogates are unrestrained by the checks and balances in the Constitution and unconstrained by the obligation to uphold the rule of law.

Relying on that philosophy, President Trump and his allies effectively delegitimized both the 2020 election and President Biden in the eyes of a large number of their followers. For these voters, regardless of the litany of evidence to the contrary, either Trump won the election or enough irregularities existed to call the results into question. Meanwhile, Trump himself continued to wave the fraudulent ballot, arguing in a June 2021 speech that "we can't have illegal aliens allowed to vote. Strong protection of poll watchers, our poll watchers, our poor, poor poll watchers. What happened to them in Philadelphia, what happened to them in Detroit, where they were literally thrown out of election for days and were actually afraid for their lives."[50] The irony here is that some individuals were, in fact, afraid for their lives, as Trump suggested. However, those fearful individuals were not Trump supporters but rather local election officials threatened by those enjoining them to "Stop the Steal."

There is also the alarming prospect that Trump's delegitimizing moves foreshadow what is to come. As then Senate Majority Leader Mitch McConnell put it after the insurrection on January 6, "If this election were overturned by mere allegations from the losing side, our democracy would enter a death spiral. We'd never see the whole nation accept an election again. Every four years would be a scramble for power at any cost."[51] In short, Trump's false voter fraud narrative has implications for both sides, and for future elections.

Pressure both from Republican elites and the grassroots will make it difficult for the Republican Party to move beyond 2020. When, after voting to impeach Trump for his role in the January 6 insurrection, Wyoming Republican Liz Cheney (R-WY) persisted in speaking against President Trump's mendacity, she was removed from her position as the conference chair by her fellow House Republicans;[52] the Wyoming GOP then voted to not recognize her as a member of the GOP, and she later lost her 2022 primary.[53] The Republican National Committee (RNC) voted to censure Representatives Cheney and Adam Kinzinger (R-IL) for participating in the House Select Committee to Investigate the January 6th Attack on the U.S. Capitol.[‡] In that censure, the RNC also called the January 6 attack "legitimate political discourse." While RNC chairwoman Ronna McDaniel later clarified that such discourse "had nothing to do with violence at the Capitol,"[54] it is hard to see the statement as anything other than an effort to downplay the significance of the storming of the Capitol that day. By mid-August 2022, eight of the ten Republican members of Congress who voted for impeachment had chosen to retire or been defeated in primaries.[55]

Especially with Trump waiting in the shadows as a potential 2024 presidential candidate, it is hard to imagine many prominent Republicans refusing to pledge fealty to his argument that 2020 was stolen from him. This reluctance has drawn criticism from the *Wall Street Journal*, which editorialized that the party "should quit chasing him [Trump] down rabbit holes [like electoral fraud]" and instead focus on opposing Biden and congressional Democrats.[56] Few prominent Republicans have taken the *Journal*'s advice.

On the bright side, in November and December 2020, state and local election officials—many of them Republicans—rebutted claims of electoral fraud and highlighted the free and fair nature of the elections they had overseen. However, some who did so faced electoral challenges[57] or have been replaced, especially in key states such as Michigan.[58] In the wake of 2020, those loyal to Trump's claims of electoral manipulation are running in large numbers for

---

‡. In the days after the January 6 attack, there was bipartisan support for an investigation of it, and party leaders eventually reached a deal to create an independent commission modeled on the one that examined the 9/11 terrorist attacks. Republicans then rejected that proposal, so House Democrats created a special committee and appointed the only two Republicans who voted in favor of it (Cheney and Kinzinger) to serve on it. For the story of the committee, see Jacqueline Alemany and Tom Hamburger, "The Jan. 6 Committee: What It Has Done and Where It Is Headed," *Washington Post*, January 4, 2022.

local office and electoral positions.[59] Of the fifteen Republicans seeking the office of secretary of state in five battlegrounds in 2021, a Reuters investigation found that ten persist in questioning whether Trump actually lost the 2020 election.[60] At the same time, local councils have passed laws—which their own lawyers admit are unenforceable—to try to prohibit voter fraud[61] even though there is no evidence confirming its existence. This suggests that the next time, there will be less resistance from these central actors.

Additionally, some in the Republican ranks who pushed back on Trump's claims in 2020 are leaving the political stage in the face of likely defeat in their party's primaries. For example, knowing that he would have faced a Trump-backed challenger had he sought reelection, Ohio representative Anthony Gonzalez (R-OH), who voted to impeach Trump, retired rather than run for reelection;[62] Adam Kinzinger of Illinois did the same.[63] Hearing about these retirements, Trump's reaction was "Two down, eight to go!"—a reference to the fate of the ten House Republicans who voted to impeach him.[64] Prior to January 6, two of the seven Republican senators who voted to convict Trump in February 2021—Richard Burr (R-NC) and Patrick Toomey (R-PA)—had already indicated their plans not to seek reelection, and were thereby insulated from Trump's electoral retribution.

Of course, many Republican leaders accept Biden's legitimacy. For example, in January 2022, the *New York Times* reported that after the November 2020 election, President Trump directed Rudy Giuliani to call the Department of Homeland Security to ask if the president had the legal authority to seize voting machines in key swing states (the officials at Homeland Security said that he did not).[65] When asked about this story several days later, Senate minority whip John Thune said, "I'm just glad that there were people in the right places and that the system worked. . . . People who had positions of responsibility held their ground even when being asked to do things that they knew they shouldn't do. Things may have bent a little bit, but they didn't break."[66] Similarly, McConnell has repeatedly noted that once the Electoral College voted, Biden was the legitimate president-elect. These leaders are, in effect, trying to walk a fine line: not supporting Trump's lies about voter fraud, but also not denouncing them too directly (likely for fear of drawing Trump's ire). But without clear statements from these leaders—ones that clearly and unambiguously denounce Trump and his falsehoods—this point gets lost in the conversation for ordinary voters.

Indeed, as political scientists Steven Levitsky and Daniel Ziblatt put it, the problem is not just with Trump but rather with elites in the Republican Party who have embraced his rhetoric about voter fraud. "In 2018, when we wrote

How Democracies Die, we knew that Donald Trump was an authoritarian figure, and we held the Republican Party responsible for abdicating its role as democratic gatekeeper," they noted. "But we did not consider the GOP to be an antidemocratic party. Four years later, however, the bulk of the Republican Party is behaving in an antidemocratic manner."[67] Of course, Trump was not the only one who pushed claims of a stolen election. A number of other Republicans, including members of Congress, did so as well.[68]

It now appears that members of Congress were involved with efforts to keep President Trump in the White House, including calling for slates of alternative electors in states where Biden won.[69] While it was clear that Trump and his associates were involved in such efforts,[70] this underscores that such efforts were broader, and involved members throughout the party, not to mention Ginni Thomas, the wife of a Supreme Court justice.[71] Trump may have been the epicenter of this effort, but he was far from an isolated actor.

Elite rhetoric matters. Bill Gates, a Republican member of the Maricopa County, Arizona, Board of Supervisors, who faced pushback from his party over his refusal to support Trump's claims, put it well: "The sad thing is that there are probably millions of people—hardworking, good Americans, maybe retired—who have paid their taxes, always followed the rules, and they truly believe this, because of what they've been fed by their leaders."[72]

There is now considerable evidence that Republican leaders knew Trump's claims were specious, yet they persisted in making them anyway.[73] After meeting with Rudy Giuliani, Senator Lindsey Graham (R-SC) allegedly said the claims Giuliani presented were suitable for the "third grade,"[74] and campaign memos confirm that many of Trump's legal team knew that their arguments were baseless as well.[75] Nevertheless, few Republicans spoke out against Trump; many continue to legitimize his false claims of voter fraud. The consequence is that ordinary voters, hearing their party's elites singing from the same hymnbook, believe the words to the chorus that they were asked to sing.[76]

Such elite rhetoric can become a self-fulfilling prophecy. For months, Trump and his allies promulgated the false claim that Democrats would use voter fraud to steal the election; Trump's voters believed them. Allaying these concerns in the mass public then became a justification for investigations of the 2020 election. When no significant fraud was uncovered, elites could then say the fact of the investigations themselves confirmed the need to tighten election security. And while this logic begged the question, the implications were clear: repeat a claim sufficiently often to make it central to the identity of a sympathetic audience, and its members will be more likely to support measures to address a nonexistent problem.

One could dismiss these machinations as just political ploys, but they remain dangerous on several levels. First, these allegations have become the basis for laws to limit voter access in states such as Texas and Georgia. More than eighteen states have enacted laws that could make it harder to vote. Some bills, such as the one in Texas, take particular aim at large urban—and hence more Democratic—counties.[77] Indeed, heading into 2022 and 2024, debates over voting access have become a central fault line in many states.[78]

Even more significant than limits to the franchise are efforts that strip power from local officials and move it to state actors, as proposed laws in Georgia[79] and Wisconsin would do;[80] a similar law was considered and killed in Arizona by the state's Republican House Speaker.[81] These proposed changes raise the prospect that a future state legislature could decide to decertify an election (or simply try to appoint different electors) if it did not like the outcome. To be clear, although this remains extremely unlikely, that scenario has gone from unthinkable to within the realm of possibility. As Jane Mayer wrote in *The New Yorker*, "Richard Hasen, a law professor at the University of California, Irvine, and one of the country's foremost election-law experts, told me, 'I'm scared shitless.' Referring to the array of new laws passed by Republican state legislatures since the 2020 election, he said, 'It's not just about voter suppression. What I'm really worried about is election *subversion*. Election officials are being put in place who will mess with the count.' "[82] According to emails obtained by *Politico*, Trump lawyer John Eastman encouraged Pennsylvania legislators to do exactly that in 2020, urging them to reject absentee ballots (claiming fraud) to swing the state to Trump and then certify a new slate of electors.[83]

The myth of voter fraud sprouted another corollary belief: that January 6 was not a fundamental challenge to our democracy. In a sign of the party's shift over time, House Minority Leader Kevin McCarthy, once critical of Trump and his role in the January 6 insurrection, now says the former president had "no involvement" in the day's events.[84] While GOP leaders privately criticized the former president, they were unwilling to do so publicly, as we noted above.[85] It is not simply that some of them are saying that Trump was uninvolved; rather, many in the Republican Party have created an alternative account of that day, as we discussed in Chapter 9. In this fictional narrative, those storming the Capitol were not Trump supporters but instead were antifa operatives in a false flag operation,[86] and the day's events were largely a "peaceful protest"[87] or were carried out by "patriots,"[88] Ashli Babbitt chief among them. Shot by Capitol police while trying to enter the House chamber, Babbitt was termed "an innocent, wonderful, incredible woman" by President

Trump.[89] By some accounts, the former president's embrace of Babbitt led others to feel that they could do the same not only with her memory but also with others involved in the riot.[90] Additionally, Arizona Republican Paul Gosar has pushed the line that Babbitt is a martyr, and grilled the FBI director over responsibility for her death.[91] From this optic, the riot at the Capitol on January 6 is not a stain on our democracy but instead a failure of the political system to acknowledge the truths that Trump is the rightful victor and that his patriotic supporters attempted to protect that deserved outcome for him and the well-being of the nation.

Finally, the arguments about voter fraud in 2020 will hover like a shadow over future elections. In 2016, Trump laid the groundwork to cast doubt on the fairness of the outcome (likely expecting that he was going to lose). In 2020, he fueled these flames again, and as we showed, the effects lingered, especially among those who actively sought out conservative media. In 2022 and 2024, these same voters will be primed at the outset to expect voter fraud, and even if it does not exist, they will seek it and claim that they have found it. That quest will further undermine their confidence in the election. While there are always partisan gaps in perceptions of the fairness of the outcome of elections, a worrisome proportion of the citizenry may now be disposed to accept an election result as legitimate only when their side wins.

This becomes even more troubling given what we now know about how President Trump behaved in the aftermath of the 2020 contest. In a post-election interview with Carol Leonnig and Philip Rucker of the *Washington Post*, the forty-fifth president of the United States reflected on his post-election strategy: "When asked whether he needed better lawyers to push his case of voter fraud, Trump replied: 'I needed better judges. The Supreme Court was afraid to take it. . . . It should have been reversed by the Supreme Court. I'm very disappointed in the Supreme Court because they did a very bad thing for the country.' Trump singled out Justice Brett Kavanaugh, suggesting that he should have tried to intervene in the election as payback for the president standing by his nomination in 2018 in the face of sexual assault allegations. 'I'm very disappointed in Kavanaugh,' he said."[92] This suggests that he considered Kavanaugh's nomination a sort of quid pro quo, and underlines why he pushed so hard to ensure that Amy Coney Barrett was appointed to the Court so soon after Ruth Bader Ginsberg's death: he would need the Court to side with him if an election case reached its docket. To be clear, the Court never took up these cases and seemed to want to stay out of the election. But Trump's expectation that they would intervene and that, when they did so, the justices he nominated would be his for the asking remains deeply problematic nonetheless.

Trump's efforts to undermine the election outcome did not stop there. Not only did he and his campaign sue and work to discredit the results in key battleground states; importuning election officials was part of his repertoire as well. Trump allegedly asked Congressperson Mo Brooks (R-AL) and others to overturn the election,[93] allegedly wanted to fire a US attorney in Georgia for not backing his claims of voter fraud,[94] tried to contact election officials in Phoenix to pressure them,[95] and harangued officials in Georgia, which became a point of contention in his second impeachment trial and for which a grand jury has been empaneled.[96] The incumbent president also pressured Department of Justice officials to declare that the election had been fraudulent.[97] The pressure on the Department of Justice is especially worrying, although officials there did refuse to intervene to try to overturn the November 2020 presidential election results in Georgia.[98] Trump and his allies also tried to pressure Mike Pence to thwart certification of the Biden-Harris win on January 6, even outlining a strategy for him to do so.[99] Even in September 2021, nine months after Biden had been sworn in as president, Trump was still urging Georgia officials to decertify Georgia's 2020 presidential results.[100]

Trump of course had a right to take his case to court; he repeatedly did so and repeatedly lost. It is his extralegal avenues that are of concern here. That's why the first and third epigraphs to this chapter are so haunting. If the Department of Justice would just declare the election illegitimate, Trump said, then he would be able to leverage the credibility of that institution to push for a different outcome. If Mike Pence would just declare that he had the constitutional authority to overturn the election, Trump could remain in office. This scenario suggests that the fears of Hasen and other experts are justified: with a different set of bureaucrats, or a different set of judges, the next Trump, or Trump himself, might succeed where in 2020 the incumbent failed. That prospect, by definition, is a tail risk: a low-probability event with a very large negative payoff. While we seek to avoid alarmism, there is a real risk of erosion of democratic bulwarks here. Indeed, reflecting that risk, in 2021 the International Institute for Democracy and Electoral Assistance listed the United States as a backsliding democracy for the first time.[101]

Nor should we underplay the important roles that bureaucrats played—or had the potential to play—in altering electoral dynamics. Here the role of the postmaster general and the director of the Cybersecurity and Infrastructure Security Agency (CISA) are particularly noteworthy. On the positive front, before he was fired by Trump, CISA director Chris Krebs debunked the electoral conspiracy claims of Trump and his surrogates, reaffirming that the 2020 election was free and fair. On the negative side of the ledger, the Trump-appointed postmaster general, Louis DeJoy, began the process of removing mail-sorting machines that could facilitate the processing of mail-in ballots. Whether as a cost-saving measure (as he claimed) or in order to thwart the on-time delivery of the mail-in ballots that Trump believed would ensure his opponent's election (as his opponents claimed), the inconvenience and delays associated with this change could have altered the outcome, especially in a year in which mail-in balloting by Democrats was widely expected to surge in numbers (as it did). Faced with outrage from Democrats and some Republicans, the postmaster general suspended those plans until after the election. But in a different year, with less outrage or a different party in control of the House or Senate, the outcome might be more problematic.

Social Media and the Spread of Misinformation

If democratic backsliding is an issue and the reach and impact of Trump's rhetoric a possible accelerant, then the roles and responsibilities of his dominant channels of influence, especially Facebook, Instagram, and Twitter, come to the fore. Shortly after the insurrection, Facebook and Twitter cited public safety as the reason for denying Trump access to their platforms.[102] "After close review of recent Tweets from the @realDonaldTrump account and the context around them . . . we have permanently suspended the account due to the risk of further incitement of violence," Twitter stated.

In a similar vein, in summer 2021 when Facebook announced an extension of Trump's suspension for two years, until at least January 7, 2023, the platform noted that it would reinstate him only "if the risk to public safety has receded."[103] "At the end of this period, we will look to experts to assess whether the risk to public safety has receded," reported Facebook's vice president of global affairs, Nick Clegg. "We will evaluate external factors, including instances of violence, restrictions on peaceful assembly and other markers of civil unrest. If we determine that there is still a serious risk to public safety, we will extend the restriction for a set period of time and continue to re-evaluate until that risk has receded."[104]

Deplatforming some individuals has effectively dampened their toxicity, as the cases of Milo Yiannopoulos and Alex Jones illustrate. Removing their megaphones greatly reduced their reach.[105] One might expect that banning Trump would have the same effect. At some level it has, in that his reach and ability to instantly hijack the news agenda with a tweet have dropped, though undoubtedly much of this effect simply reflects the fact that he is no longer in office.

One key factor differentiates Trump from others. While he may have lost the use of several of the channels he used to communicate directly with the American public, he remains the undisputed and hence powerful leader of the Republican Party. Republicans who have critiqued Trump have been sidelined, just as they were in 2016, and the party has embraced the claim that the 2020 election was illegitimate (or, at a minimum, is unwilling to dispute this claim publicly). This belief strengthens Trump's hand, as it makes him the aggrieved party seeking justice. Even without the Twitter megaphone, as long as Trump remains a potent force within the party, he has the power to make his voice heard, albeit more softly, in mainstream news and conservative media.

This means that simply deplatforming him will not sideline Trump, for two reasons. First, he can still get attention from the mainstream media (by, for example, issuing press releases or saying provocative things at rallies). As a former president and potential 2024 contender, he is inherently newsworthy. Unlike past losing candidates, Trump is undoubtedly the most significant Republican in his party writ large. Second, and more importantly, Trump's claims have survived on both Facebook and Twitter. When one influential voice is banned by some platforms, "minion accounts"—parallel, non-banned accounts—spread the message instead.[106] It is not just the algorithms but our social connections and identities that facilitate the spread of content on social media.[107] Although banning the account of an individual does deny them ready access to the followership attuned to that platform, if the person has a loyal audience, their followers can be directed to other venues featuring that person. Trump can, for example, call in to the Sean Hannity or Maria Bartiromo shows on Fox at will, and Newsmax and OANN are highly likely to carry his rallies.

If protecting the nation from the sort of violent disruption that characterized January 6 is one's goal, then Trump's rhetoric on the platforms is not the only cause for concern. The organizing capacity of allied groups is worrisome as well. Not only did a report by the Tech Transparency Project confirm a relationship between Facebook's groups feature and accelerated growth of the "Stop the Steal" movement,[108] but an investigation by the *Washington Post* and ProPublica that examined millions of posts found that in the run-up to January 6, Facebook groups daily posted more than ten thousand attacks on the integrity of the presidential election, among them a sizable number fomenting violence.[109] In the same vein, documents shared with the US Securities and Exchange Commission (SEC) and provided to Congress by former Facebook employee and whistleblower Frances Haugen confirmed an increase in social media posts inciting violence on January 6.[110]

Another worrisome platform feature is the ways in which algorithms drive viewers to increasingly extreme content. Speaking to *60 Minutes* reporter Scott Pelley on October 4, 2021, Haugen said, "Facebook has realized that if they change the algorithm to be safer, people will spend less time on the site, they'll click on less ads, they'll make less money."[111] Haugen further indicted her former employer for shutting down its Civic Integrity team and turning off election misinformation tools after the election. Documents provided by Haugen's legal counsel to the SEC not only suggest that Facebook prematurely abandoned measures in place to deal with election-tied misinformation but also confirm that, in the words of the *Washington Post,* "the company's internal research over several years had identified ways to diminish the spread of political polarization, conspiracy theories and incitements to violence but that in many instances, executives had declined to implement those steps."[112]

Testifying before the Senate Subcommittee on Consumer Protection on October 5, 2021, Haugen also stated that "Facebook's products harm children, stoke division, weaken our democracy and much more" and that the company is "accountable to no one."[113] When asked by the Senate subcommittee what she recommends, Haugen pointed to amending Section 230 of the 1996 Communications Decency Act to make Facebook liable for algorithms that promote misinformation and hate.[114]

Section 230 states that "no provider or user of an interactive computer service shall be treated as the publisher or speaker of any information provided by another information content provider,"[115] and it has been referred to the "26 words that created the internet" by cybersecurity law professor Jeff Kosseff.[116] Section 230 is the result of two landmark cases. In 1991, a federal court ruled that online service provider CompuServe was a distributor, not a publisher, and could not be held liable for the content it provided. A few years later, a 1995 New York state court ruling deemed online service provider Prodigy liable for content because the service provider moderated content that users posted.[117] These two cases created a perverse incentive: companies became liable when they tried to moderate, so the rational response would be to not do so, the opposite of what policymakers should want. To rectify this, in Section 230, Congress stipulated that companies were not responsible for user-generated content, even if they moderated it.[118] Without Section 230, the internet as we know it today and companies such as Facebook, Twitter, and YouTube would not exist in their current form, because they would potentially be liable for all user-generated content (and hence would need to regulate it much more carefully than they currently do).

Section 230 has been targeted for reform by both sides of the political aisle: it has been a "punching bag for Democrats and Republicans for years."[119] Those on the left call for reform because of widespread misinformation and hate that social media companies fail to curb, much as Haugen claimed. Those on the right seek reform because they believe that tech companies are censoring conservative voices.[120] In July 2021, Democratic senators Amy Klobuchar (D-MN) and Ben Ray Luján (D-NM) proposed the Health Misinformation Act, which would create exceptions to Section 230 if content is deemed health misinformation during times of public health emergencies.[121] On the other side, during most of 2020, Trump called for the complete dismantling of Section 230, and on May 28, 2020, he issued the Executive Order on Preventing Online Censorship, aimed at holding companies liable for content if they restrict or remove access to users.[122] The executive order, which was almost immediately challenged in court,[123] was revoked by Biden in May 2021.[124]

On Twitter, Trump called for the dismantling of Section 230 more than three dozen times.[125] Responding to Facebook deleting his post that falsely stated that the flu was more deadly than COVID-19 and to Twitter adding a warning label to a similar post, Trump tweeted "REPEAL SECTION 230!!!" on October 6, 2020, and retweeted it on October 7.[126] Trump repeatedly called on Congress to repeal Section 230 as part of the bipartisan National Defense Authorization Act (NDAA), and he threatened to veto the bill when his wish went unfulfilled. On December 8, 2020, the president tweeted, "I hope House Republicans will vote against the very weak National Defense Authorization Act (NDAA), which I will VETO. Must include a termination of Section 230 (for National Security purposes), preserve our National Monuments, & allow for 5G & troupe [*sic*] reductions in foreign lands!"[127] After vetoing the bill on December 23,[128] Trump tweeted, "Twitter is going wild with their flags, trying hard to suppress even the truth. Just shows how dangerous they are, purposely stifling free speech. Very dangerous for our Country. Does Congress know that this is how Communism starts? Cancel Culture at its worst. End Section 230!"[129] Congress overrode the veto on January 1, 2021—the only veto override of Trump's presidency.[130]

But is Haugen correct that reforming Section 230 would work? Perhaps allowing lawsuits against online content providers could incentivize them to remove false or misleading content (as it does in other media). Two challenges for social media sites, however, are the sheer volume of content and the fact that most of it is produced by amateurs, not professional journalists. It is one thing to vet a small number of claims in a newspaper or on TV generated by journalists who respect professional norms. However, doing it for social media posts involves algorithmic decisions, armies of content moderators, or both. In the past, those moderators have rebelled over work requirements and conditions, leading to a 2020 payout from Facebook.[131] Lawsuits could also have a chilling effect, handicapping smaller tech upstarts while favoring larger companies such as Facebook.

An alternative would be to have the FCC or other government bodies make these regulatory decisions, but then the question of who does the moderation—and how we ensure it is free of bias—becomes paramount. *New York Times* opinion columnist Farhad Manjoo brought this question into stark relief by asking, "Why would we choose to empower such a president's cabinet appointee as the arbiter of what's true and false during a pandemic?"[132]

Further muddling the Section 230 problem is the advent of Trump's social media platform, Truth Social,[133] which launched in 2022[134] and, like all social media sites, benefits from Section 230. The terms of service of Truth Social state, "We are not responsible for any Third-Party Websites accessed through the Site or any Third-Party Content posted on, available through, or installed from the Site, including the content, accuracy, offensiveness, opinions, reliability, privacy practices, or other policies of or contained in the Third-Party Websites or the Third-Party Content" and "As a user of the Site, you agree not to ... disparage, tarnish, or otherwise harm, in our opinion, us and/or the Site."[135] If users do not successfully contest these provisions, the protections offered by Section 230—the same ones that Trump railed against—will now protect the former president and other Truth Social users during future elections.

The development by the Trump Media and Technology Group (TMTG) of Truth Social[136] is a testament to the former president's desire to sidestep filtering of his messaging. At the same time, the launch signaled the importance Trump attaches to unfettered access to a direct channel of communication to his supporters (not to mention the financial benefits associated with monetizing their attention as well). According to Trump, Truth Social would serve as "a rival to the liberal media consortium and fight back against the Big Tech companies." "I created TRUTH Social and TMTG to stand up to the tyranny of Big Tech," he said in a statement. "We live in a world where the Taliban has a huge presence on Twitter, yet your favorite American President has been silenced."[137] TMTG also forecast the launch of "a subscription video-on-demand service which would feature 'non-woke' entertainment programming, news and podcasts."[138] Rumble, a competitor to YouTube that bills itself as an anti-cancel-culture video platform, will provide Truth Social with video and streaming services.[139] However, a May 2022 filing with the SEC reported that the Truth Social app, which has six hours of exclusive access to Trump's messages, had yet to attract paying advertisers and that TMTG expected "to incur significant losses into the foreseeable future."[140] In August 2022, Steven Brill's NewsGuard reported that "Trump, who has 3.8 million followers on Truth Social, has 'reTruthed' (Truth Social's phrase for retweeting) 30 different QAnon-promoting accounts a cumulative 65 times since first posting on the platform in April 2022. Cumulatively, the QAnon-promoting accounts boosted by Trump have approximately 772,000 followers."[141]

The Diminishment of Impeachment as a Check on Executive Power

The experiences of 2020 demonstrate that some of the presumed checks in the US governmental system are not as robust as one might have supposed. The partisan divide reflected in each of the two impeachments of Trump suggests that in these polarized times, that process is not a serious constraint on executive overreach.

In the wake of the Senate's refusal to convict Trump after his first impeachment by the House—for implying that if Ukraine wanted military aid, its leaders needed to announce an investigation of supposed wrongdoing by Joe Biden, his likely Democratic opponent—some Republicans asserted that a vote to convict was unwarranted. For example, Senators Mike Braun (R-IN), Lamar Alexander (R-TN), and, most notably, Susan Collins (R-ME) argued that Trump had learned his lesson and would rein in his behavior.[142] Speaking to Norah O'Donnell of CBS News, Senator Collins stated, "I believe that the president has learned from this case. . . . The president has been impeached. That's a pretty big lesson. . . . And there has been criticism by both Republican and Democratic senators of his call," she continued, before predicting: "I believe that he will be much more cautious in the future."[143] Collins's optimistic forecast was undercut by Trump's post-election behavior. Meanwhile, the notion that a president can act without restraint in his final weeks in office was reinforced when, during his second impeachment trial, Senate Republicans argued that he could not be convicted because he had already left office.

Indeed, the lesson of both Trump impeachments is that impeachment is a toothless check on executive overreach in most situations in contemporary politics. The two Trump impeachments realized the fears that Hamilton laid out in Federalist no. 65: "In many cases it [the impeachment] will connect itself with the pre-existing factions, and will enlist all their [senators'] animosities, partialities, influence, and interest on one side or on the other; and in such cases there will always be the greatest danger that the decision will be regulated more by the comparative strength of parties, than by the real demonstrations of innocence or guilt."[144] Cognizant that the Senate is not the perfect venue to judge impeachment cases, Hamilton nonetheless concluded it is the best option we have, as it is the only "tribunal sufficiently dignified, or sufficiently independent" to judge the president—or any other official—fairly. But the key word here is "independent."

The founders failed to anticipate what modern parties (or, really, even Jacksonian parties) would become, and the ways in which partisan bonds and party self-interest would render that independence moot. With only one Republican senator—Mitt Romney (R-UT)—voting to convict Trump in the first trial, and only seven voting to do so in the second—and every Democrat voting to convict in both—it seems hard to argue that senators are acting as impartial jurors. One can argue that previous trials, such as Bill Clinton's, revealed a similar state of affairs, and we would agree. But this suggests that except perhaps in the gravest of cases, with the most incontrovertible evidence, impeachment is only a facile check on the executive. Had Trump engaged in the same behaviors that led to Nixon's resignation in 1974, it is an open question whether Senate Majority Leader Mitch McConnell (R-KY) and House Minority Leader Kevin McCarthy (R-CA) would have done what Senate Minority Leader Hugh Scott (R-PA), House Minority Leader John Rhodes (R-AZ), and 1964 Republican Party presidential nominee Senator Barry Goldwater (R-AZ) did and gone to the White House to inform Trump that he did not have support in his own party to survive impeachment. The current state of affairs effectively removes impeachment as a check on the power of the presidency and raises questions about how to prevent executive overreach, a worrisome situation at a time of distrust in elections and a fear of democratic backsliding.

So where do we go from here? We close by featuring facets of democratic resilience in 2020.

The Citadels That Endured

In Biden's post-election victory speech, he said, "In this battle for the soul of America, democracy prevailed. We the people voted. Faith in our institutions held. The integrity of our elections remains intact, and now it's time to turn the page, as we've done throughout history."[145] Biden's speech paints the election as an unalloyed success, but in the process ignores a reality voiced by DC Circuit Court of Appeals judge Patricia Millett when she said, "The events of January 6th exposed the fragility of those democratic institutions and traditions that we had perhaps come to take for granted."[146] Our analyses highlight some of that fragility, but they also feature citadels—sometimes surprising ones—that proved to be robust: military leadership, the courts, election officials, and Fox News executives.

Military Leadership

The first is the military leadership. Some in Trump's orbit, notably his former national security advisor General Michael Flynn, hoped that the military would intervene to install Trump as the winner, or at least force close swing states to rerun the election (with the assumption that Trump would win a rerun). Speaking shortly after the election on Newsmax, Flynn noted that there "was precedent for deploying military troops for this purpose [rerunning the election] when in fact there was none. 'Number one, President Trump won on the third of November,' he said. 'He could also order, within the swing states, if he wanted to, he could take military capabilities and he could place them in those states and basically rerun the election in each of those states. It's not unprecedented. . . . These people out there talking about martial law like it's something we've never done. Martial law has been instituted sixty-four times.'"[147]

This scenario or a related one in which Trump would invoke the Insurrection Act, adopted in 1807, to deploy troops, as he considered doing in response to the summer protests, is remarkable in two regards. First, a former US military official advocated redoing an election on the basis of unsubstantiated claims of fraud, and second, the discussion transpired on Newsmax, one of the very conservative outlets that were trying to position themselves as alternatives to Fox News. Arguments such as Flynn's would be more likely to find a congenial audience in such a venue, reinforcing the argument we made throughout the book that media enclaves reinforce political predispositions.

Former General Flynn's voice was an outlier, not the norm. By training and inclination, military officers shun political and partisan entanglements. General Milley, chairman of the Joint Chiefs of Staff, was particularly insistent that the military would remain out of politics. He spoke to elected officials in the fall and noted that

> "the military's going to stay out of politics. . . . We don't determine the outcome of the election," the General said. "We don't pick the people in power. Everything's going to be okay. We're going to have a peaceful transfer of power. We're going to land this plane safely. This is America. It's strong. The institutions are bending, but it won't break." . . . "Our political leadership will be determined by the American people," Milley told another member of Congress. "We will obey lawful, legal orders from a duly constituted government, period. And at twelve o'clock on the twentieth of January, there will be a president and he will be certified by the legislature."[148]

We see Milley addressing two hazards here. First, as commander in chief, Trump might order the military to engage in extraconstitutional action of the sort envisioned by General Flynn. Milley's reference to obeying "lawful, legal orders" is a strong assertion that unlawful ones from the commander in chief would not be followed. There was ample justification for such concerns. In his book, *A Sacred Oath,* Trump's secretary of defense Mark T. Esper recounts Milley pushing back when Trump expressed the desire to deploy ten thousand active-duty troops onto the streets of the District of Columbia in response to protests following the killing of George Floyd. Esper also recalls Trump asking about the demonstrators, "Can't you just shoot them? Just shoot them in the legs or something."[149]

Second, the incumbent might refuse to relinquish the office on January 20. Milley's reference to both January 20 and duly constituted government reveals that he would have no part of such a plan. Milley publicly affirmed his determination to avoid even the appearance of involvement in politics after being burned by Trump's desire to be seen marching across Lafayette Square, military leaders at his side, to a photo op in front of a nearby church during the summer protests in Washington, DC.[150] "The country's top military official apologized on Thursday for taking part in President Trump's walk across Lafayette Square for a photo op after the authorities used tear gas and rubber bullets to clear the area of peaceful protesters," noted the *New York Times* of Milley's response to that incident. "'I should not have been there,' Gen. Mark

A. Milley, the chairman of the Joint Chiefs of Staff, said in a prerecorded video commencement address to National Defense University. 'My presence in that moment and in that environment created a perception of the military involved in domestic politics.'"[151]

It was not just the military but other civilian leaders of Defense Departments past as well who reiterated that the military had no role in the electoral process. All ten living former defense secretaries penned an op-ed in the *Washington Post* on January 3, 2021, arguing that "efforts to involve the U.S. armed forces in resolving election disputes would take us into dangerous, unlawful and unconstitutional territory. Civilian and military officials who direct or carry out such measures would be accountable, including potentially facing criminal penalties, for the grave consequences of their actions on our republic."[152] This was another clear marker by those who wanted to keep the civilians, not the military, in control.

But of course, with different generals, ones less committed to civilian control, the situation might have looked different. In May 2021, 124 retired military officers, calling themselves "Flag Officers 4 America," signed a letter supporting Trump's fraudulent claims of a stolen election and calling into question Biden's fitness for office. They argued that Biden's presidency represented "a fight for our survival as a Constitutional Republic like no other time since our founding in 1776."[153] This language of unprecedented challenges is a sobering rhetorical ploy, signaling that the letter writers think a military coup would be preferable to the status quo, opening up a space where the military would need to overthrow the government to save democracy. Had some of these individuals been in charge, would the military have signaled so clearly that it was remaining out of politics? Perhaps not. This fear of a different military intervening was reinforced when three retired generals wrote a *Washington Post* op-ed calling for the military to prepare itself to prevent such a scenario from playing out in 2024.[154]

The Courts

The second institution that withstood the test was the courts. Nearly all of the Trump lawsuits were dismissed. It is also telling that the fantastic claims Sidney Powell, Rudy Giuliani, and other Trump surrogates made about election fraud online and in their press conferences were rarely made in court. Instead, under oath, they made much narrower pleadings. One can be critical of the US legal system for many reasons, but here is an example of its strength: rule-governed standards of argument and evidence that disallow innuendo and hearsay. When Trump's team could not produce evidence to back their claims, judges were easily able to dismiss the lawsuits. Moreover, contrary to Trump's expectation, the Supreme Court chose not to intervene. Nonetheless, the claim of Trump's that we noted earlier—that he needed better judges—should be a chilling reminder that performing in a fashion consistent with his idea of a "better judge" might inform future nominations to the courts should he regain the presidency.

Election Officials

Another institutional cadre that withstood the challenge of 2020 consisted of election officials. Local election officials worked diligently to allow Americans to vote safely and securely during an unprecedented global pandemic, assisted by many private and charitable organizations.[155] Chastened by successful Russian penetration of the nation's voting infrastructure in 2016,[156] election officials and secretaries of state coordinated with one another in new and unprecedented ways. In the process they ensured that paper backups existed for votes and took other steps needed to ensure a free and fair election. Statements from the Cybersecurity and Infrastructure Security Agency, as well as from many state secretaries of state, undercut the credibility of Trump's claims of election fraud. The Republican-controlled Michigan Senate Oversight Committee found no evidence of fraud after hearing twenty-eight hours of testimony from more than ninety people and examining thousands of documents. It concluded that "citizens [should] use a critical eye and ear toward those who have pushed demonstrably false theories for their own personal gain."[157] In effect, there was a "deep state," but it was the thousands of local election officials who worked to ensure that the election was safe, free, and fair, contrary to Trump's claims.

It is also worth highlighting the reality that many of these individuals were Republicans, not Democrats. The key players in Arizona, Michigan, and Georgia, as well as in thousands of smaller jurisdictions around the country, discharged their duties with honor and duly certified Joe Biden's victory in their jurisdiction. So even if many elected Republicans perpetuated the myth of electoral fraud, many other Republican officeholders did not, a fact that cuts against the narrative of the totalizing effect of party, even in our current moment. The important role that they played highlights the importance of having people of integrity and honor in these positions.

For their service, many of these public servants were repaid with harassment and even death threats, as we document in Chapter 9. As a result, it should not be surprising that an unprecedented number reportedly are leaving these positions,[158] and those who embraced the myth of voter fraud are stepping up to replace them. "After facing threats and intimidation during the 2020 presidential election and its aftermath, and now the potential of new punishments in certain states, county officials who run elections are quitting or retiring early,"[159] noted the Associated Press in June 2021. Indeed, Trump and his allies have been working to recruit and elect candidates for these positions across the country, but especially in key states such as Michigan.[160] What happens in the future remains to be seen.

Fox News Executives

Perhaps the most surprising of the institutions that helped protect perceptions of the integrity of the outcome was Fox News and its executives. One could be critical of Fox News for many reasons, but they deserve praise for one key decision. Fox News's decision desk (and its partner, the Associated Press) made what we now know was an aggressive call to say Biden would win Arizona at 11:20 PM Eastern time on election night (because of the closeness of the Arizona race, the other major networks did not project the Arizona call until days later).[161] When pressured to retract the call by the Trump campaign, Fox executives stood firm.[162] Fox, along with all of the other networks, then projected Biden as the winner on November 7. "Only an hour after Donald Trump falsely tweeted that he had won the 2020 election by 'A LOT,' his preferred network, Fox News, joined others in projecting Joe Biden as the winner and next president of the United States," noted *Slate*.[163]

Angered by Fox's decisions, Trump encouraged his followers to flee to OANN and Newsmax, more conservative outlets whose view of the election's outcome was more hospitable to the incumbent's. "They forgot the Golden Goose," Trump tweeted about Fox News.[164] A spike in Newsmax's viewership suggested the power of those Trump appeals.[165] But here is a guardrail that is perhaps less likely to play the same role in 2024 as it did in 2020. For unexplained reasons, by January 2021, Bill Sammon, senior vice president and managing editor at Fox's Washington bureau, had announced that he was retiring, and Fox's politics editor Chris Stirewalt had been let go.[166] Will future executives be as willing to protect the decision desk and its independence?

In the end, then, perhaps the biggest takeaway is that the guardrails survived a crash test. However, that is not a reason to assume that they will hold in 2024 and beyond. Whether they will break depends on the success or failure of efforts to place congenial rather than dispassionate election officials in key offices in consequential battleground states—a decision that is up to voters; the willingness of judges to honor the norms of evidence and argument codified by the court system; and the commitment and the capacity of platforms to thwart the spread of lies about the conduct of elections and incitements to violence. It also depends on whether journalists at partisan media outlets will forswear conspiracy theories and deceptions peddled by the hosts of their opinion shows. Unknowns in the equation include the extent to which platforms that refuse to embrace the norms to which the major ones such as Facebook and Twitter at least aspire manage to build comparably sized audiences and whether the new Trump venture is able to as well. And if they do, it matters whether or not whatever content is posted or played there is amplified in mainstream news.

We do not yet know whether the crises of 2020 will be the new normal. Nor do we know whether a person with Trump's talents and temperament could create the same level of institutional disruption without commanding the power and bullhorn that come with being the incumbent president. We do know that Trump's efforts to delegitimize the 2020 outcome were hampered by lawyers who even his closest allies thought did his case more harm than good. As Peter Meijer, one of the ten House Republicans who voted to impeach Trump in 2021, put it: "The real threat isn't Donald Trump; it's somebody who watched Donald Trump and can do this a lot better than he did."[167] It is up to all of us to determine whether Meijer's claim is correct.

Appendix: Our Data and Analytical Strategy

Josh Pasek, Ken Winneg, and Matthew Levendusky

We've got tons of evidence. It's so much, it's hard to pull it all together.

—Trump lawyer Sidney Powell speaking about the voter fraud lawsuits filed by the president and his legal team[1]

Digging into the mechanics of the election was labor intensive, but very revealing.

—Michigan State Senate Oversight Committee Report on the 2020 Election in Michigan[2]

To understand how our four crises (reviewed in Chapter 1) and the fundamental factors (reviewed in Chapter 2) shaped the election and its aftermath, we need data that track citizens' attitudes, vote choice, and turnout intention, as well as their experiences with, and perceptions of, the crises that shaped 2020. To obtain this critical knowledge, we empaneled more than 9,000 Americans in four key states and interviewed them up to fifteen times across a seventeen-month period (November 2019–February 2021). Throughout the book, we used this data, but in the interest of the narrative flow of the book, we have relegated the details of how we gathered this data, and our analytical strategy, to this Appendix. Here, we explain how we designed and implemented the survey that is the backbone of the analyses in the book. Details of that process can be found in the Online Appendix (see the Open Science Framework at https://osf. io/487jk/). More importantly, it also lays out the analytical strategy that we used to present and analyze the evidence offered throughout the book. We explain the types of analyses we used (especially graphical analyses), and why we used them, to make sense of this tumultuous year. We do this to help orient readers to the types of analyses encountered throughout the book.

A Brief Overview of Our Survey Data

This book analyzed a probability sample survey of panelists recruited and collected by the Annenberg Public Policy Center (APPC) through the research firm SSRS. Samples of individuals from each of four swing states and five targeted counties were recruited in late 2019 and early 2020 and were asked to complete up to fifteen survey waves that we analyzed throughout the book. In this section, we provide some very basic details on our sampling procedure and design choices, but encourage readers interested in the details to consult our Online Appendix (https://osf.io/487jk/) for the full details.

More specifically, respondents were recruited via address-based sampling, and were sent an invitation letter asking them to join our panel (to join, individuals went to a website constructed for the panel; that was the portal they used to take all of the surveys).* We targeted four battleground states that, ex ante, were likely to be pivotal to the outcome: Florida, Michigan, Pennsylvania, and Wisconsin. All four had backed Obama in 2008 and 2012 but then flipped to Trump in 2016. Within each state, we also targeted a specific county that was likely to serve as an electoral bellwether: Pinellas County in Florida, Macomb County in Michigan, Luzerne County in Pennsylvania, and both Kenosha and Racine Counties in Wisconsin.[†] As with our states, these counties all backed Obama twice but then flipped to Trump, and we suspected (correctly) that all of them would be heavily targeted by both campaigns in 2020.

Of the 258,099 invitations that were sent to addresses, there were 20,085 responses (reflecting 7.8 percent of invitations sent). Among these responses, 1,816 were incomplete, and 1,405 were deemed ineligible (largely because the respondents were younger than eighteen years of age or because they reported that they were not US citizens). A total of 16,864 eligible respondents completed the recruitment survey wave. Subsequently, 156 of these individuals decided they did not want to participate in the study before the first wave of the survey panel, yielding a total of 16,708 panelists. This reflected a 6.5 percent overall response rate (AAPOR RR1) or an estimated 7.0 percent response rate among eligible respondents (AAPOR RR3; $e = .92$).[‡] We provide further details on our panelists, and some responsive sampling decisions made as a result of the coronavirus pandemic, in the Online Appendix.

The first wave of our study began in April 2020; participation in this wave was required for respondents to remain in the study. Of the 13,826 initial panelists invited to complete the first election wave, 10,434 did so (75.5 percent), yielding a cumulative response rate of 5.3 percent with panel recruitment (CUMRR3).[3] All respondents who completed the first election wave were eligible for all subsequent waves of the survey, but not all eligible respondents answered any given wave. Retention rates for subsequent waves were between 79 percent and 84 percent of the individuals invited. To better

---

*. While we encouraged respondents to take the studies online, some respondents chose to take the study over the phone (3.3 percent of panelists).

†. Kenosha and Racine Counties were jointly selected due to their similar composition and location to expand the size of the targeted Wisconsin sample.

‡. For more on AAPOR (American Association for Public Opinion Research) response rate (RR) calculations, see the AAPOR Standard Definitions, https://www.aapor.org/Standards-Ethics/Standard-Definitions-(1).aspx.

understand how attitudes and behaviors were changing over time, each respondent was randomly assigned to answer the survey in one of three replicates. Summary information for each wave, including the number of completed interviews, the response rate, the cumulative response rate, and differences by recruitment phases and replicates, is shown in Appendix Table A1.1.§

We invited everyone who completed wave 1 to all subsequent waves, even though not all panelists responded to every subsequent wave.** Because of our interest in understanding election dynamics, we focus our analyses on the 9,056 respondents who completed at least one of the two immediate post-election waves (waves 8 and 9), in which we asked about how they had voted. This represented a retention rate of 86.7 percent of the respondents who had completed wave 1 and yielded a final cumulative response rate of 4.6 percent (CUMRR3).[4]

As the table makes clear, we have eleven waves of data on which we focus throughout the book (though we do, in a few instances, draw on the recruitment survey or the brief engagement surveys we gave to subjects between our recruitment survey and our first main election study wave).†† Using these eleven waves, we explain the story of the 2020 election by tracing how our respondents reacted to the four crises that shaped that tumultuous year.

Dates for the waves and replicates along with notable dates in the campaign are illustrated in Appendix Figure A1.1. As that figure also illustrates, there was a consistent pattern of when responses were received for each of the survey waves, with the majority of responses coming in the first few days, and a slight bump in responses occurring on day five, after respondents were typically sent a reminder email. Since respondents tended to maintain a consistent response latency across the panel, the distribution of respondents within the weeks was consistent over time, although the composition of earlier and later responses differed slightly.

In the Online Appendix we explain in far more detail how we constructed our sample, the types of surveys we administrated, how we constructed the weights used throughout the book (to match both demographics and final election results), and how and why we imputed missing data in our analyses. We also describe a series of additional types of data we used in our analyses. Interested readers are referred there for the relevant details.

---

§. Recruitment was conducted in three phases, as described in the Online Appendix. The Online Appendix also includes details about how respondents were assigned to three replicates and why some initial panelists were not asked to continue in the study.

**. After the first wave, 227 respondents told us they did not wish to continue in the study, so we did not invite them to any subsequent waves. Because not all respondents answered all waves, we use multiple imputations in our analyses; see the Online Appendix for more details.

††. The careful reader will note that we said that there are fifteen total waves of data, but only eleven main survey waves. That is because we have the eleven main waves of data, plus the initial recruitment survey, and three engagement surveys sent to respondents between recruitment (November 2019–April 2020) and our first main survey wave (April–May 2020). For more details on these different types of surveys, see the Online Appendix.

Table A1.1 Information about Survey Waves

Wave	Type	Date Range	Population Invited	Start Dates by Phase/Replicate	Ns by Phase/Replicate	Response Rate Among Invited (%)	Cumulative Response Rate (CUMM RR3; %)
Recruit[a]	Recruitment	Nov 25 2019–Apr 21 2020	All sampled households	Nov 25/Feb 13/Mar 20	32000/151970/74129	7.0/6.7/6.0	7.2/7.0/7.2
E1	Engagement	Jan 03–Feb 24 2020	Recruited panelists in phase 1[b]	Jan 03/—/—	1776/—/—	83.0/—/—	6.0/—/—
E2	Engagement	Feb 19–Mar 28 2020	Recruited panelists in phase 1	Feb 19/—/—	1531/—/—	76.9/—/—	5.5/—/—
E3	Engagement	Mar 17–Apr 27 2020	Recruited panelists	Mar 17/Mar 18/Apr 03	1790/8019/3604	81.3/79.8/83.2	5.8/5.6/6.0
W1	Election	Apr 29–May 19 2020	Subsample of recruited panelists	Apr 29/May 06/May 13	3535/3532/3367	76.8/76.5/73.1	5.5/5.4/5.3
W2	Election	Jun 10–Jul 01 2020	All W1 respondents	Jun 10/Jun 17/Jun 24	2991/2971/2783	84.6/84.1/82.7	4.7/4.5/4.3
W3	Health	Jul 01–Jul 22 2020	All W1 respondents	Jul 01/Jul 08/Jul 15	2909/2921/2755	82.3/82.7/81.8	4.5/4.4/4.3
W4	Election	Jul 27–Aug 17 2020	All W1 respondents	Jul 27/Aug 03/Aug 10	2838/2829/2675	80.3/80.1/79.4	4.4/4.3/4.2

Wave	Type	Dates	Sample	Start dates	Ns	Response rates	
W5	Election	Aug 28–Sep 18 2020	All W1 respondents	Aug 28/Sep 04/Sep 11	2883/2874/2746	81.6/81.4/81.6	4.5/4.4/4.3
W6	Health	Sep 22–Oct 15 2020	All W1 respondents	Sep 22/Sep 30/Oct 08	2840/2833/2740	80.3/80.2/81.4	4.4/4.3/4.3
W7	Election	Oct 16–Nov 03 2020	All W1 respondents	Oct 16/Oct 23/Oct 27	2854/2859/2743	80.7/80.9/81.5	4.5/4.3/4.3
W8	Post-election	Nov 04–Nov 25 2020	All W1 respondents	Nov 04/Nov 11/Nov 18	2868/2866/2727	81.1/81.1/81.0	4.5/4.3/4.3
W9	Post-election	Dec 02–Dec 23 2020	All W1 respondents	Dec 02/Dec 09/Dec 16	2824/2820/2674	79.9/79.8/79.4	4.4/4.3/4.2
W10	Post-election	Jan 08–Feb 04 2021	All W1 respondents	Jan 08/Jan 21/Jan 28	2826/2856/2694	79.9/80.9/80.0	4.4/4.3/4.2
W11	Post-election	Feb 16–Feb 23 2021	All W1 replicate 1 respondents	Feb 16/—/—	2804/—/—	79.3/—/—	4.4/—/—
Analytic Dataset					3068/3066/2920	86.8/86.8/86.7	4.8/4.6/4.6

[a] For recruitment and initial engagement waves, start dates, Ns, and response rates are reported by phase; for all other waves, they are reported by replicate.

[b] A small number of panelists were not invited to each of the engagement surveys even though they were otherwise eligible. This included 69 respondents recruited in phase 1 for E1, 218 respondents recruited in phase 1 for E2, and 129 respondents across all phases for E3.

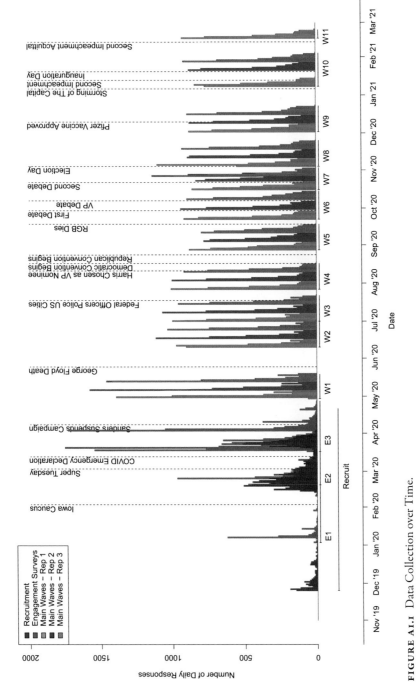

FIGURE A1.1 Data Collection over Time.

Data show daily survey responses collected, with wave and replicate indicated. Key events of 2020 are shown with dashed lines.

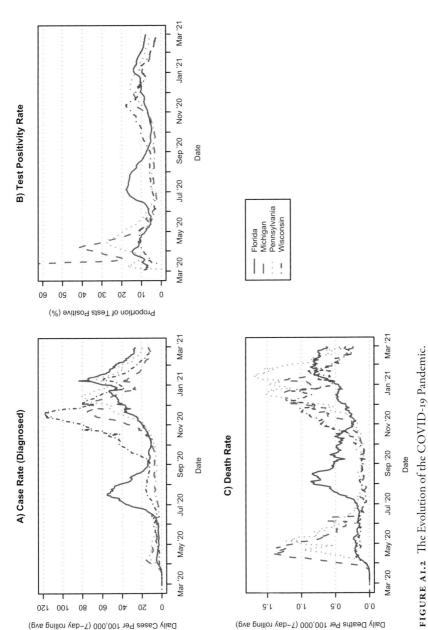

FIGURE A1.2 The Evolution of the COVID-19 Pandemic.

Data show the diagnosed case rate (panel A), test positivity rate (panel B), and death rate (panel C), by state, across the course of our study. Data provided by COVID Act Now.

In addition to these recruitment-related details, we have two additional pieces of information to provide to the reader. First, we noted in Chapter 1 that our study is not a national study, but is instead a study of four key battleground states; how should the reader think about this distinction? Second, what analytical approach did we take to analyze the data? We now turn to these tasks in order.

How We Treat Our Four States

When we designed our study in 2019, we were blissfully unaware of the four interlocking crises that would soon beset the United States and shape 2020. We therefore initially designed our survey instrument to focus on four pivotal swing states, and swing counties within each state, with the aim of using this tighter geographic focus to narrow in on the locales that would actually decide the election (thinking the story of 2020 would be a more typical one focusing on traditional campaign activities). As it turns out, we did, in fact, pick states that would help to decide the election: had Biden not won Wisconsin, Michigan, and Pennsylvania, he would not have become the forty-sixth president.

But once the four crises struck, we realized that 2020 was not just any other election, but instead would be unique, and so we shifted our focus to focus on these crises. Throughout the design and analysis of the study, we expected that the crises might well play out quite differently across our four states. And in some ways they did. The COVID-19 pandemic was perhaps the starkest confirmation of this expectation, as we see in Appendix Figure A1.2. In it, we can see the diagnosed case rate (panel A), test positivity rate (panel B), and death rate (panel C) in each of these states over time. We show multiple metrics here in part because testing was severely limited early in the pandemic, meaning that many cases in the first few months of the pandemic went undiagnosed. Test positivity can provide a window into the extent of underdiagnosis, and there are reasons to think that coronavirus deaths were particularly likely to be diagnosed, though the latter tend to be a lagging indicator and can be influenced by the quality of care.[‡‡]

Although all states were affected by the pandemic, they were affected at different times and to different extents. Early on, Michigan was hit the hardest, with the areas around Detroit particularly affected. Over the summer, as the second wave of the virus raced through the southern United States, Florida was hit hard. As the election approached, all four of our states saw significant increases in cases, though this trend started earlier and was especially pronounced in Wisconsin. As we show in Chapter 6, the economic fallout in each of our states was distinct as well, with Michigan's economy being especially hard-hit by the pandemic.

[‡‡]. There were moderate improvements in care for COVID patients in the early months of the pandemic that improved outcomes among the sickest patients over time (see, e.g., Jim Dwyer, "What Doctors on the Front Lines Wish They'd Known a Month Ago," *New York Times*, April 14, 2020).

But the different experiences across these states during the pandemic failed to translate to residents' attitudes toward the pandemic, let alone to their electoral preferences. Instead, a consistent pattern emerged: rather than having a different election in each state, things played out quite similarly across all four. When respondents in our states were asked how worried they were about a family member getting sick or whether the worst of COVID was behind us (see the results in Chapter 5), state differences were small and were easily overwhelmed by other factors (such as age and partisanship). As a result, separating out the different states typically obscured more than it clarified. This finding is consistent with claims that the American electorate and elections have become highly nationalized.[5] There are, of course, fifty-one different presidential elections—one in each state and the District of Columbia to determine the electors each will send to the Electoral College—but in 2020, at least in our states, they played out in very similar ways. In the Online Appendix, we provide some additional analyses of more micro-level trends. But the story of the 2020 election and its aftermath is a much more national one than a local one, at least across our states. Given this, except in a limited number of cases that we clearly identify in the chapters in the book, we pool respondents across states and analyze them together.

This raises the question of how closely what we observed matches what we would have obtained had we constructed a national sample (i.e., by drawing voters from every state). At some level that's an unanswerable question, because we did not construct that panel (again, because we initially wanted to focus on battleground states, thinking it would be a more traditional year/campaign). That said, our data and story are highly consistent with other national-level analyses, so it is unlikely that this choice changed our results very much. But ultimately, it is up to the reader to assess our results and decide for themselves.

Our Empirical Strategy

Throughout the book, we largely rely on graphical displays of our data to convey our substantive results. While regressions and other techniques underlie almost all of these analyses, these plots make the results much easier and more straightforward to understand.

Throughout the book, our primary analytical tool is the generalized additive model (GAM), which is a type of regression.[6] The advantage of a GAM is that the effects of variables do not need to be linear, unlike in most regression models, such as ordinary least squares regression. In a GAM, in lieu of linearity, the mapping between the independent and dependent variables is given by a series of smoothed splines, allowing researchers much greater flexibility. As readers will see throughout the book, many of our variables had highly nonlinear effects, so not accounting for that fact would have led us astray.

Because readers may not be familiar with GAMs, we present several examples to help clarify the intuition behind them. To begin, consider a relatively straightforward example: how does age map onto electoral behavior?

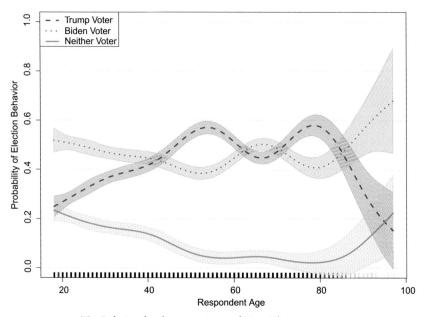

FIGURE A1.3 The Relationship between Age and Vote Choice.

Lines show the estimated proportion of respondents at each age voting for Trump (dashed red line), for Biden (dotted blue line), or for neither (solid green line) based on a GAM regression, with 95% confidence intervals shaded.

In Appendix Figure A1.3, we see how voting for each type of candidate is nonlinear across respondent age.[7] The youngest individuals in our sample tended to vote for Biden much more frequently than for Trump. This can be seen in the fact that the dotted blue line on the left side of Appendix Figure A1.3 is above the dashed red line. Individuals in their forties and fifties, in contrast, were somewhat more likely to vote for Trump than for Biden, as were respondents in their seventies. However, the oldest respondents (those older than about eighty) also tended to prefer Biden over Trump by a considerable margin, though of course there were not that many of these individuals in our sample and hence we are more uncertain about their preferences (i.e., we have large standard errors). At the same time, this figure reveals age differences in the propensity to vote for the major-party candidates. The solid green line shows that many of the youngest individuals in our sample did not vote for either Trump or Biden, a pattern that diminished with age, though it does increase again for the oldest respondents.

If we were to use a standard linear model (such as ordinary least squares), we would obscure much of this important nonlinear variation. In contrast, our approach allows us to observe the effects of partisan imprinting across generations as well as potential age effects on participation.[8]

As another example, consider an item we discuss in Chapter 5 on the COVID-19 pandemic. Starting in wave 4 (July–August 2020), we asked our respondents whether

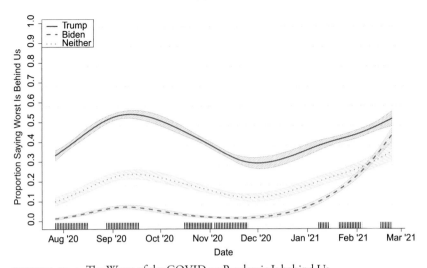

FIGURE A1.4 The Worst of the COVID-19 Pandemic Is behind Us.

Lines show the estimated proportion of Trump voters (dashed red line), Biden voters (dotted blue line), and those who voted for neither Trump nor Biden (solid green line) who said the worst of the pandemic was behind us over time. As in all over-time graphs, interview dates are visible from the rug on the *x*-axis.

they thought the worst of the COVID-19 pandemic was behind us, or whether the worst was yet to come. In many ways, as we discuss in Chapter 5, this maps onto how Trump and Biden talked about the pandemic during the campaign: in Trump's estimation, the nation had rounded the corner and the virus would soon be a memory, whereas Biden emphasized that cases were increasing throughout the fall and that much more was needed to bring the pandemic to heel. In Chapter 5, we analyzed this item in more detail, but for now, consider how those who eventually voted for Trump or Biden responded to this item. Appendix Figure A1.4 shows the proportion of Trump voters (solid red line), Biden voters (dashed blue line), and those who did not vote for either candidate (dotted green line) who thought that the worst of the pandemic was behind us at any given time. As in all such graphs throughout the book, we provide the interview dates on the rug along the *x*-axis (i.e., the horizontal lines along the *x*-axis indicate when, chronologically, we were conducting interviews).

The trend here is strikingly nonlinear. The gap between the groups was growing at some points in time (e.g., early in the fall) and was shrinking at other times (e.g., once vaccines became available to the general public early in 2021). As we show in Chapter 5, the pattern is actually even more complicated than this, as there are important nuances among Trump and Biden supporters. For now, however, the key point is that our GAM-based approach allows us to model nonlinear dynamics, both across respondents (as in Appendix Figure A1.3) and over time, exploiting the panel nature of our data (as in

Appendix Figure A1.4).[§§] This allows us to capture nuance and subtlety in our analyses that would be missed by more traditional approaches.

In the end, perhaps the best argument for our approach is that although the underlying modeling is somewhat technical and complicated, the results are easy to understand. Throughout the book, we present graphs such as Appendix Figures A1.3 and A1.4 that allow readers to see how our variables vary over time and how they map onto key outcomes such as candidate preference. Interpretation of these models does not require that readers understand the technical details, instead, the key patterns are directly reflected in the graphs. They not only make clear the extent to which different groups perceive our crises differently but also chart changes over time. Rather than asking respondents to wade through a lot of regression coefficients, which is rarely, if ever, helpful, we instead ask them to look at the graphs and then judge for themselves the importance of the trends we discuss.

A Model for Vote Choice

While we use this analytical strategy throughout the book, it is also worth discussing in greater detail the models we use to understand voters' ultimate vote choices. To be clear, our goal in the book was not simply to uncover what ultimately drove voters to pick Trump or Biden, but rather to understand the scope and impact of the year's crises on a wide range of outcomes. Indeed, what happens *after* the election is fundamental to understanding the story of 2020. But given the centrality of the presidential election, we do spend considerable time throughout the book analyzing how various factors relate to vote choice.

But one challenge of studying vote choice in recent elections is that most voters have made up their minds long in advance of Election Day. As we discuss in Chapter 3, many of our panelists knew whom they would vote for even when we recruited them, months before Joe Biden became the Democratic Party's nominee (see the discussion of Table 3.1). This has an important, and subtle, implication: most variables will have a relatively modest effect on vote choice.

But to say that effects are modest is not to say that they do not exist at all. Indeed, as we show in later chapters, there are a number of key factors—including both some

---

§§. Because we impute missing data and weight the data to yield identical demographic compositions for each replicate, as well as to match the final election results (see the Online Appendix), changes over time in these models reflect changes in the population that this study is designed to represent. Because multiple measures from various individuals are included in these over-time analyses, we present both the number of observations and the number of unique individuals that provided data for each model. We also considered calculating these over-time models with a random effect for each respondent but declined to adopt that approach because it was enormously computationally intensive (changing model run time from minutes to days for each analysis), had no effect on the trendlines themselves, and had a negligible influence on the standard errors of the models.

of the fundamental factors discussed in Chapter 2 and our crises—that *do* shape voting behavior. To model these influences, we take two different but related approaches. First, we estimate vote choice as a function of standard demographic variables, plus measures of baseline partisanship and/or past vote choice, and the explanatory factors of interest (for example, retrospective economic evaluations, which we examine in Figure 6.5). The idea here is to assess the unique role of the key explanatory factor in predicting voting while controlling for these other variables.

To see an example of this type of plot, Appendix Figure A1.5 presents a plot of standardized regression coefficients from logistic regressions predicting voting for Trump, voting for Biden, or not voting for either one in 2020 as a function of demographic variables (top panels) and demographic variables as well as partisanship (measured in our recruitment wave) and 2016 vote choice (as reported in early 2020; this second set of coefficients is presented in the bottom panels).

Here, we model voting for each candidate separately because some of the same factors that influence choice between the two candidates also influence whether individuals vote for one of them at all. We see that in the top panel, without controlling for political variables, most demographic variables are correlated with eventual vote choice. Once we control for political variables—such as 2016 vote choice and partisanship—our ability to predict election outcomes improves markedly and these demographic effects fade dramatically (as one would expect). The value of this sort of model, then, is that it helps us understand how various factors matter to eventual vote choices while controlling for other plausible explanations.

In Appendix Figure A1.5, and in the other regressions used throughout the book, we present standardized coefficients rather than unstandardized regression outputs. We do this for two reasons, one pragmatic and one substantive. First, unstandardized coefficients in regressions vary depending on how predictors are coded, meaning that readers would need to know how each variable is scaled to interpret the coefficients of the regression. So to understand unstandardized regressions, we would need to explain coding rules for *every* variable in all of our models. For example, when it comes to coding for age, does a one-unit change in age represent the effect of one additional year of age, or does it instead reflect the effect of moving from one age category to another (i.e., going from the 18–29 category to the 30–45 category)? Using standardized coefficients allows us to sidestep this issue, though we also present unstandardized coefficients, along with coding rules, in our Online Appendix.

Second, and more importantly, standardized coefficients better approximate what it is we want to know about the predictors in the model. They tell us about how much of the variation in the population can be accounted for with each predictor—that is, they indicate what mattered at scale and what did not. One effect of this is that standardization reduces the apparent importance of variables that have large individual impacts but are rare in prevalence. Because our goal in the book is to understand not the predictors of individual behavior but instead the factors that account for collective preferences, the use of standardized numbers provides a better approximation of the quantity of

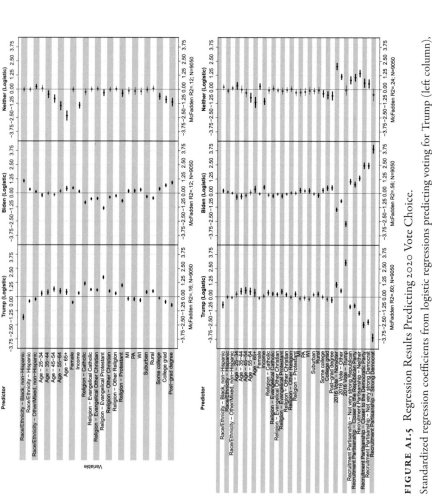

FIGURE A1.5 Regression Results Predicting 2020 Vote Choice.

Standardized regression coefficients from logistic regressions predicting voting for Trump (left column), Biden (center), or neither (right). The top row uses only demographic variables, the bottom row also includes political predictors. For each variable, standardized coefficient estimates are given as circles with 95% confidence intervals as black lines. Bolded coefficients are statistically significant ($p < 0.05$).

interest. In each figure, statistically significant predictors are given in bold: significant predictors have thick bold lines and solid circles, those that are not statistically significant have thin lines with open circles.

Beyond this multiple regression approach, we also employ a second type of model, especially when trying to understand the effects of the crises on outcomes. For example, one potential way the coronavirus pandemic might shape vote choice is if a voter knows someone who dies of COVID: seeing a friend or relative pass away from the virus might lead a voter to punish Trump for his handling of the pandemic (we take up this question in Chapter 5). To know whether this is the case, we model a respondent's eventual vote choice as a function of their initial candidate preference (Trump/Biden/someone else), the event of interest (here, whether they report knowing someone who died from COVID-19), and the interaction of these two variables. The interaction is important for two reasons. First, interacting these terms allows us to ascertain whether the effect depends on one's baseline preferences. For example, if someone who initially supports Biden has a friend die from COVID, this might strengthen their belief that Trump has mismanaged the crisis, and heighten their conviction to vote for Biden. In contrast, if that person had instead initially supported Trump, their friend's death might change their vote choice: perhaps now they might consider voting for Biden, or perhaps just not turning out at all. The second benefit to using interactions is that it helps to isolate factors that are related to changing vote choices and thus indicate the things that were likely to influence electoral behaviors rather than those that simply correspond with already-existing preferences. Collectively, then, this approach allows us to examine how the different dimensions of our crises—experiences with COVID-19, the economic fallout of the virus, and the racial reckoning—shape voter behavior, and how those effects differ throughout the electorate.

To see this in practice, consider an example: are younger or older voters more loyal to their candidates? To study this, we can model eventual vote choice as a function of initial vote choice (from wave 1), age, and their interaction. When considering these models, we plot the predicted probabilities of supporting Trump or Biden to show how these variables map onto eventual candidate support.[***]

We see that younger individuals who initially said that they supported Trump (dashed red line on the left side of Appendix Figure A1.6, panel A) were less likely to vote for him in November than were older early supporters. In contrast, older individuals who initially did not express a preference for either candidate were more

---

[***]. We estimate these using GAM models as well to account for nonlinearity in the relationships between variables. In general, we plot these interactions without controlling for other variables that could predict vote choice. This renders easily interpretable conclusions—for example, that a twenty-five-year-old who supported Biden in wave 1 had an approximately 80 percent chance of voting for him. Because of the conditional nature of the effects (i.e., the interaction with wave 1 preferences), this decision did not influence the conclusions that we reached about how key predictors and outcomes were related.

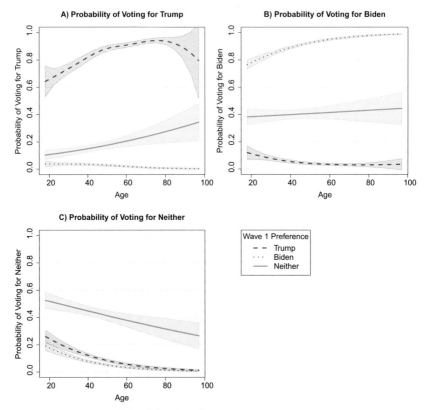

FIGURE A1.6 Age and Candidate Loyalty.

Each panel presents the predicted probability of voting for Trump (panel A), Biden (panel B), or neither (panel C), as a function of age, wave 1 candidate support, and their interaction. In each panel, the effects are shown separately for those who supported Trump (dashed red line), Biden (dotted blue line), or neither (solid green line) in wave 1.

likely to eventually vote for Trump than younger individuals (solid green line on the right side of panel A), although many more individuals across all age groups who had not initially expressed a preference ended up voting for Biden than for Trump (solid green line in panel B). In contrast, among Biden's voters, the age effect was considerably smaller, with most initial supporters remaining loyal even in the youngest age groups (dotted blue line in panel B). We can also see that younger voters were disproportionately likely to end up voting for neither major-party candidate, whatever their initial preferences (panel C).[†††] More generally, however, this broad empirical strategy allows

_____

[†††]. Because the lines of each color in panels A, B, and C in Appendix Figure 6 collectively comprise all voters with some initial preference (and thus add to 100 percent), we only include this final panel when it is especially illuminating. In most graphs, we simply present the results for voting for Biden or Trump.

us to examine how various factors are associated with change (or the lack thereof) in candidate preferences.

Together, these models allow us to see how a variety of different factors shape vote choice and offer important insights into how various factors helped to produce the outcome we observed in November, as we detail in chapters throughout the book. But it is also important to remember a fundamental limitation of any such analysis: voting is overdetermined. As we show in Chapter 3 (see also Appendix Figure A1.4), you can explain nearly all of our panelists' ultimate decisions by knowing how they voted four years before. You also can explain those same decisions effectively by asking them about their general partisan preferences. Predicting vote choice is quite easy.

But *explaining* vote choice is hard; it is impossible to know why a given voter ballots the way that they do. For example, Democrats and Republicans perceived the pandemic differently and voted differently. To what extent did these pandemic perceptions drive vote choice? Because partisanship shapes both pandemic perceptions and vote choice, there is no easy way to untangle these effects. So, while we can talk about the kinds of beliefs, attitudes, experiences, and people associated with particular choices in the election or associated with particular preference shifts, it is impossible to isolate the unique impact of each of these factors independently from one another.

For this reason, we contend that it is much more interesting to study *voters* than it is to study *voting* in the contemporary United States. Voting is so overdetermined that, while important, it ultimately becomes quite reductive. But tracking such phenomena as how Americans' views of the pre- and post-electoral crises change over time and how citizens process events to get to their voting decision is informative. To that end, throughout the book, we structured our analysis around understanding how voters behaved before, during, and after the 2020 election.

Notes

CHAPTER 1

1. Stephen Collinson, "A Nation in Crisis Faces a Critical Moment in History This Election," CNN, November 1, 2020, https://www.cnn.com/2020/11/01/politics/election-2020-donald-trump-joe-biden-history/index.html.

2. Matt Pearce, "Chanting 'Blood and Soil' and 'White Lives Matter,' White Nationalists March in Charlottesville," *Los Angeles Times*, August 11, 2017, https://www.latimes.com/nation/la-na-white-virginia-rally-20170811-story.html.

3. Adam Gabbatt, "'Jews Will Not Replace Us': Vice Film Lays Bare Horror of Neo-Nazis in America," *Guardian*, August 16, 2017, https://www.theguardian.com/us-news/2017/aug/16/charlottesville-neo-nazis-vice-news-hbo.

4. Paul Duggan and Justin Jouvenal, "Neo-Nazi Sympathizer Pleads Guilty to Federal Hate Crimes for Plowing Car into Protesters at Charlottesville Rally," *Washington Post*, April 1, 2019, https://www.washingtonpost.com/local/public-safety/neo-nazi-sympathizer-pleads-guilty-to-federal-hate-crimes-for-plowing-car-into-crowd-of-protesters-at-unite-the-right-rally-in-charlottesville/2019/03/27/2b947c32-50ab-11e9-8d28-f5149e5a2fda_story.html.

5. Angie Drobnic Holan, "In Context: Donald Trump's 'Very Fine People on Both Sides' Remarks (Transcript)," Politifact, April 26, 2019, https://www.politifact.com/article/2019/apr/26/context-trumps-very-fine-people-both-sides-remarks/.

6. Eric Bradner and Maeve Reston, "Joe Biden Takes Trump Head-On over Charlottesville in Announcement Video," CNN, April 25, 2019, https://www.cnn.com/2019/04/25/politics/joe-biden-charlottesville-trump-2020-launch/index.html.

7. Brennan Center for Justice, "It's Official: The Election Was Secure," December 11, 2020, https://www.brennancenter.org/our-work/research-reports/its-official-election-was-secure; Andrew Eggers, Haritz Garro, and Justin Grimmer, "No Evidence for Systematic Voter Fraud: A Guide to Statistical Claims About

the 2020 Election," *Proceedings of the National Academy of Sciences* 118, no. 45 (2021): e2103619118.

8. Brian Naylor, "Read Trump's Jan. 6 Speech, a Key Part of Impeachment Trial," NPR, February 10, 2021, https://www.npr.org/2021/02/10/966396848/read-tru mps-jan-6-speech-a-key-part-of-impeachment-trial.

9. Zachary Petrizzo, "Right-Wing Erupts After Biden Declares Jan. 6 'Worst Attack on Democracy Since Civil War,'" Salon, April 2021, https://www.salon.com/2021/04/28/right-wing-erupts-after-biden-declares-jan-6-worst-attack-on-democracy-since-civil-war/.

10. Andrew Solender, "Trump Says Jan. 6 Defendants 'Persecuted So Unfairly' Ahead of Capitol Rally," *Forbes*, September 16, 2021, https://www.forbes.com/sites/and rewsolender/2021/09/16/trump-says-jan-6-defendants-persecuted-so-unfairly-ahead-of-capitol-rally/?sh=58916520ccba.

11. "Transcript: Joe Biden's DNC Speech," CNN, August 20, 2020, https://www.cnn.com/2020/08/20/politics/biden-dnc-speech-transcript/index.html.

12. "Full Text: President Trump's 2020 RNC Acceptance Speech," NBC News, August 28, 2020, https://www.nbcnews.com/politics/2020-election/read-full-text-presid ent-donald-trump-s-acceptance-speech-rnc-n1238636.

13. Margaret Humphreys, *Marrow of Tragedy: The Health Crisis of the American Civil War* (Baltimore: Johns Hopkins University Press, 2013).

14. Drew Gilpin Faust, *This Republic of Suffering: Death and the American Civil War* (New York: Vintage Books, 2009).

15. G. Edward White, "Looking Backward and Forward at the Suspension Clause," *Michigan Law Review* 117, no. 6 (2019): 1313–1332, doi:10.36644/mlr.117.6.looking.

16. Centers for Disease Control and Prevention, "1918 Pandemic (H1N1 Virus) | Pandemic Influenza (Flu)," last reviewed March 20, 2019, https://www.cdc.gov/flu/pandemic-resources/1918-pandemic-h1n1.html.

17. Nadège Mougel, "World War I Casualties," US Census Bureau, 2011, https://www.census.gov/history/pdf/reperes112018.pdf.

18. Robert Barro, José Ursúa, and Joanna Weng, "The Coronavirus and the Great Influenza Pandemic: Lessons from the 'Spanish Flu' for the Coronavirus's Potential Effects on Mortality and Economic Activity," National Bureau of Economic Research, Cambridge, MA, April 2020, doi:10.3386/w26866.

19. Erick Trickey, "When America's Most Prominent Socialist Was Jailed for Speaking Out Against World War I," *Smithsonian Magazine*, June 2018, https://www.smithso nianmag.com/history/fiery-socialist-challenged-nations-role-wwi-180969386/.

20. Trickey, "When America's Most Prominent Socialist Was Jailed for Speaking Out Against World War I."

21. Michaeleen Doucleff, "WHO Points to Wildlife Farms in Southern China as Likely Source of Pandemic," NPR, March 15, 2021, https://www.npr.org/sections/goatsandsoda/2021/03/15/977527808/who-points-to-wildlife-farms-in-southw est-china-as-likely-source-of-pandemic.

22. Matthew J. Belvedere, "Trump Says He Trusts China's Xi on Coronavirus and the US Has It 'Totally Under Control,'" CNBC, January 22, 2020, https://www.cnbc.com/2020/01/22/trump-on-coronavirus-from-china-we-have-it-totally-under-control.html.

23. Domenico Cucinotta and Maurizio Vanelli, "WHO Declares COVID-19 a Pandemic," *Acta Bio-Medica: Atenei Parmensis* 91, no. 1 (March 2020): 157–160, doi:10.23750/abm.v91i1.9397.

24. National Conference of State Legislators, "President Trump Declares State of Emergency for COVID-19," March 25, 2020, https://www.ncsl.org/ncsl-in-dc/publications-and-resources/president-trump-declares-state-of-emergency-for-covid-19.aspx.

25. Sarah Mervosh, Denise Lu, and Vanessa Swales, "See Which States and Cities Have Told Residents to Stay at Home," *New York Times*, April 20, 2020, https://www.nytimes.com/interactive/2020/us/coronavirus-stay-at-home-order.html.

26. Andy Newman, "What N.Y.C. Sounds Like Every Night at 7," *New York Times*, April 10, 2020, https://www.nytimes.com/interactive/2020/04/10/nyregion/nyc-7pm-cheer-thank-you-coronavirus.html.

27. Bobby Allyn, "Fauci Estimates That 100,000 to 200,000 Americans Could Die from the Coronavirus," NPR, March 29, 2020, https://www.npr.org/sections/coronavirus-live-updates/2020/03/29/823517467/fauci-estimates-that-100-000-to-200-000-americans-could-die-from-the-coronavirus.

28. Aaron Rupar, "Trump Says 200,000 Americans Could Die from Coronavirus, Because He's Done 'A Very Good Job,'" *Vox*, March 30, 2020, https://www.vox.com/2020/3/30/21199586/us-coronavirus-deaths-trump-200000-good-job.

29. Adam Martin, "Daily U.S. Coronavirus Cases Second-Highest on Election Day," *Wall Street Journal*, November 4, 2020, https://www.wsj.com/livecoverage/covid-2020-11-04.

30. Will Feuer, "Here's Why New Cases of the Coronavirus Are Down Across Most of the U.S.," CNBC, August 25, 2020, https://www.cnbc.com/2020/08/25/new-cases-of-the-coronavirus-are-falling-in-most-of-the-us.html.

31. "USA Coronavirus: News Summary for 31 October," AS.com, October 31, 2020, https://en.as.com/en/2020/10/31/latest_news/1604138137_072079.html.

32. Josh Dawsey and Yasmeen Abutaleb, "'A Whole Lot of Hurt': Fauci Warns of Covid-19 Surge, Offers Blunt Assessment of Trump's Response," *Washington Post*, October 31, 2020, https://www.washingtonpost.com/politics/fauci-covid-winter-forecast/2020/10/31/e3970eb0-1b8b-11eb-bb35-2dcfdab0a345_story.html.

33. Damian Paletta and Yasmeen Abutaleb, "Inside the Extraordinary Effort to Save Trump from Covid-19," *Washington Post*, June 24, 2021, https://www.washingtonpost.com/politics/2021/06/24/nightmare-scenario-book-excerpt/.

34. "US President Donald Trump Calls COVID-19 'Plague from China,'" YouTube, posted by ANI News, July 2, 2020, https://www.youtube.com/watch?v=OT0WFHbHomQ.

35. Biden-Harris Democrats, "The Biden Plan for an Effective Re-Opening That Jumpstarts the Economy," Joe Biden for President: Official Campaign Website, 2021, https://joebiden.com/reopening/.

36. US Bureau of Labor Statistics, "19.2 Percent of the Unemployed Had Been Jobless for 27 Weeks or More in February 2020," March 11, 2020, https://www.bls.gov/opub/ted/2020/19-point-2-percent-of-the-unemployed-had-been-jobless-for-27-weeks-or-more-in-february-2020.htm.

37. Reality Check Team, "US 2020 Election: The Economy Under Trump in Six Charts," BBC News, November 3, 2020, https://www.bbc.com/news/world-45827430.

38. Lydia Saad, "Trump's Economic Ratings No Longer Best in Class," Gallup, June 29, 2020, https://news.gallup.com/poll/313070/trump-economic-ratings-no-longer-best-class.aspx.

39. Sarah Nassauer and Harriet Torry, "Coronavirus Closures Froze Swaths of U.S. Economy in March," *Wall Street Journal*, April 15, 2020, https://www.wsj.com/articles/march-retail-sales-plunged-8-7-as-coronavirus-shutdowns-took-hold-11586954353.

40. "How Does the Pandemic Recession Stack Up Against the Great Depression?," Federal Reserve Bank of St. Louis, October 19, 2020, https://www.stlouisfed.org/on-the-economy/2020/october/pandemic-recession-stack-great-depression.

41. "World Economic Outlook Update," International Monetary Fund, Washington, DC, June 24, 2020, https://www.imf.org/en/Publications/WEO/Issues/2020/06/24/WEOUpdateJune2020.

42. Stephen Gandel, "Goldman Sachs Expects Unemployment Rate to Drop to Lowest Level Since Korean War," CBS News, December 2, 2019, https://www.cbsnews.com/news/goldman-sachs-says-unemployment-rate-to-drop-to-lowest-since-korean-war/.

43. AJ Willingham, Renée Rigdon, and Curt Merrill, "Understanding the Massive Scale of Coronavirus in the US," CNN, September 22, 2020, https://www.cnn.com/interactive/2020/health/coronavirus-us-deaths-milestones/.

44. In February 2020, 19.2 percent of the unemployed had been jobless for twenty-seven weeks or more. US Bureau of Labor Statistics, "19.2 Percent of the Unemployed Had Been Jobless for 27 Weeks or More in February 2020," 2.

45. Samantha Fields and Mitchell Hartman, "How Many Jobs Will Come Back After the COVID-19 Pandemic Ends?," *Marketplace*, May 8, 2020, https://www.marketplace.org/2020/05/08/how-many-jobs-will-come-back-after-the-covid-19-pandemic-ends/.

46. Quoctrung Bui and Emily Badger, "In These Neighborhoods, the Jobless Rate May Top 30 Percent," *New York Times*, August 5, 2020, https://www.nytimes.com/interactive/2020/08/05/upshot/us-unemployment-maps-coronavirus.html.

47. Jim Sergent, Ledyard King, and Michael Collins, "4 Coronavirus Stimulus Packages. $2.4 Trillion in Funding. See What That Means to the National Debt,"

USA Today, May 8, 2020, https://www.usatoday.com/in-depth/news/2020/05/08/national-debt-how-much-could-coronavirus-cost-america/3051559001/.

48. US Bureau of Economic Analysis, "Gross Domestic Product, Third Quarter 2020 (Advance Estimate)," October 29, 2020, https://www.bea.gov/news/blog/2020-10-29/gross-domestic-product-third-quarter-2020-advance-estimate.

49. Congressional Budget Office, "An Update to the Economic Outlook: 2020 to 2030," Congressional Budget Office, July 2, 2020, https://www.cbo.gov/publication/56442.

50. Congressional Budget Office, "An Update to the Economic Outlook: 2020 to 2030."

51. Rebecca Rainey, "Unemployment Claims Fell Slightly to 1 Million Last Week," *Politico*, August 27, 2020, https://www.politico.com/news/2020/08/27/unemployment-claims-fell-slightly-403465.

52. US Bureau of Labor Statistics, "The Employment Situation—September 2021," https://www.bls.gov/news.release/archives/empsit_10082021.pdf.

53. Greg Iacurci, "Trump Touts V-Shaped Economic Recovery, While Biden Sees It K-Shaped," CNBC, October 16, 2020, https://www.cnbc.com/2020/10/16/trump-touts-v-shaped-economic-recovery-while-biden-sees-it-k-shaped.html.

54. Iacurci, "Trump Touts V-Shaped Economic Recovery, While Biden Sees It K-Shaped."

55. Catarina Saraiva, "How a 'K-Shaped' Recovery Is Widening U.S. Inequality," Bloomberg, December 10, 2020, https://www.bloomberg.com/news/articles/2020-12-10/how-a-k-shaped-recovery-is-widening-u-s-inequality-quicktake.

56. Raj Chetty et al., "The Economic Tracker," Opportunity Insights, 2020, https://tracktherecovery.org/.

57. Raj Chetty, John N. Friedman, and Michael Stepner, "Who Spent Their Last Stimulus Checks?," *New York Times*, February 8, 2021, https://www.nytimes.com/interactive/2021/02/08/opinion/stimulus-checks-economy.html.

58. Juliana Menasce Horowitz, Ruth Igielnik, and Rakesh Kochhar, "Trends in U.S. Income and Wealth Inequality," Pew Research Center, Social and Demographic Trends Project, January 9, 2020, https://www.pewresearch.org/social-trends/2020/01/09/trends-in-income-and-wealth-inequality/.

59. US Census Bureau, "Week 18 Household Pulse Survey: October 28–November 9," November 18, 2020, https://www.census.gov/data/tables/2020/demo/hhp/hhp18.html. See also: Anne Price, "Where Do We Go from Here?," *Insight Center* (blog), December 1, 2020, https://insightcced.medium.com/where-do-we-go-from-here-4fd2370591b7.

60. Ailsa Chang, Rachel Martin, and Eric Marrapodi, "Summer of Racial Reckoning," NPR, August 16, 2020, https://www.npr.org/2020/08/16/902179773/summer-of-racial-reckoning-the-match-lit.

61. Chris Williams, "Darnella Frazier's Video of George Floyd's Death Changed Everything: 'History Should Remember,'" Fox 10 Phoenix, April 20, 2021, https://

www.fox10phoenix.com/news/darnella-fraziers-video-of-george-floyds-death-changed-everything-history-should-remember.

62. Jenna Wortham, "A 'Glorious Poetic Rage,'" *New York Times*, June 5, 2020, https://www.nytimes.com/2020/06/05/sunday-review/black-lives-matter-protests-floyd.html.

63. Larry Buchanan, Quoctrung Bui, and Jugal K. Patel, "Black Lives Matter May Be the Largest Movement in U.S. History," *New York Times*, July 3, 2020, https://www.nytimes.com/interactive/2020/07/03/us/george-floyd-protests-crowd-size.html.

64. Armed Conflict Location and Event Data Project and Bridging Divides Initiative, "A Year of Racial Justice Protests: Key Trends in Demonstrations Supporting the BLM Movement," Princeton University, May 25, 2021, https://acleddata.com/2021/05/25/a-year-of-racial-justice-protests-key-trends-in-demonstrations-supporting-the-blm-movement/.

65. Tim Craig, "Proud Boys and Black Lives Matter Activists Clashed in a Florida Suburb. Only One Side Was Charged," *Seattle Times*, February 2, 2021, https://www.seattletimes.com/nation-world/proud-boys-and-black-lives-matter-activists-clashed-in-a-florida-suburb-only-one-side-was-charged/.

66. Jemima McEvoy, "Proud Boys Leader Who Burned BLM Flag at Trump Protest Sentenced to Five Months In Jail," *Forbes*, August 23, 2021, https://www.forbes.com/sites/jemimamcevoy/2021/08/23/proud-boys-leader-who-burned-blm-flag-at-trump-protest-sentenced-to-five-months/?sh=5524686c6ce0.

67. Karma Allen, "Man Who Helped Ignite George Floyd Riots Identified as White Supremacist: Police," ABC News, July 29, 2020, https://abcnews.go.com/US/man-helped-ignite-george-floyd-riots-identified-white/story?id=72051536.

68. Anti-Defamation League, "Disinformation: Antifa Planning Violent Attacks on White Suburbs," 2021, https://www.adl.org/disinformation-antifa-planning-violent-attacks-on-white-suburbs.

69. Danielle Wallace, "Twitter Shuts Down Fake Antifa Account Linked to White Nationalists, Misinformation Tied to George Floyd Protests Spreads," Fox News, June 2, 2020, https://www.foxnews.com/us/twitter-misinformation-dc-blackout-white-nationalist-group-antifa.

70. Mark Hosenball, "A Trump Security Chief Acknowledges Role of White Supremacist Extremists in U.S. Urban Violence," Reuters, September 9, 2020, https://www.reuters.com/article/us-usa-homeland-supremacists-idUSKBN26031F.

71. Barbara Sprunt, "The History Behind 'When The Looting Starts, The Shooting Starts,'" NPR, May 29, 2020, https://www.npr.org/2020/05/29/864818368/the-history-behind-when-the-looting-starts-the-shooting-starts.

72. Centers for Disease Control and Prevention, "Risk for COVID-19 Infection, Hospitalization, and Death by Race/Ethnicity," September 2021, https://www.cdc.gov/coronavirus/2019-ncov/covid-data/investigations-discovery/hospitalization-death-by-race-ethnicity.html.

73. Crystal Johnson-Mann, Monique Hassan, and Shaneeta Johnson, "COVID-19 Pandemic Highlights Racial Health Inequities," *The Lancet Diabetes and Endocrinology* 8, no. 8 (August 2020): 663–664, doi:10.1016/S2213-8587(20)30225-4.

74. Carla Cerami et al., "High Household Transmission of SARS-CoV-2 in the United States: Living Density, Viral Load, and Disproportionate Impact on Communities of Color," *MedRxiv: The Preprint Server for Health Sciences*, March 2021, 2021.03.10.21253173, doi:10.1101/2021.03.10.21253173.

75. "US Election 2016: Trump Says Election 'Rigged at Polling Places,'" BBC News, October 17, 2016, https://www.bbc.com/news/election-us-2016-37673797.

76. Marina Villeneuve, "Report: Trump Commission Did Not Find Widespread Voter Fraud," Associated Press, August 3, 2018, https://apnews.com/article/north-america-donald-trump-us-news-ap-top-news-elections-f5f6a73b2af546ee97816bb35e82c18d.

77. David Cottrell, Michael C. Herron, and Sean J. Westwood, "An Exploration of Donald Trump's Allegations of Massive Voter Fraud in the 2016 General Election," *Electoral Studies*, March 2017, doi:10.1016/j.electstud.2017.09.002.

78. Kathy Frankovic, "Belief in Conspiracies Largely Depends on Political Identity," YouGov, December 27, 2016, https://today.yougov.com/topics/politics/articles-reports/2016/12/27/belief-conspiracies-largely-depends-political-iden.

79. Nick Corasaniti, Reid J. Epstein, and Jim Rutenberg, "The Times Called Officials in Every State: No Evidence of Voter Fraud," *New York Times*, November 10, 2020, https://www.nytimes.com/2020/11/10/us/politics/voting-fraud.html.

80. Eric Tucker and Frank Bajak, "Repudiating Trump, Officials Say Election 'Most Secure,'" Associated Press, November 13, 2020, https://apnews.com/article/top-officials-elections-most-secure-66f9361084ccbc461e3bbf4286105705.

81. Michael Balsamo, "Disputing Trump, Barr Says No Widespread Election Fraud," Associated Press, December 1, 2020, https://apnews.com/article/barr-no-widespread-election-fraud-b1f1488796c9a98c4b1a9061a6c7f49d.

82. Kathleen Hall Jamieson and Doron Taussig, "Disruption, Demonization, Deliverance, and Norm Destruction: The Rhetorical Signature of Donald J. Trump," *Political Science Quarterly* 132, no. 4 (2017): 618–649, doi:10.1002/polq.12699.

83. Michael Bender, *Frankly, We Did Win This Election: The Inside Story of How Donald Trump Lost* (New York: Twelve Books, 2021), 78–79.

84. Hope Yen and Calvin Woodward, "AP Fact Check: Trump Falsely Claims Mueller Exonerated Him," Associated Press, July 24, 2019, https://apnews.com/article/ap-fact-check-donald-trump-ap-top-news-politics-russia-130932b573664ea5a4d186f752bb8d50.

85. David Smith, "Robert Mueller Breaks Silence to Insist He Did Not Exonerate Trump," *Guardian*, May 29, 2019, https://www.theguardian.com/us-news/2019/may/29/mueller-says-trump-was-not-exonerated-by-his-investigation.

86. Elizabeth Dias, "Pence Reaches Out to Evangelicals. Not All of Them Reach Back," *New York Times*, June 13, 2018, https://www.nytimes.com/2018/06/13/us/polit ics/southern-baptist-convention-pence.html.

87. "Democratic Presidential Candidates Debate," April 26, 2007, C-SPAN, https:// www.c-span.org/video/?197847-1/democratic-presidential-candidates-debate.

88. Evan Osnos, "Why Biden Didn't Run," *New Yorker*, October 21, 2015, http://www. newyorker.com/news/news-desk/why-biden-didnt-run.

89. Jerry Smith, "Biden Would Be the Oldest Sitting President if Elected in 2020," *Delaware News Journal*, March 8, 2019, https://www.delawareonline.com/story/ news/2019/03/08/joe-biden-would-oldest-sitting-president-if-elected-2020/301 3336002/.

90. Casey Tolan, "Kamala Harris Grabs Spotlight in Big First Week as Presidential Candidate," *Mercury News*, January 29, 2019, https://www.mercurynews.com/ 2019/01/29/kamala-harris-president-iowa-des-moines-cnn-town-hall/.

91. Joe Scarborough, "Kamala Harris Has What It Takes," *Washington Post*, January 28, 2019, http://www.washingtonpost.com/opinions/kamala-harris-has-what-it-takes/2019/01/28/afb117be-2338-11e9-ad53-824486280311_story.html.

92. Kevin Breuninger, "Kamala Harris Attacks Joe Biden's Record on Busing and Working with Segregationists in Vicious Exchange at Democratic Debate," CNBC, June 27, 2019, https://www.cnbc.com/2019/06/27/harris-attacks-bidens-record-on-busing-and-working-with-segregationists.html.

93. Niels Lesniewski, "The Legislative Record of Kamala Harris Shows a Loyal Democrat and Trump Counterpuncher," Roll Call, August 12, 2020, https://www. rollcall.com/2020/08/12/the-legislative-record-of-kamala-harris-shows-a-loyal-democrat-and-trump-counter-puncher/.

94. Li Zhou, "Joe Biden Chooses Kamala Harris as His Running Mate," *Vox*, August 11, 2020, https://www.vox.com/2020/8/11/21346506/joe-biden-kamala-harris-vice-president.

95. Osita Nwanevu, "Low Black Turnout May Have Cost Clinton the Election," *Slate*, May 8, 2017, https://slate.com/news-and-politics/2017/05/low-black-turnout-may-have-cost-clinton-the-election.html.

96. Zhou, "Joe Biden Chooses Kamala Harris as His Running Mate."

97. Adam Edelman, Deepa Shivaram, and Kristen Welker, "Kamala Harris Named by Joe Biden as His VP Pick," NBC News, August 11, 2020, https://www.nbcnews. com/politics/2020-election/joe-biden-selects-kamala-harris-his-running-mate-n1235771.

98. Chris Cillizza, "Here's Why Joe Biden Chose Kamala Harris as His VP," CNN, August 11, 2020, https://www.cnn.com/2020/08/11/politics/joe-biden-kamala-harris-vp/index.html.

99. Edelman, Shivaram, and Welker, "Kamala Harris Named by Joe Biden as His VP Pick."

100. Christopher Cadelago and Caitlin Oprysko, "Biden Picks Kamala Harris as VP Nominee," Politico, August 11, 2020, https://www.politico.com/news/2020/08/11/joe-biden-vp-pick-kamala-harris-393768.

101. Adam Carlson, "Joe Biden and Kamala Harris' First Joint Interview: 'Audacity' of Partnering and Their 'Modern Family' Values," *People*, August 18, 2020, https://people.com/politics/joe-biden-and-kamala-harris-first-joint-interview/.

102. Barbara Sprunt, "Harris, As Biden's Running Mate, Says Case Against Trump Is 'Open And Shut,'" NPR, August 12, 2020, https://www.npr.org/2020/08/12/901462712/biden-and-harris-to-introduce-their-presidential-ticket-in-delaware.

CHAPTER 2

1. "Video: Watch the Full Speech: Biden Accepts the Democratic Nomination," *New York Times*, August 20, 2020, https://www.nytimes.com/video/us/elections/100000007299879/joe-biden-full-speech.html.

2. "Fact Check: Trump's Address to the Republican Convention, Annotated," NPR, August 27, 2020, https://www.npr.org/2020/08/27/901381398/fact-check-trumps-address-to-the-republican-convention-annotated.

3. Douglas A. Hibbs, "Bread and Peace Voting in U.S. Presidential Elections," *Public Choice* 104, nos. 1/2 (2000): 149–180, http://www.jstor.org/stable/30026466; Ruth Dassonneville and Charles Tien, "Introduction to Forecasting the 2020 US Elections," *PS: Political Science and Politics* 54, no. 1 (January 2021): 47–51, doi:10.1017/S104909652000147X.

4. Robert S. Erickson and Christopher Wlezien, *The Timeline of Presidential Elections: How Campaigns Do (and Do Not) Matter* (Chicago: University of Chicago Press, 2012), https://press.uchicago.edu/ucp/books/book/chicago/T/bo13948250.html; Lynn Vavreck, *The Message Matters: The Economy and Presidential Campaigns* (Princeton, NJ: Princeton University Press, 2009).

5. Morris P. Fiorina, *Retrospective Voting in American National Elections* (New Haven, CT: Yale University Press, 1981).

6. Douglas A. Hibbs Jr., *The American Political Economy: Macroeconomics and Electoral Politics* (Cambridge, MA: Harvard University Press, 1989); Hibbs, "Bread and Peace Voting in U.S. Presidential Elections."

7. Vavreck, *The Message Matters*.

8. Eric Guntermann, Gabriel S. Lenz, and Jeffrey R. Myers, "The Impact of the Economy on Presidential Elections Throughout US History," *Political Behavior* 43, no. 2 (June 2021): 837–857, doi:10.1007/s11109-021-09677-y; D. Roderick Kiewiet, *Macroeconomics and Micropolitics: The Electoral Effects of Economic Issues* (Chicago: University of Chicago Press, 1983).

9. James E. Campbell, Bryan J. Dettrey, and Hongxing Yin, "The Theory of Conditional Retrospective Voting: Does the Presidential Record Matter Less in

Open-Seat Elections?," *Journal of Politics* 72, no. 4 (2010): 1083–1095, doi:10.1017/s0022381610000054x.

10. Carol Leonnig and Philip Rucker, *I Alone Can Fix It: Donald J. Trump's Catastrophic Final Year* (New York: Penguin, 2021).

11. See, among others, Andrew Healy and Gabriel S. Lenz, "Substituting the End for the Whole: Why Voters Respond Primarily to the Election-Year Economy," *American Journal of Political Science* 58, no. 1 (2014): 31–47, https://www.jstor.org/stable/24363467; Christopher Wlezien, "The Myopic Voter? The Economy and US Presidential Elections," *Electoral Studies* 39 (September 2015): 195–204, doi:10.1016/j.electstud.2015.03.010; Hibbs, *The American Political Economy*.

12. Patrick Thomas, Sarah Chaney, and Chip Cutter, "New Covid-19 Layoffs Make Job Reductions Permanent," *Wall Street Journal*, August 2020, https://www.wsj.com/articles/new-covid-19-layoffs-make-job-reductions-permanent-11598654257; Harriet Torry, "U.S. Consumer Spending Rose More Slowly in July," *Wall Street Journal*, August 28, 2020, https://www.wsj.com/articles/consumer-spending-likely-grew-in-july-as-labor-market-improved-11598607000.

13. Ben Levisohn, "The Stock Market Just Erased All Its Covid Losses. The Economy Is Still a Problem," *Barron's*, August 18, 2020, https://www.barrons.com/articles/s-p-500-closes-at-record-high-heres-what-could-happen-next-51597781672.

14. Richard Johnston, Michael G. Hagen, and Kathleen Hall Jamieson, *The Dynamics of Election: The 2000 Presidential Election and the Foundations of Party Politics* (Cambridge, UK: Cambridge University Press, 2004); Vavreck, *The Message Matters*.

15. Esther Castillejo, "Joe Biden Clarifies 'Shutdown' Comments Made to ABC News' David Muir," ABC News, September 3, 2020, https://abcnews.go.com/Politics/joe-biden-clarifies-shutdown-comments-made-abc-news/story?id=72798117.

16. Gerald H. Kramer, "The Ecological Fallacy Revisited: Aggregate- Versus Individual-Level Findings on Economics and Elections, and Sociotropic Voting," *American Political Science Review* 77, no. 1 (March 1983): 92–111, doi:10.2307/1956013.

17. Justin De Benedictis-Kessner and Christopher Warshaw, "Accountability for the Local Economy at All Levels of Government in United States Elections," *American Political Science Review* 114, no. 3 (May 2019): 660–676, doi:10.1017/S0003055420000027; Andrew Healy and Gabriel S. Lenz, "Presidential Voting and the Local Economy: Evidence from Two Population-Based Data Sets," *Journal of Politics* 79, no. 4 (October 2017): 1419–1432, doi:10.1086/692785; Martin Bisgaard, Kim Mannemar Sønderskov, and Peter Thisted Dinesen, "Reconsidering the Neighborhood Effect: Does Exposure to Residential Unemployment Influence Voters' Perceptions of the National Economy?," *Journal of Politics* 78, no. 3 (July 2016): 719–732, https://doi.org/10.1086/685088.

18. Quoctrung Bui and Emily Badger, "In These Neighborhoods, the Jobless Rate May Top 30 Percent," *New York Times*, August 5, 2020, https://www.nytimes.com/interactive/2020/08/05/upshot/us-unemployment-maps-coronavirus.html.

19. US Department of Health and Human Services, "Report to Congress: COVID-19 Strategic Testing Plan," May 2020, https://www.democrats.senate.gov/imo/media/doc/COVID%20National%20Diagnostics%20Strategy%2005%2024%202020%20v%20FINAL.pdf.

20. Rick Rojas, "Trump and Allies Push Toward Reopening Economy, but Governors Urge Caution.," *New York Times*, April 12, 2020, https://www.nytimes.com/2020/04/12/us/when-lockdown-ending-coronavirus.html.

21. "Federal Coronavirus Testing Plan Puts Burden on States," Associated Press, May 25, 2020, https://apnews.com/article/understanding-the-outbreak-virus-outbreak-donald-trump-nancy-pelosi-ap-top-news-95b4123551de95bbab96ec4c82e1ee4d.

22. Steven Rogers, "National Forces in State Legislative Elections," *Annals of the American Academy of Political and Social Science* 667, no. 1 (September 2016): 207–225, doi:10.1177/0002716216662454; De Benedictis-Kessner and Warshaw, "Accountability for the Local Economy at All Levels of Government in United States Elections."

23. Donald J. Trump (realDonaldTrump), "'China Has Been Working Very Hard to Contain the Coronavirus. The United States Greatly Appreciates Their Efforts and Transparency. It Will All Work out Well. In Particular, on Behalf of the American People, I Want to Thank President Xi!,'" Twitter, January 24, 2020, 1:18 PM, https://web.archive.org/web/20200426013814/https://twitter.com/realdonaldtrump/status/1220818115354923009?lang=en.

24. Michelle L. Holshue et al., "First Case of 2019 Novel Coronavirus in the United States," *New England Journal of Medicine* 382 (2020): 929–936, doi:10.1056/NEJMoa2001191.

25. "Pfizer and BioNTech Announce Vaccine Candidate Against COVID-19 Achieved Success in First Interim Analysis from Phase 3 Study," Pfizer, November 9, 2020, https://www.pfizer.com/news/press-release/press-release-detail/pfizer-and-biontech-announce-vaccine-candidate-against.

26. David Karol and Edward Miguel, "The Electoral Cost of War: Iraq Casualties and the 2004 U.S. Presidential Election," *Journal of Politics* 69, no. 3 (2007): 633–648, http://emiguel.econ.berkeley.edu/assets/miguel_research/33/_Paper__Electoral_Cost_of_War.pdf.

27. Maegan Vazquez, "Trump Invokes Defense Production Act for Ventilator Equipment and N95 Masks," CNN, April 3, 2020, https://edition.cnn.com/2020/04/02/politics/defense-production-act-ventilator-supplies/index.html.

28. Michael S. Schmidt and Maggie Haberman, "Trump Aides Prepared Insurrection Act Order During Debate over Protests," *New York Times*, June 25, 2021, https://www.nytimes.com/2021/06/25/us/politics/trump-insurrection-act-protests.html.

29. Factbase, "Speech: Donald Trump Delivers a Campaign Speech in Manchester, New Hampshire—August 28, 2020," https://factba.se/transcript/donald-trump-speech-campaign-rally-manchester-nh-august-28-2020.

30. Glenn Thrush, "Full Transcript: President Trump's Republican National Convention Speech," *New York Times*, August 28, 2020, https://www.nytimes.com/2020/08/28/us/politics/trump-rnc-speech-transcript.html.

31. Carrie Dann, "Fact-Check: Did Kellyanne Conway Say Violence and Chaos 'Help [Trump's] Cause?,'" NBC News, October 2, 2020, https://www.nbcnews.com/politics/2020-election/blog/first-presidential-debate-trump-biden-n1241282.

32. "Biden: I Support 'Law and Order, Where People Get Treated Fairly,'" YouTube, posted by NBC News, September 30, 2020, https://www.youtube.com/watch?v=mopQrNH5WK0.

33. Lee Sigelman, "Presidential Popularity and Presidential Elections," *Public Opinion Quarterly* 43, no. 4 (1979): 532–534, https://www.jstor.org/stable/2748551. Sigelman; Michael S. Lewis-Beck and Tom W. Rice, "Presidential Popularity and Presidential Vote," *Public Opinion Quarterly* 46, no. 4 (1982): 534, doi:10.1086/268750.

34. Josh Clinton et al., "2020 Pre-Election Polling: An Evaluation of the 2020 General Election Polls," American Association for Public Opinion Research, Washington, DC, 2021, https://www.aapor.org/Education-Resources/Reports/2020-Pre-Election-Polling-An-Evaluation-of-the-202.aspx.

35. Donald R. Kinder and D. Roderick Kiewiet, "Sociotropic Politics: The American Case," *British Journal of Political Science* 11, no. 2 (April 1981): 129–161, doi:10.1017/S0007123400002544; Gerald H. Kramer, "Short-Term Fluctuations in U.S. Voting Behavior, 1896–1964," *American Political Science Review* 65, no. 1 (1971): 131–143, doi:10.2307/1955049.

36. D. Roderick Kiewiet and Douglas Rivers, "The Economic Basis of Reagan's Appeal," in *The New Direction in American Politics* (Washington, DC: Brookings Institution, 1985), 69–90.

37. James Campbell and James Garand, eds., *Before the Vote: Forecasting American National Elections* (Thousand Oaks, CA: SAGE Publications, 2000).

38. John Sides, "Why Trump Isn't Getting Credit from Voters for Good Economic News," *Washington Post*, December 26, 2019, https://www.washingtonpost.com/outlook/2019/12/26/why-trump-isnt-getting-credit-voters-good-economic-news/.

39. Jeffrey M. Jones, "Presidential Job Approval Related to Reelection Historically," Gallup, May 29, 2020, https://news.gallup.com/poll/311825/presidential-job-approval-related-reelection-historically.aspx.

40. Angus Campbell et al., *The American Voter* (Chicago: University of Chicago Press, 1960), https://press.uchicago.edu/ucp/books/book/chicago/A/bo24047989.html.

41. Larry M. Bartels, "Partisanship and Voting Behavior, 1952–1996," *American Journal of Political Science* 44, no. 1 (2000): 35–50, doi:10.2307/2669291.

42. "How Groups Voted in 2016," Roper Center, November 2016, https://ropercenter.cornell.edu/how-groups-voted-2016.

43. "Exit Polls—Election Results 2008," *New York Times*, November 5, 2008, https://www.nytimes.com/elections/2008/results/president/national-exit-polls.html.

44. "President Exit Polls," *New York Times*, 2012, https://www.nytimes.com/elections/2012/results/president/exit-polls.html.

45. "National Exit Polls: How Different Groups Voted," *New York Times*, November 3, 2020, https://www.nytimes.com/interactive/2020/11/03/us/elections/exit-polls-president.html.

46. Michael B. MacKuen, Robert S. Erikson, and James A. Stimson, "Macropartisanship," *American Political Science Review* 83, no. 4 (December 1989): 1125–1142, doi:10.2307/1961661.

47. James Campbell, "Presidential Election Campaigns and Partisanship," in *American Politics Parties: Decline or Resurgence*, edited by Jeffrey Cohen, Richard Fleishner, and Paul Kantor (Washington, DC: Congressional Quarterly Press, 2001), 304.

48. Andrew Gelman and Gary King, "Why Are American Presidential Election Campaign Polls So Variable When Votes Are So Predictable?," *British Journal of Political Science* 23, no. 4 (October 1993): 409–451, doi:10.1017/S0007123400006682.

49. Corwin D. Smidt, "Dynamics in Partisanship During American Presidential Campaigns," *Public Opinion Quarterly* 78, no. S1 (2014): 303–329, https://doi.org/10.1093/poq/nfu014.

50. Donald Green, Bradley Palmquist, and Eric Schickler, *Partisan Hearts and Minds: Political Parties and the Social Identities of Voters* (New Haven, CT: Yale University Press, 2004).

51. B. Pablo Montagnes, Zachary Peskowitz, and Joshua McCrain, "Bounding Partisan Approval Rates Under Endogenous Partisanship: Why High Presidential Partisan Approval May Not Be What It Seems," *Journal of Politics* 81, no. 1 (January 2019): 321–326, doi:10.1086/700572.

52. Jeffrey M. Jones, "U.S. Party Preferences Have Swung Sharply Toward Democrats," Gallup, July 16, 2020, https://news.gallup.com/poll/315734/party-preferences-swung-sharply-toward-democrats.aspx.

53. YouGov and CBS, "CBS News Battleground Tracker—August 19–21, 2020," Google Docs, accessed October 13, 2021, https://drive.google.com/file/d/11UTgWRN1SvFmO3W9PVVOnPyGYqea4X6H/view?usp=embed_facebook.

54. Robert S. Erickson and Christopher Wlezien, *The Timeline of Presidential Elections: How Campaigns Do (and Do Not) Matter* (Chicago: University of Chicago Press, 2012), https://press.uchicago.edu/ucp/books/book/chicago/T/bo13948250.html.

55. Lynn Vavreck, *The Message Matters: The Economy and Presidential Campaigns* (Princeton, NJ: Princeton University Press, 2009).

56. Johnston, Hagen, and Jamieson, *The Dynamics of Election*.

57. Mark Boukes, Alyt Damstra, and Rens Vliegenthart, "Media Effects Across Time and Subject: How News Coverage Affects Two out of Four Attributes of

Consumer Confidence," *Communication Research* 48, no. 3 (April 2021): 454–476, doi:10.1177/0093650219870087.

58. Kim Fridkin et al., "Capturing the Power of a Campaign Event: The 2004 Presidential Debate in Tempe," *Journal of Politics* 69, no. 3 (August 2007): 770–785, doi:10.1111/j.1468-2508.2007.00574.x.

59. Kathleen Hall Jamieson, *Cyberwar: How Russian Hackers and Trolls Helped Elect a President: What We Don't, Can't, and Do Know* (New York: Oxford University Press, 2018).

60. Stephen Chaffee and J. L. Hochheimer, "The Beginnings of Political Communication Research in the United States: Origins of the 'Limited Effects Model,'" in *Mass Communication Review Yearbook*, edited by Michael Gurevitch and Mark Levy, vol. 5 (Thousand Oaks, CA: SAGE Publications, 1985); Alexander Coppock, Seth J. Hill, and Lynn Vavreck, "The Small Effects of Political Advertising Are Small Regardless of Context, Message, Sender, or Receiver: Evidence from 59 Real-Time Randomized Experiments," *Science Advances* 6, no. 36 (2020), doi:10.1126/sciadv. abc4046.

61. Seth J. Hill et al., "How Quickly We Forget: The Duration of Persuasion Effects from Mass Communication," *Political Communication* 30, no. 4 (October 2013): 521–547, doi:10.1080/10584609.2013.828143; Johnston, Hagen, and Jamieson, *The Dynamics of Election*; John Sides, Michael Tesler, and Lynn Vavreck, *Identity Crisis: The 2016 Presidential Campaign and the Battle for the Meaning of America* (Princeton, NJ: Princeton University Press, 2018).

62. Johnston, Hagen, and Jamieson, *The Dynamics of Election*.

63. William L. Benoit, Glenn J. Hansen, and R. Lance Holbert, "Presidential Campaigns and Democracy," *Mass Communication and Society* 7, no. 2 (May 2004): 177–190, doi:10.1207/s15327825mcs0702_3.

64. Markus Prior, *Post-Broadcast Democracy: How Media Choice Increases Inequality in Political Involvement and Polarizes Elections* (New York: Cambridge University Press, 2007).

65. Matthew Levendusky, *How Partisan Media Polarize America*, Chicago Studies in American Politics (Chicago: University of Chicago Press, 2013), https://press.uchicago.edu/ucp/books/book/chicago/H/bo16468853.html; Kathleen Hall Jamieson and Joseph N. Cappella, *Echo Chamber: Rush Limbaugh and the Conservative Media Establishment* (New York: Oxford University Press, 2010).

66. James N. Druckman, "Media Matter: How Newspapers and Television News Cover Campaigns and Influence Voters," *Political Communication* 22, no. 4 (October 2005): 463–481, doi:10.1080/10584600500311394.

67. Nolan McCarty, *Polarization: What Everyone Needs to Know* (New York: Oxford University Press, 2019).

68. Marc J. Hetherington, "Resurgent Mass Partisanship: The Role of Elite Polarization," *American Political Science Review* 95, no. 3 (2001): 619–631; Matthew

Levendusky, *The Partisan Sort: How Liberals Became Democrats and Conservatives Became Republicans* (Chicago: University of Chicago Press, 2009).

69. Milton Lodge and Charles S. Taber, *The Rationalizing Voter*, Cambridge Studies in Public Opinion and Political Psychology (Cambridge, UK: Cambridge University Press, 2013), doi:10.1017/CBO9781139032490.

70. Philip Jones, "Partisanship, Political Awareness, and Retrospective Evaluations, 1956–2016," *Political Behavior* 42, no. 2 (December 2020): 1–23, doi:10.1007/s11109-019-09543-y; Larry M. Bartels, "Beyond the Running Tally: Partisan Bias in Political Perceptions," *Political Behavior* 24, no. 2 (2002): 117–150, https://www.jstor.org/stable/1558352.

71. See, among others, Christopher Wlezien, Mark Franklin, and Daniel Twiggs, "Economic Perceptions and Vote Choice: Disentangling the Endogeneity," *Political Behavior* 19, no. 1 (March 1997): 7–17, doi:10.1023/A:1024841605168; Geoffrey Evans and Robert Andersen, "The Political Conditioning of Economic Perceptions," *Journal of Politics* 68, no. 1 (2006): 194–207, doi:10.1111/j.1468-2508.2006.00380.x.

72. On this sort of argument more generally, see, e.g., Martin Bisgaard, "Bias Will Find a Way: Economic Perceptions, Attributions of Blame, and Partisan-Motivated Reasoning During Crisis," *Journal of Politics* 77, no. 3 (July 2015): 849–860, doi:10.1086/681591.

73. Gerald H. Kramer, "Short-Term Fluctuations in U.S. Voting Behavior, 1896–1964," *American Political Science Review* 65, no. 1 (1971): 131–143, doi:10.2307/1955049; Andreas Kayser and Christopher Wlezien, "Performance Pressure: Patterns of Partisanship and the Economic Vote," *European Journal of Political Research* 50, no. 3 (May 2011): 365–394, doi:10.1111/j.1475-6765.2010.01934.x.

74. Kathleen Donovan et al., "Motivated Reasoning, Public Opinion, and Presidential Approval," *Political Behavior* 42, no. 4 (December 2020): 1201–1221, doi:10.1007/s11109-019-09539-8.

75. Bernard R. Berelson, Paul F. Lazarsfeld, and William N. McPhee, *Voting: A Study of Opinion Formation in a Presidential Campaign*, reprint ed. (Chicago: University of Chicago Press, 1986).

76. Christopher H. Achen and Larry M. Bartels, *Democracy for Realists* (Princeton, NJ: Princeton University Press, 2017), https://press.princeton.edu/books/paperback/9780691178240/democracy-for-realists.

77. Natalie Jomini Stroud, *Niche News: The Politics of News Choice* (New York: Oxford University Press, 2011), doi:10.1093/acprof:oso/9780199755509.001.0001.

78. Lodge and Taber, *The Rationalizing Voter*.

79. Leonie Huddy, "From Social to Political Identity: A Critical Examination of Social Identity Theory," *Political Psychology* 22, no. 1 (2001): 127–156, doi:10.1111/0162-895X.00230.

80. Ashley Jardina, *White Identity Politics*, Cambridge Studies in Public Opinion and Political Psychology (Cambridge, UK: Cambridge University Press, 2019), doi:10.1017/9781108645157.

81. Sides, Tesler, and Vavreck, *Identity Crisis*.

82. Diana C. Mutz, "Status Threat, Not Economic Hardship, Explains the 2016 Presidential Vote," *Proceedings of the National Academy of Sciences* 115, no. 19 (May 2018): E4330–E4339, doi:10.1073/pnas.1718155115.

83. Jonathan N. Wand et al., "The Butterfly Did It: The Aberrant Vote for Buchanan in Palm Beach County, Florida," *American Political Science Review* 95, no. 4 (December 2001): 793–810, doi:10.1017/S000305540040002X.

84. Edward B. Foley and Charles Stewart III, "Explaining the Blue Shift in Election Canvassing," Social Science Research Network, March 2020, doi:10.2139/ssrn.3547734; Marshall Cohen, "Deciphering the 'Red Mirage,' the 'Blue Shift,' and the Uncertainty Surrounding Election Results this November," CNN, September 1, 2020, https://edition.cnn.com/2020/09/01/politics/2020-election-count-red-mirage-blue-shift/index.html.

85. Libby Cathey and Meghan Keneally, "A Look Back at Trump Comments Perceived by Some as Inciting Violence," ABC News, May 30, 2020, https://abcnews.go.com/Politics/back-trump-comments-perceived-encouraging-violence/story?id=48415766.

CHAPTER 3

1. Jeremy Diamond, "Trump: I Could 'Shoot Somebody and I Wouldn't Lose Voters,'" CNN, January 23, 2016, https://www.cnn.com/2016/01/23/politics/donald-trump-shoot-somebody-support/index.html.

2. Shanto Iyengar et al., "The Origins and Consequences of Affective Polarization in the United States," *Annual Review of Political Science* 22, no. 1 (2019): 129–146, doi:10.1146/annurev-polisci-051117-073034.

3. Kathleen Donovan et al., "Motivated Reasoning, Public Opinion, and Presidential Approval," *Political Behavior* 42, no. 4 (December 2020): 1201–1221, doi:10.1007/s11109-019-09539-8.

4. Liliana Mason, *Uncivil Agreement: How Politics Became Our Identity* (Chicago: University of Chicago Press, 2018), https://press.uchicago.edu/ucp/books/book/chicago/U/bo27527354.html; Matthew Levendusky, *The Partisan Sort* (Chicago: University of Chicago Press, 2009), https://press.uchicago.edu/ucp/books/book/chicago/P/bo8212972.html.

5. Marc Hetherington, *Why Trust Matters* (Princeton, NJ: Princeton University Press, 2004), https://press.princeton.edu/books/paperback/9780691128702/why-trust-matters; Marc J. Hetherington and Thomas J. Rudolph, *Why Washington Won't Work: Polarization, Political Trust, and the Governing Crisis* (Chicago: University of Chicago Press, 2015), doi:10.7208/9780226299358.

6. Jonathan Rodden, *Why Cities Lose: The Deep Roots of the Urban-Rural Political Divide* (New York: Basic Books, 2019).

7. Matthew S. Levendusky, "Why Do Partisan Media Polarize Viewers?," *American Journal of Political Science* 57, no. 3 (2013): 611–623, doi:10.1111/ajps.12008; Natalie Jomini Stroud, *Niche News: The Politics of News Choice* (New York: Oxford University Press, 2011), doi:10.1093/acprof:oso/9780199755509.001.0001.

8. Magdalena E. Wojcieszak and Diana C. Mutz, "Online Groups and Political Discourse: Do Online Discussion Spaces Facilitate Exposure to Political Disagreement?," *Journal of Communication* 59, no. 1 (2009): 40–56, doi:10.1111/j.1460-2466.2008.01403.x.

9. R. Kelly Garrett, "Politically Motivated Reinforcement Seeking: Reframing the Selective Exposure Debate," *Journal of Communication* 59, no. 4 (2009): 676–699, doi:10.1111/j.1460-2466.2009.01452.x.

10. Mason, *Uncivil Agreement: How Politics Became Our Identity*.

11. Michael S. Lewis-Beck et al., *The American Voter Revisited* (Ann Arbor, MI: University of Michigan Press, 2008), https://www.press.umich.edu/338457/american_voter_revisited.

12. Lewis-Beck et al.; Angus Campbell et al., *The American Voter* (Chicago, IL: University of Chicago Press), accessed October 13, 2021, https://press.uchicago.edu/ucp/books/book/chicago/A/bo24047989.html.

13. Nicholas A. Valentino and David O. Sears, "Old Times There Are Not Forgotten: Race and Partisan Realignment in the Contemporary South," *American Journal of Political Science* 49, no. 3 (2005): 672–688, doi:10.1111/j.1540-5907.2005.00136.x.

14. David E. Campbell, James R. G. Kirk, and Geoffrey C. Layman, "Religion and the 2020 Presidential Election: The Enduring Divide," *The Forum* 18, no. 4 (December 2020): 581–605, doi:10.1515/for-2020-2104.

15. Bernard R. Berelson, Paul F. Lazarsfeld, and William N. McPhee, *Voting: A Study of Opinion Formation in a Presidential Campaign*, Reprint edition (Chicago: University of Chicago Press, 1986).

16. Morris P. Fiorina, *Retrospective Voting in American National Elections* (New Haven, CT: Yale University Press, 1981).

17. Scott Horsley, "From Jobs to Homeownership, Protests Put Spotlight on Racial Economic Divide," NPR, June 1, 2020, https://www.npr.org/2020/06/01/866794025/from-jobs-to-homeownership-protests-put-spotlight-on-economic-divide.

18. Centers for Disease Control and Prevention, "Risk for COVID-19 Infection, Hospitalization, and Death By Race/Ethnicity," September 2021, https://www.cdc.gov/coronavirus/2019-ncov/covid-data/investigations-discovery/hospitalization-death-by-race-ethnicity.html.

19. National Institutes of Health, "Factors Contributing to Higher Incidence of Diabetes for Black Americans," January 9, 2018, https://www.nih.gov/news-events/nih-research-matters/factors-contributing-higher-incidence-diabetes-black-americans.

20. Crystal Johnson-Mann, Monique Hassan, and Shaneeta Johnson, "COVID-19 Pandemic Highlights Racial Health Inequities," *The Lancet Diabetes and Endocrinology* 8, no. 8 (August 2020): 663–664, doi:10.1016/S2213-8587(20)30225-4.

21. Carla Cerami et al., "High Household Transmission of SARS-CoV-2 in the United States: Living Density, Viral Load, and Disproportionate Impact on Communities of Color," MedRxiv: The Preprint Server for Health Sciences, March 12, 2021, 2021.03.10.21253173, doi:10.1101/2021.03.10.21253173.

22. Douglas S. Massey and Nancy A. Denton, *American Apartheid: Segregation and the Making of the Underclass* (Cambridge, MA: Harvard University Press, 1998), https://www.hup.harvard.edu/catalog.php?isbn=9780674018211.

23. Bruce E. Keith et al., *The Myth of the Independent Voter* (Berkeley: University of California Press, 1992); John Richard Petrocik, "Measuring Party Support: Leaners Are Not Independents," *Electoral Studies* 28, no. 4 (December 2009): 562–572, doi:10.1016/j.electstud.2009.05.022.

24. Dave Leip, "2020 Presidential Predictions," Dave Leip's Atlas of U.S. Presidential Elections, 2020, https://uselectionatlas.org/PRED/PRESIDENT/2020/pred.php; Michael McDonald, "2020 General Election Early Vote Statistics," U.S. Elections Project, November 2020, https://electproject.github.io/Early-Vote-2020G/index.html.

25. Kat Stafford, "Voters Approve Proposal 3, Bringing Sweeping Changes to Michigan's Election Law," *Detroit Free Press*, November 6, 2018, https://www.freep.com/story/news/politics/elections/2018/11/06/michigan-voting-proposal-3-results/1885266002/.

26. Marie Albiges, "Pandemic, Partisan Attacks Exposed Gaps in Pa.'s New Mail-in Voting Law," Spotlight PA, December 3, 2020, https://www.spotlightpa.org/news/2020/12/pennsylvania-election-2020-act-77-mail-voting-republican-audit/.

27. Ledyard King and Rebecca Morin, "Trump's Campaign Has a Massive Door-Knocking Campaign. Biden's Is Just Getting Started. Will It Matter?," *USA Today*, October 1, 2020, https://www.usatoday.com/story/news/politics/elections/2020/10/01/election-2020-donald-trump-joe-biden-voter-outreach-has-big-differences/3486819001/.

28. Charlotte Alter, "Joe Biden's Invisible Campaign in All-Important Michigan," *Time*, September 15, 2020, https://time.com/5889093/joe-biden-michigan-campaign/.

29. Joshua P. Darr, "In 2020, the Ground Game Is All Trump," Mischiefs of Faction, October 9, 2020, https://www.mischiefsoffaction.com/post/2020-ground-game.

CHAPTER 4

1. Jeff Horwitz and Keach Hagey, "Parler Makes Play for Conservatives Mad at Facebook, Twitter," *Wall Street Journal*, November 15, 2020, https://www.wsj.

com/articles/parler-backed-by-mercer-family-makes-play-for-conservatives-mad-at-facebook-twitter-11605382430.

2. "Trump Supporters Chant down a Fox News Reporter in Downtown Phoenix," *Arizona Central*, November 5, 2020, https://www.azcentral.com/videos/news/politics/elections/2020/11/05/trump-supporters-harass-fox-news-reporter-downt own-phoenix/6170694002/.

3. Jonathan J. Cooper and Terry Tang, "Arizona Certifies Biden's Narrow Victory over Trump," Associated Press, November 30, 2020, https://apnews.com/article/joe-biden-donald-trump-arizona-phoenix-elections-9638adedbe826b31b5d172ba3 a1c7c3a.

4. Brian Stelter, "Trump Voters Are Flocking to a TV Channel That Claims Biden Is Not President-Elect," CNN, November 12, 2020, https://www.cnn.com/2020/11/12/media/fox-news-newsmax-reliable-sources/index.html.

5. Michael M. Grynbaum and John Koblin, "Newsmax, Once a Right-Wing Also-Ran, Is Rising, and Trump Approves," *New York Times*, November 22, 2020, https://www.nytimes.com/2020/11/22/business/media/newsmax-trump-fox-news.html.

6. John Shiffman, "How AT&T Helped Build Far-Right One America News," Reuters, October 6, 2021, https://www.reuters.com/investigates/special-report/usa-oneamerica-att/.

7. Shiffman, "How AT&T Helped Build Far-Right One America News."

8. Susanna Dilliplane, Seth K. Goldman, and Diana C. Mutz, "Televised Exposure to Politics: New Measures for a Fragmented Media Environment," *American Journal of Political Science* 57, no. 1 (2013): 236–248, doi:10.1111/j.1540-5907.2012.00600.x.

9. Seth K. Goldman, Diana C. Mutz, and Susanna Dilliplane, "All Virtue Is Relative: A Response to Prior," *Political Communication* 30, no. 4 (October 2013): 635–653, doi:10.1080/10584609.2013.819540; Seth K. Goldman and Stephen Warren, "Debating How to Measure Media Exposure in Surveys," in *The Oxford Handbook of Electoral Persuasion*, edited by Elizabeth Suhay, Bernard Grofman, and Alexander H. Trechel (New York: Oxford University Press, 2020), https://doi.org/10.1093/oxfordhb/9780190860806.013.28.

10. Andrew M. Guess, "Measure for Measure: An Experimental Test of Online Political Media Exposure," *Political Analysis* 23, no. 1 (2015): 59–75, doi:10.1093/pan/mpu010.

11. For more on the Democracy Fund + UCLA Nationscape Project, see https://www.voterstudygroup.org/nationscape.

12. Michael J. LaCour and Lynn Vavreck, "Improving Media Measurement: Evidence from the Field," *Political Communication* 31, no. 3 (July 2014): 408–420, doi:10.1080/10584609.2014.921258.

13. Kim Andersen, Claes H. de Vreese, and Erik Albæk, "Measuring Media Diet in a High-Choice Environment—Testing the List-Frequency Technique," *Communication Methods and Measures* 10, nos. 2–3 (April 2016): 81–98, doi:10.1080/19312458.2016.1150973.

14. Markus Prior, *Post-Broadcast Democracy: How Media Choice Increases Inequality in Political Involvement and Polarizes Elections* (New York: Cambridge University Press, 2007).

15. Andreas Nanz and Jorg Matthes, "Learning from Incidental Exposure to Political Information in Online Environments," *Journal of Communication* 70, no. 6 (December 2020): 769–793, doi:10.1093/joc/jqaa031; Kjerstin Thorson, "Attracting the News: Algorithms, Platforms, and Reframing Incidental Exposure," *Journalism* 21, no. 8 (2020): 1067–1082, doi:10.177/1464884920915352; Brian E. Weeks and Daniel S. Lane, "The Ecology of Incidental Exposure to News in Digital Media Environments," *Journalism* 21, no. 8 (2020): 1119–1135, doi:10.1177/1464884920915354.

16. For related uses of this measurement strategy, see Joseph Hilgard and Kathleen Hall Jamieson, "Does a Scientific Breakthrough Increase Confidence in Science? News of a Zika Vaccine and Trust in Science," *Science Communication* 39, no. 4 (August 2017): 548–560, doi:10.1177/1075547017719075; Kathleen Hall Jamieson et al., "The Role of Non–COVID-Specific and COVID-Specific Factors in Predicting a Shift in Willingness to Vaccinate: A Panel Study," *Proceedings of the National Academy of Sciences* 118, no. 52 (December 2021): e2112266118, doi:10.1073/pnas.2112266118; Daniel Romer and Kathleen Hall Jamieson, "Conspiracy Theories as Barriers to Controlling the Spread of COVID-19 in the U.S.," *Social Science and Medicine* 263, no. 113356 (October 2020), doi:10.1016/j.socscimed.2020.113356; Daniel Romer and Kathleen Hall Jamieson, "Patterns of Media Use, Strength of Belief in COVID-19 Conspiracy Theories, and the Prevention of COVID-19 from March to July 2020 in the United States: Survey Study," *Journal of Medical Internet Research* 23, no. 4 (April 2021): e25215, doi:10.2196/25215.

17. Tim Groseclose and Jeffrey Milyo, "A Measure of Media Bias," *Quarterly Journal of Economics* 120, no. 4 (November 2005): 1191–1237, doi:10.1162/003355305775097542.

18. See, for example, Jamieson et al., "The Role of Non–COVID-Specific and COVID-Specific Factors in Predicting a Shift in Willingness to Vaccinate."

19. Kathleen Hall Jamieson and Joseph N. Cappella, *Echo Chamber: Rush Limbaugh and the Conservative Media Establishment* (New York: Oxford University Press, 2010); Andrew M. Guess, "(Almost) Everything in Moderation: New Evidence on Americans' Online Media Diets," *American Journal of Political Science* 65, no. 4 (2021): 1007–1022, doi:10.1111/ajps.12589.

20. Cass R. Sunstein, *#Republic: Divided Democracy in the Age of Social Media* (Princeton, NJ: Princeton University Press, 2017); Eli Pariser, *The Filter Bubble* (New York: Penguin, 2012), https://www.penguin.co.uk/books/181/181850/the-filter-bubble/9780241954522.html; Jamieson and Cappella, *Echo Chamber*.

21. Eytan Bakshy, Solomon Messing, and Lada A. Adamic, "Exposure to Ideologically Diverse News and Opinion on Facebook," *Science* 348, no. 6239 (June 2015): 1130–1132, doi:10.1126/science.aaa1160; Elizabeth Dubois and Grant

Blank, "The Echo Chamber Is Overstated: The Moderating Effect of Political Interest and Diverse Media," *Information, Communication and Society* 21, no. 5 (2018): 729–745, doi:10.1080/1369118X.2018.1428656; Axel Bruns, *Are Filter Bubbles Real?* (New York: Polity Press, 2019), http://www.wiley.com/en-us/Are+Filter+Bubbles+Real%3F-p-9781509536443; Pablo Barberá et al., "Tweeting from Left to Right: Is Online Political Communication More than an Echo Chamber?," *Psychological Science* 26, no. 10 (October 2015): 1531–1542, doi:10.1177/0956797615594620.

22. John Sands, "Local News Is More Trusted than National News—but That Could Change," Knight Foundation, October 29, 2019, https://knightfoundation.org/articles/local-news-is-more-trusted-than-national-news-but-that-could-change/.

23. Gregory Eady et al., "How Many People Live in Political Bubbles on Social Media? Evidence From Linked Survey and Twitter Data," *SAGE Open* 9, no. 1 (2019), doi:10.1177/2158244019832705.

CHAPTER 5.1

1. Rem Rieder, "Trump's Statements About the Coronavirus," FactCheck.org, last updated March 19, 2020, https://www.factcheck.org/2020/03/trumps-statements-about-the-coronavirus/.

2. "Transcript: Joe Biden's DNC Speech," CNN, August 20, 2020, https://www.cnn.com/2020/08/20/politics/biden-dnc-speech-transcript/index.html.

3. "A Timeline of COVID-19 Developments in 2020," *American Journal of Managed Care*, January 2021, https://www.ajmc.com/view/a-timeline-of-covid19-developments-in-2020.

4. Eliott C. McLaughlin and Steve Almasy, "CDC Official Warns Americans It's Not a Question of if Coronavirus Will Spread, but When," CNN, February 25, 2020, https://www.cnn.com/2020/02/25/health/coronavirus-us-american-cases/index.html.

5. "Transcripts, CNN Newsroom (February 25, 2020)," CNN, February 25, 2020, http://www.cnn.com/TRANSCRIPTS/2002/25/cnr.01.html.

6. Pam Belluck and Noah Weiland, "C.D.C. Officials Warn of Coronavirus Outbreaks in the U.S.," *New York Times*, February 25, 2020, https://www.nytimes.com/2020/02/25/health/coronavirus-us.html.

7. Bill Barrow, "Democrats Confirm Plans for Nearly All-Virtual Convention," Associated Press, June 24, 2020, https://apnews.com/article/virus-outbreak-joe-biden-ap-top-news-elections-politics-09785e274676e46351c70644d2b77215.

8. Amanda Moreland, "Timing of State and Territorial COVID-19 Stay-at-Home Orders and Changes in Population Movement—United States, March 1–May 31, 2020," *Morbidity and Mortality Weekly Report* 69, no. 35 (2020): 1198–1203, doi:10.15585/mmwr.mm6935a2.

9. Brett Samuels and Rebecca Klar, "Trump: 'We Can't Let the Cure Be Worse than the Problem Itself,'" *The Hill*, March 23, 2020, https://thehill.com/homenews/administration/488965-trump-hints-at-changes-to-restrictions-we-cant-let-the-cure-be-worse.

10. Jim Tankersley, Maggie Haberman, and Roni Caryn Rabin, "Trump Considers Reopening Economy, over Health Experts' Objections," *New York Times*, March 23, 2020, https://www.nytimes.com/2020/03/23/business/trump-coronavirus-economy.html.

11. Peter Baker, "Trump's New Coronavirus Message: Time to Move On to the Economic Recovery," *New York Times*, May 6, 2020, https://www.nytimes.com/2020/05/06/us/politics/trump-coronavirus-recovery.html.

12. Craig Mauger and Beth LeBlanc, "Trump Tweets 'Liberate' Michigan, Two Other States with Dem Governors," *Detroit News*, April 17, 2020, https://www.detroitnews.com/story/news/politics/2020/04/17/trump-tweets-liberate-michigan-other-states-democratic-governors/5152037002/.

13. David D. Kirkpatrick and Mike McIntire, "'Its Own Domestic Army': How the G.O.P. Allied Itself with Militants," *New York Times*, February 8, 2021, https://www.nytimes.com/2021/02/08/us/militias-republicans-michigan.html.

14. Abigail Censky, "The Boiling Resentment Behind the Foiled Plan to Kidnap Gov. Whitmer," NPR, October 10, 2020, https://www.npr.org/2020/10/10/922610152/the-boiling-resentment-behind-the-foiled-plan-to-kidnap-gov-whitmer.

15. Amber Phillips, "Was the Stock Market the Object of Trump's 'Don't Create a Panic' Coronavirus Approach?," *Washington Post*, September 10, 2020, https://www.washingtonpost.com/politics/2020/09/10/was-stock-market-object-trumps-dont-create-panic-coronavirus-approach/.

16. Joe Biden, "My Plan to Safely Reopen America," *New York Times*, April 12, 2020, https://www.nytimes.com/2020/04/12/opinion/joe-biden-coronavirus-reopen-america.html.

17. Esther Castillejo, "Joe Biden Clarifies 'Shutdown' Comments Made to ABC News' David Muir," ABC News, September 3, 2020, https://abcnews.go.com/Politics/joe-biden-clarifies-shutdown-comments-made-abc-news/story?id=72798117.

18. Castillejo, "Joe Biden Clarifies 'Shutdown' Comments Made to ABC News' David Muir."

19. Libby Cathey, Lauren King, and Stephanie Ebbs, "RNC 2020 Day 4: Trump Accepts Nomination from White House," ABC News, August 28, 2020, https://abcnews.go.com/Politics/rnc-2020-day-trump-accept-nomination-white-house/story?id=72577769.

20. Claire Sanford, "Donald Trump & Joe Biden Final Presidential Debate Transcript 2020," Rev, October 22, 2020, https://www.rev.com/blog/transcripts/donald-trump-joe-biden-final-presidential-debate-transcript-2020.

21. Sanford, "Donald Trump & Joe Biden Final Presidential Debate Transcript 2020."

22. Nicholas Wu and David Jackson, "Trump: CDC Recommends Voluntary Use of Face Masks for Public to Stem Spread of Coronavirus," *USA Today*, April 3, 2020, https://www.usatoday.com/story/news/politics/2020/04/03/coronavirus-trump-says-cdc-recommending-voluntary-use-face-masks/2938705001/.

23. Claire Sanford, "Donald Trump & Joe Biden 1st Presidential Debate Transcript 2020," Rev, September 29, 2020, https://www.rev.com/blog/transcripts/donald-trump-joe-biden-1st-presidential-debate-transcript-2020.

24. Dartunorro Clark, "Fauci Calls Amy Coney Barrett Ceremony in Rose Garden 'Superspreader Event,'" NBC News, October 9, 2020, https://www.nbcnews.com/politics/white-house/fauci-calls-amy-coney-barrett-ceremony-rose-garden-supers preader-event-n1242781.

25. Andrew Restuccia, "Trump and His Aides Have Long Played Down Importance of Face Masks, Distancing," *Wall Street Journal*, October 2, 2020, https://www.wsj.com/articles/trump-and-his-aides-have-long-downplayed-importance-of-face-masks-distancing-11601655164.

26. Martin Pengelly, "Trump Tested Positive for Covid Few Days Before Biden Debate, Chief of Staff Says in New Book," *Guardian*, December 1, 2021, https://www.theguardian.com/us-news/2021/dec/01/trump-tested-positive-covid-before-biden-debate-chief-staff-mark-meadows-book.

27. Jake Lahut, "A Timeline of Trump's Public Events Between His Previously Undisclosed Positive COVID Test on September 26 and His Hospitalization on October 2," *Business Insider*, December 1, 2021, https://www.businessinsider.com/trump-covid-positive-test-timeline-debate-mark-meadows-hospital-2021-12.

28. "Trump Campaign Adviser Defends First Family Refusing to Wear Masks at Debate," Axios, October 4, 2020, https://www.axios.com/trump-campaign-advi ser-family-debate-05cbfa4f-2a26-4a6f-bf35-872f1b268e4d.html.

29. Noah Weiland et al., "Trump Was Sicker than Acknowledged with Covid-19," *New York Times*, February 11, 2021, https://www.nytimes.com/2021/02/11/us/politics/trump-coronavirus.html.

30. Damian Paletta and Yasmeen Abutaleb, "Inside the Extraordinary Effort to Save Trump from Covid-19," *Washington Post*, June 24, 2021, https://www.washingtonpost.com/politics/2021/06/24/nightmare-scenario-book-excerpt/.

31. Yashwant Raj, "'Feel Better than I Did 20 Years Ago,' Says Donald Trump, to Leave Hospital Later Today," *Hindustan Times*, October 6, 2020, https://www.hindustantimes.com/world-news/covid-19-feel-better-than-i-did-20-years-ago-says-donald-trump-to-leave-hospital-later-in-the-day/story-1VMdB89z5TfNflpCRho xfL.html.

32. Ken Thomas and Sabrina Siddiqui, "Biden Says Trump Failed Americans on Coronavirus," *Wall Street Journal*, June 30, 2020, https://www.wsj.com/articles/biden-says-trump-failed-americans-on-coronavirus-11593546742.

33. Biden-Harris Democrats, "The Biden Plan to Combat Coronavirus (COVID-19) and Prepare for Future Global Health Threats," Joe Biden for President: Official Campaign Website, 2020, https://joebiden.com/covid-plan/.

34. Matthew J. Belvedere, "Trump Says He Trusts China's Xi on Coronavirus and the US Has It 'Totally Under Control,'" CNBC, January 22, 2020, https://www.cnbc.com/2020/01/22/trump-on-coronavirus-from-china-we-have-it-totally-under-control.html.

35. Claire Sanford, "Donald Trump & Bob Woodward Covid Conversation Transcript: Trump 'Playing It Down,'" Rev, September 2020, https://www.rev.com/blog/transcripts/donald-trump-bob-woodward-conversation-transcript-trump-playing-down-coronavirus.

36. Brad Brooks, "Like the Flu? Trump's Coronavirus Messaging Confuses Public, Pandemic Researchers Say," Reuters, March 13, 2020, https://www.reuters.com/article/us-health-coronavirus-mixed-messages-idUSKBN2102GY.

37. Joe Biden (@JoeBiden), "Donald Trump knew that COVID-19 was dangerous. He knew it was deadly. And he purposely downplayed it. Now, nearly 200,000 Americans are dead. It's unconscionable," Twitter, September 9, 2020, 9:28 PM, https://twitter.com/JoeBiden/status/1303867788759568384.

38. Veronica Stracqualursi, "Biden Attacks Trump's Covid-19 Response in South Korean Op-Ed and Promises 'Principled Diplomacy' with North Korea," CNN, October 30, 2020, https://www.cnn.com/2020/10/30/politics/joe-biden-north-korea-trump-op-ed/index.html.

39. Sanford, "Donald Trump & Joe Biden 1st Presidential Debate Transcript 2020"; Sanford, "Donald Trump & Joe Biden Final Presidential Debate Transcript 2020."

40. Sanford, "Donald Trump & Joe Biden 1st Presidential Debate Transcript 2020."

41. "Herman Cain, Ex-Presidential Candidate Who Refused to Wear Mask, Dies after COVID-19 Diagnosis," Reuters, July 30, 2020, https://www.reuters.com/article/us-health-coronavirus-usa-cain-idUSKCN24V2OD.

42. Erin Mansfield, Josh Salman, and Dinah Voyles Pulver, "Trump's Campaign Made Stops Nationwide. Coronavirus Cases Surged in His Wake in at Least Five Places," *USA Today*, October 22, 2020, https://www.usatoday.com/story/news/investigations/2020/10/22/trumps-campaign-made-stops-nationwide-then-coronavirus-cases-surged/3679534001/.

43. "Timeline—In His Own Words: Trump and the Coronavirus," Reuters, October 2, 2020, https://www.reuters.com/article/us-health-coronavirus-usa-trump-comments-idUKKBN26N0U5.

44. Donald G. McNeil and Andrew Jacobs, "Blaming China for Pandemic, Trump Says U.S. Will Leave the W.H.O.," *New York Times*, May 29, 2020, https://www.nytimes.com/2020/05/29/health/virus-who.html.

45. ANI, "Donald Trump 'Playing Down' Covid-19 in US Is Almost Criminal: Biden," *Business Standard India*, September 11, 2020, https://www.business-standard.

com/article/us-elections/donald-trump-playing-down-covid-19-in-us-is-almost-criminal-biden-120091100779_1.html.

46. Executive Office of the President, "Suspension of Entry as Immigrants and Nonimmigrants of Persons Who Pose a Risk of Transmitting 2019 Novel Coronavirus and Other Appropriate Measures to Address This Risk," Federal Register, February 5, 2020, https://www.federalregister.gov/documents/2020/02/05/2020-02424/suspension-of-entry-as-immigrants-and-nonimmigrants-of-pers ons-who-pose-a-risk-of-transmitting-2019.

47. "Full Text: President Trump's 2020 RNC Acceptance Speech," NBC News, August 28, 2020, https://www.nbcnews.com/politics/2020-election/read-full-text-presid ent-donald-trump-s-acceptance-speech-rnc-n1238636.

48. Sanford, "Donald Trump & Joe Biden 1st Presidential Debate Transcript 2020."

49. Thomas J. Bollyky and Jennifer B. Nuzzo, "Trump's 'Early' Travel 'Bans' Weren't Early, Weren't Bans and Didn't Work," *Washington Post*, October 1, 2020, http://www.washingtonpost.com/outlook/2020/10/01/debate-early-travel-bans-china/.

50. "The Trump Administration and the Media," *Committee to Protect Journalists*, April 16, 2020, https://cpj.org/reports/2020/04/trump-media-attacks-credibil ity-leaks/.

51. Jordan Williams, "Trump Downplays Spike in COVID-19 Cases, Blames Media, Increased Testing for High Numbers," *The Hill*, October 24, 2020, https://theh ill.com/homenews/administration/522581-trump-downplays-spike-in-covid-19-cases-blames-media-increased.

52. Aaron Rupar, "Trump Wants You to Believe Coronavirus Cases Are 'Up Because We TEST.' He's Wrong," *Vox*, October 26, 2020, https://www.vox.com/2020/10/26/21534380/trump-coronavirus-cases-spike-testing.

53. Kathleen Hall Jamieson and Dolores Albarracin, "The Relation Between Media Consumption and Misinformation at the Outset of the SARS-CoV-2 Pandemic in the US," *Harvard Kennedy School Misinformation Review* 1, no. 2 (2020), doi:10.37016/mr-2020-012.

54. Andrey Simonov et al., "The Persuasive Effect of Fox News: Non-Compliance with Social Distancing During the Covid-19 Pandemic," National Bureau of Economic Research, Working Paper no. 27237, Cambridge, MA, May 2020, http://www.nber.org/papers/w27237.

55. Daniel Wolfe and Daniel Dale, "'It's Going to Disappear': A Timeline of Trump's Claims That Covid-19 Will Vanish," CNN, last updated October 31, 2020, https://www.cnn.com/interactive/2020/10/politics/covid-disappearing-trump-comm ent-tracker/.

56. "Remarks by President Trump in Meeting with African American Leaders," Trump White House Archives, February 28, 2020, https://trumpwhitehouse.archives.gov/briefings-statements/remarks-president-trump-meeting-african-american-leaders/.

57. Andrew Solender, "Trump Said U.S. Was 'Rounding the Final Turn' on Aug. 31—And on 39 of the 57 Days Since," *Forbes*, October 27, 2020, https://www.forbes.com/sites/andrewsolender/2020/10/27/trump-said-us-was-rounding-the-final-turn-on-aug-31-and-on-39-of-the-57-days-since/.

58. Noah Higgins-Dunn and Berkeley Lovelace, "Top US Health Official Says the Coronavirus Is 10 Times 'More Lethal' than the Seasonal Flu," CNBC, March 11, 2020, https://www.cnbc.com/2020/03/11/top-federal-health-official-says-coronavirus-outbreak-is-going-to-get-worse-in-the-us.html.

59. Toluse Olorunnipa, Ariana Eunjung Cha, and Laurie McGinley, "Drug Promoted by Trump as Coronavirus 'Game Changer' Increasingly Linked to Deaths," *Washington Post*, May 15, 2020, https://www.washingtonpost.com/politics/drug-promoted-by-trump-as-coronavirus-game-changer-increasingly-linked-to-deaths/2020/05/15/85d024fe-96bd-11ea-9f5e-56d8239bf9ad_story.html.

60. Philip Bump, "Trump's Stunning Claim That He's Taking Hydroxychloroquine Could Trigger a Cascade of Negative Effects," *Washington Post*, May 18, 2020, https://www.washingtonpost.com/politics/2020/05/18/trumps-stunning-claim-that-hes-taking-hydroxychloroquine-could-trigger-cascade-negative-effects/.

61. Wesley H. Self, Matthew W. Semler, and Lindsay M. Leither, "Effect of Hydroxychloroquine on Clinical Status at 14 Days in Hospitalized Patients with COVID-19: A Randomized Clinical Trial," *JAMA* 324, no. 21 (November 2020): 2165–2176, doi: 10.1001/jama.2020.22240.

62. Maggie Haberman, "Trump Has Given Unusual Leeway to Fauci, but Aides Say He's Losing His Patience," *New York Times*, March 23, 2020, https://www.nytimes.com/2020/03/23/us/politics/coronavirus-trump-fauci.html.

63. Chandelis Duster, Jim Acosta, and Kevin Liptak, "Trump Retweets Call to Fire Fauci amid Coronavirus Criticism," CNN, April 13, 2020, https://www.cnn.com/2020/04/13/politics/donald-trump-anthony-fauci-tweet/index.html.

64. Andrew Solender, "Biden Says He Would Ask Fauci to Stay On," Forbes, June 30, 2020, https://www.forbes.com/sites/andrewsolender/2020/06/30/biden-says-he-would-ask-fauci-to-stay-on/.

65. James N. Druckman et al., "Affective Polarization, Local Contexts and Public Opinion in America," *Nature Human Behaviour* 5, no. 1 (January 2021): 28–38, doi:10.1038/s41562-020-01012-5.

66. Grace Panetta, "Trump Is Reportedly Rattled by Dr. Fauci's High Approval Ratings Compared to His Own Poor Polling on COVID-19," *Business* Insider, July 13, 2020, https://www.businessinsider.com/trump-is-spooked-by-faucis-high-approval-ratings-on-coronavirus-wapo-2020-7.

67. "CNN: Fauci Says His Words 'Taken Out of Context' in Trump Campaign Ad," VOA, October 11, 2020, https://www.voanews.com/a/2020-usa-votes_cnn-fauci-says-his-words-taken-out-context-trump-campaign-ad/6197001.html.

68. Tim Murtaugh (@TimMurtaugh), "Dr. Fauci has repeatedly said the Trump Administration did everything possible to save lives," Twitter, October 11, 2020, 4:35 PM, https://twitter.com/TimMurtaugh/status/1315390685068120066.

69. Kaitlan Collins, "CNN Exclusive: Fauci Says He Was Taken out of Context in New Trump Campaign Ad Touting Coronavirus Response," CNN, October 11, 2020, https://www.cnn.com/2020/10/11/politics/fauci-trump-campaign-ad-out-of-context/index.html.

70. Alana Wise, "Trump Rails Against 'Fauci and These Idiots' in Campaign Call," NPR, October 19, 2020, https://www.npr.org/2020/10/19/925435610/trump-rails-against-fauci-and-these-idiots-in-campaign-call.

71. Josh Dawsey and Yasmeen Abutaleb, "'A Whole Lot of Hurt': Fauci Warns of Covid-19 Surge, Offers Blunt Assessment of Trump's Response," *Washington Post*, October 31, 2020, https://www.washingtonpost.com/politics/fauci-covid-winter-forecast/2020/10/31/e3970eb0-1b8b-11eb-bb35-2dcfdab0a345_story.html.

72. Dawsey and Abutaleb, "'A Whole Lot of Hurt': Fauci Warns of Covid-19 Surge, Offers Blunt Assessment of Trump's Response."

73. Rebecca Shabad, "Trump Suggests He Might Fire Fauci after the Election," NBC News, November 2, 2020, https://www.nbcnews.com/politics/2020-election/trump-suggests-he-might-fire-fauci-after-election-n1245735.

74. Peter Wade, "Politically Appointed Trump Aides Lie About 'Deep State Motives,' Alter CDC Virus Reports," *Rolling Stone*, September 12, 2020, https://www.rollingstone.com/politics/politics-news/trump-aides-lie-about-deep-state-motives-alter-cdc-virus-reports-1058778/.

75. Laurie McGinley, Carolyn Y. Johnson, and Josh Dawsey, "Trump Without Evidence Accuses 'Deep State' at FDA of Slow-Walking Coronavirus Vaccines and Treatments," *Washington Post*, August 22, 2020, https://www.washingtonpost.com/health/2020/08/22/trump-without-evidence-accuses-deep-state-fda-slow-walking-coronavirus-vaccines-treatments/.

76. Fadel Allassan, "Trump Tags FDA Chief in 'Political Hit Job' Complaint over Vaccine Rule," Axios, October 6, 2020, https://www.axios.com/trump-fda-commissioner-political-23de8d63-e1f6-4d2f-89e2-004020377442.html.

CHAPTER 5.2

1. Neil Malhotra and Alexander G. Kuo, "Attributing Blame: The Public's Response to Hurricane Katrina," *Journal of Politics* 70, no. 1 (January 2008): 120–135, doi:10.1017/S0022381607080097; James Druckman et al., "How Affective Polarization Shapes Americans' Political Beliefs: A Study of Response to the COVID-19 Pandemic," *Journal of Experimental Political Science*, August 2020, 1–20, doi:10.1017/XPS.2020.28.; Gary C. Jacobson, *A Divider, Not a Uniter: George W. Bush and the American People* (Boston: Pearson Longman, 2007).

2. Alex Isenstadt, "Trump Pollster's Campaign Autopsy Paints Damning Picture of Defeat," Yahoo Finance, February 1, 2021, https://finance.yahoo.com/news/trump-pollsters-campaign-autopsy-paints-204625903.html; Carol Leonnig and Philip Rucker, *I Alone Can Fix It: Donald J. Trump's Catastrophic Final Year* (New York: Penguin, 2021).

3. For more on this battery, see Kate Kenski, Bruce W. Hardy, and Kathleen Hall Jamieson, *The Obama Victory: How Media, Money, and Message Shaped the 2008 Election* (New York: Oxford University Press, 2010).

4. Diana Mutz, *Hearing the Other Side: Deliberative vs. Participatory Democracy* (Cambridge, UK: Cambridge University Press, 2006).

5. Jaclyn Kettler, Luke Fowler, and Stephanie Witt, "Democratic Governors Are Quicker in Responding to the Coronavirus than Republicans," The Conversation, April 2020, http://theconversation.com/democratic-governors-are-quicker-in-responding-to-the-coronavirus-than-republicans-135599.

6. P. Sol Hart, Sedona Chinn, and Stuart Soroka, "Politicization and Polarization in COVID-19 News Coverage," *Science Communication* 42, no. 5 (October 2020): 679–697, doi:10.1177/1075547020950735.

7. Colby Itkowitz, "Wisconsin Supreme Court Strikes Down Governor's Extension of Stay-at-Home Order," *Washington Post*, May 13, 2020, https://www.washingtonpost.com/politics/2020/05/13/wisconsin-supreme-court-strikes-down-governors-extension-stay-at-home-order/.

8. Eric Merkley et al., "A Rare Moment of Cross-Partisan Consensus: Elite and Public Response to the COVID-19 Pandemic in Canada," *Canadian Journal of Political Science/Revue Canadienne de Science Politique* 53, no. 2 (June 2020): 311–318, doi:10.1017/S0008423920000311.

9. George E. Marcus, W. Russell Neuman, and Michael MacKuen, *Affective Intelligence and Political Judgment* (Chicago: University of Chicago Press, 2000), https://press.uchicago.edu/ucp/books/book/chicago/A/bo3636531.html.

10. Shana Kushner Gadarian and Bethany Albertson, "Anxiety, Immigration, and the Search for Information," *Political Psychology* 35, no. 2 (2014): 133–164, doi:10.1111/pops.12034.

11. Colin Dwyer and Allison Aubrey, "CDC Now Recommends Americans Consider Wearing Cloth Face Coverings In Public," NPR, April 3, 2020, https://www.npr.org/sections/coronavirus-live-updates/2020/04/03/826219824/president-trump-says-cdc-now-recommends-americans-wear-cloth-masks-in-public.

12. Katherine Schaeffer, "Despite Wide Partisan Gaps in Views of Many Aspects of the Pandemic, Some Common Ground Exists," Pew Research Center, March 24, 2021, https://www.pewresearch.org/fact-tank/2021/03/24/despite-wide-partisan-gaps-in-views-of-many-aspects-of-the-pandemic-some-common-ground-exists/.

13. For example, on political coverage, see Matthew Levendusky and Neil Malhotra, "Does Media Coverage of Partisan Polarization Affect Political Attitudes?,"

Political Communication 33, no. 2 (April 2016): 283–301, doi:10.1080/10584609.2015.1038455.

14. Hunt Allcott et al., "Polarization and Public Health: Partisan Differences in Social Distancing during the Coronavirus Pandemic," *Journal of Public Economics* 191 (November 2020): 104254, doi:10.1016/j.jpubeco.2020.104254; James N. Druckman et al., "Affective Polarization, Local Contexts and Public Opinion in America," *Nature Human Behaviour* 5, no. 1 (January 2021): 28–38, doi:10.1038/s41562-020-01012-5; Austin Hegland et al., "A Partisan Pandemic: How COVID-19 Was Primed for Polarization," *Annals of the American Academy of Political and Social Science* 700, no. 1 (March 2022): 55–72; Kathleen Hall Jamieson et al., "The Role of Non-COVID-Specific and COVID-Specific Factors in Predicting a Shift in Willingness to Vaccinate: A Panel Study," *Proceedings of the National Academy of Sciences* 118, no. 52 (December 2021): e2112266118, doi:10.1073/pnas.2112266118.

15. Martin Bisgaard, "Bias Will Find a Way: Economic Perceptions, Attributions of Blame, and Partisan-Motivated Reasoning During Crisis," *Journal of Politics* 77, no. 3 (July 2015): 849–860, doi:10.1086/681591.

16. US Department of Health and Human Services, "Trump Administration Announces Framework and Leadership for 'Operation Warp Speed,'" May 15, 2020, https://public3.pagefreezer.com/browse/HHS%20%E2%80%93%C2%A0About%20News/20-01-2021T12:29/https://www.hhs.gov/about/news/2020/05/15/trump-administration-announces-framework-and-leadership-for-operation-warp-speed.html.

17. Claire Sanford, "Donald Trump & Joe Biden Final Presidential Debate Transcript 2020," Rev, October 22, 2020, https://www.rev.com/blog/transcripts/donald-trump-joe-biden-final-presidential-debate-transcript-2020.

18. Lauran Neergaard and Linda A. Johnson, "Pfizer Says COVID-19 Vaccine Is Looking 90% Effective," Associated Press, November 9, 2020, https://apnews.com/article/pfizer-vaccine-effective-early-data-4f4ae2e3bad122d17742be22a2240ae8.

19. Neergaard and Johnson, "Pfizer Says COVID-19 Vaccine Is Looking 90% Effective."

20. Hope Yen and Lauran Neergaard, "Fact Check: Trump Wrongly Takes Full Credit for Pfizer's COVID-19 Vaccine," *Baltimore Sun*, November 13, 2020, https://www.baltimoresun.com/coronavirus/ct-nw-coronavirus-vaccine-fact-check-20201113-pkzbkcfd5bcalpgkvbavqfi5iq-story.html.

21. Yen and Neergaard, "Fact Check: Trump Wrongly Takes Full Credit for Pfizer's COVID-19 Vaccine."

22. Andreu Casas Salleras et al., "Trump Supporters Have Little Trust in Societal Institutions," The Conversation, February 18, 2020, http://theconversation.com/trump-supporters-have-little-trust-in-societal-institutions-131113.

23. Bert N. Bakker, Yphtach Lelkes, and Ariel Malka, "Understanding Partisan Cue Receptivity: Tests of Predictions from the Bounded Rationality and Expressive

Utility Perspectives," *Journal of Politics* 82, no. 3 (July 2020): 1061–1077, doi:10.1086/707616.

24. Cameron Peters, "Trump Officials Are Reportedly Manipulating the CDC's Covid-19 Reports," Vox, September 12, 2020, https://www.vox.com/2020/9/12/21433844/trump-officials-manipulating-cdc-covid-19-reports.

25. Rich Mendez, "Trump Officials Bragged About Pressuring CDC to Alter Covid Reports, Emails Reveal," CNBC, April 9, 2021, https://www.cnbc.com/2021/04/09/trump-officials-bragged-about-pressuring-cdc-to-alter-covid-reports-emails-reveal-.html.

26. Dan Diamond, "Trump Officials Muzzled CDC on Church COVID Guidance, Emails Confirm," *Washington Post*, April 29, 2022, https://www.washingtonpost.com/health/2022/04/29/trump-administration-cdc-interference-religious-groups/.

27. Dan Diamond, "Messonnier, Birx Detail Political Interference in Last Year's Coronavirus Response," *Washington Post*, November 12, 2021, http://www.washingtonpost.com/health/2021/11/12/messonnier-birx-coronavirus-response-interference/.

28. Deidre McPhillips and Devan Cole, "Outgoing NIH Director Says Trump and Other Republicans Pressured Him to Endorse Unproven Covid-19 Remedies and to Fire Fauci," CNN, December 19, 2021, https://www.cnn.com/2021/12/19/politics/francis-collins-trump-political-pressure-republicans/index.html.

CHAPTER 6.1

1. Carol Leonnig and Philip Rucker, *I Alone Can Fix It: Donald J. Trump's Catastrophic Final Year* (New York: Penguin, 2021).

2. USA Today Staff, "Read the Full Transcript from the First Presidential Debate Between Joe Biden and Donald Trump," *USA Today*, September 30, 2020, https://www.usatoday.com/story/news/politics/elections/2020/09/30/presidential-debate-read-full-transcript-first-debate/3587462001/.

3. Lydia Saad, "Trump's Economic Ratings No Longer Best in Class," Gallup, June 29, 2020, https://news.gallup.com/poll/313070/trump-economic-ratings-no-longer-best-class.aspx.

4. Lydia Saad, "Americans' Take on the U.S. Is Improved, but Still Mixed," Gallup, January 27, 2020, https://news.gallup.com/poll/284033/americans-improved-mixed.aspx.

5. Leonnig and Rucker, *I Alone Can Fix It*, 51–52.

6. Jeanna Smialek, "The U.S. Entered a Recession in February," *New York Times*, June 8, 2020, https://www.nytimes.com/2020/06/08/business/economy/us-economy-recession-2020.html.

7. Smialek, "The U.S. Entered a Recession in February."

8. "Read President Trump's Speech on Coronavirus Pandemic: Full Transcript," *New York Times*, March 11, 2020, https://www.nytimes.com/2020/03/11/us/polit ics/trump-coronavirus-speech.html.

9. Asher Stockler, "President Donald Trump Announces Declaration of National Emergency Due to Coronavirus," *Newsweek*, March 13, 2020, https://www.newsw eek.com/donald-trump-coronavirus-emergency-stafford-1492275.

10. Andrea Salcedo, "Racist Anti-Asian Hashtags Spiked after Trump First Tweeted 'Chinese Virus,' Study Finds," *Washington Post*, March 19, 2021, http://www.was hingtonpost.com/nation/2021/03/19/trump-tweets-chinese-virus-racist/.

11. National Conference of State Legislators, "President Trump Declares State of Emergency for COVID-19," March 25, 2020, https://www.ncsl.org/ncsl-in-dc/publications-and-resources/president-trump-declares-state-of-emerge ncy-for-covid-19.aspx.

12. AJ Willingham, Renée Rigdon, and Curt Merrill, "Understanding the Massive Scale of Coronavirus in the US," CNN, September 22, 2020, https://www.cnn. com/interactive/2020/health/coronavirus-us-deaths-milestones/.

13. Amanda Moreland, "Timing of State and Territorial COVID-19 Stay-at-Home Orders and Changes in Population Movement—United States, March 1–May 31, 2020," *Morbidity and Mortality Weekly Report* 69, no. 35 (2020): 1198–1203, doi:10.15585/mmwr.mm6935a2.

14. Celine McNicholas and Margaret Poydock, "Who Are Essential Workers? A Comprehensive Look at Their Wages, Demographics, and Unionization Rates," Economic Policy Institute, May 19, 2020, https://www.epi.org/blog/who-are-essential-workers-a-comprehensive-look-at-their-wages-demographics-and-union ization-rates/.

15. US Employment and Training Administration, "Initial Claims," FRED, Federal Reserve Bank of St. Louis, 2021, https://fred.stlouisfed.org/series/ICSA.

16. US Bureau of Labor Statistics, "Unemployment Rate," FRED, Federal Reserve Bank of St. Louis, October 2021, https://fred.stlouisfed.org/series/UNRATE.

17. Willingham, Rigdon, and Merrill, "Understanding the Massive Scale of Coronavirus in the US"; Quoctrung Bui and Emily Badger, "In These Neighborhoods, the Jobless Rate May Top 30 Percent," *New York Times*, August 5, 2020, https://www. nytimes.com/interactive/2020/08/05/upshot/us-unemployment-maps-coronavi rus.html.

18. US Bureau of Economic Analysis, "Real Disposable Personal Income," FRED, Federal Reserve Bank of St. Louis, 2021, https://fred.stlouisfed.org/series/A067 RL1A156NBEA.

19. Christina Maxouris et al., "As of Wednesday, Every State Will Be Somewhere Along the Road Toward a Full Reopening," CNN, May 19, 2020, https://www.cnn.com/ 2020/05/19/health/us-coronavirus-tuesday/index.html.

20. Harriet Torry and Josh Mitchell, "For Economy, Worst of Coronavirus Shutdowns May Be Over," *Wall Street Journal*, May 25, 2020, https://www.wsj.com/articles/for-economy-worst-of-coronavirus-shutdowns-may-be-over-11590408000.

21. Claire Sanford, "Donald Trump Addresses Economic Club of New York Transcript October 14," Rev, October 14, 2020, https://www.rev.com/blog/transcripts/donald-trump-addresses-economic-club-of-new-york-transcript-october-14.

22. According to data from the Pew Research Center, among families with incomes under $35,000, only about 20 percent owned stocks, and the median amount was under $10,000. By contrast, among households earning more than $100,000 annually, 88 percent owned stocks, with a median value of over $130,000. See Kim Parker and Richard Fry, "More than Half of U.S. Households Have Some Investment in the Stock Market," Pew Research Center, March 25, 2020, https://www.pewresearch.org/fact-tank/2020/03/25/more-than-half-of-u-s-households-have-some-investment-in-the-stock-market/.

23. Hamza Shaban, "U.S. Stocks Come Close, but Fall Short of Record High," *Washington Post*, August 13, 2020, https://www.washingtonpost.com/business/2020/08/13/stocks-record-bear-market/.

24. Jeff Stein, "Stock Market Slide Muddles Trump's Economic Message Days before 2020 Election," *Washington Post*, October 28, 2020, https://www.washingtonpost.com/us-policy/2020/10/28/trump-stock-market-2020/.

25. Victor Reklaitis, "Trump Says His Executive Actions Led to Stock Market's Gain, as Briefing Gets Interrupted by Shooting," MarketWatch, August 10, 2020, https://www.marketwatch.com/story/trump-says-his-executive-actions-led-to-stock-markets-gain-as-briefing-gets-interrupted-by-shooting-2020-08-10.

26. Claire Sanford, "Donald Trump & Joe Biden Final Presidential Debate Transcript 2020," Rev, October 22, 2020, https://www.rev.com/blog/transcripts/donald-trump-joe-biden-final-presidential-debate-transcript-2020.

27. Sanford, "Donald Trump & Joe Biden Final Presidential Debate Transcript 2020."

28. Ben Steverman, "Harvard's Chetty Finds Economic Carnage in Wealthiest ZIP Codes," Bloomberg, September 24, 2020, https://www.bloomberg.com/news/features/2020-09-24/harvard-economist-raj-chetty-creates-god-s-eye-view-of-pandemic-damage.

29. Ella Koeze, "A Year Later, Who Is Back to Work and Who Is Not?," *New York Times*, March 9, 2021, https://www.nytimes.com/interactive/2021/03/09/business/economy/covid-employment-demographics.html.

30. Jerome H. Powell, "Speech by Chair Powell on Community Development," Federal Reserve, May 3, 2021, https://www.federalreserve.gov/newsevents/speech/powell20210503a.htm.

31. Nicholas Kulish, "'Never Seen Anything Like It': Cars Line Up for Miles at Food Banks," *New York Times*, April 8, 2020, https://www.nytimes.com/2020/04/08/business/economy/coronavirus-food-banks.html.

32. Simone Silvan, "Almost 20% of U.S. Households Lost Entire Savings During Covid," Bloomberg, October 13, 2021, https://www.bloomberg.com/news/artic les/2021-10-13/almost-20-of-u-s-households-lost-entire-savings-during-covid.

33. Ese Olumhense and Ed Mahon, "A Huge Spike in Medicaid Enrollment in Pa. Shows How Devastating the Coronavirus Has Been," *Philadelphia Inquirer*, March 22, 2021, https://www.inquirer.com/health/coronavirus/spl/pa-coronavi rus-medicaid-enrollment-increase-map-20210322.html.

34. Associated Press, "'K-Shaped' Economic Recovery Shows Pandemic's Uneven Impact, Even a Year Later," CBS News, March 10, 2021, https://www.cbsnews. com/news/economy-k-shaped-recovery-covid-pandemic-impact-uneven/.

35. Claire Sanford, "Donald Trump & Joe Biden 1st Presidential Debate Transcript 2020," Rev, September 29, 2020, https://www.rev.com/blog/transcripts/donald-trump-joe-biden-1st-presidential-debate-transcript-2020.

36. Sanford, "Donald Trump & Joe Biden Final Presidential Debate Transcript 2020."

37. Sanford, "Donald Trump & Joe Biden Final Presidential Debate Transcript 2020."

38. Richard Johnston, Michael G. Hagen, and Kathleen Hall Jamieson, *The Dynamics of Election: The 2000 Presidential Election and the Foundations of Party Politics* (Cambridge, UK: Cambridge University Press, 2004).

1. Larry M. Bartels, "Beyond the Running Tally: Partisan Bias in Political Perceptions," *Political Behavior* 24, no. 2 (2002): 117–150, https://www.jstor.org/stable/1558352; Christopher Wlezien, Mark Franklin, and Daniel Twiggs, "Economic Perceptions and Vote Choice: Disentangling the Endogeneity," *Political Behavior* 19, no. 1 (March 1997): 7–17, doi:10.1023/A:1024841605168; Geoffrey Evans and Robert Andersen, "The Political Conditioning of Economic Perceptions," *Journal of Politics* 68, no. 1 (2006): 194–207, doi:10.1111/j.1468-2508.2006.00380.x.

2. Andrew Healy and Gabriel S. Lenz, "Presidential Voting and the Local Economy: Evidence from Two Population-Based Data Sets," *Journal of Politics* 79, no. 4 (October 2017): 1419–1432, doi:10.1086/692785.

3. See, among others, Douglas A. Hibbs Jr., *The American Political Economy: Macroeconomics and Electoral Politics* (Cambridge, MA: Harvard University Press, 1989); Christopher Wlezien, "The Myopic Voter? The Economy and US Presidential Elections," *Electoral Studies* 39 (September 2015): 195–204, doi:10.1016/j.electstud.2015.03.010; Andrew Healy and Gabriel S. Lenz, "Substituting the End for the Whole: Why Voters Respond Primarily to the Election-Year Economy," *American Journal of Political Science* 58, no. 1 (2014): 31–47, https:// www.jstor.org/stable/24363467.

4. Raj Chetty et al., "The Economic Tracker," Opportunity Insights, 2020, https:// tracktherecovery.org/.

5. Ella Koeze, "A Year Later, Who Is Back to Work and Who Is Not?," *New York Times*, March 9, 2021, https://www.nytimes.com/interactive/2021/03/09/busin ess/economy/covid-employment-demographics.html.

6. Robert Griffin and John Sides, "In the Red," Democracy Fund Voter Study Group, September 2018, https://www.voterstudygroup.org/publication/in-the-red; John Sides, Michael Tesler, and Lynn Vavreck, *Identity Crisis: The 2016 Presidential Campaign and the Battle for the Meaning of America* (Princeton, NJ: Princeton University Press, 2018).

7. Steven J. Rosenstone, "Economic Adversity and Voter Turnout," *American Journal of Political Science* 26, no. 1 (February 1982): 25–46, doi:https://doi.org/10.2307/2110 837; Matt Stevens, "Poorer Americans Have Much Lower Voting Rates in National Elections than the Nonpoor, a Study Finds," *New York Times*, August 11, 2020, https://www.nytimes.com/2020/08/11/us/politics/poorer-americans-have-much-lower-voting-rates-in-national-elections-than-the-nonpoor-a-study-finds.html.

8. Christopher Wlezien, Mark Franklin, and Daniel Twiggs, "Economic Perceptions and Vote Choice: Disentangling the Endogeneity," *Political Behavior* 19, no. 1 (March 1997): 7–17, doi:10.1023/A:1024841605168; Geoffrey Evans and Robert Andersen, "The Political Conditioning of Economic Perceptions," *Journal of Politics* 68, no. 1 (2006): 194–207, doi:10.1111/j.1468-2508.2006.00380.x.

9. A. H. Maslow, "A Theory of Human Motivation," *Psychological Review* 50 (1943): 370–396, doi:10.1037/h0054346.

10. Olivier Coibion, Yuriy Gorodnichenko, and Michael Weber, "How Did U.S. Consumers Use Their Stimulus Payments?," Working Paper no. 27693, National Bureau of Economic Research, Cambridge, MA, August 2020, https://www.nber.org/system/files/working_papers/w27693/w27693.pdf.

11. Hamza Shaban and Heather Long, "The Stock Market Is Ending 2020 at Record Highs, Even as the Virus Surges and Millions Go Hungry," *Washington Post*, December 31, 2020, https://www.washingtonpost.com/business/2020/12/31/stock-market-record-2020/.

12. Kathleen Hall Jamieson and Joseph N. Cappella, *Echo Chamber: Rush Limbaugh and the Conservative Media Establishment* (New York: Oxford University Press, 2010).

13. Lynn Vavreck, *The Message Matters: The Economy and Presidential Campaigns* (Princeton, NJ: Princeton University Press, 2009).

14. Andrew Scott and Stephanie Sigafoos, "Fracking, an Industry Employing Thousands in Pennsylvania, Again in Spotlight in Final Presidential Debate," Morning Call, October 23, 2020, https://www.mcall.com/news/elections/mc-nws-vice-presidential-debate-fracking-20201023-gf744wlhgjg6zkxi4vutyotsem-story.html.

15. Susan Phillips, "Trump Pounds Fracking as a Wedge Issue in Pa. But If It's Not Voters' Top Concern, How Much Can It Help?," WHYY, October 9, 2020,

https://whyy.org/articles/trump-pounds-fracking-as-a-wedge-issue-in-pa-but-if-its-not-voters-top-concern-how-much-can-it-help/.

16. "Debate Transcript: Trump, Biden Final Presidential Debate Moderated by Kristen Welker," *USA Today*, October 23, 2020, https://www.usatoday.com/story/news/politics/elections/2020/10/23/debate-transcript-trump-biden-final-presidential-debate-nashville/3740152001/.

17. William Watts, "Stock-Market Performance Under Trump Trails Only Obama and Clinton," MarketWatch, January 20, 2021, https://www.marketwatch.com/story/stock-market-performance-under-trump-trails-only-obama-and-clinton-11611161 401. Trump's performance ranks him fourth overall for growth in the Dow Jones Industrial Average (behind Coolidge, Clinton, and Obama), third for growth in the S&P 500 (behind Clinton and Obama), and first for growth in the NASDAQ.

18. Anneken Tappeq, "Trump Leaves Office with a Good—but Not Historically Great—Stock Market Record," CNN, January 20, 2021, https://www.cnn.com/2021/01/20/investing/dow-stock-market-trump-presidency/index.html.

CHAPTER 7.1

1. Claire Sanford, "Donald Trump & Joe Biden 1st Presidential Debate Transcript 2020," Rev, September 29, 2020, https://www.rev.com/blog/transcripts/donald-trump-joe-biden-1st-presidential-debate-transcript-2020.

2. Larry Buchanan, Quoctrung Bui, and Jugal K. Patel, "Black Lives Matter May Be the Largest Movement in U.S. History," *New York Times*, July 3, 2020, https://www.nytimes.com/interactive/2020/07/03/us/george-floyd-protests-crowd-size.html.

3. Camila Domonoske, "Report: 59 Confederate Symbols Removed Since George Floyd's Death," NPR, August 12, 2020, https://www.npr.org/2020/08/12/901771780/report-59-confederate-symbols-removed-since-george-floyds-death.

4. Cheyenne Haslett, "Fact Check: Both Biden and Trump Say Their Rival Wants to Defund the Police," ABC News, August 23, 2020, https://abcnews.go.com/Politics/fact-check-biden-trump-rival-defund-police/story?id=72554629.

5. Haslett, "Fact Check."

6. Haslett, "Fact Check."

7. John Eligon, Matt Furber, and Campbell Robertson, "Appeals for Calm as Sprawling Protests Threaten to Spiral Out of Control," *New York Times*, May 30, 2020, https://www.nytimes.com/2020/05/30/us/george-floyd-protest-minneapolis.html.

8. Larry Buchanan et al., "Bird's Eye View of Protests Across the U.S. and Around the World," *New York Times*, June 7, 2020, https://www.nytimes.com/interactive/2020/06/07/us/george-floyd-protest-aerial-photos.html.

9. Derrick Bryson Taylor, "George Floyd Protests: A Timeline," *New York Times*, November 5, 2021, https://www.nytimes.com/article/george-floyd-protests-timeline.html.

10. ACLED (Armed Conflict Location and Event Data Project) and BDI (Bridging Divides Initiative), "Demonstrations and Political Violence in America: New Data for Summer 2020," https://acleddata.com/2020/09/03/demonstrations-political-violence-in-america-new-data-for-summer-2020/.

11. ACLED and BDI, "Demonstrations and Political Violence in America."

12. Associated Press, "Associated Press Tally Shows at Least 9,300 People Arrested in Protests Since Killing of George Floyd," June 3, 2020, https://apnews.com/article/c51f66bd298157c52520ef56026e4857.

13. Jack Arnholz, Ivan Pereira, and Christina Carrega, "US Protests Map Shows Where Curfews and National Guard Are Active," ABC News, June 4, 2020, https://abcnews.go.com/US/locations-george-floyd-protests-curfews-national-guard-deployments/story?id=70997568.

14. ACLED and BDI, "Demonstrations and Political Violence in America."

15. Executive Office of the President, "Protecting American Monuments, Memorials, and Statues and Combating Recent Criminal Violence: Executive Order 13933," Federal Register, July 2, 2020, https://www.federalregister.gov/documents/2020/07/02/2020-14509/protecting-american-monuments-memorials-and-statues-and-combating-recent-criminal-violence.

16. Trevor Hunnicutt, "Biden: Confederate Monuments Belong in Museums, Not Public Squares," Reuters, June 20, 2020, https://www.reuters.com/article/us-usa-election-biden-statues-idUSKBN2413DQ.

17. Riley Beggin, "Trump Signs an Executive Order on Prosecuting Those Who Destroy Monuments," *Vox*, June 27, 2020, https://www.vox.com/policy-and-politics/2020/6/27/21305396/trump-confederate-monuments-executive-order.

18. "DHS Announces New Task Force to Protect American Monuments, Memorials, and Statues," Department of Homeland Security, July 1, 2020, https://www.dhs.gov/news/2020/07/01/dhs-announces-new-task-force-protect-american-monuments-memorials-and-statues.

19. ACLED and BDI, "Demonstrations and Political Violence in America."

20. Shaila Dewan and Mike Baker, "Facing Protests over Use of Force, Police Respond with More Force," *New York Times*, June 31, 2020, https://www.nytimes.com/2020/05/31/us/police-tactics-floyd-protests.html.

21. Rose Minutaglio, "Pool Noodle Shields, Undercover Feds, and Walls of Moms: This Is Portland Right Now," *Elle*, July 22, 2020, https://www.elle.com/culture/a33392479/portland-secret-police-athena-protest/.

22. ACLED and BDI, "Demonstrations and Political Violence in America."

23. ACLED and BDI, "Demonstrations and Political Violence in America."

24. Jemima McEvoy, "Nearly 20% of U.S. Schools with Confederate Names Are Ditching Them," *Forbes*, July 15, 2020, https://www.forbes.com/sites/jemimamcevoy/2020/07/15/nearly-20-of-us-schools-named-after-confederates-are-rebranding/.

25. Hunnicutt, "Biden."

26. Barbara Sprunt, "The History Behind 'When the Looting Starts, the Shooting Starts,'" NPR, May 29, 2020, https://www.npr.org/2020/05/29/864818368/the-history-behind-when-the-looting-starts-the-shooting-starts.

27. Eric Bradner and Jeff Zeleny, "Biden Defends Crime Bill amid Criticism from Democratic Foes and Trump," CNN, June 6, 2019, https://www.cnn.com/2019/06/06/politics/joe-biden-crime-bill-2020-campaign/index.html.

28. Rashawn Ray and William A. Galston, "Did the 1994 Crime Bill Cause Mass Incarceration?," Brookings Institution, *FixGov* blog, August 28, 2020, https://www.brookings.edu/blog/fixgov/2020/08/28/did-the-1994-crime-bill-cause-mass-incarceration/.

29. Bradner and Zeleny, "Biden Defends Crime Bill amid Criticism from Democratic Foes and Trump."

30. Bradner and Zeleny, "Biden Defends Crime Bill amid Criticism from Democratic Foes and Trump."

31. Max Greenwood, "Biden Says Crime Bill Was a 'Mistake' During ABC Town Hall," *The Hill*, October 15, 2020, https://thehill.com/homenews/campaign/521326-biden-says-1994-crime-bill-was-a-mistake-during-abc-town-hall.

32. Amanda Holpuch et al., "The Tasks Joe Biden Faces: From Racial Justice to Restoring Faith in Science," *Guardian*, November 10, 2020, https://www.theguardian.com/us-news/2020/nov/10/joe-biden-presidency-white-house-racial-justice-covid-science.

33. Katherine Miller, "Joe Biden Told a Voter He'll 'Go Further' than Cutting Incarceration by 50%," BuzzFeed News, July 9, 2019, https://www.buzzfeednews.com/article/katherinemiller/joe-biden-incarceration-prison-population-cut-aclu.

34. Sheryl Gay Stolberg and Astead W. Herndon, "'Lock the S.O.B.s Up': Joe Biden and the Era of Mass Incarceration," *New York Times*, June 25, 2019, https://www.nytimes.com/2019/06/25/us/joe-biden-crime-laws.html.

35. Spence Purnell, "President Biden Says Drug Users Shouldn't Go to Jail," Reason Foundation, March 10, 2021, https://reason.org/commentary/president-biden-says-drug-users-shouldnt-go-to-jail/.

36. Joe Biden, "Biden: We Must Urgently Root Out Systemic Racism, from Policing to Housing to Opportunity," *USA Today*, June 10, 2020, https://www.usatoday.com/story/opinion/2020/06/10/biden-root-out-systemic-racism-not-just-divisive-trump-talk-column/5327631002/.

37. Jan Ransom, "Trump Will Not Apologize for Calling for Death Penalty over Central Park Five," *New York Times*, June 18, 2019, https://www.nytimes.com/2019/06/18/nyregion/central-park-five-trump.html.

38. Michael Barbaro, "Donald Trump Clung to 'Birther' Lie for Years, and Still Isn't Apologetic," *New York Times*, September 17, 2016, https://www.nytimes.com/2016/09/17/us/politics/donald-trump-obama-birther.html.

39. Josh Pasek et al., "What Motivates a Conspiracy Theory? Birther Beliefs, Partisanship, Liberal-Conservative Ideology, and Anti-Black Attitudes," *Electoral Studies* 40 (2015): 482–489, https://doi.org/10.1016/j.electstud.2014.09.009.

40. Amber Phillips, "'They're Rapists.' President Trump's Campaign Launch Speech Two Years Later, Annotated," *Washington Post*, June 16, 2017, https://www.washingtonpost.com/news/the-fix/wp/2017/06/16/theyre-rapists-presidents-trump-campaign-launch-speech-two-years-later-annotated/.

41. Gretchen Frazee and Joshua Barajas, "Trump Says Walls Work. It's Much More Complicated," *PBS NewsHour*, January 9, 2019, https://www.pbs.org/newshour/nation/trump-says-walls-work-its-much-more-complicated.

42. Glenn Kessler, "The 'Very Fine People' at Charlottesville: Who Were They?," *Washington Post*, May 8, 2020, https://www.washingtonpost.com/politics/2020/05/08/very-fine-people-charlottesville-who-were-they-2/.

43. Ta-Nehisi Coates, "The First White President," *Atlantic*, September 2017, https://www.theatlantic.com/magazine/archive/2017/10/the-first-white-president-ta-nehisi-coates/537909/.

44. "Biden: Charlottesville Was the 'Moment I Knew I Had to Run,'" August 21, 2020, https://www.nbcboston.com/news/politics/decision-2020/biden-charlottesville-was-the-moment-i-knew-i-had-to-run/2181248/.

45. "Trump to African-Americans: What Do You Have to Lose?," CNN, August 19, 2016, https://www.cnn.com/videos/politics/2016/08/19/donald-trump-african-americans-what-have-you-got-to-lose-sot.cnn.

46. Maggie Fitzgerald, "Black and Hispanic Unemployment Is at a Record Low," CNBC, October 4, 2019, https://www.cnbc.com/2019/10/04/black-and-hispanic-unemployment-is-at-a-record-low.html.

47. Ben Chu and Richard Hall, "Trump Claims to Have Improved the Lives of Black People. The Numbers Say Otherwise," *Independent*, October 7, 2020, https://www.independent.co.uk/news/world/americas/us-election/trump-black-african-americans-economy-us-election-voting-unemployment-poverty-b599945.html.

48. Astead W. Herndon and Sheryl Gay Stolberg, "How Joe Biden Became the Democrats' Anti-Busing Crusader," *New York Times*, July 15, 2019, https://www.nytimes.com/2019/07/15/us/politics/biden-busing.html.

49. German Lopez, "The Controversial 1994 Crime Law That Joe Biden Helped Write, Explained," *Vox*, June 20, 2019, https://www.vox.com/policy-and-politics/2019/6/20/18677998/joe-biden-1994-crime-bill-law-mass-incarceration.

50. "Top 10 Joe Biden Gaffes," *Time*, January 31, 2007, http://content.time.com/time/specials/packages/article/0,28804,1895156_1894977_1644536,00.html.

51. Matt Stevens, "Joe Biden Says 'Poor Kids' Are Just as Bright as 'White Kids,'" *New York Times*, August 9, 2019, https://www.nytimes.com/2019/08/09/us/politics/joe-biden-poor-kids.html.

52. Stolberg and Herndon, "'Lock the S.O.B.s Up': Joe Biden and the Era of Mass Incarceration."

53. "Pope Francis: No Tolerance for Racism, but without Violence," Vatican News, June 3, 2020, https://www.vaticannews.va/en/pope/news/2020-06/pope-francis-usa-george-floyd-protests-no-racism-violence.html.

54. Maggie Astor, "What Trump, Biden and Obama Said About the Death of George Floyd," *New York Times*, July 29, 2020, https://www.nytimes.com/2020/05/29/us/politics/george-floyd-trump-biden-obama.html.

55. Adam Edelman, "Biden Calls for 'Racial Justice' During Emotional George Floyd Funeral Speech," NBC News, June 9, 2020, https://www.nbcnews.com/politics/2020-election/biden-calls-racial-justice-during-emotional-george-floyd-funeral-speech-n1228566.

56. Astor, "What Trump, Biden and Obama Said About the Death of George Floyd."

57. Paul Farhi and Elahe Izadi, "'Race and Violence in Our Cities'? A Topic for the First Presidential Debate Draws Criticism," *Washington Post*, September 23, 2020, https://www.washingtonpost.com/lifestyle/media/debate-topic-chris-wallace-race-violence/2020/09/23/729e6bc4-fd0c-11ea-8d05-9beaaa91c71f_story.html.

58. "Read the Full Transcript from the First Presidential Debate between Joe Biden and Donald Trump," *USA Today*, September 30, 2020, https://www.usatoday.com/story/news/politics/elections/2020/09/30/presidential-debate-read-full-transcript-first-debate/3587462001/.

59. Joe Biden, "Better America | Joe Biden for President 2020," YouTube, posted by Joe Biden, August 6, 2020, https://www.youtube.com/watch?v=VyJk3H2MtzI.

60. Donald J. Trump, "President Trump Will Uphold the Law," YouTube, posted by Donald J. Trump, October 27, 2020, https://www.youtube.com/watch?v=EDP9iqcvZuU.

61. Joe Biden, "Rising | Joe Biden for President 2020," YouTube, posted by Joe Biden, October 27, 2020, https://www.youtube.com/watch?v=PDJWvAKZWqQ.

62. Jennifer Peltz, "Federal Conspiracy Charges for 2 Proud Boys in Capitol Riot," Associated Press, January 30, 2021, https://apnews.com/article/capitol-siege-new-york-indictments-riots-arrests-d2d9c7709c124c6098d46741a734ae64.

63. Matt Zapotosky, "Trump Threatens Military Action to Quell Protests, and the Law Would Let Him Do It," *Washington Post*, June 1, 2020, https://www.washingtonpost.com/national-security/can-trump-use-military-to-stop-protests-insurrection-act/2020/06/01/c3724380-a46b-11ea-b473-04905b1af82b_story.html.

64. Joe Biden, @JoeBiden, "He's using the American Military against the American People. He tear-gassed peaceful protesters and fired rubber bullets. For a photo. For our children, for the very soul of our country, we must defeat him. But I mean it when I say this: we can only do it together," Twitter, June 1, 2020, 9:49 PM, https://twitter.com/JoeBiden/status/1267634400080117761.

65. Ashley Parker, Josh Dawsey, and Rebecca Tan, "Inside the Push to Tear-Gas Protesters Ahead of a Trump Photo Op," *Washington Post*, June 1, 2020, https://www.washingtonpost.com/politics/inside-the-push-to-tear-gas-protest

ers-ahead-of-a-trump-photo-op/2020/06/01/4b0f7b50-a46c-11ea-bb20-ebf0921 f3bbd_story.html.

66. Ken Dilanian, "Trump Photo Op Not Why Police Chased Protesters from Park, Report Says," NBC News, June 9, 2021, https://www.nbcnews.com/politics/don ald-trump/police-did-not-clear-d-c-s-lafayette-park-protestors-n1270126.

67. Julia Azari, "From Wallace to Trump, the Evolution of 'Law and Order,'" FiveThirtyEight, March 13, 2016, https://fivethirtyeight.com/features/from-wall ace-to-trump-the-evolution-of-law-and-order/.

68. CBS News, "Trump Says He's 'President of Law and Order,' Declares Aggressive Action on Violent Protests," CBS News, June 2, 2020, https://www.cbsnews.com/ news/trump-protest-president-law-and-order/.

69. Michael Schmidt and Maggie Haberman, "Trump Aides Prepared Insurrect Act Order During Debate Over Protests," *New York Times*, June 25, 2021, https://www. nytimes.com/2021/06/25/us/politics/trump-insurrection-act-protests.html.

70. Mike Allen, "Scoop: Esper Says Trump Wanted to Shoot Protestors," Axios, May 2, 2022, https://www.axios.com/mark-esper-book-trump-protesters-24e93272-2af5-423d-be3b-164daab7b43d.html.

71. "Kenosha Guard Leader Stands by Call to Arms," *Kenosha News*, August 27, 2020, https://www.kenoshanews.com/news/local/kenosha-guard-leader-stands-by-call-to-arms/article_805394dc-e50d-53b5-997f-aef00beof8c8.html.

72. Eric Litke, "No, Trump Doesn't Deserve Credit for Kenosha De-Escalation," Politifact, September 1, 2020, https://www.politifact.com/factchecks/2020/sep/ 01/donald-trump/heres-why-trump-vastly-overreaches-claiming-credit/.

73. Craig Gilbert, "Five Takeaways from a Peaceful (and Highly Political) Visit to Kenosha by President Donald Trump," *Milwaukee Journal Sentinel*, September 1, 2020, https://www.jsonline.com/story/news/politics/analysis/2020/09/01/ trump-visits-kenosha-5-takeaways-presidents-speech-reaction/5685419002/.

74. Rachel Wetts and Robb Willer, "Who Is Called by the Dog Whistle? Experimental Evidence That Racial Resentment and Political Ideology Condition Responses to Racially Encoded Messages," *Socius* 5 (January 2019): 1–20, doi:10.1177/ 2378023119866268.

75. Gilbert, "Five Takeaways from a Peaceful (and Highly Political) Visit to Kenosha by President Donald Trump."

76. Charles Davis, "Trump Defended Kyle Rittenhouse, a 17-Year-Old Supporter of His Charged with Killing 2 People in Kenosha," *Business Insider*, August 31, 2020, https://www.businessinsider.com/trump-defends-kyle-rittenhouse-charged-with-homicide-in-kenosha-2020-8.

77. Peter Wade, "DHS Officials Given Talking Points Supportive of Kyle Rittenhouse, Report Says," *Rolling Stone*, October 1, 2020, https://www.rollingstone.com/polit ics/politics-news/homeland-security-officials-given-talking-points-supportive-of-kyle-rittenhouse-1069621/.

78. Patrick Marley et al., "Joe Biden Meets with Jacob Blake Family, Says Trump Rhetoric 'Legitimizes the Dark Sides of Human Nature,'" *Milwaukee Journal Sentinel*, September 3, 2020, https://www.jsonline.com/story/news/politics/elections/2020/09/03/joe-biden-meets-jacob-blake-family-visits-kenosha/570 2199002/.

79. Marley et al., "Joe Biden Meets with Jacob Blake Family, Says Trump Rhetoric 'Legitimizes the Dark Sides of Human Nature.'"

80. Joe Biden, @JoeBiden, "There's no other way to put it: the President of the United States refused to disavow white supremacists on the debate stage last night," Twitter, September 30, 2020, 7:35 AM, https://twitter.com/JoeBiden/status/1311 268302950260737.

81. Becky Sullivan, "Kyle Rittenhouse Is Acquitted of All Charges in the Trial over Killing 2 in Kenosha," NPR, November 19, 2021, https://www.npr.org/2021/11/19/1057288807/kyle-rittenhouse-acquitted-all-charges-verdict.

CHAPTER 7.2

1. ACLED (Armed Conflict Location and Event Data Project) and BDI (Bridging Divides Initiative), "Demonstrations and Political Violence in America: New Data for Summer 2020," https://acleddata.com/acleddatanew/wp-content/uploads/2020/09/ACLED_USDataReview_Sum2020_SeptWebPDF_HiRes.pdf.

2. Michael Tesler, "Priming Predispositions and Changing Policy Positions: An Account of When Mass Opinion Is Primed or Changed," *American Journal of Political Science* 59, no. 4 (2015): 806–824, https://www.jstor.org/stable/24582949.

3. Andrew M. Engelhardt, "Racial Attitudes Through a Partisan Lens," *British Journal of Political Science* 51, no. 3 (July 2021): 1062–1079, doi:10.1017/S0007123419000437.

4. Donald R. Kinder and Lynn M. Sanders, *Divided by Color: Racial Politics and Democratic Ideals* (Chicago: University of Chicago Press, 1996), https://press.uchic ago.edu/ucp/books/book/chicago/D/bo3620441.html. Although see Michael Tesler, "The Return of Old-Fashioned Racism to White Americans' Partisan Preferences in the Early Obama Era," *Journal of Politics* 75, no. 1 (2012): 110–123, doi:10.1017/s0022381612000904.

5. Lawrence Bobo, "Group Conflict, Prejudice, and the Paradox of Contemporary Racial Attitudes," in *Eliminating Racism: Profiles in Controversy*, edited by Phyllis A. Katz and Dalmas A. Taylor, 85–114 (New York: Plenum, 1988), https://scho lar.harvard.edu/files/bobo/files/1988_group_conflict_in_eliminating_racism. pdf?m=1452698121.

6. Ange-Marie Hancock, *The Politics of Disgust: The Public Identity of the Welfare Queen* (New York: New York University Press, 2004).

7. Rose M. Brewer and Nancy A. Heitzeg, "The Racialization of Crime and Punishment: Criminal Justice, Color-Blind Racism, and the Political Economy of

the Prison Industrial Complex," *American Behavioral Scientist* 51, no. 5 (January 2008): 625–644, doi:10.1177/0002764207307745.

8. Tali Mendelberg, "Executing Hortons: Racial Crime in the 1988 Presidential Campaign," *Public Opinion Quarterly* 61, no. 1 (1997): 134–157, https://www.jstor.org/stable/2749515.

9. Michael Tesler and David O. Sears, *Obama's Race: The 2008 Election and the Dream of a Post-Racial America* (Chicago: University of Chicago, 2010), https://press.uchicago.edu/ucp/books/book/chicago/O/bo10443910.html.

10. Lawrence D. Bobo, "Somewhere Between Jim Crow and Post-Racialism: Reflections on the Racial Divide in America Today," *Daedalus* 140, no. 2 (2011): 11–36, doi:10.1162/DAED_a_00091.

11. Vincent L. Hutchings and Nicholas A. Valentino, "The Centrality of Race in American Politics," *Annual Review of Political Science* 7, no. 1 (2004): 383–408, doi:10.1146/annurev.polisci.7.012003.104859.

12. Tesler and Sears, *Obama's Race*.

13. Paul M. Sniderman and Edward G. Carmines, *Reaching Beyond Race* (Cambridge, MA: Harvard University Press, 1997), https://www.hup.harvard.edu/catalog.php?isbn=9780674145795.

14. Li Zhou, "Kamala Harris Has Been Criticized for Her Criminal Justice Record. She's Just Begun to Offer a Response," *Vox*, January 21, 2019, https://www.vox.com/2019/1/21/18191864/kamala-harris-2020-criminal-justice.

15. Kate Kenski, Bruce W. Hardy, and Kathleen Hall Jamieson, *The Obama Victory: How Media, Money, and Message Shaped the 2008 Election* (New York: Oxford University Press, 2010).

16. Stacy G. Ulbig, "The Appeal of Second Bananas: The Impact of Vice Presidential Candidates on Presidential Vote Choice, Yesterday and Today," *American Politics Research* 38, no. 2 (2010): 330–355, doi:10.1177/1532673X09358950.

17. Kevin Breuninger, "Trump Signs Executive Order Urging Police Reform, Says Cops Need More Funding," CNBC, June 16, 2020, https://www.cnbc.com/2020/06/16/trump-signs-executive-order-urging-police-reform-says-cops-need-more-funding.html.

18. Rem Rieder, "Trump's False, Recurring Claim About Biden's Stance on Police," FactCheck.org, July 21, 2020, https://www.factcheck.org/2020/07/trumps-false-recurring-claim-about-bidens-stance-on-police/.

19. ACLED and BDI, "Demonstrations and Political Violence in America."

20. Jennifer A. Kingson, "Exclusive: $1 Billion-Plus Riot Damage Is Most Expensive in Insurance History," Axios, September 16, 2020, https://www.axios.com/riots-cost-property-damage-276c9bcc-a455-4067-b06a-66f9db4cea9c.html.

21. Yotam Ophir et al., "News Media Framing of Social Protests Around Racial Tensions During the Donald Trump Presidency," *Journalism*, August 2021, 1–19, doi:10.1177/14648849211036622.

22. Mia Bloom, "Far-Right Infiltrators and Agitators in George Floyd Protests: Indicators of White Supremacists," May 30, 2020, 5, https://docs.house.gov/meetings/JU/JU00/20200610/110775/HHRG-116-JU00-20200610-SD019.pdf.

23. "National Tracking Poll #2005131: May 31–June 01, 2020," Morning Consult, June 1, 2020, https://assets.morningconsult.com/wp-uploads/2020/06/01190233/2005131_crosstabs_POLICE_Adults_FINAL_LM.pdf/. See table MC6.

24. Andrew W. Lehren et al., "Protests Renew Debate About Police Use of Armored Vehicles, Other Military Gear," NBC News, June 20, 2020, https://www.nbcnews.com/news/us-news/floyd-protests-renew-debate-about-police-use-armored-vehicles-other-n1231288.

25. "George Floyd: 'Unacceptable' Attacks on Reporters at Protests," BBC News, June 2, 2020, https://www.bbc.com/news/world-us-canada-52880970.

26. Maggie Koerth and Jamiles Lartey, "Why So Many Police Are Handling the Protests Wrong," The Marshall Project, June 1, 2020, https://www.themarshallproject.org/2020/06/01/why-so-many-police-are-handling-the-protests-wrong.

27. Rosette Royale, "Seattle's Autonomous Zone Is Not What You've Been Told," *Rolling Stone*, June 19, 2020, https://www.rollingstone.com/culture/culture-features/chop-chaz-seattle-autonomous-zone-inside-protests-1017637/.

28. Jonathan Levinson et al., "Federal Officers Use Unmarked Vehicles to Grab People in Portland, DHS Confirms," NPR, July 17, 2020, https://www.npr.org/2020/07/17/892277592/federal-officers-use-unmarked-vehicles-to-grab-protesters-in-portland.

29. Ophir et al., "News Media Framing of Social Protests Around Racial Tensions During the Donald Trump Presidency."

30. Donald J. Trump and Ben Carson, "We'll Protect America's Suburbs," *Wall Street Journal*, August 16, 2020, https://www.wsj.com/articles/well-protect-americas-suburbs-11597608133.

31. Donald J. Trump, "Why would Suburban Women vote for Biden and the Democrats . . . ," *Twitter*, August 22, 2020, https://www.thetrumparchive.com/?searchbox=%22why+would+suburban+women+vote+for+biden%22/.

32. "Trump Pleas with Suburban Women: 'Please Like Me,' " YouTube, posted by Associated Press, October 13, 2020, https://www.youtube.com/watch?v=ebsapmo4flQ.

33. Philip Bump, "The Dramatic Shifts in the 2020 Election, Visualized," *Washington Post*, November 10, 2020, https://www.washingtonpost.com/politics/2020/11/10/dramatic-shifts-2020-election-visualized/?no_nav=true.

34. Denise Lu and Karen Yourish, "How Did Trump Do in Counties That Backed Him in 2016?," *New York Times*, November 9, 2020, https://www.nytimes.com/interactive/2020/11/09/us/politics/2016-election-trump-counties.html?referringSource=articleShare.

35. William H. Frey, "Biden's Victory Came from the Suburbs," Brookings Institution, November 13, 2020, https://www.brookings.edu/research/bidens-victory-came-from-the-suburbs/.

36. Trevor Hunnicutt and Joseph Ax, "Biden Faces Balancing Act as Activists Call to 'Defund the Police,'" Reuters, June 8, 2020, https://www.reuters.com/article/usa-election-biden-police-idINKBN23G07R.

37. "Read the Full Transcript from the First Presidential Debate Between Joe Biden and Donald Trump," *USA Today*, September 30, 2020, https://www.usatoday.com/story/news/politics/elections/2020/09/30/presidential-debate-read-full-tra nscript-first-debate/3587462001/.

38. "National Voter Surveys: How Different Groups Voted," *New York Times*, November 3, 2020, https://www.nytimes.com/interactive/2020/11/03/us/electi ons/ap-polls-national.html.

CHAPTER 8

1. Donald J. Trump, "Remarks by President Trump at the White House Conference on American History," The White House, September 17, 2020, https://trumpwhi tehouse.archives.gov/briefings-statements/remarks-president-trump-white-house-conference-american-history/.

2. Chelsea James, "Mispronouncing 'Kamala': Accident or Message?," *Washington Post*, October 23, 2020, https://www.washingtonpost.com/politics/mispronouncing-kamala-accident-or-message/2020/10/23/5927f120-13b3-11eb-ad6f-36c93e6e94fb_story.html.

3. David Neiwert, "When White Nationalists Chant Their Weird Slogans, What Do They Mean?," Southern Poverty Law Center, October 10, 2017, https://www.splcen ter.org/hatewatch/2017/10/10/when-white-nationalists-chant-their-weird-slog ans-what-do-they-mean.

4. Meg Wagner, "'Blood and Soil': Protesters Chant Nazi Slogan in Charlottesville," CNN, August 12, 2017, https://www.cnn.com/2017/08/12/us/charlottesville-unite-the-right-rally/index.html.

5. Tara Isabella Burton, "This Weekend's Charlottesville Rally Represents an Alliance Between pro-Confederates and Nazis," *Vox*, August 12, 2017, https://www.vox.com/2017/8/12/16138352/this-weekends-charlottesville-rally-shows-how-close-good-old-boys-and-nazis-really-are.

6. Elana Schor, "Christianity on Display at Capitol Riot Sparks New Debate," Associated Press, January 28, 2021, https://apnews.com/article/christianity-capitol-riot-6f13ef0030ad7b5a6f37a1e3b7b4c898.

7. Stephanie K. Baer, "Trump Supporters Who Attempted the Coup at the US Capitol Flaunted Racist and Hateful Symbols," BuzzFeed News, last updated January 7, 2021, https://www.buzzfeednews.com/article/skbaer/trump-supporters-racist-symbols-capitol-assault.

8. Schor, "Christianity on Display at Capitol Riot Sparks New Debate."

9. Luke Broadwater and Alan Feuer, "House Jan. 6 Committee Subpoenas White Nationalist Figures," *New York Times*, January 19, 2022, https://www.nytimes.com/2022/01/19/us/politics/jan-6-committee-subpoena-white-nationalists.html.

10. Michael Gerson, "How Do We Tame Trumpism's Virulent Nostalgia for an Old Status Quo?," *Washington Post*, April 26, 2018, https://www.washingtonpost.com/opinions/how-do-we-tame-trumpisms-virulent-nostalgia-for-an-old-status-quo/2018/04/26/f96e13de-4977-11e8-9072-f6d4bc32f223_story.html.

11. Samuel P. Huntington, *Who Are We? The Challenges to America's National Identity* (New York: Simon and Schuster, 2004).

12. Kate Zernike and Megan Thee-Brenan, "Poll Finds Tea Party Backers Wealthier and More Educated," *New York Times*, April 15, 2010, https://www.nytimes.com/2010/04/15/us/politics/15poll.html.

13. Matt A. Barreto et al., "The Tea Party in the Age of Obama: Mainstream Conservatism or Out-Group Anxiety?," in *Rethinking Obama*, edited by Julian Go, Political Power and Social Theory, vol. 22, 105–137 (Bingley, UK: Emerald Group, 2011), doi:10.1108/S0198-8719(2011)0000022011.

14. "Trump's Staunch GOP Supporters Have Roots in the Tea Party," Pew Research Center, May 16, 2019, https://www.pewresearch.org/politics/2019/05/16/trumps-staunch-gop-supporters-have-roots-in-the-tea-party/.

15. Diana C. Mutz, "Status Threat, Not Economic Hardship, Explains the 2016 Presidential Vote," *Proceedings of the National Academy of Sciences* 115, no. 19 (May 2018): E4330–E4339, doi:10.1073/pnas.1718155115.

16. John R. Hibbing, *The Securitarian Personality: What Really Motivates Trump's Base and Why It Matters for the Post-Trump Era* (New York: Oxford University Press, 2020).

17. Ted Brader, Nicholas A. Valentino, and Elizabeth Suhay, "What Triggers Public Opposition to Immigration? Anxiety, Group Cues, and Immigration Threat," *American Journal of Political Science* 52, no. 4 (2008): 959–978, doi:10.1111/j.1540-5907.2008.00353.x; Alan I. Abramowitz, "Transformation and Polarization: The 2008 Presidential Election and the New American Electorate," *Electoral Studies* 29, no. 4 (December 2010): 594–603, doi:10.1016/j.electstud.2010.04.006; Mutz, "Status Threat, Not Economic Hardship, Explains the 2016 Presidential Vote"; Eric D. Knowles and Linda R. Tropp, "The Racial and Economic Context of Trump Support: Evidence for Threat, Identity, and Contact Effects in the 2016 Presidential Election," *Social Psychological and Personality Science* 9, no. 3 (April 2018): 275–284, doi:10.1177/1948550618759326.

18. Karen Stenner, *The Authoritarian Dynamic* (New York: Cambridge University Press, 2005), https://www.cambridge.org/core/books/authoritarian-dynamic/7620B99124ED2DBFC6394444838F455A; Stanley Feldman and Karen Stenner, "Perceived Threat and Authoritarianism," *Political Psychology* 18, no. 4 (1997): 741–770.

19. John T. Jost et al., "Political Conservatism as Motivated Social Cognition," *Psychological Bulletin* 129, no. 3 (2003): 339–375, doi:10.1037/0033-2909.129.3.339.

20. Feldman and Stenner, "Perceived Threat and Authoritarianism."

21. Ashley Jardina, *White Identity Politics*, Cambridge Studies in Public Opinion and Political Psychology (New York: Cambridge University Press, 2019).

22. Clara L. Wilkins and Cheryl R. Kaiser, "Racial Progress as Threat to the Status Hierarchy: Implications for Perceptions of Anti-White Bias," *Psychological Science* 25, no. 2 (December 2013): 439–446, doi:10.1177/0956797613508412.

23. Walter S. Stephan and Cookie White Stephan, "An Integrated Threat Theory of Prejudice," in *Reducing Prejudice and Discrimination*, edited by Stuart Oskamp (New York: Psychology Press, 2000), pp. 23–46.

24. Iain Walker and Thomas F. Pettigrew, "Relative Deprivation Theory: An Overview and Conceptual Critique," *British Journal of Social Psychology* 23, no. 4 (November 1984): 301–310, doi:10.1111/j.2044-8309.1984.tb00645.x.

25. Rogers M. Smith, *Civic Ideals: Conflicting Visions of Citizenship in U.S. History* (New Haven, CT: Yale University Press, 1999), https://yalebooks.yale.edu/book/9780300078770/civic-ideals; Elizabeth Theiss-Morse, *Who Counts as an American?: The Boundaries of National Identity* (Cambridge, UK: Cambridge University Press, 2009), doi:10.1017/CBO9780511750717.

26. Theiss-Morse, *Who Counts as an American?*; Thierry Devos and Mahzarin R. Banaji, "American = White?," *Journal of Personality and Social Psychology* 88, no. 3 (2005): 447–466, doi:10.1037/0022-3514.88.3.447.

27. Richard L. Zweigenhaft and G. William Domhoff, *Diversity in the Power Elite: How It Happened, Why It Matters* (Lanham, MD: Rowman & Littlefield, 2006).

28. William H. Frey, "The US Will Become 'Minority White' in 2045, Census Projects," *The Avenue* blog, Brookings Institution, March 14, 2018, https://www.brookings.edu/blog/the-avenue/2018/03/14/the-us-will-become-minority-white-in-2045-census-projects/.

29. Sabrina Tavernise, "Why the Announcement of a Looming White Minority Makes Demographers Nervous," *New York Times*, November 22, 2018, https://www.nytimes.com/2018/11/22/us/white-americans-minority-population.html.

30. Mark J. Perry, "Women Earned Majority of Doctoral Degrees in 2019 for 11th Straight Year and Outnumber Men in Grad School 141 to 100," American Enterprise Institute, October 15, 2020, https://www.aei.org/carpe-diem/women-earned-majority-of-doctoral-degrees-in-2019-for-11th-straight-year-and-outnumber-men-in-grad-school-141-to-100/.

31. Jan Van Bavel, Christine R. Schwartz, and Albert Esteve, "The Reversal of the Gender Gap in Education and Its Consequences for Family Life," *Annual Review of Sociology* 44, no. 1 (2018): 341–360, doi:10.1146/annurev-soc-073117-041215.

32. Kathryn Edin et al., "The Tenuous Attachments of Working-Class Men," *Journal of Economic Perspectives* 33, no. 2 (Spring 2019): 211–228, doi:10.1257/jep.33.2.211.

33. Anne Case and Angus Deaton, *Deaths of Despair and the Future of Capitalism* (Princeton, NJ: Princeton University Press, 2020), https://press.princeton.edu/books/hardcover/9780691190785/deaths-of-despair-and-the-future-of-capitalism.

34. Gregory A. Smith, "About Three-in-Ten U.S. Adults Are Now Religiously Unaffiliated," Pew Research Center, December 14, 2021, https://www.pewforum.org/2021/12/14/about-three-in-ten-u-s-adults-are-now-religiously-unaffiliated/.

35. "An Examination of the 2016 Electorate, Based on Validated Voters," Pew Research Center, August 9, 2018, https://www.pewresearch.org/politics/2018/08/09/an-examination-of-the-2016-electorate-based-on-validated-voters/.

36. "Election 2020: Voters Highly Engaged, but Nearly Half Expect Difficulties Voting," Pew Research Center, August 13, 2020, https://www.pewresearch.org/politics/2020/08/13/election-2020-voters-are-highly-engaged-but-nearly-half-expect-to-have-difficulties-voting/.

37. David E. Campbell, Geoffrey C. Layman, and John C. Green, *Secular Surge: A New Fault Line in American Politics*, Cambridge Studies in Social Theory, Religion and Politics (Cambridge, UK: Cambridge University Press, 2020), doi:10.1017/9781108923347.

38. Arlie Russell Hochschild, *Strangers in Their Own Land* (New York: New Press, 2016), https://thenewpress.com/books/strangers-their-own-land.

39. Robert Farley, "Trump Retweets Bogus Crime Graphic," FactCheck.org, last updated November 24, 2015, https://www.factcheck.org/2015/11/trump-retweets-bogus-crime-graphic/.

40. Chris Cillizza, "Donald Trump's New Message to Suburban Women? I Fixed the Dishwasher!," CNN, October 19, 2020, https://www.cnn.com/2020/10/19/politics/donald-trump-dishwasher-nevada/index.html.

41. Cillizza, "Donald Trump's New Message to Suburban Women? I Fixed the Dishwasher!"

42. "Donald Trump 'Proud' to Be a Birther," *The Laura Ingraham Show*, Fox News, posted by Laura Ingraham, March 30, 2011, https://www.youtube.com/watch?v=WqaS9OCoTZs.

43. Leila Fadel, "Majority of Muslims Voted for Biden, but Trump Got More Support than He Did in 2016," NPR, December 4, 2020, https://www.npr.org/2020/12/04/942262760/majority-of-muslims-voted-for-biden-but-trump-got-more-not-less-support.

44. Elizabeth Dias, "'Christianity Will Have Power,'" *New York Times*, August 9, 2020, https://www.nytimes.com/2020/08/09/us/evangelicals-trump-christianity.html.

45. Annie Karni, "Trump Denounces Anti-Catholic Bias Even as He Attacks Biden's Faith," *New York Times*, September 28, 2020, https://www.nytimes.com/2020/09/28/us/politics/trump-biden-catholics.html.

46. Peter Glick and Susan T. Fiske, "The Ambivalent Sexism Inventory: Differentiating Hostile and Benevolent Sexism," *Journal of Personality and Social Psychology*

70, no. 3 (1996): 491–512, doi:10.1037/0022-3514.70.3.491; Peter Glick and Susan T. Fiske, "An Ambivalent Alliance: Hostile and Benevolent Sexism as Complementary Justifications for Gender Inequality," *American Psychologist* 56, no. 2 (2001): 109–118, doi:10.1037/0003-066X.56.2.109; Ange-Marie Hancock, *Intersectionality: An Intellectual History* (New York: Oxford University Press, 2016), doi:10.1093/acprof:oso/9780199370368.001.0001.

47. Paul LeBlanc, "Trump Uses Outdated Thinking in Attempt to Woo Suburban Women: I'm 'Getting Your Husbands Back to Work,'" CNN, October 27, 2020, https://www.cnn.com/2020/10/27/politics/trump-suburban-women-2020-elect ion/index.html.

48. Jenna Johnson and Ryan Van Velzer, "Donald Trump Says It's 'Not Nice' to Call Women 'Tough,'" *Washington Post*, June 18, 2016, https://www.washingtonpost. com/news/post-politics/wp/2016/06/18/donald-trump-says-its-not-nice-to-call-women-tough/.

49. Juana Summers, "Trump Calls Harris a 'Monster,' Reviving a Pattern of Attacking Women of Color," NPR, October 9, 2020, https://www.npr.org/2020/10/ 09/921884531/trump-calls-harris-a-monster-reviving-a-pattern-of-attack ing-women-of-color.

50. "Trump: Clinton Such a Nasty Woman," YouTube, posted by CNN, October 19, 2016, https://www.youtube.com/watch?v=Q2KOQfZoZdo.

51. Poppy Noor, "Trump Called Kamala Harris 'Nasty'—Is It Because She Grills Powerful Men?," *The Guardian*, August 12, 2020, https://www.theguardian.com/ us-news/2020/aug/12/trump-kamala-harris-nasty.

52. Chris Cillizza, "Donald Trump's Vague Attack on Kamala Harris Has a Clear Point," CNN, September 9, 2020, https://www.cnn.com/2020/09/09/politics/ donald-trump-kamala-harris/index.html.

53. Erin C. Cassese and Tiffany D. Barnes, "Reconciling Sexism and Women's Support for Republican Candidates: A Look at Gender, Class, and Whiteness in the 2012 and 2016 Presidential Races," *Political Behavior* 41, no. 3 (September 2019): 677–700, doi:10.1007/s11109-018-9468-2.

54. Kristen Kobes Du Mez, *Jesus and John Wayne* (New York: Liveright, 2020), https://wwnorton.com/books/9781631495731.

55. Louisa Thomas, "America First, for Charles Lindbergh and Donald Trump," *The New Yorker*, July 24, 2016, https://www.newyorker.com/news/news-desk/amer ica-first-for-charles-lindbergh-and-donald-trump.

56. Mutz, "Status Threat, Not Economic Hardship, Explains the 2016 Presidential Vote."

57. Maureen A. Craig and Jennifer A. Richeson, "On the Precipice of a 'Majority-Minority' America: Perceived Status Threat from the Racial Demographic Shift Affects White Americans' Political Ideology," *Psychological Science* 25, no. 6 (April 2014): 1189–1197, doi:10.1177/0956797614527113.

58. Xanni Brown, Julian M. Rucker, and Jennifer A. Richeson, "Political Ideology Moderates White Americans' Reactions to Racial Demographic Change,"

Group Processes and Intergroup Relations 25, no. 3 (November 2021): 642–660, doi:10.1177/13684302211052516.

59. Brenda Major, Alison Blodorn, and Gregory Major Blascovich, "The Threat of Increasing Diversity: Why Many White Americans Support Trump in the 2016 Presidential Election," *Group Processes and Intergroup Relations* 21, no. 6 (2018): 931–940, doi:10.1177/1368430216677304.

60. Samuel P. Huntington, *American Politics: The Promise of Disharmony* (Cambridge, MA: Belknap Press of Harvard University Press, 1981), https://www.hup.harvard.edu/catalog.php?isbn=9780674030213.

61. Jake Silverstein, "The 1619 Project and the Long Battle over U.S. History," *New York Times*, November 9, 2021, https://www.nytimes.com/2021/11/09/magazine/1619-project-us-history.html.

62. Jake Silverstein, "Why We Published the 1619 Project," *New York Times*, December 20, 2019, https://www.nytimes.com/interactive/2019/12/20/magazine/1619-intro.html.

63. J. Brian Charles, "The New York Times 1619 Project Is Reshaping the Conversation on Slavery. Conservatives Hate It," *Vox*, August 19, 2019, https://www.vox.com/identities/2019/8/19/20812238/1619-project-slavery-conservatives.

64. "We Respond to the Historians Who Critiqued the 1619 Project," *New York Times*, December 20, 2019, https://www.nytimes.com/2019/12/20/magazine/we-respond-to-the-historians-who-critiqued-the-1619-project.html.

65. Nicole Gaudiano, "Trump Creates 1776 Commission to Promote 'Patriotic Education,'" *Politico*, November 2020, https://www.politico.com/news/2020/11/02/trump-1776-commission-education-433885.

66. Trump, "Remarks by President Trump at the White House Conference on American History."

67. The President's Advisory 1776 Commission, "The 1776 Report," The White House, January 2021, https://trumpwhitehouse.archives.gov/wp-content/uploads/2021/01/The-Presidents-Advisory-1776-Commission-Final-Report.pdf.

68. Michael Crowley and Jennifer Schuessler, "Trump's 1776 Commission Critiques Liberalism in Report Derided by Historians," *New York Times*, January 18, 2021, https://www.nytimes.com/2021/01/18/us/politics/trump-1776-commission-report.html.

69. Frank E. Lockwood, "Bill by Sen. Tom Cotton Targets Curriculum on Slavery," Arkansas Online, July 26, 2020, https://www.arkansasonline.com/news/2020/jul/26/bill-by-cotton-targets-curriculum-on-slavery/.

70. Clare Foran, "GOP Sen. Tom Cotton Pitches Bill to Prohibit Use of Federal Funds to Teach 1619 Project," CNN, July 24, 2020, https://www.cnn.com/2020/07/24/politics/tom-cotton-1619-project-bill/index.html.

71. Lockwood, "Bill by Sen. Tom Cotton Targets Curriculum on Slavery."

72. Rogers M. Smith and Desmond King, "White Protectionism in America," *Perspectives on Politics* 19, no. 2 (May 2020): 460–478, doi:10.1017/S1537592720001152.

73. Douglas J. Ahler and Gaurav Sood, "The Parties in Our Heads: Misperceptions About Party Composition and Their Consequences," *Journal of Politics* 80, no. 3 (July 2018): 964–981, doi:10.1086/697253.

74. Ruth Igielnik, "Men and Women in the U.S. Continue to Differ in Voter Turnout Rate, Party Identification," Pew Research Center, August 18, 2020, https://www.pewresearch.org/fact-tank/2020/08/18/men-and-women-in-the-u-s-continue-to-differ-in-voter-turnout-rate-party-identification/.

75. Lawrence Glickman, "3 Tropes of White Victimhood," *Atlantic*, July 20, 2021, https://www.theatlantic.com/ideas/archive/2021/07/three-tropes-white-victimhood/619463/.

76. "Tucker Carlson Calls Biden's Immigration Policy 'the Great Replacement' and 'Eugenics,'" Media Matters for America, September 22, 2021, https://www.mediamatters.org/tucker-carlson/tucker-carlson-calls-bidens-immigration-policy-great-replacement-and-eugenics.

77. "'The Great Replacement': An Explainer," Anti-Defamation League, accessed January 13, 2022, https://www.adl.org/resources/backgrounders/the-great-replacement-an-explainer.

78. Trump, "Remarks by President Trump at the White House Conference on American History."

79. Data on frequency and placement of airing from Advertising Analytics. Ad transcribed from digital version aired in Philadelphia.

80. "Don't Let Them Ruin America," YouTube, posted by Donald J. Trump, August 15, 2020, https://www.youtube.com/watch?v=G7AU5cHpl_U.

81. Amos Tversky and Daniel Kahneman, "Availability: A Heuristic for Judging Frequency and Probability," *Cognitive Psychology* 5, no. 2 (September 1973): 207–232, doi:10.1016/0010-0285(73)90033-9.

82. Trump, "Remarks by President Trump at the White House Conference on American History."

83. Trump, "Remarks by President Trump at the White House Conference on American History."

84. "Full Text: President Trump's 2020 RNC Acceptance Speech," NBC News, August 28, 2020, https://www.nbcnews.com/politics/2020-election/read-full-text-president-donald-trump-s-acceptance-speech-rnc-n1238636.

85. Ayesha Rascoe, "Reelection Campaign Launches 'Black Voices for Trump' Initiative," NPR, November 8, 2019, `https://www.npr.org/2019/11/08/777466954/reelection-campaign-launches-black-voices-for-trump-initiative.

86. C. Isiah Smalls, "New Donald Trump Ad Taps Herschel Walker, Rep. Vernon Jones to Recruit Black Voters," *Miami Herald*, September 11, 2020.

87. "Vice President Joe Biden Remarks on Extremism and Terrorism," C-SPAN, February 17, 2015, https://www.c-span.org/video/?324394-2/vice-president-joe-biden-remarks-extremism-terrorism.

88. Clara L. Wilkins and Cheryl R. Kaiser, "Racial Progress as Threat to the Status Hierarchy: Implications for Perceptions of Anti-White Bias," *Psychological Science* 25, no. 2 (December 2013): 439–446, doi:10.1177/0956797613508412.

89. Felicia Pratto et al., "Social Dominance Orientation: A Personality Variable Predicting Social and Political Attitudes," *Journal of Personality and Social Psychology* 67, no. 4 (1994): 741–763, doi:10.1037/0022-3514.67.4.741.

90. Morris Levy and Dowell Myers, "Racial Projections in Perspective: Public Reactions to Narratives About Rising Diversity," *Perspectives on Politics* 19, no. 4 (December 2021): 1147–1164, doi:10.1017/S1537592720003679.

91. Ashley Jardina, *White Identity Politics*, Cambridge Studies in Public Opinion and Political Psychology (New York: Cambridge University Press, 2019).

92. P. J. Henry and David O. Sears, "The Crystallization of Contemporary Racial Prejudice Across the Lifespan," *Political Psychology* 30, no. 4 (2009): 569–590, doi:10.1111/j.1467-9221.2009.00715.x.

93. Peter K. Enns and Ashley Jardina, "Complicating the Role of White Racial Attitudes and Anti-Immigrant Sentiment in the 2016 US Presidential Election," *Public Opinion Quarterly* 85, no. 2 (October 2021): 539–570, doi:10.1093/poq/nfab040.

94. Enns and Jardina, "Complicating the Role of White Racial Attitudes and Anti-Immigrant Sentiment in the 2016 US Presidential Election"; Daniel J. Hopkins, "The Activation of Prejudice and Presidential Voting: Panel Evidence from the 2016 U.S. Election," *Political Behavior* 43, no. 2 (June 2021): 663–686, doi:10.1007/s11109-019-09567-4.

95. Dan Cassino and Yasemin Besen-Cassino, *Gender Threat: American Masculinity in the Face of Change* (Stanford, CA: Stanford University Press, 2021); Andrew L. Whitehead and Samuel L. Perry, *Taking America Back for God: Christian Nationalism in the United States* (New York: Oxford University Press, 2020).

CHAPTER 9.1

1. Felicia Sonmez, Tom Hamburger, and Paulina Firozi, "'I Concede NOTHING!' Trump Says Shortly After Appearing to Acknowledge Biden Won the Election," *Washington Post*, November 15, 2020, https://www.washingtonpost.com/politics/2020/11/15/i-concede-nothing-trump-says-shortly-after-appearing-acknowledge-biden-won-election/.

2. Jonathan Allen, "'They're not here to hurt me': Former Aide Says Trump Knew Jan. 6 Crowd Was Armed," *NBC News*, June 28, 2022, https://www.nbcnews.com/politics/congress/jan-6-panel-looks-trump-white-house-cassidy-hutchinson-testimony-rcna35550.

3. Joe Manchin, "Senate Resolution 718," 116th Congress, 2020, https://www.congress.gov/116/bills/sres718/BILLS-116sres718ats.pdf.

438 *Notes*

438 *Notes*

4. Allison Pecorin and Trish Turner, "Unanimous Senate Commits to Peaceful Transfer of Power After Trump Refuses," ABC News, September 24, 2020, https://abcnews.go.com/Politics/unanimous-senate-commits-peaceful-transfer-power-trump-refuses/story?id=73216758.

5. Pecorin and Turner, "Unanimous Senate Commits to Peaceful Transfer of Power After Trump Refuses."

6. "October 19, 2016 Debate Transcript," Commission on Presidential Debates, October 19, 2016, https://www.debates.org/voter-education/debate-transcripts/october-19-2016-debate-transcript/.

7. "Trump Claims Millions Voted Illegally in Presidential Poll," BBC News, November 28, 2016, https://www.bbc.com/news/world-us-canada-38126438.

8. "Read the Trump Campaign's Internal Memo," *New York Times*, September 21, 2021, https://www.nytimes.com/interactive/2021/09/21/us/trump-campaign-memo.html.

9. David Cottrell, Michael C. Herron, and Sean J. Westwood, "An Exploration of Donald Trump's Allegations of Massive Voter Fraud in the 2016 General Election," *Electoral Studies*, March 2017, doi:10.1016/j.electstud.2017.09.002.

10. Claire Sanford, "Donald Trump and Joe Biden 1st Presidential Debate Transcript 2020," Rev, September 29, 2020, https://www.rev.com/blog/transcripts/donald-trump-joe-biden-1st-presidential-debate-transcript-2020.

11. David Wasserman, "Beware the 'Blue Mirage' and the 'Red Mirage' on Election Night," NBC News, November 3, 2020, https://www.nbcnews.com/politics/2020-election/beware-blue-mirage-red-mirage-election-night-n1245925.

12. "'We Did Win This Election,' U.S. President Donald Trump Claims, Despite Votes Still Being Counted," YouTube, posted by CTV News, November 4, 2020, https://www.youtube.com/watch?v=wOVs-r968qg.

13. Sam Gringlas, Scott Neuman, and Camila Domonoske, "'Far from Over': Trump Refuses to Concede as Biden's Margin of Victory Widens," NPR, November 7, 2020, https://www.npr.org/sections/live-updates-2020-election-results/2020/11/07/932062684/far-from-over-trump-refuses-to-concede-as-ap-others-call-election-for-biden.

14. Jacob Shamsian and Sonam Sheth, "Trump and His Allies Filed More than 40 Lawsuits Challenging the 2020 Election Results. All of Them Failed," *Business Insider*, February 2021, https://www.businessinsider.com/trump-campaign-lawsuits-election-results-2020-11.

15. Tom Hals, "In Fresh Blow to Trump, U.S. Court Rejects Pennsylvania Election Case," Reuters, November 27, 2020, https://www.reuters.com/article/uk-usa-election-lawsuit-pennsylvania-idUKKBN2872BA.

16. Matthew Brann, "Donald J. Trump for President, Inc. v. Kathy Boockvar, et al.," Memorandum Opinion, United States District Court for the Middle District of Pennsylvania, November 21, 2020, https://pacer-documents.s3.amazonaws.com/147/127057/15517440654.pdf.

17. Eric Tucker and Frank Bajak, "Repudiating Trump, Officials Say Election 'Most Secure,'" Associated Press, November 13, 2020, https://apnews.com/article/top-officials-elections-most-secure-66f9361084ccbc461e3bbf42861057a5.

18. Donald J. Trump, "Donald J. Trump on Twitter: 'The Recent Statement by Chris Krebs on T . . .' [Tweet]," Archive.is, November 2020, http://archive.is/1gN5x.

19. See, among others, Sharad Goel et al., "One Person, One Vote: Estimating the Prevalence of Double Voting in U.S. Presidential Elections," *American Political Science Review* 114, no. 2 (2020): 456–469, doi:https://doi.org/10.1017/S00030 5541900087X; Cottrell, Herron, and Westwood, "An Exploration of Donald Trump's Allegations of Massive Voter Fraud in the 2016 General Election."

20. Nick Corasaniti, Reid J. Epstein, and Jim Rutenberg, "The Times Called Officials in Every State: No Evidence of Voter Fraud," *New York Times*, November 10, 2020, https://www.nytimes.com/2020/11/10/us/politics/voting-fraud.html.

21. Reid J. Epstein, "Michigan Republicans Debunk Voter Fraud Claims in Unsparing Report," *New York Times*, June 23, 2021, https://www.nytimes.com/2021/06/23/us/politics/michigan-2020-election.html.

22. Andrew C. Eggers, Haritz Garro, and Justin Grimmer, "No Evidence for Systematic Voter Fraud: A Guide to Statistical Claims About the 2020 Election," *Proceedings of the National Academy of Sciences* 118, no. 45 (2021): e2103619118, doi:10.1073/pnas.2103619118.

23. Jaclyn Peiser, "Pennsylvania Man Admits He Voted for Trump with His Dead Mom's Name: 'I Listened to Too Much Propaganda,'" *Washington Post*, May 4, 2021, https://www.washingtonpost.com/nation/2021/05/04/pennsylvania-bruce-bartman-voter-fraud/.

24. "Four Seasons Total Landscaping Press Conference—Long Version," YouTube, posted by AP Archive, November 17, 2020, https://www.youtube.com/watch?v=7QTRO9MG6z8.

25. Rem Rieder, "Trump Tweets Conspiracy Theory About Deleted Votes," FactCheck.org, November 13, 2020, https://www.factcheck.org/2020/11/trump-tweets-con spiracy-theory-about-deleted-votes/.

26. Alison Durkee, "Dominion Sues Newsmax, OANN and Ex-Overstock CEO Byrne in New Defamation Suits over Election Conspiracy Theory," *Forbes*, August 10, 2021, https://www.forbes.com/sites/alisondurkee/2021/08/10/dominion-sues-newsmax-oann-and-ex-overstock-ceo-byrne-in-new-defamation-suits-over-election-conspiracy-theory/.

27. Casey Tolan, Curt Devine, and Drew Griffin, "MyPillow Magnate Mike Lindell's Latest Election Conspiracy Theory Is His Most Bizarre Yet," CNN, August 5, 2021, https://www.cnn.com/2021/08/05/politics/mike-lindell-mypillow-ceo-election-claims-invs/index.html.

28. Phil Goldstein, "How State and Local Governments Kept the 2020 Election Secure," *StateTech*, November 11, 2020, https://statetechmagazine.com/article/2020/11/how-state-and-local-governments-kept-2020-election-secure.

29. For an exploration of the role of Russian hackers and trolls in the 2016 election, see Kathleen Hall Jamieson, *Cyberwar: How Russian Hackers and Trolls Helped Elect a President: What We Don't, Can't, and Do Know* (New York: Oxford University Press, 2018), https://www.amazon.com/Cyberwar-Russian-Hackers-Trolls-President/dp/0190915811.

30. Michael T. McCaul, "Cybersecurity and Infrastructure Security Agency Act of 2018," H.R. 3359, 2018, https://www.congress.gov/bill/115th-congress/house-bill/3359.

31. Chris Krebs, @CISAKrebs, "Seeing #disinfo that some isolated voting day issues are tied to some nefarious election hacking and vote manipulation operation. Don't fall for it and think twice before sharing! Check out Rumor Control for more info on the security safeguards built into elections. #Protect2020," Twitter, November 7, 2020, 3:50 PM, https://twitter.com/CISAKrebs/status/1325178780722196480.

32. Chris Krebs, @CISAKrebs, "To be crystal clear on ⬇, I'm specifically referring to the Hammer and Scorecard nonsense. It's just that—nonsense. This is not a real thing, don't fall for it and think 2x before you share. #Protect2020," Twitter, November 7, 2020, 4:29 PM, https://twitter.com/CISAKrebs/status/1325188644966117376.

33. Kathleen Hall Jamieson, "How Conspiracists Exploited COVID-19 Science," *Nature Human Behaviour* 5, no. 11 (November 2021): 1464–1465, doi:10.1038/s41562-021-01217-2.

34. William Barr, "Office of the Attorney General to President Donald J. Trump," December 14, 2020, https://int.nyt.com/data/documenttools/attorney-general-william-barr-resignation-letter/b82836cf0fe20bf8/full.pdf.

35. Stephen Fowler, "'This Was a Scam': In Recorded Call, Trump Pushed Official to Overturn Georgia Vote," NPR, January 3, 2021, https://www.npr.org/2021/01/03/953012128/this-was-a-scam-in-recorded-call-trump-pushed-official-to-overturn-georgia-vote.

36. Carol Leonnig and Philip Rucker, *I Alone Can Fix It: Donald J. Trump's Catastrophic Final Year* (New York: Penguin, 2021), esp. chap. 20.

37. "Capitol Hill Siege," Program on Extremism, George Washington University, 2022, https://extremism.gwu.edu/Capitol-Hill-Cases.

38. Julia Jacobo, "This Is What Trump Told Supporters Before Many Stormed Capitol Hill," ABC News, January 7, 2021, https://abcnews.go.com/Politics/trump-told-supporters-stormed-capitol-hill/story?id=75110558.

39. Calvin Woodward, "AP Fact Check: Trump's Call to Action Distorted in Debate," Associated Press, January 13, 2021, https://apnews.com/article/fact-check-trump-us-capitol-remarks-221518bc174f9bc3dd6e108e653ed08d.

40. Robert A. Pape and Keven Ruby, "The Face of American Insurrection: Right-Wing Organizations Evolving into a Violent Mass Movement," University of Chicago, Division of the Social Sciences, January 2021, https://d3qi0qp55mx5f5.cloudfront.

net/cpost/i/docs/americas_insurrectionists_online_2021_01_29.pdf?mtime=161
1966204.

41. Michael S. Schmidt, "Trump Says Pence Can Overturn His Loss in Congress. That's Not How It Works," *New York Times*, January 5, 2021, https://www.nytimes. com/2021/01/05/us/politics/pence-trump-election.html.

42. *United States of America vs. Dawn Bancroft and Diana Santos-Smith*, No. 1:21-mj-00182, United States District Court for the District of Columbia, January 28, 2021.

43. Zolan Kanno-Youngs, "F.B.I. Director Warns of Russian Interference and White Supremacist Violence," *New York Times*, September 17, 2020, https://www.nyti mes.com/2020/09/17/us/politics/fbi-russia.html.

44. "Proud Boys," Southern Poverty Law Center, 2021, https://www.splcenter.org/ fighting-hate/extremist-files/group/proud-boys.

45. "First 2020 Presidential Debate Between Donald Trump and Joe Biden," YouTube, posted by C-SPAN, September 29, 2020, https://www.youtube.com/watch?v= wW1lY5jFNcQ.

46. Ben Collins and Brandy Zadrozny, "Proud Boys Say They Are 'Standing Down and Standing By' After Trump's Debate Callout," NBC News, last updated September 30, 2020, https://www.nbcnews.com/tech/tech-news/proud-boys-celebrate-after- trump-s-debate-call-out-n1241512.

47. Pape and Ruby, "The Face of American Insurrection."

48. Tim Sullivan and Adam Geller, "Increasingly Normal: Guns Seen Outside Vote-Counting Centers," Associated Press, November 7, 2020, https://apnews.com/arti cle/protests-vote-count-safety-concerns-653dc8f0787c9258524078548d518992.

49. Sullivan and Geller, "Increasingly Normal."

50. Tony Romm, Isaac Stanley-Becker, and Elizabeth Dwoskin, "Facebook Bans 'STOP THE STEAL' Group Trump Allies Were Using to Organize Protests Against Vote Counting," *Washington Post*, November 5, 2020, https://www.washingtonpost. com/technology/2020/11/05/facebook-trump-protests/.

51. Shannon Bond and Bobby Allyn, "How the 'Stop the Steal' Movement Outwitted Facebook Ahead of the Jan. 6 Insurrection," NPR, October 22, 2021, https://www. npr.org/2021/10/22/1048543513/facebook-groups-jan-6-insurrection.

52. Romm, Stanley-Becker, and Dwoskin, "Facebook Bans 'STOP THE STEAL' Group Trump Allies Were Using to Organize Protests against Vote Counting."

53. Benjamin Fearnow, "Michigan Secretary of State's Home Surrounded by Election Protesters Shouting Obscenities," *Newsweek*, December 7, 2020, https://www. newsweek.com/michigan-secretary-states-home-surrounded-election-protesters- shouting-obscenities-1552875.

54. Brakkton Booker, "Michigan AG Investigating Threats Made Against Wayne County Election Officials," NPR, November 24, 2020, https://www.npr.org/secti ons/biden-transition-updates/2020/11/24/938550750/michigan-ag-investigating- threats-made-against-wayne-county-election-officials.

55. Pat Ralph, "Philly Election Officials Received Death Threats over Ballot Counting, City Commissioner Says," Philly Voice, November 9, 2020, https://www.phillyvo ice.com/philadelphia-city-commissioners-al-schmidt-pennsylvania-60-minutes-interview-cbs/.

56. Virginia Chamlee, "Election Officials Detail Death Threats Received After Trump Loss," *People*, October 27, 2021, https://people.com/politics/top-election-officials-detail-death-threats-received-after-trump-election-loss/.

57. Lauren Aratani, "Donald Trump Releases Video Statement Repeating Baseless Vote Fraud Claims," *Guardian*, December 2, 2020, https://www.theguardian.com/us-news/2020/dec/02/donald-trump-video-statement-baseless-vote-fraud-claims.

58. Bill McCarthy, "No Evidence for Viral Claim That '22 Million Illegal Aliens' Are 'Voting Illegally,'" Politifact, July 27, 2021, https://www.politifact.com/factchecks/2021/jul/27/facebook-posts/no-evidence-viral-claim-22-million-illegal-aliens-/.

59. Sanford, "Donald Trump & Joe Biden 1st Presidential Debate Transcript 2020."

60. Jane C. Timm, "Fact Check: Trump's Bogus Claim of More Votes in Detroit than People," NBC News, November 18, 2020, https://www.nbcnews.com/polit ics/2020-election/fact-check-trump-s-bogus-claim-more-votes-detroit-people-n1248121.

61. Tali Mendelberg, *The Race Card* (Princeton, NJ: Princeton University Press, 2001), https://press.princeton.edu/books/paperback/9780691070711/the-race-card.

62. Antoine J. Banks and Melissa A. Bell, "Racialized Campaign Ads: The Emotional Content in Implicit Racial Appeals Primes White Racial Attitudes," *Public Opinion Quarterly* 77, no. 2 (Summer 2013): 549–560, doi:10.1093/poq/nft010.

63. Claire Sanford, "Donald Trump Des Moines, Iowa Rally Speech Transcript October 9," Rev, October 9, 2021, https://www.rev.com/blog/transcripts/donald-trump-des-moines-iowa-rally-speech-transcript-october-9.

64. Khalil Gibran Muhammad, *The Condemnation of Blackness: Race, Crime, and the Making of Modern Urban America* (Cambridge, MA: Harvard University Press, 2019), https://www.hup.harvard.edu/catalog.php?isbn=9780674238145.

65. Haaretz and Associated Press, "Gingrich Pushes 'Soros Stole the Election' Conspiracy Theory on Fox News," *Haaretz*, November 9, 2020, https://www.haar etz.com/jewish/gingrich-soros-election-fox-news-1.9297734.

66. Reuters Staff, "Fact Check: George Soros Has Not Been Arrested for 'Election Interference,'" Reuters, November 27, 2020, https://www.reuters.com/article/uk-factcheck-soros-not-arrested-idUSKBN2872B6.

67. Dylan Stableford, "Giuliani, Flailing, Says Venezuela, Clinton and Soros Hatched 'Centralized Plan' to Steal Election for Biden," Yahoo!, November 19, 2020, https://www.yahoo.com/now/giuliani-flailing-says-venezuela-clinton-and-soros-hatched-centralized-plan-to-steal-election-for-biden-202122663.html.

68. Ali Swenson, "AP Fact Check: Trump Legal Team's Batch of False Vote Claims," Associated Press, November 19, 2020, https://apnews.com/article/fact-check-trump-legal-team-false-claims-5abd64917ef8be9e9e2078180973e8b3.

69. Chelsey Cox, "Fact Check: Claim That Voting Noncitizens Affected 2020 Election Outcome Is Unverified," *USA Today*, November 19, 2020, https://www.usatoday.com/story/news/factcheck/2020/11/19/fact-check-claim-voting-noncitizens-2020-election-unverified/6237115002/.

70. Brian Naylor, "Read Trump's Jan. 6 Speech, a Key Part of Impeachment Trial," NPR, February 10, 2021, https://www.npr.org/2021/02/10/966396848/read-trumps-jan-6-speech-a-key-part-of-impeachment-trial.

71. Daniel Dayan and Elihu Katz, *Media Events: The Live Broadcasting of History* (Cambridge, MA: Harvard University Press, 1994), https://www.hup.harvard.edu/catalog.php?isbn=9780674559561.

72. Matthew Rosenberg, Jim Rutenberg, and Michael M. Grynbaum, "The Next Big Lies: Jan. 6 Was No Big Deal, or a Left-Wing Plot," *New York Times*, January 6, 2022, https://www.nytimes.com/2022/01/06/us/politics/jan-6-lies.html.

73. Michael M. Grynbaum, Davey Alba, and Reid J. Epstein, "How Pro-Trump Forces Pushed a Lie About Antifa at the Capitol Riot," *New York Times*, March 1, 2021, https://www.nytimes.com/2021/03/01/us/politics/antifa-conspiracy-capitol-riot.html.

74. Bill McCarthy, "How Fox News Hosts' Jan 6 Texts, On-Air Comments Told Different Stories of Attack," Politifact, December 16, 2021, https://www.politifact.com/article/2021/dec/16/how-fox-news-hosts-jan-6-texts-air-comments-told-d/.

75. Phillip Bump, "Trumpland Has a New Favorite Jan. 6 Conspiracy Theory," *Washington Post*, December 23, 2021, http://www.washingtonpost.com/politics/2021/12/23/trumpland-has-new-favorite-jan-6-conspiracy-theory/.

76. Colby Itkowitz, "'Normal Tourist Visit': Republicans Recast Deadly Jan. 6 Attack by Pro-Trump Mob," *Washington Post*, May 12, 2021, http://www.washingtonpost.com/politics/trump-riot-capitol-republicans/2021/05/12/dcc03342-b351-11eb-a980-a60af976ed44_story.html.

77. Frank E. Lockwood, "6 GOP Lawmakers Lament Treatment of Jan. 6 Suspects," *Arkansas Democrat Gazette*, July 28, 2021, https://www.arkansasonline.com/news/2021/jul/28/6-gop-lawmakers-lament-treatment-of-jan-6-suspects/.

78. Alan Feuer, "Debunking the Pro-Trump Right's Claims About the Jan. 6 Riot," *New York Times*, September 17, 2021, https://www.nytimes.com/2021/09/17/us/politics/capitol-riot-pro-trump-claims.html.

79. Alanna Durkin Richer, Michael Kunzelman, and Jacques Billeaud, "Records Rebut Claims of Unequal Treatment of Jan. 6 Rioters," Associated Press, August 30, 2021, https://apnews.com/article/records-rebut-claims-jan-6-rioters-55adf4d46aff57b91af2fdd3345dace8.

80. Aaron Morrison, "Race Double Standard Clear in Rioters' Capitol Insurrection," Associated Press, January 7, 2021, https://apnews.com/article/congress-storming-black-lives-matter-22983dc91d16bf949efbb60cdda4495d.

81. David Folkenflik, "Tucker Carlson's Capitol Insurrection Series Promotes Disproved Conspiracy Theories," NPR, November 2, 2021, https://www.npr.org/

2021/11/02/1051577596/tucker-carlsons-capitol-insurrection-series-promotes-disproved-conspiracy-theori.

82. Stephen Battaglio, "Fox Nation Streams Tucker Carlson Doc Pushing Conspiracy Theory That Government Agents Spurred Insurrection," *Los Angeles Times*, November 1, 2021, https://www.latimes.com/entertainment-arts/business/story/2021-11-01/tucker-carlson-documentary-suggest-jan-6-insurrection-was-manipulated-by-the-government.

83. Scott Pelley, "Whistleblower: Facebook Is Misleading the Public on Progress Against Hate Speech, Violence, Misinformation," CBS News, October 3, 2021, https://www.cbsnews.com/news/facebook-whistleblower-frances-haugen-misinformation-public-60-minutes-2021-10-03/.

84. Julia Carrie Wong, "Facebook Removes Pro-Trump Stop the Steal Group over 'Calls for Violence,'" *Guardian*, November 5, 2020, https://www.theguardian.com/us-news/2020/nov/05/facebook-trump-stop-the-steal-group-removed.

85. Wong, "Facebook Removes Pro-Trump Stop the Steal Group over 'Calls for Violence.'"

86. Craig Silverman, Ryan Mac, and Jane Lytvynenko, "Facebook Knows It Was Used to Help Incite the Capitol Insurrection," BuzzFeed News, April 22, 2021, https://www.buzzfeednews.com/article/craigsilverman/facebook-failed-stop-the-steal-insurrection.

87. Silverman, Mac, and Lytvynenko, "Facebook Knows It Was Used to Help Incite the Capitol Insurrection."

88. Guy Rosen and Monika Bickert, "Our Response to the Violence in Washington," Facebook press release, last updated January 7, 2021, https://about.fb.com/news/2021/01/responding-to-the-violence-in-washington-dc/.

89. Rosen and Bickert, "Our Response to the Violence in Washington."

90. Rosen and Bickert, "Our Response to the Violence in Washington."

91. "Letter to Twitter," Select Committee to Investigate the January 6th Attack on the United States Capitol, January 13, 2022, https://january6th.house.gov/sites/democrats.january6th.house.gov/files/2022-1-13.BGT%20Letter%20to%20Twitter%20-%20Cover%20Letter%20and%20Schedule_Redacted.pdf.

92. "Letter to Alphabet," Select Committee to Investigate the January 6th Attack on the United States Capitol, January 13, 2022, https://january6th.house.gov/sites/democrats.january6th.house.gov/files/2022-1-13.BGT%20Letter%20to%20Alphabet%20-%20Cover%20Letter%20and%20Schedule_Redacted.pdf.

93. Jamie Corey, "Republican Attorneys General Dark Money Group Organized Protest Preceding Capitol Mob Attack," Documented, January 7, 2021, https://documented.net/2021/01/republican-attorneys-general-dark-money-group-organized-protest-preceding-capitol-mob-attack/.

94. Grand Jury Sworn In on January 8, 2021, *United States of America vs. Elmer Stewart Rhodes III*, United States District Court for the District of Columbia, January 12, 2022.

CHAPTER 9.2

1. Joshua D. Clinton et al., "Trumped by Trump? Public Support for Mail Voting in Response to the COVID-19 Pandemic," *Election Law Journal: Rules, Politics, and Policy* 21, no. 1 (September 2021): 15, doi:10.1089/elj.2020.0671.

2. Shaun Bowler et al., *Losers' Consent: Elections and Democratic Legitimacy* (Oxford: Oxford University Press, 2007); Andrew M. Daniller and Diana C. Mutz, "The Dynamics of Electoral Integrity: A Three-Election Panel Study," *Public Opinion Quarterly* 83, no. 1 (May 2019): 46–67, doi:10.1093/poq/nfz002.

3. Bowler et al., *Losers' Consent*; Daniller and Mutz, "The Dynamics of Electoral Integrity."

4. It is very likely that the gaps in confidence are larger in this election than in earlier elections. See Robert Griffin and Mayesha Quasem, "Crisis of Confidence: How Election 2020 Was Different," Democracy Fund Voter Study Group, June 2021, https://www.voterstudygroup.org/uploads/reports/Final-Reports/Crisis-of-Confidence_June2021.pdf. Because our data cover only the 2020 election, however, we cannot compare to earlier years.

5. Bowler et al., *Losers' Consent*.

6. Miles Parks, "Trump, While Attacking Mail Voting, Casts Mail Ballot Again," NPR, August 19, 2020, https://www.npr.org/2020/08/19/903886567/trump-while-attacking-mail-voting-casts-mail-ballot-again.

7. Skyler Swisher, "No Longer a 'Flori-Duh' Laughingstock: How Florida's Vote Came In So Fast," *Sun Sentinel*, November 5, 2020, https://www.sun-sentinel.com/news/politics/elections/fl-ne-election-2020-florida-fast-vote-reporting-20201105-4vecbsq2tffkfpzd25avu3zz4i-story.html.

8. Edward B. Foley and Charles Stewart III, "Explaining the Blue Shift in Election Canvassing," SSRN Scholarly Paper, Social Science Research Network, March 2020, doi:10.2139/ssrn.3547734.

9. Marshall Cohen, "'Things Could Get Very Ugly': Experts Fear Post-Election Crisis as Trump Sets the Stage to Dispute the Results in November," CNN, July 20, 2020, https://www.cnn.com/2020/07/20/politics/disputed-election-crisis-trump/index.html; Jonathan Lai, "How Does a Republican Lead on Election Night and Still Lose Pennsylvania? It's Called the 'Blue Shift,'" *Philadelphia Inquirer*, January 27, 2020, https://www.inquirer.com/politics/election/pennsylvania-2020-election-blue-shift-20200127.html.

10. Aamer Madhani and Kevin Freking, "In Video, Trump Recycles Unsubstantiated Voter Fraud Claims," Associated Press, December 2, 2020, https://apnews.com/article/joe-biden-donald-trump-media-social-media-elections-71d5469ac0bbccbfe601528a2517b239.

11. Madhani and Freking, "In Video, Trump Recycles Unsubstantiated Voter Fraud Claims."

12. Emily Previti, "State Election Officials Urge Swift Legislative Action on Voting Reforms," Penn Live, August 4, 2020, https://www.pennlive.com/news/2020/08/state-election-officials-urge-swift-legislative-action-on-voting-reforms.html.

13. Cynthia Fernandez, "The Months-Long Political Saga That Guaranteed a Long Vote Count in Pennsylvania," *Philadelphia Inquirer*, November 4, 2020, https://www.inquirer.com/politics/election/spl/pennsylvania-election-2020-counting-results-delays-mail-ballots-20201104.html.

14. Brian F. Schaffner and Samantha Luks, "Misinformation or Expressive Responding? What an Inauguration Crowd Can Tell Us About the Source of Political Misinformation in Surveys," *Public Opinion Quarterly* 82, no. 1 (March 2018): 135–147, doi:10.1093/poq/nfx042.

15. Adam J. Berinsky, "Telling the Truth About Believing the Lies? Evidence for the Limited Prevalence of Expressive Survey Responding," *Journal of Politics* 80, no. 1 (January 2018): 211–224, doi:10.1086/694258; Ariel Malka and Mark Adelman, "Expressive Survey Responding: A Closer Look at the Evidence and Its Implications for American Democracy," PsyArXiv, December 2021, doi:10.31234/osf.io/nzy9e.

16. Gabriel Abraham Almond and Sidney Verba, *The Civic Culture: Political Attitudes and Democracy in Five Nations* (Princeton, NJ: Princeton University Press, 2016), https://press.princeton.edu/books/hardcover/9780691651682/the-civic-culture; Pippa Norris, *Democratic Deficit: Critical Citizens Revisited* (Cambridge, UK: Cambridge University Press, 2011), doi:10.1017/CBO9780511973383.

17. Bill Keveney and Maria Puente, "How Conservative Media Stoked Baseless Election-Fraud Claims That Motivated DC Rioters," *USA Today*, January 11, 2021, https://www.usatoday.com/story/entertainment/tv/2021/01/11/dc-riots-how-newsmax-oan-conservative-outlets-fueled-mob/6589298002/.

18. Mark Jurkowtiz, Amy Mitchell, Elsas Shearer, and Mason Walker, "U.S. Media Polarization and the 2020 Election: A Nation Divided," Pew Research Center Report, January 24, 2020, https://www.pewresearch.org/journalism/2020/01/24/u-s-media-polarization-and-the-2020-election-a-nation-divided/.

19. Andrew Guess, "(Almost) Everything in Moderation: New Evidence on Americans' Online Media Diets," *American Journal of Political Science* 65, no. 4 (October 2021): 1007–1022.

20. Larry Bartels, "Ethnic Antagonism Erodes Republicans' Commitment to Democracy," *Proceedings of the National Academy of Sciences* 117, no. 37 (September 15, 2020): 22752–22759.

21. Bartels, "Ethnic Antagonism Erodes Republicans' Commitment to Democracy."

22. John Gramlich, "A Look Back at Americans' Reactions to the Jan. 6 Riot at the U.S. Capitol," Pew Research Center, January 4, 2022, https://www.pewresearch.org/fact-tank/2022/01/04/a-look-back-at-americans-reactions-to-the-jan-6-riot-at-the-u-s-capitol/.

23. Betsy Woodruff Swan, "DHS Draft Document: White Supremacists Are Greatest Terror Threat," *Politico*, September 2020, https://www.politico.com/news/2020/09/04/white-supremacists-terror-threat-dhs-409236.

24. See, e.g., Michael Kenney and Colin Clarke, "What Antifa Is, What It Isn't, and Why It Matters," War on the Rocks, June 23, 2020, http://warontherocks.com/2020/06/what-antifa-is-what-it-isnt-and-why-it-matters/.

CHAPTER 10

1. Katie Benner, "Trump Pressed Justice Dept. to Declare Election Results Corrupt, Notes Show," *New York Times*, July 30, 2021, https://www.nytimes.com/2021/07/30/us/politics/trump-justice-department-election.html.

2. National Public Radio, Transcript of the House Jan. 6 Committee Hearing, June 28, https://www.npr.org/2022/06/28/1108396692/jan-6-committee-hearing-transcript/.

3. Scott MacFarlane, @MacFarlaneNews, "Trump tonight: 'Mike Pence did have the right to change the outcome,'" Twitter, January 30, 2022, 7:05 PM, https://mobile.twitter.com/MacFarlaneNews/status/1487940101816864769.

4. Donald J. Trump, "Videotaped Remarks on the Attack on the United States Capitol, the Certification of the Electoral College Results, and the Transition to a New Administration," The American Presidency Project, January 7, 2021, https://www.presidency.ucsb.edu/documents/videotaped-remarks-the-attack-the-united-states-capitol-the-certification-the-electoral.

5. Dan Balz, "This Was the Week When Trump Revealed All," *Washington Post*, February 5, 2022, https://www.washingtonpost.com/politics/2022/02/05/sundaytake-trump-jan6-election/.

6. Lynn Vavreck, *The Message Matters: The Economy and Presidential Campaigns* (Princeton, NJ: Princeton University Press, 2009).

7. Jonathan Allen and Amie Parnes, *Lucky: How Joe Biden Barely Won the Presidency* (New York: Crown, 2021).

8. Carol Leonnig and Philip Rucker, *I Alone Can Fix It: Donald J. Trump's Catastrophic Final Year* (New York: Penguin, 2021).

9. Marc Fisher, "Donald Trump: 'I Am the Least Racist Person,'" *Washington Post*, June 10, 2016, http://www.washingtonpost.com/politics/donald-trump-i-am-the-least-racist-person/2016/06/10/eac7874c-2f3a-11e6-9de3-6e6e7a14000c_story.html.

10. Josh Dawsey, "Trump Derides Protections for Immigrants from 'Shithole' Countries," *Washington Post*, January 11, 2018, http://www.washingtonpost.com/politics/trump-attacks-protections-for-immigrants-from-shithole-countries-in-oval-office-meeting/2018/01/11/bfc0725c-f711-11e7-91af-31ac729add94_story.html.

11. Benjamin Swasey, "Trump Retweets Video of Apparent Supporter Saying 'White Power,'" NPR, June 28, 2020, https://www.npr.org/sections/live-updates-prote

sts-for-racial-justice/2020/06/28/884392576/trump-retweets-video-of-apparent-supporter-saying-white-power.

12. Brent Kendall, "Trump Says Judge's Mexican Heritage Presents 'Absolute Conflict,'" *Wall Street Journal*, last updated June 3, 2016, https://www.wsj.com/articles/don ald-trump-keeps-up-attacks-on-judge-gonzalo-curiel-1464911442.

13. Niraj Chokshi, "Trump Accuses Clinton of Guiding Global Elite Against U.S. Working Class," *New York Times*, October 14, 2016, https://www.nytimes.com/ 2016/10/14/us/politics/trump-comments-linked-to-antisemitism.html.

14. Bianca Quilantan and David Cohen, "Trump Tells Dem Congresswomen: Go Back Where You Came From," *Politico*, July 14, 2019, https://www.politico.com/ story/2019/07/14/trump-congress-go-back-where-they-came-from-1415692.

15. Eric Bradner, Sarah Mucha, and Arlette Saenz, "Biden: 'If You Have a Problem Figuring Out Whether You're for Me or Trump, Then You Ain't Black,'" CNN, May 22, 2020, https://www.cnn.com/2020/05/22/politics/biden-charlamagne-tha-god-you-aint-black/index.html.

16. Glenn Thrush, "President Biden's Full Inauguration Speech, Annotated," *New York Times*, January 20, 2021, https://www.nytimes.com/2021/01/20/us/politics/ biden-inauguration-speech-transcript.html.

17. Chloe Foussianes, "Amanda Gorman's Poem Stole the Show at the Inauguration. Read It Again Here," *Town and Country*, January 21, 2021, https://www.townan dcountrymag.com/society/politics/a35279603/amanda-gorman-inauguration-poem-the-hill-we-climb-transcript/.

18. Sarah Mucha and Jeff Zeleny, "Michelle Obama Releases Closing Campaign Message Calling Trump's Actions 'Morally Wrong' and 'Racist,'" CNN, October 6, 2020, https://www.cnn.com/2020/10/06/politics/michelle-obama-vote-joe-biden-closing-message/index.html.

19. Samuel P. Huntington, *American Politics: The Promise of Disharmony* (Cambridge, MA: Harvard University Press, 1983), https://www.hup.harvard.edu/catalog. php?isbn=9780674030213.

20. Rogers M. Smith, *Civics Ideals: Conflicting Visions of Citizenship in U.S. History* (New Haven, CT: Yale University Press, 1999), https://yalebooks.yale.edu/book/ 9780300078770/civic-ideals.

21. William O. Douglas, *Points of Rebellion* (New York: Random House, 1970).

22. Alan Feuer, "Oath Keepers Leader Sought to Ask Trump to Unleash His Militia," *New York Times*, May 4, 2022, https://www.nytimes.com/2022/05/04/us/polit ics/oath-keepers-jan-6-riot.html.

23. Jordan Williams, "Trump Told McCarthy That Rioters 'More Upset About the Election than You Are,'" *The Hill*, February 12, 2021, https://thehill.com/homen ews/house/538714-trump-told-mccarthy-that-rioters-more-upset-about-the-elect ion-than-you-are.

24. Kevin Liptak, "Trump's Presidency Ends with American Carnage," CNN, January 6, 2021, https://www.cnn.com/2021/01/06/politics/donald-trump-capitol-mob/index.html.

25. Alana Wise, "Trump Condemns Capitol Hill Violence, Ignores His Role in Inciting the Mob," NPR, January 7, 2021, https://www.npr.org/sections/insurrection-at-the-capitol/2021/01/07/954587997/white-house-condemns-violence-on-capitol-hill-without-addressing-trumps-role.

26. Colby Itkowitz, "Trump Falsely Claims Jan. 6 Rioters Were 'Hugging and Kissing' Police," *Washington Post*, March 26, 2021, https://www.washingtonpost.com/politics/trump-riot-capitol-police/2021/03/26/0ba7e844-8e40-11eb-9423-0407992 1c915_story.html.

27. Dan Mangan, "Trump Says of Capitol Rioters Who Sought to Overturn Biden's Win: 'What I Wanted Is What They Wanted,'" CNBC, July 19, 2021, https://www.cnbc.com/2021/07/19/trump-says-he-and-capitol-rioters-wanted-same-thing-overturning-biden-win.html.

28. Mangan, "Trump Says of Capitol Rioters Who Sought to Overturn Biden's Win: 'What I Wanted Is What They Wanted.'"

29. Laurie Roberts, "'How Many Elections Are They Going to Steal Before We Kill These People?,'" *Arizona Republic*, October 27, 2021, https://www.azcentral.com/story/opinion/op-ed/laurieroberts/2021/10/27/when-do-we-get-use-guns-tpusa-owns-and-others-too/8570812002/.

30. Clare Foran et al., "Most House Republicans Silent over Violent Marjorie Taylor Greene Comments as Democrats Condemn Them," CNN, January 27, 2021, https://www.cnn.com/2021/01/27/politics/marjorie-taylor-greene-comments-reaction/index.html.

31. Melissa Quinn, "House Votes to Censure Congressman Paul Gosar for Violent Video in Rare Formal Rebuke," CBS News, November 18, 2021, https://www.cbsnews.com/news/paul-gosar-censure-committees-house-aoc-video/.

32. Paul Kane, Marianna Sotomayor, and Jacqueline Alemany, "Fear, Anger and Trauma: How the Jan. 6 Attack Changed Congress," *Washington Post*, January 3, 2022, https://www-washingtonpost-com.proxy.library.upenn.edu/politics/2022/01/03/january-6-congress/ics/2022/01/03/january-6-congress/.

33. Catie Edmondson and Mark Walker, "One Menacing Call After Another: Threats Against Lawmakers Surge," *New York Times*, February 9, 2022, https://www.nytimes.com/2022/02/09/us/politics/politician-death-threats.html.

34. Lisa Lerer and Astead W. Herndon, "Menace Enters the Republican Mainstream," *New York Times*, November 12, 2021, https://www.nytimes.com/2021/11/12/us/politics/republican-violent-rhetoric.html.

35. Joan E. Greve, "'A Core Threat to Our Democracy': Threat of Political Violence Growing Across US," *Guardian*, November 27, 2021, https://www.theguardian.com/us-news/2021/nov/27/political-violence-threats-multiplying-us.

36. Brett Murphy and Letitia Stein, "How the CDC Failed Public Health Officials Fighting the Coronavirus," *USA Today*, January 16, 2021, https://www.usatoday.com/in-depth/news/investigations/2020/09/16/how-cdc-failed-local-health-officials-desperate-covid-help/3435762001/.

37. Dina Temple-Raston, "CDC Report: Officials Knew Coronavirus Test Was Flawed but Released It Anyway," NPR, November 6, 2020, https://www.npr.org/2020/11/06/929078678/cdc-report-officials-knew-coronavirus-test-was-flawed-but-released-it-anyway.

38. Laurie McGinley and Carolyn Y. Johnson, "FDA Pulls Emergency Approval for Antimalarial Drugs Touted by Trump as Covid-19 Treatment," *Washington Post*, June 15, 2020, https://www.washingtonpost.com/health/2020/06/15/hydroxychloroquine-authorization-revoked-coronavirus/.

39. Ashley Kirzinger et al., "KFF COVID-19 Vaccine Monitor: The Increasing Importance of Partisanship in Predicting COVID-19 Vaccination Status," Kaiser Family Foundation, November 16, 2021, https://www.kff.org/coronavirus-covid-19/poll-finding/importance-of-partisanship-predicting-vaccination-status/.

40. Melina Delkic, "Arkansas' Governor Says It 'Was an Error' to Ban Mask Mandates," *New York Times*, August 8, 2021, https://www.nytimes.com/2021/08/08/world/asa-hutchinson-arkansas-mask-mandate.html.

41. David Leonhardt, "U.S. Covid Deaths Get Even Redder," *New York Times*, November 8, 2021, https://www.nytimes.com/2021/11/08/briefing/covid-death-toll-red-america.html.

42. Shane Goldmacher, "G.O.P. Governors Fight Mandates as the Party's Covid Politics Harden," *New York Times*, August 31, 2021, https://www.nytimes.com/2021/08/31/us/politics/republican-governors-covid-19.html.

43. Julia Harte and Sharon Bernstein, "Some U.S. Hospitals Forced to Ration Care amid Staffing Shortages, COVID-19 Surge," Reuters, September 17, 2021, https://www.reuters.com/world/us/some-us-hospitals-forced-ration-care-amid-staffing-shortages-covid-19-surge-2021-09-17/.

44. Patricia Mazzei, "As G.O.P. Fights Mask and Vaccine Mandates, Florida Takes the Lead," *New York Times*, November 17, 2021, https://www.nytimes.com/2021/11/17/us/florida-coronavirus-covid-19.html.

45. Sheryl Gay Stolberg, "Republicans, Wooing Trump Voters, Make Fauci Their Boogeyman," *New York Times*, February 7, 2022, https://www.nytimes.com/2022/02/07/us/politics/fauci-republicans-trump.html.

46. Harry Enten, "Flu Shots Uptake Is Now Partisan. It Didn't Use to Be," CNN, November 14, 2021, https://www.cnn.com/2021/11/14/politics/flu-partisan-divide-analysis/index.html.

47. David Schwartz and Nathan Layne, "'Truth Is Truth': Trump Dealt Blow as Republican-Led Arizona Audit Reaffirms Biden Win," Reuters, September 24, 2021, https://www.reuters.com/world/us/arizona-republicans-release-findings-widely-panned-election-audit-2021-09-24/.

48. CNN, "READ: Trump Lawyer's Memo on Six-Step Plan for Pence to Overturn the Election," CNN, September 21, 2021, https://www.cnn.com/2021/09/21/polit ics/read-eastman-memo/index.html.

49. "Transcript of David Frost's Interview with Richard Nixon," edited by Jeremy D. Bailey, 1977, Teaching American History, accessed 2021, https://teachingamer icanhistory.org/document/transcript-of-david-frosts-interview-with-richard-nixon/.

50. Ryan Taylor, "Donald Trump Speech Transcript at North Carolina GOP Convention Dinner June 5," Rev, June 5, 2021, https://www.rev.com/blog/tran scripts/donald-trump-speech-transcript-at-north-carolina-gop-convention-din ner-june-5.

51. CBS Evening News, @CBSEveningNews, "'If this election were overturned by mere allegations from the losing side,' Sen. Mitch McConnell says, 'our democ-racy would enter a death spiral. We'd never see the whole nation accept an election again. Every four years, there'd be a scramble for power at any cost,'" January 6, 2021, 1:48 PM, https://twitter.com/CBSEveningNews/status/1346891518825668608.

52. Barbara Sprunt, "GOP Ousts Cheney from Leadership over Her Criticism of Trump," NPR, May 12, 2021, https://www.npr.org/2021/05/12/995072539/gop-poised-to-oust-cheney-from-leadership-over-her-criticism-of-trump.

53. "Wyoming GOP Votes to Stop Recognizing Cheney as a Republican," Associated Press, November 15, 2021, https://apnews.com/article/donald-trump-liz-cheney-wyoming-casper-1966d793df2baa85e0fecad4026b0e99.

54. Jonathan Weisman and Reid Epstein, "G.O.P Declares Jan. 6 Attack 'Legitimate Political Discourse,'" *New York Times*, February 4, 2022, https://www.nytimes.com/2022/02/04/us/politics/republicans-jan-6-cheney-censure.html.

55. Ken Bredemeier, "Of 10 Republicans Who Voted to Impeach Trump After Capitol Riot, Only 2 Might Remain in Congress," *VOA News*, August 17, 2022, https://www.voanews.com/a/republicans-voted-to-impeach-trump-after-capitol-riot-but-only-2-will-remain-in-congress-/6705694.html.

56. Editorial Board, "Trump Loses Arizona—Again," *Wall Street Journal*, September 25, 2021, https://www.wsj.com/articles/donald-trump-loses-arizona-again-maric opa-county-recount-2020-election-11632604370.

57. Riley Snyder, "Nevada Republicans Vote to Censure SOS Cegavske over Voter Fraud Allegations," *Nevada Independent*, April 10, 2021, https://thenevadainde pendent.com/article/nevada-republicans-vote-to-censure-sos-cegavske-over-voter-fraud-allegations.

58. Samuel Dodge, "Gov. Whitmer Replaces GOP Canvasser Who Certified Election with Conservative Activist," M Live, January 19, 2021, https://www.mlive.com/public-interest/2021/01/gov-whitmer-replaces-gop-canvasser-who-certified-election-with-conservative-activist.html; NPR, "Republicans in Michigan Have Replaced Election Officials Who Certified Biden's Win," May 4, 2022, https://

www.npr.org/2022/05/04/1096641003/republicans-in-michigan-have-replaced-election-officials-who-certified-bidens-wi?t=1652161467900.

59. Isaac Arnsdorf et al., "Heeding Steve Bannon's Call, Election Deniers Organize to Seize Control of the GOP—and Reshape America's Elections," ProPublica, September 2, 2021, https://www.propublica.org/article/heeding-steve-bannons-call-election-deniers-organize-to-seize-control-of-the-gop-and-reshape-americas-elections.

60. Tim Reid, Nathan Layne, and Jason Lange, "Special Report: Backers of Trump's False Fraud Claims Seek to Control Next Elections," Reuters, September 22, 2021, https://www.reuters.com/world/us/backers-trumps-false-fraud-claims-seek-control-next-us-elections-2021-09-22/.

61. Andrew Seidman, "A Pa. Town's 'Election Integrity Law' Shows How Trump's Lies Can Hijack Local Politics and Government," *Philadelphia Inquirer*, August 15, 2021, https://www.inquirer.com/politics/pennsylvania/voter-fraud-gop-lehigh-northampton-pennsylvania-election-20210815.html.

62. Eric Beech, "Republican Congressman Who Voted to Impeach Trump Won't Seek Re-Election," Reuters, September 17, 2021, https://www.reuters.com/world/us/republican-congressman-who-voted-impeach-trump-wont-seek-re-election-2021-09-17/.

63. Ally Mutnick, Olivia Beavers, and Quint Forgey, "Kinzinger Retiring from Congress, Vows 'Broader Fight Nationwide' Against Trumpism," *Politico*, October 29, 2021, https://www.politico.com/news/2021/10/29/rep-adam-kinzinger-wont-seek-reelection-next-year-517599.

64. Max Greenwood, "Trump Touts Kinzinger's Retirement: '2 Down, 8 to Go,'" *The Hill*, October 29, 2021, https://thehill.com/homenews/campaign/579115-trump-touts-kinzingers-retirement-2-down-8-to-go.

65. Alan Feuer, Maggie Haberman, Michael Schmidt, and Luke Broadwater, "Trump Had Role in Weighing Proposals to Seize Voting Machines," *New York Times*, January 31, 2022, https://www.nytimes.com/2022/01/31/us/politics/donald-trump-election-results-fraud-voting-machines.html.

66. Alexander Bolton, "No. 2 Senate Republican Praises Election Official for Standing Up to Trump," *The Hill*, February 1, 2022, https://thehill.com/homenews/senate/592349-no-2-senate-republican-praises-election-official-for-standing-up-to-trump.

67. Steven Levitsky and Daniel Ziblatt, "The Biggest Threat to Democracy Is the GOP Stealing the Next Election," *Atlantic*, July 2021, https://www.theatlantic.com/ideas/archive/2021/07/democracy-could-die-2024/619390/.

68. Katie Benner et al., "Meadows and the Band of Loyalists: How They Fought to Keep Trump in Power," *New York Times*, December 15, 2021, https://www.nytimes.com/2021/12/15/us/politics/trump-meadows-republicans-congress-jan-6.html.

69. Luke Broadwater and Alan Feuer, "New Details Underscore House G.O.P. Role in Jan. 6 Planning," *New York Times*, April 26, 2022, https://www.nytimes.com/2022/04/26/us/politics/jan-6-texts-mark-meadows.html.

70. Alan Feuer, Maggie Haberman, and Luke Broadwater, "Memos Show Roots of Trump's Focus on Jan. 6 and Alternative Electors," *New York Times*, February 2, 2022, https://www.nytimes.com/2022/02/02/us/politics/trump-jan-6-memos.html.

71. Danny Hakim, Luke Broadwater, and Jo Becker, "Ginni Thomas Pressed Trump's Chief of Staff to Overturn 2020 Vote, Texts Show," *New York Times*, March 24, 2022, https://www.nytimes.com/2022/03/24/us/politics/ginni-thomas-trump-mark-meadows.html.

72. Jane Mayer, "The Big Money Behind the Big Lie," *The New Yorker*, August 9, 2021, https://www.newyorker.com/magazine/2021/08/09/the-big-money-behind-the-big-lie.

73. Doug Bock Clark, Alexandra Berzon, and Kristen Berg, "Building the 'Big Lie': Inside the Creation of Trump's Stolen Election Myth," ProPublica, April 26, 2022, https://www.propublica.org/article/big-lie-trump-stolen-election-inside-creation#1319228.

74. Isaac Stanley-Becker, "Lindsey Graham and Mike Lee Personally Vetted Trump's Fraud Claims, New Book Says. They Were Unpersuaded," *Washington Post*, September 20, 2021, https://www.washingtonpost.com/politics/2021/09/20/peril-woodward-costa-graham-lee-fraud/.

75. Alan Feuer, "Trump Campaign Knew Lawyers' Voting Machine Claims Were Baseless, Memo Shows," *New York Times*, September 21, 2021, https://www.nytimes.com/2021/09/21/us/politics/trump-dominion-voting.html.

76. Kevin Arceneaux and Rory Truex, "Donald Trump and the Lie," *Perspectives on Politics*, forthcoming.

77. J. David Goodman, Nick Corasaniti, and Reid J. Epstein, "Texas G.O.P. Passes Election Bill, Raising Voting Barriers Even Higher," *New York Times*, August 31, 2021, https://www.nytimes.com/2021/08/31/us/politics/texas-voting-rights-bill.html.

78. Nick Corasaniti, "Voting Battles of 2022 Take Shape as G.O.P. Crafts New Election Bills," *New York Times*, December 4, 2021, https://www.nytimes.com/2021/12/04/us/politics/gop-voting-rights-democrats.html.

79. Benjy Sarlin, "What's Keeping Democracy Experts up Most at Night? An Overturned Election," NBC News, July 5, 2021, https://www.nbcnews.com/politics/politics-news/what-s-keeping-democracy-experts-most-night-overturned-election-n1272971.

80. Reid J. Epstein, "Wisconsin Republicans Push to Take Over the State's Elections," *New York Times*, November 19, 2021, https://www.nytimes.com/2021/11/19/us/politics/wisconsin-republicans-decertify-election.html.

81. Andy Rose and Veronica Stacqualursi, "Arizona Republican House Speaker Effectively Dooms GOP Bill to Allow State Legislature to Reject Election Results," CNN, February 3, 2022, https://edition.cnn.com/2022/02/03/politics/arizona-bill-reject-election-results-effectively-blocked/index.html.

82. Mayer, "The Big Money Behind the Big Lie," emphasis in original.

83. Kyle Cheney, "'Provide Some Cover': Batch of Eastman Emails Sheds Light on Contacts with State Legislatures," *Politico*, May 10, 2022, https://www.politico.com/news/2022/05/10/eastman-emails-pennsylvania-legislators-biden-00031668.

84. Amy B. Wang, "Jan. 6 Committee Leaders Blast McCarthy's 'Baseless' Claim about Trump's Innocence," *Washington Post*, September 4, 2021, https://www.washingtonpost.com/politics/2021/09/04/jan-6-committee-leaders-blast-mccarthys-baseless-claim-about-trumps-innocence/.

85. Alexander Burns and Jonathan Martin, " 'I've Had It with This Guy': G.O.P. Leaders Privately Blasted Trump After Jan. 6," *New York Times*, April 21, 2022, https://www.nytimes.com/2022/04/21/us/politics/trump-mitch-mcconnell-kevin-mccarthy.html.

86. Michael M. Grynbaum, Davey Alba, and Reid J. Epstein, "How Pro-Trump Forces Pushed a Lie About Antifa at the Capitol Riot," *New York Times*, March 1, 2021, https://www.nytimes.com/2021/03/01/us/politics/antifa-conspiracy-capitol-riot.html.

87. Dominick Mastrangelo, "Ron Johnson: Jan. 6 Capitol Riot Was a Largely 'Peaceful Protest,'" *The Hill*, May 20, 2021, https://thehill.com/homenews/senate/554548-ron-johnson-jan-6-capitol-riot-was-largely-peaceful-not-an-insurrection.

88. Shant Shahrigian, "Trump Praises Jan. 6 Rioters as 'Patriots' and 'Peaceful People,'" Yahoo News, July 11, 2021, https://news.yahoo.com/trump-praises-jan-6-rioters-211400473.html.

89. Shahrigian, "Trump Praises Jan. 6 Rioters as 'Patriots' and 'Peaceful People.' "

90. Paul Schwartzman and Josh Dawsey, "How Ashli Babbitt Went from Capitol Rioter to Trump-Embraced 'Martyr,'" *Washington Post*, July 30, 2021, https://www.washingtonpost.com/dc-md-va/2021/07/30/ashli-babbitt-trump-capitol-martyr/.

91. Julian Mark, "Paul Gosar Demands Name of Capitol Officer Who Killed Rioter Ashli Babbitt, Saying She Was 'Executed,'" *Washington Post*, June 16, 2021, https://www.washingtonpost.com/nation/2021/06/16/paul-gosar-capitol-riot-babbitt/.

92. Leonnig and Rucker, *I Alone Can Fix It*, 512–513.

93. Luke Broadwater and Shane Goldmacher, "House Republican Says Trump Asked Him to Illegally 'Rescind' 2020 Election," *New York Times*, March 23, 2022, https://www.nytimes.com/2022/03/23/us/politics/trump-mo-brooks-senate.html.

94. Katie Benner, "Former U.S. Attorney in Atlanta Says Trump Wanted to Fire Him for Not Backing Election Fraud Claims," *New York Times*, August 11, 2021, https://www.nytimes.com/2021/08/11/us/politics/byung-pak-trump-atlanta-election-fraud.html.

95. Michael Wines and Reid J. Epstein, "Trump Is Said to Have Called Arizona Official After Election Loss," *New York Times*, July 2, 2021, https://www.nytimes.com/2021/07/02/us/politics/trump-arizona-hickman-2020-election.html.

96. Richard Fausset, "Georgia Jury to Consider Whether Trump Illegally Interfered in 2020 Election," *New York Times*, May 2, 2022, https://www.nytimes.com/2022/05/02/us/trump-election-georgia-grand-jury.html.

97. Katie Benner, "Trump Pressed Official to Wield Justice Dept. to Back Election Claims," *New York Times*, June 15, 2021, https://www.nytimes.com/2021/06/15/us/politics/trump-justice-department-election.html.

98. Katherine Faulders and Alexander Mallin, "DOJ Officials Rejected Colleague's Request to Intervene in Georgia's Election Certification: Emails," ABC News, August 3, 2021, https://abcnews.go.com/US/doj-officials-rejected-colleagues-request-intervene-georgias-election/story?id=79243198.

99. Jamie Gangel and Jeremy Herb, "Memo Shows Trump Lawyer's Six-Step Plan for Pence to Overturn the Election," CNN, September 20, 2020, https://edition.cnn.com/2021/09/20/politics/trump-pence-election-memo/index.html.

100. Alia Shoaib, "Trump Wrote to Georgia's Secretary of State Asking Him to Consider 'Decertifying' the 2020 Election Result," September 18, 2021, https://news.yahoo.com/donald-trump-wrote-georgia-secretary-091241802.html.

101. Miriam Berger, "U.S. Listed as a 'Backsliding' Democracy for First Time in Report by European Think Tank," *Washington Post*, November 22, 2021, http://www.washingtonpost.com/world/2021/11/22/united-states-backsliding-democracies-list-first-time/.

102. Twitter, "Permanent Suspension of @realDonaldTrump," January 8, 2021, https://blog.twitter.com/en_us/topics/company/2020/suspension; Salvador Rodriguez, "Facebook Says Donald Trump to Remain Banned for Two Years, Effective from Jan. 7," CNBC, June 4, 2021, https://www.cnbc.com/2021/06/04/facebook-says-donald-trump-to-remain-banned-from-platform-for-2-years-effective-from-jan-7.html.

103. Shannon Bond, "Trump Suspended from Facebook for 2 Years," NPR, June 4, 2021, https://www.npr.org/2021/06/04/1003284948/trump-suspended-from-facebook-for-2-years.

104. Nick Clegg, "In Response to Oversight Board, Trump Suspended for Two Years; Will Only Be Reinstated if Conditions Permit," Meta, June 4, 2021, https://about.fb.com/news/2021/06/facebook-response-to-oversight-board-recommendations-trump/.

105. Shagun Jhaver et al., "Evaluating the Effectiveness of Deplatforming as a Moderation Strategy on Twitter," *Proceedings of the ACM Human-Computer Interaction* 5, no. CSCW2 (October 2021): 30, doi:10.1145/3479525.

106. H. Innes and M. Innes, "De-Platforming Disinformation: Conspiracy Theories and Their Control," *Information, Communication and Society*, October 2021 (pre-print), doi:10.1080/1369118X.2021.1994631.

107. Wen Chen et al., "Neutral Bots Probe Political Bias on Social Media," *Nature Communications* 12, no. 1 (September 2021): 5580, doi:10.1038/s41467-021-25738-6; Eytan Bakshy, Solomon Messing, and Lada A. Adamic, "Exposure to Ideologically Diverse News and Opinion on Facebook," *Science* 348, no. 6239 (June 2015): 1130–1132, doi:10.1126/science.aaa1160.

108. "Capitol Attack Was Months in the Making on Facebook," Tech Transparency Project, January 19, 2021, https://www.techtransparencyproject.org/articles/capitol-attack-was-months-making-facebook.

109. Craig Silverman et al., "Facebook Groups Topped 10,000 Daily Attacks on Election before Jan. 6, Analysis Shows," *Washington Post*, January 4, 2022, http://www.washingtonpost.com/technology/2022/01/04/facebook-election-misinformation-capitol-riot/.

110. Chris Looft and Layla Ferris, "Facebook Whistleblower Documents Offer New Revelations About Jan. 6 Response," ABC News, October 25, 2021, https://abcnews.go.com/Technology/facebook-whistleblower-documents-offer-revelations-jan-response/story?id=80694096.

111. Scott Pelley, "Whistleblower: Facebook Is Misleading the Public on Progress Against Hate Speech, Violence, Misinformation," CBS News, October 3, 2021, https://www.cbsnews.com/news/facebook-whistleblower-frances-haugen-misinformation-public-60-minutes-2021-10-03/.

112. Craig Timberg, Elizabeth Dwoskin, and Reed Albergotti, "Inside Facebook, Jan. 6 Violence Fueled Anger, Regret over Missed Warning Signs," *Washington Post*, October 22, 2021, https://www.washingtonpost.com/technology/2021/10/22/jan-6-capitol-riot-facebook/.

113. Olivia Solon and Teaganne Finn, "Facebook Whistleblower Tells Congress Social Network Is 'Accountable to No One,'" NBC News, October 5, 2021, https://www.nbcnews.com/politics/congress/facebook-whistleblower-tell-congress-social-network-accountable-no-one-n1280786.

114. Marguerite Reardon, "Section 230: How It Shields Facebook and Why Congress Wants Changes," CNET, October 6, 2021, https://www.cnet.com/news/section-230-how-it-shields-facebook-and-why-congress-wants-changes/.

115. Christopher Cox and Ron Wyden, "Communications Decency Act," 47 USC § 230 (1996), https://www.law.cornell.edu/uscode/text/47/230.

116. Jeff Kosseff, *The Twenty-Six Words That Created the Internet* (Ithaca, NY: Cornell University Press, 2019), https://www.cornellpress.cornell.edu/book/9781501714412/the-twenty-six-words-that-created-the-internet/.

117. Jeff Kosseff, "The Gradual Erosion of the Law That Shaped the Internet," *Science and Technology Law Review* 18, no. 1 (2017), doi:10.7916/stlr.v18i1.4011.

118. Steve Randy Waldman, "The 1996 Law That Ruined the Internet," *Atlantic*, January 2021, https://www.theatlantic.com/ideas/archive/2021/01/trump-fighting-section-230-wrong-reason/617497/.

119. Farhad Manjoo, "Facebook Is Bad. Fixing It Rashly Could Make It Much Worse," *New York Times*, October 27, 2021, https://www.nytimes.com/2021/10/27/opin ion/facebook-regulation-section-230.html.

120. Nandita Bose, "Democrats Prefer 'Scalpel' over 'Jackhammer' to Reform Key U.S. Internet Law," Reuters, October 2020, https://www.reuters.com/article/us-usa-tech-liability/democrats-prefer-scalpel-over-jackhammer-to-reform-key-u-s-inter net-law-idUSKBN27E1IA.

121. "Klobuchar, Luján Introduce Legislation to Hold Digital Platforms Accountable for Vaccine and Other Health-Related Misinformation," news release, July 22, 2021, https://www.klobuchar.senate.gov/public/index.cfm/2021/7/klobuchar-luj-n-introduce-legislation-to-hold-digital-platforms-accountable-for-vaccine-and-other-health-related-misinformation.

122. "Preventing Online Censorship—Executive Order," Federal Register, May 28, 2020, https://www.federalregister.gov/documents/2020/06/02/2020-12030/ preventing-online-censorship.

123. "CDT Suit Challenges President's Executive Order Targeting First Amendment Protected Speech," Center for Democracy and Technology, June 2, 2020, https:// cdt.org/press/cdt-suit-challenges-presidents-executive-order-targeting-first-amendment-protected-speech/; "Rock the Vote v. Trump," Electronic Frontier Foundation, August 2020, https://www.eff.org/cases/rock-vote-v-trump.

124. Joseph R. Biden, "Executive Order on the Revocation of Certain Presidential Actions and Technical Amendment," The White House, May 14, 2021, https:// www.whitehouse.gov/briefing-room/presidential-actions/2021/05/14/execut ive-order-on-the-revocation-of-certain-presidential-actions-and-technical-amendment/.

125. Brendan Brown, "Search on Trump Twitter Archive for 'Section 230,'" Trump Twitter Archive V2, January 2022, https://www.thetrumparchive.com/?search box=%22section+230%22.

126. Shirin Ghaffary, "Facebook Deleted a Trump Post That Falsely Claimed the Flu Can Be More Deadly than Covid-19," *Vox*, October 2020, https://www.vox.com/ recode/2020/10/6/21504307/facebook-deleted-trump-post-flu-deadly-covid-19-twitter.

127. Brown, "Search on Trump Twitter Archive for 'Section 230.'"

128. Amanda Macias, "Trump Vetoes Colossal $740 Billion Defense Bill, Breaking with Republican-Led Senate," CNBC, December 23, 2020, https://www.cnbc. com/2020/12/23/trump-vetoes-740-billion-ndaa-defense-bill.html.

129. Brown, "Search on Trump Twitter Archive for 'Section 230.'"

130. "U.S. Senate: Vetoes by President Donald J. Trump," United States Senate, 2021, https://www.senate.gov/legislative/vetoes/TrumpDJ.htm.

131. Kari Paul, "Facebook to Pay $52m for Failing to Protect Moderators from 'Horrors' of Graphic Content," *Guardian*, May 12, 2020, https://www.theguard

ian.com/technology/2020/may/12/facebook-settlement-mental-health-mod erators.

132. Manjoo, "Facebook Is Bad. Fixing It Rashly Could Make It Much Worse."

133. "TRUTH Social," Truth Social, 2021, https://truthsocial.com/.

134. Kate Park, "Trump to Launch His Own Social Media Platform, Calling It TRUTH Social," TechCrunch, October 2021, https://social.techcrunch.com/ 2021/10/20/trump-launches-his-own-social-media-platform-truth-social/.

135. "Truth Social Terms of Service," Truth Social, September 2021, https://truthsoc ial.com/terms-of-service/.

136. Park, "Trump to Launch His Own Social Media Platform, Calling It TRUTH Social."

137. Park, "Trump to Launch His Own Social Media Platform, Calling It TRUTH Social."

138. MacKenzie Sigalos, "Trump Announces Social Media Platform Launch Plan, SPAC Deal," CNBC, October 20, 2021, https://www.cnbc.com/2021/10/20/ trump-announces-social-media-platform-launch-plan-spac-deal.html.

139. Ailan Evans, "Trump's Media Company Strikes Deal with Anti-'Cancel Culture' Video Platform Rumble," Daily Caller, December 2021, https://dailycaller.com/ 2021/12/14/donald-trump-tmtg-truth-social-rumble/.

140. Aimee Picchi, "With No Ad Revenue, Truth Social Parent Sees Losses for 'the Foreseeable Future,'" CBS News, May 17, 2022, https://www.cbsnews.com/news/ truth-social-donald-trump-digital-world-trump-media-technology-group/.

141. Jack Brewster, Coalter Palmer, and Shayeza Walid, "Misinformation Monitor: August 2022," NewsGuard, August 28, 2022, https://www.newsguardt ech.com/misinformation-monitor/august-2022/.

142. Steve Benen, "A Fresh Look at the 'Big Lesson' Collins Wanted Trump to Learn," MSNBC, January 4, 2021, https://www.msnbc.com/rachel-maddow-show/ fresh-look-big-lesson-collins-wanted-trump-learn-n1252727.

143. John Bowden, "Collins: Trump Has Learned 'a Pretty Big Lesson' from Impeachment," *The Hill*, February 4, 2020, https://thehill.com/homenews/sen ate/481486-collins-trump-has-learned-a-pretty-big-lesson-from-impeachment.

144. Alexander Hamilton, "The Avalon Project: Federalist No. 65" (March 1788), The Avalon Project, https://avalon.law.yale.edu/18th_century/fed65.asp.

145. Matt Viser, "Joe Biden's Speech to America: 'It Is Time to Turn the Page,'" *Washington Post*, December 14, 2020, https://www.washingtonpost.com/polit ics/joe-biden-address/2020/12/14/80c04d02-3e35-11eb-8db8-395dedaaa036_st ory.html.

146. *Donald J. Trump v. Bennie G. Thompson*, no. 21-5254, United States Court of Appeals for the District of Columbia Circuit, December 9, 2021.

147. Leonnig and Rucker, *I Alone Can Fix It*.

148. Leonnig and Rucker, *I Alone Can Fix It*, 434.

149. Mark Esper, *A Sacred Oath: Memoirs of a Secretary of Defense During Extraordinary Times* (New York: William Morrow, 2022).

150. Leonnig and Rucker, *I Alone Can Fix It*.

151. Helene Cooper, "Milley Apologizes for Role in Trump Photo Op: 'I Should Not Have Been There,'" *New York Times*, June 11, 2020, https://www.nytimes.com/2020/06/11/us/politics/trump-milley-military-protests-lafayette-square.html.

152. Ashton Carter et al., "All 10 Living Former Defense Secretaries: Involving the Military in Election Disputes Would Cross into Dangerous Territory," *Washington Post*, January 3, 2021, https://www.washingtonpost.com/opinions/10-former-defense-secretaries-military-peaceful-transfer-of-power/2021/01/03/2a23d52e-4c4d-11eb-a9f4-0e668b9772ba_story.html.

153. Bryan Bender, "'Disturbing and Reckless': Retired Brass Spread Election Lie in Attack on Biden, Democrats," *Politico*, May 11, 2021, https://www.politico.com/news/2021/05/11/retired-brass-biden-election-487374.

154. Paul D. Eaton, Antonio M. Taguba, and Steven M. Anderson, "3 Retired Generals: The Military Must Prepare Now for a 2024 Insurrection," *Washington Post*, December 17, 2021, http://www.washingtonpost.com/opinions/2021/12/17/eaton-taguba-anderson-generals-military/.

155. Molly Ball, "The Secret History of the Shadow Campaign That Saved the 2020 Election," *Time*, February 4, 2021, https://time.com/5936036/secret-2020-election-campaign/.

156. See Kathleen Hall Jamieson, *Cyberwar: How Russian Hackers and Trolls Helped Elect a President: What We Don't, Can't, and Do Know* (New York: Oxford University Press, 2018), https://www.amazon.com/Cyberwar-Russian-Hackers-Trolls-President/dp/0190915811.

157. Adam Brewster, "GOP-Led Michigan State Senate Committee Finds No Evidence of Widespread Fraud in 2020 Election," CBS News, June 24, 2021, https://www.cbsnews.com/news/michigan-senate-no-election-fraud-2020/.

158. Ivana Saric, "Election Workers Departing in Droves After 'Partisan Rancor' in 2020," Axios, June 13, 2021, https://www.axios.com/2021/06/13/election-workers-left-jobs-2020.

159. Anthony Izaguirre, "Exodus of Election Officials Raises Concerns of Partisanship," Associated Press, June 13, 2021, https://apnews.com/article/election-officials-retire-trump-2020-threats-misinformation-3b810d8b3b3adee2ca409689788b863f.

160. Amy Gardner, Tom Hamburger, and Josh Dawsey, "Trump Allies Work to Place Supporters in Key Election Posts Across the Country, Spurring Fears about Future Vote Challenges," *Washington Post*, November 28, 2021, http://www.washingtonpost.com/politics/trump-allies-election-oversight/2021/11/28/3933b3ce-4227-11ec-9ea7-3eb2406a2e24_story.html.

161. Stephen Battaglio, "Why Fox News Analyst Arnon Mishkin Called Arizona for Biden on Election Night," *Los Angeles Times*, November 5, 2020, https://www.lati

mes.com/entertainment-arts/business/story/2020-11-05/fox-news-arnon-mish kin-election-2020-arizona-trump-biden.

162. Annie Karni and Maggie Haberman, "Fox's Arizona Call for Biden Flipped the Mood at Trump Headquarters," *New York Times*, November 4, 2020, https://www.nytimes.com/2020/11/04/us/politics/trump-fox-news-arizona.html.

163. Rachelle Hampton and Marissa Martinelli, "Here's the Moment Fox News Called the Election for Biden," *Slate*, November 7, 2020, https://slate.com/news-and-politics/2020/11/fox-news-biden-winner-presidential-election.html.

164. Jason Silverstein, "Trump Posts Flurry of Anti-Fox News Tweets: 'They Forgot What Made Them Successful,'" CBS News, November 13, 2020, https://www.cbsnews.com/news/trump-fox-news-tweets/.

165. Associated Press, "Two Fox News Executives Depart in Wake of Arizona Election Night Call," *Guardian*, January 19, 2021, https://www.theguardian.com/media/2021/jan/19/two-fox-news-executives-involved-in-election-night-ariz ona-call-are-out.

166. Associated Press, "Two Fox News Executives Depart in Wake of Arizona Election Night Call."

167. Tim Alberta, "What the GOP Does to Its Own Dissenters," *Atlantic*, January/February 2021, https://www.theatlantic.com/magazine/archive/2022/01/peter-meijer-freshman-republican-impeach/620844/.

APPENDIX

1. Alexandra Garrett, "Trump Lawyer Sidney Powell Says Georgia Election Lawsuit 'Will Be Biblical,' Suggests GOP Governor Helped Biden," Newsweek, November 22, 2020, https://www.newsweek.com/trump-lawyer-sidney-powell-says-geor gia-election-lawsuit-will-biblical-suggests-gop-governor-1549333.

2. Edward McBroom et al., "Report on the November 2020 Election in Michigan," Michigan Senate Oversight Committee, 2020, https://misenategopcdn.s3.us-east-1.amazonaws.com/99/doccuments/20210623/SMPO_2020ElectionRepor t_2.pdf.

3. Mario Callegaro and Charles DiSogra, "Computing Response Metrics for Online Panels," *Public Opinion Quarterly* 72, no. 5 (December 2008): 1008–1032, doi:10.1093/poq/nfn065.

4. Callegaro and DiSogra, "Computing Response Metrics for Online Panels."

5. Daniel J. Hopkins, *The Increasingly United States: How and Why American Political Behavior Nationalized*, Chicago Studies in American Politics (Chicago: University of Chicago Press, 2018), https://press.uchicago.edu/ucp/books/book/chicago/I/bo27596045.html.

6. Nathaniel Beck and Simon Jackman, "Beyond Linearity by Default: Generalized Additive Models," *American Journal of Political Science* 42, no. 2 (1998): 596–627, doi:10.2307/2991772.

7. Simon Wood, *MGCV: Mixed GAM Computation Vehicle with Automatic Smoothness Estimation*, version 1.8-36, 2021, https://CRAN.R-project.org/package=mgcv.

8. Gary C. Jacobson, "The Obama Legacy and the Future of Partisan Conflict: Demographic Change and Generational Imprinting," *Annals of the American Academy of Political and Social Science* 667, no. 1 (September 2016): 72–91, doi:10.1177/0002716216658425; Larry M. Bartels and Simon Jackman, "A Generational Model of Political Learning," *Electoral Studies* 33 (March 2014): 7–18, doi:10.1016/j.electstud.2013.06.004.

Index

For the benefit of digital users, indexed terms that span two pages (e.g., 52–53) may, on occasion, appear on only one of those pages.